COGNITIVE DEVELOPMENT

Neo-Piagetian Perspectives

COGNITIVE DEVELOPMENT

Neo-Piagetian Perspectives

Sergio Morra
University of Genoa

Camilla Gobbo
University of Padua

Zopito Marini
Brock University

Ronald Sheese
York University

Lawrence Erlbaum Associates
Taylor & Francis Group

New York   London

Cover design by Kathryn Houghtaling Lacey

Cover art: Image of sculpture by Fausto Melotti
Theme II with seven variations (1969)
From the Barilla Collection of Modern Art, Parma, Italy

Lawrence Erlbaum Associates
Taylor & Francis Group
270 Madison Avenue
New York, NY 10016

Lawrence Erlbaum Associates
Taylor & Francis Group
2 Park Square
Milton Park, Abingdon
Oxon OX14 4RN

© 2008 by Taylor & Francis Group, LLC
Lawrence Erlbaum Associates is an imprint of Taylor & Francis Group, an Informa business

Printed in the United States of America on acid-free paper
10 9 8 7 6 5 4 3 2 1

International Standard Book Number-13: 978-0-8058-6350-5 (Softcover)
978-0-8058-4358-3 (Hardcover)

Visit the Taylor & Francis Web site at
http://www.taylorandfrancis.com

To the memory of Robbie Case—
a master researcher, a friend,
a model for all of us.

Contents

Preface   xiii

1   **From Piaget to the Neo-Piagetians**   **1**

    Still "Neo-"? *1*
    Two Piagets *6*
        Piaget as Theorist of Logical Competence *7*
        Piaget's Dialectical View of Development *8*
    Problems for the Developmental Theory of Logical Competence *13*
        Synchrony and "Horizontal Décalage" *14*
        ✓ Adults' Errors of Logic *15*
        Precocious Logical Reasoning in Children *16*
        Cross-Cultural Differences in Developmental Pathways *17*
    Who Killed Genetic Epistemology? *18*
        The Evidence *18*
        The Verdict *21*
    Setting the Stage for Neo-Piagetian Theories *22*
        Information Load and Task Complexity *22*
        Representation and Its Development *25*
        Strategies and Control Processes *29*
    On the Dialogue Between Epistemological Traditions *32*
    Conclusion *38*

2   **The Theory of J. Pascual-Leone**   **40**

    Cognitive Development and Cognitive Style *40*
        Field Dependence/Independence *40*

Field Dependence and Piagetian Tasks *42*

Schemes and Processing Capacity *43*

    Processing Capacity: Hypotheses Regarding
        Its Limits and Development *43*

    Research on the CSVI Task *44*

Schemes: Definitions and Properties *45*

    The Components of Schemes *45*

    The Properties of Schemes *46*

Scheme Classification *47*

    Examples *49*

Second Level Operators *50*

    Learning Effects *51*

    Attentional Energy *53*

    The Inhibition of Irrelevant Information *54*

    Field Effects *57*

    Automatic Encoding of Space and Time *58*

    Emotion-Based Activation *59*

The TCO and Task Analysis *59*

    General Characteristics of the TCO *59*

    Task Analysis *61*

A Classical Piagetian Problem: The Control of Variables *63*

    Task Analysis *63*

    Experiment *64*

Is the Water Level Horizontal? *65*

    Task Analysis *66*

    Correlational and Experimental Research *67*

A Psycholinguistic Problem: The Comprehension of Metaphors *69*

    Task Analysis *70*

    Experimental and Correlational Research *72*

Planning and Production of Children's Drawings *73*

    Drawing a Partial Occlusion: Task Analysis *74*

    Experimental and Correlational Research *75*

Cognitive Development and Motor Ability *77*

    Rho Task Analysis *78*

    Research on the Rho Task *79*

Research on Inhibitory Processes *81*

    Comparing Inhibitory Processes Across Tasks *83*

Conclusion *86*

3 **Structuralist Approaches to Developmental Stages** **88**

Piaget's Structuralist Approach *88*

    The Concept of Structure *89*

    Piaget and Structuralism in Psychology *89*

A Neo-Piagetian Reformulation of Structuralism *90*

    The Symbolic Nature of Thought *91*

    Cognitive Systems *91*

    Relational Complexity *93*

Experiments on the Comprehension of Systems of Rules *94*
Conservation and Transitivity Research *97*
The Question of Information Load *99*
    The Problem *99*
    An Attempted Solution *100*
    Problems and Prospects *102*
An Attempt at a Synthesis of Two Theories *103*
    Methodological Problems and Theoretical Responses *104*
    Experimental Studies *105*
Structuralist Approaches to Individual Differences *106*
    Analogical Representations, Concrete Operations
        and Individual Décalages *107*
    Studies on Individual Décalages *108*
    Experiential Structuralism *110*
Conclusion *113*

4   **Problem Solving in Children**   **115**

The Use of Heuristics in the Solution of Well-Defined
        Problems *116*
    Heuristics in the Solution of Well-Defined Problems *118*
    The Use of Heuristics in Children's Problem Solving *119*
Problem Solving and Learning by Analogy *125*
    Children's Understanding of Analogy *130*
    Advantages and Limitations of the Analogical Procedure
        in Problem Solving *133*
Instruction and Problem Solving *135*
    Siegler's Model; the Balance Problem *136*
    The Balance Problem and Training *139*
    The Role of Instruction in the Use of Analogical Procedures *142*
Conclusion *147*

5   **The Cyclical Nature of Skill Development**   **148**

The Development of Dynamic Skills in the Theory
        of K. Fischer *149*
    Methodology *152*
    Optimal and Functional Level *154*
The Cyclical Shape of Development *157*
    The Structural Levels of Skill: An Example *159*
    Upper Limit on Skill Level Development *163*
Change Processes *165*
    Transition Processes and Individual Differences *173*
Generalization and Specificity *177*
Some Methodological Notes on the Epigenetic Approach
        of Skill Theory *182*
Conclusion *188*

6   Structures and Processes in Case's Theory
    of Development   190

    General Characteristics of the Theory 191
    Outlining Cognitive Development in Case's Theory:
            The Balance Beam Task 194
        The Development of Sensorimotor Control Structures
            in Infancy (1–18 Months) 194
        The Development of Interrelational Control Structures
            in Preschoolers (1–5 Years) 196
        Dimensional Control Structures in Middle Childhood
            (5–11 Years) 198
        The Development of Vectorial Control Structures
            in Adolescence (11–19 Years) 200
    Processes of Change in Executive Control Structures 201
    Working Memory and Operational Efficiency 202
        Measuring WM: Problems and Solutions 203
        Does Operational Efficiency Play a Role in the Size of WM? 204
        Role of Maturation on WM and Link With Cognitive
            Development 207
    Central Conceptual Structures and Their Development 208
        Central Numerical Structure: The Development of the
            "Mental Number Line" 210
        Central Narrative Structure: The Development of
            "Mental Story Line" 215
        Is There Support for the Existence of CCSs? 217
    Processes of Change in CCS Development and Relationship
            With ECS 220
    Factors Influencing the Development of Central Conceptual
            Structures 222
        Role of WM on Central Conceptual Structures 222
        Role of Experience in Development of CCS 223
    Conclusion 225

7   Cognitive Development as Change in Representations   229

    General Changes in Representation: Mounoud's Qualitative
            Developmental Progression 230
        General Form of Mounoud's Developmental Model 231
        Phases in Mounoud's Developmental Model 233
        Empirical Support for the Model 237
    Specific Changes in Knowledge Representation
            in A. Karmiloff-Smith 239
        From Procedural Knowledge to the Construction
            of Theories: The RR Model 240
        Empirical Support for the RR Model 243
    Development: What Is Innate in Karmiloff-Smith's Theory? 245
        Representation and Neuroconstructivism 246

Comparing the Two Theories *250*
Change or Enrichment of Children's Theories? *253*
Conclusion *257*

8 **Cognitive Development and Emotional Development**   **260**

Daggers Drawn With Psychoanalytic Accounts *260*
    Fischer's Oedipus Conflict and the Unconscious *261*
    Childhood Amnesia *264*
Emotions, Skills, Social Roles, and Attachment *267*
A Theory of Emotional Development *270*
    The Emergence of Emotions and Control Structures *270*
    Appraisals, Moods, and Personality Development *273*
The Horizon of Wisdom *276*
Conclusion *281*

9 **Applications**   **284**

Psychometric Applications *284*
Educational Applications *288*
    Curriculum Planning and Individualized Instruction *289*
    An Example: The Missing Addend Problem *291*
    Teaching Central Conceptual Structures *293*
    Other Broad Educational Goals *297*
    Toward a New Foundation of Cognitive Educational
        Research? *300*
Heuristic Tools for Task Analysis *302*
    Identifying the Cognitive Units *303*
    Process Modeling *306*
Conclusion *309*

10 **In Conclusion**   **310**

The Shape of Development *310*
    The Issue of Generality and Specificity in Stage
        Development *310*
    Continuity and Discontinuity in Stage Development *317*
Variability in Development *322*
    U-Shaped Behaviors *323*
    Variability as a Cue to Multiple Levels of Cognitive
        Functioning *325*
    Role of Variability in General Developmental Theories *329*
    Some Notes on Individual Differences *332*
Information Load and Working Memory *336*
    Models of Working Memory *339*
    Capacity and Speed *344*
    Capacity and Its Interaction With Other Constructs *347*

Maturation and Environment *347*
    The Issue of Precocious Abilities *347*
    Neurological Maturation and Limits of Environmental
        Influence *351*
    Summary *359*
Toward an Integration *360*
    Points of Agreement *360*
    Controversies and Possible Solutions *362*
    Again on Dialectic *365*
    Prospects *368*
Conclusion *371*

References   373

Author Index   413

Subject Index   425

Preface

This book ties together almost four decades of neo-Piagetian research. Neo-Piagetian theorists share many similarities with Piaget—they take a constructivist approach to cognitive development, they are broad in their scope, and they assume that cognitive development can be divided into stages with qualitatively different characteristics. They also assume that the complexity of children's thinking increases across these stages, but unlike Piaget, they define the complexity of the stages in accordance with features of the child's information processing system rather than in terms of logical properties. An integration of the various neo-Piagetian theories now seems possible and in this book we outline the directions in which the next generation of researchers might proceed in order to create a unified, general neo-Piagetian theory of cognitive development.

Therefore, the intended audience of this book includes both the present and the next generation of researchers in cognitive development as well as those with broader developmental and educational interests. Our intended audience includes as well all those who study cognitive development from other theoretical points of view and wish to compare the respective perspectives and to enter into a fruitful dialogue about them. Our greatest hope is that the graduate students in developmental programs around the world will find this book emphasizing broad theoretical perspectives a stimulating and useful means for orienting their future research. The book should certainly be valuable for graduate teaching.

The book is focused on both theory and research, and a unique feature is our constant critical analysis and comparison of concepts across theories. This feature, of course, is a necessary one in view of our desire to work toward an integration of neo-Piagetian approaches.

The neo-Piagetian authors most often cited through the book are Robbie Case, Andreas Demetriou, Kurt Fischer, Graeme Halford, Pierre Mounoud, Juan Pascual-Leone, Anik de Ribaupierre, and Bob Siegler (listed in alphabetic order), and their co-workers. We include in the list Bob Siegler, who likes to call himself an 'atypical neo-Piagetian' because he shares only some, not all of the prototypical features of a 'mainstream neo-Piagetian.' A few of these researchers (namely, Mounoud, Pascual-Leone, and de Ribaupierre) have worked at Geneva for at least a few years, which is another (albeit less important) origin of the term neo-Piagetian.

Although she does not define herself as neo-Piagetian, we also discuss some work of Annette Karmiloff-Smith—on the contrary, she has expressed serious reservations on the whole neo-Piagetian enterprise. Nevertheless, given the importance of her studies, the close relationship of her epistemological and theoretical tenets with those of the neo-Piagetians, and her Genevan academic roots, we feel the book would be incomplete if we did not discuss her work.

Some theories are presented more extensively in the book than others. This is not intended to diminish the importance of the proposals that are presented more briefly, but only to avoid redundancy on points on which some theories are similar. As well, we discuss numerous studies that are not neo-Piagetian. Human information processing and dynamic systems concepts are among the most important sources neo-Piagetian theory has drawn on in a dialogue that will hopefully continue with theorists based in other conceptual frameworks. We intend this book, among other things, to be an instrument for that dialogue.

The book has 10 chapters. The first section of chapter 1 calls the reader's attention to the relevance of the topic, while the bulk of the chapter is a historically oriented introduction to the major neo-Piagetian issues. Chapters 2, 3, 5, and 6 discuss some of the main theories or groups of theories. Chapters 4, 7, 8, and 9 are devoted to specific topic areas and their relation to neo-Piagetian research. Chapter 10 presents our conclusions and our views on possibilities for an integrated neo-Piagetian approach to cognitive development.

The order of the chapters is in part chronological and in part content-based. Chapter 2 is devoted to Pascual-Leone's Theory of Constructive Operators and chapter 3 to the structuralist neo-Piagetian approaches—most notably Halford's theory, followed by Chapman's, Demetriou's, and the work of the so-called "French connection" (Lautrey, de Ribaupierre, and Rieben). The theories of Pascual-Leone and Halford were the first two to come into the world, and for this reason we present them first (even though, as the reader will note, these two theories have been considerably reworked and improved over the years). Consequently, in chapter 2 we also present in some detail several specific lines of research in order to show how the theory 'works.' Chapter 4 deals with problem solving and children's use of heuristics, analogies, and strategies; we consider studies by Siegler, Halford, and Fischer along with several non-Piagetian authors as a means of preparing the ground for chapters 5 and 6. These chapters are devoted to two major neo-Piagetian theories, those of Fischer and Case, respectively. We deemed it appropriate to place these chapters in sequence because the two theories share the assumption of a cyclical recursion in cognitive development. Chapter 7 deals with the role of representation in cognitive development; of course, representation also arises in earlier chapters, but here we focus on theories, such as Mounoud's and Karmiloff-Smith's, in which this aspect is more prominent than in others. We also consider here some authors who are more distant from the constructivism that characterizes the Piagetian and neo-Piagetian tradition. Chapter 8 ties together several contributions on the intertwining of emotional and cognitive development; in addition to authors also cited in other parts of the book, we also cover the work of emotion specialists with a neo-Piagetian background, such as Marc Lewis, Michael Mascolo, and Sheldon White and David Pillemer. Chapter 9 deals briefly with some applications of neo-Piagetian theories in the psychometric and educational domains and with task-analytic methods that readers might wish to apply in their own field.

The final chapter presents our evaluation of the neo-Piagetian theories from the point of view of broad theoretical issues of developmental psychology. These issues include the shape of development (continuous or discontinuous? domain-specific or general?), the explanation of variability in development, the modelling of working memory or processing capacity (a very important issue for most of the neo-Piagetian theories), and the influence of innate and maturational components on development. Finally, in the last section of chapter 10, we outline some perspectives for a possible theoretical integration.

Like neo-Piagetian psychology, the writing of this book has been a collective enterprise. Fortunately email makes communication between Italian and Canadian authors easy today, so that in any given moment we could readily give feedback to one another on all parts of the book. We share the responsibility for the entire book, but the various authors had different responsibilities in drafting and revising each chapter. Chapter 1 was written collectively by Morra, Gobbo, Marini, and Sheese. Morra took responsibility for writing chapters 2, 3, 8, and 9, and Gobbo for chapters 4 and 5. Chapters 6 and 7 were written by Gobbo, Marini, and Morra, and chapter 10 by Gobbo and Morra. Sheese revised material throughout the work and took responsibility for its final editing.

We thank the publisher Il Mulino for allowing us to adapt material from an earlier book by Gobbo and Morra, *Lo Sviluppo Mentale: Prospettive Neopiagetiane*. We thank Marco Dondi, Corrado Federici, Marc Lewis, Yukari Okamoto, Marion Porath, Robert Sandieson, and Robert Siegler for reading and giving valuable comments on preliminary versions of some chapters; Janice Johnson and Juan Pascual-Leone for useful and stimulating discussions; Marinella Parisi for trusting so much our work; and our reviewers, including Ellin Scholnick of the University of Maryland. We also thank the support staff of our four departments who were so helpful (thanks in particular to Stefano Andriolo, Valeria Gazzea, Derek Hope, Amanda Noble, Carol Penner, Liliana Piccoli, and Fabio Spinelli). We are also very grateful to our relatives and friends, who accepted so well the amount of time and effort that we devoted to this book.

Regardless of whether you are a novice or an expert in neo-Piagetian studies, we sincerely hope you will find reading the book worthwhile; above all we hope that you will become engaged in fruitful and rewarding dialogue about the issues we discuss.

—*Sergio Morra*
—*Camilla Gobbo*
—*Zopito Marini*
—*Ronald Sheese*

1

From Piaget to the Neo-Piagetians

STILL "NEO-"?

Taking up this book a potential reader might think skeptically: "Why *neo-*?" It was the early 1970s when the first neo-Piagetian theories were published as a new integration of Piagetian concepts with ideas originating from Human Information Processing and other classical psychological frameworks. "That was indeed new some 30 years ago," our skeptical reader might object, "but is there anything in neo-Piagetian theories that is still new and current?"

Let us start from what could well be the conclusion of this book and answer: Yes, neo-Piagetian research has not only anticipated issues that have recently become hot, but has also continued, over the decades, to produce results and models that can usefully inform the current debates. Indeed, developmentalists and cognitive researchers of any theoretical leaning should pay closer attention to neo-Piagetian models—this book is aimed precisely to assist such focusing of attention.

Our first chapter is devoted primarily to history, that is, to the origin of the neo-Piagetian approach. However, in this first section we wish to briefly indicate—merely as examples—some of the current, lively debated proposals in developmental psychology to which neo-Piagetian approaches are relevant. These proposals raise theoretical and epistemological issues that are very similar to those raised by the neo-Piagetian approaches; and, thus, a dialogue between the two should be very fruitful. We shall mention, in turn: (a) microdevelopment; (b) discontinuity and nonlinear models of development; (c) connectionist modeling and issues of representational change; (d) working memory capacity, intelligence, and cognitive development; (e) inhibition and executive control. Though brief, we intend to convey here the idea that neo-Piagetian authors have much to say about these widely debated topics—and about many other theoretical and applied topics as well. This section, in other words, seeks to persuade the initially skeptical reader to go beyond a browse through the first pages and to pay deep attention to the rest of the book. It is in the following chapters, of course, that more substantive theoretical arguments and support from empirical research are presented.

Microdevelopment refers to the process of change in cognition or ability on a short-time scale; it is an approach focused on the construction of abilities, rather than on their stabilized state (Granott & Parziale, 2002a, 2002b). Some researchers within the Piagetian tradition (Inhelder, Sinclair, & Bovet, 1974; Karmiloff-Smith & Inhelder, 1974/1975) considered the benefits of this approach back in the 1970s; in recent years, it has become a basic instrument to study detailed developmental changes and reorganizations (see Siegler, 2006). Because the approach itself is methodological rather than theoretical, it can yield new theoretical insights, but it also needs to draw on existing theory. A clear theoretical language is necessary to describe the initial ability patterns and the differences between the cognitive structures that underlie the initial responses and the subsequent ones. It is also necessary to explain how microdevelopment fits in and interacts with long-term development, which, in turn, needs a theory of cognitive development that is systematic enough to account for cognitive change on different time scales. Neo-Piagetian theories are excellent candidates for that job, and actually, have already offered theoretical insights into microdevelopmental research (e.g., Fischer & Immordino-Yang, 2002; Granott, Fischer, & Parziale, 2002; Siegler, 1996b, 2006; see also chap. 5 in this book).

Discontinuity is a theoretical problem that includes the vexed question of stages in development, but it is broader than that. Developmental discontinuities may be global, such as Piagetian stages, or local, such as a rule shift in a specific task (e.g., Siegler, 1981). Sometimes, sophisticated nonlinear mathematical models have been proposed to account for developmental discontinuities; for instance, van der Maas and Molenaar (1992) have suggested use of the nonlinear models of catastrophe theory; and, indeed, Jansen and van der Maas (2001) offered an excellent account, based on the cusp catastrophe, of rule transition in the "balance scale problem." However, such models of discontinuity are often only descriptive. They provide a clear mathematical formulation of the relations between independent variables and observed behaviors, but they need to be complemented by psychologically explanatory accounts, that is, by theoretical insights on what the independent variables stand for in the child's mind and why they would account for the observed behaviors in the mathematically described way. Neo-Piagetian research has given considerable attention to issues of developmental discontinuity, both to explain those aspects of Piagetian stages that still retain some descriptive validity, and to model change in specific tasks (see especially chaps. 2 through 6 in this book). Therefore, we argue, there can be only benefit in dialogue between researchers who use nonlinear models, such as the catastrophe or the dynamic systems approaches, and the neo-Piagetians; the former provide new insight on the form of transitions and changes, and the latter provide theoretically grounded insights on the psychological mechanisms that underlie such transitions and changes.

Connectionist models have become increasingly popular in psychology, although there has been debate on which aspects of cognition do or do not lend themselves well to connectionist modeling (e.g., Fodor & Pylyshyn, 1988; Page, 2000), and strong arguments for connectionist modeling of cognitive development have been put forward by Elman et al. (1996) and Thomas and Karmiloff-Smith (2002). Connectionist models are composed of units or nodes, each of which has a variable degree of activation, and connections among units; also the strength of connections can change over time. One of the reasons why connectionist models are considered useful is that they include nonlinear relations among the model's parts, which, in turn, may account for nonlinearity and discontinuity in behavioral change. However, cognitive development might not be explained well just by changes that are internal to a given connectionist architecture (e.g., changes in the strength of its connections). The overall architecture itself may change, and it has been argued that, for a developing system, it may be convenient to "start small," learn simple concepts and rules, and then grow to have a larger architecture or processing capacity, which, in turn, can use the already-learned simple rules in order to learn more complex concepts (Elman, 1993). What is the nature of such changes in the architecture of the system and its processing capacity? Does it have anything to do with the developmental changes in working memory capacity (or similar constructs) that have been posited by neo-Piagetian theories? Probably yes, and at least one approach has systematically related connectionist modeling of representational change to a neo-Piagetian account of processing capacity (Halford, Wilson, & Phillips, 1998; see also chaps. 3 and 7).

Working memory capacity (that is, the capacity to hold various pieces of information simultaneously and to use them for further processing) is a critical feature of several models of human cognition, and it is widely recognized that it affects performance on many tasks. It has also been claimed that individual differences in working memory capacity account well for differences in measures of fluid intelligence (Engle, Tuholski, Laughlin, & Conway, 1999; Kyllonen, 2002). If so, working memory development should be highly relevant to the development of cognitive abilities in children—as neo-Piagetian authors have long been claiming (e.g., Case, 1995; Case & Okamoto, 1996; Halford, 1993a; Pascual-Leone & Johnson, 2005; see chaps. 2, 3, and 6). Cognitive researchers are now shifting to a theoretical paradigm that views working memory as the subset of long-term memory that is in the focus of attention at a given moment (Cowan, 2001, 2005; Engle, Kane, & Tuholski, 1999). This recent shift, if anything, makes more evident the need for students of cognitive development to use the abundant neo-Piagetian literature on working memory development, which is closely related to the attentional approach to working memory. Furthermore, there is an ongoing debate on the relationship among intelligence, working memory capacity, and speed of processing (Conway, Cowan, Bunting, Therriault, & Minkoff, 2002) as well as on the role of processing speed in cognitive development (e.g., Kail, 2000). Neo-Piagetian contributions are available on the speed/capacity issue (e.g., Demetriou, Christou, Spanoudis, & Platsidou, 2002; Halford, Maybery, O'Hare, & Grant, 1994) and more will presumably appear in the next years.

Inhibition and *executive control*, as psychological constructs, are complementary to those of activation and capacity; activating representations and focusing attention on them or, vice versa, withdrawing attention from them can be considered opposite functions. Executive processes are often understood as the ones involved in selecting, planning, organizing and monitoring action or thought (Lehto, Juujärvi, Kooistra, & Pulkkinen, 2003; Shallice & Burgess, 1993).[1] Zelazo and his colleagues have proposed a theory of executive function development, called Cognitive Complexity and Control (CCC) theory, according to which there is an age-related increase in the hierarchical complexity of the rules that children can use. A child who has performed a task following one set of rules could shift to other rules, conflicting with the previous ones, only if able to combine them into a (more complex) superordinate rule (Zelazo, Müller, Frye, & Marcovitch, 2003a, 2003b).[2] Others emphasize, instead, the role of other aspects of executive function, for example, the ability to inhibit a prepotent response tendency that, if not inhibited, would prevent children from using their knowledge (e.g., Kirkham, Cruess, & Diamond, 2003; Southgate, Gomez, & Meints, 2005) or from taking into account the task instructions in deceiving tasks

---

[1]Incidentally we note, as Shallice and Burgess (1993) remark, that Norman and Shallice's (1986) well-known model of the supervisory attentional system draws heavily on the Piagetian concept of scheme—which is another point of contact between neuropsychology, experimental psychology, and Piagetian developmental psychology, much in the same spirit of neo-Piagetian theories.

[2]Zelazo, Craik, and Booth (2004) extend the CCC theory to account also for the decline of executive function in ageing.

(Hughes, 1998; Russell, Mauthner, & Tidswell, 1991). Kirkham et al. (2003) give the name "attentional inertia" to children's (and also adults') difficulty to disengage attention from previously attended task features. Although there is debate on the nature of the processes involved in executive control, there is agreement (e.g., Diamond, 2002; Kirkham & Diamond, 2003; Lehto et al., 2003; Zelazo et al., 2003b) that the development of executive function involves development of both memory activation and inhibitory functions. We wish to note, too, that several types of inhibition have to be distinguished: (a) the mutual inhibition between competing schemes or representations, also called lateral inhibition, or "contention scheduling" by Norman and Shallice (1986); (b) automatic inhibition of representations of previously attended information that does not conflict with the current task requirements; (c) effortful selective inhibition of representations of currently salient information that conflicts with the task requirements; (d) effortful inhibition of previously active rules or procedural knowledge, which seems to be involved in paradigms that require children or adults to overcome attentional "inertia" (Allport & Wylie, 2000; Kirkham et al., 2003); and (e) response-withholding, such as in the stop-signal paradigm (e.g., Logan & Irwin, 2000). Valuable insights on the nature of inhibitory functions, and on the relationship between speed of processing, activation, and different forms of inhibition, have been provided by neo-Piagetian authors (e.g., Johnson, Im-Bolter, & Pascual-Leone, 2003). It is also important when analyzing children's performance on cognitive tasks to clarify the interaction between working memory or activation capacity on one side, and inhibition or selective attention on the other; on these matters, see chapters 2 and 9 in particular.

We have outlined some theoretically salient topics on which debate is currently lively and pointed to how neo-Piagetian research has been contributing ideas and results relevant to the issues involved. It would have been equally possible for us to focus on content domains (such as problem solving, language development, or the relationship between cognitive and emotional development), specific age ranges, or fields of applied research, and to argue that neo-Piagetian research continues to offer valuable contributions in those areas. Classical Piagetian theory, no doubt, also still has something to say. Even though several of its major claims have been superseded (as we argue in the following sections), reflection on Piaget's work keeps stimulating worthy efforts and useful clarifications (e.g., Amin & Valsiner, 2004; Beilin, 1992a; Desrochers, 2003; Niaz, 1998; Shayer, 2003). Nevertheless, one could hardly say—in Lakatos' (1970) terms—that the classical Piagetian research program is still progressive (see also Roth, Slone, & Dar, 2000). We hope to have persuaded the reader that neo-Piagetian research, however, with its history of some decades is still today quite a progressive program.

TWO PIAGETS

A book on neo-Piagetian research must certainly take Piaget as its point of departure, at the very least in order to clarify connections to his work by neo-Piagetians as well as their distinction from it. For this purpose we partition Piaget's work, distinguishing the logical Piaget from the dialectical Piaget. By "the logical Piaget," we mean his view of cognitive development as a sequence of stages defined in terms of logical competence; the "dialectical Piaget," instead, is concerned with developmental processes that generate new cognitive structures. This separation is partly arbitrary; the works of Piaget that present dialectical models of child development always express cognitive abilities in terms of logic. And vice versa, those texts that model the child's logical competence always display an implicit dialectical conception of development. By splitting Piaget in two, obviously we simplify and schematize. However, the rhetorical advantage of this strategy is to underline our argument that although the logical Piaget was superseded some time ago, the dialectical Piaget has great currency and remains fundamental to neo-Piagetian theory.

Piaget's research in the 1920s, presented in five volumes,[3] explored the child's representation of the world, of natural phenomena and of mechanical causation; the development of moral judgment and of verbal reasoning; and the relationship between language development and cognitive development. In these first works, Piaget was not yet formulating models of children's thought, but he was informally describing its characteristics in terms of "egocentrism" (inability to consider points of view different from one's own in the present moment), "transduction" (proceeding not from the general to the particular or vice versa, but from one particular to another, often on the basis of similarity), and insensitivity to contradictions along with vicious circles.

The first studies used verbal questions and responses almost exclusively. Although aware of the insufficiency of a verbal approach to cognition, only in the 1930s did Piaget study preverbal forms of intelligence in research on the first 2 years of life. The three volumes that present these studies describe in functional terms, with little formalization, the relations that the child progressively establishes with the world. The main theoretical constructs (discussed in subsequent chapters) introduced by Piaget in this period were *scheme, coordination of schemes, assimilation, accommodation,* and *organization* of the individual's mind as a totality. But in this same decade, for the first time, Piaget (1937/1959) introduced a formalization, based on the algebraic concept of *group*, to describe the development of the conception of space.

---

[3]See Flavell (1963) for a discussion of Piagetian research from the 1920s to the 1950s.

Piaget as Theorist of Logical Competence

The period from the 1940s to the 1960s was Piaget's most productive stage. He returned systematically to reasoning in childhood and preadolescence without limiting himself to verbal interviews, but also asking children to manipulate a variety of materials. In this period, he developed formal models of child cognition based on abilities of a logical nature. Consideration of such models is beyond the scope of this book; see instead Piaget (1952/1957, 1972), Inhelder and Piaget (1955/1958), Flavell (1963), Sheppard (1978). In particular, regarding preschoolers' logical abilities in the preoperational period (the "constituent functions"), the reader should consult Piaget, Grize, Szeminska, and Vinh Bang (1968/1977). To clarify what one means by a logical model of child cognition, we limit ourselves here to describing a single example.

Piaget and Szeminska (1941/1952) studied the development of the concept of number by means of a series of techniques. The best known of these consists of arranging two groups of objects in front of a child in parallel rows, in a manner such that their numerical equality is clear; then, one of the two rows is rearranged and the child's awareness of the persistence of the numerical equality is assessed. Examples of other techniques adopted include asking the child to reproduce an arrangement of objects exactly; to order a series of dolls and a series of sticks and then choose the stick corresponding to each doll; or to say whether, among two sets of clearly visible objects, there are more objects in a set arranged as 4 + 4 or in another arranged as 7 + 1. Different techniques, such as those just discussed, serve to explore different aspects of the concept of numbers (e.g., one-to-one correspondence, cardinality, ordinality, etc.). According to Piaget and Szeminska's data, the ability to count the number of objects in each arrangement did not play a crucial role in the solution of these problems, whereas the development of logical abilities was essential, as clarified in the following section. The latter were absent in the youngest children who responded on the basis of perceptual cues, such as the length of the row or the proximity of the objects to one another. Children in a subsequent stage succeeded in constructing a correspondence or a series, but "only believe in the established relationship as long as it is actually perceived" (Piaget & Szeminska, 1941/1952, p. 148). By the age of 6 to 7 years old, such logical competencies were well acquired. According to Piaget and Szeminska, in this later stage of development, children use a system of mental operations independent of the arrangement of the objects, and a series or a correspondence would be given in advance by a "logical act" that coordinates the relationship.

The comprehension of number presupposes, according to the authors: (a) logical operations of classification, by means of which classes can be included hierarchically one within another and subdivided into subclasses while keeping track of the broader class of which they are a part; (b) logical operations of seriation, such that the nth element can be considered both as the element that precedes the one in position $n + 1$ and, simultaneously, as the element that follows the one in position $n - 1$; (c) an equivalence relation among the elements that constitute a class, units that are distinct but interchangeable; (d) a logical operation of multiplication of asymmetric relations, by which if two rows of objects contain the same number of units, the longer row is also necessarily the less dense.

Perhaps it is not surprising that Piaget has described the psychological conception of number in terms of logical categories; number is a concept particularly suited to such analysis. According to Piaget, however, the *logical properties* of part–whole relations and of ordinal relations are also fundamental to mental operations of the sort that he calls "infra-logical," such as the conceptual representation of time and of space (Piaget & Inhelder, 1947/1967).

The theory that every normal individual's cognition develops across the sensorimotor, preoperational (or intuitive), concrete operational and formal operational stages took form in the 1940s. Each of these stages is characterized by logical capabilities of growing generality and complexity.[4] The abilities of the last two stages in particular are characterized by logical operations, or, in psychological terms, *internalized* and *reversible actions*. According to Piaget (1972), "a psychologically equilibrated structure is, at the same time, a logically formalizable structure. . . . Logic is the axiomatics of the operational structures, whose actual functioning is studied by cognitive psychologists and sociologists" (p. 15). Similarly, Piaget (1952) states, "Operational logic is an algebraic theory of structures, and it is in the functioning of these that actual thought displays a logic" (p. 81).

Piaget's Dialectical View of Development

In what sense then do we portray a dialectical Piaget alongside the logical Piaget? In philosophical language the term *dialectic* refers to the constant transformation of reality by means of contradictions among contrasting processes. Such contradictions produce qualitative leaps or syntheses

---

[4]The passage from the sensorimotor stage to the preoperational stage is characterized by the ability to establish symbolic representations; therefore, one cannot speak of logical competence in the sensorimotor stage. Even when Piaget introduces an algebraic notation for this stage, he only intends to formally represent practical competencies. We list here, for readers who have some familiarity with logic, the logical competencies of the subsequent stages. At the preoperational stage the child's logical competences do not go beyond function. Those of the concrete operational stage are expressed by "groupings" (similar to algebraic groups, in which however the associative property is not general). The competencies of the formal operational stage are characterized by propositional calculus, with group and lattice structures defined over the set of 16 binary propositions.

qualitatively different from each of the two preexisting elements of the contradiction. Thus, the development of any particular aspect of reality is not understood as a gradual, linear accumulation of small or large changes adding on to that which preexisted. Rather, development is viewed as a conflictual process by means of which the gradual, cumulative processes give rise to qualitative changes, to new situations that cannot be compared to the preceding ones simply in terms of quantitative differences. By this account, the new situations will, in their turn, become characterized by new contradictions, and for this reason, it is not possible to conceive of a final state of development that is not subject to contradiction.

The question of how close Piaget's conception of mental development is to the dialectical philosophy worldview has given rise to interesting debates, although with little communication among them, in France (Bronckart & Parot-Locatelli, 1977; Goldmann, 1966, 1970; Jalley, 1977; Le Ny, 1977), in North America (Buck-Morss, 1975; Buss, 1977; Lawler, 1975; Moessinger, 1977; Wozniak, 1975), also with a Genevan contribution to the American debate (Sinclair, 1978), and in Italy (Amann Gainotti, 1980).

Controversy exists on the relationship between Piaget and dialectic because the philosophical influences on Piaget were actually multiple and heterogeneous. In the introduction to *The Origins of Intelligence in Children*, Piaget (1936/1952) makes clear the postulates from which his research program begins. There one finds an interactive conception of intelligence, understood as adaptation to the environment by means of exchanges (exchanges of information, as we would call them today). These exchanges are constituted by processes of assimilation of external reality and accommodation to it, with the complementarity of these regulated by the "organization" function of the individual. But together with this interactive, dialectical view of intelligence, one finds Aristotelian and Kantian echoes, including a dozen *a priori* categories of reasoning (structured whole, relation, end, means, quality, class, quantity, number, object, space, causality, and time). These categories, pre-established in a manner somewhat at odds with Piaget's usual depth of thought, actually constitute a considerable portion of his research's field of inquiry. Thus the contrast between the dialectical idea of an organism that develops through interacting with the environment and the metaphysical idea of categories of reasoning that are "in a certain sense preformed" (Piaget, 1936/1952, p. 16) runs through Piaget's own philosophical presuppositions. No wonder then that different judgments are expressed with regard to the dialectical, or nondialectical, character of Piagetian theory in the interdisciplinary discussions among psychologists and philosophers.

Bidell (1988) suggests that Piaget and Vygotsky share dialectical conceptions in common, conceptions that are of considerable importance (if made explicit) for research methodology in developmental psychology. In particular, Bidell maintains that the study of interrelationships between cognitive development's social aspects and its individual aspects is the most fertile ground for the elaboration of theories that might develop the dialectical position of both the Piagetian approach and of the Vygotskian approach, extending the scope of both.

Piaget (1964/1967) discusses mental development in terms of *genesis* and *structure*. He defines mental structure as a system (for example, a system of mental operations) endowed with its own laws, but partial with respect to the totality of the psyche. Genesis is defined as a transformation beginning from a state A and concluding in a more stable state B. In contrast with the Gestalt conceptions, which he considered "a structuralism without genesis" and with the behaviorist conceptions, "genesis without structures" (p. 145), Piaget argues that the two aspects are inseparable and formulates two theses: (1) "Genesis emanates from a structure and culminates in a structure" (p. 147); and (2) "Every structure has a genesis" (p. 149). In such a way, Piaget formulates a theory of qualitative leaps in mental development. Even if the genesis of new structures is attributed to factors that act in a relatively continuous manner (maturation, experience, and an equilibration factor, to be discussed in the following section) their outcome is not a uniform development, a "genesis without structures," but a development through discontinuous stages. Each successive phase restructures the concepts and operations of the previous phases and confers on them a new meaning, placing them in a qualitatively different and more complex structure.

It is characteristic of Piaget to seek the roots of logic in *action*, presenting sensorimotor intelligence as the point of departure for a process that, through successive restructurings, leads to operational intelligence. The logical operations themselves are conceptualized as interiorized actions.

In the 1970s, Piaget closely investigated the role of action in cognitive development; (in particular, he studied by means of practical problems of some complexity "the affiliation of knowing to doing" (Piaget, 1974/1978, p. v). For example, children were asked to steer a boat with a jammed rudder or to construct a bridge with bits and pieces of wood. The latter task requires a practical understanding of the concept of weight (not as a general force that somehow restrains objects, but as a direct downward force), of counterweight, of a force's point of application, of the effects of differences in weight, as well as an intuition of the location of an object's center of gravity. It is not necessary that the children understand conceptually these notions, but they cannot commit practical errors with respect to them lest their constructions collapse, as sometimes happened to the youngest children. Obviously, it is not easy to analyze the nature of this practical knowledge. In brief, Piaget believes that the results of actions on objects provoke, as feedback, regulations of the actions themselves, and that becoming cognizant of such regulations makes the acquisition of concepts possible. The composition, in turn, of regulations that deal with the same set of actions makes possible the "inferential coordinations" (preoperational functions and concrete operations).

Piaget (1974/1978) considers action as "know-how" (p. 213), which precedes conceptual knowledge: "Cognizance . . . start[s] from the external results of the action, later engage[s] in the analysis of the means employed and finally bear[s] on the general coordinates (reciprocity, transitivity, etc.)," but on the other hand, "from a certain level onwards, there is a reverse effect of conceptualization on action" (p. 214). The role of action in the development of knowledge as proposed by Piaget is reminiscent of the role of praxis (goal-directed human action) in knowledge of the external world according to an important thread of dialectical philosophy (e.g., the "Theses on Feuerbach" of the young Marx, 1845/1976).

The central problem of any theory of cognitive development is to specify the mechanisms that allow new acquisitions. In Piagetian terms, it is necessary to explain the genesis of the preoperational and operational cognitive structures. In a work that presents a thoroughly dialectical interpretation of mental development, Piaget (1975/1985) confronts the problem of the "process that leads from a state near equilibrium to a qualitatively different state at equilibrium by way of multiple disequilibria and reequilibrations" (p. 3). Roth et al. (2000) regard the concept of equilibration as the hard core of Piaget's research program, and Flavell (1996, p. 201) remarks: "In elaborating his equilibration model, Piaget was one of the first psychologists to make a serious try at explaining as well as describing cognitive development." According to Piaget, a cognitive system is in equilibrium when it can assimilate external reality to its schemes, or it can easily accommodate these schemes to reality by means of already acquired compensatory mechanisms. A system in equilibrium tends to conserve itself; and thus, disequilibria, which "alone force the subject to go beyond his current state," (Piaget, 1975/1985, p. 10) are a source of progress in the development of knowledge. They set in motion reequilibration processes, understood not as a return to the preceding equilibrium, but as the achievement of a new one.

There are two types of disturbances or perturbations, and subjects can react to these with regulations, that is, by modifying their way of acting. The first type, for Piaget, is composed of the resistances that objects present to the accommodation of schemes. These resistances result in failure or error that constitutes negative feedback for subjects. The second type of perturbation is found in the insufficient assimilations of reality on the part of the already activated schemes or in their unsatisfied needs. These could provoke a search for new information and therefore, with the prolongation of the same scheme's assimilative activity, give rise to positive feedback. In each case, "it is always when a lacuna turns up, and because of the perturbations that are either its source or its result, that a new endeavor is undertaken" (Piaget, 1975/1985, p. 139). The subject seeks to avoid incoherence (a concept that neo-Piagetians, too, accept in various ways) and therefore tends toward forms of equilibrium, which are achieved, however, only occasionally and temporarily. Each achievement opens onto new problems owing to the potential operations it is always possible to construct on the basis of the preceding ones.

Piaget describes three ways in which the subject could react in order to compensate perturbations. The simplest reaction is to ignore the perturbation, deforming the interpretation of reality in such a way as to be able to constrain it within one's schemes. Reactions of this type are only partially compensatory and lead to a rather unstable equilibrium. For example, consider a length seriation task, in which a young child has been able to arrange only a pair of sticks or a triad (short, middle, long). On receiving more sticks to be placed into the series, that child might use them to arrange more pairs or triads and ignore the experimenter's request to make a single series with all of the sticks.

A second type of response is to modify the cognitive system, introducing new relations that permit an integration of the perturbations into the system and an assimilation of the unexpected circumstance. For instance, a child who has already arranged three sticks in order of length, on receiving more sticks could undo that arrangement and, perhaps by way of trial and error, take into account the relations among them and eventually succeed in placing a larger number of elements in the appropriate order.

Finally, the most advanced reaction is to anticipate the possible variations (which, by such anticipation, lose their status as perturbations and become part of the cognitive system as potential transformations). To keep with the length seriation example, a child who has just ordered three sticks, on receiving more, could compare their length with those already arranged and place the new ones directly in the appropriate serial positions.

The problem, of course, is to explain how the subject moves from the elementary reactions to the more advanced ones. Though we cannot describe it in detail here, Piaget's general model of the equilibration process consists of a series of interactions between "observables" (observations that subjects make with respect to their actions and operations or with respect to external objects) and "coordinations" (inferences that subjects draw with respect to their activity, or causal relationships that they are able to establish among external objects). These interactions give rise to "a succession of states indicating progressive equilibration" (Piaget, 1975/1985, p. 47).

New schemes also derive from the equilibration process. That is because regulations, in addition to compensating the perturbations that resist the activation of an already existing scheme, also produce new observables and coordinations concerning the subject's activity. In their turn, these new observables and coordinations permit attributions of new causal relationships in the external world. As for the initially activated scheme, "either it was acquired, and therefore itself proceeded from similar developmental processes, or it was innate. In the latter case it would be the product of regulations or compensations of an organic nature" (Piaget, 1975/1985, p. 68).

However, the nature of "regulation" remains rather indeterminate in Piaget's model. By definition, regulation consists of each repercussion from the effects of an action A on its new execution A'. But how do these repercussions come about? If the previously acquired schemes only permit an assimilation of reality that is full of gaps (lacunae), if they produce systematic errors, how is it possible that the individual, on the basis of these schemes and their regulations, builds new schemes or cognitive structures? If we say that the regulations consist of feedback mechanisms, we simply give the process another name without explaining it. In fact, one could pose the question as: How does the subject manage not only to be sensitive to the feedback (noticing errors, lacunae, and perturbations) but also to benefit from it in constructing new schemes and more equilibrated cognitive structures?

Piaget (1975/1985) suggests that lacunae on the perceptual or representational level are "characterized by the impossibility of dealing with everything at once, owing to the limitations of the field of . . . attention" (p. 114). The scheme that a child is using "retains certain characteristics of objects" (p. 115), but exerts a negative pressure on elements that have cognitive "contradictions or incompatibilities" with it (p. 115)—elements that are then omitted or repressed. It is actually those elements "that up to then have been omitted" that give rise to feedback mechanisms: perturbation will form from the "tendency for an element initially 'repressed' to penetrate the field of observables" (p. 116). The hypothesized process has a dialectical character; as Inhelder (1982) observed, two originally independent systems become integrated into a new whole that goes beyond each of them. Yet, what is it that confers on the "initially repressed" elements the power "to penetrate the field of observables," to cause new coordinations and inferences, to expand the field of attention, to introduce new relations in the cognitive system and finally to provide a new, more stable equilibrium?

The attempt to answer these questions, to shed light on the "causal mechanisms of Piaget's mysterious regulations" (Pascual-Leone, 1988, p. 431), forms a considerable part of the neo-Piagetian research program.

PROBLEMS FOR THE DEVELOPMENTAL THEORY OF LOGICAL COMPETENCE

In the preceding section we have pointed out the contrast between the Piagetian theory of *logical competence* and the Piagetian theory of *equilibration*, the former defined by logico-mathematical structures in which the principle of noncontradiction is fundamental, whereas in the latter contradictions are the engine of cognitive development. The contrast is not irresolvable: according to Piaget at each level of cognitive development, the contradictions among the products of mental operations trigger equilibration processes that create more general logico-mathematical structures capable of resolving these contradictions. We have pointed out, as well, an incompleteness in the theory of equilibration that neo-Piagetian approaches seek to fill in. Now we intend to evaluate the Piagetian theory of cognitive competencies: indeed, the Piaget that one finds most often in the textbooks is still the Piaget of logical operations.

Today it is widely recognized that logic is not an adequate model for the cognitive abilities of children, nor is it adequate for adults (Evans, 2002; Flavell, 1982; Gobbo, 1991a). In his final works, Piaget himself (1977, 1980) recognized that the operational theory is too strongly tied to classical extensional logic and that its truth tables lead to paradoxes on the psychological level. He mentions, as an alternative, a "logic of meanings" (Piaget, 1980, p. 3) that, unfortunately, he was not able to fully develop. A posthumous book (Piaget & Garcia, 1987/1991) presents his ideas on inferences as implications between meanings (which are attributed to objects, to their properties, and to the actions themselves), and on the early formation, at the level of actions and their meanings, of operations that are isomorphic to the 16 binary operations of propositional logic. Therefore, the solution Piaget was striving for was founding psycho-logic on meaning, and meaning on action. Despite the interest of that attempt, it seems unlikely that it could save Piaget's theory of operational logic from mounting criticism.

Synchrony and "Horizontal Décalage"

Some anomalies[5] faced by the operational theory were already widely debated in the 1970s and 1980s. First of all, let us consider the holistic nature of operational structures: for example, the concrete operations reduce to eight logical forms ("groupings") with equally general properties (Piaget, 1952/1957). For this reason, they should be acquired more or less simultaneously. Researchers who have examined the development of different concrete operational structures in the same individuals have, however, painted a more complex picture (Jamison, 1977; Lautrey, de Ribaupierre, & Rieben, 1985; Toussaint, 1974).[6]

---

[5]Kuhn (1962) designates as anomalies those data that, without appearing immediately as a falsification of a theory, do not clearly conform to it, and in fact require *ad hoc* explanations.

[6]Comparing the time of acquisition of different logical structures requires equating the materials, the information load, the response modality, and so on, varying only the logical structure of the tasks. The studies that fulfill these requirements to a satisfactory degree provide contra-

A glaring anomaly is provided by the temporal displacements in the acquisition of logically equivalent concepts, called "horizontal *décalages*" in the Piagetian jargon. The best-known example is that of the "conservation" of mass, weight, and volume. If two equal balls of clay are presented to a 7-year-old, and if one of them is pressed flat or rolled out, the child will probably recognize that they still contain the same quantity of clay after the transformation. Yet prior to age 9, few will recognize that they still have the same weight, and only around age 11 will the child comprehend that they continue to fill the same volume (Piaget & Inhelder, 1941/1974). Given that the logical abilities required of the child are the same in all three cases (very similar to those required in order to grasp numerical invariance, which was mentioned previously), Piaget and Inhelder have to appeal to extralogical concepts to explain the *décalage*. They maintain that different objects, or different properties of the same objects, present different "resistances" to assimilation by the operational structure. Although there is certainly nothing absurd in this explanation, it is not theoretically satisfying because the theory specifies only the logical operations, not the object properties that "resist" those operations, nor the psychological mechanism of such resistance (Legrenzi, 1975). Thus, each time that some theoretical prediction fails, the theory can be saved by reference to the resistance of the objects; but this argument puts one in the embarrassing situation of proposing an unfalsifiable theory.

According to some authors (Fischer, 1980a; Flavell, 1963; Klahr & Wallace, 1976; Siegler, 1981) temporal displacements in mid-childhood are the rule rather than the exception. Chapman and Lindenberger (1988), for example, present a systematic study of *décalages* in the operation of seriation. It is worth noting that the horizontal *décalages* appear not only in the acquisition of logically equivalent concepts, but also in the solution of practical problems.[7]

Adults' Errors of Logic

Another source of anomalies is given by the performance of adults in reasoning problems. For Piaget (1952/1957), formal operations are the final stage of cognitive development. Adults and adolescents, according to the theory (Inhelder & Piaget, 1955/1958), should be able to reason in a hypothetico-deductive manner about propositions, using the 16 binary combina-

dictory results. However, according to some authors the synchronization hypothesis is not essential to Piaget's theory (de Ribaupierre, 1993).

[7]For example, Piaget (1974/1978) asks children to direct an automobile with its steering wheel already turned, or a boat with a turned rudder, toward a finish line directly ahead of the starting point. The solution of letting the model go from an oblique position is achieved around 7 years for the steering wheel, around 9 years for the rudder.

tions of the propositions p, not-p, q, not-q.[8] Thanks to the acquisition of these competencies they should also understand proportionality and be able to verify hypotheses by systematically isolating the variables as necessary.

From many studies, however, it emerges that normal, well-educated adults do not reason in a manner as logical as that predicted by the Piagetian theory, and not because of a lack of carefulness, but rather because they follow systematic strategies or biases (adequate in certain cases, inadequate in others) that are not describable in logical terms (see Johnson-Laird, 1983, on adult reasoning; see Keating, 1979, on adolescent reasoning; Neimark, 1979;).

A good example, although it is not a Piagetian one, is found in Wason's (1968) four-card problem. Each card has a letter on one side and a number on the other. Presented first is the sentence "If there is a vowel on one side of the card, then there is an even number on the other," a sentence that has the logical form of implication, one of the 16 binary propositions. Then four cards, on which one might see, for example, an E, an M, a 4, and a 7, are presented and the individual is asked which cards must be turned over in order to determine whether the sentence is true or false. Numerous experiments indicate that adults do not usually represent the sentence according to the truth table for implication, and that they rarely consider the cases that could falsify the rule (e.g., see Evans, 2002). For this reason, to propose the presence of particular logical structures is not a valid explanation of adult competence, given the results from the many studies that demonstrate the fallaciousness of adult reasoning. Of course, one can defend Piaget's theory by objecting that logical competence could be present but not manifest itself with equal ease in all contexts or tasks. However, like in the case of "horizontal *décalage*," one would like to know what reasons make this task so difficult for persons who should have acquired formal operations. Once again, the Piagetian theory seems to be, at best, incomplete.

Precocious Logical Reasoning in Children

Another important anomaly, in a sense opposite to the previous one, is seen in correct solutions to some problems by children who, according to Piaget, should not yet have developed the logical competencies necessary to find those solutions. Precocious solutions are reported, for example, in problems of seriation (Halford, 1989), conservation (Field, 1987) and inclusion (Rabinowitz, Howe, & Lawrence, 1989; Wilkinson, 1976; Winer, 1980). In

---

[8]According to Inhelder and Piaget (1955/1958), the formal logical properties of the INRC group and the lattice can actually be found in adolescents' verbal explanations of their responses.

general, these studies show that manipulating logically irrelevant variables can facilitate solution.

Even Wason's four-card problem can be modified in its administration by teaching the correct interpretation of the sentence and placing the question in a context that makes the search for counterexamples plausible. In doing so, correct solutions are obtained even from 6-year-olds (Legrenzi & Murino, 1974). Even though the form of the problem is the same, that is, testing an *if–then* rule, a rule with "deontic" content (such as a permission or obligation) elicits "pragmatic schemes" and renders the task much easier (Cheng, Holyoak, Nisbett, & Oliver, 1986). Evidence of correct reasoning with deontic rules has also been found in preschoolers (e.g., Harris & Nuñez, 1996).

In line with Piaget, some authors, among them Halford (1989) and Case (1985, 1992), argue that often the precociousness of solutions is only an appearance, and they criticize the inadequate procedures that alter the nature of the problems in some studies. Nevertheless, they also maintain that the solution of many concrete operational problems can be advanced to about 5 years of age.

These findings tell us more than the fact that children between 5 and 7 years old have abilities unrecognized by Piaget and that it is difficult to determine whether a child has entered the concrete operational stage. As Legrenzi (1975) notes, the most important theoretical implication of the influence of a multiplicity of heterogeneous variables, such as the linguistic form of the instructions, the nature of the materials, the information load and the familiarity of the task, is to raise the difficult problem of completing the Piagetian theory by specifying psychological processes or information processing mechanisms that can account for the gap between children's logical competence and their performance. This idea is also shared and supported by many neo-Piagetians.

Cross-Cultural Differences in Developmental Pathways

A final source of anomalies is found in cross-cultural research. There are universal aspects, independent from cultural context, in the Piagetian stages and, in particular, in the sensorimotor stage (Dasen & Heron, 1981; Parker, 1978); but there are also aspects strongly influenced by the cultural context. Dasen (1975), for example, reports a very interesting fact: spatial concepts of the concrete-operations level develop at a much earlier age among Inuit children growing up in a nomadic Arctic hunting and fishing culture than among Ebrié children in a settled African farming culture or among European children. On the other hand, the Ebrié children acquire conservation concepts earlier than do the Inuit children. From this and other data (Dasen & Heron, 1981; Heron & Dowel, 1973, 1974; Peluffo, 1967) showing that two concepts that develop in lockstep in Geneva may develop at very different paces in other cultures where one of the concepts is more relevant or useful for survival; one could then conclude that the structured wholes (*structures-d'ensemble*) posited for Genevan children are not necessarily valid elsewhere.

Strictly speaking, none of the research cited here constitutes by itself a falsification of the Piagetian stage theory of operational development; often *ad hoc* explanations are possible (e.g., by considering how a particular operational ability will manifest itself in different contexts). But a large body of such studies appeared in the 1970s and, taken together, they convinced some researchers that the stage concept was inadequate for describing cognitive development. Flavell (1982) suggests that if there are stage-like aspects of cognitive development, they should be sought in other, non-Piagetian directions—for example, in the acquisition of broadly applicable schemes and scripts, in the development of the ability to process an increasing quantity of information, and perhaps in adults' social expectations for children of a given age.

As becomes clear as we proceed, neo-Piagetian theories retain an idea of stage, but not one based on logical competences. The neo-Piagetian theories, however, better specify the mechanisms of development and provide explicit accounts of the phenomenon of *décalage*.

WHO KILLED GENETIC EPISTEMOLOGY?

A host of research results, some of which have been cited here, cast into doubt the logical Piaget. But what has become of the dialectical Piaget? What can we say today about the concepts of genesis and structure, of practical success and grasp of consciousness, of equilibration, perturbations, and regulation? Has the nature of regulation been cleared up? Has cognitive research surpassed the dialectical Piaget as well as the logical Piaget?

The Evidence

In our opinion, the research results are not mortal blows against the dialectical Piaget, but rather the dialectical Piaget has simply been forgotten or ignored. Reese (1993) traces the history of child psychology in North America, where, in the 1950s and 1960s, experimental research revolved around the work of behaviorist researchers. After a brief interlude during which Piagetian theory was in vogue, the cognitive revolution of the 1970s (analogously with the behaviorist one of the 1950s) imported a theoretical framework from general psychology—the Human Information Processing approach. We think that, within that framework, the dialectical Piaget's questions about developmental processes were extraneous—even if from a structuralist and constructivist point of view, they were indeed crucial.

Whereas, in the 1970s, American and English experimenters, although critical of stage theory, explored classical Genevan research themes (logical operations, number, space, time, etc.) there was a move in the opposite direction within the Piagetian school. As Brown and Weiss (1987) observed, a result of other schools' attacks on the concepts of stage and *structures d'ensemble* was that research in Geneva during that period focused on such themes as contradictions, equilibration, reflective abstraction and the psychological mechanisms of regulation. Berthoud and Ackermann-Valladao (1980) dedicate an entire article to demonstrating that the problems proposed by genetic epistemology can be studied with the methods of experimental psychology. Nevertheless, different research groups often seemed deaf to one another, or better, there seemed to be a case of "incommensurable paradigms" (Kuhn, 1962) within a scientific discipline.

A well-known case of this apparent deafness at that time is provided by Brainerd's (1978) analysis of the stage concept. Brainerd argues that the Piagetian concept of stage could possibly have descriptive value for indicating behaviors typical of more or less arbitrarily delimited developmental periods, but could not have explanatory value. In fact, according to Brainerd, an explanatory construct requires identification of *antecedent* variables (for example, maturational plateaus or reinforcement contingencies) that are *independently measurable* and that produce the described changes in the dependent variable (the behavioral stages). Moreover, he sees equilibration as "the vaguest and most tentative" of the criteria for identifying stages, because Piaget did not specify its "exact empirical consequences" (pp. 179–180). However, it seems that Brainerd interprets equilibration as existence of an initial period within a stage, characterized (perhaps for biological reasons) by rapid and numerous acquisitions, followed by a period of greater stability of the cognitive structure.[9] It is against this conception of equilibration that Brainerd directs the debate and cites evidence of incompatible results.

Brainerd's essay attracted a number of heated responses. Some objected that the concepts of atom or gene, certainly created in the absence of procedures for their identification or measurement, have an explanatory value because they provide an account of a number of facts (Ennis, 1978; Kurtines, 1978). Others (Bickhard, Cooper, & Mace, 1985; Wetherick, 1978) ob-

---

[9]It seems likely, according to this view, that Brainerd (1978) confused equilibration with another Piagetian concept, namely stage consolidation. What is more, some of the other authors taking part in the debate on Brainerd (1978) seem to be suffering from a similar misunderstanding.

served that Brainerd was not espousing "the" scientific conception of *explanation*, but rather "a" conception, one strongly influenced by Humean empiricism and by the first formulations of logical positivism. Some accused him of misinterpreting or distorting essential aspects of Piagetian thought (Karmiloff-Smith, 1978; Klahr, 1978b). Undoubtedly, Brainerd represents an extreme point of view, which, however, seems to us emblematic of the manner in which genetic epistemology has been criticized *more on metatheoretical bases than on factual ones*, especially in influential American research centers. Of course, our observation does not imply the validity of the Piagetian theses regarding knowledge development, but does point to the way in which they have been abandoned without adequate attempts to verify them.

We have underlined here the weight of researchers' metatheoretical views. Does that mean, perhaps, that observations and experimental data have little importance or that they are, so to speak, only a corollary of *a priori* convictions? No, we believe that the ultimate measure of a research program's value always lies in the facts it is able to produce and explain. What we wish to point out, nevertheless, is that a scientist's philosophical preconceptions (explicit or implicit) considerably influence the way in which that scientist poses problems and defines both theoretical concepts and the experimental variables themselves.

Because of this, Reese (1993) recommends teaching developmental psychology students a variety of theoretical approaches and providing them with a solid base in philosophy of science as well, given that different theoretical approaches "reflect different philosophies, or world views" (p. 519). American experimental child psychology, Reese observes further, has had a mechanistic approach, as opposed to the Piagetian organic approach. In spite of the influence of English translations of Piaget, Luria, and Vygotsky, and despite some important exceptions (such as Riegel, 1979) dialectic "was not appreciated by most United States developmentalists" (Reese, 1993, p. 519).

Also Voyat (1980) noted that Piaget was interpreted in the United States either as a neomaturationist or as a neobehaviorist, clearly pointing out American culture's difficulty, at that time, with the concept of interaction between individual and environment and with the idea of internal regulation leading to new constructions. Indeed, we are dealing with concepts that although completely comprehensible within the frame of dialectical conceptions in the European philosophical tradition, are extraneous to empiricism from which the North American philosophical culture derives.

Among the motives that have led cognitive research, *de facto*, to dismiss the dialectical Piaget, we find both philosophical resistance and the rapid passage (with psychology's cognitive revolution) from the rat-in-the-cage metaphor to the computer metaphor, neglecting other possible metaphors preferred by Piaget: for example, the organism that interactively adapts to its environment, or the scientist who modifies his knowledge through verification and restructuring of hypotheses. Although simplistic, perhaps the computer metaphor (propositional symbolic representations, serial or parallel processing models) was necessary at the beginning of the cognitive revolution as an intelligible, culturally acceptable alternative to the philosophical conceptions of the behaviorists.

It is possible that the lasting success of the computer metaphor is also associated with the general cultural climate of the times. The predominance in the Western world of a cultural model based on individual consumption and status symbols, and that above all requires efficiency, competitiveness and conformity renders culturally irrelevant (in a certain sense) any discourse on the critical attitude and on the self-modification of knowledge, both of which have been emphasized by Piagetian-oriented educators. Thus, the computer metaphor may have enjoyed a certain ideological support: that psychologists study the efficiency of the human computer's architecture or its ability to represent knowledge seems relevant, whereas study of contradictions, dialectic and other "old-fashioned" matters seems out of place.

It should be noted in this regard that the most important neo-Piagetian authors, although acknowledging the merits of metaphors that compare the mind's architecture to that of a computer, have strongly argued for a theoretical synthesis between Human Information Processing concepts and Piagetian ones. We also note that, after misunderstanding Piaget, a number of authors have inappropriately interpreted the neo-Piagetian theories exclusively in terms of information processing, often treating them as if they were models of the development of a short-term memory store. In this sense, even though the neo-Piagetian theories offer a bridge between Human Information Processing and genetic epistemology, not many researchers have been able to cross that bridge—the majority held back by the philosophical resistance that hinders understanding of both Piaget and the neo-Piagetians.

The Verdict

The Piagetian legacy is manifold (see also Beilin, 1992b; Flavell, 1996). First of all, it includes the discovery of an impressive variety of phenomena as well as explanations of these phenomena that according to some reviews (e.g., Bond, 1998; Halford, 1989) are, in good part, still valid. It also includes a theory of logical competence and of its stage-wise development, which, however, is now widely considered inadequate. Finally, it includes a theory of equilibration processes and transitions in cognitive development. Despite incompleteness on certain points (for example, the concept of regulation seems insufficiently specified), it is our opinion that this theory has a certain plausibility and could still be fruitful; yet, it has been unduly neglected in experimental research. Smith (1993) concludes a broad analysis of critical evaluations of Piaget's work recognizing that his theory remains a fundamental reference point for identifying questions concerning development, and that it will not be possible to call a developmental theory adequate unless it is able to answer such questions better than Piaget's theory does.

The solutions proposed by the neo-Piagetians are substantially different from those offered by Piaget, and as we see, they also differ somewhat among themselves. Nevertheless, neo-Piagetians, in contrast to other contemporary scholars, mean to formulate theories *at least as general* as Piaget's. With respect to transitions in cognitive development, the innovations in the proposed solutions do not imply a dismissal of the critical questions raised by Piaget. In fact, not only the major neo-Piagetian theorists, but also some perhaps wrongly considered minor, have explicitly tried to maintain, like Piaget, a fully constructivist concept of cognitive development.

In short, our verdict is that although a certain short-sightedness on the part of cognitive psychology (its empiricist presuppositions, its contradiction-free flowcharts) has nearly resulted in the death of genetic epistemology, viable possibilities for a vibrant life are clearly visible. Accordingly, in the following chapters we shall examine how neo-Piagetian researchers have drawn key ideas from the psychology of Human Information Processing and proposed new solutions to the problems left open by the dialectical Piaget.

SETTING THE STAGE FOR NEO-PIAGETIAN THEORIES

In this section we consider some concepts that were emerging in cognitive and developmental research in the 1960s and 1970s, and that have contributed in important ways to the start of neo-Piagetian theories. We focus, in turn, on information load, representation, and cognitive strategies, and deal with those concepts not as they are seen currently by cognitive researchers, but rather, as they were discussed at the time when neo-Piagetian research was taking its first steps.

Information Load and Task Complexity

The capacity to process an increasing quantity of information with age is one of the principal starting points of neo-Piagetian approaches to cognitive development. Piaget had already considered the phenomenon early on, noting the "narrowness of the field of attention" in children.

... a far wider field of attention is required to handle a relational judgment than to handle a predicative judgment. ... Every relation requires that the subject be conscious of at least two objects at the same time. ... But ... it still remains to be explained why the child has a narrower field of attention than ours. (Piaget, 1924/1965, pp. 218–219)

The explanation proposed by Piaget is that the narrower field of attention and egocentrism both derive "from primitive habits of thought, which consist in taking immediate personal perception as something absolute, and both bring in their wake an inability to handle the logic of relations" (Piaget, 1924/1965, p. 221). So the child keeps in mind a lesser quantity of information than the adult does, but Piaget views this narrowness as a consequence of "primitive habits" of thought, that is, as a consequence (rather than the cause) of the limited generality of the child's acquired structures (see Chapman, 1987, for a discussion; see also Piaget, 1975/1985).

As soon as doubts arise regarding the account of cognitive development in terms of logical competencies, the idea that the explanation of children's limited attentional capacity might be reversed also emerges. Perhaps the growth of what Piaget called the *field of attention* is a cause (rather than consequence) of the development of logical and infra-logical competence. The earliest neo-Piagetian investigations are clearly characterized by hypotheses of this kind (Case, 1974a; Halford, 1970b; Pascual-Leone & Smith, 1969).

The growth of cognitive psychology created a favorable climate in this regard. Miller (1956) had suggested measuring human processing capacity by means of *subjective* measures (units measured not by any of their intrinsic properties, but rather by the meaning they acquire in the coding process, that is, in the experience of the *subject*). Certainly an important problem to resolve is how to identify such subjective units, units to which Miller gave the name *chunks*. Taking Miller's chunks, along with Piaget's schemes, as the basic units of cognition is one of the first important ideas in the founding of a neo-Piagetian approach. Pascual-Leone (1970) suggests that older children are able to hold in mind simultaneously a greater number of chunks or schemes, and therefore can also solve Piagetian problems better.

We briefly describe here two studies (Frith & Frith, 1978; Scardamalia, 1977) that exemplify well the idea of such an age-related increase in the amount of information that a child can process.

Scardamalia (1977) reconsiders a combinatorial reasoning problem that Piaget and Inhelder (1951/1975) studied and which they considered to be classified as formal operational. Although the logical structure of the task is a generalization of the multiplication of classes (a typical concrete operation; see Piaget, 1952/1957), they consider it a formal problem because it requires reasoning about combinatorial possibilities (rather than givens), with a potentially infinite number of dimensions. Piaget and Inhelder (1951/

1975) note that children of 12–13 years, in contrast to older ones, only succeed in using a systematic strategy with a reduced number of variables. By way of explanation they suggest that the 12-year-olds have not yet consolidated the formal structure.

However, Scardamalia (1977) suggests that this is an example of *horizontal décalage* and that the decisive factor determining the difficulty of the task is its *information load*. She demonstrates it with an experiment in which she asks children of different ages to solve problems based on an increasing number of dimensions. Using materials that vary along several dimensions (e.g., shapes, colors, background symbols; in all, there were up to eight dimensions in the hardest items) children are asked to construct all possible combinations that can be made with one value of each dimension (for instance, given the just-mentioned dimensions, make a green square with a background of little crosses, a blue square with a background of little crosses, and so on). She found that children of 8 to 9 years of age succeed on problems with four dimensions, those of age 11 succeed with five dimensions, and adults even with seven dimensions. These results show that success on this combinatorial reasoning problem does not depend on having reached the formal operational stage; in fact, even 8-year-olds are able to do it. Instead consideration of information load becomes fundamental. In fact, the children in this experiment, although capable of solving the problem with a particular number of dimensions, *no longer succeed* when the problem is posed with *one* additional dimension.

Frith and Frith (1978) study a different problem, one of classification; and their point of departure is that classification studies typically employ materials that do not allow analysis of the mental processes involved. If objects are selected from the everyday environment, many of their features are uncontrolled and it is difficult to know which features children are considering in their classification operations. If instead well-controlled stimuli are used, they are often abstract and too simple, such as geometric shapes of various colors.

Frith and Frith seek to determine which of two hypotheses can account for development of the ability to classify, (a) an increase with age in the *number* of stimulus characteristics taken into consideration, or, (b) a greater *accuracy and consistency* in the use of each characteristic considered.

These authors employ three types of meaningful stimuli in their research. The stimuli are relatively complex, differentiated by nine characteristics that vary in a graduated manner; yet, at the same time, they are well controlled. One series of stimuli, for example, consists of imaginary animals varying with respect to the shape of the head, the position of the eyes, the shape of the neck, the shape of the forelegs, and so on. Each of these characteristics assumes one of ten different values along a continuum; the forelegs, for example range from very spiky to very smooth. For each type of material the authors utilize 30 figures constructed according to systematic criteria that we do not report here. Children and adolescents varying in age from four to sixteen are each presented with one of the three types of material (e.g., animals) and asked to sort the stimuli on the basis of their similarity.

Two aspects of the results are of interest to our discussion. The results concerning the first hypothesis are very clear: with age the number of characteristics taken into account increases. The groups formed when 4-year-olds sort the figures differ, to a significant extent, on the basis of only two of the stimuli's characteristics. The groups created by 16-year-olds differ, however, on the basis of seven characteristics on average. Between these extremes regular increments are found.

As for the second hypothesis, with respect to the precision with which each of the characteristics employed is effectively maintained as a classification criterion, only between the ages of 4 and 6 does one witness a substantial improvement. In short, what increases with age is the *number of properties* of an object that the child holds in mind; the ability to use such information regularly and accurately also grows within the period up to 6 years of age.

Scardamalia (1977) studied a Piagetian problem within the framework of a specific neo-Piagetian model, whereas Frith and Frith (1978) explored classification from a classic information-processing point of view. Nevertheless, those two studies are highly consistent in demonstrating the importance of the number of distinct pieces of information that children succeed in considering simultaneously, a number that determines both performance in combinatorial problems and the processes of classifying complex materials. In both cases this number increases regularly with age.

These two studies can give the reader an idea of the meaning of *information load imposed by a problem* and of *increasing capacity to process information*. Indeed these two concepts are complementary: a key idea, developed in various ways by neo-Piagetian theorists is that the development of processing capacity permits the solution of problems that impose an increasing demand in terms of information load.

Representation and Its Development

Another key idea is that new and more abstract forms of mental representation emerge with age. In the 1970s, many researchers began to investigate the manner in which we represent and organize knowledge in our minds. With respect to the organization of concepts, for example, it was proposed that we form semantic networks in long-term memory, that is, an interconnected set of propositions in which the concepts can be connected to their attributes and to other concepts (Anderson & Bower, 1973; Collins & Loftus, 1975). This proposed organization favors the formation of conceptual schemes by means of which, for example, we understand that the verb "to break" not only refers to the action, but also includes the agent who performs it, an instrument with which it is performed, an object on which it is performed, and a passage from an unbroken to a broken object (Rumelhart & Ortony, 1977). The child also learns to select the attributes of a concept and to form hierarchically superordinate classes including elements from different subclasses.

In addition, the child extracts regularities underlying sequences of events in everyday life and composes scripts (Schank & Abelson, 1977) such as "taking a bus" or "going to a restaurant." These scripts allow the child to foresee the order of occurrence of crucial events and thereby to adjust to diverse situations. Because scripts are drawn from experience, individual differences can operate in their formation (Nelson, 1986).

Furthermore, attention has been dedicated to the different forms in which the world might be represented, not only language and mental imagery, but also action. The objective has been to study not only representation of *declarative* knowledge (concepts and facts), but also representation of *procedural* knowledge (how to use concepts and act on facts).

One crucial problem for those who study development is to determine what type of knowledge children possess in order to decide when one can properly speak of representation. As Mandler (1983) has illustrated, researchers have given two different meanings to the term *representation*. On the one hand, representation refers to the knowledge that the individual has formed from the world, a position that leads to the study of its coding and organization. On the other hand, a narrower meaning is that representation corresponds to symbolic activity: the individual creates an image or a symbol that "stands for" and is distinct from an aspect of reality.

Piaget (1936/1952, 1945/1962) introduces the term *representation* in both the "broad" and the "narrow sense," as he called them. Piaget identifies representation in the broad sense with conceptual thought, in which the act of intelligence is dependent on neither immediate perceptions of the world, nor on actions that the subject takes with respect to it. Representation in the narrow sense is understood as forming and using images, symbols or signs based on their capacity to evoke absent objects or events. In Piaget's view, one cannot attribute representational ability (in either sense) to the child prior to the sixth stage of the sensorimotor period, which begins at about 18 months. Prior to that stage the Piagetian infant can recognize an object, but not evoke an absent object; the infant can anticipate or foresee an event, but only if the context provides perceptible indices that activate a direct connection with the event itself.

During the sixth stage the first forms of symbolization appear: the infant begins to make believe, assigning to one object (signifier) the function of another (signified), imitates events that occurred previously (deferred imitation), and no longer uses language simply as an accompaniment to action. Only at this point does Piaget speak of "mental representation."

Bruner, however, proposed that child development is marked by changes in the modes available for representing information. Representation, for Bruner and Anglin (1973), refers to a system of rules by means of which individuals mentally store the recurring characteristics of their environment in an economic manner, a process that permits them to go "beyond the information given." In particular, three modes of representation develop in the course of early childhood:

1. *Enactive representation*, characterized by actions, constitutes a way to represent past events by means of appropriate motor responses. The knowledge is procedural and consists in actions required by the environment and in manipulations of the environment. The ability to reflect on this knowledge is minimal.

2. *Iconic representation* constitutes a way of processing the world by means of images. Iconic representation is analogical and, in contrast to language, is not arbitrary: given an image, one can recognize the associated object, which is not the case with a word. In contrast to enactive representation that is serial, the image is simultaneous and atemporal. For this reason, it is difficult to represent an event such as tying a knot iconically, whereas it is easy to represent it by a series of ordered actions. Iconic representation first appears around 12 months of age and is well established by 5 to 7 years. It constitutes an advancement for the child in that it permits the formation of foundational schemes: no longer dependent on action, knowledge can be internalized. However, the knowledge remains dominated by the spatial and perceptual characteristics of the world and permits only a limited degree of inferential processing.

3. *Symbolic representation* first appears around 18 months of age and is typically mastered in adolescence. Language is its most important form, permitting the highest levels of cognition. In agreement with Vygotsky (1934/ 1962), Bruner takes the position that there is a close connection between language and thought. Language is arbitrary and provides links to remote referents. These symbolic links allow one to process information and aspects of the world indirectly, to produce transformations and combinations and to make inferences.

These three representational modes do not constitute stages; they make their appearance in sequence, but remain available to the individual continuously. During development there is an interaction among the modes in the sense that information first coded according to one mode of representation can later be translated into another mode.

Each of the three modes of representation provides models that express one's knowledge of the world. These models are selective. They do not incorporate all the specific characteristics of each encounter that one has with a particular event. Rather, by means of more economical rules they preserve the characteristics of like events.

Let us consider in which sense, according to Bruner, one can speak of representation as early as infancy. The child makes use of the experiences that flow from his actions, and representations of these guide the child in adjusting to new situations and in building more complex and more advanced knowledge. With the growth of competence, behaviors become flexible and productive; the child can substitute one behavior for another in order to achieve a particular goal and can combine behaviors to accomplish a new purpose. The construction of a particular competence requires an internal representation of its purpose; it is not simply trial and error learning. It is similar to the process of solving a problem and, as such, requires an *intention*, the use of *feedback* to reduce the difference between the current state and the final state, and a *structure* constituted by acts or subroutines that are modular (in the sense of being less variable and more automatized) and serially ordered according to hierarchical rules.

Bruner studies, for example, the developing ability of the infant to grasp an object while looking at it, and observes that the infant moves from disorganized sequences involving movements of the mouth, the arms, the shoulders, and the hands to a reorganized set of actions that permit subroutine substitution. Initially, for example, the hand may close before touching the object, but later remains open until making contact. This leads to further refinements, for example, as the hand approaches the object it gradually begins to close, anticipating the object's size and shape. As the subroutines consolidate, the grasping becomes rapid and smooth.

Modularization—a term used by Bruner with the meaning of automatization of subroutines—decreases the amount of time and attention required for execution of the subroutines. By freeing attention modularization makes it possible to include a subroutine in a more complex sequence of actions. The ability to drink from a cup provides an example of the construction of such a new sequence. Initially the child brings the cup to the mouth with a single movement, making no adjustments in the trajectory; then, the child inserts pauses in this action, during which the cup is oriented to keep the contents level. Eventually the child's monitoring of the level is constant and the movement becomes smooth and controlled at the same time.

Bruner has studied the development of various abilities, for example the capacity to go around an obstacle or to hold up a box's lid with one hand in order to grasp an object with the other. These are abilities that Bruner himself has called "pathetically simple" (Bruner & Anglin, 1973, p. 245). Yet, they shed light on the kind of progress that the child makes thanks to forming enactive representations, which are employed in information processing and mark the attainment of hierarchically more complex levels of activity.

The debate on whether or not representations exist in infancy has gone further, focusing on the possibility that procedural knowledge expressed in contextually adapted actions is not the only form of knowledge constructed in the sensorimotor period. Perhaps there is also a declarative type of knowledge expressed in the ability to form object concepts. Some studies with such techniques as *habituation*, which started about three decades ago, support the idea that in addition to a discrimination ability, the infant knows how to construct classes or distinct categories of objects (see Haith & Benson, 1998, for a critical review). For example, Fagan and Singer (1979) demonstrate that the young infant is able to distinguish faces belonging to different categories, such as male and female faces or child and adult faces. Ross (1980) shows that already at 1 year of age a child repeatedly presented with exemplars of one category (e.g., animals) reacts to the change when an object belonging to a different category is presented, as opposed to another from the same category. Mandler (1983, 1992) maintains that data of this sort indicate the existence of knowledge that develops simultaneously with procedural knowledge.

Strategies and Control Processes

Genetic epistemology deals with the construction of knowledge from action, given that "reality is continually restructured through the subject's own activities" (Inhelder, 1978, p. 122); it is the subject's actions that, from a constructivist viewpoint, create new structures and new forms of organization.

There has been a period in the cognitive sciences during which, in contrast to interest in knowledge construction, the prevailing concern has been with *how* one is able to solve the problems. Cellérier (1979) asserted, for example, that the cognitive sciences examine the application of knowledge, how internal knowledge structures control action. For his part, Piaget made a distinction between structures and procedures, but privileges study of the first. Nevertheless, at the end of the 1970s, Inhelder and her collaborators began to focus their work on the study of procedures, directing their interest to discovery and invention processes, to the procedures that the individual enacts in order to solve *a particular problem in a particular situation* (e.g., Karmiloff-Smith & Inhelder, 1974/1975). In his last works, although affirming that structures and procedures are antithetical, Piaget has considered them two inseparable aspects of cognitive activity: the use of each procedure refers back to structural knowledge, and the formation of structures is in turn derived from the application of procedures (Inhelder & Piaget, 1979).

Although cognitive psychologists, in contrast with the Genevan group, may have disregarded the dialectic of knowledge structures and procedures; they have greatly expanded the study of cognitive strategies, as a brief description of this work shows. The term *strategy* is used for a process or cognitive operation aimed at achieving a predetermined goal such as understanding a text, remembering something, or solving a problem. Strategies are often deliberate and may be carried out through either mental or physical action. Strategies are often activated when we realize that strategic action will minimize the cognitive effort required to achieve the predetermined goal. The term strategy is general and includes not only activity that, if followed appropriately, leads to success, but also processes or general problem solving methods called *heuristics* that narrow the search for possible solutions. According to the distinction made by Cellérier (1979), the use of heuristics deals with pragmatic transformations, a type that lacks the obligatory nature that characterizes epistemic transformations. It is in this wide sense that we refer to strategies.

Specific strategies for carrying out tasks in diverse settings have been identified and studied with respect to their development in children. The idea of these studies has been to determine whether differences of strategy or of strategy regulation can explain developmental differences in children's performance. Certainly among the first to begin work in this area was Bruner, who, considering cognition as a product of the tools made available by culture, initiated a fruitful line of research on strategies and errors in reasoning (Bruner, Goodnow, & Austin, 1956; Bruner, Olver, & Greenfield, 1966). For example, he studied concept formation by observing individuals' attempts to discover a rule, asking them to make choices among examples that might or might not verify hypotheses about the rule. He also observed how the strategies people used to make their choices varied according to task variables such as the number of trials available and the consequent evaluation of risk.

Often an individual's knowledge in the specific domain of a problem plays a considerable role in weighing the given variables and defining what would represent a solution. For this reason, differences in the strategies adopted and in the solutions identified have been found between experts and novices as well as between adults and children. Particular types of problems have been designed to permit study of the use of cognitive strategies while avoiding confounds due to differences in knowledge among those studied. A variety of generic strategies and heuristics have been studied including, for example, "means–ends analysis," which consists of searching within the legal moves for those that advance one toward the solution step by step (see chap. 4).

Much research on strategic behavior has been concentrated in the area of memory (Flavell, 1970). Processing strategies such as rehearsal can increase short-term memory capacity and keep information active. One can remember all the more if one elaborates the meaning of the material to be remembered, rather than leaving it unaltered as happens with simple rehearsal. For instance, one can associate two words (e.g., *pipe* and *whale*) in a single image (a *whale* smoking a *pipe*), or repeat the items by composing a story linking them to one another—items can be retrieved later from the story framework. One who has to learn a list of numbers may discover that they form a historic date or the date of a birthday. Regrouping items in these ways into larger meaningful units or chunks (Chase & Ericsson, 1982; Miller, 1956) allows one to keep a greater number of items in mind. Categorizing items is another form of organization. For example, one can regroup items from a grocery list according to the superordinate category to which they belong (vegetables, beverages, meats, etc.) and perhaps order them sequentially according to one's path through the supermarket.

Strategies used in complex tasks such as studying and understanding a text have also been widely studied. For example, one may seek to understand the general sense of a passage by scanning it, making use of section titles to see how the content is organized. One may also use techniques or external aides strategically, for example, underlining key concepts or drawing diagrams.

When a wide variety of strategies are possible, the one adopted must be functional for the task. Helpful in strategy selection is metacognitive ability, that is, knowledge about one's mental processes and the ability to reflect on and control them (self-regulation and executive control). Both the knowledge and the ability to use it are important and interrelated with one another (Brown, 1978; Flavell & Wellman, 1977). Knowing how our mind functions tells us about the limits of our abilities and the need to act on information to avoid its loss and reduce its cognitive load. Executive control of processes permits one to carry out regulatory activities: planning, predicting one's performance, monitoring one's comprehension, monitoring the solution stages of a problem, and calibrating one's actions.

A strict relationship between metacognition and cognitive performance has not been established, in part because of methodological problems involved in the measurement of such a relationship, for example, inappropriate verbal questionnaires (see Cornoldi, Gobbo, & Mazzoni, 1991). Also playing a part is the fact that awareness of one's processes only occurs in situations in which it is not possible to employ automatized procedures. Nevertheless, it remains fundamental to examine this relationship, as a potential factor contributing to the explanation of developmental differences.

Various studies demonstrate development in strategic activity on the part of children. For example, the rehearsal strategy, which in its simplest form is used by 6-year-olds after a bit of prompting, is not learned in its more complex form until later (Ornstein, Nauss, & Liberty, 1975). It has also been shown that 4- and 5-year-olds have difficulty using categorization to organize material (Lange, 1978). Other strategies appear even later: for example, identifying the most important ideas in a text, utilizing a theme in order to give coherence to a text, or recording each trial undertaken in a task designed to identify the variables that influence a particular phenomenon. These are all strategies that are applied under the individual's conscious control and that are acquired later in childhood or even during adolescence (Brown, Bransford, Ferrara, & Campione, 1983; Siegler & Liebert, 1975).

Metacognitive ability, like cognitive ability, is not an all-or-none phenomenon. A child can display early control abilities such as glancing every so often toward the place where an experimenter has hidden an interesting object to be retrieved later (Wellman, 1983), but not be able to say what to do in order to remember to take an object to school the next morning. (Kreutzer, Leonard, & Flavell, 1975).[10]

These few examples suffice to highlight some important points from cognitive psychologists' study of strategic processing: (a) young children possess fewer strategies than do older children or adults; (b) older children can use strategies in a more elaborate way; (c) task experience is indispensable for the development of some strategies, for example, those appropriate to school materials and tasks; (d) the child is not always able to adopt strategies spontaneously—the so-called production deficit (Flavell, 1970; Hagen, Hargrave, & Ross, 1973)—emphasizing the importance of both instruction and development of metacognitive abilities; and (e) applying a strategy does not always lead to success—other variables can have an effect, including poor problem representation, lack of familiarity with the material, lack of mastery of the strategy or the inappropriateness of the strategy to the child's difficulty. Strategic and regulatory ability increase with age; knowledge of how one's mind functions increases as does the ability to keep track of feedback and of the differences among various task situations.

ON THE DIALOGUE BETWEEN EPISTEMOLOGICAL TRADITIONS

We have argued that the rise of neo-Piagetian theories was stimulated to a large extent by concepts like *chunk, information load, limited capacity, representation, symbol, strategy,* and *control,* which were formulated in the first

---

[10]In an interesting study Gauvain and Rogoff (1989) find that planning abilities, which are absent in 5- and 6-year-olds working alone, make an appearance when the children work in pairs: Sharing responsibility for the successful completion of a task seems to favor the explication of a plan.

decades of cognitive psychology and often had a counterpart in Piagetian concepts. This correspondence would seem to create an ideal situation for a dialogue between cognitive, Piagetian and neo-Piagetian psychologists. However, things turned out differently.

Piagetian research was generally praised for having discovered important phenomena and posed fundamental problems (e.g., Flavell, 1996; Smith, 1993), but criticized for its emphasis on logical structure. It also met resistance from many cognitive researchers because it was not framed in accordance with their explicit or implicit empiricist philosophical presuppositions. As we noted, the questions and models of the dialectical Piaget were often overlooked. In addition, cognitive researchers (unsatisfied with the failure of general late-behaviorist theories) often held the presupposition that a psychological theory should not be too general, but limit itself to modeling a specific task or ability; this presupposition turned against Piaget, too. And it also turned against neo-Piagetian theories, which aim to be no less general than Piaget's, and no less dialectical.

The dissatisfaction with stages defined by logical competence tended to spread over the whole notion of developmental stages—whereas the idea of an incremental increase in specific skills and domain-specific knowledge seemed to fit better the underlying empiricist epistemology of many North American and British researchers (see also Goswami, 2001). In short, despite the points of contact between Piagetian, neo-Piagetian, and information-processing theories, the dialogue between those approaches has stunningly decreased between the 1970s and 1980s.

Among neo-Piagetian theorists, Case is probably the one who emphasizes most the need for a dialogue among researchers working within different frameworks, with an aim to integrate the historical and philosophical roots of the epistemological traditions that have contributed to the study of cognitive development. Case (1991, 1996a, 1996c, 1998; for a similar classification see also Gopnik, 1996) discusses three broad epistemological frameworks that exerted, and continue to exert, a far-reaching influence on developmental psychology: the empiricist, the rationalist, and the sociohistorical tradition. Although it is outside the scope of this chapter to undertake a detailed analysis (see Case, 1998), it is helpful to provide a brief outline of the interactions between these traditions and their possible evolution.

Case (1998) points to the long-lasting influence of empiricism and in particular logical positivism on behaviorism and learning theory; like other authors (e.g., Legrenzi, 1975; Reese, 1993) he notes how Piaget has often been read with empiricist glasses by American researchers and traces the history of reciprocal criticism between empiricist learning researchers and Piagetian researchers. However, Case (1998), as well as other neo-Piagetians (Fischer & Bidell, 1998, 2006), also note the strong points of the empiricist tradition, such as carefully controlled experiments, observations of learning in multi-trial tasks, and attention to the knowledge acquisition processes by which children discriminate, encode, and retrieve information. More recently, within an epistemological framework, which must still be considered empiricist, new methodological approaches emerged, such as microgenetic studies of learning and development (Siegler, 1887a), and new views of conceptual development as an acquisition of expertise (e.g., Chi & Koeske, 1983). For expertise theories, the growth of knowledge is still seen as being under the control of local learning factors. Although this latter assumption may be simplistic, the models of knowledge proposed within this tradition have become increasingly sophisticated, also as a result of developments in cognitive science.

The second epistemological tradition highlighted by Case is generally called rationalist—with Kant as the most prominent ancestor. Developmental psychologists who have adopted this paradigm tend to focus on quite different issues than the empiricists do. For example, there is a great deal of interest in the unfolding of children's knowledge, with particular focus on its structures. Thus, there is interest in finding out what abilities children appear to have early in their lives, even from birth, and what kind of "initial" structures they use to make sense of the world. In sharp contrast to the empiricists, the rationalists have maintained that knowledge is acquired by a process whereby the individual imposes order on data through such systems as, for instance, logic. A basic assumption is that, without any preexisting system in place, such as the understanding of rudimentary causal relationships, numbers, or time, it would be difficult to make sense of the world, as children do.

Baldwin (1906/1968) was the first developmental theorist to adopt this framework, proposing that children progress through four general stages (sensorimotor, quasi-logical, logical, and hyperlogical) and maintaining that new experiences are "assimilated" into existing schemata. Piaget owes much to Baldwin's early insights, and, as just noted, the dialectical Piaget who introduces components from biology and dialectical philosophy into developmental psychology coexists with a Kantian soul who believes in *a priori* categories and incorporates the notion of "logical structures" into Baldwin's framework. Of course, the strengths of rationalist approaches are different from those of the empiricist, also in methodology. Although the empiricist tends to focus on a single task that involves some form of learning, and systematically vary its parameters, the rationalistically oriented researcher often focuses on children's understanding across a number of tasks, tasks in which the effects of empirical learning often have to be overcome by the child. Piagetian methods, such as the "clinical interview" that probes children's reasoning by proposing counter-suggestions to their explanations, aim to bring to light children's broad knowledge structures and their change over time.

More recent developments of the rationalist tradition in psychology include the so-called "theory theory," that is, an approach according to which children have a naïve theory of some domain, which eventually they change through a radical restructuring, similar to the theoretical revolutions that occur in the history of science. A well-known example is Carey's (1985) view of children's naive theories of biology (see also chap. 7, this volume). According to Case (1998), these theories remain squarely in the rationalist tradition by characterizing children's conceptual development as a series of qualitative transformations in internal structures, which have a rather broad field of application and are relatively impervious to task-specific experience. However, contrary to Piaget and the neo-Piagetians, some of these theories propose that the conceptual change takes place within modules that are domain-specific and innate. The models of children's conceptual understanding proposed within the "theory theory" approach have enriched remarkably the field of cognitive developmental psychology. Despite the deep differences in underlying epistemology and in the proposed explanation of change, a dialogue is possible between this approach, the expertise approach, and the neo-Piagetian approach, because of their common concern for detailed modeling of children's knowledge structures.

The third epistemological tradition used to study children's conceptual development is generally referred to as *sociohistorical epistemology*. According to this view, knowledge does not reside in the structure of the object, as empiricists would claim—nor within the structure of the subject, as the rationalist would claim; rather it has its origins in the social and historical elements of culture, such as the tools and concepts created to facilitate interactions between people and their environment. Vygotsky (1934/1962), generally regarded as the best-known proponent of the sociohistorical approach, suggested that children's thinking must be seen in a much larger context, one that includes biological, psychological, and sociological components, where the development of language, tools, and heuristics to transmit knowledge from one generation to the next must be studied and understood. Within this tradition, issues such as literacy, numeracy, and schooling are central concerns.

The work of such researchers as Jerome Bruner, Michael Cole, Patricia Greenfield and David Olson has provided, on the one hand, evidence of the powerful effects of formal schooling on promoting abstract thinking. On the other hand, they have provided descriptions of the remarkable complexity of various skills and conceptual systems in use in some illiterate cultures. The view of a contextually based cultural "apprenticeship" of children may sometimes overlook the cognitive developmental prerequisites of such cultural transmission (although Vygotsky himself, with his conceptualization of children's "zone of proximal development," does not fall under this criticism). Nevertheless, researchers in the sociohistorical tradition have made, and are still making, important contributions to the study of different forms of cultural praxis and learning, and to our understanding of children's knowledge and its intertwining with the culture of a society.

Although the landscape of developmental psychology is still characterized by large differences separating different epistemological traditions and theoretical currents, there are signs of an effective dialogue taking place. There now seems, in comparison with the 1970s, to be a sense that each approach had a major contribution to make to the study of children's thinking; on some points, even agreement seems to have emerged. The main point of convergence seems to be that children's cognitive structures should be viewed neither as system-wide (e.g., Piaget's *structures d'ensemble* of logical operations), nor merely as task-specific elements and associations (as in early empiricist models). Rather they should be seen as systems for making meaning in a rather broad domain. According to Case (1998), "For theorists in the empiricist tradition, the move to this middle ground meant a move . . . toward a view where broad structural and/or disciplinary coherences are considered as well. For theorists in the rationalist tradition, the move to this middle ground has meant a move . . . toward a detailed consideration of factors that are domain specific" (p. 764).

Indeed, there are other signs that dialogue among different traditions is becoming more fruitful. For instance, there is increasing awareness that Piaget's and Vygotsky's views were not so opposite as they have for a long time been portrayed. Both shared a dialectical view of the developing child, endowed with internal cognitive structures and actively interacting with the environment. In this sense, in several respects, the contributions of Piaget and Vygotsky can be regarded as complementary (Bidell, 1988; Pascual-Leone, 1996a; Shayer, 2003; Smith, 1996); van Geert (1998) has also proposed a relevant integration of Piaget's and Vygotsky's basic ideas within a dynamic systems approach.

The neo-Piagetian approach, as a whole, can also be regarded as a particular form of dialogue among traditions, as we see in more detail throughout the book. Accepted from the rationalist tradition are the broad scope of theorizing, the structural modeling that spans over tasks or domains, a notion of general stages as a heuristic to describe the structure of development, and a methodological preference for testing predictions derived from general theories. Accepted from the empiricist tradition are aspects such as the use of well-controlled experiments, a careful modeling of domain-specific knowledge, and occasional use of learning paradigms. Finally, accepted from the sociohistorical tradition are the interest in symbol systems and some attention to the child's opportunities to acquire knowledge in the cultural context. As just mentioned in the earlier section, the neo-Piagetian movement started with the assumption of the need for a theoretical synthesis between preexisting approaches, in particular (but not exclusively) between classical Piagetian and Human Information Processing concepts. For instance, Pascual-Leone (1970) proposes a redefinition of Piaget's "schemes" in a manner that is compatible with the *S-R* tradition (see chap. 2, this volume). Pascual-Leone and Sparkman (1980) argue that rationalist and empiricist methodologies should be viewed as complementary, rather than incompatible. In a similar vein, Halford (1970b) provides a neo-Piagetian, structuralist framework to account for the possibility of children *learning* conservation concepts (see chap. 3); Demetriou and Efklides (1987) call their approach "experiential structuralism" (see chap. 3); and Fischer, by adopting a dynamic systems approach, reconciles the role of endogenous and environmental influences on development (see chap. 5). Moreover, Vygotsky's approach has also been taken into account by neo-Piagetians, especially by Case and Fischer.

Such an attempt at theoretical synthesis was not accepted with great enthusiasm by the scientific community during the 1970s and 1980s. Rather, during that time neo-Piagetian theories were often perceived as a repainted version of Piaget's old stage theory, conceptually obsolete with an unnecessary philosophical tone. In addition, their scope was often deemed too general to be taken seriously by empiricist researchers, accustomed as they were to task-specific models.

But, as we have argued here, the growing dialogue between different traditions combined with a renewed interest in far-reaching theoretical approaches would seem to open the possibility for neo-Piagetian research to be reevaluated more seriously. New approaches are also emerging as a result of this developing dialogue and an interest in "grand theories." Consider, for instance, the neuroconstructivist approach (Elman et al., 1996; Oliver, Johnson, Karmiloff-Smith, & Pennington, 2000; Scerif & Karmiloff-Smith, 2005; see also chap. 7, this volume). This approach definitely starts from a synthesis between nativist (*a priori*, rationalist) assumptions and connectionist (associationist, empiricist) assumptions, and it frames such a synthesis along the lines of Piagetian constructivism. Such an approach is epistemologically very close to the neo-Piagetian approach.

Another interesting attempt to synthesize Piagetian and information-processing concepts, rationalist and constructivist assumptions is proposed by Russell (1999). His main thesis is that cognitive development involves monitoring one's actions and intentions together with an increasing ability to inhibit prepotent responses. Russell accepts from Piaget the idea of the child's mental action or praxis as the basis for cognitive development; but he objects to Piaget's underestimation of the nativist position, and argues that one must posit the existence of an innate symbolic capacity that, rather than being constructed, would mature at an age of about 12–18 months. However, although Russell criticizes neo-Piagetian authors for departing too much from the classical Piagetian views,[11] he seems to overlook how the growth of working memory capacity could account for the emergence of symbolization and construction of various types of symbols, including language (e.g., see Case, 1985; Pascual-Leone & Johnson, 1999).

Thus, we return to the starting point of the chapter. The current debates on topics such as microdevelopment, developmental discontinuities, connectionist models, and executive functions (but we could also have mentioned topics like emotion and hot cognition, giftedness, specific impairments, transfer of learning—all topics on which neo-Piagetian authors have offered valuable contributions) are debates that cut across the traditional boundaries among schools. Now the limitations of a classical information-processing approach are as widely acknowledged as are those of the classical Piagetian one. Broad theories are attracting the interest of the scientific community again. When trying to study broad issues, one can hardly be satisfied with strictly empiricist, rationalist, or sociohistorical assumptions, and one strives for some sort of interpenetration of such opposites. Thus, by aiming at a synthesis of opposites, researchers tend to rediscover dialectic—even though they may not use this term. Though they are complex, neo-Piagetian theories and models can find more fertile ground today than in previous decades. Of course, a good outcome also requires a continuous sensitivity to the current debate from neo-Piagetian theoreticians, and, of course, neo-Piagetian theorizing can, in turn, benefit from an increasing dialogue among the epistemological traditions and theoretical approaches. The following chapters of this book can be taken not only as an invitation to greater knowledge of the details of neo-Piagetian theories but also as a contribution to the dialogue among the different traditions and to the dialogue among neo-Piagetian theories themselves.

CONCLUSION

The following chapters of this book tie together almost four decades of neo-Piagetian research. More specific than "post-Piagetian," the adjective neo-Piagetian does not allude simply to research that deals in some innovative way with issues or tasks that Piaget studied. Neo-Piagetian theories all have the following features:

1. like Piaget, they take a constructivist approach to cognitive development,
2. similarly to Piaget, they are broad in scope, and they assume that cognitive development can be divided in periods or stages with qualita-

---

[11]A similar criticism has also been expressed by Karmiloff-Smith (1993).

tively different characteristics (though the age ranges of these periods may not coincide with those proposed by Piaget),

3. similarly to Piaget, they assume that children's thinking increases in complexity from one stage to the next; however, differently from Piaget, it is not logic from which they borrow the criteria that define the complexity of each stage. Rather, in neo-Piagetian theories these criteria correspond to particular features of the child's information processing system.

Having relinquished reliance on a logical system, neo-Piagetian theories have also been able to incorporate a variety of other issues, such as individual differences and aspects of emotional development.

Before commencing our discussion of specific neo-Piagetian theories and lines of research, we must mention another major attempt in these four decades at comparing and discussing the whole range of neo-Piagetian theories. A special issue of the *International Journal of Psychology*, republished in 1988 as a book edited by Andreas Demetriou, presented five general theories of cognitive development as well as contributions on specific topics and some discussion articles comparing different theories. On that occasion Demetriou (1987) noted that "Piagetian psychology, though the psychology of 'the Giant,' was above all a one man psychology . . . In contrast, neo-Piagetian psychology is a collective enterprise in the true sense of the word" (p. 503). In the introduction to that book, Sternberg (1987) lightheartedly described the enterprise as a horse race in which every theoretician was breeding and riding his theoretical horse—a race the end of which was still unforeseeable.

But since that time great progress has been made, in theory refinement, in available evidence, and in dialogue among researchers. At this point, after nearly 40 years of "collective enterprise," it is certainly time to draw a balance. Now, not only can we discuss similarities and differences among theories and present research supporting one or another of them, but we also feel able to boldly title the last section of the last chapter "Toward an Integration." Not our own integration—we are not bold to that point—but, as the reader will see, we outline the directions in which research might proceed in order to create a unified, general neo-Piagetian theory of cognitive development.

2

The Theory of J. Pascual-Leone

COGNITIVE DEVELOPMENT AND COGNITIVE STYLE

The first systematic neo-Piagetian theory, the Theory of Constructive Operators (TCO), arose as an integration of two lines of inquiry: the Piagetian study of cognitive development and Witkin's study of field dependence. Juan Pascual-Leone (1969), hypothesizing that individual differences in cognitive style influence the appearance of Piagetian operations, proposed construction of a psychological theory compatible with the data of both schools. Pascual-Leone sought not simply to juxtapose the constructs of the two theories, but also to introduce new theoretical constructs allowing redefinition of the basic ideas of both theories *in the same language*. He sought as well to point out the structural analogies (where they exist) between Piagetian tasks and those created by Witkin.

Field Dependence/Independence

The concept of *cognitive style* refers to a dimension of cognitive processing along which people differ from one another. Examples include reflective and impulsive styles, convergent and divergent thinking, and the preference for use of broad or narrow categories. People tend to remain more or less faithful across diverse situations to their characteristic cognitive style. The concept of cognitive style is different from that of cognitive ability. Individual differences in cognitive style occur with respect to a bipolar scale;

therefore, saying that one person is "more reflective" than another is equivalent to saying that person is "less impulsive." One cannot call either the impulsive end or the reflective end of the bipolar scale "positive," given that in different situations, both the impulsive style and the reflective style have adaptive value. Individual differences in cognitive ability, however, occur with respect to a unipolar scale; and, clearly, it is more adaptive to be more able rather than less.

The specific cognitive style studied by Witkin et al. (Witkin, Dyk, Faterson, Goodenough, & Karp, 1974; Witkin, Goodenough, & Oltman, 1979; Witkin et al., 1954) is field-dependence/independence. According to Witkin, *field-dependent* perception is ruled by the overall organization of the surrounding perceptual field, the parts of which are dealt with as though fused together. In *field-independent* perception, however, one experiences the elements of the field as distinct from one another, even though the field has an overall structure. Witkin et al. (1954) primarily studied cognitive style differences in perceptual tasks. For example, participants were placed in a tilted room and asked to rotate their chair to bring themselves to a vertical position. Some individuals (labelled *field-independent*) reached the vertical almost exactly. Others were influenced by the surrounding perceptual field, that is by the inclination of the floor, walls and ceiling, to the extent that they positioned their seat obliquely such as to be leaning in the same direction as the incline of the walls. In another case, participants had to position a rod vertically within a perceptual field formed by an inclined frame. Another example, the embedded figures task, requires finding a simple figure within a larger more complex figure that is meaningful and designed in such a way as to reduce the saliency of the simpler figure. Field-dependent individuals find it difficult to disregard the complex figure and locate the requested detail rapidly.

Further studies (Witkin et al., 1974) demonstrate that field dependence is not simply a perceptual style, but a cognitive one in the full sense of that term.[1] Field-independent persons perform better on some intelligence test items that require analyzing and restructuring the stimulus field, for example, Wechsler's picture arrangement, block design, and picture completion. Moreover, field-independent individuals prove more adept at solving verbal problems that require restructuring the terms of the problem, that is, an insight that disregards a knowledge field composed of rules learned in a similar context, or a field based on "functional fixity" in the use of objects.

---

[1]Despite the correlation with tests of ability, field-dependence/independence is considered a cognitive *style*. In fact, some perceptual tasks and certain social situations favor field-dependence (Witkin et al., 1974; Witkin, Goodenough, & Oltman, 1979). Skill in visual arts probably requires a set of abilities, some global in nature and others analytic.

Field-Dependence and Piagetian Tasks

Pascual-Leone (1969) hypothesizes a precise relationship between field dependence and certain Piagetian tasks. According to his hypothesis, tests of field dependence (and other tasks correlated with them) involve a cognitive conflict: prior knowledge or the perceptual characteristics of the stimuli tend to activate inappropriate strategies. Thus, one must exert attentional effort to activate appropriate knowledge and strategies as well as to overcome the effect of the misleading information. Many Piagetian tasks, according to Pascual-Leone, present the same type of conflict, and therefore should correlate with tests of field dependence.

Consider, for example, the classic Piagetian conservation tasks. In these, the child views two equal balls of clay, one of which is then flattened or elongated. After the transformation, the child is asked to judge whether one of the two contains more clay than the other, or if one is heavier, or if one would cause the water level in a container to rise more. The perceptual salience of the difference between the visible surfaces or the heights of the two objects and the child's past experience (which suggests that a wider or taller object is also heavier, contains more matter, etc.) constitute misleading information and tend to activate a strategy based on a perceptual comparison between the two objects as they appear in the moment. In order to provide a correct response, the child must instead attend simultaneously to several pieces of information: the initial equality of the balls, the transformation conducted, the fact that it did not involve adding or subtracting clay, and the fact that if two objects contain the same quantity of matter then their weights are also the same.

Similar considerations apply for other Piagetian tasks. When one asks children to compare the length of two zigzag paths, the straight-line distance between their end points constitutes a perceptually salient dimension that permits a rapid, but often incorrect, judgment. A correct strategy requires instead an integration of the lengths of the differently directed path segments.

The most salient information sometimes prompts responses that conflict with the correct one. For example, consider a child looking through a small window at a cylinder on which some pictures are drawn such that these pictures appear in the window one at a time (Piaget & Inhelder, 1966). Rotating the cylinder to the left, the child will say that the picture to be seen next is the picture that is to the left of the currently visible one. The child is fooled by the salience of rotation direction. In this case, too, discovering a correct rule requires coordination of various items of information: the order of the pictures, their cyclical positioning, and the direction of rotation of the cylinder with respect to the window.

In agreement with his hypotheses, Pascual-Leone finds that the performance of 10-year-olds on a set of Piagetian tasks, including those described here, correlates with their performance on tests of field independence and on the analytic tasks of Wechsler's test. Moreover, the experimental manipulation of salient but misleading pieces of information suggests that the field-dependent children are particularly influenced by these pieces. Pascual-Leone (1969) finds that field-dependent adults also commit occasional errors in these cognitive tasks.

Pascual-Leone's results, confirmed by further research (Huteau, 1980; Neimark, 1981; Pascual-Leone, 1989; Pascual-Leone & Morra, 1991) support the hypothesis of a structural similarity between field-independence tasks and certain Piagetian tasks. In both cases, a cognitive conflict must be resolved by coordinating relevant information that is not salient, rather than using information that is more salient or is familiar from past experience.

SCHEMES AND PROCESSING CAPACITY

As we have seen, Pascual-Leone emphasizes that success on Piagetian tasks requires keeping in mind various pieces of information simultaneously and coordinating them. Although Piaget explains cognitive development with changes in logical competence, Pascual-Leone suggests instead that the stage aspects of cognitive development are to be explained by increases in the capacity to coordinate information.

Processing Capacity: Hypotheses Regarding Its Limits and Development

The relevant pieces of information obviously differ from one task to another, and for this reason it is not possible to make comparisons among different tasks by defining units of information in an "objective" manner, for example, by analyzing stimulus attributes. It is from *the subject's point of view* that units of information are to be defined, namely by considering which mental operations or chunks of information constitute functional units. The concept of *scheme*, which Piaget (1936/1952, 1967) characterizes as a functional whole, is particularly suitable for this purpose.

The concept of scheme is elaborated in the following section. Here we note only that, reinterpreting the corpus of Piagetian data, Pascual-Leone hypothesizes that with development children are able to coordinate an increasing number of schemes. In particular, for the cognitive acquisitions of the late preoperational period (5–6 years) the coordination of two schemes is required; most of the abilities typical of concrete operations

(7–8 years) require coordination of three schemes. The number becomes four for abilities acquired later (about 9 years) and five or more for the operations that Piaget called formal (de Ribaupierre & Pascual-Leone, 1979; Pascual-Leone, 1980; Pascual-Leone & Smith, 1969).[2] Pascual-Leone (1970) hypothesizes a mechanism that is able to attend to a certain number of schemes simultaneously, and this capacity increases one unit on average every 2 years up to the age of 15. At that age, the number is seven, which according to Miller (1956) characterizes the capacity of the human information processing system.

Research on the CSVI Task

In order to verify such hypotheses, which at that time constituted an interpretation of the Piagetian data that was both new and against the current, Pascual-Leone (1970) devised a new task substantially different from the Piagetian ones. In Pascual-Leone's task, the schemes are clearly defined *a priori* and are learned in the same manner by all the participants. These "artificial" schemes are constituted by stimulus–response pairings, such as: red—clap your hands, large figure—open your mouth, and so on. Once such pairs are learned, the main experimental task begins using complex visual stimuli (CSVI, *Compound Stimuli Visual Information task*). Children, between the ages of 5 and 11, are shown cards with a patterned drawing displaying two or more of the features for which they have learned paired responses. To minimize the possible influence of short-term memory the patterns are presented for a sufficiently long period (5 seconds) and the children can respond during the presentation, as well as immediately after. Pascual-Leone hypothesizes that children will respond to one or more features of a compound stimulus, in accordance with a probabilistic model.[3] The model has two parameters: the number of relevant features in the drawing, and the children's "central computing space," that is, the number of schemes that they are able to coordinate. Pascual-Leone (1970, 1978) finds that, as hypothesized, this number is two at 5 years of age and increases by one unit every 2 years. These results have been confirmed by several experiments with procedural variations (such as using response buttons rather than a set of motions, using sequential rather than simultaneous presentation of the characteristics for responding, and varying the duration of presentation; e.g., see de Ribaupierre et al., 1990; Globerson, 1983a; Miller, Bentley, & Pascual-Leone, 1989; Pascual-Leone, 1970).

---

[2]The reference here is to the "classical" version of the Piagetian tasks. As seen in the first chapter, their experimental versions can involve different information loads.

[3]The model adopted is the Bose-Einstein distribution. Instead, Case and Serlin (1979) consider the distribution of Maxwell-Boltzmann more appropriate. These are described in various textbooks of probability theory (e.g., Feller, 1968).

Trabasso and Foellinger (1978) reexamined Pascual-Leone's (1970) model employing a short-term memory task involving gestures rather than the CSVI. Their results were sharply different from those of Pascual-Leone, and their experiment provoked an interesting and lively debate on the epistemological level (Pascual-Leone, 1978; Pascual-Leone & Sparkman, 1980; Trabasso, 1978). A comparison between the results of Pascual-Leone (1970, 1978) and those of Trabasso and Foellinger (1978) demonstrates that the CSVI is *not* a short-term memory task and that *limited processing capacity* and *short-term memory* are not synonymous concepts.

One variable that considerably influences performance on the CSVI is the task's familiarity, a characteristic that permits development of suitable attentional strategies (de Ribaupierre, 1993; Miller, Bentley et al., 1989; Pascual-Leone, 1970; see also the following section of this chapter).

SCHEMES: DEFINITIONS AND PROPERTIES

To this point in the chapter, we have considered the research with which Pascual-Leone developed the basic insights of his theory. Now we consider how the formal aspects of the TCO have been developed. These aspects include two types of constructs: schemes (or subjective operators) and second-order (or metasubjective) operators.

The Components of Schemes

In this theory, the *scheme* is conceived as the unit of analysis of cognitive processes. Because this concept is fundamental, it is necessary to define it in more precise terms than those of Piaget. Also necessary are practical rules (see chap. 9) for identifying the schemes involved in a mental process.

A scheme, according to Piaget, is a set of the organism's reactions that are not necessarily observable, and that are tightly connected in a totality or whole. Activation of a scheme is possible in diverse situations ("assimilation" of reality by a scheme), but modification or differentiation ("accommodation") is also possible. Some schemes are innate, but the vast majority result from experience, from the capacity of human beings to abstract invariant properties from their activities and perceptual experiences. Accommodation and coordination of existing schemes are processes that normally lead to the acquisition of new schemes.

Pascual-Leone (1969, 1970; Pascual-Leone & Goodman, 1979; Pascual-Leone & Johnson, 1991) redefines more precisely the Piagetian concept, by postulating that each scheme has two, or in some cases three, components. The two essential components of every scheme are called the *releasing component* and the *effecting component.* The first is made up of the set of conditions that, *even if minimally satisfied*, initiate the scheme's activation. The second consists of the effect of its activation. The third component, called the *terminal component*, is found only in schemes that are organized according to a temporal sequence and is constituted of the conditions that bring the activation to an end.

Schemes can be, and usually are, organized hierarchically and recursively; one scheme could be made up of schemes that are in turn made up of schemes and so on. Often both the releasing component and the effecting component of a scheme are formed of lower level schemes.

The Properties of Schemes

Because even partial satisfaction[4] of the conditions of a scheme's releasing components is sufficient to activate that scheme, the tendency in any particular situation is toward the activation of many schemes. For example, on encountering the word *horse* while reading a book, the scheme of the corresponding lexical unit is activated. Its primary effect is to activate a representation of the word's pronunciation and meaning. But schemes corresponding to other lexical units orthographically similar to *horse* and sharing a certain number of activation conditions are also activated. Other schemes will have been activated by the phrase preceding the word *horse*, others by the differing significances associated with encountering the word in a novel as opposed to a zoology textbook, and still others by recent thoughts or experiences. The meaning of the activated lexical units could, in turn, be a part of the activating conditions of other more complex, higher level schemes—for example, schemes representing knights in chivalrous battle. Only a subset of the schemes is compatible with one another, however, and their compatibility enhances their activation, whereas the incompatible schemes inhibit one another. Thus, if an opera-loving reader encounters the word horse while a radio in the background is playing the music of Monteverdi, that reader may begin imagining Tancredi and Clorinda's duel, even if the word appears in a zoology text.

The preceding example illustrates several postulates proposed by Pascual-Leone and Goodman (1979), which we reformulate liberally as follows:

- Each activating condition included in a scheme's releasing component carries its own "activation weight." If a salient condition of a scheme or if a condition for which particular relevance has been learned is satisfied, the scheme's activation increases more than would occur with the

---

[4]Other theories postulate cognitive units, such as the "productions" of Newell and Simon (1972), which are activated only if their conditions are completely satisfied.

satisfaction of a less salient condition whose importance had not been learned.[5]

- Activation of a scheme tends to diminish the activation of other schemes that are incompatible with it.[6]

- Activation of a scheme induces activation of higher level schemes for which that scheme is a condition of activation.[7]

- Activation of a scheme tends to increase the activation of other schemes that are compatible with it.[8]

- A person's mental processes and behavior are codetermined by the set of compatible schemes that are most active at a given moment. This final postulate is fundamental for the theory and is called the *schematic overdetermination principle*.

SCHEME CLASSIFICATION

Pascual-Leone (1976a, 1984, 1995; Pascual-Leone et al., 1978; Pascual-Leone & Johnson, 1991) classifies schemes according to three criteria: *modality, level*, and *type*.

Modality of Schemes. Classification by *modality*[9] is the most obvious. It refers to the scheme's content: visual schemes, auditory schemes, and so on, for recognizing stimuli in each sensory modality; linguistic schemes for understanding and producing language; affective schemes and personality schemes (conceptualized as complex, superordinate structures that coordinate a number of cognitive and affective schemes). In the affective schemes, according to the TCO, the effecting component is made up of

---

[5]For example, if one has a scheme for puffin, seeing a puffin's beak (very salient) will be sufficient to recognize the bird. If the bird is too far away to allow identification of the beak, a condition with high activation weight could be the manner of flying, but only for a person who has had sufficient opportunity to learn this bird's flight. On the other hand, it is likely that the activation weight will be low for the feet because these are similar in other marine birds and not very salient.

[6]For example, schemes for eating and for blowing out the candles both tend to activate in the presence of a birthday cake, yet they are incompatible with each other in as much as their effecting components require movements that can not be carried out simultaneously.

[7]For example, activation, for whatever reason, of the scheme that represents the concept "cod" tends to activate the schemes for "fish," "animal," and "food."

[8]For example, for a person with a scheme for Macbeth's temptation, the schemes for "dagger," "darkness," and "witches" increment each other's activation because all three are constituents of that superordinate scheme.

[9]One of the main issues in neuropsychology and cognitive science is the study of representations of knowledge and the way in which these representations form modules, semantic areas or, at the least, cognitive domains. This issue is discussed more extensively in chapters 5–7.

physiological reactions (to turn pale with fear, to blush with embarrassment) or motivational reactions (for example, a motivational effect of fear is
the activation of motor and cognitive schemes connected to flight). Cognitive schemes are divided into two broad categories, akin to the distinction
usually made in cognitive psychology between propositional and analog
representations.[10]

Abstraction Level. The second criterion of scheme classification is the
level of abstraction. This criterion is based in the postulate that schemes are
organized in a hierarchical and recursive manner, that is, that any scheme
may be composed of other schemes. Thus, it is possible to order schemes according to successive levels of complexity and abstraction with the simplest
perceptual and motor schemes (such as those that encode single visual input
characteristics) at the base of the hierarchy. Pascual-Leone (1984) proposes
detailed, though speculative, hypotheses on such a hierarchy. He suggests
that in each cognitive domain there is a habitual, or *zero*, level, of representation (e.g., representations of objects) and that to activate schemes at levels
more complex or more abstract than the zero level requires attentional effort. Similarly, he proposes that such effort would also be required in order
to pay attention to components or features at a level more elementary than
the habitual one; in other words, only with analytical effort would it be possible to activate elementary representations separately from the zero-level representations of which they are a habitual part.

Scheme Type. The third classification criterion, *types (or modes) of
schemes*, concerns the distinction between figurative and operative knowledge[11] (Piaget & Inhelder, 1966). In brief, figurative schemes represent
states and operative schemes represent transformations. Objects, configurations, concepts, meanings, mental states are represented in the mind as
figurative schemes, whereas operative schemes represent actions, processes, operations, and transformations that beginning from one state generate another (Pascual-Leone et al., 1978; Pascual-Leone & Johnson, 1991).

---

[10]Pascual-Leone (1976a, 1984, 1995) refers to these as *logological* (conceptual) and
mereological (experiential) structures, respectively. The first would be formed of concepts, relations and propositions connected by rules with a syntactic form. It would involve substantial reduction of information with respect to the experiential data that it represents. The second, however, would be perceptual, spatial, temporal, motor, and intentional representations reflecting
experiential knowledge, that includes much of the detail that one notices and the constraints
that one meets in interactions with the realities in the environment. Conceptual and experiential
structures tend to be stored respectively in the left and right hemisphere.

[11]Similar to this distinction between figurative and operative knowledge is Anderson's (1983)
distinction between declarative and procedural knowledge (see also Pascual-Leone, 1995).

Of course, both figurative and operative schemes may be found at any level of abstraction and within any modality.

Certain schemes, as previously mentioned, are organized according to a temporal sequence and include an ending component. When a scheme contains a representation of time, it is called a *fluent*, a term taken from artificial intelligence. In figurative fluents, the time representation appears as an expectation (that a state x is followed by a state y, and finally a state z, etc.). In operative fluents, representation of time could appear in the form of a temporally sequenced series of operations, parts of a procedure, or steps of a program.

Executive schemes are an important subclass of operative fluents, involved in the plans and control functions of the mind. *Plans* are operative fluents that represent procedures or procedure segments, strategic moves, and sequences of steps that a person's behavior or thoughts might follow. Executive schemes with *control* functions do the work of monitoring mental activity, which is, using and regulating an organism's attentional resources, verifying that those schemes necessary for a plan's execution are active in each moment. In this way, the executive schemes regulate the combination and the temporal order of schemes activated to attain a purpose or to put into action a strategy (Pascual-Leone, 1976a; Pascual-Leone et al., 1978). Thus, one sees that executive schemes can be quite sophisticated, especially in an educated adult.[12] However, even a young child will already have developed its first executive schemes, though they will be rudimentary and based only on analogical representations, for example, plans for exploring objects and the environment.[13]

Examples

A few illustrative examples may provide a clearer sense of this threefold system for classifying schemes. The mental representation of how to tighten a screw would be an operative scheme at the zero level in the motor modality. The mental representation of the verb "go" is an operative fluent at the zero level in the linguistic modality. In the case of a person for whom the rules for solving an algebraic system with two unknowns were well

---

[12]Contrary to theories that posit one central executive system (e.g., Baddeley, 1986), the TCO postulates a great multiplicity of specialized executive schemes.

[13]The first, simple executives would be developed between 1½ to 2 years of age (e.g., Pascual-Leone, 1996b). For instance, they could organize a sequence of actions in symbolic play, a plan for producing a two-word sentence, or the invention of new means to a certain goal. Pascual-Leone and Johnson (1999), however, adopt a different terminology and call "executive" practically any coordination of sensory-motor schemes, even at the age of 6 months. We believe, however, that this difference is only due to an attempt at simplifying language in the latter chapter and that the actual claim made by the TCO is that executives appear late in the second year of life.

learned, the mental representation of this set of rules would be an operative scheme in the conceptual-propositional modality. The scheme's level would be superordinate with respect to the variables and the individual rules. The scheme that allows one to recognize a rose would be a figurative scheme at the zero level in the visual modality. The mental image of a rose would itself be composed of subordinate level schemes that are also figurative and in the analogical modality. Activation of these schemes representing various parts of the rose would require some mental effort. An example of a figurative fluent (in the analogical-conceptual modality) might be the *frame* that generically represents the "Hollywood comedy": a set of prototypical roles, characters and interactions within which the developments of each scene carry more or less detailed expectations for the following scenes.

Clearly, individuals develop their own repertoire of schemes different from that of any other person. In the TCO, schemes are also referred to as *subjective operators*: "operators" in the sense that when applied to a particular mental state (a perceptual input or other previously activated schemes) they produce a new mental state; "subjective" in the sense that they are specific to every individual and that the process of their successive activation constitutes the content of one's subjective experience. It is the experiences that individuals have in their own environments that allow the formation and coordination of schemes. For example, the concept of orthogonal projection or the procedure for making coffee are unitary schemes only for those persons having sufficient experience with orthogonal projection or making coffee. For the inexpert, to discriminate an orthogonal projection from other types of drawings or to prepare coffee would require the coordination of several schemes.

Although having stimulated little specific research, the TCO system of classifying schemes has a theoretical importance as a guide in construction of models concerned with identifying the schemes involved in a task or mental activity.

SECOND-LEVEL OPERATORS

Another fundamental construct in the Theory of Constructive Operators is that of second-level or *metasubjective operators*. The TCO treats schemes of the first level as "subjective" operators, in part because every individual possesses a large personal repertoire of these. Even though a person is not aware of which individual schemes are active in one's mind, it is the activation of sets of schemes that determines the content of subjective experience. Metasubjective operators, instead, cannot be a part of subjective experience because, unlike schemes, they do not have their own information content. These second-level operators are information processing mechanisms that act on the first level operators (i.e., schemes). Also in contrast to the subjective operators, those of the second level constitute a small number of general resources common to all people. Although there are quantitative differences among people in the strength or efficiency of the metasubjective operators, there are no qualitative differences in the repertoire. It would be impossible for a person to have a metasubjective operator not possessed by others.

Metasubjective operators serve the function of increasing or decreasing the activation levels of schemes, and they enable the formation of new schemes. As just stated, when a scheme is activated it tends, in turn, to activate other compatible schemes and to inhibit incompatible ones. However, if a scheme's activation level depended solely on the perceptual input and on the activation or inhibition received from other schemes, then in each moment we would be prisoners of our current repertoire of schemes, of the greater or lesser salience of the stimuli, and of the propagation of activation among the schemes most closely connected to one another. Thus, it is necessary to posit the existence of other mechanisms distinct from the schemes that enable processing and integration of information, so that one can go beyond the information given and beyond the current scheme repertoire. One of these mechanisms, called "central computing space" in early writings, has already been mentioned in the section entitled "Schemes and Processing Capacity." Here we describe the metasubjective operators included in the theory, though we also note that it is certainly possible to hypothesize other operators or to discover that the functions now attributed to a single mechanism depend instead on two or three different ones. In such cases, of course, the theory would have to be modified.

Learning Effects

The psychological mechanisms that enable the formation of new schemes, that is, the *C, LC* and *LM operators*, have been inferred from numerous Piagetian, cognitive and behaviorist studies of learning.

The *C operator* (for Content learning) corresponds to Piaget's accommodation of schemes (Pascual-Leone & Goodman, 1979). Accommodation occurs when one's experience violates one's expectations; that is, when a scheme *x* is strongly activated in a situation, but *x* leads to the activation of some schemes that are incompatible with other ones activated in that situation.[14] At that point, the repertoire of schemes can be enriched by the

---

[14]For example, a plastic apple might activate schemes for grasping and biting, but one's tactile experience will activate other schemes incompatible with biting. In this way, from the scheme that represents apples one could differentiate a scheme that represents artificial apples, that is, something with the appearance of an apple that does not, however, lend itself to being eaten.

formation of a new scheme x' that is similar to the one already strongly activated but different in some feature. In addition to Piagetian accommodation, the C operator mechanism for forming schemes also seeks to explain discriminative learning as described by behaviorists.

The two L operators (for structural *L*earning) provide an account of other types of learning that involve the formation of a superordinate scheme. In these cases the formation of the new scheme derives not from the modification of an existing scheme, but from the coordination of two or more schemes activated simultaneously (Pascual-Leone, 1976a, 1976b; Pascual-Leone & Goodman, 1979). The activation of any one of the schemes coordinated within the superordinate scheme would automatically result in the activation of all the others. The phenomenon of automatization of cognitive processes provides a notable example of the coordination of schemes.

The L operators are labelled LC and LM. The LC operator involves slow, gradual learning processes based on the frequent coactivation in a given context of two or more schemes already formed by means of the C operator. Complex schemes are the result, and they are often analogical representations of experiential content that are not readily transferable beyond the context in which they were acquired. Nevertheless, they make up a dense associative network (that could produce interference effects if one had to activate only one of the component schemes).

LM learning, on the other hand, is rapid and abrupt. It is produced with the use of attentional resources (see the M operator in the following section), sometimes with conscious learning strategies. It leads to structures that are hierarchically organized and do not include a representation of the context in which they are learned (hence, it is sometimes called logical-structural learning), and thus are less susceptible to interference. LM learning could produce representations of various sorts, from concepts to complex procedures or symbolic rules. Although the LC and LM distinction has important theoretical and practical consequences (Pascual-Leone, 1976a, 1995; Pascual-Leone & Goodman, 1979; Pascual-Leone & Johnson, 1999), it is not essential for most of the matters we consider in this book, and we often speak simply of the L operator.

The work of Miller and his colleagues (Miller, Bentley & Pascual-Leone, 1989; Miller, Pascual-Leone, Campbell, & Juckes, 1989) is important to illustrate learning of executives. These authors have repeatedly administered the CSVI and other measures of the central computing space to low socioeconomic level African (Zulu) children. In a control condition, in which attentional strategies had little importance because of lengthy duration of the stimulus and a prohibition on responding prior to its discontinuation, they showed that the capacity of these children was equivalent of Canadian children participating in other studies. On tests for which success also depended on adequate executive schemes (e.g., schemes for controlling attention in a tachistoscopic version of the CSVI), performance by Zulu children on the *first presentation* was inferior to that of Canadian children of the same age. However, on *successive presentations* of parallel forms of these tests, the same children obtained higher scores. Miller and colleagues attribute the improved results to the formation and partial automatization, while performing the tests, of appropriate executive schemes. Bentley, Kvalsig, and Miller (1990) reached the same conclusion in a similar experiment with a different type of test (the FIT; see chap. 9).

Attentional Energy

The M operator (for Mental energy), also metaphorically called "central computing space,"[15] has the function of incrementing activation of schemes that are relevant to a task, but that are not sufficiently activated by the perceptual input or by other operators. Thus, the M operator is an attentional resource, similar to Kahneman's (1973) well-known energetic model of attention. But, in contrast to Kahneman's theory, the TCO specifies the M operator's capacity in quantitative terms, expressing it as the maximum number of schemes that the M operator could activate simultaneously.

Pascual-Leone (1974, 1980, 1987; Pascual-Leone & Johnson, 2005) suggests a possible neuropsychological base for the M operator. He views the executive schemes, localized in the frontal and prefrontal lobes, as utilizing the energy resources of the reticular system to activate schemes localized in other cortical areas; and he suggests that the increase with age of the M operator's capacity is due to the maturation of the neuronal structures on which it depends. Maturation, and therefore the increase in the available reserve of mental energy, would be a continuous phenomenon with increasing age; however, the discontinuous, stage-like aspects of mental development would be due to "qualitative leaps" that occur every time that the increase in energy is sufficient to activate one more scheme.

Many studies, including those on the CSVI just cited, support the hypothesis of an increase in the capacity of the M operator (or M capacity) of one scheme every 2 years, from 3 to 15 years of age. Pascual-Leone and Johnson (1991) extend the study of the M operator's development to the first years of life, considering experiments with linguistic tasks (Benson, 1989) and memory tasks (Alp, 1988, 1991; Benson, 1989) in addition to the Piagetian literature. They maintain that less mental energy is required to activate a sensorimotor scheme than to activate a scheme at the symbolic representation level; and they suggest that the number of sensorimotor schemes that

---

[15]The expression "central computing space" has often misled readers to believe that the M operator functions like a short term memory similar to the one hypothesized by Atkinson and Shiffrin (1968). In order to avoid this misinterpretation, this metaphoric term has fallen a bit into disuse.

the M operator can activate simultaneously increases from one at the age of about 1 month to seven at about 3 years (for further discussion of the development of M capacity in the sensorimotor period, see Pascual-Leone & Johnson, 1999).

In a chapter on aging, Pascual-Leone (1983) suggests that the available capacity of mental energy declines with advancing age and that, on average, 60-year-olds have at their disposal an M operator functionally equivalent to that of children in the 11–12-year-old range (see Morra, Vigliocco, & Penello, 2001, for new supporting evidence).

M capacity is expressed by the formula $e + k$, in which e represents the executive schemes and k the number of operative and figurative schemes that can be activated simultaneously. The suggestion is that the amount of energy necessary for activation of the executive schemes is modest, given that these are well-learned operations and control processes. Moreover, it is assumed that the quantity of mental energy required to activate executive schemes is approximately equivalent to the M capacity of a 2-year-old child (Pascual-Leone & Goodman, 1979), this is why executive schemes begin to appear around 2 years of age. For these reasons, e is treated as a constant in the expression of the M capacity for children of 3 years and older.[16] Of course, an adult's executive schemes are more complex than those available to a young child, but this aspect of development is attributed to learning and automatization. Execution of the complex operations provided for by adult executive schemes requires holding several items of information in mind, but it is to these items that the M operator must dedicate most of its resources (i.e., those represented by the k parameter). Table 2.1 summarizes the maturation of M capacity according to this theory.

The Inhibition of Irrelevant Information

The *I operator* (for *I*nterrupt) carries out functions complementary to the M operator; it is a central attentional mechanism that inhibits (disactivates) irrelevant schemes in a top-down way. It may be easiest to see its role in the context of selective attention.

Consider, for example, the Stroop effect (Mac Leod, 1991; Stroop, 1935), which involves stimuli that have mutually contradictory properties. Adults are able to read the name of a color, for example the word "red," more quickly than they are able to respond "red" when presented with a figure of this color. And when presented with the names of colors written in different

---

[16]In older children and adults, executives (i.e., plans and controls) would monitor task performance and regulate allocation of M capacity to content schemes. In infants, who still lack appropriate executives, task performance would be motivated by either a need or a nonmediated affect, which triggers the arousal necessary to mobilize M energy that activates one or more sensorimotor schemes.

TABLE 2.1
Development of the Capacity of the *M* Operator According to the TCO

Age	*M Capacity*	
	e	*e + k*
0–1 month	0	
1–4 months	1	
4–8 months	2	
8–12 months	3	
12–18 months	4	
18–26 months	5	
26 months–3 years	6	
3–5 years	7?	
5–7 years		*e + 1*
7–9 years		*e + 2*
9–11 years		*e + 3*
11–13 years		*e + 4*
13–15 years		*e + 5*
15 years–adult		*e + 6*
after 35–40 years		*e + 7*
		in decline

Note. The ages indicated are approximate values and relative to the population average. Certainly individual differences exist related to early or late maturation. The figure "7?" in the *e* column indicates that how *M* Capacity grows in terms of sensorimotor tasks after 3 years of age is not clearly determined.

colors, for example the word "red" written in yellow, they do not find it particularly difficult to read the word. However, they do demonstrate difficulties (slower answers and occasional errors) in naming the color in which such words are written. Being overlearned and more accessible, the information about the word's meaning interferes with the use of the incompatible information about its color. The fact that, nevertheless, one almost always succeeds in answering correctly suggests the existence of a process that discards the incorrect information.

The *negative priming* paradigm (e.g., Houghton & Tipper, 1994; Tipper, 2001) is another case that suggests the existence of an *I* operator. We have mentioned that the Stroop effect involves a delayed response to a stimulus because of irrelevant features of that stimulus, which must be inhibited. By contrast, negative priming involves a delayed response to a stimulus because of irrelevant features of a preceding one, features that in the current stimulus are present and relevant. A widely accepted interpretation of negative priming is that, after having inhibited a representation of an irrelevant aspect of the first stimulus, longer time is required to activate it when it becomes relevant for responding to the stimulus that follows (see Tipper, 2001, for a discussion).

Experimental research on inhibitory control processes has gained increasing importance, and several other paradigms have also been used both with adults (e.g., Friedman & Miyake, 2004; Mitchell, Macrae & Gilchrist, 2002) and in the course of development (e.g., Christ, White, Mandernach, & Keys, 2001; Wolfe & Bell, 2004).

Neuropsychology also indicates the existence of inhibitory cognitive mechanisms (e.g., Shallice, 1988). Patients with frontal lesions tend toward perseveration (they are unable to efficiently interrupt ongoing mental activities and processes), are easily distractible and have difficulty when it is necessary to ignore salient information. Brain imaging studies suggest that maturation of the frontal lobes is involved in acquisition of inhibitory control (e.g., Durston et al., 2002).

Pascual-Leone (1983, 1984; Pascual-Leone et al., 1978) suggests that inhibition of irrelevant information plays a role in many cognitive activities, including Piagetian problems and field-independence tasks. The reason is that these situations often require not only that one attend to relevant information, but also that one not be deceived by perceptually salient features or by well learned (but misleading) rules.

Pascual-Leone (1984; see also Dempster, 1992) hypothesizes that a central inhibitory mechanism is involved in selective attention, in Piagetian problems, in field dependence tasks, and in the control of those behaviors found lacking in frontal patients. Moreover, Pascual-Leone et al. (1978) maintain that in certain situations such as free recall or divergent thinking, for which an easy and rapid succession of ideas is valuable, one's performance depends on executive control schemes—*interruption and dis-interruption controls*—that regulate the activity of the I operator. Because the I and M operators act in synergy, their development might be intertwined in some way also (Pascual-Leone & Johnson, 2005). Besides controlled inhibition, automatic inhibition would also occur following each allocation of M capacity, to suppress activation of those schemes that are not under the focus of attention (e.g., Pascual-Leone, 1984, 1987, 1997).

Although these hypotheses are suggestive, it must be recognized that within the TCO the properties and functioning of the I operator are not yet completely formalized. Among the important claims are that the I and M operators are co-functional, as they are both under the control of executive schemes localized in the frontal and prefrontal lobes; that they both develop during infancy and decline in advanced age; and that in both of them there are individual differences (i.e., inhibitory processes are less efficient in field-dependent individuals). A further specification of the I operator's properties would constitute an important development of the theory. Some empirical evidence supports these views (see the section entitled "Research on Inhibitory Processes" for examples) and, at the same time, opens the way to further refinements.

Field Effects

The *F operator* (for *F*ield) represents field effects in information processing. Such effects can influence the activation of figurative schemes (in perception, this is the case of the Gestalt laws, that is, the principles of closure, proximity, similarity, symmetry, etc.; see Kanizsa, 1979). Field effects can also influence the activation of operative schemes (e.g., the attentional phenomenon of spatial stimulus–response compatibility: a task is facilitated if the organization of responses is congruent with that of the stimuli).[17]

Expressed in intuitive terms, the function of the *F* operator is to facilitate the activation of the simplest possible representation of the stimulus configuration. However, as Pascual-Leone recognizes, it is not easy to formalize the concept "simple representation of a configuration" and thereby express in a precise, yet comprehensive way the role of the *F* operator in cognitive processes. The problem remains open notwithstanding the frequent informal use of similar concepts by psychologists of all orientations, and some valuable attempts to specify models of them (e.g., Hochberg, 1988; Kornblum, Hasbroucq, & Osman, 1990).

According to Pascual-Leone (1976b, 1980) one tends to assimilate the conceptual structure of a problem to its perceptual structure. The *F* operator is the organism's tendency to simplify the pattern of activated figurative schemes, and to structure its operative processes in such a way as to make them congruent with this simplified organization of the figurative schemes.[18]

This informal, but intuitively clear, definition can be illustrated with respect to some Piagetian problems.[19] For example, Inhelder et al. (1974) presented children with a zig-zag line constructed from sticks and asked them to construct from other sticks a straight line of the same length as the model. The global configuration of the model led the children to consider the start and end points of the line rather than the number or length of the sticks from which it was composed. They tended, therefore, to construct a straight line with its start and finish aligned side by side with those of the model line. Although such a line is clearly shorter and constitutes an incorrect solution, it is nonetheless a solution that satisfies the *F* operator's requirement of simplicity (Pascual-Leone, 1976b).

---

[17]Even in such a simple task as discrimination of whether a stimulus appears in a higher or lower position, one performs better if the response involves pushing buttons that are placed higher and lower, respectively, rather than in other arbitrary positions.

[18]Pascual-Leone and Johnson (1999, p. 181) further specify that this operator "minimizes the number of schemes that directly apply to inform the performance (including perception or representation) . . . while maximizing the set of distinctive, salient features of experience (activated low-level schemes)."

[19]Piaget and Inhelder (1959, 1966) list a "figural factor" among the causes of the horizontal *décalages* that have the ability to interfere with or facilitate operative thought. However, within the framework of Piagetian theory such a factor has never been studied thoroughly.

This same factor can also induce incorrect judgments in the conservation problems (Pascual-Leone, 1980). For example, in a conservation of volume problem, asked which object's immersion will result in the greatest rise of the water level, children tend to predict a rise based on the height of the object itself.

The F operator can induce incorrect judgments not only in problems in which perception plays a role, but also in problems of a purely symbolic nature. When asked to produce all possible permutations of a set of symbols, naïve participants (who are unfamiliar with the mathematical concept of permutation) produce responses that appear different from one another, rather than following a systematic approach (de Ribaupierre, 1989). Also in the four-card problem described in chapter 1, people's tendency to choose (incorrectly) the cards with the explicitly mentioned symbols seems to be a case of responding in a manner compatible with the stimulus configuration.

In the cases considered thus far, the F operator induces formulation of incorrect or inappropriate judgments. As the reader may have already realized, the F and the I operators may act in a reciprocal antagonism. Problematic situations are problematic because the solution that seems most obvious and intuitive is, in fact, wrong. But this doesn't mean that the F operator is always, or even generally, misleading. On the contrary, in most everyday circumstances it is useful for producing judgments that are consistent with the structure of the surrounding world. Often, for example, a judgment based on salient perceptual characteristics is effective and more economical than an accurate assessment. The F operator also plays a facilitating role in abstract or symbolic tasks provided that they are constructed in such a way that the correct answer is congruent with the emergent structure of the stimuli. Pascual-Leone (1980) suggests that conditions for Piagetian equilibration processes are optimal when the simplest synthesis of the information activated by a problem constitutes a correct solution.

Automatic Encoding of Space and Time

The S operator (for Space) is composed of the cognitive mechanisms that compute the location of objects in the physical environment and the spatial relations among them; neuropsychologists call it the "where" system and locate it in the dorsal-parietal pathway. Its does not carry out a conscious calculation, but rather, there are automatic parallel processes involving information on spatial positions[20] (Pascual-Leone & Johnson, 1999, 2005). Possibly, acquisition of basic spatial concepts, such as the horizontal and vertical coordinates, may also involve S operator processes.

---

[20]There is a debate about what spatial information is automatically encoded also in memory and what is not (e.g., Farrell & Robertson, 1998; Schumann-Hengsteler, 1992; Walker, Hitch, Doyle, & Porter, 1994). Neo-Piagetian theories could benefit from that debate in order to specify which aspects of spatial information processing tax limited attentional resources.

In addition, Pascual-Leone hypothesizes the existence of a T operator (for *Time*): not a conceptual representation of time but a process of automatic encoding of real time. It would be involved in automatic structuring of currently evolving states of experience and in episodic memory encoding (and therefore also in the construction of the self), but also in the acquisition and use of the sequential structures of language, in the acquisition of rhythms, in learning expectancies about objects, and in structuring simple executive plans and strategies. Also the literature on the "psychological moment" of the first half of the 20th century could be interpreted in this light. The conjectures on the T operator (e.g., Pascual-Leone & Johnson, 1999), however, still require further development.

Emotion-Based Activation

The A operator (for *Affect*) represents emotion-based contributions to the activation of schemes. As described previously, the Theory of Constructive Operators posits specific *affective schemes* that embody the physiological components and motivational effects of emotions, and *personality schemes* that coordinate affective with cognitive schemes. One possible consequence of the activation of affective schemes is the temporary flow into the cognitive system of a quantity of energy capable to activate a certain number of cognitive schemes beyond those already activated from other sources. In certain cases, this activation might favor better performance (e.g., Miall, 1989, discusses the role of affect in the comprehension of literary texts); in other cases the activated schemes might be irrelevant or involve strategies incompatible with rational performance (e.g., in panic the representation of a target is so strongly activated that it may inhibit representation of alternative routes). The A operator is particularly important during infancy, when the M operator and other endogenous sources of scheme activation are still rather weak.

THE TCO AND TASK ANALYSIS

Up to this point we have considered in detail the various constructs of the Theory of Constructive Operators. Let us turn now to a consideration of the overall picture they form.

General Characteristics of the TCO

The TCO is a complex theory that proposes a clear distinction between two levels of constructs, namely the subjective operators and the metasubjective operators. One of the purposes of the TCO is to account for *cognitive conflicts*. The theory posits that the knowledge and strategic processes activated in a situation are multiple, and possibly contradictory; and further, that in such cases, various metasubjective operators favor the activation of one or another set of schemes.

The TCO also provides a coherent approach to *cognitive styles*. According to Pascual-Leone (1974, 1989; see also de Ribaupierre, 1989; Globerson, 1989; Pascual-Leone & Goodman, 1979) cognitive styles derive from different balances among the mental operators that act in contrast with one another. For example, he suggests that in field-dependent individuals the F, L, and C operators tend to prevail over the I and M operators (and over the executive schemes that control them) and that the opposite holds for field-independent individuals. Thus, the difference among persons of various types is not a deficiency or difference with respect to a single variable, but rather is a matter of a different balance among numerous variables.

Extensive research (e.g., Baillargeon, Pascual-Leone, & Roncadin, 1998; Case & Globerson, 1974; Globerson, 1983a, 1983b, 1985, 1987, 1989; Goode, Goddard & Pascual-Leone, 2002; see also Pulos, 1997, and related commentaries) shows that field independence and M capacity are different constructs, and that field-dependent persons need not have lesser M capacity than field-independent ones. Rather, the two cognitive styles differ in terms of processing strategies, perceptual biases, or allocation of attention, such that performance turns out to be different on some measures of M capacity and working memory as well.

The TCO also suggests a solution to the *learning paradox* (e.g., Juckes, 1991). Pascual-Leone criticizes theories in which one's new and creative performances (such as succeeding for the first time in one's life in solving a conservation problem) are explained by the acquisition of logical competencies, inference rules, production systems (Klahr & Wallace, 1976) or other specific knowledge that is transferable to new problems. If such explanations were correct, it would be necessary to ask how one had acquired these logical competencies or other specific knowledge that had never before been demonstrated or used. Could learning without experience be possible? Bereiter (1985) expresses the learning paradox as follows: according to some theories, in order to acquire a new ability or piece of knowledge an individual must already implicitly possess a cognitive structure at least equal in complexity to that of the new acquisition, but this requirement is paradoxical.

There are two possibilities for resolving the paradox. One approach is to avoid a need for learning experiences by adopting (like Beilin, 1971) an extreme innateness hypothesis, a possibility that is coherent but not very plausible. The other assumes, like Pascual-Leone (1980), that creative and novel performances do not depend on preexisting knowledge alone, but also on the intervention of general mechanisms (the metasubjective operators). For example, in the case of solving a conservation problem, the *M* operator and the *I* operator are certainly involved: *M* to activate relevant knowledge and *I* to inhibit the tendency to respond on the basis of a salient dimension. Also involved is the *F* operator that releases a simple representation and a response that is consistent with the activated knowledge. In this case, the participation of the *M* and *F* operators constitutes the process that Piaget calls *equilibration*. By means of these new or creative performances one could also learn specific knowledge, competencies, or rules that are transferable, though only subsequently, to similar situations or problems. Thus, the metasubjective operators hypothesis provides a resolution of the paradox of acquiring knowledge without prior experience (which would be equivalent to saying: knowledge learned without having learned it).

Finally, the TCO makes an important contribution to task analysis, that is, to the identification of all the knowledge and abilities required for successful execution of a task.

Task Analysis

The TCO is a complex and multifaceted theory, and its approach to *task analysis* and to the formulation of processing models for specific situations reflects its complex, articulated form. From the point of view of the TCO, task analysis requires the psychologist to perform the following operations:

1. Identify the strategy, or the various strategies (also the incorrect ones) that one can implement in a given task. If more than one strategy is identified, then identify also the factors that might lead an individual to follow one strategy rather than another (e.g., metasubjective factors, experimental or situational variables, or prior experience).
2. Describe the temporal unfolding of each strategy analyzed, decomposing it in a sequence of operations or successive steps.
3. Specify the set of schemes that are activated[21] in order to carry out each of the described steps.
4. Indicate the causes of each scheme's activation; that is, whether it is activated by perceptual input or by one or more subjective operators.

These four points, however, describe the final result of a task analysis, not how the task analysis is conducted. The latter is discussed in chapter 9.

---

[21]The theory posits hierarchies of schemes in which those schemes that are more complex have less complex ones as components. In a task analysis it is appropriate to list the highest level activated schemes, because in this way the activation of the components of the superordinate schemes is also granted.

Task analysis is theory guided and affords various inferences and predictions. For example, if one concludes that in order to implement a certain strategy a person must activate five schemes by means of the M operator, then one can predict that children with an M capacity less than $e + 5$ will not be able to carry out the strategy and that attempts to do so will lead to imprecise and inadequate outcomes. Or suppose an analysis recognizes two alternative strategies, one of which is facilitated by the F operator whereas the other employs the I operator; then one could predict that the first strategy is more likely to be adopted by field-dependent individuals whereas the second is more likely among field-independent individuals. Or if, in an experiment or instructional situation, certain linguistic or perceptual variables are manipulated in such a way as to increase or decrease the salience of some aspect of a problem, this manipulation could increase the probability of particular relevant schemes being activated without any intervention of the M operator. The task is thus facilitated and becomes performable by a person with an M capacity smaller (by a quantifiable amount) than that required for the standard version of the task. Finally, if one introduces learning phases that automatize the activation of a scheme or coordinate previously separated schemes, the L operator will replace or cooperate with the M operator, thereby facilitating the task to a degree corresponding to the number of schemes involved.

One may note that task analysis permits both qualitative and quantitative predictions. Qualitative examples include predictions on the effects of information salience, or the relations between cognitive style and performance. Quantitative ones include predictions regarding the M capacity required to follow a given strategy, or the degree of task facilitation that occurs when one is able to specify the schemes activated as a result of manipulating particular variables. In some cases, particularly precise quantitative predictions have been made; for example, for performance in a memory task (Burtis, 1982, exp. 1) or for school-age children's planning of their drawings (Morra, Moizo, & Scopesi, 1988).

Either for practical reasons or simply due to excessive difficulty, it is not always possible to carry out a detailed analysis of all the aspects of a task. For example, the temporal breakdown of a strategy into successive steps might be uncertain, and for this reason the psychologist might be limited to analyzing one or two of its crucial moments. As another example, there might be doubts about the sources of activation for certain schemes and these would limit a psychologist to approximate evaluations. In both of these cases, predictions and inferences would be less accurate.

We turn now to describing some of the research carried out within the TCO framework that provides examples of task analysis and of the methods used to test the predictions based on this theory.

A CLASSICAL PIAGETIAN PROBLEM:
THE CONTROL OF VARIABLES

A problem studied by Inhelder and Piaget (1955/1958), variously translated from the French as "dissociation of factors," "separation of variables," or "control of variables," involves determining the variables that influence the flexibility of a rod. Several rods are laid out horizontally and fixed at one end. The rods vary in terms of material (wood, brass, steel), length, cross-sectional form (round, square) and thickness; and dolls of different weights are placed on the free end of each rod. A basin of water lying beneath the free end allows a practical evaluation of the flexibility concept in terms of whether the rod approaches or touches the water. This simple situation reveals the children's ability to determine the individual dimensions along which the rods vary as well as their ability to use a basic principle of experimental method, namely varying one factor at a time while holding all the others constant.

Up to about 6 years of age, Inhelder and Piaget found prelogical performance; between 7 and 11 years they found an increasing ability to classify the observed facts, but without any systematic approach; and only in the oldest children did they find an ability to vary all the factors independently (still with some uncertainty up to 14 years). According to the authors, the task is certainly a formal operations one as it requires a propositional reasoning that involves implication and a systematic combinatorial calculus.

Task Analysis

Case (1974a) made the prediction, counterintuitive at the time of the research, that the scheme for control of variables could be made accessible to 8-year-olds. We now review the essential features of his analysis.

According to Case, a child whose repertoire includes the appropriate executive scheme would be able to adopt a systematic comparison strategy. Thus the child would be able to verify whether a rod with a certain characteristic bends more than another that does not have the characteristic while simultaneously making sure that the rods do not differ with respect to any of the other characteristics.

This demanding operation requires that four schemes be activated. Suppose, for example, that a child has noted that one of the long rods bends more than one of the short ones, and seeks to verify whether longer rods are more flexible in general. The schemes that are *simultaneously* involved are: (1) a figurative scheme representing the observation that the long rod bends more; (2) an operative scheme corresponding to the rule "if there ʹ also some difference between the rods other than length, mark it"; ͡ urative scheme representing a relevant property (for example, the thickness) of rod A; and (4) a figurative scheme representing the corresponding property of rod B. To carry out this check the child must alternately direct attention to rods A and B, and for these rods *one* of the schemes indicated by (3) and (4) would be activated, in turn, by perceptual input. The operation would then be repeated for each of the relevant variables.

If this strategy requires simultaneous activation of four schemes, one of which is activated by the input, then it is possible to conclude that the required M capacity is $e + 3$. Therefore, the normal child of 7–8 years should be able to implement it. According to Case, the reason why success is not usually attained before 11 years is that younger children do not possess adequate executive schemes relating to the concept of "rigorous proof," a concept for which occasions to acquire it are rare. Nevertheless, according to Case, acquisition of such a concept is possible with an M capacity of $e + 3$; and therefore, it should be possible to teach it to 8-year-olds who meet the following conditions:

1. they are cognitively normal, and in particular they have acquired the M capacity typical of their age;
2. they are given the opportunity to learn the concept of rigorous proof; and
3. they have at least a minimal degree of field independence.

Experiment

To test this analysis, Case (1974a) selects 6 groups of children, three of which are trained with respect to the rigorous proof concept whereas the other three act as control groups. In each condition (training and control) there are: a group of 8-year-old field-independent children, a group of 8-year-old field-dependent children, and a group of 6-year-old field-independent children.

Beginning with the demonstration of a nonrigorous proof, the experimental groups receive instruction that is systematically guided toward understanding the concept of interest. They are asked to compare an aluminum rod inserted in a black block (in which a weight is hidden) with a brass rod inserted in a white block and to decide whether the aluminum or brass rod weighs more. The deception is then revealed and the researcher demonstrates that the proof should be carried out by comparing two rods within equivalent blocks. The training continues with different tasks and materials, alternating explicit explanations and invitations to explore, verbal questions and practical experience.

Subsequently all the children, both from the training groups and the control groups, undertake criterion tasks (the control of variables) both with Piagetian materials (the flexible rods) and with another kind of stimuli.

Among the 8-year-olds, those who are field-independent and are trained produce, as predicted, a higher number of correct responses. Comparing the four groups of 8-year-olds one sees that *both* instruction *and* field independence yield significant effects. Trained or not, the 6-year-olds perform poorly on the criterion task. This result is also consistent with the theoretical predictions: the task analysis indicates, in fact, that the 6-year-olds are not yet endowed with the M capacity that is necessary in order to take advantage of the training.

Case concludes that Piagetian structural analysis, in terms of formal operations, can not explain the results of his experiment, but that the neo-Piagetian, functional approach does yield a satisfactory analysis.

IS THE WATER LEVEL HORIZONTAL?

The TCO has also contributed to the analysis of another classical Piagetian problem, the representation of water level (Piaget & Inhelder, 1947/1967). The child is asked to indicate on a real bottle, or to draw on paper the level that water would assume if an empty bottle was refilled about halfway. The bottles are presented in various positions: upright, upside down, placed horizontally on a side, or tilted at various angles.

Piaget and Inhelder describe errors of various types (see also Fig. 2.1). Up to 3–4 years of age, children succeed only in indicating the presence of water in the bottle, for example with a scribble inside the bottle outline. Most 5-year-olds can represent the water level with a line, but they draw it parallel to the bottom of the bottle irrespective of its position, as though the water remained attached to the bottom. An advance is seen around 7 years: with sideways or capsized bottles the line is drawn horizontally, but with a tilted one the line is often drawn approximately parallel to the bottom. At age 9, with tilted bottles, in addition to correct horizontal responses some curious errors are also seen: lines inclined midway between the horizontal and parallel to the bottom, nearly vertical lines, and even some curved lines. Only at age 11–12 do Piaget and Inhelder find a majority of correct answers with inclined bottles. For a review of subsequent research, which also reports the frequency of errors at each age, see Pascual-Leone and Morra (1991).

Piaget and Inhelder (1947/1967) explain the ability to represent water level by the development of spatial and geometric competence, in particular, the understanding of a system of horizontal and vertical coordinates.

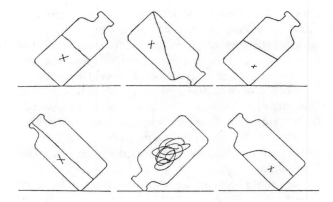

FIG. 2.1. Examples of errors on the water-level problem with tilted bottles. The child is asked to draw a line representing the water's level and to mark that portion of the bottle that contains water with an X. *Source:* Adapted from Pascual-Leone and Morra (1991).

However, this account seems inadequate or incomplete given the occurrence of errors even in samples of adults, who have presumably already acquired the concepts of horizontal and vertical.

Task Analysis

Let's summarize Pascual-Leone's (1969) task analysis. The youngest children's responses are elementary because of their limited M capacity. They can activate simple executives related to instructions such as "imagine water in the bottle," "point with your finger" or "take a pencil and draw." With $M = e + 1$, however, they are able to activate only one symbolic scheme beyond the executive. For this reason they are typically limited to activating the figurative scheme for the concept of *inside*. The outcome is a gross gesture of pointing at any position in the bottle, or a scribble that indicates simply that the water is to be found in the bottle.

Acquisition around age 5 of the strategy of drawing the water parallel to the bottom is also a fruit of experience with bottles and other containers, which usually are positioned upright and thus tend to activate (LC operator) an image of water on the bottom of the container. The regular "good form" of this image makes likely (F operator) that the child accepts it as the correct answer. The strategy carried out at 5 years of age also demands an M capacity of $e + 2$; the two schemes required in addition to the executive are the mental representation of a *line* as a boundary of the water in the bottle and a representation of the *position* of the water, namely at the bottom.

Two reasons would account for the progress that occurs around 7 years of age. First, the acquisition of the scheme of water as a fluid (that falls and accumulates in the lower part of a container) seems necessary in order to overcome the earlier strategy of drawing water as if it adhered to the bottom. Second, the development of an M capacity of $e + 3$ makes it possible to activate, in addition to the executive schemes, three units of information: namely, the representation of a *line* (also required by the previous strategy), the scheme just described of water as a *fluid* that falls toward the lower part of a container, and the mental representation of the *position* of the water, that is, at least a rough assessment of which part of the bottle is lowest.

According to Pascual-Leone, however, an M capacity of $e + 4$, or in some cases even of $e + 5$, is necessary in order to respond correctly when the bottle is in a tilted position. Those children who don't yet have the necessary M capacity seek in imprecise ways, as suggested by the errors just described, to indicate that the water falls to the bottom. The five schemes that must be activated together include the same three required by the preceding strategy, and in addition, the mental representations of two points, one for each side of the bottle, positioned "equally low," that is, at the same height from the table or the support that holds the bottle. In connecting these points, one obtains a horizontal line under which one can draw the water. The children with more sophisticated physical and geometric knowledge, however, could succeed with an M capacity of $e + 4$ by activating the same three schemes required by the previous strategy plus a mental representation of the horizontal coordinate.

Although it is possible to achieve the correct solution by coactivating the four or five necessary schemes, there are, at the same time, important error factors that continue to influence even the responses of older children and of adults (especially field-dependent individuals lacking adequate physical knowledge). The F operator, in particular, induces errors in persons of every age, both because of the "good form" of the (mental or graphic) representation of water at the bottom of the bottle, and also because the motor response most compatible with the presented stimuli consists of producing right angles with respect to the sides of the bottle, in other words a line parallel to the bottom.

Correlational and Experimental Research

Pascual-Leone (1969) reports, both for 9–10-year-olds and for adults, correlations between the water level task and tests of field dependence, as well as experimental research yielding outcomes consistent with the analysis just discussed. He also reports that, among field-dependent adults, one finds not only more errors than among the field-independent, but also a greater variability among each person's responses; that is, field-dependent adults often oscillate between correct and incorrect responses. Numerous studies confirm the relationship between field dependence and the water level task, and others (De Avila, Havassy, & Pascual-Leone, 1976; Pennings, 1991) show a relationship between M capacity and the water level problem. Furthermore, numerous studies provide evidence that physical knowledge also explains, at least in part, the variability in performance. This result is also consistent with the task analysis just presented.

Pascual-Leone and Morra (1991) provide a detailed review of research on the water level task and its relevance to neo-Piagetian models. For the sake of brevity we only mention here one experiment (Howard, 1978) with a method that is notable in this context. In contrast to many studies in which the participants must produce a motor response (such as to draw a line), Howard asks adults to evaluate whether the photographs presented (in which water is either horizontal or inclined at varying angles) are actual or artificial. Those who do not recall the principle of horizontality of liquids make numerous errors. But, although the typical error in the studies that require a motor response is to incline the water line in the same direction as the bottom, Howard reports that the average error is in the opposite direction, though only by a few degrees. We are able to conclude that even if the physical knowledge is important, in adults the error of representing the water as leaning in *the same direction* as the bottom is *not* due to lack of physical knowledge, but precisely to that which Howard's method has eliminated: a field effect, inherent in the production of a graphic or motor response.

A recent study with more than 300 participants aged 5–13 (Morra, in press-a) tests several predictions (explicitly stated by Pascual-Leone & Morra, 1991), on the roles of M capacity, field dependence, and physical knowledge in performing the water level task. All predictions are satisfied except one, that is, it turns out that with horizontal stimulus bottles the minimum M capacity necessary for drawing a horizontal line is not $e + 3$, but instead, $e + 2$. This discrepancy can be accounted for by suggesting a minor correction in the task analysis: with horizontal bottles one scheme, representing the straight line, may be boosted by the F operator and, therefore, does not need to be activated by the M operator. This is because the vertical bottom and the horizontal sides and neck create a perceptual field of horizontal and vertical straight lines that facilitates a horizontal motor response. All other predictions, concerning either group mean performance, or prevailing error patterns, or minimum M capacity necessary for correct performance, or individual differences in degrees of angular error are supported by the data.

It seems remarkable that the model of the water level problem proposed by Pascual-Leone (1969) stands the challenge of time so well and still gains direct or indirect support from research by many authors who in some cases have a different theoretical orientation.

It is not possible to review here all studies of the other Piagetian tasks framed within the TCO; we only mention some research on concrete (Case, 1975a, 1977; Toussaint, 1976) and formal operations (de Ribaupierre, 1980; de Ribaupierre & Pascual-Leone, 1979; Scardamalia, 1977), and on social and moral cognition (Chapman, 1981; Stewart & Pascual-Leone, 1992).

A PSYCHOLINGUISTIC PROBLEM: THE COMPREHENSION OF METAPHORS

The two preceding sections consider tasks that Piaget himself studied extensively. The remainder of the chapter is devoted to themes and research paradigms that are innovative with respect to the Piagetian tradition.

Language is an important area to which the Geneva school has dedicated only a few studies (e.g., Piaget, 1923; Sinclair, 1967). Despite Piaget's interest (1968) in structuralist linguistic theories, his conviction that language development is essentially a consequence of intellectual development (Piaget, 1954, 1970b) prevented his research group from investigating the development of language ability as such.

Decades of psycholinguistic research have clearly demonstrated, however, the specificity of language development, to the point that until recently an approach to language development that also takes into account the influence of general aspects of cognitive development could be seen as unusual or dissonant (for a debate, see Johnsonn et al., 1989; Johnson & Pascual-Leone, 1989b; Karmiloff-Smith, 1989).

The point made by Johnson, Fabian, and Pascual-Leone (1989) is that language development not only depends on specific acquisitions, but is also constrained by general aspects of cognitive processing, that is, by the development of such components of the human information processing system as the second-level operators of the TCO. Johnson, Fabian, and Pascual-Leone (1989) study, in particular, the role of the M, F and L operators in the understanding and production of subordinate clauses between 5 and 12 years of age.

Here we consider the research on metaphor comprehension, a problem that has been analyzed in some detail within the TCO framework. A metaphor transfers the meaning of one or more words from its literal sense to a figurative sense. For example, the phrase "Our school is a paradise" does not mean that it is literally a place where the spirits of the departed gather, but rather that it has such pleasant features that one could compare it to paradise. Richards (1936) distinguishes two elements of metaphor, the tenor (the primary subject to which the rhetorical figure refers) and the vehicle[22] (the expression adopted as an instrument of figurative expression). Metaphor permits a creative use of language, but at the same time involves a wider degree of ambiguity than the usual use of terms based on denotative exactness. For example, consider Robert Frost's metaphor regarding the road "less traveled by": within it the reader can find *multiple* clues for its interpretation, some of which are mutually compatible and some, perhaps, which are pertinent to the context of the poetry in which the metaphor appears.

One should not be surprised to learn that the ability to comprehend metaphors is another subject of dispute among psychologists. Some maintain that this ability is acquired at a relative early age, others in preadolescence. In fact, as with other abilities, metaphor comprehension proves more or less difficult depending on variations in experimental method, and there is debate as to the methods most appropriate for assessing it. In addition, the causes that allow children acquisition of metaphor comprehension are debated. Some authors recognize a possible role for general cognitive ability, such as logical competence in the Piagetian sense; but usually the explanations make reference to specific linguistic or conceptual knowledge (see Johnson et al., 1989; Vosniadou, 1987).

Task Analysis

Johnson and Pascual-Leone (1989a) observe that few studies have examined in detail the interpretations that children give to metaphors. Often the responses are only categorized as right or wrong, but in this way metaphor is treated as though it were not by nature ambiguous, susceptible to multiple interpretations. According to these authors the ability to understand metaphors should not be considered in all-or-none terms; rather, the few studies that attend to the content of the responses suggest a gradual acquisition of the ability to provide interpretations less and less tied to the literal meaning of the vehicle. Johnson and Pascual-Leone's theoretical proposal considers five types or "developmental levels" of metaphor interpretation.

The first level simply consists of inappropriate responses that deny any meaning to the metaphorical expression, or that understand it in a literal sense, or that distort the interpretation in a nonmetaphorical way. For a metaphor such as "my sister was a mirror" the response "she was standing in front of a mirror" would be considered inadequate for these reasons.

The subsequent levels require an *M* capacity that increases in accordance with the connection to be found between the tenor and the vehicle.

---

[22]For example, in the metaphor considered, "our school" is the tenor and "a paradise" is the vehicle.

The second level, called *identity*, requires an M capacity of $e + 3$ in that it involves the activation of a figurative scheme that represents the vehicle, another that represents the tenor, and an operative scheme for identifying identical aspects of the two objects. At this level, our example metaphor might be interpreted as "one could see oneself in her eyes." This interpretation is not a literal one; however, it is based on a shared property of mirrors and human pupils (the optical reflection of images) and does not involve any semantic transformation.

The third level, called *analogy*, involves the semantic transformation of some aspect or property of the vehicle. With the same metaphor, the response "my sister resembles me" is also based on a mirror's property of reproducing images but here is understood in two different senses: the optical reflection in the mirror and the similarity of the two siblings' faces. A person with an M capacity of $e + 4$, seizing on a possible identity (an aspect with respect to which the two objects might be equal) could produce an analogy by activating four schemes: three figurative ones corresponding to the tenor, the vehicle and the just-formed identity meaning, and an operative one to transform the first provisional interpretation, adapting it to the characteristics of the tenor.

The fourth level of responses is called *concrete experiential predicate*. It takes the form of a description of a prototype, an event or a concrete example regarding the tenor. This type of response also requires that one consider some property or aspect of the vehicle, but only as a clue to evoke pertinent aspects of the tenor. In the sister/mirror metaphor, the response "you were playing Simon Says and your sister would copy you" would be classified as a concrete experiential predicate.

The fifth level is called *generic conceptual predicate*. Also in this case the respondent's verbal expression must refer only to the tenor and not to the vehicle. In comparison to the fourth level, which involves an aspect or a concrete example of the tenor, responses at this level involve a more general or more abstract concept or property attributable to the tenor such as in, "my sister takes me as an example."

The responses classified as predicates presuppose that the respondent has identified an analogy that leads to the choice of properties of the tenor that allow reinterpretation of the analogy in a more elaborate way. The generic conceptual predicate requires an M capacity of $e + 5$ as it entails four figurative schemes (tenor, vehicle, the provisionally established meaning for the analogy, and at least one concept that is more abstract relative to the tenor), plus one operative scheme that changes the analogy in a way that is closely relevant to the tenor. The concrete experiential predicate could be formed in the same way, with the only difference being that in place of the abstract concept a figurative scheme is activated that represents some experiential knowledge of the tenor. At least occasionally even those with an M capacity of $e + 4$ can produce responses at this level in situations for which experiential knowledge is sufficiently well learned as to be activated by the LC operator rather than requiring attentional energy.

In short, an M capacity of $e + 3$ is required for identity, $e + 4$ for analogy, $e + 5$ or on occasion $e + 4$ for concrete experiential analogy, and $e + 5$ for generic conceptual predicate. Obviously one must also possess the necessary conceptual figurative schemes and linguistic operative schemes. Finally, Johnson and Pascual-Leone maintain that a metaphor is better interpreted and the M capacity required is reduced when the context (both linguistic and nonverbal) facilitates one's attention to relevant properties of the tenor.

Experimental and Correlational Research

In their primary experiment Johnson and Pascual-Leone (1989a) ask the participants (children from 6 to 13 years of age, plus an adult group) to give all the interpretations that come into mind for the six metaphors made up from the possible combinations of two tenors (my sister and my shirt) and three vehicles (a rock, a mirror, and a butterfly). For each metaphor, the highest level interpretation that each person is able to produce is noted. Each also completes an intelligence test with measures of both verbal and nonverbal reasoning, a verbal test of divergent thinking, and two nonverbal measures of M capacity: the figural intersection task (see chap. 9) and a variation of the CSVI.

The results conform to the predictions made on the basis of the task analysis. With 6-year-olds, inappropriate answers are most prevalent; at 7 years and above, the majority of responses can be classified at least as identity; from 9 years, at least half of the responses are analogies or predicates; and from 11 years, the majority of responses are classified as predicates. If instead of assessing the results from the point of view of age, one considers the growth of M capacity from $e + 2$ to $e + 5$, one observes just as clearly the predicted pattern of responses, There is a strong correlation between the ability to understand metaphors and performance on the measures of M capacity, even though these measures are nonverbal and do not share any content or specific knowledge with the metaphors.[23]

---

[23]The correlation between M capacity and metaphor comprehension remains significant even with age and intelligence test scores partialled out. This result is a particularly stringent verification of the hypothesis. The effects of the content of metaphors and of its interaction with age or M capacity have been studied by means of the combinations of two tenors and three vehicles. Elaborating the vehicle by means of adjectives has also been studied. The results replicate those obtained with the whole cited set of six metaphors; no interaction of content with age or M capacity is found; and the presence of one or more adjectives has no effect. It appears that the vehicle constitutes a single concept, independent of its linguistic extension and from the richness of detail provided by adjectives.

Johnson (1989) studies the comprehension of metaphors presented in Spanish and in English to bilingual children from 7 to 12 years of age, whose mother tongue is Spanish, and who are progressing normally in an English-language Canadian school. This research employs many tests, for the most part verbal, for the purpose of distinguishing the tasks that depend on specific abilities in a particular language from those that, beyond the verbal content, involve more general cognitive resources.

The results show that the metaphor comprehension tasks in English and in Spanish are highly correlated; and, moreover, the correlation between the Figural Intersection Test and metaphor composition in each language is significant and remains so even when a compound index of ability in that specific language is partialled out. This data provides further support for the conclusion of the previous research, namely, for the role of the M operator in the interpretation of metaphor.

In conclusion, the TCO seems capable of generating a valid analysis of at least some aspects of language such as metaphor and subordinate clauses (Johnson et al., 1989).[24]

PLANNING AND PRODUCTION OF CHILDREN'S DRAWINGS

Drawing is another form of symbolic representation that Piaget did not investigate extensively. He was interested in drawings mainly as converging evidence for his theory of geometrical knowledge, and accepted Luquet's classical theory of stages in drawing competence, characterized by different levels of realism. Research on drawing takes off again within a Human Information Processing framework (e.g., Freeman, 1980; Willats, 1987). In this context, Morra (1995) proposes a neo-Piagetian account of development of children's drawing.

Children's drawings are usually schematic; early graphic schemes are formed in the context of scribbling, and their potential meaning is sometimes discovered accidentally or figured out on the spot. Within a few years (roughly between the ages of 3 and 5), however, children acquire a repertoire of graphic schemes that have a meaning for them, or can be used as components of more complex, meaningful drawings. Morra (1995) suggests that a graphic scheme is a hierarchically organized figurative scheme that represents the visual aspect of a previous satisfactory solution that the child has found to a pictorial problem; for instance, a child's graphic

---

[24]Also tasks with a nonverbal symbolic content have been studied from the point of view of the TCO: for example, Bell and Kee (1984), Bereiter and Scardamalia (1979), Case (1972, 1974b), Pascual-Leone and Smith (1969).

scheme for a house is derived from the visual aspect of some satisfactory outcome of that child's attempts to draw houses (see also van Sommers, 1984). Also operative schemes are involved in drawing, such as motor schemes, procedures (e.g., for modifying a habitual graphic scheme), drawing systems (e.g., the practical rules of oblique projection, for an older child who masters it, constitute an *LM* structure of operative schemes). Most important in drawing are the operative schemes for spatial placement of items on the page; for example, a young child may draw a circle for the mouth carefully under the circles that represent the eyes; a 4-year-old may acquire a rule to draw figures aligned with the bottom of the page; an older child may arrange the various elements of a scene in selected parts of a sheet.

Metasubjective operators (especially learning and field operators) also have an important role that cannot be reviewed in detail here. Drawing often involves planning and problem-solving, and in such situations the role of the *M* operator comes to the fore. To exemplify drawing research based on the TCO, we report here some studies of partial occlusion (Morra, 2002; in press-b; Morra, Angi, & Tomat, 1996).

Drawing a Partial Occlusion: Task Analysis

How can a child draw an object that is partly visible, and partly hidden behind something else? Preschoolers tend to draw a partly occluded object as if it were fully visible; this strategy is overcome by a majority of children at an age that varies, across experimental conditions, between 5 and 8 years (see Cox, 1991). A major finding from previous research is the similarity effect; children show a stronger tendency to draw an integral shape for the partly occluded object when the occluding and occluded objects have similar shapes (Cox, 1991).

Morra et al. (1996) suggest that this task involves two misleading factors. One is learning; a child who has a graphic scheme for the object that is partly occluded tends to apply that graphic scheme. The other is a field factor, only involved when the occluding and occluded object are similar; in this case, they are perceptually encoded according to the Gestalt law of grouping, which, in turn, enhances the child's tendency to draw a group of similar forms. Therefore, children may draw clearly separate figures for the two objects, or at best, to convey the idea of the objects' spatial proximity, draw two contiguous but integral figures.

There are two strategies that can yield graphic representation of a partial occlusion. One strategy involves the plan to draw the occluded object's scheme without those lines or components that would usually represent the currently hidden part. This "hidden line elimination" strategy requires activation of three schemes: (a) a figurative graphic scheme for the occluded object, (b) a figurative representation of its hidden part, and (c) an operative scheme that "mentally deletes" from the graphic scheme (a) those components that correspond to the part (b). Therefore, the M demand of this strategy is $e + 3$. Moreover, due to the previously mentioned error factors, its use should be correlated with field independence, especially for the case in which the two objects are similar.

The other strategy that can lead to the successful drawing of a partial occlusion requires activation of only two schemes: (a) an operative scheme for placing a graphic scheme on the page in an appropriate position, that is, connected to the drawing of the occluding object; and (b) a figurative graphic scheme for the visible part of the occluded object. The M demand in this case would be only $e + 2$; however, this strategy is made difficult not just by the same error factors that hinder the other one, but also by the possibility that the graphic scheme (b) is not easily available, and a child might even need to create it on the occasion.

Therefore, certain predictions follow: first, that the M capacity required for partial occlusion drawing is $e + 2$, which is the minimum demand of a successful strategy, and that an increase in partial occlusions occurs when an M capacity of $e + 3$ makes both strategies accessible; second, that partial occlusion drawing is also correlated with field independence; and third, that the demands for M capacity and field independence are higher in case of similar objects, because in this case, the F operator also turns into a misleading factor. One further prediction regards a particular error pattern (called "transparency" because the two objects are drawn partly superimposed, as if the occluding object were transparent). This outcome is assumed to be a consequence of faulty implementation of the hidden line elimination strategy by children who don't yet have the required M capacity. Consider the case of a child with a capacity of $e + 2$, who is able to activate only the first two schemes involved in that strategy, but not the third one; the likely outcome would be a "transparency" drawing. Thus, it is predicted that this particular sort of drawing is only produced by children with a capacity of $e + 2$.

Experimental and Correlational Research

Morra et al. (1996) manipulate in an experiment the similarity of the model objects (e.g., a ball behind another ball, versus a pyramid behind a cube) and the visibility of the model while drawing (i.e., for half of the participants the model objects were screened before the child started to draw). The similarity effect proves equally strong with a screened model as with a visible model, which implies that this effect is due to initial perceptual encoding—

rather than, for instance, to observing the model during the drawing process. A second experiment suggests that the similarity effect is actually associated with the Gestalt phenomenon of perceptual grouping.

Further experiments (Morra, 2002; Morra et al., 1996) confirm that, as predicted, partial occlusions are not drawn by children with an M capacity of $e + 1$, that children with $M = e + 3$ draw more partial occlusions than those with $M = e + 2$, and that partial occlusion drawing is correlated with field independence. Morra et al., with a sample of first-graders, find that partial occlusion drawing is related to M capacity and field independence only for model pairs of similar objects; however, with a sample of children in a broader age range (5 to 8), Morra (2002) finds that the drawing of partial occlusions is related to M capacity and field independence with any pair of model objects. In both studies "transparency" drawings are associated with an M capacity of $e + 2$ (Morra, in press-b). In contrast, for children with an M capacity of $e + 1$, the most common outcome by far is a drawing of integral and clearly separate shapes of the two objects (Morra, 2002); this simple solution requires mental activation of only one scheme, namely, the one that represents the identity of the partly hidden object.

Pascual-Leone (1989) makes a distinction between the field-dependence tests that are particularly sensitive to figural field factors (e.g., the Embedded Figures test, in which the misleading field derives from perceptual cohesiveness of a meaningful figure, which hinders detection of a smaller figure embedded in it) versus those that are more sensitive to stimulus–response compatibility (e.g. the Rod and Frame test, in which one is biased to align the rod according to the frame's inclination). Based on this distinction, Morra (2002) also studies which tests better predict performance in the drawing task and determines that the single best predictor is the Children's Embedded Figures Test—a test that is sensitive to field factors in perceptual encoding.

A number of other studies examine drawing from the point of view of the TCO. Morra et al. (1988) investigate how children plan in advance the drawing of a complex scene. Morra, Caloni and D'Amico (1994) study children's ability to modify the graphic scheme of a human figure, a tree, or a ship in order to convey an intended emotional meaning. Morra (2005) explores other modifications in the human figure, such as those that represent a particular movement. On the whole, this work accounts well for the drawing tasks under consideration, thus supporting the theoretical view of drawing development suggested by Morra (1995). Other studies have considered a task that involves representation of complex spatial relations, but not in the domain of drawing (Morra, 2001a; Morra, Pascual-Leone, Johnson, & Baillargeon, 1991). These studies add further evidence of the TCO's ability to generate useful analyses of spatial tasks.

COGNITIVE DEVELOPMENT AND MOTOR ABILITY

Execution of complex movements may require mental programming, at least until they are sufficiently well practiced as to become automatized. Motor programming is an area of research quite distinct from sensorimotor intelligence and practical intelligence as studied by Piaget. Many argue that the limits of working memory influence the ability to program movements: Smyth and Pendleton (1990) studied the representation of movements in working memory, and Allard and Burnett (1985) studied the formation of complex cognitive units (chunking) that represent sports actions. Developmental research in this area is not extensive; Todor (1975, 1979) opened the way to exploration of this territory.

The motor task that Todor studied is not very complex; it is made up of two component movements, one circular and the other straight. The form of the combined movements resembles an upside down Greek letter *rho*, and thus the name "rho task." The rho task requires not only rapidity, but also coordination of movements. The apparatus itself looks like a rectangular box with a handle close to the person operating it that can be moved circularly to a point where it meets a bumper. On the opposite side of the box there is a target. The task consists of making the circular movement so that the handle hits the bumper, then letting go of the handle and hitting the target with one's hand, all as rapidly as possible (see Fig. 2.2).

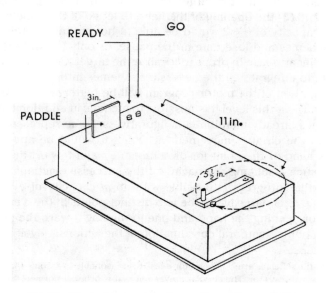

FIG. 2.2. Rho task apparatus. *Source:* Pascual-Leone (1987).

A set of sensors and timers breaks the movement into four phases: the *reaction time* from the "go!" signal to the beginning of the movement; the *rotation time* corresponding to 330 degrees of circular motion; the *pause time* in which the child opens his or her hand, releases the handle to continue of its own inertia, and prepares the movement toward the target; and the *linear time* involved in the straight motion toward the target.

Rho Task Analysis

The analysis of the rho task has been perfected in a series of studies (Pascual-Leone, 1987; Todor, 1975, 1977, 1979). The reaction time and the rotation time are of little psychological interest because they involve only the initiation and execution of a movement and do not require coordination of additional information or motor schemes. However, in the subsequent pause phase and linear phase, someone lacking the ability to form coordinations of the movements would have to first complete the rotation, then decide to open his or her hand and finally to direct the hand toward the target. The more able one is with respect to mentally integrating these components of the complex movement, the more time that can be saved in these phases.

A minimal integration of the components requires an M capacity of $e + 3$ given that, while carrying out the circular movement, one must activate[25] simultaneously three operative motor schemes that represent: (1) the arm's movement toward the target, (2) the direction of one's gaze toward the target, and (3) the opening of the hand to let go of the handle. Children with an M capacity of $e + 2$ would be able to hold in mind either only the first two schemes and lose time in the pause, or only (1) and (3) and lose time in the linear phase in order to localize the target. Certainly they would not be able to integrate all the necessary schemes into a single program.

The integration of the motor program will be better with an M capacity of $e + 4$ because at this level it is possible to include, in addition to the operative schemes already mentioned, a figurative scheme representing either the point in the circular movement at which it would be appropriate to open one's hand or the point for directing one's aim toward the target. By employing such a scheme the pacing of the successive actions can be improved. Further progress is possible with an M capacity of $e + 5$. At this level, one can attend to each of the two distinct points in the circular movement, one for opening the hand and one for aiming toward the target, thus permitting optimal temporal coordination of the actions. Development of M

---

[25]Although the schemes are simple motor ones, it is reasonable to assume that their activation involves the M operator. The circular movement that is being performed and the instruction to do it rapidly induce in their own right a concentration of attention on the movement being executed in that moment. Therefore effortful mental attention is necessary for advance planning of the subsequent movements.

capacity to the higher levels of $e + 6$ or $e + 7$ would have no influence on motor coordination in the rho task.

Research on the Rho Task

Todor (1975) compares three groups of children aged 6, 11, and 18. Performance of the 18-year-olds is the fastest, and they require only a few trials to reach the optimal level of performance, after which practice has minimal effect. In the early trials the speed of the 11-year-olds is not as great, but by the final trials their performance is as rapid as that of the 18-year-olds. Although initially low, the correlation between the times for the various components of the movement in the final block of trials is positive, as is also true for the 18-year-olds. With the experience of just a few dozen trials, the 11-year-olds achieve a speed and a degree of integration among the movements similar to that of the 18-year-olds.

The slowest group on the task is the 6-year-olds; but the most notable result in this group is that even though their times improve over the course of the experiment, the correlation between the components of their movements does not improve with practice; in fact, it declines almost to zero. It appears that 30 practice trials are sufficient for these children to accelerate each of the components of the rho movement but not to integrate them into a single program. The results of this research motivated the task analysis described in the previous section and subsequent research was carried out to test it.

Todor (1977, 1979) compares eight groups of children ranging from 5 to 12 years of age and chosen by means of the CSVI so that their M capacity is normal for their age. Each child completes 25 practice trials on the rho task followed by five trials for which the times are analyzed statistically.

The results support the hypothesis that with each increment of one in M capacity there should be a decrease in the pause times and in the linear phase. It is in alternate years that these decreases are observed. Also confirmed is the hypothesis that a particularly large difference should be found with respect to both pause times and linear times between children with an M capacity of $e + 2$ and those with $e + 3$ as a result of the inability of the first group to integrate the various actions into a single motor program.[26]

---

[26]The increase in M capacity from $e + 2$ to $e + 3$ leads to a decrease of 160 milliseconds in the performance time of interest while each successive increase in M capacity permits a savings of another 80 milliseconds. One might object that in the year in which the M capacity increases from $e + 2$ to $e + 3$, a child's motor speed also increases and that the latter could be the true cause of the obtained result. In order to counter this objection Todor (1979) reports an analysis of covariance in which variability in rotation time is statistically controlled. The differences between the $e + 2$ and the $e + 3$ groups in statistically corrected pause time and linear time remain significant.

As the task analysis predicts, rotation time does improve with age but not as a function of M capacity. These results, therefore, demonstrate that the developmental improvement in pause time and linear time, indicative of the degree of motor integration, has a different cause from the improvement in rotation time.

Pascual-Leone (1987) reports another study with 7- to 12-year-olds in which he considers the role of M capacity, practice and hemispheric specialization. Each child completes two series of trials on the rho task, first with the right hand and then with the left. After 2 weeks the task is repeated with the left and then with the right. Two hypotheses guide the research. First, some authors suggest that the development of M capacity derives primarily from automatization of cognitive processes. If this were so, then Todor's results would be replicated in the first series of trials but not in the fourth as practice would have automatized the components of the motor program. If, however, M capacity develops as a function of maturation, Todor's results should be replicated in both the first and fourth series.

Second, Pascual-Leone (1987) wishes to examine whether the executive schemes that control the use of M capacity are found in both hemispheres or localized in the dominant one. If the former is the case Todor's results should be replicated with both hands, but in the latter case these results would be found only when (right-handed) children complete the task with the right hand.

The results show a clear relation of pause time and linear time with M capacity in the first and fourth series of trials (completed with the right hand). In the second and third series, however, the improvement with age is gradual from 8 years and up. The effect of M capacity in the fourth series contrasts with the hypothesis that automatization of processes is the basis of M capacity development. The different outcome for the series involving the left hand suggests that the executive schemes regulating *M-capacity* use are lateralized in the dominant hemisphere.

An improvement with practice is found among the youngest children (7–8 years) and may be explained by learning processes (*LC* operator): the children might gradually learn to use proprioceptive feedback for motor coordination in the task. For the older children, who quickly acquire an optimal integration thanks to an M capacity of $e + 5$, the additional practice yields little or no benefit.

The research described in this section points at interesting possibilities for the study of motor programming (see also Gerson & Thomas, 1977, 1978). One may ask whether a neo-Piagetian approach is also suitable for more complex motor tasks, important to the children (or adults) who learn them, such as complex sports or dance movements. According to Russell (1990) it is difficult to define cognitively the "problems" in sports, or to identify appropriate units of analysis. Thus, research is often limited to rather abstract laboratory tasks. There are ecologically valid studies on the acquisition of ability in basketball (French & Thomas, 1987) and tennis (McPherson & Thomas, 1989; Williams, Ward, Knowles & Smeeton, 2002) and on memory for movement sequences in modern dance (Starkes, Caicco, Boutilier, & Sevsek, 1990), but these consider only a single cognitive variable, namely the degree of knowledge of the studied activity on the part of the participants. Tallir, Musch, Valcke, and Lenoir (2005), in a study with 10-year-olds, showed that field-independent children were more able at decision making in basketball. Corbett and Pulos (1999) presented a preliminary study, framed within the TCO, of skills like hopping and jumping a rope. There are ample possibilities in this field, and the methods described here could be extended to research on the acquisition of other motor abilities.

RESEARCH ON INHIBITORY PROCESSES

The concept of inhibitory processes in human cognition was not yet popular at the beginning of the Eighties, when so-called "oil-pump" or flowchart models were still the most credited accounts of information processing, except perhaps in language comprehension and memory for narratives. In particular, bottom-up or data-driven models dominated the field of backward pattern masking (see Felsten & Wasserman, 1980, for a review). Backward pattern-masking is a paradigm in visual perception, that consists in brief presentation of a stimulus (e.g., a letter), which after a short interval is replaced by a "mask" (e.g., a random arrangement of letter fragments) that impairs stimulus recognition. Pascual-Leone, Johnson, Goodman, Hameluck, and Theodor (1981) proposed a series of masking experiments, with children aged from 6 to 12 and young adults, as a test of the I operator, followed by further experiments with adults of different ages (Pascual-Leone, Johnson, Hameluck, Skakich, & Jedrzkiewicz, 1987).

The basic idea of Pascual-Leone et al. (1981, 1987) is that, on presentation of the mask, a conflict arises between the task executive (a plan to follow the experimenter's instructions and detect the letters) and the orienting reflex (an innate operative scheme that directs attention to any new stimulus, such as the mask). Therefore, stimulus recognition involves suppression of the mask representation, in order to extract relevant stimulus features from the stimulus–mask compound. The better a person is able to ignore the mask—either because of experimental manipulation or individual differences—the more effectively the stimuli will be recognized.

Pascual-Leone et al. (1981, 1987) manipulate an apparently minor aspect of the materials, that is, the fixation stimulus that is presented at the beginning of every trial to direct the participant's attention where the target stimulus will appear. Different fixation stimuli are used; the two main ones are either a single point at the center of the display, or four points arranged in a square pattern demarcating the area where a letter appears. The basic hypothesis is that the four-dot fixation stimulus cues the I operator to the area where one must inhibit processing of the irrelevant features displayed in the mask. In agreement with this prediction, all of the experiments showed better performance with the four-dot fixation stimulus. One could object that it is not an inhibitory process that causes this result, but rather automatic activation (i.e., priming) of a certain area in visual space. To test this possibility, Pascual-Leone and colleagues use a five-dot fixation stimulus, that is, the four-dot square configuration plus the single dot in the center. The priming interpretation predicts that the five-dot pattern would yield at least as good performance as would the four-dot pattern, because it would prime the same area with an even greater quantity of materials. According to the I operator hypothesis, however, the four-dot fixation stimulus should yield better performance than the five-dot one, because the latter could lead participants to attend either to the square pattern or to the central point. The results support the inhibitory account, because performance with the five-dot fixation stimulus turns out to be intermediate between those with the single dot and those with the four-dot pattern.

The results suggest that (notwithstanding different overall performance at various ages) the advantage for the four-dot pattern over the single dot is roughly constant from 6-year-olds to young adults. (This, incidentally, is another clue that the four-dot advantage is not related to the M operator, which develops considerably during this age range.) One experiment also tests Pascual-Leone's (1983) claim that the I operator declines in elderly subjects, by comparing different age groups from 20 to 70 years. The results show a decrease with age of the four-dot pattern advantage, and the difference is not significant for the oldest age group. Two experiments, respectively with 11- to 12-year-olds and young adults, also test the effect of individual differences in cognitive style. The results show that field-independent participants perform better and, in particular, are better able to take advantage of the four-dot pattern than field-dependent participants. This result rules out the possibility that the advantage of the four-dot stimulus is due to the F operator (otherwise the outcome would have been quite the opposite); it cannot be accounted for by traditional, bottom-up models of visual masking, and provides further support to Pascual-Leone's model, which predicts that in situations of cognitive conflict field-independent people are more efficient in using the I operator or the executive schemes that control it.

It is unfortunate that those experiments were not published in major journals; perhaps they were too much ahead of their time. Although they do not clarify every property of the I operator, they provided evidence in favor of such a construct, when it was not obvious at all. Recent research has undertaken the study of the *I* operator again, comparing different experimental paradigms in which it may be involved.

Comparing Inhibitory Processes Across Tasks

Johnson et al. (2003) consider two different speeded tasks in which the *I* operator might be involved: a Stroop task and a spatial location task, both designed according to the logic of negative priming. These tasks are given (along with other measures[27]) to samples of children in the age range from 6 to 11.

The Stroop task has three conditions: (a) A control condition, in which rows of X's in various colors are presented for color naming; (b) An interference condition, in which color names written in a different color are presented for color naming, and consecutive items have no feature in common; for example, the word "blue" written in orange is followed by the word "green" written in yellow, and the child must respond "orange" to the first item and "yellow" to the second; and (c) A negative priming condition, similar to (b), except that each item is printed in the same color that was the meaning of the word in the previous item; for example, the word "blue" written in orange is followed by the word "green" written in blue, then by the word "black" written in green, and so on. It is known from previous research (e.g., Tipper et al., 1989) that responses in condition (b) are slower than in condition (a) because of the interference of word reading on color naming, and that condition (c) is even slower, because responses are delayed not only by interference, but also by negative priming. When response times (RTs) show a relatively *small* difference between conditions (b) and (a) this is taken as an indicator of efficient inhibition, that is, resistance to interference. When RTs show a relatively *large* difference between conditions (c) and (b) this, too, is taken as an indicator of efficient inhibition, because a large negative priming effect suggests that the irrelevant features of the previous item had been strongly inhibited.

The spatial location task uses a display with four squares, located up, down, left, and right on a screen. In each item, a colored patch appears in the center of the screen and two X's (one in the same color as the central patch and one in a different color) appear in two of the four squares. The child's task is to rapidly move a joystick to the location of the X cued by the color of the central patch. Items appear in pairs, that is, a prime and a probe item. There are actually four conditions defined by the prime–probe

---

[27]These are: two tests of *M* capacity (the CSVI and the FIT), some measures of processing speed, and a test (called Trail Making) that involves planning an unfamiliar sequence. An important outcome, that here cannot be reported in detail, is that three constructs are clearly distinguished. *M* capacity is not accounted for by either speed or inhibition. Also inhibition is not accounted for by speed.

relationship, but describing two is sufficient here: (a) a control condition, in which the two squares used in the probe are those that were not used in the prime; (b) a negative priming condition, in which the distracter X is presented in a square that was not used in the prime, but the target X appears in the same square where the distracter appeared in the prime item. Note that in this task there is no condition defined as interference. In the Stroop task, each stimulus has two features that tend to elicit different responses, so that a person must select the relevant feature and suppress the salient but irrelevant one. In this task each stimulus also has two features (a color and a location), but these two features of the same stimulus do not elicit different responses; rather, the color cues target selection, and then one can respond to the target's location. Previous research (e.g., Milliken, Tipper, & Weaver, 1994) shows that, even though this task involves no interference, it does yield a negative priming effect, that is, responses are slower when the probe target appears in the same place as the prime distracter. Moreover, negative priming in response to location seems to be manifest at an earlier age (e.g., Simone & McCormick, 1999) than in the context of a Stroop task (e.g., Tipper, Bourque, Anderson, & Brehaut, 1989). The study by Johnson et al. (2003) attempts to solve the puzzle of why negative priming emerges at different ages in these tasks.

The results for the two tasks considered separately are consistent with those of previous research. In the spatial location task a negative priming effect is found (of about 50 msec), that is highly significant and independent of age. In the Stroop task, a large interference effect is found; it is significant in both younger (6–8) and older (9–11) children, but is larger in the younger group. At the same time the negative priming effect is significant in the older group (having a magnitude of about 80 msec per item), but is negligible and nonsignificant in the younger group.

The correlations among these effects shed some light on different forms of negative priming. There is a negative correlation between interference and negative priming effects in the Stroop task. This result is in agreement with the view that, in that paradigm, those children who can better inhibit the irrelevant features in a Stroop stimulus and, thus, show a smaller interference in one condition, also show a larger negative priming in another condition where inhibition of irrelevant features of the previous item turns into residual inhibition of relevant features of the subsequent item. However, negative priming in the spatial location task is clearly uncorrelated with both negative priming in the Stroop task, and with interference in it. That is, the Stroop and the spatial location paradigms tap two different and unrelated forms of negative priming.

Johnson et al. (2003) interpret the results according to Pascual-Leone's (1984) distinction between effortful and automatic interruption. The Stroop task would require effortful inhibition because of its misleading nature (the presence of contradictory features in each stimulus, which requires the subject to filter out the most salient but irrelevant of them). Therefore, considering individual differences, negative priming is associated with reduced interference; and considering age-group differences, it is not possible for children younger than a certain age (that in this paradigm turns out to be 9 years) to apply successful interruption in the task. The spatial location task, instead, can be described as distracting (because two stimuli appear and only one must be responded to) but not misleading (because the two stimuli are easily distinguished and their properties make clear which one must be responded to). Hence, no effortful inhibition is needed. Instead, automatic inhibition is produced (at all ages, and without any specific relation to task difficulty) as a consequence of the choice to respond to the stimulus in a particular location—and ignore the other one.

A further study with adults (Johnson et al., 2005) has a similar design. It includes three tasks that are known to produce negative priming, that is, the Stroop task and the spatial location task just described, and a paradigm that involves letter naming under different memory loads (from Engle, Conway, Tuholski, & Shisler, 1995). In this task two superimposed letters are presented, one red and one green, and the participant must name aloud quickly the red letter while ignoring the green one. Items are arranged in pairs, that is, a prime and a probe. In the control condition, both letters in the probe are different from the two in the prime. In the negative priming condition, the distractor (green letter) in the prime becomes the target (red) in the probe. Furthermore, the letter naming task is embedded within a word memory task. A prime–probe sequence can be presented under different memory loads; that is, a variable number of words, ranging from 0 to 4, are presented before the prime, and the participant encodes them for recall after responding to the probe. Engle et al. (1995) suggest that naming the red letter while ignoring the superimposed green one demands effortful selection, and therefore, inhibition is maximally efficient without a memory load, but less efficient with increasing memory load because a person has less resources available. Therefore, Johnson et al. (2005) assume that negative priming under load = 0 is an index of effortful inhibition, but negative priming under load = 4 is not.

Four negative priming measures (i.e., RTs in the negative prime condition with RTs in an appropriate comparison condition partialled out) in this study are of interest here: (1) in the Stroop task, (2) in the spatial location task, (3) in the letter naming task without memory load, (4) in the letter naming task under load = 4. The results show that (1) and (3) are positively correlated, which is consistent with the view that they both represent the outcome of effortful interruption. Also (2) and (4) are positively correlated, consistent with the view that they both represent the outcome of automatic interruption that follows selection. All other correlations, instead, are negative (although only one of them is significant); Johnson, Im-Bolter, and Pascual-Leone et al. (2005) suggest that, at the very least, automatic and effortful inhibitory processes are unrelated to each other, and that they may possibly even be two negatively related styles—in the sense that people who are most efficient in effortful, strategic interruption might be less prone to automatic interruption.

These studies seem to mark a progress in the study of the properties of the I operator, and its individual and developmental differences. Furthermore, they are carried out in closer connection with "mainstream" information-processing research (that was not the case of early neo-Piagetian studies of inhibitory processes as mainstream cognitive psychology at that time had not yet begun to study inhibition directly), with more than a chance that such reciprocal influence can benefit both sides.

CONCLUSION

The TCO was the first theory to define itself neo-Piagetian; it inaugurated the unification of Piagetian, information-processing, and individual-differences approaches in a single theory of cognitive development. It includes different learning mechanisms for the formation of new schemes; it regards maturation of an attentional resource (the M operator) as a precondition for developmental transitions, and it considers the interplay of various "metasubjective operators" as a dynamic factor of conflict resolution, which sometimes develops into a new equilibrium. The merits of the TCO, however, are not just historical. As we have shown throughout the chapter, it has evolved considerably from the first formulations (Pascual-Leone, 1969, 1970; Pascual-Leone & Smith, 1969).

Some of the main ideas of the TCO were long disregarded by mainstream researchers. According to Pascual-Leone's (1987) own recollection, "In 1963 I proposed to Piaget the concept of a mental capacity, or mental-attention mechanism, capable of boosting a limited number of schemes . . . Piaget understood very well this idea . . . but did not like it" (pp. 532–533). For decades, this idea was given little consideration by orthodox Piagetians, empiricist learning-oriented researchers, or proponents of flowchart models. At best, it was misunderstood as a concept akin to short-term memory. Today, however, many researchers accept the view of attentional resources that limit working memory capacity and constrain cognitive development. Similarly, the idea of an inhibitory mechanism—not just an attentional filter that excludes aspects of the perceptual input from processing, but a cognitive resource also involved in thinking and problem solving—was foreign to the mainstream models of cognitive psychology. But the idea of inhibitory attentional resources is now common. The idea of multiple metasubjective operators that could interact and also conflict with one another originally sounded almost science-fiction, but from the 1990s, a similar approach has been proposed, for instance, within dynamic systems models and connectionist models of executive control.

The TCO is still evolving; research on what is termed M or I operator in the TCO now feeds into the current lines of mainstream research on the basic mechanisms of cognition, and the TCO's dialectical models of development in various cognitive domains are accepted with much less skepticism. Aspects of the TCO still need to be developed further; for instance, formalization of the I operator mechanisms is very much a work in progress. Some other metasubjective operators and the interactions among them also need further elaboration, either in general conceptual terms or in the specific way they affect performance on particular tasks. And perhaps the development of computational models based on the TCO could improve the conceptual precision of its constructs.

Current research on such topics as giftedness (Johnson et al., 2003; Johnson, Pascual-Leone, Im-Bolter, & Verrilli, 2004; Pascual-Leone, Johnson, Verrilli, & Calvo, 2005), specific language impairment (Im-Bolter, Johnson, & Pascual-Leone, 2006), vocabulary learning (Morra & Camba, 2005), reading comprehension in the life span (Borella & de Ribaupierre, 2006), and arithmetical ability (Agostino, Im-Bolter, Johnson, & Pascual-Leone, 2005) shows that this theoretical approach is productive and capable of exploring new areas. This chapter has presented the overall structure of the TCO and some lines of research carried out in this framework. In the following chapters (particularly chaps. 6, 8, and 9), we mention other contributions of the TCO and highlight its similarities and differences with other neo-Piagetian theories.

3

Structuralist Approaches
to Developmental Stages

The theory of Pascual-Leone, presented in the previous chapter, adopts the Piagetian concept of scheme, but radically reinterprets the concept of stage. According to Pascual-Leone (1987) developmental stages result from increases in the capacity of the M operator, and stages are to be observed only in those tasks for which activation of the appropriate schemes is not facilitated by field effects or prior learning.

Other neo-Piagetian theories, however, approach stages in a more Piagetian manner. These theories connect stages to the concept of *structure* as conceptualized by Piaget, which is basing each developmental stage in a particular type of structure. In this chapter, we consider theories taking this approach; of particular importance is the contribution of Graeme Halford. We also discuss some research that steps a bit further away from its Piagetian origins, but that maintains a structuralist point of view on the problem of individual differences. First, however, we consider in general terms the fundamental characteristics of Piagetian structuralism.

PIAGET'S STRUCTURALIST APPROACH

Structuralism is a theoretical approach not only within psychology, but within social science generally (e.g., see Chomsky, 1959; Piaget, 1968). According to structuralism, scientific explanation consists in the identification of a formalizable structure to which the facts to be explained are subject and from which they may be interpreted deductively.

The Concept of Structure

Piaget (1968) defines a structure as "a system of transformations. . . . It is a system and not a mere collection of elements and their properties" (p. 5). Every structure is characterized by *laws* of the *whole*, of *transformation* and of *self-regulation*. The transformations themselves preserve or enrich the structure without employing or producing elements external to the system.

A structure is defined on a set of elements, each of which has their own particular characteristics or properties. However, laws of the whole concern the relations among these elements rather than the properties of the individual elements themselves. The concept of structure is thus distinct from that of set or aggregate, neither of which is defined by relations among its elements. The set of integers can serve to illustrate laws of the whole. Although each integer has the individual property of being odd or even, positive or negative, prime or nonprime, the integers do not exist in isolation and were not discovered in just any order. Such structural properties as numerical succession and algebraic group structure express relations among the elements of the set and, thus, are ingrained in the whole set of integers rather than in the individual numbers.

The concept of transformation concerns one broad aspect of the wholeness of structures. The laws of transformation specify, given certain elements of the whole, which other elements derive from them.

Self-regulation involves a structure's preservation across transformations. For example, the structure of an algebraic group is "closed" with respect to the operations that define it, that is, there is no operation that yields an element not belonging to the structure. A biological structure behaves in a manner that regulates its imbalances and maintains homeostasis by means of transformations. Piaget (1968, 1970b) notes that the concept of self-regulation, when applied to structures with transformations that develop temporally (as in biology, sociology, or psychology), provides a means to avoid postulates of innateness or of pre-established harmony between thought and the universe. Piaget (1968) says that harmonies are actually established by successive self-regulated transformations of structures, even that "there is no coherent structuralism apart from constructivism" (p. 135). He is also explicit regarding the compatibility between structuralism and dialectic (see also Piaget, 1970b).

Piaget and Structuralism in Psychology

As a psychologist, the structures that Piaget finds most interesting are those of intelligence (Piaget, 1964/1967, 1968, 1970b, 1975/1985). Logical structures are not conscious; rather, the person is considered as the locus of the biological functioning that permits psychological structures to exist, to self-regulate and assimilate external reality, and to generate new, better equilibrated structures. Psychology, according to Piaget, does not study the inner experience of individuals but rather the structures that are common to all individuals.

Piaget recognizes that structuralist ideas have been presented many times in the history of psychology, usually contraposed to atomistic theories or empiricist associationist theories. Piaget (1968) believes that this is the case of the Gestalt school that, notwithstanding the historical merits of having refuted the idea of elementary sensations, proposes structures that are without history and without genesis, without functions and without relations to the subject, and in which no role is found for that subject's *active perception.*

Piaget (1964/1967, 1968, 1975/1985) maintains that every structure is the result of a genesis and every genesis is formed by the passage from a simpler to a more complex structure. The processes of equilibration and abstractive reflection have the child constructing his/her own structures, though not in a manner that is free or arbitrary. By means of reflective abstraction, simpler or less equilibrated structures of thought that are applicable to various contents generate more complex or more equilibrated structures. The construction process for psychological structures proceeds in a necessary way according to a principle of consecutive equilibration until the child reaches the stage of formal operations. The necessity is not *a priori*, but rather consists in the fact that every phase of development, passing from the simplest to the most complex, renders the following phase highly probable. For example, the formal operations derive from the concrete operations and take them over as their own content.

Thus structure and genesis are closely connected concepts in Piaget's thought, as are stage and reflective abstraction. The problem posed for contemporary research is whether having abandoned formal logic as a model for the structure of thought, it is also necessary to abandon the concept of structure and the associated one of genesis; or, whether it is "only" necessary to find a more appropriate model for cognitive structure than is provided by formal logic.

A NEO-PIAGETIAN REFORMULATION OF STRUCTURALISM

Many neo-Piagetian theories employ ideas and concepts taken from Piagetian structuralism. Some authors speak of neostructuralism (for example, Case & Edelstein, 1993) or of experiential structuralism (Demetriou, Efklides, & Platsidou, 1993). The theoretical conception that is most continuous with Piagetian structuralism is that expressed by Halford (1978a, 1982,

1987; Halford & Wilson, 1980) first described in terms of "symbol systems" and subsequently reframed in terms of "relational complexity" (Halford, 1993a, 1999; Halford, Wilson et al., 1998).

The Symbolic Nature of Thought

Halford (1982) takes up the distinction between a presymbolic stage of cognitive development (i.e., Piaget's sensorimotor stage) and subsequent stages in which the child is capable of symbolic representations and, thus, of true thought. For Halford a *symbol* is any internal representation that is applicable to diverse aspects of reality and transferable from one situation to another. For example, the concept of length has a symbolic character because it can be related to the different lengths of various objects and used in the solution of various types of problems.

Halford (1982) agrees with Piaget that the first symbolic functions are deferred imitation, symbolic play, mental imagery, drawing, and language. On the grounds of an extensive literature review, he concludes that most of the research suggests an average age between 21 and 28 months for the onset of symbolic representation.

The use of symbols, by itself, does not assure accuracy and efficiency of thought; even adults can relate symbols to reality in uneconomical or incoherent ways, as decades of research on the psychology of thinking have documented. But even though thought can lead to incorrect conclusions, it has a generative nature, in that other symbolic representations are generated from some initial symbolic representation.

Cognitive Systems

Halford's early theoretical proposal hinged on the concept of *cognitive system*. By definition a cognitive system is constituted of a *problem*, a *symbolic representation* of that problem and a set of *correspondences* between the problem and the symbolic representation. Halford and Wilson (1980) develop the formal aspects of the theory; we present here only the essential ones.

Symbolic representations are viewed as *systems* of symbols. A symbol system is a structure constituted by a set of elements (the symbols) and a function that from certain combinations of a specified number of symbols generates another specific symbol. A simple example of a symbol system is the structure constituted by the integers under the operation of addition. Addition is the system's function, and it generates a specific symbol from combinations of other given symbols.

The rules that interconnect the symbols of a system may sometimes possess certain mathematical properties (for example, a symbol system might be an algebraic group as is true of the set of integers under addition), but this is not necessarily the case. To define a symbol system it is sufficient to know, given a certain combination of symbols, what other symbol is generated.

Of course, the hypothesis that cognition employs symbol systems does not imply that the thinker is conscious of the formal properties of such systems. Just as with Piaget's operational structures, Halford's symbol systems presuppose simply that the individual has available some kind of representation with the desired properties.

A cognitive system also involves the representation of the problem, that is, a mental model of some portion of the environment with which the subject is interacting.

Finally, a cognitive system involves rules of correspondence between the problem of interest and its symbolic representation. These rules associate each element of the environment with a symbol. Halford says that cognition produces valid conclusions when there is an isomorphism between the symbol system employed and the environmental system to which it corresponds.[1] Such an isomorphism implies that each symbol always corresponds to the same environmental element and vice versa. Also, each relation among symbols corresponds to a relation among the corresponding environmental elements. Without this isomorphism, the conclusions reached are not valid. Halford observes, however, that the psychologically interesting question is: *How does a person come to notice* that a conclusion is not valid?

The answer is that people are able to avoid erroneous reasoning when they are able to determine whether they have assigned symbols to environmental elements in a coherent manner. In order to achieve this, symbol systems of different complexity can be needed (Halford, 1978a, 1982; Halford & Wilson, 1980). The complexity of symbol systems is not discussed here, because more recently Halford (1993a, 1999; Halford, Wilson et al., 1998) reframed that problem in terms of the complexity of relations. The complexity of symbol systems can be taken as a particular case of relational complexity (e.g., Halford, Wilson et al., 1998).

Adequate processing capacity would be a necessary condition for solving problems, but not a sufficient one. The subject must also have available a symbol system appropriate for the problem and must be able to encode the environmental elements relevant to an adequate representation of the

---

[1]Halford here seems to assume that there are actually laws regulating environmental systems, whether or not the subject knows them or science has discovered them. This *realist* epistemological assumption regarding scientific laws distances him from the *constructivist* epistemological thesis of Piaget.

problem. Only learning content-appropriate codes allows satisfaction of these conditions. In other words, cognitive structures are *learned*, and sufficient processing capacity is a *prerequisite* for learning. In short, Halford's theory is centered on the idea that in the succession of developmental stages children are able to *acquire* (i.e., to learn or to construct in problem-solving situations) concepts, representations, and mental abilities that require cognitive systems of increasing complexity.

Relational Complexity

According to Halford (1999), a representation of a relation includes a relation symbol or predicate, the argument(s) of the predicate, and the binding between the two. For instance, the binary relation BIGGER-THAN(horse, dog) is a binding between the predicate BIGGER-THAN and the arguments "horse" and "dog." Representing the arguments alone is insufficient, because it fails to specify the relation; but also adding a symbol for the predicate would be insufficient, because it would not specify whether the horse or the dog is bigger. A binding is necessary to integrate the components and indicate which entity fills each role. In turn, higher order relations have relations as arguments. For instance, BECAUSE(BIGGER-THAN(horse, dog), AVOIDS(dog, horse)) is a higher order relation, the arguments of which are BIGGER-THAN(horse, dog) and AVOIDS(dog, horse).

Relational knowledge has some important properties. One is systematicity (certain relations can imply other relations). Another is decomposability, that is, some relations can be composed of simpler relations; for example, the ternary relation MONOTONICALLY-LARGER(a, b, c) can be decomposed into LARGER(a, b), LARGER(b, c), and LARGER(a, c). Still another is omnidirectional access, that is, given all but one of the components of a relation, we can access or retrieve the remaining component. Because of the importance of such properties in human thinking, Halford (1993a, 1999; Halford, Wilson et al., 1998) grounded his theory on mental representation of relations.

In this context, the most important property of relations is their *dimensionality*, which is considered a major determinant of the complexity of higher cognition. Halford suggests that processing capacity is limited not by the number of items, but by the number of entities that have to be related. *Unary relations* are the simplest ones; they have two components (a predicate and an argument) that are bound together. Instances of unary relations are propositions that express attributes, for example BIG(horse), or class membership, such as ANIMAL(horse).[2] *Binary relations* have three linked, but dis-

---

[2]More precisely, BIG(x) and ANIMAL(y) are unary relations, whereas BIG(horse), or ANIMAL(horse), are relational instances that belong to those relations. Similarly, BIGGER-THAN(x, y) is a binary relation, and BIGGER-THAN(horse, dog) is one of its relational instances.

tinct components (a predicate and two arguments). Examples are BIGGER-THAN(horse, dog) and AVOIDS(dog, horse). Univariate functions, such as $f(a) = b$, can also be represented at this level. Binary relations are the grounds for the processing of analogies; for example, understanding that

woman : baby :: sheep : lamb

would not entail processing a quaternary relation, but only two instances of the same binary relation, MOTHER-OF(x, y).

Ternary relations have the form $R(x, y, z)$; that is, they include a predicate and three arguments, bound together. A concept based on a ternary relation is the "love triangle," in which two persons, x and y, both love a third person, z. Also transitivity involves representation of a ternary relation. Bivariate functions, like $f(x, y) = z$, can also be represented at this level. Binary operations are special cases of bivariate functions; for example, the binary operation of arithmetic addition consists of the set of ordered triples (2, 3, 5), (6, 2, 8), and so on, that is, all the instances of the relation $+(x, y, z)$, in which the third term is the sum of the first two.

Quaternary relations have the form $R(w, x, y, z)$. An example would be proportion $a/b = c/d$, that expresses a relation between four variables. They also include trivariate functions, like $f(w, x, y) = z$. A composition of binary operations, such as $(a + b) \times c = d$ is another case of quaternary relation.

According to Halford (1993a) children can process unary relations at least by 1 year, binary relations by 2 years, ternary relations by 5 years, and quaternary relations by 11 years. In principle, one can define representations of higher relational complexity. However, Halford (1999) treats their psychological existence as speculative, and notes that quinary relations could be available only for a minority of adults.

Halford and colleagues suggest that a relation can be represented in a neural network by means of a tensor product of vectors, in which each vector represents one component of a relation. This proposal is interesting because it reconciles symbolic representation with connectionist modelling. There is evidence that computational models of this sort can simulate experimental data, thus showing that specific models framed within Halford's theory are computable. However, detailed consideration of these aspects goes beyond the scope of this book (see instead Halford, Wilson et al., 1998, and related commentary).

EXPERIMENTS ON THE COMPREHENSION OF SYSTEMS OF RULES

An essential step for verifying this theory is research on understanding cognitive systems under well controlled conditions of learning. Halford (1978b; Halford & Wilson, 1980) carried out important experiments, framed then in terms of symbol systems; but we present them here using Halford's newer and more general terminology, that is relational complexity.

In a series of experiments (Halford, 1978b), children were trained to associate symbols (e.g., geometrical figures) with rules. In one case, each child was presented in a learning phase with a toy truck to be moved among 4 small white houses placed at the corners of a square table. The child was shown cards with a symbol (e.g., a geometrical figure). A different symbol was paired with each of 4 rules for moving the truck: move the truck one step in the clockwise direction (rule C), move one step in the anticlockwise direction (rule A), move diagonally (rule D), do not move the truck (rule N). The child was not told the meaning of each symbol, but rather had to learn it by trial and error. This game was repeated several times, using different sets of symbols to represent the same rules, until the child had learned the rules perfectly. The test phase then began with the experimenter placing a house and the truck in one corner of the table while another 3 houses of different colors were given to the child. Then the child was given a series of cards with geometrical figures, and with each figure the child was told the color of the house to which that symbol would direct the truck. The child's task was to arrange the houses at appropriate corners and determine the moving rule associated with each symbol (as explained later in this section).

Some of the problems require the child to process binary relations; these can be solved by considering only a single pairing between a geometrical figure (symbol) and a color (object). Other problems demand consideration of two pairs in order to achieve a coherent solution, and these require processing of ternary relations.

The "binary" problems involve rules C, A, and N. In these cases consideration of a single symbol–color pair is sufficient to yield a congruent arrangement of the houses. Suppose, for instance, that the truck is initially located at the red house and that the symbol X (e.g., a star) calls for a movement to the yellow house. If the child decides that the symbol X represents rule C, then the yellow house has to be placed in the next position clockwise from the red house. The symbol Y that doesn't change the house color clearly represents rule N (in this case, too, a single symbol–color pairing permits identification of the representation of N). The symbol Z, which does require a movement of the truck, then necessarily represents rule A. Of course, if the symbols interpreted as C and A are interchanged (e.g., if the star is taken as representing rule A), the circular order of the houses around the table will be reversed, but still coherent and correct. Thus, a relational instance such as X(red, yellow) is sufficient to allow arrangement of the houses in a coherent manner, interpreting X as the symbol for rule C or rule A, as desired.

Problems that use the rules C, D and N require, instead, a ternary relation. The difficulty is not due to rule N; a symbol that prescribes a move-

ment to the same-colored house as the one where the truck is already located could not represent any rule other than N. A single symbol–color pair
is, thus, enough to decode this symbol. But with respect to rules C and D, a
single pair provides ambiguous information and is insufficient for deciding
on an arrangement of the houses.

If the symbol X calls for moving the truck from the red to the yellow
house, one can not interpret it as representing rule C or rule D arbitrarily;
examination of another pairing of that symbol with a color is necessary. If
the first presentation of X indicates a movement from red to yellow and the
second presentation of X calls for moving from yellow back to red, then one
can infer that the symbol X represents rule D (and the yellow house must
be placed at the corner opposite to the red one). If, instead, the second
presentation of X requires moving from yellow to blue (let's suppose), then
it is clear that X represents rule C; the yellow house must be placed at the
angle adjacent to the red house (thereby allowing completion of the movements in accordance with the rules indicated by each symbol).

So we see that consideration of a relational instance such as X(red, yellow, red), or X(red, yellow, blue), as in the examples here, is necessary in
these problems in order to decide whether a certain symbol represents
rule C or rule D and, consequently, to determine a coherent way of arranging the houses.

Another of Halford's (1978b) experiments uses other types of problems,
similar in their superficial form and, therefore, quite comparable to one another. However, these problems are constructed so as to require ternary
and quaternary relations. Halford and Wilson (1980) conduct experiments
involving similarly structured problems on a table that is hexagonal instead
of square.

The results with children from 3 to 6 show that in the learning phase
even the youngest children learn the rules, though more slowly than the
oldest do. Learning the rules for "binary" and "ternary" problems is not different in difficulty; this is consistent with theoretical predictions, because
learning each rule only involves processing a binary relation. As predicted
by the theory, the "ternary" problems prove more difficult in the test phase,
because it is in the test problems that processing ternary relations is necessary for interpreting the symbols. A high rate of correct responses on "binary" problems can already be seen among 4-year-olds; although notable
progress on "ternary" problems is observed only after age 5 (Halford,
1978b; Halford & Wilson, 1980). A similar result is found with children between the ages of 8 and 13: all the children easily solve the "ternary" problems, whereas a majority of correct answers is not found for "quaternary"
problems until age 11 (Halford, 1978b) or age 10 (Halford & Wilson, 1980).

Experiments with fairly abstract materials, in which the information load
can be manipulated in a manner that eliminates, as far as possible, the im-

portance of the meanings and of the knowledge acquired from daily experience, are necessary in order to test the predictions of the theory in a stringent and controlled way. This is the case for the research described here just as it is for Pascual-Leone's research with composite visual stimuli described previously.

A subsequent study (Halford, Bain, et al., 1998) uses problems similar to those described in this section to investigate the acquisition of learning sets and the induction of relational schemes in adults. Further research with adults suggests that the ability to interpret graphic representations of statistical interactions is also limited by the interaction's relational complexity, defined as the number of variables involved in an interaction (Halford, Baker, McCredden, & Bain, 2005).

CONSERVATION AND TRANSITIVITY RESEARCH

The main studies connecting Halford's theory to the Piagetian literature involve the concepts of number and quantity (e.g., Halford, 1970b, 1993a; Halford & Boyle, 1985; Halford & Fullerton, 1970), the concept of transitivity (e.g., Andrews & Halford, 1998, 2002; Halford, 1984; Halford & Kelly, 1984), and the balance scale (Halford, Andrews, Dalton, Boag, & Zielinski, 2002).[3] This work tends to associate at least some of the Piagetian concrete operational structures with ternary relations. For example, whereas Piaget places understanding of the invariance of number at 6–7 years of age and Bryant (1972) much earlier at 3 years of age, Halford suggests that children younger than 5 could not understand whether a give transformation entails number invariance or not. Consistent with this prediction, Halford and Boyle (1985) show that prior to age 5, children's errors are nonsystematic and show lack of understanding of numerical invariance after a spatial transformation, whereas older children do understand it. Further, when experimental conditions induce errors in numerosity judgments, their errors show a consistency between pre- and post-transformation responses, which presume that they understand the numerical invariance of a set of objects when their spatial arrangement is altered.

Halford (1982, 1989) suggests that conservation of number can be acquired around age 5, because, in contrast to Piaget, he examines children's responses in situations that either create no conflict between perception and reasoning, or that feature compensation for such conflicts by means of training that directs the child's attention to the relevant dimensions of the task. Nevertheless, he acknowledges that the acquisition mechanisms for conservation are not yet clear. "A wide range of training techniques have been used, but the outcome does not appear to favor any one teaching method.

---

[3]This task shall be considered in chapters 4 and 6.

Any technique works at least sometimes, and no technique consistently succeeds. . . . Thus, training studies have failed to isolate a *single process* underlying conservation acquisition" (Halford, 1993a, p. 404; italics added).

Clearer results are provided by experiments on transitive inference.
Transitive inference refers to situations in which, given two premises that
can be expressed as $a < b$ and $b < c$, one must draw the conclusion $a < c$.
Controversy exists regarding the age at which children are capable of transitive inference. Piaget and Inhelder (1959) give an age of about 7, whereas
other studies point to an earlier age, such as 3 or 4 years (Bryant &
Trabasso, 1971; Pears & Bryant, 1990). These authors hypothesize that it is
not transitive inference of which the young children are incapable, but
rather that they are simply not able to retrieve the information to be used
as premises for the inference.

Halford (1984) distinguishes tasks that can be performed correctly on
the basis of information regarding a single pair of elements from those that
require integrating the information from two premises, and suggests that
only the former could be performed by a majority of 4-year-olds. As Andrews and Halford (1998) note, integration of two premises involves forming an ordered triple, that is, processing a ternary relation. Several studies
(e.g., Andrews & Halford, 1998, 2002; Halford, 1984, 1993a; Halford & Kelly,
1984) provide experimental criticism of the proposal that young children
master transitivity, and support the view that children younger than 5 years
of age can approach serial order only by means of isolated binary relations.

For instance, in the final experiment of Andrews and Halford (1998), children are presented with four "premises" that consist in pairs of colored
squares, one above the other. These pairs can be indicated as *ab*, *bc*, *cd*,
and *de*; they are all displayed on a page, in a random fashion, and refer to
the order, *abcde*, of five colors in a tower. In binary relation items, a child is
given two squares (e.g., *b* and *c*), and has to arrange them in a tower; then,
another square (e.g., *d*) is handed to the child, who must place this, too, in
the tower, in a way that is consistent with the "premises." Such items can
be solved by considering one pair at a time. In ternary relation items, a
child is given two squares that are not included in the same premise (*b* and
d), and has to arrange them; then, the square *c* is also given to the child,
who must place it in the correct (i.e., middle) position. To achieve success,
one must represent mentally the order of all three squares (*b*, *c*, *d*). The results show that binary items are much easier than ternary items. More important, 4-year-olds perform much better than chance in binary items, but
in ternary items, the great majority of them either performs randomly, or
follows strategies based on a single binary relation. In contrast, 5- and 6-
year-olds perform ternary relation items much better than chance, and also
much better than a baseline that represents performance based on processing isolated binary relations.

THE QUESTION OF INFORMATION LOAD

We have seen that Halford's theory postulates a particular type of structure related to cognitive processes, namely, relations; and that measuring their complexity enables one to specify the type of structure required by a task. The Piagetian stages are reinterpreted in terms of the child's ability to process relations of increasing complexity. Moreover, the theory hypothesizes that relations of increasing complexity pose an increasing information load on the child's processing. In general, the neo-Piagetian theories make assertions regarding the information load imposed by cognitive processes. This particular theory views processing capacity as the ability to process relations of a given complexity (e.g., Halford, Wilson et al., 1998).

Although the studies discussed so far in this chapter support the predictions of Halford's theory regarding the relative difficulty of tasks and the age at which children begin to respond correctly, most of them do not include any measure of processing capacity.[4]

The Problem

Initially, Halford (1978a, 1978b, 1982; Halford & Wilson, 1980) hypothesized that the achievement of a short-term memory span of 2, 4 and 6 units, respectively, would be indicative of having achieved the ability to process binary, ternary, and quaternary relations (or more precisely, in Halford's earlier terminology, to use symbol systems of Levels 1, 2, and 3). Halford suggested that the ability to verify the coherence of cognitive systems depends on short-term memory capacity, in the sense that if a person is not able to keep $2 \times n$ elements in short-term memory (i.e., n symbols and n environmental elements), neither will that person be able to verify the coherence of a Level n cognitive system. This view elaborated on an idea of McLaughlin (1963) on digit span and Piagetian stages. But experimental evidence relevant to this hypothesis is scarce (Halford & Wilson, 1980) and sometimes problematic (Halford, 1969) if not completely negative (Halford 1993a; Halford, Bain & Maybery, 1984).

The hypothesis was abandoned as a result of such studies. Halford (1987) recognized after having conducted dozens of studies seeking to demonstrate that short-term memory is the "workspace" in thinking, that his ex-

---

[4]Halford, Maybery and Bain (1986) find a relation between transitive reasoning and information processing capacity in 3- to 5-year-old children; however, they use a technique that poses particular problems and that is discussed later in this chapter. Halford and Wilson (1980) use digit span, and report significant correlations between it and the ability to resolve problems involving movement rules. Only one study on conservation examines its relationship with short-term memory (Halford, 1969); in this case, however, no correlation is found.

periments lead inexorably to the conclusion that such is not the case.[5] The hypothesis that short-term memory is the site of thought implies that a strong reciprocal interference should exist between reasoning processes and the simultaneous maintenance of information (such as a brief series of digits or words) in short-term memory; but this interference has not been demonstrated. For instance, Halford, Maybery, O'Hare and Grant (1994) rule out the hypothesis of a trade off between short-term memory and performance in various cognitive tasks (such as counting, subtraction, and transitive inference). Even when an interference is observed, it is not disruptive, nor larger in younger children than in older ones. A similar conclusion follows from research conducted in other laboratories (Baddeley & Hitch, 1974; Klapp, Mashburn, & Lester, 1983). Halford (1993a) points out that the experiments carried out to develop the theory that connects information processing capacity to short-term memory capacity have, instead, demonstrated the untenability of the hypothesis.

An Attempted Solution

In place of simple measurement of short-term memory span, Halford (1993a) proposes the "easy-to-hard" research method (Hunt & Lansman, 1982) as a means to study whether the difficulty of cognitive tasks derive, at least in part, from their information-processing load. The easy-to-hard paradigm involves the use of two versions of the task to be studied, an easy one and a hard one. The two versions are as similar as possible except for their information-processing load, and the assumption is that the limits of a child's processing capacity influence performance on the difficult version but not on the easy one. As just described, pairings of tasks from different levels correspond well to this requirement. (For example, let the task under study, henceforth called primary task, be classification; then, the easy version could involve problems in which subclasses are compared, and the hard version could ask for comparing a subclass with a superordinate class.) A secondary task is also used (such as coding a series of to-be-recalled stimuli or a simple signal-detection task in which the response time is measured). This task uses a different stimulus presentation modality and a different response modality than the primary task does in order to avoid interference due to sharing of the input or output channel (for instance, if the primary task involves visual presentation of classification problems, the secondary task may involve auditory presentation of signals to be detected). The purpose is to guarantee that the interference between the pri-

---

[5]Recall from chapter 2 that Pascual-Leone has used the term *central computing space*, but he does *not* consider it synonymous with "short-term memory." Therefore, he does not meet the problem of explaining independence of thinking from short-term memory; instead, the problem for him is to devise measures of capacity that are not based on short-term memory tasks.

mary and secondary tasks is indeed due to the sharing of a limited processing capacity, rather than for other reasons. A further assumption is that neither the secondary task nor the easy version of the primary task exceeds the child's processing capacity when administered separately. It is also assumed, however, that the capacity is exceeded when the tasks are carried out simultaneously, and, therefore, interference between them is expected.

The research paradigm requires 4 experimental conditions: (1) simultaneous performance of the secondary task and the easy version of the primary task, (2) the difficult version of the primary task alone, (3) the easy version of the primary task alone, and (4) the secondary task alone. The fact that the difficult primary task is always carried out in isolation and never concurrently with the secondary task excludes the possibility that performance on the difficult version is influenced in uncontrolled ways by interference from the secondary task.

The logic of the easy-to-hard method is as follows: if the children's performance on the difficult version of the principal task depends on their limited information-processing capacity, and if simultaneous performance of the easy version and the secondary task is impeded by these same capacity limits, then a correlation will be found between measures of the children's performance in experimental conditions (1) and (2).

Yet, if one does find the predicted correlation, it could also be because the difficult and easy versions of the primary task share similar characteristics (as may also be true of the difficult primary version and the secondary task). To control for this possibility, partial correlation is used: the possible influence of similarity with conditions (3) or (4) is eliminated statistically by partialling out the measures of performance in these conditions from the correlation between performance in conditions (1) and (2); if this partial correlation is still significant, then one may conclude that limited processing capacity influences performance on the difficult version of the primary task.

Some studies have actually employed the easy-to-hard method. In this way, Halford, Maybery, and Bain (1986) showed that one cause of the difficulty of transitive inference for 3- to 6-year-olds is their limited information processing capacity. Halford and Leitch (1989) reached a similar conclusion studying classification in children from 3 to 7. Both of these studies employed easy and difficult tasks involving binary and ternary relations, respectively; the secondary task in one study was to repeat color names, and in the other it was to respond rapidly to a signal.[6] It is also

---

[6]Previous studies employing a typical dual-task methodology reported that a secondary task results in more interference with a Level 2 task than with a similar Level 1 task (Halford et al., 1984; Halford, Brown, & Thomson, 1986). Even though this method presents greater problems for interpreting the results, the fact that both methods produce converging results provides further credibility for the conclusions described here.

worth mentioning that the easy-to-hard paradigm has also been used to validate a measure of M capacity, the Digit Placement Task (Foley & Berch, 1997).

Problems and Prospects

The experiments of Halford and his colleagues provide support for the idea that structures (cognitive systems) that involve relations of increasing complexity are acquired in the course of development, and that there is a connection between relational complexity and the limits of information-processing capacity. The question remains, however, *how much* capacity is required to process relations of different complexity.

Studies with the easy-to-hard methodology provide correlations among diverse measures including response times and accuracy scores. The correlations among these are certainly interpretable as stemming from a limited processing capacity, but none of the measures can be considered as a measure of processing capacity itself.

The case is different for memory span or measures of *M* capacity. Certainly one can debate whether they are valid constructs for determining a person's information-processing capacity (as we have seen, Halford has abandoned his hypotheses regarding memory span); but if one assumes that they are, then it would not be difficult to assert, for example, that a span of 5 digits indicates a short-term memory capacity of 5 units.

But in the case of a partial correlation of (let us suppose) .40 between response time on a secondary task and accuracy on a difficult primary task, all that one can conclude is that, in a certain population of children, 16% (.40 squared) of the variance in the difficult task is explainable in terms of limited processing capacity. Neither the response time nor the percentage of correct responses, or any other measure used in these experiments can be considered in itself as a measure of processing capacity.

Paradoxically, just when Halford had so elegantly demonstrated the effect of limited processing capacity on children's cognition, he seems to have given up on defining a unit of measurement for that capacity (which was the capacity of short-term memory in a preceding version of the theory). Although the previous theory formulated the hypothesis (erroneous, but clear and testable) that a short-term memory capacity of 2, 4, or 6 units was necessary to acquire cognitive systems of Level 1, 2, or 3, respectively, subsequently (in the absence of a unit of measurement) how much processing capacity is required is not clear. Therefore, it is impossible to know whether a child has the necessary capacity to learn systems of a specific level; neither can the relation between available resources and performance on a cognitive task be studied, given that the value of the first variable can not be known.[7]

More recently, Halford, Wilson et al. (1998) defined processing capacity in terms of relational complexity itself. Andrews and Halford (2002) compared performance of 3- to 8-year-olds in several tasks that involve processing relational information. The results showed significant correlations among these tasks, which loaded on a single factor, and acceptable correspondences among their developmental patterns. This can be taken as support for the relational complexity metric. Similarly, Halford and Andrews (2004) shows consistency in the relational complexity of inferences made by children in different domains. However, so far, the study of individual differences does not go beyond prediction from one reasoning task to another. One can expect that processing resources and their measurement are a topic that Halford's research group will investigate more deeply in the future.

AN ATTEMPT AT A SYNTHESIS OF TWO THEORIES

Halford's theory is built on structuralist epistemological assumptions; the explanation of processes resides in abstract structures, namely cognitive systems and relations. Laws of the whole regulate such structures and their coherence, and the degree of complexity of these laws (i.e., the relational complexity) is explanatory with respect to thought processes. Cognitive tasks are classified according to the formal structures, that is, by the complexity of the types of relations that they involve.

The TCO, considered in the previous chapter, is also a structuralist-influenced theory in the sense that it is certainly not atomistic or associationistic. The individual schemes are (for Pascual-Leone as for Piaget) functional totalities; and the interaction among metasubjective operators is not random, but rather follows its own laws of the whole. Pascual-Leone, however, places lesser theoretical importance than Halford on structured

---

[7]As possible indicators of resources Halford (1993a) considers processing speed, primary memory, M capacity, the number of units present in a network of distributed representations, and Miller's (1956) concept of chunk, but he does so in terms that are completely open with respect to future research developments. He acknowledges the imprecision of the approach, but sets the problem aside: "The concept of resources has been criticized because it includes no specification of mechanisms but, although a process theory is desirable, it complements rather than replaces a resource theory" (Halford, 1993a, p. 103). However, Halford's theory is a theory not only of resources, but also of cognitive processes, and it hypothesizes a connection between limited resources and the processes of thinking. As such, it seems to need a specification of mechanisms and a definition of measures of available resources.

wholes while emphasizing the temporal unfolding of information processing, and the consecutive activation of different schemes.

Chapman (1987, 1990) notes that these neo-Piagetian theories have inspired a considerable amount of research and, over a wide variety of cognitive tasks, have provided considerable data favoring a relationship between
processing capacity and ability. He proposes a theoretical revision that
leads to a synthesis between the two theories.

Methodological Problems and Theoretical Responses

According to Chapman (1987) a problem of the Theory of Constructive Operators is its failure to specify sufficiently rigorous rules for task analysis. In
particular, it is difficult to determine precisely which schemes are involved
in a cognitive process, their respective sources of activation, and, in particular, which schemes are activated by the M operator at any given moment.
For Chapman (1990), if with respect to the analysis of a task the theory is
open to too many different possibilities, or if its application requires too
many specific assumptions, there is a risk that the same theory, on the basis of different assumptions, could permit contradictory predictions, and
thus become unfalsifiable.

Chapman (1987, 1990) finds Halford's approach more rigorous as it extracts predictions regarding information load from quantitative analysis of
a cognitive task's formal properties. Like Halford, Chapman (1987) considers it appropriate to calculate the information load associated with a task
on the basis of the number of variables that must be considered for its successful completion. But Halford's approach is not exempt from criticism.
For example, why propose (as in his earlier theory) distinct units for symbols and for their corresponding environmental elements? It is plausible
that the child considers only the content of the problem rather than simultaneously considering both the general form of the variables and their concrete values as present in the problem. Moreover, the cognitive load in a
reasoning task is constituted not only by the premises, but also by the representation of the conclusion.

The solution to this problem proposed by Chapman is structuralist in
the extreme, namely to return to Piaget's operational structures and to
count the number of representations that one must coordinate in order to
apply each of them.

On the other hand, Chapman (1987, 1990) considers Halford's solution to
the measurement of processing capacity unsatisfactory. A theory of information processing that is modeled in sufficient detail and is sufficiently general in its domain of application requires commensurability between the
tests used to measure the child's cognitive resources and the analyzed cog-

nitive tasks. This is to say that the units for measuring capacity must be the same for the cognitive tasks under study and for the test of capacity. Chapman (1990) notes that Halford's methods of task analysis are so tied to the types of reasoning tasks that he studies that it is difficult to see how they could apply to tests of capacity.

Without excluding other possibilities, Chapman (1987) suggests using measures of M capacity proposed by Pascual-Leone, Case, and collaborators. These have the advantage that they can be analyzed in terms of the number of representations that must be considered simultaneously.

Experimental Studies

For the purpose of testing experimentally the proposed theoretical synthesis, Chapman and Lindenberger (1988) study the acquisition of transitive inference including the role of the number of premises and their content in determining the horizontal *décalages*. Transitivity problems involving length and weight are presented to children between 6 and 9 years old. The number of premises varies from 2 to 4 for length and from 2 to 3 for weight.

Up to 6–7 years of age the children succeed on items that only appear to be transitivity problems, but can actually be solved on perceptual grounds.[8] Only a minority of these children succeed in solving even transitivity problems with only two premises. Moreover, an increase in the number of premises results in an increasing difficulty in the problems; this result supports the hypothesis that ability with transitive inference is limited by processing capacity.

As regards the content variable, an interesting result is found in the length and weight comparison. In a first experiment the weights are in the form of spheres of different sizes, such that one sphere could be heavier than another but, at the same time, also smaller. In this situation some children (who are known to be able to solve length problems) respond that the larger object is heavier based on the misleading size cue; and for this reason, the weight problems seem more difficult than the length problems. Yet in a second experiment in which the weights are spheres of the same size (thus eliminating the misleading size cue) problems of length and of weight are of equal difficulty; only the number of premises, and not the content, remains as a significant cause of *décalages*.

Another study (Chapman & Lindenberger, 1989) tests the relation between "attentional capacity" (i.e., M capacity, defined operationally by the

---

[8]Such an experimental condition was introduced for the purpose of criticizing research of Brainerd and Kingma (1984) that we do not report here. We note the convergence between Halford's results and those of Chapman and Lindenberger in falsifying the hypothesis that young children are able to carry out transitive inference. For further arguments, see Chapman and Lindenberger (1992a, 1992b).

Figural Intersection Test and backward digit span; see chap. 9) and the Piagetian classification and seriation tasks. These tasks require consideration of the values of at least 3 variables and, thus, would seem to require at least 3 units of attentional capacity. The results confirm that the measures of attentional capacity correlate with the Piagetian tasks, and in particular, that an attentional capacity of at least 3 units is required in order to give operational-level responses to these tasks.

The results presented here agree with Chapman's (1987, 1990) proposed theoretical synthesis and suggest that it merits serious consideration. We observe, however, that they can not be taken as unambiguous support as two of the other theories we consider (those of Pascual-Leone and of Case, the latter in chap. 6) lead to the same predictions as those of Chapman and Lindenberger (1988, 1989). Finally we wish to note that Chapman and Lindenberger's results do contribute to falsifying the hypotheses of those radical critics of Piaget who attribute a rather precocious logical ability to preschool children; this lends further support to Halford's (1989) argument.

STRUCTURALIST APPROACHES TO INDIVIDUAL DIFFERENCES

Piaget applied himself exclusively to the study of universal cognitive structures, whereas neo-Piagetian authors (e.g., Pascual-Leone, 1969, 1989; Shafrir & Pascual-Leone, 1990) have initiated research programs dedicated both to the universal development of increasingly complex structures and to individual differences in cognitive style. Other researchers have also brought interest in individual differences to the foreground (see Case & Edelstein, 1993). For example, Demetriou and Efklides (1987) make use of factor analysis for the study of individual differences and, in contrast to the American psychometric tradition, interpret their results in a structuralist frame. Andrews and Halford (2002) take an individual differences approach to the study of relational complexity. Edelstein, Keller and Schröder (1990) define cognitive abilities in structural terms and consider the effects of social structure on individual differences. Larivée, Normandeau, and Parent (2000) offer a review of how the internal development of Genevan and French research on individual differences met with and flowed into the neo-Piagetian current. In this section, we discuss some of these approaches.

De Ribaupierre (1993) considers structuralist concepts as descriptive, that is, they represent abstract descriptions of aspects of behavior shared by a certain group of individuals. Lautrey (1993) argues that an adequate explanation of individual differences, including different developmental pathways, is possible only if one admits that (in addition to the structuralist discontinuities between successive levels of development) there are dis-

tinct modalities of information processing, such as propositional and analogical processes. We consider here this hypothesis by reviewing a number
of lines of research.

Analogical Representations, Concrete Operations and Individual *Décalages*

Now classic in psychology is the distinction between propositional mental
representations (concept definitions, semantic networks, logical and syn-
tactical rules) and analogical ones (mental models of time, space and causality, mental images, vivid experiential memories with rich sensorial quali-
ties). The term *analogical* indicates that the properties of analogical
representations (in contrast to those of propositional representations) resemble the properties of the processes involved in perceiving the world or
acting on it. Some authors (Johnson-Laird, 1983; Kosslyn, 1980; Logie &
Denis, 1991) have highlighted the advantages that derive from combining
the use of both types of representation.

Also Piaget has addressed mental images, viewing them (Piaget & Inhelder, 1966) as composed of *figurative schemes*, a construct that is particularly
suitable for representing aspects of a *static* configuration. In this conception, it is only with the advent of concrete operational thinking that mental
images become capable of also representing *transformations* adequately.
Particularly relevant to Piaget's view of mental images is his distinction between *logical* operations and *infralogical*[9] operations. The latter are very
similar to the former (including their formal properties) with the exception
that they refer to aspects of reality with a continuous nature such as time
and space, and, in particular, to spatial configurations. Infralogical operations involve an application to the spatial or temporal continuum of the
same operations that can be applied to qualitative similarities or differences among objects.

Piaget's conception of mental images does not require any adjustment to
his theory of operational development as he hypothesizes that logical and
infralogical structures develop at the same rate; the claim is that "they begin to take shape at the same ages ... and in a closely parallel fashion"
(Piaget & Inhelder, 1963, p. 180; see also Piaget & Inhelder, 1966; Piaget,
Inhelder, & Szeminska, 1948). However, one could ask whether analogical
representations may not be adequate for representing some transformations of reality, perhaps in children who have yet to master the "concrete"
logical operations completely.

Lautrey, de Ribaupierre, and Rieben (1985) study analogical representations and concrete operations from the point of view of individual differ-

---

[9]This term does not signify prelogic or inferiority to logic in any way; rather it marks a relation to a domain that is physical or otherwise less abstract than that associated with logic.

ences. They agree with Piaget that infralogical wholes can be difficult to decompose, and therefore children could have initial difficulties in applying
operational thinking to those domains. If so, then one should find collective
horizontal décalages, that is, a general developmental delay of infralogical
operations (and in particular, of those that involve physical or geometrical
spatial representations) with respect to the corresponding logical operations. On the other hand, mental images in which space is represented analogically could be advantageous for carrying out concrete operations on
spatial concepts. If representation of transformations by mental images is
possible at a purely analogical level, that is, *without* the intervention of
propositional-type logical operations, then the possibility of collective *décalages* would not necessarily occur. Further, if some children were more inclined to use mental images and others to use propositional representations, one might find a phenomenon of *individual décalages* not predicted by
Piaget. This is to say that some children could be at a more advanced level
in logical than spatial tasks, whereas just the opposite could be the case for
other children.

Studies on Individual *Décalages*

To test their hypotheses this same research group (which Larivée et al.,
2000, dubbed "the French connection") presented a large sample of children ranging from 6 to 12 years in age with two logical tasks and six spatial
ones (two geometric tasks, two tasks dealing with physical concepts, and
two primarily imaginative). For example, one of the logical tasks involved
probabilistic reasoning problems (Piaget & Inhelder, 1951/1975). All the
tasks involved trials varying in difficulty. The simplest of these problems
asks whether the likelihood of selecting a red chip would be greater when
drawing from a sack containing 1 red chip and 1 blue one, or from another
sack containing 2 reds and no blues. The most difficult problem compares a
sack containing 2 red chips and 4 blue ones with a sack containing 3 red
and 5 blue.

The two geometric tasks involved, for various geometric solids, cross-
sectional forms and the unfolding of surfaces (Piaget & Inhelder, 1947/1967).
The physical concept tasks included trials involving conservation of substance, weight and volume as well as the construction of solids that differ in
size while remaining equivalent in volume (Piaget & Inhelder, 1941/1974,
1947/1967). The imaginative tasks (Piaget & Inhelder, 1966) required imagining and drawing such things as the holes that would be found in a piece of
paper after folding it in various ways and cutting it along one of the folds.

Different techniques for data analysis are used in different studies (de
Ribaupierre, Rieben, & Lautrey, 1985; Lautrey, de Ribaupierre, & Rieben,
1985, 1987; Rieben & de Ribaupierre, 1988; Rieben, de Ribaupierre, & Lau-

trey, 1986, 1990). Lautrey et al. (1987) score the responses to each individual item as correct or incorrect and submit these data to a correspondence analysis. Two dimensions emerge; one is related to the degree of difficulty or complexity of the item, the other is related to whether the item content is logical or spatial. One can then evaluate each child's performance with respect to these dimensions in such a way as to identify some children who perform better with logical or with spatial items, respectively.

The correlations among the 8 tasks are positive and significant but not particularly high (de Ribaupierre et al., 1985). This suggests that, although there are general factors that partially explain cognitive development involved in this set of tasks, the tasks also involve specific characteristics.

Rieben et al. (1986, 1990) examine children's performance (measured on an ordinal scale) on each pair of the 8 tasks, a total of 28 pairs. For each pair they consider three hypotheses: (1) *synchrony*, the majority of the children respond at the same level on both tasks; (2) *horizontal décalage*, children tend to give higher level responses on one of the two tasks, which, thus, is considered easier; (3) *individual décalage*, there are both a considerable number of children who give better responses for the first task and a considerable number who give better responses for the second.

The authors find that synchrony is the best model in 15 of the 28 cases and argue that these results indicate the considerable importance of general factors in development. In nine cases, horizontal *décalage* is the best model, and this result is indicative of factors related to differences in the complexity of the problems. Finally, there are four cases for which the best model is individual *décalage*. Though not many, Rieben et al. (1990) note with interest that these cases involve a comparison between a logical task and a spatial task. This fact suggests that, at least in some cases, the spatial content of the problems is a source of difficulty for some children while being a facilitating factor for others, an outcome that differs from that hypothesized by Piaget.

The research described here confirms the existence of general cognitive developmental factors that permit children to solve increasingly complex problems, in accordance with the views of Piaget and many neo-Piagetians. At the same time, however, there is evidence of a role for mental representations that goes beyond Piaget's thesis involving figurative schemes, mental images and infralogical operations. Lautrey et al. (1985), in fact, find that the infralogical (spatial) content of the problems can in certain cases hinder solving the problem whereas in other cases facilitating it, especially if the spatial, perceptual characteristics are important for solving the problem. Moreover, there are individual differences in the ability to make use of representations of one or the other type.

In short, the reported research demonstrates that a structuralist approach to cognitive processes can be reconciled with the study of individual differences. As de Ribaupierre (1993) notes, the propositional and ana-logical processing modalities coexist in every child, and the use of one or the other depends on the context as well as on individual differences. The structural levels, which describe the children's performance in such a way as to make their responses comparable across different tasks, permit distin-guishing between general developmental factors and individual differences; Rieben et al. (1990) and de Ribaupierre (1993) call this approach a "mini-mal" structuralism.

Experiential Structuralism

Andreas Demetriou and his colleagues (e.g., Demetriou & Efklides, 1987; Demetriou et al., 1993) have characterized their view as *experiential struc-turalism*. This term conveys the idea that, although the mind's structures are partly innate (at least in their basic architecture and in some kernel ele-ments), only experience enables the mind's structures to develop and take shape, so that they can meet the structures of the specific tasks that a per-son encounters in the environment. Demetriou has proposed a full-blown theory of cognitive development (e.g., Demetriou & Raftopoulos, 1999), but because the methods of analysis most widely used by this research group are, by far, those based on individual differences, we consider this as the best point for presenting their work.

This theory posits that the mind has a three-layered architecture. Each of the three layers, in turn, has a complex organization. The first layer in-cludes Specialized Structural Systems (SSS—sometimes also called Special-ized Capacity Systems, or SCS). At least five SSSs have been identified, respectively specialized for the processing of (1) categorical or qualitative-analytic, (2) quantitative-relational, (3) spatial-imaginal, (4) causal-experi-mental, and (5) verbal-propositional information. These systems are envi-ronment-oriented, and each is specialized for a specific domain and a specific set of operations to be performed on a specific set of cognitive units. Each SSS would include a few kernel elements (e.g., depth perception could be a perceptual kernel element of the spatial SSS), which are innate and modular (i.e., informationally encapsulated in the sense of Fodor, 1983). Then, an SSS would also include rules, processing skills, and operations that evolve as a result of the application of the kernel elements over time. Finally, an SSS would include products of its past operations, which consti-tute a person's conceptions and beliefs about that domain. Thus, each SSS is regarded as a complex network of component processes and operations, which represent and process the different aspects of a given domain.

The second layer of the mind is called the Hypercognitive System; Deme-triou et al. (1993) argue that the term *metacognition* carries the meaning (in the prefix "meta") that self-understanding and self-management come after cognition, whereas the prefix "hyper" does not entail this assumption. This system enables self-mapping of the mind, recording and comparing one's own experiences, and constructing a theory of the mind and a representation of the cognitive self. It involves, first, self-monitoring and self-regulation processes used during problem solving or decision making. Furthermore, it involves models and representations of past cognitive experiences that come as a result of the functioning of online self-monitoring and self-regulation.

The third layer of the mind is called the Processing System. It is assumed to be connected both with the various SSSs and with the hypercognitive system. Three dimensions of the processing system are deemed to be relevant: speed, storage, and control. These refer, respectively, to the maximum speed at which a given mental operation can be executed, the maximum number of information units and mental acts that can be activated simultaneously, and the maximum efficiency at which a decision can be made about the right operation to be performed.

Demetriou and Raftopoulos (1999) suggest a number of forms and mechanisms of cognitive change. In general terms, they assume that different components and subcomponents of the architecture of a person's mind can develop at a different pace; however, they will not develop completely independently of one another, because development of each component is constrained by the others. It is also suggested that a change in any component of the mind triggers a whole set of changes in the rest of the system. Thus, "when the changes in one of the systems accumulate to a certain level," a change in *another* system may function "as a catalyst triggering the reorganization of the intellect as a whole, at a new representational or structural level" (Demetriou et al., 1993, p. 137).

For instance, according to Demetriou and Raftopoulos (1999), changes in both speed and control of processing between 9 and 11 years, followed by improvements in self-monitoring and self-regulation at the age of 11 or 12, might account for the turn from concrete to abstract representations at about 12 years of age.

Demetriou makes explicit that his approach to structural task analysis bears a resemblance to Halford's: "To understand what a problem is about, one must be able to represent for oneself the minimum connections between the elements that define its identity. . . . In Halford's terms, this constitutes the dimensionality of a problem" (Demetriou et al., 1993, p. 25). Because of this similarity, we do not discuss in detail the problems used by Demetriou and his colleagues in their empirical research, nor the criteria according to which they evaluate a priori the level of complexity of such tasks.

Generally speaking, most of their studies aim at validating different constructs of the theory by applying exploratory or confirmatory factor analysis (or other techniques based on individual differences) to large batteries of tests, though occasionally other research methods have been used as well (e.g., learning studies). Thus, for instance, Demetriou, Platsidou, Efklides, Metallidou, and Shayer (1991) study the structure of the quantitative-relational SSS; Efklides, Demetriou, and Metallidou (1994) focus on the propositional SSS; Demetriou, Kazi, and Georgiou (1999) explore the hypercognitive system; Demetriou et al. (1993) document the distinction among the various SSS and their relationship with the hypercognitive system; Demetriou, Spanoudis, Christou, and Platsidou (2002) propose a regression model of the Stroop effect; and Demetriou, Christos et al. (2002) investigate the processing system and its development.

As a specific example of this large-scale research program, let's consider a cross-cultural study of quantitative abilities (Demetriou, Pachaury, Metallidou, & Kazi, 1996). This study uses a battery of arithmetic operations, one of proportional reasoning, and one of algebraic reasoning, each of which includes items at four developmental levels. These batteries are administered to more than 500 participants, partly Greek and partly Indian, in the age range of 10–16 years old. Confirmatory factor analyses show that, in both cultures, three factors that represent the three batteries plus one general factor can account for covariance among the tests. Rasch scale analyses showed that also the developmental levels of the items constituted good scales in both cultures. The authors suggest that these results provide evidence for cross-cultural validity of their model of the quantitative-relational SSS. At the same time, cross-cultural differences are also found, that is, the Indian subjects as a group lag behind the Greek, and the Greek group shows higher structural coefficients for the battery-specific factors and lower structural coefficients for the general factor, in comparison with the Indians. Demetriou et al. (1996) interpret these differences as showing that, when relevant domain-specific skills are not strong enough, the mind's general systems carry a larger portion of the responsibility for coping with the task demands.

Given the similarity among the domains of Demetriou's SSSs, Case's central conceptual structures (see chap. 6), and the group factors of classic psychometrics, Case, Demetriou, Platsidou and Kazi (2001) designed a study that may contribute to bridging cognitive-developmental and differential psychology. This study uses tests that were previously validated for Demetriou's five SSSs and for Case's spatial, numerical, and verbal-narrative conceptual structures, along with seven subtests of the WISC; this battery is administered to children in the age range of 7–10 years old. As expected, five domain-specific factors plus one general factor[10] can account

---

[10]The selection of tests used in this study does not enable the authors to distinguish which psychological constructs (e.g., within Demetriou's theory, which properties of the hypercognitive or of the processing system) are represented by the general factor.

for performance in the whole battery. Every test, either taken from Demetriou's or Case's previous research or from the WISC, is loaded by the factor that represents the predicted SSS, with only one exception, that is, Demetriou's test of deductive reasoning does not group as expected with the tests of Case's verbal-narrative conceptual structure and the verbal subtests from the WISC, but instead it is loaded by the qualitative-analytic factor. This exception may suggest that the boundaries between SSSs are not so clear-cut as previous research had suggested. Case et al. (2001) suggest redefining one of the factors as more purely verbal, rather than propositional or inferential; and to consider another factor to stand for logical and inferential processes in general, rather than for categorical reasoning only. Although this unexpected result may point to a need of further research to map more precisely the specific domains of cognition (and their development), all the other findings are in agreement with the predictions.

A recent cross-cultural study (Demetriou et al., 2005) provides further support for the cultural universality of processing domains or SSSs. The overall success of these studies shows that, in general, the various SSSs are not an idiosyncratic finding due to particular tests used by Demetriou and colleagues, and therefore, the issue of domain specificity has to be taken seriously in attempting to build a comprehensive theory of cognitive development.

CONCLUSION

The extreme structuralist rigor of early models (e.g., Chapman, 1987; Halford, 1987) seems to carry a price, namely the bracketing of the role of strategies and goals in the regulation of cognitive processes, and neglect of the temporal flow in information processing. More recent models (e.g., Halford, Wilson et al., 1998), however, clarify the role of relational complexity of representations as a resource, and accept the need to complement structural analysis of representations with consideration of strategies and processes. Thus, the research presented in this chapter seems to indicate that a structuralist approach still has value when the goal is to identify qualitatively different and increasingly complex levels of representations or mental operations. It seems to us that de Ribaupierre's (1993) descriptive and minimalist vision of structuralism, in limiting its explanatory value, makes the most of its actual potential.

In light of these considerations a structuralist approach can be considered useful and important, but insufficient in itself for constructing an adequate theory of cognitive development. As we shall see in the following chapters of this book, all neo-Piagetian theories and models satisfy the requirements of "minimal structuralism" as intended by de Ribaupierre (1993) and Rieben et al. (1990), but structuralism is a major feature for only some of them. We shall take this point further in chapter 9 when discussing the contribution of structuralist descriptions to task analysis and process modeling. Of course, neo-Piagetian researchers converge in pointing out that more complex structures require greater attentional resources or processing capacity. However, the nexus between structural complexity and quantity of resources is not always made fully explicit; this nexus remains an open problem for some of the theories discussed in this chapter.

The study of individual differences is not specific to structuralist approaches only; for instance, it has long been a major issue also for the TCO. Whereas the studies of individual differences reviewed in this chapter focus primarily on issues of representation, Pascual-Leone focuses more on issues of cognitive style, which can be studied in terms of the interplay among metasubjective operators. The work of Lautrey, de Ribaupierre, and Rieben points at the possibility of different developmental courses in the field of propositional and analogical representations, and Demetriou extends this view to no less than five representational domains. As Larivée et al. (2000) note, the pluralistic and multidimensional approach of the "French connection," with its emphasis on the propositional versus analogical distinction, can be seen as complementary to the main neo-Piagetian models. The same can probably be said of the "Greek connection." That is, the individual-difference studies reviewed here are not merely concerned with issues of measurement, but aim at elucidating the existence of different representational domains and their role in cognitive development, possibly in interaction with more general mechanisms. This is an issue on which Robbie Case developed particularly important theoretical views (see chap. 6).

Finally, we note that, although all structuralist neo-Piagetian approaches share with Piaget the assumption that tasks can be ordered according to their level of structural complexity, this does not imply that they also share with Piaget a strong belief in developmental stages. The concept of "stage" is softened, in Halford's theory, by the role of learning, that is made possible but does not necessarily follow the ability to process relations of a given level of complexity; in Demetriou's theory, as well as in the view of Lautrey and colleagues, the concept of stage is softened by consideration of the representational domain and the processing demands of the tasks.

4

Problem Solving in Children

Neo-Piagetian models contribute to the study of children's problem solving by fostering an understanding of the cognitive processes that underlie the generation of solutions, both correct and incorrect. These models permit study of the processes leading to specific acquisitions, that is, study of the step-by-step development of the procedures and strategies used by children. The purpose of such study is to evaluate the contribution of these specific acquisitions to an account of change and developmental progress in problem solving generally.

Problem solving is a topic that has attracted researchers from such diverse theoretical perspectives as Gestalt, associationist and information processing. The method of study adopted and the type of problem studied varies with each approach, and concomitant differences are found in conceptions of what a problem is, of what processes are employed in solving a problem and of what variables influence reaching a solution. Typical of the Gestalt theory, for example, might be study of insight problems, which require a restructuring of the problem situation; associationists may study variables influencing the associative strength between the correct response and the problem situation, whereas information processing proponents would consider the strategies children adopt in relation to the representation of the problem that they form. These diverse perspectives, however, share the idea that a situation is considered a problem when it poses obstacles and the idea that if a problem has a well-defined solution, then once it is found, it is considered the right one by all solvers (given all factors are under control).

In the first portion of the chapter, we consider studies that examine problems of the type that require constructive actions leading step by step to achievement of a pre-established goal. Our interest is how the reasoning processes and strategies underlying children's solution attempts develop. Subsequently we examine the use of analogy in problem solving, and consider its advantages and limitations. Finally, the role of instruction in problem solving is examined.

THE USE OF HEURISTICS IN THE SOLUTION OF WELL-DEFINED PROBLEMS

Many situations are characterized by an initial state and a final or goal state that is to be achieved by means of operations that step by step transform the initial state into the final one. Such situations become problems to the extent that some restriction limits the number of moves or the type of operations allowed. Situations with these characteristics are termed *well-defined* problems within a classical perspective and are of various types. One type includes actual problems of daily life that require planning ability, for example, the problem of arriving at a certain place within certain time limits while taking account of a restriction on the use of particular streets and the need to complete specific errands along the way. Another type of problem involves identifying the rule or principle appropriate for a specific case. These problems are common in, but not limited to, the school environment, as in algebra, geometry, physics, and so on. Puzzles such as the Tower of Hanoi represent yet another type. In these problems, elements of a configuration must be moved in such a way as to transform it to a desired state by means of a limited number of legal moves. Another type is the insight problem, so called for the sudden arrival of the solution as if from a flash of inspiration (an example is the 9-points problem[1] of Maier, 1931). The characteristic of these problems is that the representation initially formed of the problem contains unnecessary restrictions that impede solution, and it is only when this initial representation is abandoned that the solution becomes available.

In some types of problems specific domain knowledge plays a role, including, for example, many problems connected with school subjects such as mathematics or science. Domain knowledge allows access to concepts, principles, rules and procedures that are stored in long-term memory and

---

[1]Given a 3 by 3 square matrix of points, the problem is to connect all 9 points without lifting one's pencil from the paper. The typical initial problem representation, which limits the connecting lines to the area delimited by the matrix of points, must be abandoned in order to achieve a solution.

that differentiate the performance of experts from non-experts. In the game of chess, for example, the knowledge built up through years of experience regarding typical position patterns of the pieces allows the expert to reduce the problem space in any particular situation, thereby enabling recognition of which moves are best and execution of a more extended simulation of future moves (Chase & Simon, 1973; deGroot, 1966).

The role of knowledge is critical in another class of problems called *ill-defined*. In these problems, differently from well-defined problems, one or more of the problem characteristics (initial state, restrictions on the permissible operations, the final state to be attained) is unclear. Such problems are common both in everyday life and in disciplinary fields such as economics and medicine (e.g., Lesgold, 1985, studied the role of specific knowledge in radiology diagnosis). Voss, Greene, Post, and Perner (1983), for example, asked both experts in political economy and non-experts to decide what might be done to improve agricultural production in the former Soviet Union. This problem is ill-defined in that detailed information is not provided on the existing level of productivity and the factors influencing it; restrictions related to geography and climate are not clear; and the desired degree of improvement in productivity is also unspecified. Often problem-solvers are unsatisfied by the solutions to ill-defined problems, and different problem-solvers, even experts in the domain, do not necessarily agree on a solution. Domain knowledge is important in these problems as a means of identifying subproblems within which a number of factors converge and can, therefore, be addressed in a global manner. Attempts to eliminate the role of individual factors in isolation, a common approach by non-experts, often result in incompatible suggestions for solution and an unconvincing final solution.

Knowledge also plays a part in insight problems, in this case as a factor in the kind of situational representation activated. Existing schematic knowledge can lead to a univocal representation of presented material or of instructional elements in a manner that may often be inadequate for attaining the desired goal. Domain knowledge is not a factor in problems of the puzzle type such as the Tower of Hanoi, and it is this characteristic that has attracted the attention of researchers to them. Using these problems it is possible to study the various strategies children employ and their effectiveness without concern that different levels of knowledge may interfere in the solving process.

Algorithms are available for some well-defined problems and their application will proceed smoothly within a given processing system, reduce searching of the problem space to a minimum and, most importantly, "guarantee solution of problems of the class in question" (Newell & Simon, 1972, p. 822). Yet, in some problems the algorithms can only be applied with the aid of a computer, given that the number of alternatives to examine exceeds the capacity of the human mind. For example, in solving an 8-letter anagram one could generate more than 40,000 letter combinations to be checked for semantic plausibility. The problem-solver, thus, often makes use of heuristics, short cuts that limit the number of alternatives to examine, but that do not always result in success.

We now consider one of the well-defined problems for which no algorithm is available. This problem, therefore, requires the use of heuristics, or general strategies, that can facilitate the problem-solver's search for the desired solution.

Heuristics in the Solution of Well-Defined Problems

The utility of heuristics depends on the type of problem involved. For example, a very simple heuristic, *generate and test* (generate a possible solution and test whether it is the desired one) is useful in situations presenting a relatively small number of possibilities. As Newell and Simon (1972) note, if the problem is to find the name of a fruit that begins with the letter "o," use of this heuristic proves more helpful if the correct answer is a prototypical, highly salient fruit (such as orange) than if it is a nonprototypical one (such as olive).

Depending on the problem, heuristics do yield knowledge in some cases. In medical diagnosis, for example, the fact that a hypothesis based on a series of symptoms is not confirmed can assist generation and testing of another hypothesis by pointing to initially neglected symptoms or by minimizing the weight given to symptoms initially considered critical.

One limit to this strategy lies in the fact that the test is applied to the complete solution with no possibility to consider and check the validity of its parts. This same limit applies to another heuristic (*depth-first searching*), which involves following a selected solution path exhaustively; if it does not lead to the desired goal, one needs to abandon the attempt and begin again with a new path.

Among the most studied heuristics are *means–ends analysis* and *subgoal decomposition*. When using means–ends analysis the problem-solver plans the sequence of moves or operators to apply, working forward from the initial state or backward from the end state. The solver proceeds cyclically through two phases: (a) identify the difference between the current state of the problem and the final state, and (b) apply a legal operator useful for reducing the difference. When the final goal cannot be reached directly, this strategy is used together with subgoal decomposition, which reduces the problem space with progressive movement toward the goal; it does so through intermediate moves that may temporarily distance one from the final goal.

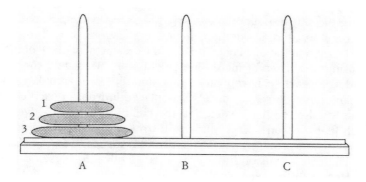

FIG. 4.1. Three-disk tower of Hanoi problem. *Source:* Klahr (1978a).

These strategies work well with the Tower of Hanoi (TOH) problem (see Fig. 4.1), a well-defined problem that has been studied primarily in adults as well as through simulations with production systems (Simon, 1979). The initial state of the problem consists of a set of successively smaller disks (typically 3 disks) stacked on one of three available pegs. The final or goal state is a similar stack on one of the other pegs, and it is to be reached by a series of moves that are subject to two restrictions: only one disk may be moved at a time and a larger disk may never be placed on top of a smaller one.

To solve this problem one uses means–ends analysis, planning the moves to be made and creating hierarchically connected subgoals that lead toward the desired solution. As the number of disks to be moved increases; thus, the number of subgoals to establish and keep in mind also increases; and, thus, the problem becomes more difficult.

The Use of Heuristics in Children's Problem Solving

Klahr and Robinson (1981) studied the development of problem-solving ability focusing on the Tower of Hanoi problem. Earlier studies (Byrnes & Spitz, 1977; Piaget, 1974) showed that only a portion of 6-year-olds succeed in correctly performing even the simplest version of the task involving only two disks and a minimum of three moves. Piaget found that children proceed by trial and error, showing no logical capacity for understanding the task or for planning what moves to make in order to achieve the desired goal. Klahr and Robinson reconsidered this problem not so much to verify the previous results as to learn about the development of strategic behavior in 4- to 6-year-olds, including, for example, planning sequences of moves in advance and formulating subgoals for the purpose of moving toward the goal state.

To make the situation more interesting, the problem was presented in the context of a story, and, in addition, some modifications were introduced in the materials and in the display of initial and final states. In place of the disks of decreasing size, cans of increasing height were used, and the children were told that each can represented a different-sized monkey (daddy, mommy, and baby). A series of cans was placed in front of each child (see Fig. 4.2) in the desired final order, and the child was asked to give instructions such that a second series of cans in front of the experimenter would end up in the same arrangement. The described moves were not actually carried out. The restrictions on the moves were identical to those for the standard problem with the exception that to make it more meaningful and simpler for the child it was smaller cans that were not to be placed on larger ones. If such a move were actually made, the smaller can would slide off.

Different versions of the problem involved different arrangements of the cans with respect to both the initial state and the final state (the pegs on which the cans were to be placed and the number of cans per peg). The minimum number of moves required (based on the optimal solution) ranged from 2 to 7. Because not all of the versions were beyond their ability, it was possible to observe the children's capacity for planning.

The types of moves to be carried out varied (Klahr, 1978) according to the state of the display at any given time and, therefore, the subgoal to be achieved. The simplest move—move a disk directly to the final peg—could

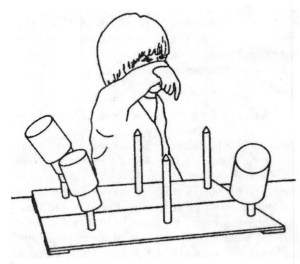

FIG. 4.2. Apparatus used by Klahr for the monkey story problem. The child is asked to anticipate the sequence of moves that the researcher must make in order to reproduce the arrangement on the child's side of the apparatus. *Source:* Klahr (1978a)

only be used in solving problems that required two moves. More complicated moves were useful in problems with a higher minimum: Remove a can from a peg in order to pick up the can beneath it, and remove a can from a peg in order to move another can onto it.

In addition to presenting the initial and final states of the problem as towers, as in the standard problem, a "flat-ending" version of the problem was used in which the final state consisted of one can on each peg. The goal was to observe generalization to a problem involving a different representation.

According to the authors' analysis, the Tower of Hanoi problem requires that one be able: (a) to plan and carry out a series of moves that satisfies subgoals leading to attainment of the main goal, something children often do spontaneously, such as "getting a chair to reach a cabinet containing a string to tie on a doll" (Klahr & Robinson, 1981, p. 115); and (b) to remove an obstacle that interferes with reaching an object, something that infants are able to do within their first year. The authors' revision of the standard problem intentionally made the context meaningful for the child so as to allow formation of an adequate representation while leaving the structure of the problem unaltered. The problems were presented in increasing order of difficulty so as to observe early abilities and the development of strategy learning and generalization.

Children's moves and verbal planning were analyzed in different ways. One consideration was the number of moves that children were able to plan with different types of problems and according to whether the final configuration was to be flat or towered. The maximum length of planning attributed to a child was based on the restrictive criterion of success with the entire set of problems requiring a given number of moves. Consistent with analyses of the standard problem, few 6-year-olds were successful with 7-move tower problems; but analysis also showed that almost half of 4-year-olds successfully completed 3-move problems and that the majority succeeded with 2-move problems.

These results show adoption of the subgoal decomposition strategy and planning ability that would not come to light by means of the analysis typically employed in previous studies, nor by a classical Piagetian assessment of development in terms of full attainment of a concept. The study also shows that the materials involved can greatly influence the strategies that the child adopts (Simon & Hayes, 1979). In comparison to the tower-ending version of the problem, performance with the flat configuration of cans is poor: this version lacks information about the order in which to move elements into the final state, and this lack hinders the use of the subgoaling strategy, even though it is in the child's repertoire.

For problems that require more than two moves, analysis of first moves provides another means of examining planning. Because the complete sequence of a child's planning is evaluated without actually carrying out any of the planned moves, the child faces the difficulty of maintaining the changing intermediate arrangements in memory. First moves are not subject to this difficulty and, thus, analysis of these can provide useful information about a child's strategies. This analysis of moves demonstrated the children's ability to set subgoals, even when the results were not effective. Illegal first moves, such as moving a can directly to its final position without regard to the game's restrictions were rare among 5-year-olds but more common among 4-year-olds. That more illegal moves were found in the flat-ending than in the tower-ending version of the problem provides additional evidence that the children's procedure was guided by their representation of the final configuration.

Based on an analysis of each child's protocol, Klahr and Robinson (1981) formed theoretical models to account for the strategic abilities observed in each age group. These are summarized in the three decision principles that follow in the following section. The theoretical models for move selection are sequenced on the basis of increasingly sophisticated combinations of these decision principles (Klahr & Robinson, 1981).

1. Subgoal selection. A child might seek first to move the smallest can to its target peg, but one could also conduct a forward search to find a subgoal achievable in a single move and begin with that one.
2. Obstructor detection and removal: If the can to be moved is under one or two other cans, a child who is able to identify such an obstruction can then adopt recursive procedures to remove it.
3. Depth of search: If the length of the forward search necessary for subgoal planning exceeds the child's capacity, the child may apply a more direct (but possibly erroneous) heuristic or reduce the depth of search by changing subgoals.

Klahr and Robinson's research demonstrated that at age 6, children already possess a vast repertoire of problem-solving strategies that they apply even in relatively unfamiliar environments. These strategies develop rapidly between ages 4 and 6, and they allow children to solve problems of increasing difficulty that require ability to plan and set subgoals. The most advanced of the non-optimal models identified by the authors corresponded to the behavior of almost half of the children. This model allows solution of 6-move (and less) problems and it anticipates a search depth of three moves.

Similar results by Blumberg (1978) showed that even 5-year-olds whose incorrect moves have led them into blind alleys are able to move out of them. Over successive trials the children learned from their experience, slowly adapting their general planning ability to a new context. Children know how to plan both locally and remotely, that is, they are able to anticipate both the consequences of a next move and the moves that should be taken or avoided subsequently. In comparison to adults and 11-year-olds, the younger children are able to plan sequences working forward but not working backward; that is, they are not able to start from the solution and go back to the moves that lead to the initial state. From these results and those provided by Klahr and Robinson's sophisticated analysis, it seems that by the time they enter elementary school, children know how to make plans involving up to six moves.

How do children build this ability? Fischer is among those who address this question concerning the development of planning. As described in chapter 5, he characterizes development as a series of small steps (involving not only progress but also regression) and sudden qualitative spurts, recurring in cycles, which define new levels of development. His interest is in qualitative changes marking advancements in the skill organization, an organization characterized by a growing complexity of relations among skill components. Investigating children's ability to solve Tower of Hanoi problems in the classical three disks format, Fischer proposes that planning follows the same developmental course as any other skill (Bidell & Fischer, 1994).

Having learned to anticipate simple means–end actions, a precursor of planning, children first achieve the ability to move a disk from one place to another and replace it with another disk (single representation), that is, they use one set of actions to evoke the other set. At the next level, 4-year-olds represent the dependency of one action on another (mapping relation), such as when they understand that it is necessary first to remove the disk on the top in order to move the one beneath. At the next level (system), 6- to 7-year-olds realize that relational mapping is not enough and become able to hierarchically coordinate two relational mappings into a more complex system. In other terms, children are able to represent a two-dimensional relation, by mentally anticipating the relations between two dependent systems. This occurs, for example, when placing a disk temporarily on a platform different from its final position in order to free the disk under it to place it in the final post and then go back to the first disk and place it in another position.

Support for Fischer's proposed developmental phases is offered by Welsh, Pennington, and Groisser (1991) who show that children's Tower-of-Hanoi performance spurts at the times and with the levels of complexity predicted by Fischer's theory. Not only is the development of planning similar to that of other cognitive skills, but also the processes activated for building higher level planning are those identified for the construction of other skills (Fischer & Bidell, 2006; Parziale, 2002). One example is shifting attention from one single representation to another: although this is a simple process, eventually it allows one to bring together two different representations and to coordinate them into a one-dimensional mapping. Moreover, the use of the reiteration process after a spurt consolidates the level achieved taking into account small variations in the tasks.

According to Fischer, planning ability is best observed when children are actually trying to solve a problem, rather than by asking them to anticipate the behaviors without actually making the moves, as in Klahr's study. This method allows one to study planning in a context in which the child takes into account the external feedback. Children, aged 6 to 11 years, are videotaped while solving the first of a series of Tower of Hanoi problems, and analysis of both macro and microdevelopmental processes is conducted. According to Fischer's theory, the macrodevelopmental processes are built on planning skills that are consolidated through the microprocesses of a previous lower level and that, at the same time, set the limit to the higher level that can be achieved. Observation of the children's movements captures not only the number of moves to reach the solution but also the relations among consecutive moves.

During the first trial on a problem, variables such as number of moves, pauses between moves, and rule violations inform about transition patterns occurring while attempting the problem solution. One can ask such questions as whether planning depends on duration of pause time. Spitz, Minsky, and Besselieu (1985) found that although retarded children showed a lower performance on Tower of Hanoi problems than non retarded, this difference was not related to the initial pause in the first trial. However, this study's consideration of only the initial pause time is a limitation. In fact, Fischer showed that planning may occur not only in the initial phase but also during the subsequent moves. How is pause time during the trial related to performance? Typical patterns emerged: Compared to efficient solvers, less efficient ones were characterized by longer pauses and more erroneous moves during the first phase. In this phase their level of representation was below the one needed to be successful, but its consistency indicated that it was, indeed, directed by planning rather than by chance. In fact, their difficulty in the initial phase was to be attributed to inability to hold in working memory a representation at an even lower level (one-dimensional relations) than that needed for the solution. The time spent on this phase, therefore, was useful to build the basic skill components and allowed transition to a higher level. In fact, their moves proceeded more rapidly and more efficiently in the second phase, once transition to the higher level occurred. This phase was characterized by a more complex representation, marking a qualitative increase in working memory (see chap. 5).

Studies of this sort suggest that the type of representation that children form of a problem changes with development. There is a change in the type of encoding that the children are able to carry out on the goal, the material and the information given. Moreover, as processing capacity increases with development, so does ability to decompose the final goal into subgoals while holding in mind the restrictions on the moves and the order in which they can be made. Advanced solution performance is, at least in part, a function of the relevant dimensions that a child is able to encode and keep in mind; we will see this by considering analogical problem solving tasks in the subsequent section. First, however, we wish to turn briefly to a model recently proposed by Siegler (2006), which promises to contribute considerably to our understanding of how children discover and acquire new strategies.

Siegler's model is presented in the context of domain-specific problems such as arithmetic and uses the metaphor of overlapping waves to represent his proposal that at any given point in time a child's thinking is characterized by multiple approaches. The model suggests that children have various representations and strategies available and use them in an increasingly adaptive manner, exhibiting temporary progress or regression depending on the phase of learning. Siegler says that adaptive choice seems to be related to a conceptual structure, a goal sketch, that outlines the goals to be met by a strategy and that is formed by the child even before discovery of the strategy. On the basis of several microgenetic studies in various problem domains (Alibali, 1999: Chen & Siegler, 2000; Perry & Lewis, 1999; Siegler & Jenkins, 1989) importance is given to distinguishing between the discovery of a strategy in terms of its first use and in terms of the time required for uptake or consolidation that may require variable experience and/or time (Siegler & Stern, 1998; Siegler & Svetina, 2002). Having different strategies available and using them is a potent means for consolidating a new strategy, particularly in the initial phases of discovery. With experience and age, old strategies may be dismissed and new adaptive strategies selected, but these strategic behaviors will vary depending on environmental factors, learning history in previous sessions or trials, and the type of problem (Siegler, 1995; Siegler, 2006).

PROBLEM SOLVING AND LEARNING BY ANALOGY

Human reasoning is conceived as essentially analogical rather than logical (Halford & Mccredden, 1998; Hofstadter, 2001; Holyoak & Thagard, 1995). Use of analogical procedures is one of the means adopted spontaneously by those who set out to learn in a new domain and to solve new problems (Greeno, 1978). Analogical reasoning is a common resource when addressing a new problem or situation in diverse fields such as scientific, political, creative, and everyday thinking (Dunbar, 2001). Noticing similarities between situations encountered in known domains and those arising in a new domain, a person activates already existing schemata that are relevant to solve new problems. According to Rumelhart and Norman (1981), these schemata are packets of knowledge "embedded in specialized procedures that are employed in the interpretation events in our environment" (p. 357). Further, ". . . the means whereby this knowledge is extended is, we believe, best viewed as an analogical process" (p. 343). These schemata are activated and applied implicitly—that is, not necessarily consciously—within a specific context and taking account of its specific aspects. Because direct application is rare, new schemata are created through a process of "tuning" that modifies the existing ones to be used adequately in the new specific context.

Analogical reasoning can be used also in solving logical problems such as transitivity according to Halford and McCredden (1998), through a process of schema formation. Transitivity tasks, such as "A greater (nicer, more clever) than B and B greater than C" are typically solved when we conceptualize the three (or more) terms of the premises as an ordered series. When the task is new, this is accomplished through a mental model in which a base schema is activated as an analog to arrange the terms in an ordering array from top to bottom (or from left to right). Thus, a mental model based on an established schema is activated from a context, adapted and applied to a new transitive context, as a specific procedure. However, use of such a schema would not reduce processing load given that both premises need to be processed jointly to locate the relative position of each term in the array without ambiguity (Halford, 1998). This fact indicates that use of analogical schemata can favor understanding of a logical problem but would not accelerate development.

Reasoning by analogy involves finding a correspondence between the base or source (known problem or domain of departure) and the target (on which the transfer operates and which becomes known by inference). It involves processes that permit comprehension of what relation between elements of the source is appropriate between those of the target. A possible use of analogy consists in noting the similarity between a story presenting a problem with its solution and a second story posing only a problem for a child to solve. For example, in a study by Holyoak, Junn, and Billman (1984) the child must recognize information in the base story regarding the means to reach a goal and generalize it to the target problem. In the story the protagonist reaches the goal, consisting in transferring material from one container to another, by rolling up a magic carpet and placing the material inside in such a way that it can be transported from a near into a far container. Attempting to solve the subsequent problem (involving different material and different containers), the child could note a correspondence with the previous story and generalize its solution method to the problem. In this example, having analyzed the various objects available, the child may recognize a piece of paper as analogous with the carpet in that both can be rolled up and used to transport material placed inside the roll. The results of this research showed that, to some extent, 4-year-old children are able to operate a relational mapping and solve the analogical problem.

This correspondence is not a matter of the properties of the base and the target separately, but rather of the relationship existing between them. Consider, for example, an analogy studied by Gentner (1983), namely, Rutherford's analogy between the solar system (base) and the structure of the hydrogen atom (target) "the sun is to planet as the nucleus is to electron." The sun's attributes (yellow, hot, etc.) are not the relevant matter to consider; rather it is the relations that exist between the sun and the planets that are relevant, given that some of these relations also connect nucleus and electron (e.g., planets circle the sun and electrons circle the nucleus; the sun and a planet attract one another as do the nucleus and an electron).

Two components of this process of searching for correspondence are particularly important. One is *encoding*, which permits activation of a mental representation that includes *inferring* the base's attributes and relations. The other is the comparison of representations resulting in a process of *mapping*, which allows finding a correspondence with the second pair, and *implementing* the relation, such that the missing element respects the same relation as the one found between the elements of the first pair (Chen, 1996; Gentner, 1983; Sternberg, 1985). As shown in these examples, analogy involves correspondence between relational properties of the two concepts not necessarily between surface attributes.

From this brief illustration it follows that knowledge of the base domain is an essential requisite for understanding analogy and attaining transfer. If one does not know enough about the solar system it is not possible to identify and map the relations to the new target domain. Knowledge may reduce the processing load by permitting a conceptual chunking (Halford, 1993, see chap. 3 for illustration of his theory). Take, for example, the analogy between heat-flow and water-flow. First, information relating to concepts such as temperature difference and heat flow is represented in chunks, within which the single details, irrelevant to process the analogy itself, are compressed into single higher order concepts (Halford & McCredden, 1998). In the analogy, each can be used as a chunk without further need to process their components and this enables their relation (temperature difference causing heat flow) to be represented in a higher level dimensionality as a binary relation within processing capacity. Use of conceptual chunking supports the relevance of both specific knowledge and general abilities as critical requisites for solving analogies.

Furthermore, the examples just discussed point out that analogy is characterized by other dimensions, one being systematicity (Gentner, 1983;

Gentner & Toupin, 1986). Systematicity is something like a measure of conceptual coherence, such as making explicit the causal structure in a story provided as a base. It involves the extent to which relations in the base are mutually constrained, thus forming a higher order system that is relationally consistent with the target. In Rutherford's analogy between sun and hydrogen atom, the fact that the sun is hotter than a planet is a relation that is not connected to the higher order system of interconnected relations involving mass, attractive force and distance. Gentner suggests that such unconnected relations are less likely to be applied to a target than those that are part of a coherent structure. The likelihood of processing structural relations is affected by structural coherence.

Systematicity is also a dimension of analogy complexity. According to Halford (1993) a simple analogy such as "cat : kitten :: horse : foal" involves a *relational mapping*, that is a single relation ("parent of") connecting base and target. A single relation is involved also in the following examples from Halford (1993) "John pushes Bill : Bill collides with Mike :: Judy provokes Marie : Marie hits Jenny." In both cases, each element of the base can be separately mapped to a corresponding element of the target: "pushes" is similar and can be directly mapped to "provokes," as is the case for "collides" and "hits." Thus, in both examples each of the two elements of the base involves one relation that can be processed separately from the other: it does not entail higher order coherence. In contrast with the examples just noted, a *system mapping* involves a higher order structure formed by at least two relations. The structural coherence of the causal chain connecting the two parts of the base validates the relational correspondence with the two parts of the target. For example, consider the following example, superficially similar to that just reported: "John pushes Bill : Bill collides with Mike :: Wendy helps Anne : Anne smiles at Jenny." The analogy is validated because a *higher order relation*, "cause," connects the two parts of the analogy: the action of John on Bill and the resulting action of Bill on Mike is analogous to the relation between the action of Wendy on Anne and the resulting action of Anne toward Jenny. There is not a surface similarity between "pushes" and "helps": they become connected in a system through operating in parallel on the correspondences between each element of the base and each element of the target through a higher order relation. The abstract dimension "cause" connects the elements of the base and, coherently, the elements of the target.

Complexity is a function of the number of arguments involved in the structural relation that are to be processed *in parallel*. According to the relational complexity analysis, "Representation of both source and target does not increase processing complexity . . . because relational representations can be superimposed without increasing complexity, provided the relation between the source and the target does not have to be explicitly represented" (Halford & Andrews, 2004, p. 139). Consequently, level of systematicity or structural similarity also affects the processing capacity needed for solving. In the example just discussed, of a relational mapping, the single relation "parent of" (cat, kitten) has two arguments (binary relation) that are first processed in the base and *then* in the target (horse, foal), before their correspondence is matched. Consequently, according to Halford, the analogy "parent of" entails two *binary* relations processed separately, rather than in parallel (univariate function, represented by the tensor product of three vectors).

When the two parts are to be processed jointly, complexity increases. For example given a logical problem such as the transitivity problem just mentioned, the two elements in each of the two premises have to be processed in parallel if one is to order them in series, and this operation requires representation of *a system* of relations (Andrews & Halford, 1998; Halford, 1993). Thus, when the analogy involves a system mapping, as in the example in which the high-order relation *"cause"* is extracted or in transitivity, the arguments processed *in parallel* are four: this entails a ternary relation (bivariate function, represented by the tensor product of four vectors). Thus, an analogy involves a ternary relation only if it is impossible to segment the processing of the relations. When segmentation is possible and a single relation is processed at a time, the required processing capacity is reduced and the analogy is solved through a simpler relational mapping rather than a system. This analysis of systematicity has implications for development, as is specified in the following section.

Another dimension that characterizes analogy, in addition to systematicity and complexity of structural similarity, is surface similarity (transparency or semantic similarity). It is a variable that regards the extent to which the mapped elements between source and target share the same (or similar) meaning and it has to do with the superficial similarity of the base elements that are salient but often irrelevant to solution (Gentner, 1983; Gentner & Toupin, 1986; Holyoak et al., 1984; Holyoak & Thagard, 1989). Processing the correspondence between the superficial attributes of the elements may not be enough to understand the analogy if one does not map the critical elements that are structurally similar (Chen & Daehler, 1992; Gentner & Toupin, 1986; Holyoak & Koh, 1987). A study by Holyoak and Koh (1987) with adults showed that surface similarity with an already known problem could, indeed, help one notice the analogy to a new problem. However, when the known problem presents high surface but low structural similarity, it may not be useful to process the relations and find correspondence between the two concepts.

The interaction between systematicity and surface similarity was revealed also in Gentner and Toupin's (1986) study of children's understanding of analogy. Children aged 4–6 and 8–10 heard a story and then acted out a target story having different degrees of variation in characters and their assigned roles: highly similar characters and roles in the two stories would mean a high degree of object similarity (high transparency). In addition the new story might or might not have parts that point to a higher order structure, such as a brief introduction, key terms, critical elements of the story structure, or a moral. The presence of these would enhance systematicity in terms of structural coherence of the stories. This analogy could be solved simply on the basis of high surface similarity; or if transparency was lacking, a child should resort to systematicity. Although both groups of children were able to recognize the correspondence between base and target when object similarity was high, only the older children could take advantage of systematicity to gain an accurate information transfer. Thus, the importance of processing systematicity depends on the degree of transparency, and surface similarity is advantageous but not indispensable.

Recently, the relative influence of three types of similarity—surface, structural, and procedural—was further examined (Chen, 1996). The base stories, in one study, presented a high or low *surface* similarity (regarding characters, goal, and object) and a high or low *structural* similarity (action either causally connected to or isolated from the character's goal). In another study, the base stories presented different levels of *surface* similarity and of *procedural* similarity (procedures involved in the source to be used in the target; Bassok, 1990). Each type of similarity contributed to performance, but the combination of surface with structural or procedural similarity determined the highest performances. Children's verbal reports showed that, although the 8-year-olds were more likely to perceive and represent the different types of similarity, the 5-year-olds were also sensitive to different elements of similarity as resulted from their representation of the source analogue. Thus, all three types of similarity may play a role, although in different ways, in children's analogy processing.

Children's Understanding of Analogy

As knowledge of the source domain is an essential requisite for understanding analogy, children are likely to understand a greater range of analogies as their domain specific knowledge increases during development. However, knowledge is not the only factor accounting for developmental differences in understanding analogy or in using it to solve problems. Another fundamental requisite is development of a processing capacity adequate to extract the relation and connect the elements of the analogy. As neo-Piagetian theories indicate, understanding analogy, just like any other cognitive ability, is not an all-or-none phenomenon. Differently from Piaget, who sets classical analogy understanding at the formal stage of development (Piaget, Montangero, & Billeter, 1977), neo-Piagetian theories view analogies as varying in terms of the cognitive elaboration required to reach a solution (e.g., Halford, 1993).

We have seen Halford's (1993) proposal that analogies vary in their relational complexity, which depends on the number of relations to be processed simultaneously in order to map the base to the target. His theory expects relational complexity to predict the age at which different analogies are resolved. Analogies involving unary, binary or ternary relations should start to be solved at 1 year, 2 years or 5 years of age, respectively, assuming that prerequisite knowledge is available. Young preschoolers are expected to be able to solve a simple type of analogy "but their ability to integrate binary relations or process ternary relation is in dispute" (Andrews & Halford, 1998, p. 142). Furthermore, even when children are able to handle binary relations, if object similarity is too salient they may not complete a structural encoding, and their reasoning may rely on the surface similarity (Halford, 1993).

Chen, Sanchez, and Campbell (1997) demonstrated the ability of 1-year-olds to solve simple isomorphic problems using a means–end analysis task requiring two steps, to devise a tool and to use it in order to reach a final goal. The task shares similarities with one of Piaget's that involved pulling a toy closer to oneself by means of a cord attached to the support on which it was resting. The children participated in three trial tasks, the first trial being the base analog. In case of failure, the adult modeled the child's actions. In each trial the apparatus changed two surface features (toy and color of the support). Whereas the 10-month-olds did not improve over trials, the 13-month-olds' performance on the second and third trial test became better and more efficient, showing ability to transfer the solution learned in the first trial.

Singer-Freeman (2005) studied the ability of 2-year-olds to solve binary relations both in classical tasks (e.g., loose yarn : stretched yarn :: loose rubber band : stretched rubber band) and in problem-solving tasks. For example, in problem solving, first, in order to lower the load of drawing a relational inference, the experimenter demonstrated to a group of children the relation between the elements of two bases (e.g., stretching a loose rubber band between plastic poles in order to put an orange on it and make the orange roll). Then a target problem was presented for which the same relation had to be applied to different elements of the scenarios (e.g., stretching a rubber band between two different poles to put on a bird and make it fly). Children's performance increased in the second trial, meaning that familiarization with the task contributes to processing an analogy suitable to the child's age; however, some children did not solve the analogy even after explicit prompts on how to proceed. This was interpreted as meaning that young children can spontaneously draw analogies but have difficulty to do it in an intentional way. Moreover, children solving classical analogies were not the same children who solved analogical problems; according to the author, this probably suggests that with young children differential processes are involved in the two types of tasks.

The results of these two studies document the emerging ability of 1- and 2-year-olds to draw analogical inferences with increasing complexity. In both studies performance increased over trials and analogy tasks were solved by young children at a level of complexity within the reach of their processing capacity and under conditions of high contextual support. Such support included making explicit the relation in the base, ensuring understanding through modeling and feedback.

We have seen that children are able to solve logical problems such as class inclusion and transitivity at about 5 years of age (Halford, 1993). It has been suggested that the analogical use of a well-established familiar schema may favor the extraction of relevant relations and allow correct solution (Halford, 1993). In particular, solution of class inclusion problems (e.g., "in a bunch of red and white flowers, are there more red flowers or more flowers?") entails the processing of ternary relations, which is a system mapping involving the relation between a superordinate class and two subclasses. Could presentation of a pragmatic familiar schema be used analogically to draw a correct class inclusion solution? Goswami and Pauen (2005) utilize the analogy of "family" to a class inclusion task (as suggested by Halford, 1993): the base is the whole, superordinate class of "family" composed of two parents and three children, mapped into the target, say, a bunch of balloons, including a smaller and larger subset of balloons. Providing the "family" analog increased performance for the 5-year-olds compared to a control group (without such a schema), but this was not the case for the 4-year-olds. Thus, use of a pragmatic schema essentially makes the analogy relations more understandable for those children that are able to process a system of relations. However, after an explicit hint that the bunch of balloons could be a "balloon family," the 4-year-olds' performance improved, younger than expected by Halford's theory. One could question whether such contextual support preserves the core of the reasoning task. It may change the structure of the problem so that the use of simpler representational models allows processing of separate binary relations. For example, simple models may activate label-matching processes, directly accessing the notion that "family" is the whole group; or even forming other pragmatic schemata such as "pretend that the bunch of balloons is a family, the set of two are the parents, and so on." Neither of these processes entails a system of logical relation characterizing the class inclusion problem and more research is needed to control for complexity of the analogy problem actually solved by younger children.

Gentner indirectly confirms the core idea of Halford's position that during development children change the way they cognitively address analogy and that an earlier correct understanding is limited to analogies that can be resolved through less advanced processes requiring less processing capacity. She asserts that the young child is not able to use the structure of relations shared by the source and the target, and for this reason, analogy solutions are based on attributes shared by the objects, that is, on a purely superficial similarity. In particular, Gentner speaks of a relational shift occurring in two developmental phases: younger children would interpret analogies in terms of object similarity and only at a later phase would they be able to interpret them in terms of relational (structural) similarity (Gentner, 1988, Gentner & Toupin, 1986, Kotovsky & Gentner, 1996; Rattermann & Gentner, 1998). In support of this developmental shift are findings showing that young children succeed in using the analogy procedure only when the correspondence between the descriptions of the two problem situations is complete. If extraneous elements are inserted in the target story such that the correspondence between the two situations is no longer direct and complete, the younger children no longer recognize the analogy (Holyoak et al., 1984).

Although there is evidence that 3- and 4-year-olds can solve analogies entailing binary relations, it is also found that when the mapping task involves variations both in object similarity and in relation, mapping tend to be based on appearance. Thus, use of analogs in reasoning, according to many scholars, among which are Gentner, Goswami, Halford, and Holyoak, involves both general processes and domain specific knowledge and it is subject to one's processing capacity.

Advantages and Limitations of the Analogical Procedure in Problem Solving

Use of analogy can be very profitable for teaching and learning but one should also be aware of the limits of its application. New schemata constructed on the basis of existing ones are not always perfect, nor, as Rumelhart and Norman (1981) state, are they necessarily adequate to solve any kind of problem in the new domain. This is because it is not always a good analogy that is activated for the specific task at hand. Rumelhart and Norman indicate that teaching fractions using the pie analogy leads to successful abstraction of addition and subtraction operations from the specific context (e.g., subtracting one quarter from a whole pie leaves three quarters of the pie). However, it hinders the ability to divide and multiply fractions, for which it is more profitable to teach fractions in analogy to arithmetical operation, as a compounding of a division and a multiplication (e.g., dividing one number by two and multiplying it by one gives one half of a number).

Anderson, Greeno, Kline, and Neves (1981) also draw attention to some limitations of using analogies for learning to solve new geometry problems through examples presented in the text. Although this process is useful in cases of actual correspondence between examples and problems, in other cases correspondence is only apparent, being based on the similarity of a diagram that brings a particular example to mind. In fact, both children and adults resort to surface similarity when they cannot encode the deep relational structure of the problems, and this is confirmed by the behaviour of novices in the physics domain who categorize physics problems on the basis of surface elements of the problem texts (Chi, Feltovich, & Glaser, 1981). Not only may students who use examples relying on surface similarity incur negative transfer, but they may also fail to use analogically those examples sharing a poor surface correspondence to a target problem. It is precisely the necessity of processing both the similarities and differences, according to Gick and Holyoak (1983), that accounts for the greater difficulty of analogical reasoning on the basis of an example compared to analogical reasoning based on a schema.

A study by Chen and Daehler (1989; see also Gick & Holyoak, 1983) illustrates a limitation in the possibility to generalize a principle abstracted from an analogy. In their study an abstract schema could be formed from a base story, useful to transfer information for solving another problem presented subsequently. This target problem involved retrieving a bead from a container with an opening that was too small to allow one to simply reach in and pull it out. The bead was floating in a small amount of water near the bottom of the container. Two possible solution principles were illustrated in different stories, and children were trained on only one of them. The first principle was to add water to the container causing the marble to rise on the liquid's surface; the second was to connect two tinker-toy sticks to make a spoon long enough to fish the marble from the bottom. The material available to the children during the problem-solving phase permitted only one of the two solutions. The results showed that it is possible to train 6-year-olds to develop a solution principle and that forming such an abstract representation increases positive transfer, that is to say, increases the ability to apply the principle drawn from the base stories to the target problem. However, the training did not improve the ability to avoid negative transfer. That is to say, training did not help children recognize cases in which the principle is not appropriate. Children also attempted to transfer the principle learned from the story when the available material actually supported the application of the other principle.

Thus it seems that training in abstracting a principle to apply in analog problems would be useful but not sufficient for avoiding negative transfer. In the same vein, specific knowledge could help to use analogy but has some limitations: in fact experts in the domain are less likely to run into negative transfer, although it does not fully guarantee the possibility to recognize all situations in which a principle does not apply (Novick, 1988).

Consideration of the factors that influence good analogy use makes more understandable the fact that two isomorphic problems do not always yield comparable performance. A simple change in instructions or in the degree of familiarity of the context could play a role, for example, by preventing the child from representing isomorphic problems in the same way and thereby leading to failure to adopt the same procedures (Simon & Hayes, 1979).

Overall, awareness of the limits of an analogy in solving new problems is very important. As suggested by Halford (1993), analogical problem solving is useful at an initial stage of learning, when relevant features of a familiar domain may help a first conceptualization of a new domain. However, when information characterizing the new domain does not share similarity with the known domain, analogy should be dismissed and its limitations acknowledged. This explains why the use of analogies in teaching and learning "may always be a delicate course between Schylla and Charybdis" (Duit, Roth, Komorek, & Wilber, 2001, p. 299).

The following section raises the question of how problem-solving ability can be acquired and improved and considers how teachers might make good use of analogies.

INSTRUCTION AND PROBLEM SOLVING

Instructional interventions have followed from the analyses of information processing theorists, and the effects of these interventions are the first topic of this section.

According to Piaget the stage of development achieved by a child limits the effect of learning experiences; however, he has suggested that instruction seeking to increase performance will be more effective to the extent that the child's current developmental stage is close to the desired level (Piaget, 1970a) as shown by more advanced responding on a pretest (Inhelder et al., 1974). Moreover, these studies suggest that a learning experience will be more profitable to the extent that modalities and situations proposed are similar to those that the child encounters in natural learning settings.

Reflection on how others solve a problem is one typical activity when trying to understand a new problem, and it has been shown that strategy generalization is wider when one generates explanations from one's own problem solving activities or from those of others (Chi, Bassok, Lewis, Reimann, & Glaser, 1989; Chi, de Leeuw, Chiu, & LaVancher, 1994). In so doing, one gains a better understanding of the goal structure and is able to contrast competing, less adequate strategies (Crowley & Siegler, 1999). This advantage has also been found with children. For example, in conservation tasks and mathematical problems, explicit instructions to explain the correct solution of a more knowledgeable adult improves schoolchildren's performance (Siegler, 2002). The same is true of instructions asking children to explain one's own solution or the reasoning (either correct or incorrect) of other children.

Given these hints on a positive role for certain interventions, it would seem important to observe in some detail what it is that children modify as a result of instruction and how the modification comes about. The methodology of Robert Siegler (1978) allows useful insights on this matter, as we see after briefly describing his model and the balance scale problem to which it can be applied.

Siegler's Model; The Balance Problem

Siegler (1976, 1978; Siegler & Klahr, 1982) offers a potent model for generating predictions of children's performance in Piagetian problems. The model proposes that with development the child becomes able to use increasingly powerful rules allowing solution of increasingly complex problems. The *décalage* problem is explained by maintaining that development is characterized neither by the child's stage nor by the rule mastered by the child. The child can use different rules in different problems that only appear similar and for which a differentiated stock of experiences exists.

From among the various problems considered by Siegler we discuss the balance problem, a widely studied proportional reasoning problem that he has adapted from a version described by Inhelder and Piaget (1955/1958). The child is presented with a balance formed of two arms with a support post at the fulcrum. Identical metal weights can be placed onto the four pegs located at regular intervals on each arm. Depending on the number of weights used and their placement in relation to the fulcrum, the balance can remain in equilibrium or go down to one side or the other. The child's task is to observe, while both balance arms are blocked by supporting posts, a particular configuration of weights and to predict what position the balance will take when the supports are removed. Six types of balance problem have been created for the purpose of studying more precisely what it is that varies during development. Some of these problems can be solved by using the simplest rules, but others can only be solved with use of more advanced rules. The configurations associated with each of the 6 problems are shown in Figure 4.3.

Siegler's (1976, 1981) model makes precise predictions regarding which problems children should solve and what responses they will give for each of the six types of problems. The children who use the least advanced rule, Rule I, take account only of the number of weights, information that is sufficient for solving problems of Type 1, 2 and 4. In using Rule II, children also

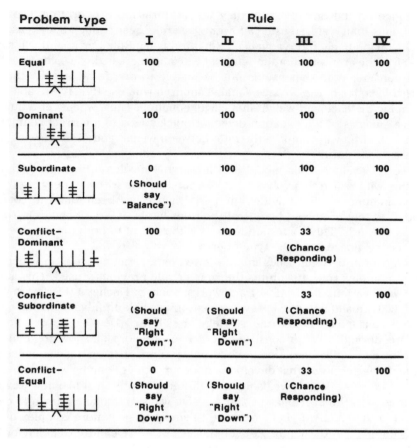

Problem type	Rule			
	I	II	III	IV
Equal	100	100	100	100
Dominant	100	100	100	100
Subordinate	0 (Should say "Balance")	100	100	100
Conflict–Dominant	100	100	33 (Chance Responding)	100
Conflict–Subordinate	0 (Should say "Right Down")	0 (Should say "Right Down")	33 (Chance Responding)	100
Conflict–Equal	0 (Should say "Right Down")	0 (Should say "Right Down")	33 (Chance Responding)	100

FIG. 4.3. Predictions of percentage of correct answers and error patterns for children using Rules I–IV on different arrangements of Siegler's balance problem. *Source:* Siegler (1981).

consider distance, but only as an alternative to weight. Thus, problems of Type 1, 2 and 4 will be solved in accordance with the weight dimension; whereas those of Type 3, which have an equal number of weights on each arm but at different distances, will be solved by considering distance. However, children using Rule II will fail problems of Type 5 and 6 because weight is what will be considered in these cases and that dimension will lead to an error. With use of Rule III, children begin to understand that both weight and distance are to be considered simultaneously. But if children are not able to compute the relationship between the two dimensions, they will fail in the so-called conflict problems where each arm has the highest value for one of the two dimensions (more weight on one arm and greater distance on the other). Thus, they will perform more poorly on Type 4 problems than children using a lower order rule, even though their reasoning is qualitatively more advanced. Children using Rule I or Rule II will say that it is the arm with more weight that will fall, whereas those using Rule III will consider both dimensions but be unable to decide among the three possible states of the balance. Finally, children who use Rule IV are able to combine distance and weight in a single equation. Thus, whenever a qualitative analysis of the situation does not quickly lead to a correct solution, these children will compare the ratio between weight and distance with respect to each arm.

Siegler evaluated his model of a hierarchy of rules of increasing complexity with research involving 3- to 17-year-olds and with a variety of problems. In support of the model, the performance has been found to correspond to that predicted by one of the rules in about 90% of children from age 5 upwards. This correspondence is with respect to both the number of correct responses and the type of errors.

Transition between rules is not viewed as a series of steps in which a more complex rule substitutes the simpler rule previously used. This is in line with various theoretical frameworks, such as Fischer's (Fischer & Bidell, 2005) maintaining that development involves both advancements and regressions (to a simpler rule, strategy or skill use). Detailed observations before, during and after construction of a new rule or skill show great inter- and intraindividual variation in children's performance on a given concept or task. Siegler noted that development occurs in overlapping waves, meaning that a rule, like a wave, is not substituted abruptly. Just like new waves overlap with the previous ones, alternative ways of thinking remain at disposal of the child who becomes able to employ a new more complex one. This entails that during the critical phases of change children's behavior is not consistent as they show switching between rules before adopting a higher rule more consistently. DeLoache, Miller, and Pierroutsakos (1998) use the metaphor of child as bricoleur to suggest that diverse processes and strategies are a resource used by the child as tools are used by the bricoleur.

Microgenetic studies show use of other rules and specify transitions with respect to the balance scale problem (Siegler & Chen, 2002). In particular, rules observed with conflict problems give an insight to the multiform guessing behavior already noticed by Siegler (1981). For example, when both weight and distance are unequal in the two arms, different rules may be employed such as those involving additive procedures with which the child calculates the sum of weights and distance in each arm and compares them, as well as compensation rules (Halford at al., 2002) such as the "buggy" rule. The latter involves shifting toward the end of the scale the pile of weights in the arm with a greater number of weights (placed closer to the fulcrum), subtracting one element as the pile moves one peg further down, until equality of either weights or distance is reached (van der Maas & Jansen, 2002; Normandeau, Larivée, Roulin, & Longeot, 1989; van Maanen, Been, & Sijstma, 1989).

van der Maas and Jansen (2003) have tested the hypothesis underlying Siegler's model with participants aged 6 to 22. They measured response time, assuming that it reflects the number of steps that a participant takes when solving a problem, hypothesizing that it is affected by the quantitative features of the problems. Performance supported the use of five rules: Siegler's Rules I to IV and the compensation rule. Furthermore, analysis of response time better specified Siegler's model. For example, differently from expectations based on the model, children using Rule II did not consider distance only when the two sides had an equal number of weights: rather, response times showed that distance was always processed, independent of equality of weights. Another important outcome of this study is the demonstration of variability in performance (Siegler, 1996; Siegler & Chen, 2002) in terms of occasional regression to a lower level, and sporadic advancement to a higher rule (see also the Fischer studies in chap. 5). It also shows more precisely that inconsistent performance (a) is related to a slower response time, and (b) appears only in some rule transitions, such as when switching from Rule I to Rule II.

Overall, while expanding Siegler's model, van der Maas and Jansen's study also provides a strong methodological suggestion to consider using response time in evaluating processes underlying problem solving in order to reveal patterns of development.

The Balance Problem and Training

An important issue considered by Siegler (1976) is whether, taking account of one's existing state of knowledge, children can be trained to use a more advanced rule. Two training procedures were compared involving groups of 5-year-olds and 8-year-olds who had been found to use Rule I on a pretest. One type of training focused on the distance dimension and had the goal of advancing from Rule I to Rule II; the other focused on the conflict between the two dimensions and had the goal of progress to Rule III or Rule IV. The training consisted of presenting problems of either the distance or conflict type and asking the children to make predictions about which arm would go down, followed by a demonstration of the actual result. Five-year-olds were found to benefit from distance training, advancing to use of Rule II; however, unlike the older children, they did not benefit from training with respect to the conflict between the two dimensions. The hypothesis put forward to explain this difference centers on *encoding*. It suggests that prior to training those who had only reached the Rule I level were spontaneously encoding only the weight dimension; but with training they learned to encode the distance dimension and, thus, advanced one level of rule use. However, the older children are likely to encode both dimensions already, even if they don't take account of both in their problem solutions. Even though incomplete, their ability to represent distance enables these children to benefit from the training regarding conflicts, which necessarily involves both dimensions, and thus move to use of Rule III.

The encoding hypothesis was supported by Siegler (1976) with data from a task in which children were shown various balance configurations and asked to reproduce them using a comparable balance and set of weights. Independently of how long the children observed the model and independently of whether the model was present when attempting to reproduce it (a variation included to control for memory load), the youngest children proved to be less accurate in reproducing distance than weight, whereas the older ones did not differ with respect to the dimensions. Halford et al. (2002) suggest that young children have greater experience with weight compared to distance. But the question is, what does experience involve. The 5-year-olds in Siegler's study improved, meaning they coded both dimensions equally well, only when the experimenter trained them to repeat the number of weights and their distance on each arm from the fulcrum. Thus, the training was successful when it involved not only "what" was to be encoded, but also "how" the encoding must be done.

A continuation of the study (Siegler, 1976) involved those 5-year-olds who as a result of the instruction on "what" and "how" to encode came to represent both distance and weight, though in post-test they used only Rule I spontaneously. The question of interest was whether these children could now benefit from training that provided feedback on conflict problems. If the encoding hypothesis is accurate, then, in comparison to a control group encoding only the weight dimension, the 5-year-olds who learned by means of instruction to code both dimensions should respond to training on conflict problems similarly to the 8-year-olds who coded both dimensions spontaneously. Results confirmed the encoding hypothesis showing that not only 8-year-olds, but also some 5-year-olds could advance to use of Rule III. As a result of successfully learning to represent both distance and weight, these children were able to further benefit from more advanced training.

Is it possible to train even younger children? The performance of children younger than 5 does not fall strictly in line with any of the rules proposed in the model. However, provided with the same type of instruction that proved effective with the 5-year-olds ("what" and "how" to code), the 4-year-olds, though not the 3-year-olds, benefited from it and succeeded to use Rule I. This result is attributed to the fact verified in independent trials that the 4-year-olds, unlike the 3-year-olds, had the ability to encode weight, an ability that thus permitted them to understand the instruction.

Halford et al. (2002) concentrate on the earliest phase of understanding the relations involved in the balance scale. Their different aim led to some methodological changes in their procedures in comparison to Siegler, who considered a rule attained when employed for at least 80% of one's responses. They made straightforward predictions regarding children's performance based on relational complexity. Given that problems requiring discrimination of weight alone or distance alone entail a binary relation involving the comparison of, say, weights in one arm with those in the other, children as young as 2 years old should be able to solve simple Rule 1 problems. Problems in which both dimensions have to be considered at once, such as conflict problems in which the correct response is "balance," are characterized by ternary relations and thus should not be solved before the age of 5.

A pretest was followed by an extended familiarization phase (Halford et al., 2002) including demonstrations and explanations regarding the effect of changing the number of weights (or distance) on pulling down an arm; then, children themselves set weights on the scale to obtain a given result (e.g., left arm down) and checked the result. After 25 minutes of training, test and posttest problems were presented. The study showed that with the detailed familiarization phase providing high contextual support, performance exceeded chance levels at the ages predicted on the base of relational complexity. Problems involving only one dimension were the easiest and were solved by age 2 or 3, whereas the most difficult conflict-balance problems were solved above chance at 6 years. A comparison with level of performance obtained on other tasks, transitivity and class inclusion, requiring either binary or ternary relations, showed positive correlation, suggesting that relational complexity is a critical feature in problem solving.

These findings are very interesting because they highlight an emerging ability under high contextual support. Performance was favored by a lengthy familiarization phase to ensure mastery of material and basic operations. However, the number of weights and distances on each side ranged from one to three, permitting the use of a simpler strategy such as subitizing. As well, in all problems that required processing of distance (weight) alone, it was always two weights (distances) that were posted. Consequently, ability on the balance scale may not be consolidated early as the demand for processing relations was minimal. Although the results are fascinating, further research would be useful to specify performance differences among the different types of conflict problems just pointed out, all involving ternary relations. In sum, the balance problem demonstrates the importance of leading the child from a global type of representation, based essentially on one dimension (weight), to a more analytic type that takes account of both dimensions (Klahr & Wallace, 1976) and their relationship.

Some conclusions follow from this line of research:

1. It is possible to improve a child's problem-solving ability.
2. A child does not benefit from instruction that is too distant from his/her state of ability and knowledge. To be effective the instruction must be close to the child's current level.
3. To devise an effective instruction, one must be able to determine how the child represents the problem. The first purpose of instruction is to lead to the use of rules just beyond those associated with the level of encoding attained prior to training.
4. Both processing capacity and knowledge play a role.
5. Changes in encoding are facilitated by instruction directed not only toward "what" is to be coded, but also "how."

The Role of Instruction in the Use of Analogical Procedures

We have seen how using analogies in learning offers the advantage of employing prior knowledge for the building of new knowledge, and that it does so by means of mapping schemata activated in the specific base domain to a target. Thus, analogy can be a powerful tool for knowledge acquisition and learning. In particular, analogical thinking is involved in learning to solve problems from examples, as demonstrated by Klahr and Nigam (2004) who asked children to assess the accuracy of examples and to hear experimenter explanations of why some were correct. It is important to consider that ". . . if children are to acquire abstractions, it is important that they learn the structure of the examples they experience. Good analogs can help here because mapping from an example to an analog forces children to pay attention to corresponding relations in the two structures" (Halford, 1993, p. 191).

What are the conditions that favor the use of correct analogical reasoning? How would children solve a problem analogically in absence of specific hints indicating that the base could be an analog to the problem? To observe the role of practice, methodological controls were introduced in a recent microgenetic study with 4-year-olds (Tunteler & Resing, 2002). The spontaneous use of analogies, in absence of specific hints indicating that the base could be an analog to the problem, was studied by simply asking children to physically solve a problem after listening to a base story. Specific contextual support was not offered: the experimenter did not make explicit the causal relation between the problem to be solved (target) and the story (base), the target shared low surface similarity with the base, and available tools presented functions either consistent or inconsistent with the story. In addition, the story protagonist's goal was motivated by a precipitating event whereas the target problem was presented as a task without justifying the request to solve it. These procedures may well disfavor the possibility of perceiving structural similarity.

The children in the practice condition received two different analogies per week for 6 weeks. In the final session they were more likely to solve the problems using a tool consistent with the story than were the children in a control group who completed only the first and last session. However, in spite of such improvement at the end of the practice training, they still showed little ability to verbally acknowledge the analogy or to reason about their solution choice (even though such performance seems within the child's linguistic ability). Thus, practice may place children within an analogy context and induce spontaneous use of analogy; however such practice may not be enough to foster awareness about the source of their behavior nor to accelerate the ability to give a verbal account.

The level of an analogy's complexity depends on "the minimum information required to establish the validity of the mapping, rather than on the total information in the structures of source or target" (Halford, 1993, p. 234). Thus, researchers and educators who aim to test ability on logical problems involving relational systems should be aware that a possible methodological artifact could change the nature of the task. In particular if intervention would turn a system mapping problem into one that can be solved by processing relations in series rather than in parallel, then level of complexity decreases and the problem can be solved at a younger age (Halford et al., 1998). It is on this ground that Halford objects to Goswami's (1995) claim that 3- and 4-year-olds can understand transitive analogies involving ternary relations. He suggests that the problems utilized in that study could be segmented into steps and solved by using simpler strategies, for example, by initially placing the two terms of the first premise and then simply appending the third term by processing the second relation separately. As a single premise is processed each time, the task requires handling only a binary relation rather than a system mapping (Halford, 1984; Halford et al., 1998).

Although in some analogy contexts, the correspondence is such that one can usefully activate schemata that are already consolidated, in others analogy use may be limited because the existing schemata do not contain all the procedures for which the new schemas must provide. For example, in the geometry case just described (Anderson et al., 1981), the problem analysis remains superficial if one considers only the presented diagrams. For this reason, Anderson proposes other means of proceeding; among these the most fruitful is termed *subsumption*, a method involving "meaningful learning" as contrasted, in accord with Wertheimer (1945), to mechanical learning. With this approach the solution to a proffered geometry example is not sought on the basis of a simple characteristic; rather, the child seeks to understand the relevant spatial relations subsumed by the application of a general structure or principle. In so doing the child can employ available schemes to form a meaningful representation of the problem.

Although there is evidence of successful analogy transfer, this is not the rule. What is responsible for a good transfer? Many studies confirm that the representations relevant to solving a problem impact transfer. For example, students learning a new domain (human circulatory system) could profit from an analogy with a familiar domain (the mail delivery system) depending on the level of conceptual understanding of the familiar domain and awareness of how the analogy is to be applied in integrating knowledge in the new domain (Mason, 1994). Type of representation will depend on the context in which the knowledge transfer is useful and could involve processes of schema construction, such as forming a goal structure or abstracting a principle. Thus, a fruitful way to approach the transfer question is to consider the type of representation children form of the base and the representation they apply to the target. For example, in one study (Brown, Kane, & Echols, 1986) the base and target given to children of ages 3 to 5 consisted of isomorphic stories differing in superficial features but sharing a common goal structure in which the protagonist solves a problem. Those children who were able to report a common goal structure when asked to recall the base and those who were prompted to form such a representation succeeded in transferring the solution to a new target story. Thus, representing the relations in the base appears to be a condition to solve a problem analogically.

In the Brown et al. study both base and target were stories sharing a relatively concrete goal structure; the representation formed was rather specific and may have favored a simple level of analogical transfer. Sometimes the difficulty in analogical reasoning is to notice that the solution involved in the base can be represented in the target. In a recent study (Pauen & Wilkening, 1997), 7- and 9-year-old children were trained on a rule for the balance scale problem. The goal was to observe whether the learned solution principle would be applied to a different problem involving the interaction between two unequal forces, called a "force table" task. The analogy of the balance scale was chosen because in a previous study focusing on ability to solve force table tasks, young children spontaneously generated such an analogy. Some children were trained on a balance scale (base task) to use a rule that focused on a single force and that was inadequate for the force table (target task). Others learned a base-task rule that focused on an integration of forces and that did afford positive transfer. The older children trained on the integration rule tended to transfer it to the new problem more than the single-force group and an untrained control. The younger children, instead, considered only a single force in the target problem, even though they had successfully used the integration rule in the balance scale problems and were able to recall all the parts of the rule. Their poor performance seems to be due to the type of representation they formed of the target in comparison to the base. In fact, although they recalled the parts of the integration rule on request, they mentioned spontaneously only the first part (regard for a single force) when comparing the force table task and the balance scale. The interpretation is that the younger children represent the two problems differently and that their mapping includes only the aspects considered relevant in their representation.

How is it possible to foster transfer? Given that a critical requirement for using analogy in problem solving is to make a good mapping between base and target, it is important to notice their similarities in order to use the analog as a tool to apply to new domains. At the same time, one must acknowledge their differences in order to avoid negative transfer (see also chap. 9). Addressing in general terms the question of how to make the mapping task easier and more efficient, a recent study (Kurtz, Miao, & Gentner, 2001) suggested the process of mutual alignment, which involves a focus on comparisons carried out in two analogous, partially understood situations. This is a useful encoding process and can be an important tool in learning new knowledge. The base and target scenarios were presented simultaneously and could be symmetrically mapped favoring an extraction of parallel structures. Participants (undergraduate students) had to describe the two scenarios, rate their similarities, and list their differences. Explicitly asking students to give a joint interpretation of these scenarios presented side by side and to find the one-to-one correspondence between the specific elements of the two situations produced a deep understanding. Students in this condition were better able to derive the structural relation common to both scenarios when compared to students in conditions with a joint interpretation alone, with a correspondence alone, or with no explicit request for comparison.

Other means to improve analogical reasoning have been investigated, such as experience with sequences of easy-to-hard analogy problems and extended experience. In classical analogies, practicing simpler problems aids solution of more difficult ones. For example, solving simple analogies involving perceptual pattern problems before having to solve proportional analogies entailing a part–whole relation (presented in the form of geometrical figures) increases the solution of the latter compared to presentation in the reverse order (Goswami, 1989). According to Gick and Holyoak (1983), abstracting a general principle from a source is more difficult for adult participants when only one source story is presented rather than two. Consider, for example, the problem in which the radiation required in order to destroy a tumor is so strong that its use will also destroy healthy tissue. The solution to this problem (use a large number of low intensity rays that pass through different healthy tissues and converge on the tumor) is found more easily when it is preceded by other stories involving analogous problems and there is encouragement to make the resemblance clear. This procedure helps problem-solvers to abstract the underlying principle and ignore the specific content of the different problems.

Multiple experience with the base or source is a relevant factor. However, experience with problems presenting the *same* type of specific procedure, formula, or rule has a profound limitation in that it favors transfer to problems asking for the same procedure, but not to target requiring a different, novel procedure (Chen, 1999; Kotovski & Gentner, 1996). Thus, variability in the source situations is a critical element. For example, Chen (1999) used classical water jug problems (Luchins, 1942), in which a specific quantity of water has to be poured into a jar using three containers of different sizes to arrive at the desired quantity. Transfer with 10- and 11-year-olds was positively affected by both of two types of source variation in procedure (in comparison to sources with invariant procedural features). One type was problems of the same class (water jug) involving different procedural rules; the second was problems belonging to a different class (e.g., involving length) but solvable with analogous procedural rules. However, 8-year-olds' performance did not improve with variant source procedures compared to invariant, showing developmental differences in the ability to profit from differentiated multiple sources. Whereas younger children learned procedures welded to specific situations (to use the author's term), older children taking advantage of the different bases were able to abstract the principle; at the same time, they understood that solving an analog problem requires searching the appropriate procedure.

Taking account of the components involved in solving analogy problems, it is possible to make some suggestions for their use in the acquisition of new knowledge. First of all, the domain from which the analogy is drawn must be highly familiar so that the student can easily activate already existing relevant schemata. In this respect the studies just mentioned have important implications for education; for example they indicate the importance of adopting child-generated analogies and of controlling the relevance of the causal structures in the child's representation of both base and target. We have seen that when the relevant representation doesn't occur spontaneously, the student must be supported in a search for similarities and differences between the well-known domain and the one to be learned. Such support leads to greater benefits if the representation is abstracted rather than welded to the specific situation of the given base. This process is important with respect to applying analogous procedures only in problems that require the same type of reasoning.

Finally, given the pervasiveness of analogy in learning, it could also be used as a tool to tap student knowledge of specific domains and to identify possible naive conceptions or even alternative representations (Alexander, Murphy, & Kulikowich, 1998), which, according to Fischer, are "alternative pathways of understanding, often based in a schema or metaphor that frames a range of skills and can lead to better understanding" (Schwartz & Fischer, 2004, p. 169).

CONCLUSION

In this chapter we have illustrated models of children's strategies and processes in solving problems and provided examples of different types of problems. A central issue for learning and development is the ability to transfer a solution to new problems. Some studies show that children initially acquire and adopt the strategies within specific task situations and rely heavily on a degree of contextual support; they show that it is only gradually that the strategies become general in the sense they are for adults in most situations. We have seen that one of the factors responsible for incorrect solutions is the type of representation that the child initially forms of the problem. In particular we have identified the child's difficulty in encoding the relevant dimensions of a problem.

Recently direct instruction has been evaluated as a tool to foster transfer in students' learning and development of scientific reasoning (Chen & Klahr, 1999; Klahr & Nigam, 2004). We have considered the benefit of giving appropriate instructions to children to encode a complete representation of the relevant dimensions in both problem solving and analogical reasoning.

In particular, prior knowledge, relational complexity and processing load are identified in the literature on children's problem solving as having important roles. In the case of analogy, other factors are important and these include representation of the base and the target and degree of structural and surface similarity. Environmental support is seen as relevant to the daily use of analogy. It is related to experience with different types of problems and solutions, use of familiar schemata, and salience of a focus on the structural relations.

Overall, issues of domain-specific knowledge, skill building and learning, and their interaction with capacity limitations, have been highlighted throughout this chapter. These same issues are central in the next two chapters devoted to two major, cyclical theories of cognitive development.

CHAPTER

5

The Cyclical Nature of Skill Development

As described in previous chapters, the neo-Piagetian theories of Pascual-Leone and Halford seek to resolve many of the challenges posed to Piaget's developmental theory. Their resolutions retain, however, several fundamental Piagetian assumptions, including the stage conception of development and the emphasis on *general* processes as accounting for developmental acquisitions within different domains and areas of knowledge. Within the information processing approach, other models (see chap. 4) have been developed and are associated with research methods that track the processes enacted in an individual's problem solving. These methods provide detailed, precise data on solution paths for specific problems.

Although some theories we have discussed emphasize a general vision of development, other theories and models partition development into domain specific acquisitions. Both general and specific theories have difficulties accounting for certain important aspects of development: the former do not explain the variability in progress that many observers feel characterizes development across and within domains, the latter do not succeed in accounting for the generalization of abilities resulting from the synchronous developments acknowledged by researchers and practitioners.

From the early 1980s Kurt Fischer (1980, 1987; Fischer, Knight, & Van Parys, 1993) has developed a theory that seeks to mediate between developmental continuity and discontinuity. His approach is epigenetic and makes explicit the possibility of both synchronous and sequential developments. According to his model, acquisitions occur within task domains, but the model adopts a conciliatory stance between empiricist and nativist positions. Like other neo-Piagetian theories it locates the child within a process of knowledge construction, though in contrast to other models, it more deeply examines the impact of multiple environmental factors on developmental progress.

In recent times, Fischer's theory has been revised in a manner that provides a greater specification of the mechanisms underlying synchrony and variability and that pays greater attention to both large scale and small scale developments. This has become possible through the use of methodologies that enable observations and analyses at both microdevelopmental (Siegler, 1995, 2002) and macrodevelopmental levels.

THE DEVELOPMENT OF DYNAMIC SKILLS IN THE THEORY OF K. FISCHER

Fischer's theory, originally called skill theory, was laid out systematically in an article that appeared in *Psychological Review* in 1980. In a recent presentation of the theory (Fischer & Bidell, 2006), development is identified as a *constructive dynamic web*, a phrase suggestive of the theory's distinctive emphasis on a contextual consideration of children's skill development.

We begin with a definition of the concept of skill because of its central role in the theory. "A skill is a capacity to act in an organized way in a specific context" (Fischer & Bidell, 2006, p. 321). The skill construct illustrates important features of Fischer's approach to psychological structures. He views the latter as systems of relations among parts that are actively seeking equilibrium; and thus, he considers skills and other structures to be dynamic rather than static. His view of psychological structure as "the actual organization of dynamic systems of activity" (Fischer & Bidell 2006, p. 320) contrasts with a traditional view of structure as a form that preexists, that is separate from the (cognitive) activity and that is independent of the content actualizing the activity. Fischer's premise is that a person constructs skills dynamically in specific contexts, very often in social situations, which are obviously not static and that, for this reason, demand constant adaptation and reorganization. It follows from the definition that skills, at least up to young adulthood, do not have a general significance comparable to Piaget's scheme. Due to sources of task variation such as time, content, characteristics of the individual, presence of coparticipants, or cultural values, different activities may exhibit different levels of performance. Thus, "A skill is the ability to control variation in specific domains and contexts" (Parziale, 2002, p. 162) adapting to the variability of the object to which it applies.

A skill is composed of one or more components or sets of actions (or thoughts). Lower level skills function as subsystems when integrated to form a higher level skill. In order for components to combine and become a skill, each of the individual components and their interrelations must be mastered and undergo differentiation and coordination, based on qualitatively new integration and mutual participation of previously independent components. A skill draws from several systems: For example, Fischer points out that telling a story requires the collaboration of systems such as memory, emotion, language, cultural meaning, scripted knowledge, and narrative abilities. Thus, dynamic skills require integration of related systems, each participating in and contributing to the functioning of the others.

Processes of self-organization and self-regulation are involved in skill construction. To illustrate the nature of these processes, an analogy with the cardiovascular system is used. Each component of the system self-regulates in relation to variation in other components such that the overall system is internally organized. Likewise, a skill organizes and reorganizes itself to adapt to variations. Its functioning involves continuous control of its components by means of self-regulating the interparticipation of the component systems (Fischer & Bidell, 2006). For example, children who have worked on a task with collaborating adults assisting them to focus on specific parts of the problem need to adapt to the new requirements, self-regulating and reorganizing their perspective and activity on the task, when they are left to solve the problem alone (Bidell & Fischer, 2000). These processes in part account for variability in skill development, operating in service of both skill maintenance and construction of new skills.

Skills are dynamic in the sense that, being interparticipatory, they are integrated and they reciprocally influence each other, showing variations depending on both internal conditions and external situations. For example, a child temporarily disturbed by emotional events might not be able to focus on a specific cognitive task, or one's social context could be more or less favorable—the developing child might work alone or with others, or coparticipants might vary in their level of expertise and their cooperative attitude.

This observation relates not only to a "pervasive variability" of human behavior generally, but also to the variability of children's performance on tasks used to measure development. Fischer constantly reminds us of the dynamic nature of development for two reasons: On the one hand, from a theoretical point of view, it sets the basis for studying the role of context as a source of multiple influences on the child's performance. On the other, from an applied perspective, it is useful to everyone dealing with children to know that stability across trials in children's responses to test questions, although possible, is not to be expected.

Given the variability in the individual's conditions and of the supportive context, a child cannot at a given time show the same level of logical structure in every task, nor can a child be said to "belong to" a certain stage in all domains; rather, performance can show both variability and synchrony. As a consequence, development is not a linear increase of skills (abilities, capacities) relating to thought, action and emotion, but is rather a *nonlinear, dynamic growth in a constructive web*. In a growth curve, both continuity and discontinuities (spurts) can be observed, and these involve change processes that reciprocally affect development, as is specified in the following section. In fact, the metaphor of a "constructive dynamic web" replaces that of a "ladder" so as to highlight the dynamic feature in skill construction of continuous adjustment to different conditions. Changes could be both small *steps* at a microlevel and qualitative long-term changes at a macrolevel.

Each segment or "strand" of a web as visualized by Fischer (see Fig. 5.1) represents a skill domain (it could be a domain concept or a dimension in problem solving) and connections among strands represent relations among skills; they can form groupings or clusters of skill domains. Take, for example, a constructive web representing skill building for concepts relating to three domains—mathematics, self-in-relationship, reflective judgment—in adolescence and young adulthood. Sequences of small steps are visualized, and the strands are drawn parallel when the steps develop at the same time. Because of short-term and long-term variability within each strand,

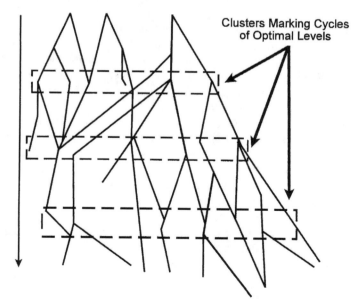

FIG. 5.1. A developmental web of many strands with clusters of discontinuities for three skill levels. *Source:* Fischer (in press).

the strands are not predetermined. Like the strands of a spider's web, their position and interconnections may vary according to the different constructive activities produced by the person (situated in a physical and social environment). This indicates that different persons can take different pathways during development and learning of concepts in different domains.

Strands can be drawn with solid or dashed and dotted lines, the former representing skills that are consolidated, the latter those under construction and that need further consolidation. A dotted line might, for example, represent a skill resulting from a single instance of optimal support by a coparticipant and that still needs to be consolidated and generalized to the point of adjusting to task variability before it would be drawn as a solid line. The strands composing the web can be represented through growth curves (based on mathematical equations) and may show different shapes depending on personal characteristics, contextual support, and type of measurement.

Methodology

Fischer and his collaborators contribute to solving the issue of continuity and discontinuity and that of variability by adopting suitable methodologies, considering the nature of variability and how it is measured, as well as bringing about a closer interaction between models and data (Fischer & Rose, 1999). The underlying idea is that differences in intraindividual performance on repeated measurements are not due to a random error in measurement but constitute a phenomenon characterizing development. In this sense, pulling data together to calculate a mean performance would not be appropriate. Viewing variability as part of a developmental process, it becomes important to note the range of variations and to ask whether this range itself may vary during development.

Nonlinear dynamic models (in particular, catastrophe theory) predict that variability tends to be higher when the system is approaching a qualitative change (Thelen & Smith, 1998; van Geert & van Dijk, 2002). In this sense, an increase in variability is a precursor to a major change that, once consolidated, predicts a relative stability. Scholars of development and education need to take this idea into account in order to attend to characteristics of an individual's process and to predict phases in development.

Suitable methodologies to assess development present two features: (a) the use of multiple assessment conditions and repeated testing, (b) online observations during performance. Instead of a single task, sets of tasks are devised and proposed to the participants (see also chap. 10). This allows the analysis of both small variations occurring on a task performance in a short time and spurts that take place under optimal performance, when a skill changes level of complexity. A multiple assessment may involve a multiple-task method, that is, a set of tasks (e.g., on conservation) similar in complexity useful to gain independent measures at each predicted developmental phase (van der Maas & Molenaar, 1992). Another possibility is the scalogram technique that involves a set of tasks of the same type but increasing in complexity (Fischer et al., 1993). Moreover, observations may involve a person working alone or with a coparticipant, either a peer or an expert. In this way, the effect of different types of social contexts on performance can be examined.

Several tools are available to assess continuity and discontinuities in development. One type employs Guttman scales involving a set of tasks within a domain. Utilizing similar content and differing only in complexity; they measure one sequence of linear developments in the web. An important technique of this type is POSI, which stands for Partially Ordered Scaling of Items. This statistical technique proves useful for Fischer's study of developmental sequences. It involves a set of tasks that can be presented to a child in increasing order of difficulty in order to establish variations in performance. This scaling method substitutes for (or complements) longitudinal studies in which a child repeatedly completes the same or similar tasks, thus raising the problem of practice effects. The name POSI follows from the fact that the ordering of difficulty is partial in the sense that within a phase more than one task could be constructed and their solution orders might not be consistent. However, if the predictions regarding the sequence of phases are correct, then one should find that a child located in a particular phase succeeds on all of the tasks associated with the preceding phases, but fails all those associated with subsequent ones (Fischer et al., 1993).

Rasch scaling based on nonlinear development models allows identification of both continuous developments and pathways pointing to individual differences such as those shown by children learning to read a single word. It allows detection of sequences and makes it possible to examine whether items conform to predicted hierarchical sequences, considering both person performance and item difficulty. Rasch analysis enables the use of a common scale across domains and examination of hierarchical skill complexity. For example, in a recent study (Dawson-Tunik, Commons, Wilson, & Fischer, 2005) moral judgment interviews from a wide lifespan sample (5 to 86 years) were first analyzed with a domain-general tool to identify level of complexity in development. However, as with other tools providing mean scores to compare group performance on task sequences, questions relating to difficulty associated with transitional phases and to confidence level on person and item estimates could not be addressed. Thus, a Rasch analysis was applied to gain information on item difficulty and individuals' performance complexity, allowing an answer to the question of the level of task difficulty at which a movement in performance can be observed from a lower level to a higher level and vice versa.

Another useful tool for identifying the trajectory of progress across domains or developmental levels involves the grouping of tasks with similar complexity in various domains to form developmental scales. This type of assessment enables identification of task variability in terms of short-term changes and long-term reorganization and skill clustering. A further benefit of using multiple assessment conditions is the possibility to observe different growth patterns depending on what is assessed.

Granott (2002) describes a methodology that closely attends to micro-developments in skill construction and generalization as people work together on a task for which new skills are to be developed. For example, a dyad working together to solve a novel problem (what causes a robot's movements) was observed in terms of their actions on the object and their communicative exchanges during problem solving. Their communication was at a high level from the beginning and showed little variation during the solution process. On the contrary, their understanding, as evidenced by their activities on the robot and their attempts to explain it to others, showed a nonlinear growth. It exhibited regressions to a lower level before reconstructing a more solid higher level skill. This variability is very important from a theoretical point of view in that it reinforces the idea that learning is a multidimensional activity showing relative stability, spurts, and even regressions in some aspects but not in others.

As becomes clear in the next section, looking at development by averaging the performance data of a group of children obscures understanding of its nature (see also Siegler, 1987a). Looking at the profile of a developing person, characterized by spurts and plateaus showing different variability according to different internal and external support conditions, is more promising.

Optimal and Functional Level

That variability is a feature of development from infancy is documented by De Weerth, van Geert, and Hoitink's (1999) study on emotion behaviors such as fussing and smiling during the first year of life. In this study variability is explained as adaptation to the context while attempting to draw the mother's attention, until, with the development of more advanced strategies, radical changes in those behaviors take place. Variability takes two forms: it may be a temporary adaptation to differences in contextual factors, but it may also underline a different pattern of development.

Variations in performance on successive task presentations occur within a *developmental range*, which is the interval within which task performance can vary in situations of high or low contextual support. For example, Fischer and Ayoub (1994) examined in relation to various contextual factors children's ability to narrate stories about positive and negative social interactions. For example, a 5-year-old girl narrated either a very complex or a simplified story that was produced either immediately after modeling by an adult or at a short time delay. It was found that when the girl changed her personal affective state, as a result of the initiation of a negative interaction with the adult, the story she narrated showed a shift in content, passing from describing a positive social interaction to a negative one.

In another study (Fischer, Rotenberg, Bullock, & Raya, 1993), the representation of social peer interactions was observed through the production of stories by a group of eight 7-year-olds with or without contextual support. The most complex stories were produced under a condition of high support in which the experimenter provided the gist of the story, but it dropped to a lower level when the stories were produced spontaneously, in a condition of low support. The results of these studies provide important insights into development and learning. Depending on variations in external conditions or level of contextual support, performance profiles differ, showing either little variation or qualitative discontinuity. Fischer et al. (1993) found that the participants themselves evidenced a similar pattern of variability.

The number of components constituting a skill and the types of relations among them increase with development. Given that the components are always applied to specific objects, which may differ for specific trials, children succeed in their interaction with the environment in gaining progressively better control of the external sources of behavioral variability, by means of self-regulation ability.

The overall shape of development is illustrated in the following discussion with respect to the development of a sample skill (see "The Structural Levels of Skill: An Example," this chapter). Skills develop across a series of levels. Within a level, the development of a skill is slow and gradual, albeit not characterized by a linear performance. It involves short-term changes, small *steps* in which the relations between components expand to include more elements. For example, a skill may develop from involving an interaction with one person to include interaction with two persons.

However, in the shift from one level to another, there are spurts that stand out in a series of skills. There are two critical sources for developing a skill. One is internal: it involves self-regulation and self-organization and it relates to the mastering of the lower level skills that are the components contributing to the construction of a higher level skill. The other element is external, and involves both physical and social aspects. The external context contributes to development in part by providing a base for one to practice a particular skill, practice that is regulated by the object on which one acts. The context also offers a base of direct, *optimal level* support that, when present, leads to a more advanced understanding of problematic aspects than could be achieved spontaneously.

Thus Fischer draws from Vygotsky's (1962) concept of a zone of proximal development (ZPD), stating that the level of support offered by the social environment determines whether an individual's potential is maximally expressed. Typical forms of contextual support are *modeling* and *prompting*, realized when the social environment provides a model who displays a higher level of skill and/or demonstrates in some way (e.g., by means of questions) the key concepts crucial to a given situation. The highest support is provided by *scaffolding*, when an expert adult directly participates in the task, sharing the control of activity with the child. For example, it is possible for children to reach a higher level on a task when they work together with an adult in solving a problem beyond their *functional* level and the adult intervenes directly in a portion of the process. With low support the individual's performance is at a lower functional level, whereas with high support their performance moves to an *optimal* level (the educational aspects of optimal level support are briefly discussed in chap. 9).

The difference between performances at functional and at optimal level has been observed in several studies considering various ages, in different domains and with different cultures. Some examples include studies just mentioned relating to positive and negative social interactions in school children (Fischer et al., 1993), development of reflective judgment in adolescents and young adults (Fischer & Pruyne, 2002; Kitchener, Lynch, Fischer, & Wood, 1993), conception of the self in various relationships conducted with Korean and U.S. adolescents (Fischer & Kennedy, 1997), understanding arithmetic concepts from childhood to adolescence (Fischer, Kenny, & Pipp, 1990). In the latter study, for example, participants were asked to complete a series of tasks: to solve arithmetic problems, to define the four operations relating to the solved arithmetic problems, and to explain the relationship between each of two pairs of operations. First the participants provided spontaneous answers (low support); then the experimenter gave a well worked-out response and the subjects were asked to give their own answer (high-support condition). They were told to think about the task and to return 2 weeks later at which time a second session took place, first with spontaneous answers (low support) and then again with high support. With low support, a slow increase of performance took place not before age 16–17 (functional level). Two distinct curves, characterized by little or considerable practice, were evidenced for both high and low support sessions. Although about 60% passed the task at 17 years in the first session, 88% were successful 1 year earlier in the second high-support session (Fischer, Kenny, & Pipp, 1990).

The concept of optimal level of performance is important in Fischer's theory from various points of view. First consider that at a given point in development one's performance regarding a skill could be at different levels depending on the degree of support at the moment of its production. If generated spontaneously and influenced solely by practice, performance might be at a *functional level* and appear less coherent, affected by multiple factors characterizing that particular context. Yet if produced in the presence of favorable physical and social support, a skill moves toward the *optimal level* (for that person in that context). Thus, in Fischer's terms, the ZPD is the interval between the person's highest performances with and without social support, that is, the difference between optimal and functional (current) levels.

Another important aspect of introducing the concept of optimal level is that it justifies the introduction of qualitative changes in development, which could be observed as a result of a sudden discontinuity with a previous approach to the task, as seen in catastrophe models. This new level involves a new interpretation of the task or problem. The reaching of a new optimal level follows a previously slow development at a functional level, characterized by nonsystematic change or monotonic growth depending on the context. Great variability is shown immediately before and after the new developmental spurt (Fischer & Kennedy, 1997). The succession of optimal levels derives not only from environmental influences such as high support but also from the child's maturation (see the following section). The optimal level establishes for a child the "most complex type of skill that he or she can manage" (Fischer & Pipp, 1984b, p. 47).

Progress at the optimal level does not necessarily involve a definitive change at the current, functional level. Lack of consolidation or interferences such as emotional problems can still lower performance subsequently to the functional level.

THE CYCLICAL SHAPE OF DEVELOPMENT

According to Fischer, the child goes through a series of 10 *levels* divided into 3 *tiers* in the course of development. A fourth tier relating to action components spanning the first 3 months of life (called the reflex tier) was formerly proposed (Fischer, 1980) but awaits further evidence. A new skill's level is prepared by *steps* that mark otherwise gradual changes or short-term microdevelopments occurring within a level; these are represented in Figure 5.2. A new level is characterized by a spurt or discontinuity, and it is both determined and describable according to the type of components that the child is able to control, as well as by their number and the relationships that occur among them. The major changes during development occur in cycles of reorganization: there are three of increasing complexity and they characterize the three tiers: After the first 3 months, the child moves to the *sensorimotor* (action) tier (from 3–4 months to about 2 years), then to the *representational* tier (from 2 to 12 years), and finally, to the *abstract* tier (from 12 to 25 years).

Progress among the various levels follows the same form within each of the three tiers. The development is cyclical in nature in the sense that progress in each tier is through four levels, where the final level constitutes the first level of the subsequent tier. Successive levels are composed by and coordinate the structures of the previous level, but they add to the structure of the components (or sets) and elaborate their interactions, as shown in Figure 5.2. In passing through the levels of a given tier, one moves from control of isolated sets (first-level structure: *single sets*), to placement of two or more sets in relation to each other (second level: *mapping*), to differentiation of subsystems and their relations (third level: *system*), to relations among systems (fourth level: *system of systems*). Such a system of systems then is reorganized to constitute a new single higher level unit, resulting from integration and coordination of its subcomponents.

Reorganizing skills into a new, higher level unit renders them simpler, and such a unit is the most elementary structure in the subsequent, more advanced tier. Each tier represents a radical qualitative, discontinuous, change in psychological behavior, ranging from sensorimotor actions in the first tier to abstract levels of thought in the third. Fischer and Bidell (1998, 2006) propose that the last level of the abstract tier is integrated into a new level called "principles" (although they note absence of evidence for further levels based on single principles).

A similar layout of cyclical development had been accepted also by Case (1985, 1992; see chap. 6), although, differently from Fischer, he described the model as the "staircase of development." Fischer uses the term *tier* instead of *stage* because the target referent in his theory is the development of specific skills, for which both stability and variability are envisaged. Al-

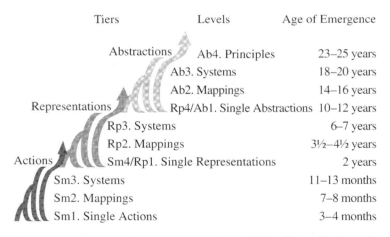

Tiers	Levels	Age of Emergence
Abstractions	Ab4. Principles	23–25 years
	Ab3. Systems	18–20 years
	Ab2. Mappings	14–16 years
Representations	Rp4/Ab1. Single Abstractions	10–12 years
	Rp3. Systems	6–7 years
	Rp2. Mappings	3½–4½ years
Actions	Sm4/Rp1. Single Representations	2 years
	Sm3. Systems	11–13 months
	Sm2. Mappings	7–8 months
	Sm1. Single Actions	3–4 months

FIG. 5.2. Developmental cycles of levels and tiers of skills. *Source:* Fischer and Bidell (2006).

though specific abilities might develop simultaneously, they do not necessarily do so in the way implied by the concept of stage and the metaphor of
a developmental ladder.

The Structural Levels of Skill: An Example

Before looking more directly at fundamental questions regarding change
processes and the generality of development in Fischer's theory, we illustrate the series of levels reached during development by making reference
to a specific skill. The example is drawn from an early study (1980) and relates to a cognitive skill similar to those examined by other neo-Piagetian
theories. This description refers to general processes that might be employed in a child's construction of such skill and its components.

Progression through the three tiers can be described with reference to
the skill of understanding a specific apparatus (adapted from Piaget et al.,
1968/1977) in relation to the *conservation of length* (see Fig. 5.3). Due to space
constraints, only the development of skills during the sensorimotor and
representational tiers are presented; the analysis is carried on through
transitions to four levels and a major qualitative shift. The apparatus consists of a cord that passes over a peg that serves to divide the cord into two
parts—a vertical segment with a weight attached at its end, and a horizontal
segment attached to a spring at its end. Variations in the weight result in ex-
pansion or contraction of the spring and a concomitant variation in the
lengths of the two cord segments—when the vertical segment becomes longer, the horizontal one becomes shorter.

Sensorimotor Tier (S): From 3–4 Months to 2 Years. Within the four
levels of this tier, it is sensorimotor sets that the child controls. The point of

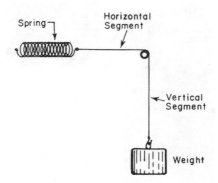

FIG. 5.3. An apparatus for the study of conservation of length. *Source:* Fischer
(1980).

departure for these actions and perceptions is the single unity of the new sensorimotor tier (level S1, probably derived from the combination of systems of reflex sets reached at the end of the reflex tier). Over the course of development of this tier, the child constructs practical skills with which he or she understands the properties of the objects and acts in a progressively more adequate manner on them so as to achieve specific effects.

Level I: SI, Single Sets (4 Months). The child deals with sensory patterns that lead to control of isolated sets (the set G, for example, in Table 5.1). In relation to the apparatus in Figure 5.3, the child looks at it when it crosses his or her visual field, or grasps the spring when it touches a hand. These are sets which, like the primary circular reactions of Piaget's theory, the child is not able to put into relationship with each other.

TABLE 5.1
Sensorimotor and Representational Levels of Skills

Level, Age and Name of Structure	Reflexes	Sensorimotor Level	Representational Level	Abstract Level
RF4/S1 (4 months) System of reflex systems/single sensorimotor set	$\begin{bmatrix} A \leftrightarrow B \\ \updownarrow \\ C \leftrightarrow D \end{bmatrix}$	$\equiv [G]$		
S2 (7–8 months) Sensorimotor mapping		[G – H]		
S3 (11–13 months) Sensorimotor system		[G ↔ H]		
S4/Rp1 (20–24 months) System of sensorimotor systems/single representational set		$\begin{bmatrix} G \leftrightarrow H \\ \updownarrow \\ I \leftrightarrow J \end{bmatrix} \equiv [M]$		
Rp2 (4–5 years) Representational mapping			[M – N]	
Rp3 (6–7 years) Representational system			[M ↔ N]	
Rp4/A1 (10–12 years) System of representational systems/single abstract set			$\begin{bmatrix} M \leftrightarrow N \\ \updownarrow \\ O \leftrightarrow P \end{bmatrix} \equiv [\zeta]$	

Note. Adapted from Fischer, 1980.

Level 2: S2, Mapping (7–8 Months). One of the most important mappings at this level is the means–ends relation, by which one action is in the service of another and the child controls their relation. At this level, the child looks at the spring in order to be able to pull it, or pulls it in order to be able to look at it. These remain two complementary mappings, not yet combined with each other.

Level 3: S3, System (11–13 Months). Continuing the same example, the child now becomes able to control a means–ends system. He or she controls variations in one of the two sets and puts them into relation with that of the other. This gives rise to active experimentation such that the child is able to put the variations in his or her actions in relation with the variations in the results. For example, the child might observe that it is possible to pull the spring in different ways and also observe each time the resulting variations in its extension.

The S4 level, described in the following section, is the culmination of the sensorimotor tier. It both initiates the successive tier and constitutes its basic unit.

Representational Tier (Rp): From 2 Years to 12 Years. The child becomes able to internally represent concrete properties of objects and persons, and thus understands that the properties of an object are independent of his or her action on it.

Level 4: S4, System of Systems/Rp1 Single Sets (20 to 24 Months). At the previous level the child controls only one system at a time, but at this level the child controls the variations of more than one sensorimotor system. Fischer cites Piaget's observation that the infant combines the sensorimotor system of swinging on a swing with the system of making a leaf sway and that their combination gives rise to the word "bimbam" applied to both. Consider again the example of the spring and weight apparatus. When it is not only the child who performs the action of pulling the spring, but also others, the child combines sensorimotor systems regarding the relation between pulling the spring and its extension (new representational set *M*). In this way, the child finally succeeds in attributing properties to the object independent of his or her actions. Among the systems of systems controlled at this level are such new skills as attributing to the attached weight the effect of pulling the vertical part of the cord.

Level 5: Rp2, Mapping (4 to 5 Years). At the previous level the combination of systems produces single sets, but at this level the infant succeeds in putting one set in relation with another, for example *M* with *N* in Table 5.1 (note the parallelism with the type of structural organization at level *S2*).

Thus, thanks to the ability to form a relation between two sets—in particular, for example, the set involving the apparatus's weight and the one involving its spring—the child can form an intuitive idea of how the amount of weight is related to the stretching of the spring or of the relation between vertical and horizontal segments of the cord.

Level 6: Rp3, System (6 to 7 Years). At the previous level intuitions regarding the relations between sets become more precise as a result of a mapping of the components of each of the sets. At the system level, the length of the vertical segment is now compensated by the length of the horizontal one, and the length of the first can be used to predict that of the second. The child is therefore able to understand that variations in weight lead to variations in the relative length of the two parts of the cord while their total length remains constant. In this way the child acquires the "conservation of length" concept, understanding that total length remains constant because the variations in one segment of the cord compensate for those in the other.

Abstract Tier (A): From 10–12 Years to 24–26 Years. As with the other tiers, the fourth level of the representational tier constitutes the first level of the abstract tier. Thanks to the combination of representational sets, the child becomes able to form abstract categories with a degree of broad generality.

Level 7: Rp4, System of Systems/A1 Single Sets (10 to 12 Years). With respect to the apparatus, the ability to put systems into relation allows the child to predict that changes in weight will result in the spring stretching in such a way that the cord's horizontal length varies in accordance with its vertical length. Control of variations in the different components of the apparatus increases; but, as Fischer states, the child also shows evidence of forming a complex meaning of the apparatus's general state. The ability to put systems in relation to one another may also permit formation of the general idea of conservation, with it no longer being limited to specific contexts (substance, liquid, etc.). This ability permits abstraction of the general rule that changes resulting from compensations along component dimensions do not influence quantity, whatever that quantity might be.

Fischer has analyzed the construction of other skills. With respect to passage from the sensorimotor to the representational tier, of particular interest is his earlier analysis, together with Corrigan, of language development (Fischer & Corrigan, 1981). This work indicates that (a) language is a skill like others and develops in accordance with the same sequence of levels, and (b) that language is not dependent on cognition as it is for Piaget and should itself be understood not as a single skill, but rather as one composed of diverse skills. Fischer and Corrigan's analysis suggests that one cannot speak of language prior to level S3, neither with respect to production nor to comprehension. Production is not yet referential if one defines a word as referential when it is used in diverse contexts and with different functions. Moreover, comprehension seems to precede production, but better performance in comprehension may benefit from a greater contextual support offered by the environment. Furthermore, the first forms of a child's language at level S3 are still sensorimotor rather than representational, given that they rely on sensorimotor actions like vocalizing and listening rather than being based on the coordination of systems as required in the representational tier.

Progress in moral reasoning has been analyzed by Dawson-Tunik et al. (2005) through interview data from kindergarten to adult participants and shows six developmental levels, from single representations to abstraction of principles of systems. This study is also valuable for showing that a pattern made of successive periods of discontinuities (spurts) and consolidations proceeds during development from childhood to adulthood forming a sequence of qualitatively different complexity levels.

The development of social roles is the focus of another important study that illustrates the sequence of levels proposed by the theory. This work is briefly mentioned in the following discussion to exemplify the processes leading to change within and between levels.

Upper Limit on Skill Level Development

We have seen how the concept of optimal level is introduced to deal with the fundamental aspects of skill construction. We have looked at the sequence of optimal levels by means of describing the recurring levels within the tiers. In these tiers, each level establishes the *upper limit* on the complexity that a skill activity can reach. What is the nature of this limit? A quick answer would be: The upper limit is set with the contribution of both contextual support and maturation, but evidence for such a claim is needed and is reported in the following section.

We have pointed out that, according to Fischer, a child can show the most complex type of skill under optimal conditions and evidence of spurts in such conditions has been mentioned. This limit does not depend on a single factor such as the number of units of information active in short-term memory or in working memory, as it does in the theories of Case and Pascual-Leone (actually both these theorists include other factors to explain development), but rather on the type of skills organization.

Two sets of constraints can be at work to establish the optimal level limit. On the one hand, the level of mastery and consolidation of the subskills, which is affected by contextual support, intrinsically posits a constraint on the complexity of the skill that can be reached by the child at a certain point and, consequently, to the level developed for that skill. On the other hand, the upper limit on level of growth is set by the capacity of a person's processing system, called the system's *carrying capacity*, which is "the limit on growth that is characteristic of this particular system in this situation" (Fischer & Bidell, 2006, p. 358). It must also be noted that the system's self-regulation is based on its upper limit. This suggests that development is accounted for by multiple factors, and theories that seek to explain development through one single mechanism, like working memory, simplify the picture of development.

The role of maturation in the progress reached at a given time during development is well illustrated in Fischer's work with the brain-cognition hypothesis (Fischer, in press; Fischer & Rose, 1999), although studies directly addressing this issue are still scarce. The hypothesis posits a close relation between neural and psychological growth, suggesting that development of action, thought, and emotion is supported by brain maturation. With each qualitative change "a new kind of control system for action emerges, supported by growth of a new type of neural network linking several brain regions and built upon lower level skills. . . . After emergence, the new systems undergo a lengthy period of consolidation, during which they . . . form efficient behavioral-neural control systems" (Fischer & Bidell, 2006, p. 385).

Fischer and Rose (1999), for example, noticed that the curve formed by the spurts in EEG energy during adolescence is similar to the curve resulting from qualitative changes observed in certain developmental studies, such as the changes in the abstract levels of development of reflective judgment or those manifested by adolescents in their conception of themselves in social relationships. In a case study Bell (1998) provides direct evidence about developmental progress in infancy mirroring brain changes. Bell observed the relation between spurts in an early language acquisition, babbling (ability to produce sounds composed of more than one syllable), and EEG coherence (where coherence assesses whether electrical wave patterns are positively correlated in different brain regions, meaning that the regions are connected). The infant under observation showed an intense effort to babbling in correspondence with an increase in coherence in the frontal-temporal left region, which is associated with language.

As Fischer pointed out, more research studies are needed that investigate directly with the same individuals and explore the nature of the relationship between brain and psychological development. It could be that brain growth sets the conditions for building higher level skills or, reciprocally, there could also be an influence of cognitive advancements and experience on aspects of brain activity.

Constructing a task skill involves microdevelopmental sequences consisting of a set of short-term changes (including small variations observed in ongoing activities and steps during short time spans). They are changes in skills involved in specific contexts. Many changes at a microlevel occur at a given time resulting in the construction of many specific skills in specific contexts, each of them dynamically following different strand patterns of a web because of variability in the contexts. Macrodevelopments are long-term qualitative changes in which skills show a clustering of discontinuities at each level of the sequence of tiers just reported, having a stage-like flavor. Macrodevelopments have their basis on continual and gradual dynamic changes and microdevelopmental steps through which the subsets or skill components were previously constructed. They result from the overall processes at microlevel, which are constituted by "the cumulative process in which all the microprocesses participate" (Fischer & Bidell, 2006, p. 363). The microdevelopments, providing the basic components for each skill construction, set a limit on macrodevelopment. Moreover, the macrolevel is limited by a person's processing system. In turn, the macrolevel puts a constraint on the level that can be reached by microprocesses. Thus, micro- and macrolevels are interdependent, and each one sets a limit on the level reached by the other.

CHANGE PROCESSES

Our sketch of a developmental sequence and of the presence of constraints in skill construction is now complete. However, we have yet to consider the important matter of the transition processes that lead the child to restructure the organization of a skill in a more complex form. We now consider how the theory accounts for both the gradual, continuous change within a level and the rapid, qualitative change between levels.

First, it must be recalled that development is dynamic, and rarely is a skill performance smooth and stable across time. At any given moment, a person does not function at a single level of competence (Fischer & Bidell, 2006). Rather, during development, performance is characterized by fluctuation occurring within a developmental range, that is, the gap between optimal and functional level. How are new skills formed? Differentiation and coordination are the chief processes allowing transition to macrodevelopmental, qualitative changes. The emergence of a new system requires ability to differentiate the subsets that compose a set to allow more articulated relations between parts. Through the process of *differentiation* low level, less adequate skills become ready for combination in a higher fashion. To exemplify, let's consider a study on the acquisition of the skill of understanding social roles (Fischer & Pipp, 1984b; Watson & Fischer, 1980). This study involved a play situation in which toy male and female puppet models were available for playing out the roles of doctor (and father), nurse, female patient and child patient (and daughter), as well as scale models of objects that are relevant to the roles. Using the models, the experimenter presented different stories varying in complexity in accordance with the various phases of acquisition and then invited the child to do the same. Differentiation of components from an undifferentiated whole, for example, operates on the male model with respect to the two possible roles, doctor in one case and father in the other. This differentiation is useful to set up the possibility of using the important process of coordination.

As already noted, *coordination* is the rule that fosters movement, in concert with optimal support, to the successive level and permits a qualitative change in the new skill construction. Coordination consists of the ability to combine and integrate two separately consolidated skills; for example, two mappings are integrated, forming a representational system. It does so in such a way that if the child is ready to increase the potential upper limit, then movement to the next level is possible. Through coordination, skills that have been differentiated become subsystems of a new more integrated system, in which the task complexity is reduced. This leads to hierarchical integration that brings along a higher order level of performance. Considering again the role acquisition study, the child first takes on the behavioral role of doctor (taking temperatures, giving shots), and separately, the role of patient (level S4, which corresponds to the first representational level Rp1). After playing with the models and considering these two roles in isolation, the situation favors the use of processes that induce putting them in relation to each other; and, thus, thanks to the coordination process, the child becomes able to process the roles of doctor and patient in a complementary manner and to combine them into the social role of doctor relating to a patient. Similarly the child creates the social role of nurse and that of father, and in this way progresses to level Rp2, demonstrating a qualitative change. For example, after considering separately and successively the two roles of doctor and father with respect to the patient, coordination foreshadows the ability to consider simultaneously the male puppet model acting both as doctor and as father to the puppet daughter, who responds herself in accordance with the role of patient and the role of child simultaneously.

So, the question becomes: Which are the processes favoring differentiation and coordination? Several transitional processes are proposed to account for skill development. Change processes occur both within and between levels. They can involve small, less complex microdevelopmental changes taking place within short time intervals, or more complex changes leading to discontinuities favoring a new developmental level or transition to a new tier. Microdevelopmental sequences and macrodevelopments share some similarity and similar mechanisms are proposed for changes with respect to both. In fact, much research by Fischer and collaborators focused on microdevelopmental changes.

The change processes are illustrated with reference to the social role acquisition study (Fischer & Pipp, 1984b) and to two studies analyzing dyads working together on understanding a task. Studying collaborative task performance affords the possibility of dealing with both actions and explicit verbalizations during the construction moves and, thus, enables a closer examination of development and learning. One collaboration study (Granott, 2002, just mentioned) considered adult dyads whose goal was to understand the functioning of a robot; the other study involved dyads of middle school children who had to construct a bridge (of a specified length) using only toothpicks and marshmallows (Parziale, 2002). We present six main processes defined through the analysis of dyadic conversational moves between participants, in addition to the activities relating to the ideas they shared. The processes are shift of focus, bridging, backward transition, reiteration, recast, and distributed cognition. Moreover, two processes (introduced in Fischer, 1980) substitution and compounding, are briefly mentioned. The process of bridging is ubiquitous, having been identified in several dyads and in various phases of skill construction. It is considered the most important process leading to skill coordination and higher level integration; thus, it is presented in more detail.

Shift of Focus (or Co-Occurrence). At the initial stage of skill building, a transition to a higher skill may start with co-occurring use of low-level skills on a task. The developing person (the problem-solver) shifts between two different representations each of which is only partially appropriate for the task. Through shifts their inadequacy is noticed and this enables attempts to differentiate those skills in order to eventually integrate them in a new, higher hierarchical skill. Shift of focus involves gradual change through the possibility of displacing the focus of attention from one set to another. Although the subskills are not yet combined with one another, in some cases this rapid movement of attention can prepare their coordination. For example, the child in the social role acquisition study concentrates first on the relation between the doctor and the patient, and then immediately following, there is a switch in attention so that the child focuses on the relation between the nurse and the same patient. These sets are already constituents of the child's skill, which in passing from one to the other, places them in temporal relation to one another.

The number of shifts is greater in the initial phase of problem solving, when the task is unfamiliar (Parziale, 2002). Subsequently, task dimensions are identified and the number of shifts decreases. Fischer reports an observation by Perry, Church, and Goldin-Meadow (1988) that serves as an exemplar of an early phase in constructing the *conservation* skill. When children could not yet integrate the two dimensions of the container, considering the relationship between height and width, they shifted from one dimension to the other, verbally expressing how tall the container was and gesturing how wide. Shifts are involved in the process of bridging (which sets a target beyond the current level of the system; see the following discussion), providing the content for broader "shells" (Parziale, 2002). In this sense co-occurrence has the potential to prepare coordination and may occur across levels, favoring a sudden idea restructuring. However, shift of focus typically operates within a level in that its common function is maintenance and preparation of a new advancement.

Bridging is an important mechanism for constructing new knowledge, a "process of leaping into the unknown." It is a notion that shares some similarity with Siegler's (2006) idea of the child having a conceptual understanding prior to discovery of a new strategy. Bridging works by setting a shell, a target or a goal that a person needs to reach, but that lies beyond one's current level of functioning. The shells are empty, carrying no, or only partial, content. Their role, however, is crucial in that they direct activity toward a new goal for learning by setting "a place-holder for missing knowledge" (Granott et al., 2002, p. 145). They work just like the pillars in an overhead highway under construction: without the pillars (shell) the road (missing knowledge) cannot be built or be stable; the pillars are the markers for the goal to construct the highway and for the direction it will take. Shells by themselves are "partial and fuzzy" (Fischer & Bidell, 2006, p. 369) and might be useless if the new content is not identified. They have a function for a skill builder analogous to that of an outline of a written document for a writer: "By outlining the missing knowledge, the shell creates a scaffold that makes the construction possible" (Granott et al., 2002, p. 146).

Initially, shells are empty in skill building; then as one progresses in skill, bridging sets partially filled shells that reorganize skills and lead to qualitative developmental changes. For example, in the Parziale study a bridging question led a dyad toward a qualitatively different representation of the construction of the bridge as a three-dimensional structure. Although the children did not yet know the strategy to build such a structure, the bridging question was the turning point for a major qualitative progress.

As just mentioned, bridging may work in alliance with shift of focus: bridging builds the shell layout and sets the direction for a shift of focus; shifts of focus provide the content, allowing integration of skill components or incomplete ideas. Suppose, for example, that one member of a dyad in the Parziale (2002) robot task notices that the object moves just subsequent to a sound and this person then says "there is a reaction on the robot." Doing so sets a shell that helps focus on the concept of causality in that context, gradually specifying the components or factors that could be cause or effect, differentiating between the role of the movements of the object and the actions of the dyad working on the task.

Bridging works both *bottom-up* from existing knowledge to new knowledge and *top-down* from the target level set by the shell and current skill. Progress is often gradual: on the one hand, observing different parts of the events may stimulate new hypotheses, and, on the other hand, events are processed and interpreted according to a different perspective. In this way bridging produces coordination.

Bridging can take five different forms, as revealed by the participants in the two dyad studies. One can express a *term* or an unfinished *statement* including a partial content to denote, for example, a change noticed in the robot's movement: this verbalization sets a marker to reach a better understanding of the current activity or to search for useful knowledge (e.g., the term "reaction" may lead to the search of specific factors causing movement). A similar function is provided by asking a *question* that is prompted by a change in the object under observation and points out the need to find the answer or to make a new hypothesis. Bridging can work also by expressing an *intention* to try out something new when suitable procedures or hypotheses have not yet worked out. Furthermore, *recast* is a process by which one reformulates one's understanding of the situation and this process may direct one to a new higher level approach.

How can bridging be activated? It is a process of self-scaffolding but it can also be done by others, as when the developing child collaborates with an adult. Scaffolding the creation of a shell can be done by suggesting any of the types of bridging. In proposing the apparent paradox that a content empty shell can lead to new understanding, the function of scaffolding is compared to the construction of the seemingly impossible ancient Roman arch. In order to place the central stone of the arch (the fulcrum) the side stones are needed; but, in turn, it is the fulcrum of the construction that sustains the sides. The problem is resolved by building a scaffold to support one part until the other is built; similarly, a shell works as a scaffold allowing the construction of new knowledge.

Lack of bridging may have a negative effect. For example, a child dyad physically constructed a part of the bridge, performing a more advanced action than the previous one; but they did so without having a clear idea of why they did it. Although it could potentially scaffold a new perspective on the bridge building problem, they were not able to utilize it to pursue the construction. This is due to the fact that their action was performed without laying out a shell that would facilitate their advance to a higher understanding.

Reiteration contributes to development by strengthening a skill within a level, across levels, and along a developmental sequence. Facing successive presentations of specific tasks, children meet variations, and their level of performance fluctuates within a developmental range. As a particular skill level is constructed, activities are reiterated with modifications and the child attends to and considers the changing relations among different parts of the task. For example, an adult dyad working on the robot problem, after an intuition prompting the bridging term "reaction," reiterated the sequence with the goal of determining the type of sound to which the robot responded. Then, during reiteration the dyad noticed that the robot changed movements. This outcome resulted in a new sequence initiated by a bridging process setting a new goal, and successive reiterations contributed toward a new understanding of causality.

Thus, reiteration is not a rote activity, but rather a necessary process through which a skill or a sequence is discovered and rediscovered by repeating actions and processes (such as bridging and shifts of focus) with modifications in different contexts. This process, resulting from self- or other-scaffolding, contributes to integration of knowledge and consolidation of a developmental sequence, favoring generalization within a range of variability.

Backward transition is another process often activated when a major change demands the construction of a new skill sequence. This process involves the regression of a skill performance. Fischer refers to a common experience of performing worse the second attempt we make when learning a new skill, a very common phenomenon (Strauss, 1982; Strauss, Stavy, & Opraz, 1979) often disregarded as "noise" in the data or "*décalage*." Paradoxically, in moving to a higher level a person often temporarily falls to a lower level, showing U-shaped patterns of development. Probably the so-called "luck of the beginner" experienced by some people could be related to this phenomenon: At the initial stage of learning (for example, playing cards or croquet), a person may defeat an opponent but then immediately show a poorer performance, as one tries to better understand and master the task parameters. A higher performance is temporarily followed by lower level activities than that shown in other tasks. When a task domain is unfamiliar, reiteration processes may not adjust to a different situation: a solution cannot be reached with the usual activities and understanding regresses to a more intuitive, less coherent level. This is a common pattern toward adaptation, based on the assumption that a higher level of understanding is built over lower level structures. In fact, regression follows a spurt occurring too rapidly, usually under high support, and it enables the reconstruction of lower level skills on the base of which later progressions are built. An example can be found in the arithmetic understanding study (Fischer et al., 1990): after a rapid increase in the two high support sessions a drop in performance was found followed by a long period of slow increase and consolidation (see Fig. 5.4).

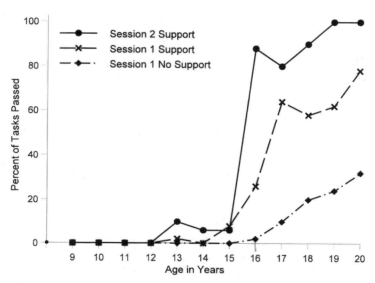

FIG. 5.4. Spurts for mappings of arithmetic operations. *Source:* Fischer (in press).

When an individual progresses in a manner not entailing understanding, a regression to an earlier interpretation may occur and thereby allow one to reset and reconstruct earlier components in order to accommodate the new task variation. Thus, backward transitions involve a reorganization of earlier components and knowledge, leading toward the perception of new relations and to a new interpretation. For this reason a backward transition often predicts a subsequent higher, more consolidated phase. Often seen in the initial phase of building a new skill, backward transition may also be triggered later when an important change occurs in the specific context and a deeper understanding is demanded involving reorganization. For example, such a transition can be activated when one tries to test a new hypothesis without adequate prior knowledge. The extent of regression is not fixed; it depends on characteristics of the person, such as her ability, and on the specific task features and context, such as familiarity. However, like advancements, regressions also occur within a developmental range.

Distributed cognition takes its name from the fact that useful information is gathered and coordinated not only in thoughts but also through actions on physical objects. Although incomplete understanding may trigger a backward transition, sometimes a person may operate on the target objects to test an idea that was not verbalized. In this way there is an implicit reasoning superior to the one openly verbalized. This process was identified, for example, in the study just mentioned about children working to build a bridge. The children achieved their intuition directly with the physical objects, and the feedback offered by observing the result on the element of construction could be used to proceed. Their performance expressed with the objects was one level above their current level as evidenced by the conversational moves. The fact that the underlying reasoning did not undergo further explicit elaboration makes Parziale think that this type of cognition is not in conscious awareness.

Finally the two processes of substitution and compounding are transformational rules operating within levels. *Substitution* is considered a simple rule and represents a simple form of generalization that applies to a single element of the task. It is often a prelude to shifts of focus. For example, during the course of level 6 (Rp3) the child in the role acquisition study shows the ability to substitute the model of the girl patient with that of a woman, thus building a broader concept of patient in terms of instances to which it could apply.

Compared to substitution, *compounding*, is more advanced and is a process leading toward skill integration. Although sets or subsystems are juxtaposed in the case of shifts of focus, with compounding the child is able to assemble more sets and does so in such a way that the sets are brought into relation with each other. For example, both the doctor and the nurse have their particular role specifications and interact with each other in treating the same patient, and the patient responds in an appropriate manner to both.

In sum, transition processes are involved any time a person faces a change in the specific task situation. They are triggered by both minor variations and major ones. Processes such as reiteration, regression and bridging may support one another and may be activated recurrently at different phases of skill building or sequence reorganization. Individuals may adopt different approaches to a problem and these differences may lead to differences in the processes activated and the path followed toward successful construction of new adequate skills.

Examination of these transition processes is important because it reveals two important assumptions with respect to development. On the one hand, higher levels of knowledge or skills are built over lower levels, and this idea is shared by many stage theories, from Piaget to Case. On the other hand, different levels coexist. For example, two levels of development are involved simultaneously in bridging: the functional level, which is the person's current level of functioning for the skill of interest, and the target level. The lower level serves as an anchor to bridge to a more advanced structure. A person can function at different levels at the same time, showing regression in one skill while maintaining a higher level functioning or even progressing in others. Once more, it is useful to recall that these assumptions have their foundation in careful methodologies that are not formalized to make attributions to one stage of development, but that aim rather at following different developmental paths that at a given point in time can exhibit different levels for different skills.

Transition Processes and Individual Differences

How are individual differences explained by the theory? Individual differences in skill acquisition derive from the type of processes employed; children do not all follow the same path in constructing skills. In fact, children do not all bring the processes or rules into use in a fixed sequence nor do they use the same processes. The path followed depends, in part, on the nature of the physical context available, in the sense that physical context can permit the child more or less opportunity to bring skill components into the kind of close proximity in which their relationships might be studied. Children's performances may well differ with respect to tasks that vary in familiarity and have not been well practiced. The path also depends on the degree of social support given by adults or peers providing models from which relations can be taken.

In addition, individual differences lead to variation in the flexibility and the frequency with which rules are applied. Therefore, the complexity and generalization of the skill constructed within each level could differ from one person to another. For example, Fischer (1980) argues that in acquiring the conservation-of-length concept the child might pass through the phases just recounted, leading to the direct construction of that specific concept and ending at the beginning of the abstract tier with its comprehension. However, it is also possible that the child could come to understand the conservation of length indirectly, rather than constructing this specific skill. The child could form the abstract concept of conservation on the basis of previously built conservation constructs, for example, number or substance, and then generalize their application to the case of length without having to elaborate it directly.

Skill theory also suggests that the performance of children who demonstrate specific learning difficulties can be analyzed on the basis of the differential gap with respect to the norm found between the optimal level and the functional level. Such a gap might be traced back to the individual having followed a different sequence in the construction of those skills. Knight and Fischer (1992; Fischer & Knight, 1990) conducted an interesting study related to this idea. It concerned the first phases of learning to read single words. They suggest that those children who do not have reading difficulty initially learn to identify letters and in parallel acquire the ability to recognize a rhyme (tested as a form of sound analysis). In a subsequent phase, these visual and sound components become integrated in reading recognition and then production of rhymes and reading production proceed in sequence. Children with reading disabilities, however, exhibit two different developmental sequences in learning to read single words, both showing pathways for which the integration phase is missing: either reading and rhyme recognition start before letter identification and these three skills are built independently of one another, or letter identification starts earlier, followed by reading recognition and production that precede and remain separate from the corresponding sound analysis tasks (see Fig. 5.5).

Predictions based on skill theory permit one to establish tasks for assessing the developmental sequence of a skill's specific components. They allow assessment of specific individual differences by reference to the developmental path followed, and, thus, create the possibility of a targeted intervention—a considerable advantage in comparison to the possibilities associated with such a vague term as developmental retardation.

Another individual characteristic is the level of knowledge held within a domain, a characteristic that is often studied in the expert–novice paradigm. In one study (Yan & Fischer, 2002) novice, intermediate, and expert students in the computer domain had to learn a specific computer tool during one semester in which their progress was assessed four times. Interestingly, although in each group some students profited from the course, increasing their initial level of performance, both individual and group differences in the growth curves were found. The performance of novices during the semester showed frequent up and down shifts in skill level and their learning curve was nonlinear and chaotic. The students starting with intermediate competence were characterized by repeated phases of brief regressions followed by advances in which they rebuilt the skill. Before any subsequent regression, their advances were more stable than those reached by the novices. Their learning was variable, showing a so-called "scalloping" curve. Experts started with a low performance but rapidly reached an adequate level; their learning curve showed a rapid increase followed by a plateau only occasionally interrupted by very small drops in the generalization process. This study not only shows that individual differences may be due to the initial level of domain knowledge but it also confirms that variability is ubiquitous, although with dramatic differences, at any phase of learning.

Another important source of individual differences is level of emotionality, a factor that exerts an influence in areas such as development of self-concept and language (for a discussion of Fischer's perspective on the development of emotions see chap. 8). For example, in general how children represent the self in positive and negative social interactions exhibits a bias toward positive interaction (Fischer & Ayoub, 1994; Fischer et al., 1997). However, in an extremely negative affective state such as that resulting from abuse or maltreatment, children may show a different developmental path with respect to how they perceive themselves in social relations. For example, abused girls interviewed in a hospital showed a negative bias in

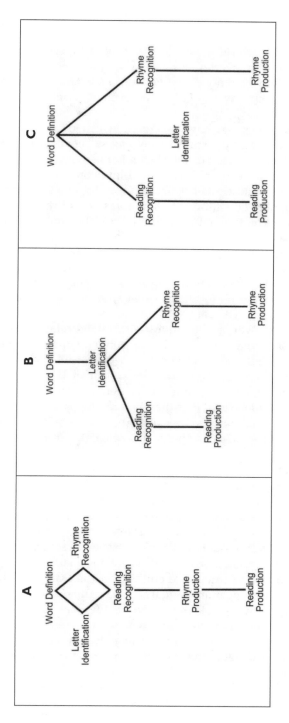

FIG. 5.5. (a) Pathway 1: Normative developmental pathway for reading single words. (b) Pathway 2: Independence of reading and rhyming. (c) Pathway 3: Independence of reading, letter identification, and rhyming. *Source*: Knight and Fischer (1992); Fischer and Bidell (2006).

their self-representation with respect to other non-abused depressed girls in the same hospital (Calverley, Fischer, & Ayoub, 1994). "Their self-descriptions were negative but not primitive. The abused girls were developing along a distinctive pathway, not failing to develop" (Fischer & Bidell, 2005, p. 119).

Individual differences may have their source also in cultural diversity. A good example is offered by a study examining self-concept in adolescents from a far-eastern country, Korea (Fischer & Kennedy, 1997), in comparison to adolescents from a western culture, the United States. In this study, Korean and American adolescents from grades 8 to 13 gave a spontaneous description (low-support condition) of themselves and of their relationships with several people (mother, father, and friends). The analysis of these self-descriptions, measuring the functional level of the participants, showed a difference between the two groups. Korean adolescents provided a simpler self-conception; and, furthermore, this conception did not show developmental changes during adolescence. However, in a second part the adult interviewer scaffolded the performance (high support). A diagram was constructed to help each participant visually represent and focus on different aspects of self. Moreover, specific questions helped relate characteristics requiring skills of increasing levels. In the optimal support condition, Korean's conceptions became more complex, with spurts visible in two age groups, and reached a level comparable to that of U.S. adolescents, although at a 1-year delay. This study documents cultural differences but more importantly it illustrates that the attention in Fischer's theory to the gap between functional and optimal performance (low- and high-support conditions) permits valuable insights regarding the developmental phenomena studied.

Sometimes culture itself sets the high support conditions for optimal performance. Cultural differences may influence the language of emotion, for example. Although Chinese share with many other Western and Eastern cultures similar ways of grouping families of emotions, differences have been found for some emotions. Shame, for example, is a critical emotion in Chinese culture, a part of children's everyday experience. In contrast to other cultures, Chinese categorize words signifying shame as a separate basic family when asked to categorize emotion words (Kitayama, Markus, & Matsumoto, 1995). Moreover, in Mandarin, 113 words relate to "shame" and are sorted out by native speakers into six families, each involving several subordinate categories. In English the same is not true; "shame" is represented only by a subcategory of another negative emotion, sadness. Similarly "guilt" is an important family in English, showing many subcategory clusters, whereas in Chinese, it is included only as a minor family of shame (Li, Wang, & Fischer, 2004). These studies are relevant because they show that cultural meaning, on the one hand, is reflected in language and emotion concept representation, and, on the other hand, it influences children's acquisition of emotion words. Emotion terms relating to shame are acquired very early by Chinese children, but not by the U.S. children.

In general, the optimal level of performance does not show important individual variability. There is the suggestion that reaching a new optimal level will have the strong effect of restricting the individual's use of transition processes and that the child will not be able to proceed rapidly in elaborating the new skill's complexity. Initially, he or she will not be able to coordinate newly constructed skills. Moreover, if two skills are already at their optimal level, they will not be coordinated immediately because doing so would exceed the upper limit of the person's carrying capacity.

Thus, individual differences would not generally be found in optimal level performance. Even those individuals who would perform at a lower level spontaneously perform at a higher level—corresponding, in fact, to their highest potential—when tested in conditions providing a high level of environmental support. That is to say, individual variability showing continuous changes is typically observed at a functional level of performance, but a high environmental support (such as scaffolding and practice in Fischer et al.'s (1990) study on arithmetic understanding) increases the performance and makes it less variable. Clearly then, optimal level is not the principal source of individual differences, although it is a common occurrence with performance measured at the functional level.

GENERALIZATION AND SPECIFICITY

One contribution of Fischer's theory is that it generates evidence of individual profiles presenting differences within short time intervals (e.g., variation in type of story complexity depending on level of support) and can also evidence commonalties in development. We should now be able to address the question of generality in development. What possibilities for generalization are implied by Fischer's theory? What relationship is envisioned between generality and the acquisition of specific skills?

Thus far we have presented Fischer's skill theory as one in which variability in performance (often called *horizontal décalage* after Piaget) is considered the rule rather than the exception. Fischer and Bidell (1991) express two fundamental developmental principles, *variability* and *graduality*, and for both the role of the environment and personal characteristics are important. These external and internal sources certainly influence the learning process, and it is for this reason that the structural construction of different skills may proceed along different paths and require different amounts of time. Indeed we have noted that learning might be specific *within a level* of development and also *within a single domain*. The application of transition processes is influenced by the context, this by virtue of the environment prompting a certain relation among the sets or components. In a situation involving environmental support, performance may reveal a skill at the optimal level relative to others in the same domain of tasks.

However, Fischer's position is not a radical one, in that it does allow for the possibility of synchrony. It is the interaction of contextual and maturational factors that contributes to this possibility (Fischer & Farrar, 1987; Fischer & Immordino-Yang, 2002). In fact, a challenge for Fischer's theory is to be able explain synchrony in light of the pervasive variability. The definition of mechanisms of development becomes very relevant in that the theory has to deal with both aspects of stability and variations and needs to consider both short-term and long-term changes within and across domains.

To state that "The organization of behavior develops systematically, and it also varies from moment to moment" means that there is "order in the variability" (Fischer & Bidell, 2006, p. 332). Variability is not random, it is patterned and involves "ordered fluctuations" (Granott, 2002) and this patterning lays down the possibility of synchronous development.

Synchrony in development derives from more than one source. On the one hand, if there is similarity in the content and/or the child has the same opportunity for practice and optimal support, then different tasks can show synchronous development. On the other, we have already seen that optimal level plays a part in producing qualitative changes across a wide range of skills. Generalization does not occur at a given point in time: synchronous developments take place within an *interval* of time.

Within a task domain, generalizations are anticipated and the sequence of their development can be observed. For example, in learning to play "make-believe," a generalization of broad importance results from coordination, the mechanism that leads the child's passage to the successive level with the aid of various transition processes. This is seen when in initially constructing the skill of make believe, the child consolidates those sets involved in knowing how to feign sleep, and then generalizes these abilities by applying them to dolls. The sequence might continue with such a microgeneralization as expanding the number of actions in a set, for example, pretending that the doll is sleeping, first lying it down on a cushion and then having it say "good night." Moreover, by application of processes such as the substitution rule, shift of focus, or reiteration, the control of a consolidated set can be extended to another set not yet in relation to the first, thus expanding the number of sets that constitute the skill. For example, the child might extend and generalize the skill of making-believe with the doll: in particular, after having acquired the actions useful for pretending to sleep, the child might expand the skill by substituting pretending to sleep with pretending to eat, thus creating a new set at the same level as the first.

Between two similar tasks, the generalization process is readily observed and is predictable from an analysis of the components involved. The greater the number of shared components in two tasks, the more easily will the child be able to use the same skill in both. Such predictions are facilitated by a good task analysis and, according to Fischer (1980, 1997), a good task analysis aims at determining the components involved in the activity under consideration, the relationships among them that are under the person's control, and the level required to work out different aspects of the activity. Thus, within a domain, synchrony is certainly predictable for tasks that share important components. A good example of generalization within a domain is found in Case and Okamoto (1996). Teaching a well-defined central conceptual structure such as "number" increases synchrony across task domains requiring the use of the same core concept (see chap. 6).

Is generalization *across domains* possible? Two perspectives are taken in Fischer's theoretical framework to introduce synchrony in development. On the one hand, generalization among diverse specific domains can occur when a skill in one domain is part of a skill in another domain. A study by Corrigan (1978) demonstrates the synchronous development of a cognitive skill and a linguistic skill in the absence of complete synchrony between the two domains. At the time of acquiring object permanence, the child also becomes able to say, "all gone" and "more." These words denoting absence and presence are in correspondence with the ability to consider an object even when it is not directly perceived. The position that synchrony between domains occurs for those specific skills that make use of the same elements is further illustrated by noting that Corrigan also found a very low correlation between performance with respect to object permanence and the production of other words. On the other hand, it has been specified that through continual processes, local skills reaching optimal level performance are consolidated and generalized, enabling skill clustering and qualitative changes. This view carries the notion that discontinuities tend to appear at the same time in different skill domains, and thus the child's thought shows not only variations during development but also similarities across a range of different domain skills, with spurts occurring at about the same time, giving the stage-like flavor to the course of development.

Thus, although skills are acquired in specific context domains, the learning process also involves the ability to generalize, and in order to evaluate the importance of this ability we must consider the restrictions that apply to it. There are clear limitations in expecting generalization. This follows from differences such as context familiarity and environmental support associated with different skills. In particular, new skills are difficult to generalize: They are not consolidated and they cannot be applied to different task situations until maintenance is reached. Although a change of optimal level may occur with respect to a wide range of skills, one does not necessarily observe homogeneity among skills belonging to different domains. The skill clustering is subjected to an upper limit set by the optimal level, and this limit is defined by a person's processing or "carrying" capacity (see the previous discussion).

Another way of looking at synchrony is van Geert's (1994) consideration of the features of a dynamic system through a nonlinear dynamic model devoted to hierarchical growth of action, thought, and emotion, and which is based on logistic growth equations. Three parameters are considered: *level of the grower* (or skill component) shown in the performance that precedes a change, *rate of the system's growth*, and *system's capacity*. Depending on the contextual support conditions, the rate of change could be either rapid or gradual. Details of the model and its application to skill development can be found in van Geert (1994, 1998), Fischer and Kennedy (1997), and Ruhland and van Geert (1998).

Because skill components are connected and all influence activity, on the one hand different growth curves are expected depending on differences in the components and the strength of their connections. For example, prior performance could be disrupted when time and effort spent for understanding a new characteristic of a task compete with time needed to consolidate a prior level understanding. On the other hand, a higher level grower may positively affect the level of another one: however this occurs within the limits of the system's carrying capacity.

The theory introduces the concept of equilibration to explain the fact that under conditions of high context support a growth in one domain is accompanied by growth in other domains. At a functional level, indeed, there is not such a tendency to seek homogeneity among skills. In the model the term "*attractor*" is introduced, in analogy with a magnet, to say that with optimal level "there seems to be something pulling the curves toward a common place," so that "the growers for different domains tend to seek the same levels" (Fischer & Bidell, 2006, p. 361). "Attraction" is a feature of dynamic models, due to the system's self-organization converging toward a stable configuration. Attraction accounts for the relative (or dynamic) stability shown by a system between phases of developmental transitions, that is, within a developmental level; whereas large variability is found around the transition (Thelen & Smith, 1998; van Geert & van Dijk, 2002).

Important processes favoring skill clustering are bridging and backward transitions, and they operate to restore equilibrium in two different cases. Bridging operates when a major advance in some skills favors a similar advancement in a cluster of skills. Bridging itself is considered an "attractor" (van Geert, 1998) that influences the way of thinking and favors convergent spurts in different skills: the shell sets a pointer to a future "relatively stable state toward which the system gravitates" (Granott et al., 2002, p. 138). Backward transition comes into play when an advance is so rapid that the entire system cannot adapt to it within its limitations. Thus, equilibrium is reestablished by a performance drop with respect to the rapid improvement. The latter phenomenon may explain the U-shape often detected in development. This situation is typically observed after training: Given the system's tendency toward equilibration, a rapid spurt in one skill would affect other ones, pulling them toward an increase, but this tendency may overcome the system's carrying capacity and result in a drop in performance. For this reason, Fischer agrees with Piaget's objections about training aimed at speeding up a specific advance beyond the natural level of development.

Maturation is also involved in synchronous developments (Fischer, in press; Fischer & Rose, 1994). The cycles of discontinuities forming developmental levels and tiers "comprise a cascade of growth changes that move through brain areas and psychological domains systematically and cyclically—a growth process systematically altering neural networks as it moves" (Fischer & Bidell, 2006, p. 385). For example, studies on EEG coherence (Thatcher, 1994), indicating level of connectivity among different cortical areas, showed discontinuities as predicted by Fischer's theory at the same age in which spurts in performance for several task domains marked transition to different levels of development. Likewise, Matousek and Petersén (1973) documented spurts in the curve of alpha EEG in the occipito-parietal area in a sample of Swedish participants ranging from 1 to 21 years (see Fig. 5.6). The spurts occurred at the same ages as those predicted by Fischer's theory for possible synchronous developmental levels (see Fig.

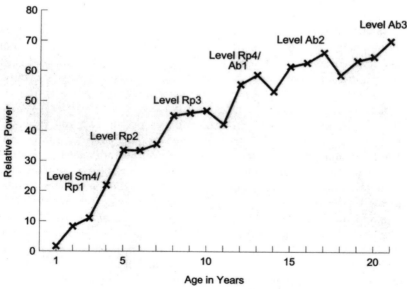

FIG. 5.6. Development of relative power in alpha EEG in occipital-parietal area in Swedish children and adolescents. *Source:* Fischer and Bidell (2006).

5.2) from Level 4 (corresponding to system of systems in the sensorimotor tier and creating a new unit at the representational tier, Sm4/Rp1) to level 10 (abstract tier, Ab3).

A more direct analysis of the relation between psychological behavior and growth of specific brain areas is offered by Bell and Fox's (1994; Bell, 1998) studies, in which the growth functions of domain skills in infants of 8 to 12 months, such as search behavior, are compared to cortical activity in specific brain regions. Concurrent growth in some regions, but not in other ones, is found. This result is taken as a sign of a relation between specific skills and brain, as there was lack of activation of those regions when an individual did not develop the related skills.

However, it has to be noted that recently Fischer (in press) has warned about drawing inferences from these results for the purpose of direct application to education. By no means are research studies investigating the link between the development of psychological behavior and the brain at a stage that would warrant inferences to school policies, such as, for example, endorsing a restriction on provision of new learning opportunities in the phase where a plateau is predicted.

SOME METHODOLOGICAL NOTES ON THE EPIGENETIC APPROACH OF SKILL THEORY

As we have seen, Fischer, like Piaget, in his approach considers the child as an active constructor of skills, and he introduces processes that are more precise than any previously proposed. In elegant ways Fischer and his collaborators indicate that the same individual may show multiple levels for the same skill due to variations in the person's internal condition and external context.

Fischer's theory places skills within phases of building and rebuilding through transition and consolidation processes; and, thereby, it imposes a precise form on the way the theory addresses important developmental issues. The recurring developmental question that asks at what level of development a particular skill or concept can be identified as present appears malformed from Fischer's theoretical perspective. The process is an epigenetic one, and the form in which a concept appears at one point is transformed by means of new relations that, in turn, become the base for subsequent restructurings. As Granott (2002) stated, different levels of knowledge structures coexist; the old lower level skills are not replaced by the new more advanced ones; they remain in the repertoire and are used in critical conditions (low contextual support) when constructing or reconstructing a skill (see also Siegler, 1996b).

One important issue concerns how the situation or research design influences our knowledge of the child's ability. Tasks may vary with respect to materials and procedures, presenting factors that could favor or disfavor the possibility of acting at a certain level. Keeping in mind the important role attributed to contextual support by Fischer's theory, it becomes clear how aspects of methodology can invite inaccurate interpretations of development, to the point of identifying false sequences, *décalages*, and even false synchronies.

Fischer (1980) provides a specific example from Bryant and Trabasso's (1971) study of the acquisition of transitivity. In that case, 5-year-olds whose spontaneous performance on transitive inference would have been at Level 5 (representational mapping, Rp2), succeeded in making level 6 (system, Rp3) when they had to memorize the single premises of each problem before being asked to draw the logical conclusion. According to Fischer, however, learning the premises favored the children's application of the *compounding rule* within level Rp2 and that mimicked performance of the next higher level, a level for which the coordination process is necessary. On this premise, Bryant and Trabasso's results could be replicated only if children learned the premises of the task in advance for the purpose of reducing their cognitive load prior to drawing the transitive inference. Generalization to other tasks is not to be expected in the way it would be if the children actually made the transition to a higher level.

There is a link here to a wider problem concerning training evaluation. We have seen that Fischer accounted for the temporarily better performance that follows training as due to a rapid optimal support spurt causing disequilibrium in the system. The need to consolidate a new level skill, through temporary regression and reconstruction explains the common experience of lack of generalization. Long-term positive effects of training, although not explicitly considered by Fischer, can be imagined within his theory's framework if the training presents two characteristics: its duration is long enough and it includes a sufficient variety of situations to permit the phases of skill consolidation and generalization to occur within the training period. In fact, examples of generalization, including far transfer tasks, are found in Case and Sandieson (1992) concerning training on abilities relating to quantitative reasoning, and in McKeough (1992) concerning training on social dimensions. In both cases the training corresponded to the characteristics just discussed: for example, in the Case and Sandieson training lasted 1 month, involving 20 sessions for about 10 minutes each.

Related to the previous question is the matter of controlling the influence of research methodologies on underevaluating or overestimating children's level of development. Methodological and theoretical implications are associated with determining what requirements a task must meet in order to be adequate to measure a certain level. According to Fischer's theory, a skill is neither present nor absent in an individual; but rather it is in a certain phase of development—a view shared by other neo-Piagetian scholars such as Case, Pascual-Leone, and Halford. By means of task analysis and by using multiple assessment and scaling procedures one can not only observe the level at which a skill is located at a given moment, but one can also determine the minimum cognitive requirement that must be involved in a task in order to derive the presence of a concept at a certain level within a tier in the child's performance. It is not always the case that a precocious performance on a skill task indicates understanding of the concept under study. Sometimes tasks are simplified with the intent of lowering cognitive complexity. However, rather than bringing to light a precocious ability on the part of the child with respect to that skill, these simplified tasks may well involve different concepts or skills. For example, Fischer and Bidell (1991), like Case (1992), suggest that Gelman's conservation of number task actually involves a different concept. Three-year-olds were successful, but they were able to solve it on the basis of strategies such as a simple counting procedure or subitizing, which do not directly involve conservation. When the task presented to the children preserved the core concept, they did not exhibit a good performance. In fact, there are also cases where elimination of factors thought of as obscuring the child's skill is not associated with a higher level of performance at an earlier age. For example, a meta-analysis of a great number of theory-of-mind studies concerning development of false belief and that incorporated variations in task materials and procedures showed that none of these variations consistently enhanced the preschoolers' level of performance (Wellman, Cross, & Watson, 2001).

The study of synchronies and of rapid changes of level does not, as we have seen, provide a full description of development. Just as fundamental is the introduction of the sequential analysis of skill development. Such analysis, in combination with task analysis, points to three important aspects of development. First is the prediction of variability (*décalages*) and synchronies within a level of development, accomplished by taking account of the skills' shared components and of the influence of contextual factors. The second is the conception of a skill's precursors in terms of lower level skills that become components to be creatively elaborated into a new, more complex structure during the acquisition process. The third is better specification of the sequences of development of one or more skills within a level, as seen, for example, in the study just described related to learning to read a single word. Profiles established from performances on various tasks that become integrated in the course of development permit insight to developmental webs or networks, rather than limiting research to single developmental sequences in isolation (Fischer et al., 1993).

Generalization is a very important question for an epigenetic theory of development to address. We have just seen that the possibility to generalize a skill to a broad range of tasks is certainly foreseen by the theory, and it is relevant to examine the processes leading to it and to make predictions about its occurrence. Generalization is the result of consolidation and gradual adaptation to context variability such that the skill becomes available to one in contexts different from that in which it was acquired. When performance exhibits a spurt reached too rapidly, these processes do not occur and the child cannot even show maintenance of the new performance level.

It appears that the meaning assigned to a within skill generalization is by definition restricted; the child does not build so-called general abilities. Each skill is applied at any time to each task and even minimal task variations may change performance. A concept needs to be worked out in each contextual situation given that task familiarity is a factor influencing the use of a skill at a given level.

Consolidation and generalization are very important concepts in learning and development and they are often introduced together in Fischer's writing. Given their salience, it would be useful to have further specification of these concepts. Although simulation is provided by van Geert's (1998) nonlinear dynamic model, it is not clear whether consolidation and generalization are two distinct phases or they involve different processes.

Further, with respect to cross domain generalization, it is not specified whether synchrony has the same sources and takes the same form whether it occurs when advancing to a higher level within a tier or when the system transformation is to a new tier. Although it is stated that coordination is the main mechanism working toward hierarchical skill integration, generalization processes between levels are not necessarily the same as those activated when starting a new tier and, in particular, it is not clear whether these processes show the same complexity.

A related issue deals with development of change processes. It is useful to address it from both a theoretical point of view and an educational perspective; in order to make adequate and insightful interventions one needs to know whether processes develop. In particular, we should know how it is that the child becomes able to use them to change performance level or a pattern of behavior.

Dawson-Tunik and her collaborators (2005) state that mechanisms of development may be similar across childhood and adulthood, with periods of consolidation at a given complexity level and periods of transition. However, from the theory it is not clear whether some processes require a more advanced cognition than others and whether specific experience is necessary to count on a set of processes. In the earlier version of the theory (1980), it was specified that some transformation rules, such as substitution, are simpler that others, but their origin remains underspecified.

Another aspect of interest is whether processes are the result of external situations, as sometimes reported in Granott's and Parziale's exemplar observations, such that direct experience with task and problem situations is the relevant factor. Or are some processes "built in" to the mind on an innate basis, in which case the question is what would be likely to trigger them? Or are they acquired during development when the external context offers the right circumstances, creating the need to build them?

Developmental processes take place within a physical and social context that allows practice and the elaboration of new aspects, and that context may perhaps include the contribution of a peer or the support of a more competent person. Yet development also requires an organism ready to enact these processes. The theory indicates that the mechanism of coordination, leading to cycles of hierarchical skill developments, is involved in the epigenetic growth of optimal levels showing similarities with the growth curves of brain activity, but other processes are not specifically discussed from this point of view. It would be important to know more on this matter: indeed individual differences may be conceptualized as diversity in the ability to use the transformation rules rapidly and flexibly for making generalizations to different contexts made available by the environment. It has been stated that "different people may show different patterns in the growth cycle" of the cortical network (Fischer, in press, p. 13): is such a difference related to the type of processes used by an individual? Or, if developmental processes are similar across life span (Dawson-Tunik et al., 2005), would the pattern of brain growth not affect process use and, consequently, individual differences?

Another question in need of deeper discussion concerns whether and how awareness is involved in the use of change processes. Fischer and collaborators insightfully have identified several processes as part of a child's mental activity during a task performance. A few times when referring to dyads working together in problem solving a participant is said to acknowledge the need to search information, and, of course, awareness accompanies explicit hypothesis formulations. Yet, not much has been proposed about whether skill building or aspects of it would involve metacognition in terms of process selection and awareness. For example, self-monitoring one's understanding was presented as critical for taking advantage of the bridging process, but what causes success or failure in adopting the process of self-monitoring itself may be difficult to clarify.

As frequently noted, a fundamental aspect of Fischer's theory lies in the specificity associated with skill development, that is, in the acquisition of independent domain-specific structures. From this perspective, it is not the child that is at a given level of development, rather it is the child's skill that in a given moment is at a certain level. Fischer sets himself in opposition to a nativist position that core domain knowledge is already present at birth. He maintains that it is not the skill that is innate, nor that there is such a thing as a predetermined (abstract) psychological structure. When stating that children build specific skills, Fischer does not place himself within a modular conception of development that can be reduced to a neurologically based processing specificity. The specificity in his theory lies in the process of skill building and in the broad role that the context plays both in variability and in the sequence of phases that occur in skill construction. In his revision of the theory Fischer does not propose an initial cycle of levels to form the reflex tier, as he did in the earlier version (1980); however, following his line of thinking, he is only awaiting more straightforward empirical evidence regarding these early developments taking place in the first 3 months of life.[1]

Does specificity have a status of its own in the theory or is it introduced functionally, for the purpose of explaining variability (the *décalages*)? In addition to account for intraindividual variability and differences across domains, the specifics of the specificity concept have been further elaborated through a deeper analysis of maturational factors in the construction of skills. In fact, the specialization of brain regions is considered crucial in development for both domain skills (e.g., language) and processes, as just mentioned. From the theory it is clear that *décalage* is anticipated and observable only (or better, principally) within a level. The movement from one level to another seems to occur in a more generalized way with numerous synchronies. Fischer views such movement as being determined by the new optimal level and this pattern is proposed to be common to individuals, so much so that he excludes it as a source of individual differences. Given the differing role of variability in different phases of development, a crucial aspect deserving further attention is the passage between levels and the transition to a new tier, seeking to account for the type of transition processes attributed to generalization as well as those attributed to specificity.

Finally, with respect to a change of level, the theory indicates that the optimal level poses an upper limit on the complexity of skill construction and, at the same time restricts the role in which the contextual support can operate. Such limit is set by the process of coordination and within the system's processing capacity. In place of the notion of an increase in working memory or in place of introducing an increase in complexity (or dimensionality) of representations (as do other neo-Piagetian theorists, who, however, do not pose a single mechanism but also introduce the role of the context), he argues for a progressive and more complex self-regulated organization of structures within the system's carrying capacity.

---

[1]Perhaps the idea of insertion of the reflex tier with its cycle of levels into the theory derives from the need to also assign a sequential development to precociously displayed skills in the infant's first period of life, in which both the child's activity and the contextual support play a role.

Fischer states that working memory (WM) plays a role in development not so much in terms of its size (number of items or chunks considered at the same time), but rather in terms of the organization or structural relation among the items. In other terms, WM is marked more by a qualitative change than by its quantitative increase during development (Bidell & Fischer, 1994). Using the representational tier as an example, what counts is not the fact that one skill at a time in Rp1 (Level 3, single representational unit) is held in working memory compared to two skill components held simultaneously in Rp2 (Level 4, representational mapping). Rather, it is the type of relation linking the components. In fact, the components held in WM are still two in Rp3 (Level 5), but they are organized in a higher level relation, from representational mappings to representational systems. Yet, theorists focused more on the role of size of WM, and this might suggest that type of relations among units is itself a countable element: for example, it may be said that bidirectional relations such as in a representational system (Rp3) require keeping in mind simultaneously one additional unit compared to one-directional relations (Rp2). Moreover, the single unit marking a change of tier is in fact a more complex, unified meaning (chunk) assigned to four units interrelated as system of systems, thus indicating that the change may be both qualitative and quantitative.

On the one hand, the idea of developmental progress as marked by greater complexity of relations among abilities, knowledge, and strategies held in mind can be widely shared. On the other hand, it is empirically demonstrated that memory span increases during development and this is viewed by some theories as a requisite enabling better chunking and more advanced interrelations among skills (abilities, concepts). Also Fischer proposes that during development skills increase in the number of composing elements and/or complexity of their interrelations, and both number and structural relations are important for working memory. However, ". . . changes to new developmental levels . . . involve qualitative changes in organization of relations among actions (and secondarily correlated quantitative changes)" (Bidell & Fischer, 1994a, p. 148). Further specification of these critical concepts would probably clarify the role attributed by Fischer to quantitative changes, whether they are conceived as a key to enable qualitative changes or, vice versa, as the result of the latter.

CONCLUSION

Kurt Fischer was the first to propose cyclical developmental levels within major stages. By placing his skill theory within a dynamic systems approach he is able to reconcile the idea of increasing skill complexity during development with that of variability in performance during skill acquisition.

Thus, Fischer is able to account for patterns of developmental sequences and different developmental profiles associated with particular characteristics of children involving conditions in which they have grown up—facing extremely emotional situations, for example—or cultural differences. In all cases, there is a difference in the path followed by skill development rather than a lack of skills.

Among the central features we have highlighted with respect to Fischer's theory is optimal level support, a key concept accounting for variability. Support is lower when a task is new or when environmental social support withdraws too quickly. We have emphasized that Fischer pays great attention to mechanisms of change, that is, to the type of processes activated in transitions both within and between tiers. Fischer and his collaborators point to specific processes relating to temporary regressions and temporary advancements and demonstrate the importance of skill consolidation. And we have illustrated how the theory deals with both specificity in task domain acquisition and with generalization, with synchronicity as well as with variability.

Despite the coherence of the theoretical proposal, some aspects require further specification. These include, for example, the source for increases in carrying capacity, the nature of the carrying capacity construct, and the role of working memory relative to that of carrying capacity. Compared to other proposals, Fischer's theory is very rich in terms of processes to account for change. However, it would be valuable to know more about the nature of transitional processes that explain change in the type of thought between different tiers (a problem noted in other theories as well) and to better understand what favors cross-domain synchrony.

Though some aspects require further specification, overall, Fischer's theory and the methodology used in his studies provide an insightful and fruitful perspective on the world of development and learning.

6

Structures and Processes
in Case's Theory of Development

Case, like many neo-Piagetians, sought to illuminate the structure as well as the process of children's thinking by combining some of the core concepts proposed in Piaget's work with more current psychological paradigms such as the insights and methodologies offered by information processing and cognitive science. As mentioned in chapter 2, during the initial phase of his research activity he worked within the framework of Pascual-Leone's theory of constructive operators (TCO; e.g., Case, 1974a; Case & Globerson, 1974), but subsequently he developed a theory that differs from the TCO in several important aspects. As his theorizing evolved, other perspectives were incorporated into the original framework, resulting in a general developmental theory of considerable range and explanatory power (Case, 1985, 1992c, 1998; Case & Okamoto, 1996). The purpose of this chapter is to provide an outline of the theory and an analysis of its current relevance.

Case's research is of particular interest because he has been able to study many controversial issues experimentally, helping to clarify important concepts pertaining to the development of children's thinking. In particular, his theory deals with crucial problems related to the role of working memory growth and experience, the identification of core or central structures, and the use of instructions in the deployment of strategies.

Case's theory preserves many salient features of the ideas of Piaget. For instance, he retains the hierarchical divisions or stages characteristic of the structures in children's thinking. However, as does Fischer (see chap. 5), Case places greater emphasis on the role of the progression through the structures, describing their development within each stage. At the same time he modifies and widens the notion of structure, identifying two types of structures: executive components (Case, 1978a, 1985) and central conceptual elements (Case, 1992c, 1998).

GENERAL CHARACTERISTICS OF THE THEORY

The general assumption of Case, much emphasized in his earlier work, is that children can be characterized as thinkers and "problem-solvers." The overarching aim of the theory is to illuminate how children develop into ever more powerful problem solvers, and into higher level thinkers.

In the first version of this theory Case (1978a, 1985) proposed that, at least in part, development can be explained on the base of two major notions, namely: (1) a functional increase in working memory, and (2) a mechanism that explains such an increase by way of a corresponding increase in operating efficiency, or automatization, through opportunities to practice. Later, this idea of a sort of mechanistic trade-off between operational efficiency and working memory size was revised by Case (1992c, 1995, 1998; Case & Okamoto, 1996). In the later version of the theory he focused on the construction of conceptual schemes in relation to the development of central conceptual structures, but he also maintained the role attributed to control structures in the earlier version.

The first part of this chapter is devoted to the information processing approach introduced in Case's theory and stresses the importance accorded to those processing elements that focus on the way children initiate, organize, and direct their cognitive activities. Thought to be largely under voluntary control, these *executive control structures (ECS)* are involved in planning and monitoring what children attend to and what strategy they implement when faced with a problem. As becomes apparent in the next section, ECSs constitute one fundamental structural aspect marking developmental changes in Case's theory.

These control structures, which are the operations used to solve problems encountered in the environment, are proposed to be constituted of three components: (1) a representation of the essential feature(s) of a class of problems (a "problem situation"); (2) a representation of the goal(s) for that particular class of problem (an "objective"); and (3) a representation of the sequence of operations to be used to move the process from the initial problem state to its final solution (a "strategy").

In facing the challenge of how best to characterize the development of children's thinking across time, Case's theory postulates that children's executive control structures progress through a sequence of four major stages and in this regard is similar to Piaget's. Case proposed that in each stage children successfully demonstrate an understanding of the predominant tasks facing them, and that these are a function of the type of mental element represented by the component schemes or elements of the structure. The four major stages are: (1) Sensorimotor, (2) Interrelational, (3) Dimensional, and (4) Vectorial (or Abstract). These are characterized by an increasing hierarchical complexity of the relations within executive control structures, starting with first-order relations in the sensorimotor stage and developing to fourth-order relations in the vectorial stage (see Fig. 6.1).

Case's theory attributes a cyclical and recurring pattern to substage development. Like Fischer, Case accounts for the developmental progression within each of the four major stages by postulating a sequence of four recurring substages. They were originally named operational coordination, unifocal coordination, bifocal coordination, and elaborated bifocal coordination. In more recent writings (Case & Okamoto, 1996; Marini & Case, 1994), however, the substages are named after the stage, for example, for the dimensional stage, the substages are: predimensional (0), unidimensional (1), bidimensional (2), and integrated bidimensional or bidimensional elaboration (3). In this book we use Case's later terminology.

The development of the substages is very much a function of the number of mental elements of a particular task that can be represented simultaneously. This complexity is defined by the number of "basic units of thought" the child is able to control. Each successive substage is characterized by the consolidation of previous units of ECS and the addition of a new basic unit or a new relationship linking earlier structures. It is proposed that the complexity of the structure achieved at the last substage of a major stage (i.e., substage 3) corresponds to a basic unit of the first substage (i.e., substage 0) of the next stage, making it possible to begin the progression at a new and higher order level of relation.

The structural aspects of the theory are illustrated in Figure 6.1. Briefly, at substage 0, various operational elements, symbolized as "A" and "B," are each consolidated, but because the child is not yet able to coordinate two elements, they are used in isolation. At substage 1, the two qualitatively different types of operations are coordinated into one structure $(A - B)$, resulting in a qualitative as well as a quantitative developmental shift. At substage 2, two pairs of similar operations, each individually available at the previous substage, are coordinated $(A_1 - B_1 \text{ and } A_2 - B_2)$, but not fully integrated (as represented with a dotted line). At substage 3, an elaborated coordination (illustrated by replacing the dotted line with a solid X) involves full integration of the previous operations in the form of compensation. As can be seen in the figure, with the transition to the next major stage, each one of these elaborated units is processed as a single element, and the entire process is repeated. The size of working memory (WM) demand, ranging from 1 to 4 within each stage, is also shown in the figure.

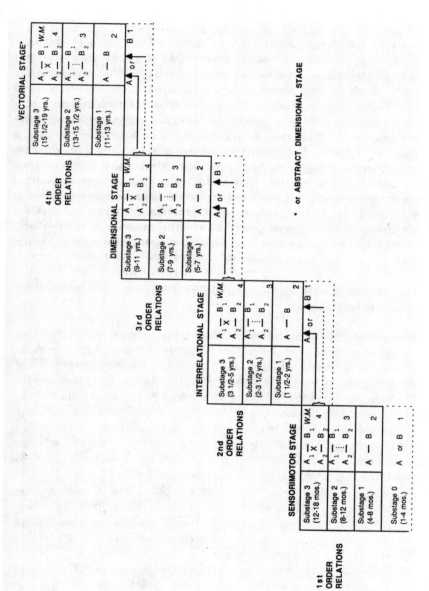

FIG. 6.1. Hypothesized cyclical structure of children's knowledge at different stages and substages of development. *Source:* Case (1992a).

OUTLINING COGNITIVE DEVELOPMENT
IN CASE'S THEORY: THE BALANCE BEAM TASK

To illustrate the developmental progression of ECSs through the four stages and substages in concrete terms, we make use of the Balance Beam task, a widely used assessment tool extensively analyzed by Piaget, Siegler and many others to investigate children's cognitive development (see also chap. 4). A significant methodological contribution of Case's research program is the development of adapted versions of the apparatus, thus permitting the study of children's cognitive development in each of the four stages (see Case, 1985, 1992c). In this section, to give a flavor of the progression within and between stages, we briefly provide a description of the balance beam problems characteristic of each stage, the executive control structures activated by children as they solve the task, and the required working memory size. The ages reported are approximate and subject to individual differences in the rate of development. The behaviors pointing to the executive control structures described for each substage should only be understood as typical or prominent ones.

The Development of Sensorimotor Control Structures
in Infancy (1–18 Months)

At the sensorimotor stage, children attempt to understand the world by using a range of perceptual experiences and motor activities, often involving vision and touch. At this stage, children are particularly interested in connecting events through a gradual understanding of some form of cause and effect linkage, such as the interesting sound of bells resulting from pushing on a lever or, in a similar fashion, the noise that results when a child drops a spoon on the floor (Case, 1992c).

To study children's cognitive progression during the sensorimotor stage, Case and Hayward (see Case, 1985; Case & Hayward, 1984; Hayward, 1986) developed a sequence of tasks using a modified Balance Beam apparatus (see Fig. 6.2). The overall goal was to make events recur in an interesting way so that infants (1 to 18 months) would be able to attend to the various problems presented to them, for example, tracking the side of a beam going up and down. To make the task more appealing a bell would ring when the appropriate end of the beam was pushed down (or up).

During *substage 0* (1 to 4 months), children consolidate abilities integrating them in single structures (A or B). Examples include schemes such as to direct the eyes to track an interesting object moved out of sight, or to move the hand toward a desired position (for example, move thumb back to mouth). In the balance task, children achieve the ability to follow the beam arm that moves up and down, by moving their head and eyes in its direc-

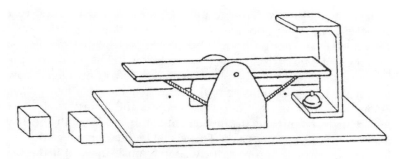

FIG. 6.2. Balance beam used by Case to study infant control structures. (* = springs). *Source:* Case (1985).

tion. They could touch the beam without looking at the bell, or look at the bell without moving their hand. Only one element at a time needs to be kept in working memory (WM = 1), that is, the scheme for following the moving object. All 4-month-old babies in the sample proved to have consolidated this scheme, although some of the 2-months-olds kept fixating the point where the beam had moved out of view.

During *substage 1* (4 to 8 months), a new executive control structure is formed (A – B) by integrating, in a means–end relation, two of the units previously consolidated and used in isolation. At this point, not only are infants able to visually track the beam set in motion by the experimenter (as in the previous substage) but they also become able to imitate the action by making the link with the experimenter's hand movement (WM = 2).

During *substage 2* (8 to 12 months) the infant's attention expands to include another action–reaction structure (A$_1$ – B$_1$ and A$_2$ – B$_2$) and the child begins to apprehend their connection. The infant achieves the ability to perform a similar but slightly more complex task in which the bell is hung over the beam at the end opposite to the child. It requires focusing on two objects at a time—coordinating the gaze on the bell at the far end of the apparatus with the hand's action on the near side of the beam. Thus, although the problem structure in this substage is not qualitatively different from the previous task, it requires a broader coordinated representation that includes monitoring on the far side of the beam the results of an event occurring on the near side. The three sensorimotor schemes that, according to Case, must be coordinated to perform this task are: (a) moving the arm to reach the beam, (b) as the hand approaches or touches the beam, turn one's head and look at the other side, and (c) push the beam as the hand makes contact with it (WM = 3).

During *substage 3* (12 to 18 months) the child is able to fully integrate the existing structures (A$_1$ – B$_1$ × A$_2$ – B$_2$). This integration produces more flexible elaboration and simultaneous activation of the two structures (WM = 4).

It enables the child to explore reversibility in pairs of action and reaction (Case, 1992c). These new, broader structures are applied to tasks involving actions and movements on both sides of the beam. For example, babies perform the same task with the bell placed below the beam at the opposite side, thus raising the near side of the beam, instead of pushing it down, in order to make it ring. In addition to the three schemes that need to be kept in WM in the previous task, this task involves the insertion of one more scheme, namely, monitoring the movement of the far side of the beam while the hand pushes up the near side. This visual feedback enables the baby to reverse direction of action and, for example, push upward if the first attempts had brought the beam to the wrong direction (a correction that younger babies are unable to make), Thus, the child shows understanding of a practical form of reversibility.

This full coordination of sensorimotor representations of actions and movements on both sides of the beam constitute an *interrelational* representation. The elements of a sensorimotor structure can be assembled and consolidated as a new, whole unit; and in this sense, substage 3 of the sensorimotor stage can also be labeled as substage 0 of the interrelational stage.

The Development of Interrelational Control Structures in Preschoolers (1–5 Years)

By the end of the sensorimotor stage, young children have consolidated their cognitive structure and this allows them to apprehend the connection between their actions and the external world. Children use this capability to enter the interrelational stage, where their mental representations are concerned with relations among objects, people, and actions.

A modified balance beam apparatus (see Fig. 6.3) was constructed (Liu & Case, 1981) to present four levels of problems with a similar goal of making

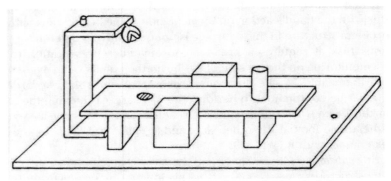

FIG. 6.3. Balance beam used by Case to study preschool control structures. *Source:* Case (1985).

a bell ring. The testing sequence starts with simple items (see sensorimotor substage 3). Subsequently, more complex items involve placing weights on the beam or removing blocks that limit its movement; the last and most difficult items require discrimination between heavy and light weights and their effects on the movement of the beam.

Consider first the origins of *substage 0* (12 to 18 Months). The elements of the sensorimotor substage 3, flexibly applied to different situations, form the basis for a new form of thinking. The structures are assembled and consolidated as new units constituting the first interrelational representation. A single interrelational representation (WM = 1) is sufficient for problems that do not involve blocks or weights to be placed on the beam's arms. Children at this age possess separate interrelational representations, such as the ability to free the movement of the balance beam by removing blocks from under the arms, or by pushing down one arm and looking at the effect on the other arm; however, they are not yet able to integrate these two structures to solve a problem.

During *substage 1* (18 to 24 months) toddlers construct a new control structure (A − B) by integrating two interrelational representations previously consolidated and used in isolation (WM = 2). This qualitative change allows solving problems in which the supports under the beam prevent its movement. For example, the child is able to remove first the blocking supports in order to move one arm of the beam up or down while monitoring the reversible effects on the other arm (Case, 1992c).

During *substage 2* (2 to 3 years) children expand their ability by representing an additional interrelational structure ($A_1 − B_1$ and $A_2 − B_2$); for instance, they can use weights as an instrument to tilt the beam. They understand, for example, that a weight must be placed on an arm of the beam in order to make the other arm move upward when the supports are removed. Thus, children are able to focus on three different interrelational units that are kept active in mind: one for the beam system, one for the effect of a weight, and one for the support removal (WM = 3).

Only during *substage 3* (3 to 5 years) do children further elaborate the elements of the control structures to include understanding of the composition between two interrelations ($A_1 − B_1 \times A_2 − B_2$). Now they can solve the most difficult problems devised for this stage, ones in which a heavier and a lighter weight must be placed appropriately on the two arms of the beam to attain the goal of ringing the bell. The light weight is handed to the child first, so he or she must refrain from placing it on the side that is to go down (as would be appropriate for items with only one weight). Instead, it must be placed on the side that is to go up, leaving the other side free for the heavier weight. A new sort of relational reversibility is involved here. A successful strategy involves keeping in mind four interrelational units: (a) which side of the beam must go up and which one down, (b) placing the heavy weight on the side that must go down, (c) placing the light weight on the side that must go up, and as in the previous cases (d) removing the supports (WM = 4).

Thus, at the end of the interrelational stage children are able to manage a system of relations. "In process terms, one could say that they can, by the end of the stage, establish a sequence of relational goals as a means to achieving a terminal goal that is itself relational in nature" (Case, 1992c, p. 27). Such coordination of relations opens the way to a qualitatively new and more complex type of cognitive unit, dimensional representations.

Dimensional Control Structures in Middle Childhood (5–11 Years)

One achievement of the interrelational stage (between 4½ to 5 years of age) is the ability to make predictions regarding the compensating effect of a heavy weight on the action of a light weight placed on the opposite side of the balance beam. Counting is another scheme structure consolidated during the interrelational stage. However, young children are not able to use this skill to quantify the number of weights and draw inferences on the balance beam behavior. The combination of a qualitative understanding of the action of a heavy versus a light weight with a quantitative understanding of number of weights or distances is characteristic of dimensional thought. As children progress through this stage they can focus on two dimensional structures simultaneously, and they begin to make finer discriminations between them. For example, children at this stage can eventually consider information related to the discrepancy between the number of weights on a beam and its distance from the fulcrum and make a prediction that the side of the beam with the greater difference will fall down.

Building on the previous work of Inhelder and Piaget (1958), as well as the research of Siegler (1976, 1981) and Furman (1981), Marini and Case (see Case, 1985; Marini, 1984, 1992) used a traditional balance beam apparatus (see Fig. 6.4). They designed sets of problems at four levels of complexity. For all tasks, the goal was to predict (and explain) which side of the beam would go down. The problems varied in terms of weight (the number of metal rings) as well as distance (the number of pegs from the fulcrum) on each side of the beam that needed to be taken into account to solve the problem.

Substage 0 (predimensional, 3½ to 5 years) coincides with substage 3 of the interrelational stage. Children consolidate representations that are building blocks of dimensional thought. On the balance beam task they can predict that, when there is a large weight difference on the two arms of the apparatus, the one that looks heavy will go down and the one that looks

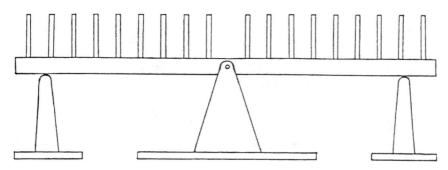

FIG. 6.4. Balance beam used by Case and Marini. *Source:* Marini (1984).

light will go up (WM = 1). Counting weight difference is not required and a single scheme is sufficient to make this prediction.

During *substage 1* (unidimensional, 5 to 7 years), children can make predictions based on the number of weights on each side, including when they differ by only one unit. As discussed in chapter 4, this understanding (identified as Rule I by Siegler, 1976, 1981) marks an important progress. The child makes the important transition, from basing his prediction solely on qualitative information to using quantitative information. The rule applied is simple and it yields correct predictions only when the distance of weights from fulcrum is equated. In order to use this rule, a child has to count the number of weights on each side and consider two pieces of information at once, that is, the outcome of both countings (WM = 2).

During *substage 2* (bidimensional, 7 to 9 years) children expand the analysis of the problem to include two different bidimensional elements (also identified as Rule II by Siegler, 1976, 1981). In other words, they can focus both on weight and distance from fulcrum, although these two dimensions are not yet well integrated. In case the number of weights on each side is the same, children often resort to distance information and predict that the beam will tilt on the side where the weights are further away from the fulcrum. To do so, they must coordinate in working memory three units of information, that is, the outcome of applying the weight rule (which is inconclusive because the weights are equal), and the distance of the weights from the fulcrum on each side (WM = 3).

During *substage 3* (integrated bidimensional, 9 to 11 years) children acquire more complex strategies, such as the one that considers both the differences between the two sides in number of weights and the difference in their distance from fulcrum; and they make their prediction according to the larger difference. This clearly involves an elaborated integration in that the two dimensions are fully integrated in a systematic way, enabling solution of problems that involve a conflict between weight and distance. To follow this strategy, a child must coordinate in working memory four pieces of dimensional information, relating to the numeric values required to compare the different numbers of weights and distances on each side (WM = 4).

The Development of Vectorial Control Structures in Adolescence (11–19 Years)

A major achievement of the dimensional stage is the ability to combine two dimensions (such as weight and distance in the balance beam problem) and to understand that one compensates the effect of the other. Moreover, at this stage children are able to compare two fractions such as 3/6 versus 1/2, and determine their equivalence by considering that the denominator 6 is double of 3 (Case, Krohn, & Bushey, 1992). However, the coordination of these two operations (causal reasoning on weight and distance and computing ratios) is not yet achieved. In the strategies just described each comparison is executed in a relatively simple manner, using addition and subtraction.

For more complex and sophisticated comparisons individuals need to form abstract control structures allowing comparisons of ratios relating to the two dimensions. At the vectorial stage this is possible because individuals can consider relations between variables and use multiplication and division schemes to derive the magnitude and direction of a compound variable (*vector*). An example would be solving and comparing two ratios to predict which side of a balance beam would go down (Marini & Case, 1994). These concepts are similar to vectors, because each of them consists not of a single value, but of a set of related dimensional values. They are abstract structures in that they do not maintain a concrete referent on the setting of the problem in the balance beam apparatus.

During *substage 0* (prevectorial, 9–10 years) children acquire the first, simple executive control structures for problems for which two dimensions (such as weight and distance) are in opposition. Also a concept of ratio is usually acquired at that substage. However, only at substage 1 (univectorial, 11–13 years) do children become able to compare two integer ratios: for instance, there are 4 weights on the right and 2 on the left, which means 2 times heavier, but there are 6 pegs on the left and 2 on the right, that is 3 on the left for each one on the right. Three times is more potent than 2 times, so the beam will tilt to the left. This decision involves holding two ratios in working memory. In the following substages, this control structure would undergo further quantitative development. Thus in *substage 2* (bivectorial, 13–15.5 years) children might consider a noninteger ratio (e.g., compare a ratio of 2 with a ratio of 2½) and in *substage 3* (integrated bivectorial, 15.5–19 years) two noninteger ratios (such as 2½ and 2¾) could be compared.

PROCESSES OF CHANGE IN EXECUTIVE CONTROL STRUCTURES

One of Case's contributions is a view of how the interaction of development and learning produces something other than a simple linear effect. What we have outlined so far suggests that both *quantitative* and *qualitative* changes are likely to occur within a stage whereas a major *qualitative* change is usually observed between stages resulting from the complex ECSs of the last substage (Case, 1985). Ability to apply increasingly complex mental structures (that are indicated in terms of knowledge restructuring by Case, 1992c) is mainly due to the development of children's working memory in combination with the opportunity and motivation to practice. Thus, before addressing the core of Case's later theoretical contribution, regarding Central Conceptual Structures, it is important: (a) to examine the processes that allow developmental change and (b) to observe the role assigned to working memory and the methodological aspects relating to its measurement. These are considered in the next two sections.

How does Case account for transition between substages and stages? In describing children's ability in each substage, Case shows that typical changes occur in the executive control structures.[1]

Three processes are introduced to explain changes and they are used alone or in combination. One process is *consolidation*: once a structure undergoes a change, it has to be consolidated before another change can occur. Another is *integration*. Its action is apparent, for example, in the transition to a higher stage: a one-unit structure already consolidated in substage 0 is integrated with another one forming a higher level integrated structure. For example, in the dimensional stage, knowledge that a heavy weight can reverse the effects of a light weight to make a beam move down is integrated with another unit, that is, knowledge of counting (where a higher number means "more"). A new structure is built so that children can predict which way a balance beam goes down by counting and comparing the number of weights on the two arms.

A new level of thinking can also result by *differentiation*. For example, once a new form of understanding achieved in substage 1 is consolidated, it can be extended and applied to other aspects of the problem. The child can now apprehend some sort of relation between aspects of the problem. Pro-

---

[1]Case (1992c) commented on the achievements during the substages both in structural terms and in process terms; the latter refer to children's increasing ability to establish subgoals as a means to achieve a final goal. In this section, we do not keep with this terminological distinction and we focus on mechanisms or processes of structural changes, regarding the type of relations between elements or units of control structures.

cedurally, differentiation is attained by the process of *shift of focus* (Bidell & Fischer, 1994b; Case, 1996a ; see also chap. 5, this volume), in that it results from frequently shifting attention back and forth from one aspect to another so that they can be considered in close succession. This corresponds to a "tentative" integration, the basis for building a more integrated system of relations.

How is it possible that two existing structures, each consolidated and used in isolation, become integrated into a higher order structure? The processes just described are better specified by the more subtle processes invoked to explain stage transition (Case, 1985, 1992c, 1998). Integration and differentiation are enabled by a process of *schematic search* where one structure remains active while a second structure is searched. As a result of the search, two structures are simultaneously active in mind (or in close succession) and their combination is evaluated (*schematic evaluation*) to determine its utility. They are then reorganized so that they can be handled as a unitized element: this new unit is labeled (*re-tagging*) with a new, higher order, symbol system representing the new scheme. Such a new scheme is, then, *consolidated*, enabling an easier access in the future (see Fig. 6.1).

According to Case, the most dramatic change occurs in stage transitions, characterized by different levels of abstraction. Such transitions occur through a process of hierarchical integration, "that is, a process in which the functional relation between two qualitatively different structures is abstracted and gradually brought under conscious control" (Case, 1996c, p. 200). This points out a difference between *implicit* understanding (apprehension), typical of earlier substages, and *explicit* understanding in substage 3. The latter entails an ability to consciously formulate the relations between elements of a system, for example, the number system and to generalize knowledge and operations within such a system (Case, 1992c; The *implicit–explicit* distinction are further elaborated in chap. 7).

In the next two sections, we illustrate the role of working memory and Central Conceptual Structures in Case's theory, after which we return to developmental change processes relating to conceptual structures.

WORKING MEMORY AND OPERATIONAL EFFICIENCY

The reader has probably noted, at this point, some similarities and some differences between Pascual-Leone's and Case's theories regarding working memory. The ages at which Case indicates a one-unit WM increase correspond to those identified by Pascual-Leone. In particular, the quantitative estimates of WM capacity during the sensorimotor stage and the dimensional stage in Case's theory are consistent with Pascual-Leone's estimates of M capacity growth during the same age ranges. However, differently from Pascual-Leone, Case introduces a cyclical increase of WM within each stage from 1 to 4 units, where the 4 units are eventually assembled into one unit. The reader may also have noted similarities and differences with Fischer's theory. Both authors view cognitive development as a recurrent, cyclical increase of complexity through major stages defined by new forms of representation; however, Case assigns a basic role to working memory as a main factor of cognitive development (e.g., Case, 1985, 1995; Case & Okamoto, 1996)—a point on which Fischer does not make particularly strong claims. Because of the major role in cognitive development that Case posited for working memory, it seems necessary to discuss in some depth this concept and the causes of development of working memory itself.

Measuring WM: Problems and Solutions

Given the fundamental role assigned to working memory, one great concern of Case and coworkers has been the creation of WM measures appropriate for different developmental stages. Case faced the problem of making sure that the object of the investigation was, in fact, the size of WM itself. In other words performance on WM tests must be attributable unambiguously to the capacity for temporary storage of representations that are typical of a certain stage, rather than to other variables such as strategy use or familiarity with operations.

Interest in the problem of strategy use, also found among other researchers in the seventies (e.g., Chi, 1978; Dempster, 1981), started with early studies based on Pascual-Leone's theory. Case (1972) used a Digit Placement Task, in which children between the ages of 6 and 10 were presented with a series of numbers in ascending order (e.g., 3, 9, 18), one at the time. When a "target" number (e.g., 11) was shown to them, the children had to determine its position in the ascending series. According to the hypothesis, children would be successful in performing tasks that matched their M capacity and would show increased variation as the tasks exceeded that capacity. In order to make the task a true test of M capacity, it was necessary to prevent children from using facilitating strategies, such as rehearsing the numbers or chunking them. Thus, the numbers were presented one at a time for only a brief time, the participants were asked to read the cards aloud, and then the numbers were quickly removed from sight. The majority of the subjects demonstrated an M capacity indicated by the theory at the predicted ages, that is, they were consistently able to process a series of as many numbers as their predicted M capacity, but made errors with longer series. However, in a subsequent study (Case, 1974b), participants were allowed to inspect numbers in the order they preferred, or even instructed to inspect the target number first. As expected, strategies based on a convenient inspection order enhanced performance; however, this was not equally true at all ages, because younger children were less able to use such strategies. Does strategy use involve some M capacity? Or, vice versa, are capacity scores somehow flawed by the younger participants' lower strategic skills or by the greater processing demand on them when a strategy is new (Bjorklund, Miller, Coyle, & Slawinski, 1997)? Or, does greater familiarity with the operations used to measure capacity increase the operational efficiency of older children? It is not easy to disentangle the respective roles of capacity, strategies and knowledge in performance on working memory tests.

Taking into account these findings, Case was methodologically cautious and set criteria that had to be fulfilled by the WM tests at each stage. These included preventing use of chunking and memory strategies that would surreptitiously reduce the number of units to be kept active in memory and controlling for familiarity. He accomplished this by presenting formally equivalent items involving a basic operation typical of each stage (counting at the dimensional stage, for example).

At the interrelational stage, two nonverbal tasks have been created to assess WM. These involve repeating the actions that the experimenter performs on each of a number of objects protruding from a board where this number increases across trials until the maximum capacity of the child is reached. As predicted, the majority of children in the substages pertaining to the interrelational period increase their *span* for both words and actions, thereby confirming that their WM increases by 1 unit until 4 units are reached at age 5 (Case, 1985; Case & Khanna, 1981). Similarly, for assessment of WM in the vectorial stage the task involves an increasing number of cards in which the relationship between green and yellow dots varies. The subjects have to indicate the number of green dots there are for each yellow dot and then remember the ratio (Case, 1985). Novel tasks have also been devised for the dimensional stage, as is described in the following section. Empirical evidence on the increase in WM size and the positive correlation among the different tests devised for each stage has been provided by several studies (e.g., Case, 1985; see also Pulos, 1997).

Does Operational Efficiency Play a Role in the Size of WM?

Case proposed in his early work that the overall capacity or total processing space (TPS) would hold constant during development. He argued that the progressive automatization of operations would require less operating space (OS), thus freeing up more and more short-term storage space (STSS), resulting in a growth of working memory capacity with age. Such trade-off was summarized in the formula TPS = OS + STSS.

Does greater operational efficiency determine an increase in WM? To address this question, a new "complex span" measure[2] was introduced, the Counting Span (Case, Kurland, & Goldberg, 1982). This measure requires the child to remember the outcome of a certain operation (counting) and also allows the researcher to measure the efficiency of this operation independently. For instance, after counting sets of 3, 8, and 4 dots the child had to recall the numbers 3, 8, 4 (see chap. 9 for further details). To test the role of operation automatization in the increase of storage space (WM) size, some studies considered the relation between counting speed (taken as an index of efficiency of this operation) and counting span scores. The average counting speed and the average counting span scores of age groups ranging from 4 to 10 years showed a clear linear function: as counting speed increased, span also increased. Furthermore, at the level of individual differences, the correlation between speed and span was significant, including when age was partialled out.

Additional confirmation of these results was obtained in studies with children and adults (Case et al., 1982). Adults were instructed to "count" in a "foreign language" (the numbers were 3-letter nonsense syllables), and they then had to perform a counting span task in that "language." Both their counting speed and their span dropped to values akin to those found with 6-year-olds counting in English. Moreover, their performance was not significantly different from the regression line representing the performance of children of various ages. Overall, the results show that: (a) speed increases with age, and (b) unfamiliar material hinders operational efficiency such that both speed and span may decrease. In the early version of the theory, the results of these experiments were interpreted as supporting the trade-off hypothesis, according to which operational efficiency or automatization would increase with age, thus leaving more resources available to keep the outcome of each operation in short-term storage.

However, this interpretation of the results is only one possibility. Correlation does not imply causation. Perhaps adults did not treat the unfamiliar syllables used in the experiment as single units of information like numbers and their difficulty encoding the less familiar materials might have slowed down the counting operation. If this is the case, the elements composing each syllable would load working memory more than would a single digit; and on that account, not only span but also speed could be impaired.

---

[2]The Counting Span can be regarded as the first of the "complex span" measures (e.g., Engle, Kane et al., 1999), that is, those tests in which one must remember a set of stimuli while performing a sequence of cognitive operations. It was developed by Case and Kurland (1978) and presented as a conference paper by Case, Kurland, and Daneman. (1979). Meredith Daneman, who had been a student of Case, subsequently contributed also to the well-known "Reading Span" test (Daneman & Carpenter, 1980), which often is thought (incorrectly) to be the forefather of the complex span measures.

How to explain the increase in speed during development? As noted by Case (1995), the studies just reported have *two* possible explanations, and they could be considered complementary: older children are faster in carrying the basic operations because they are more highly practiced; older children have more efficient neurological systems. That operational efficiency alone cannot be the only factor is supported by a study (Case & Kurland, 1980) showing that extensive practice on counting alone did not increase 6-year-olds' counting speed (although the maximum speed was reached more rapidly by trained children). Although the latter study does not directly examine the effect of counting speed on counting span, it shows that operational efficiency has clear limitations: not being remedied by practice, other factors, such as maturation, must also contribute to this limit.

Studies from other laboratories also challenged the hypothesis of a trade-off between operational efficiency and the number of operational products that can be stored simultaneously. Halford and his colleagues (see Halford, Maybery, O'Hare, & Grant, 1994) separated the counting and memory components of the counting span. They presented a list of spoken digits to be remembered followed by a number of cards with dots to be counted. Subsequently the child was required to recall the list of digits. Thus, the numbers of digits to be recalled and the cards to be counted could be varied independently. The participants' ages ranged from 5 to 12 years. Halford and colleagues reasoned as follows: because the counting operation should be more demanding for young children, then according to Case's trade-off hypothesis an interaction between age and number of countings should be expected; in particular, a loss of information from working memory due to the attentional demands of counting should be more pronounced for the younger age groups. The results did confirm that older children can recall longer digit lists, and that memory performance does decrease as a function of the number of cards presented for counting, though such a decrease can be interpreted either according to the trade-off hypothesis or in terms of retroactive interference. However, the important result is that no interaction was observed between age and number of cards presented; it seems that the counting task impairs memory performance equally at all ages. This result rules out the hypothesis that an operation (counting) takes up more working memory space when it is less automatized (i.e., in younger children).

Also Towse, Hitch, and Hutton (1998) found that a longer counting impairs counting span performance. Their counting task presented a set of cards with different number of dots. As in Case's procedure, the children had first to count the dots of the cards and then to recall the final number of each card. However, the order of the cards was manipulated such that the last card would involve counting either few dots (e.g., 3) or several (e.g., 8), and thus require more or less effort and time to count them. With a short counting the numbers previously counted and stored were reported more easily in the span test. Differently from Halford, they interpreted their findings in terms of decay over time. Again, however, it seems to us that these results also are consistent with an interference explanation. In other words, counting aloud the digits from 1 to 8 could interfere with memory of the final numbers of previous cards more than counting only the digits from 1 to 3.

Overall, it appears that the better memory performance of older children has to be explained in terms different from a simple trade-off with operational efficiency. Barrouillet and his collaborators proposed an explanation that integrates both time and resource constraints. Through several experiments, both with children (Barrouillet & Camos, 2001) and adults (Barrouillet, Bernardin, & Camos, 2004), these authors provide strong support for a model according to which performance on the counting span and other complex span tasks depends both on the difficulty of the operations performed and the rate of those operations per unit of time. Either more difficult operations or a shorter time available for executing them would increase the cognitive load of the task, which in turn would result in a lower span.[3]

In sum, even though Case et al. (1982; Case, 1985) demonstrate a relationship between working memory and speed of processing, more recent research both from Case's lab and other research groups has led to discarding the particular hypothesis of a trade-off between operational automaticity and short-term storage space. Other accounts (not mutually exclusive) seem more likely. For instance, both processing speed and working memory capacity could be constrained by maturation; or a larger capacity could enable faster processing; or, as suggested by Barrouillet, the rate of operations could be one, but only one, of the factors that determine the processing load. More research is needed to examine the complex relationship between speed of processing and working memory.

Role of Maturation on WM and Link With Cognitive Development

We turn now to the factors affecting a developmental increase of WM. Case (1985, 1992b, 1995, 1998; Case & Mueller, 2001) introduced a maturational explanation, considering several potential sources of maturational changes. Myelination increases with age and in particular in the tracts between hemispheres, favoring differentiation and integration in the two hemispheres.

---

[3]One could ask what it is that makes one operation more difficult than another. On this point Barrouillet et al. (2004) seem to rely on rather qualitative or intuitive accounts. Granted this possible limitation of the model, one should also acknowledge that it is clearly distinguishable from the time decay or the automaticity–storage trade-off models, and better supported by the data.

This is hypothesized to have an impact on cognitive abilities. There is also increasing connection in the fibers between frontal and posterior lobes, with consequent dendritic growth. Growth of activity in frontal lobes and increasing connections with the posterior lobes are thought to relate to cognitive development.

Similarly to Fischer (in press), Case discusses a series of studies by Thatcher (1992; Thatcher, Walker, & Giudice, 1987) in which cortical electrical activity measured with EEG is analyzed in different parts of the cortex. The interest is on a measure of "coherence," that is, the extent to which electro-encephalographic waves generated in different parts of the cortex are in phase (synchronous) with each other. An increase with age of EEG coherence was found between frontal and posterior lobes in children aged 4 to 9 years, which can be interpreted as an increasing control of frontal over posterior lobes activity. The pattern emerging from these studies (see also Case, 1992b; Stuss, 1992; Thatcher, 1997) suggests that greater connections between frontal and posterior lobes could affect both the speed of reactivation of neuronal circuits (schemes) in the posterior lobes and the ability to sustain them in an active state despite interference. Thatcher (1992) observed that such an increase of EEG coherence is not quite linear, but rather shows wave-like patterns of growth.

What is the relationship between frontal lobe maturation and cognitive development? As has been pointed out, frontal lobes are called "the seat" of working memory; and changes in connections between frontal and posterior regions are found to be close to the rate of WM growth during the age range under observation (Case, 1992b). In addition, the rate of increase of EEG coherence is also similar to the general increase of processing speed with age (Kail, 1991). Indeed, Case hypothesizes that frontal lobe activity is not only related to attentional capacity but also to formation of new executive control structures (ECS).

Case (1996a) identified a major spurt in frontal lobes close to the age at which the theory predicts the transition to a new stage: WM reaches 2 units allowing integration of two existing structures in a new structural mapping (unidimensional level). Thus, Case proposes that among other sources of maturation frontal lobes play a crucial role in WM size and in ability to construct a higher order pattern, both of which are necessary in forming executive structures.

CENTRAL CONCEPTUAL STRUCTURES AND THEIR DEVELOPMENT

In his revision of the theory (fully outlined in his 1992 book) Case introduced the role of conceptual structures, considered central to children's development. In so doing he fully preserved the importance assigned to control structures in previous work (see Case, 1985) and completed the picture of development taking care also of the content of the developing structures. The revised theory was refined in his later writings (Case, 1993, 1998; Case & Okamoto, 1996), following new research projects, and the nature of conceptual structures within the developing system was further elaborated.

The notion of Central Conceptual Structures (CCS) is important for many reasons. Primarily, introduction of CCS contributes to understanding the nature of the building blocks of children's thinking and how these initial structures are put together in different domains. The focus is on conceptual development, an aspect that was left aside when looking at the child as a strategic problem solver. Thus, introduction of these structures offers the opportunity to work toward a solution of the controversy over whether the developmental progression is best characterized as domain general or domain specific (Case, 1988; Case & Sandieson, 1988).

Central Conceptual Structures are integrated networks of concepts and cognitive processes that form the basis for much of children's conceptual development in the form of thinking and learning in specific-content domains (see Case, 1992c, 1998; Case & Okamoto, 1996; Case, Okamoto, Henderson, & McKeough, 1993). Over the course of development, these structures undergo several major qualitative transformations (i.e., stages) as well as minor changes (i.e., substages), permitting children to think about a range of problem situations in a more complex and advanced manner. The CCSs are best thought of as cognitive structures that do not have a system-wide influence in the same way as advocated by a Piagetian view of domain-general development driven by logical structures. At the same time, however, neither is their influence thought to be as narrow and "localized" as that advocated by domain-specific researchers (see Carey, 1985; Fodor, 1983; Gardner, 1983). This middle ground maintains that CCS allows children to understand events that have a common underpinning in terms of a similar network of concepts, across different areas.

Case defines CCSs as "central" in that they form the conceptual kernel, the "center" of children's understanding of an array of problem situations sharing similar conceptual features (Case, 1996a). These core concepts constitute the base for developmental progress: for instance, the acquisition of numeracy forms the basis for a large variety of concepts and strategies needed to solve quantitative problems. Similarly, the behaviors, norms, and expectations involved in understanding social relations can be assumed to require a conceptual structure centered on narrative thought. They tap into a social knowledge that involves an understanding of the intentions needed to address social situations (see Case, 1998). Space is another example of a CCS directly studied by Case. In essence, each CCS constitutes the conceptual "core" around which children's thinking develops in a particular domain.

Case also describes CCSs as "central" because aspects of their development remain "centrally" controlled. For instance, the theory proposes that changes in system-wide factors that have a strong biological underpinning influence working memory, which, in turn, affects CCS development, either enhancing or constraining its level of attainment at a given age. In the revision of the theory one of Case's goals is to examine the relationship between working memory and CCS, discussing its causal direction.

Although these conceptual structures are controlled by central maturational factors influencing working memory capacity, they are not general abilities, and their range of application is domain-specific. However, they are not "modular" in nature in a strictly nativist sense: they require practice and experience to develop. Thus, another goal of Case's revised theory is to account for variability due to various sources: practice, cultural differences, and a child's proneness to face learning situations. As we see in the following section, Case addressed these very important issues in various ways, and also pointed out that the varying contexts of learning may affect some aspects of CCS. However, Case maintains that such differences do not affect the rate at which development takes place.

In brief, CCSs are conceptualized as networks of concepts (and the relations amongst them), built through experience and subjected to system-wide limitations of a maturational origin. Each CCS has a wide application across different areas; for example, the conceptual structure for quantity is relevant to such diverse areas as mathematics, time, money, and music notation. The theoretical novelty associated with the introduction of CCS lies in the consideration of two structural aspects of development, executive control and conceptual structures, both viewed as essential pillars of development. On the generality–specificity issue Case takes an intermediate position, as he proposes that both general and specific factors, in different ways, influence development of the two types of structures.

Case and his colleagues investigated the nature of children's central conceptual structures in a number of domains and across various age ranges. However, for the purposes of this chapter, we focus on research in the domains of quantitative and social thought, involving children from ages 4 to 10. These domains have been intensively studied, providing solid support for the notion of CCS.

Central Numerical Structure: The Development of the "Mental Number Line"

As Case stated, the study of CCS addresses three major challenges, namely: (1) children's "core" abilities need to be identified, (2) these abilities need to be integrated into a coherent framework, and (3) new tasks need to be constructed (or old tasks reanalyzed) in such a way as to permit the testing of CCS development in the domain of interest. To achieve these goals, methodological cautions are taken. The tasks must entail the specific core concepts characterizing CCS while avoiding the circularity that is possible if one devises tasks to support a predicted CCS and theorizes about CCSs on the basis of the tasks used to validate them.

A central conceptual structure related to "numerical thought" underlies children's ability to think about and manipulate quantities. This structure reflects an understanding of core mathematical concepts such as a "number line." It allows one to count a sequence of objects, to understand that each object is to be counted only once, and, in addition, that the number assigned to the last object corresponds to the total number of objects. Other core concepts involve arithmetic operations, such as addition and subtraction. The CCS for numerical thought reflects the way these concepts are interrelated and applied to various problem situations (Case & Okamoto, 1996; Case & Sandieson, 1988; Griffin, Case, & Siegler, 1994).

Developmental Progress in Building a CCS in the Domain of Number

Construction of the numerical structure starts very early in life: by the age of 4 children already possess an intuitive understanding of two core concepts. One is an early ability to deal with non-numerical quantity: it permits one to solve problems that require understanding of such global concepts as "more" or "less" and "a lot" or "a little." At this age, the child intuitively knows that taking things away (i.e., subtraction) and adding things (i.e., addition) may change a judgment about which has more and which has less. A second core concept concerns an intuitive numerical knowledge of counting. At this age children can count sets of objects, often using a sensorimotor routine for tagging each element of the set. Thus, when asked "How many things are there?" they understand that the answer is the last number counted in each set (Gelman, 1978).

This type of conceptual number structure characterizes children at the *predimensional* level (substage 0); at this point the two core concepts are used in isolation. The limitation of 4-year-olds' knowledge resides in their inability to combine these two core structural elements each relating to either numerical or non-numerical knowledge. A great numerical difference between two sets of objects is easily detected, but they cannot yet make a specific quantity judgment using counting. For this reason they cannot judge, for example, which set is bigger, whether it is the one with four objects or the one with five. Transition to the dimensional stage takes place gradually between 4 and 6 years. During this time the two earlier structures are thought to merge into a new higher level structure, determining a major developmental change.

At the *unidimensional* level (substage 1), 6-year-olds become able to use information about the position of a number on the number line, and can make quantity judgments relative to other numbers in the sequence. Children now form a "mental number line" allowing mental mapping of number words with the position of numbers in a counting string. They also understand that moving forward or backward in a string determine a specified increase or decrease in quantity. Thus, by combining the earlier isolated core structures, children at the age of 6 reach knowledge of *cardinality*.

Details about the nature of this new conceptual structure are reported in Figure 6.5. Case considered it a prototype, a template for capturing the individual and combined aspects of the way interrelated concepts are assembled into the central concept of a domain (Case, 1998). The figure depicts the model of the new numerical structure at 6 years, and it shows critical concepts necessary to acquire knowledge of and reasoning about numbers. The key elements included in the figure relate to knowledge of: (a) written numerals (1, 2, 3, . . .); (b) word numbers (one, two, three, . . .); (c) of the fact that when counting (both physical and mental), the process of tagging objects has to be systematic, so that each object is tagged only once; (d) of the fact that each act of tagging denotes a different set size, that has its own perceptual configuration; and (e) the forming of an internal representation, understanding that movement from one number to the next is equivalent to either adding or subtracting one unit, depending on the direction of movement, and realizing the correspondence between adding or subtracting and making a quantity bigger (more) or smaller (less), respectively.

Having formed such a Central Conceptual Structure, 6-year-old children should be equipped to solve a vast range of problems requiring the unidimensional level of thought. Thus, children at this age should pass items that capitalize on the heuristic of "sequences," and on the concept of "next" (see Fig. 6.5), a central element of the model. For example, children should answer such items testing understanding of the 'next' relation as, "What comes after 7?" and "What number comes two after 7?" They should be able to move back and forth on a *single* number line to find a number that lies at a specified number of units from another given number, computing additions and subtractions such as 2 + 4 or 8 − 6. Other sets of items include "Which of two numbers, 5 or 7 is bigger (smaller)?" which taps ability to use ordinal information for deciding about cardinality (row *b* and row *e*), and "Which is closer to 5, 6 or 2?" which assesses, in a different context, knowledge of adjacency in the sequence. Children are now ready to expand their conceptual structure and move to the other two substages.

At the *bidimensional* level (substage 2), eight-year-olds expand their understanding to consideration of two numerical structures at once, each requiring a lower level structure. Thus they can understand a number system

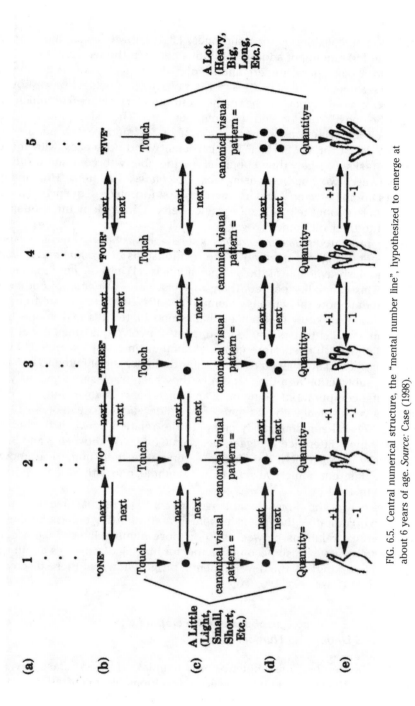

FIG. 6.5. Central numerical structure, the "mental number line", hypothesized to emerge at about 6 years of age. *Source:* Case (1998).

with base ten, considering tens and ones. Their knowledge should further include understanding of additive relations between the tens and ones columns and a conceptual understanding of a difference between numbers. Considering items parallel to those of the previous substage, they should be able to answer, "What number comes four numbers before 60?" which involves the "next" relation with two number lines. They should also solve items such as "Which number is bigger, 27 or 32?" and "Which number is closer to 24, 21, or 18?," which test cardinality and adjacency with more complex tasks. Further, they should show the ability to compute a difference between two numbers, using *double counting*. The item "How many numbers are in between 3 and 9?" involves first forming a sequence of mental objects to count the two numbers and then counting along the sequence to compute their difference (row *e*).

At the integrated *bidimensional level* (substage 3), children become capable of generalizing and integrating the relationships of *two numerical structures* (singularly available at the bidimensional level) into the entire number system. This capability permits them to construct a principle of addition, understanding how the various columns (i.e., 10s, 100s, etc.) relate to each other. Thus, they know that ten 1's makes one 10, ten 10s makes one 100, and so on. Parallel tests suitable for this level involve questions about the 'next' relation with even more complex number lines, for example, "What number comes 10 numbers after 99?" Their thought is not limited to one addition or subtraction at a time, and now they keep track simultaneously of two mental computations going back and forth between ones and tens columns. Thus they deal with two sums or two differences, instead of one (13 + 39; 301 − 7) and simultaneously compute the relation between two differences ("Which difference is bigger, between 6 and 9 or between 8 and 3?"). The theory also predicts the ability to generalize their numerical knowledge to a different numerical system, for example, one with base 60 (hours, minutes) instead of 10.

At the end of the dimensional stage the core conceptual structure pertaining to quantitative thought is fully integrated, allowing understanding of the reciprocal relations between two or more number lines. Such a core conceptual structure also becomes "a tool for making discoveries about the world . . . [marking] . . . the developmental progression that these discoveries produce" (Case, 1996a, p. 9).

Empirical Evidence Corroborating Development of a CCS Underlying Number

Using the number line sequence as a template (Fig. 6.5), Case devised sets of tasks to assess the hypothesized development of central numerical understanding in 6-, 8-, and 10-year-olds. Various tasks of increasing complexity were designed to tap understanding of the core elements character- izing the three levels of dimensional thought. Examples of the items are just reported in illustration of substage development. In brief, the tasks suitable to test the predicted levels of children's quantity thought from 6 to 10 years tap understanding of a single "mental number line" at the unidimensional level, simultaneous consideration of two mental lines at the bidimensional level, and multiple mental lines or other numerical systems at the inte- grated bidimensional level (Okamoto & Case, 1996). The results, based on item analysis examining proportions of accurate responses, showed high correspondence with the hypothesized sequence of development. Support for the model was also provided by a latent structure analysis conducted on this research data and that showed that number knowledge forms a co- herent structure at each substage. Indeed, it identified a high probability of passing items at the complexity level predicted for a given (or lower) substage but not for passing items of higher substages. Moreover, it should be noted that the task levels proposed to the children corresponded to a Guttman scale, as revealed by a scalogram analysis (Okamoto & Case, 1996).

Using a different methodology, Fan, Mueller, and Marini (1994) also pro- vide evidence in support of the predicted sequence of CCS development. They examined the strategies reported by children in solving problems along with their explanations. There is also evidence of later developments of a central numerical structure. Some studies suggest that, on the ground of a well-established core structure for natural numbers, students can sub- sequently construct the quantitative CCSs for rational numbers (Moss & Case, 1999) and mathematical functions (Kalchman & Case, 1998), which un- dergo—at later ages—a similar progression through four substages.

Altogether, these results confirm that a numerical CCS develops in dis- tinct substages characterized by increasing advancements in children's un- derstanding of core structural concepts. Moreover, the findings indicate that CCS development is subjected to a system-wide limitation in the sets of number lines and computations that children can keep track of simulta- neously in different substages (see the section entitled "Factors Influencing the Development of Central Conceptual Structures," in this chapter).

Central Narrative Structure: The Development of "Mental Story Line"

The approach to studying this domain, labeled "narrative structure," fol- lows a similar pattern as with the methods applied to the study of number structures just outlined. It begins with the identification of two core ele- ments on which the narrative structure is built. One is an understanding of the "scripts" or general rules governing typical sequences of events, particularly those involving social interactions, including common social scripts such as parent–child relationships. Scripts provide powerful guidelines and conventions for the way sequences of events tend to unfold. According to Nelson (1988), 3-year-old children have already learned simple scripts: they understand the way one event can follow another and, importantly, they can use language to describe familiar "scripts."

The second core element of the narrative conceptual structure is "theory of mind" acquisition, which involves understanding a set of concepts and their interrelationships concerning one's own and other people's mental states, relations between mental states and external behavior, and amongst mental states themselves. Studies show that 2- to 3-year-olds have only an initial understanding that people have a mental representation of the world. However, between the ages of 3 and 4, preschool children become capable of understanding that these mental states can be influenced by external events and vice versa (Astington, 1994; Wellman, 1990). It is only between 4 and 5 that children understand that other persons' mental representations of the world are different from their own.

The central narrative structure is characterized by the dimension of "intention." We consider the development of this dimension through each substage. It is hypothesized that most 4-year-olds can function at a substage referred to as *preintentional* (substage 0) wherein they can deal with each of the two social core concepts just mentioned (i.e., scripts and theory of mind) separately; however, as is the case with the development of the numerical mental line (i.e., predimensional), they are not able to integrate the two into one structure. At this age children seem to have knowledge of familiar scripts and mental states, but they are not able to introduce intentional states when telling an event or story. For example, in the "Storytelling" task, devised and extensively studied by McKeough (1992a, 1992b), the analysis of stories produced by preschoolers reveals an account of social situations that contain familiar "scripts." Most young children explained a particular behavior (e.g., the mother's response) by referring to a previous event in a familiar sequence (e.g., the child's misdeed) and, in addition, they made predictions about the behavior or event that would follow. This suggests the use of a sequence and the application of the concept of "what will come next." However, preschool children do not seem to be able to consider simultaneously internal states as possible causes of story events when making predictions nor when justifying a story character's actions (Case & McKeough, 1989; McKeough, 1992a).

A transition occurs between the ages of 5 and 6, when children become capable of coordinating the two original core concepts into a higher order structure. The theory proposes that 6-year-olds are able to understand that familiar human activities form a coordinated sequence of events based on two components: one external and the other internal. As noted by Case (1996a) the external component refers to the behavioral aspect of any sequence, what Bruner (1986) calls the "landscape of action." The internal component refers to the "intentional" aspect, or the "landscape of consciousness." Thus, this substage is appropriately labeled *uni-intentional* (substage 1), whereby children are capable of generating plots in which events unfold in familiar sequence and contain references to the story character's internal states, such as desires and goals.

At the *bi-intentional level* (substage 2), 8-year-olds are capable of generating story plots that contain a "chain" of two or more event sequences, with both usually stemming from a similar motive. However, the first sequence does not typically result in the attainment of the goal (i.e., resolve the problem faced by the main story character), whereas the last event sequence usually does.

Finally, at the *integrated bi-intentional level* (substage 3), 10-year-olds can create stories with plot structures, showing evidence of multiple attempts at resolving the problems faced by the story characters. However, unlike the plots at the previous substage, these story sequences show integration into "nested" series of events, resulting in a more coherent overall story (Case & McKeough, 1990; Case, Okamoto, Henderson, McKeough, & Bleiker, 1996; McKeough, 1992a).

Is There Support for the Existence of CCSs?

We turn now to the evidence for the three main features of CCSs: (a) each CCS characterizes a specific domain; (b) acquiring a CCS does not transfer to other CCSs; (c) all CCSs follow a similar developmental progression.

Do CCSs Exist and Are They Domain-Specific?

The first question, critical for Case's theory, addresses existence of domain-specific CCSs. To answer it, we need to observe whether, as predicted by the theory, performance is generalized to tasks of diverse areas, whenever the core concepts characterizing the CCS are involved. If numerical CCS is really the backbone of quantitative thought, it should be used to interpret a vast range of situations involving counting. These would include strictly physical ones, such as predicting which side of a balance beam would go down, as well as problems that are more social in nature but require a degree of numeracy, such as the fairest way to distribute a given resource. In particular, the tasks devised for the numerical CCS include not only number knowledge (see the section entitled "Developmental Progress in Building a CCS in the Domain of Number" in this chapter), but also tasks on: (a) scientific reasoning, such as the balance beam, (b) social understanding, such as a birthday party task that requires deciding who is the happier of two children given the number of gifts desired and received by each child (Marini, 1992), and (c) tasks tapping other applications of number knowledge, such as money knowledge (Case & Sandieson, 1988) and time telling (Case, Sandieson, & Dennis, 1986).

In the same vein, we need to see whether these predictions are confirmed, not only for development of numerical CCS but also for that of the central narrative structure. The tasks involving the central narrative structure, for example, include story telling (McKeough, 1992a), as well as other tasks, among which are: (a) empathic cognition (Bruchkowsky, 1992); (b) explaining simple (happy) and complex (e.g., embarrassed) feelings (Griffin, 1992); and (c) understanding the mother's role and motives (Goldberg-Reitman, 1992).

The idea of a CCS representing a rich network of domain specific concepts is supported by studies addressing the question in several ways. One involves studying whether it is possible to teach the CCS for number, typically mastered by 5- to 6-year-olds, to children of that age who have not yet acquired its core concepts spontaneously? As predicted, children trained in the core components do improve on problems presented in training and also solve various new quantitative problems (Griffin et al., 1994). Would the same outcome be obtained for any number training? Griffin and Case (1996) found that children taught all the core concepts of the numerical CCS identified by the theory exhibited more within-domain transfer than a control group administered a traditional teaching program relating only to some mathematical concepts.

Within domain generalization is also found in the CCS underlying social thought. Porath (2003) showed that 4- and 5-year-olds' understanding of the teacher's role and intentions (assessed with a task similar to Goldberg-Reitman's study on understanding the mother) was highly predictive of their ability to conceptualize their activities and social relations in the classroom.

Does the CCS underlying quantitative thought tap different core elements from those tapped by the CCS for social thinking? Case et al. (1996) presented two sets of numerical and narrative tasks to a sample of 6-year-olds, a critical age for constructing unidimensional and uni-intentional CCSs. A factor analysis showed that two factors were present, one involving all quantitative tasks and the other all the narrative tasks, a result favoring the existence of distinct CCSs.

After observing within domain generalization, a critical way to support the notion of domain related CCSs is to look at whether there is a limit in generalization of CCS. Case's theory, indeed, allows transfer within tasks involving a CCS but not across CCSs, and Case et al. (1993) compared a group trained on core concepts pertaining to a numerical CCS with a group trained on narrative CCS concepts. Children in each training group showed transfer only within the trained CCS and did not generalize the higher level of ability reached in one domain to the other one. This lack of transfer across CCSs speaks in favor of the specific nature of CCSs, as predicted by Case's theory.

Finally, another way to support CCS specificity is to look at children who present a particular talent in some area. One can ask whether their excellence compared to their peers is limited to the domain of their talent or whether they exhibit a generalized higher intellectual performance. Porath (1992) examined children talented in either narrative or spatial ability and found that their performance was superior to that of their nontalented peers (and similar to that of adults) only in the specific area of talent. This leads Case to infer existence of CCSs in which acquisitions are best described as specific conceptual structures that present themselves as distinct and coherent entities.

Do All CCSs Follow a Similar Sequence of Development?

A further important issue is whether development of different CCSs proceeds in parallel. Case et al. (1996; see also Okamoto & Case, 1996) studied 4- to 10-year-olds' rate of progress within and between numerical and narrative CCSs on two sets of tasks. Tasks were formulated in such a way as to test the increasingly higher level of difficulties predicted by Case's theory for the dimensional stage. The results revealed age-related advancements in solving higher level problems within each CCS. The mean scores for the two CCSs did not differ and, in addition, a high correlation between the two batteries of tasks confirmed the same developmental course for both CCSs. This finding is further strengthened when looking at individual children's performance on tasks of the two CCSs, showing high synchrony at each age in the two batteries, with the few differences limited to one substage level. A greater difference was found with 10-year-olds, but again, a difference of 1.5 levels was very rare.

Most of the studies we have presented in support of the validity of the CCS construct have involved children in the dimensional stage, whereas other stages were studied to a lesser extent. Would the hypothesized sequence in substages also be found with adolescents? Some studies have examined the developmental progression in the vectorial or abstract stage of a quantitative thought structure and/or of the narrative structure (Kalchman & Case, 1998; Marini & Case, 1994; McKeough & Genereux, 2003). For example, Marini and Case (1994) assessed development of quantitative and social understanding from 10 to 18 years, administering problems on quantitative reasoning (balance beam) and a personality diagnosis task (use personality traits to predict a story character's decision in a dilemma context). The results indicated that development follows the predicted sequence in parallel fashion in both types of tasks for the majority of subjects, as revealed by mean scores and by a high correlation between performances in the two CCSs tasks. This supports the idea that there is a capacity that permits the construction of abstract thought structures applicable to different domains; such a capacity constrains the progress within a series of substages. About one third of the subjects showed a difference of one substage, indicating that, although the progression of a child's structures can be diversified in different domains, nonetheless the pattern of growth is fairly consistent, providing solid support for the type of structures predicted by Case's theory. As Case (1998) noted, it seems that the differences are due to the influence of knowledge, and are more pronounced at older ages (see the following section).

PROCESSES OF CHANGE IN CCS DEVELOPMENT AND RELATIONSHIP WITH ECS

Case considers the processes of CCS change, and reflects further on the role of ECSs on development of Conceptual Structures. He noticed that the CCS needed to solve all problems in a domain is the same in that it includes the same set of concepts (as also indicated by the loading on a single factor), whereas the formation of an ECS is tailored to the specific problem pertaining to a CCS domain. This has two consequences: on the one hand it means that construction of ECSs is critical for the application of a conceptual structure to the vast range of specific problems it covers. "For every conceptual structure that children develop at any age, I believe that they must develop a whole family of executive control structures, if they are to deal with the full range of tasks for which their central conceptual structure is relevant" (Case, 1996c, p. 201). In some cases a conceptual advancement "serves as a sort of invitation" (Case, 1996c, p. 203) to the construction of new control structures, whereas in other cases, availability of a control structure may precede conceptualization of a problem (an issue also discussed by Fischer, although in different terms; see chap. 5). On the other hand, it also means that the general model of development (see Fig. 6.1) does not need to be changed to include the conceptual aspect.

What are the processes that account for CCS transition? How can new content be acquired and existing schemes linked, reorganized, and represented with a new symbol system and applied to new tasks? Case extends the processes of consolidation, integration and differentiation to deal with conceptual change; these are the same processes he introduced to explain changes in development of Executive Control Structures. Borrowing from Pascual-Leone, Case (1996a, 1998) assumes that two types of learning take place in CCS acquisition. These two are C-learning and M-learning, which involve associative and attention-mediated operators, respectively. For example, when playing a dice game, an *association* can be created between a highly activated scheme ("a lot") and a weak element (for example, the perceptual configuration of 6 dots). After encountering various situations of this type, this association is eventually differentiated from others (for example, five dots). Moreover, when two existing schemes are both highly activated, integration will occur (for example, the word "six" can be added to the perceptual configuration of 6 dots).

M-learning involves awareness in attending to two existing schematic elements: when both are highly activated and attended to, a new connection is rapidly created that can be consciously applied to many other contexts. Associative and attentional processes activate each other in an *"iterative feedback loop."* By strengthening existing associations, more attention is freed up and can be devoted to M-learning; in turn, by expanding attention and creating new connections, associative learning is more likely to take place. According to Case, this "sort of iterative loop is likely to be present in all children's learning, whether or not it is conceptual, and whether or not it is central" (Case, 1996a, p. 20).

Based on iterative loops, the most important mechanism concerning these two types of learning is the hierarchical integration of central conceptual structures. It involves a second feedback loop in the development of central conceptual structures, called the *hierarchical feedback loop*. It is a level of processing added to the higher system and receiving input from a lower order system, that is, from the existing schemes. It is in line with Piaget's "reflective abstraction," corresponding to a new level added to the hypercognitive system (from Demetriou et al., 1996) or a new level of hidden units (borrowing from connectionism; Case, 1998). As Case points out, specific and general understandings feed each other in an iterative way, enabling development of conceptual structures. Local changes in task specific (associative) understandings foster a small change in conceptual understanding of a more general sort permitting abstraction of the structures from many lower level tasks and their integration in a higher conceptual unit. This new general level is used to deal with a broad range of specific contexts, that fact permits an increase in specific knowledge that, in turn, through further differentiation and integration, allows a more advanced general structure.

This leads to the proposal that the hierarchical feedback loop has two effects: an averaging effect on level of performance, counteracting the specific task variability, and acceleration of development (bootstrapping) toward its limit. Thus, higher levels of conceptual structures tend to show the same rate of development across different tasks (Fischer used the notion of "attractor"): "although the content that they serve to organize is modular, the structures themselves reflect a set of principles and constraints that are system-wide in their nature and change with age in a predictable fashion. They thus possess certain general commonalities that transcend the specific domain to which they apply" (Case, 1996a, p. 5). It is the hierarchical feedback loop that has the "standardizing influence ... across different tasks" because it "connects specific and general understanding" (Case, 1996b, p. 159) resulting from change processes that are context specific (associative) and conscious processes that are more general.

These processes are a function of the growth of neurological modules and rely on a specific neurological substrate, depending on the contents of a CCS (visual number form, number words, analogical representation of number magnitude, etc.). They could be based on maturation of frontal lobes, connections between frontal and posterior lobes, connections in posterior lobes and hemispheric differentiation (Dehaene & Cohen, 1994; for further details see Case, 1998). They are also a function of experiential factors, such as, exposure to counting, different salience acquired by elements not present in the existing routine, and mastering routines to the point that they do not require attentional resources (Case, 1998), as illustrated in the following section.

FACTORS INFLUENCING THE DEVELOPMENT OF CENTRAL CONCEPTUAL STRUCTURES

A search for factors that may influence the developmental progression has led to the consideration of more biologically based explanations, including general maturational factors and specific neurological changes as well as other factors that are more dependent on socializing processes such as the effects of educational experiences. Thus, we now turn to the role of maturation and of experience in CCS acquisition.

Role of WM on Central Conceptual Structures

We have already discussed the relation between WM size and growth of Executive Control Structures, showing that ECSs increase in complexity as WM increases. With the introduction of Central Conceptual Structures, Case also addresses the question of a causal relationship between WM and CCS. We have noted that WM increase is related to cortical developments located mainly in the frontal lobes and their connections with posterior lobes. An increased "connectedness" in the fibers between frontal and posterior lobes is thought to be related to conceptual developments.

This idea suggests that WM size may set a limit on CCS development. Before jumping to this conclusion, however, one should rule out the possibility that CCS is responsible for WM increase, that is, exclude the possibility that an improved conceptual structure yields a higher operational speed and counting span. To test this possibility, 5- and 6-year-olds who had not yet spontaneously acquired a conceptual structure for numbers were given specific training. The only children able to profit from the training were those whose WM size for numbers was that predicted by Case's theory for a numerical CCS. This result suggests that WM sets a limit to learning; and, in addition, after the training those children showed a superior conceptual understanding of number than a control group. However, the treatment children did not perform better than the control group on the counting speed and counting span tests (Case, 1995). Overall, the results suggest that WM size sets a maturational constraint on CCS and confirm that an increase in working memory does not take place as a by-product of knowledge acquisition and conceptual learning.

Role of Experience in Development of CCS

System-wide constraints undoubtedly play a role in CCS development; however, specific schemes require practice and experience to develop. Case maintains that CCSs are cultural products (in Vygotskian terms): from early age task performance is influenced by local factors such as the particular context of the problems, the frequency with which problems are encountered and social models provided to solve them. Moreover, specific factors relate to the child's socioemotional and motivational states, especially mastery motivation to reach goals relating to external experience.

The sources of variability are multifaceted, and Case proposes that although they affect local performances, they do not affect the rate of conceptual structure development. A "preferred developmental pathway" is proposed "for a large class of individuals" (Case, 1996c, p. 211). Four considerations are in order:

a) Any culture offers a very broad range of opportunities, although sometimes different ones, to construct basic core concepts such as numeracy and intention;

b) Intra- and interindividual differences are often encountered. They regard performance in specific tasks or even in a conceptual structure, as in talented children (Porath, 1992). Differences are explained by the fact that "each conceptual structure has its own content, its own type of operation, and its own developmental trajectory" (Case, 1996c, p. 211). However, in normal children, differences may not be so large as to affect the overall rate of intellectual growth.

c) Children's natural curiosity to explore the environment makes it possible to develop CCS at a similar rate;

d) No matter how much experience is offered on a particular CCS content, WM sets a limit to the level of development.

Exploration in this direction comes with cross-cultural studies conducted by Case and collaborators (Okamoto, Case, Bleiker, & Henderson, 1996). For example, on numerical CCS development, Japanese children (6 to 10 years) compared to U.S. children, showed higher scores only with the 6-year-olds on a number knowledge test, mainly on items relating to the base-ten principle. This difference could be attributed either to extra training on basic mathematics in their family or to a linguistic difference in number words that makes it easier to understand the principle. However, Japanese children's performance on other quantitative tasks, such as the balance beam problem, did not differ from their U.S. peers. This result indicates that understanding a specific core element does not transfer to a more general numerical conceptual understanding, meaning that both Japanese and U.S. daily life experience and schooling offer many, although different, contexts for building the numerical CCS. Although performance of young Japanese children is higher on some tests, their level of numerical development does not push beyond the age-related limits set by working memory.

These conclusions are confirmed by other cross-cultural studies dealing with a CCS underlying space cognition (Okamoto et al., 1996). For example, although Chinese children who receive direct training on drawing a human figure do draw more complex figures compared to Canadian children, they do not construct a higher level spatial structure. The skills observed on the spatial layout of their drawings are equivalent to those of their Canadian peers.

Overall, different types of specific experience may lead to the same general level of development and a similar pattern of performance across several tasks (Case, 1996b). This is also the case for children with high and low SES, the former being highly exposed to many task situations whereas the latter are provided with low exposure. Although low-SES children exhibit a lower performance than the high-SES group, their working memory size does not vary and they show the same developmental profile. This even profile across tasks for which they may face different experience opportunities favors Case's idea of a general process involving a hierarchical feedback loop that poses a reciprocal influence between general and specific processes. Through such a process, "the profile of development is evened out because benefits obtained from high-frequency learning experiences are passed on via the mediation of the central conceptual structures, to low-frequency ones" (Case, 1996b, p. 186). As just mentioned, these processes have an "averaging" effect.

Educational experiences, thus, promote the development of children's central conceptual structures but within the limits set by neurological maturation and working memory capacity. Educational experiences must work within the range of processes enabling and controlling development of executive control and central conceptual structures (Case & Okamoto, 1996; Griffin, Case, & Capodilupo, 1995).

CONCLUSION

Robbie Case, like many neo-Piagetians, resisted the temptation to throw the proverbial baby (i.e., Piagetian theory) out with the bath water and created a synthesis of the Piagetian view and more current paradigms such as information processing. These theoretical and empirical efforts can be detected in the evolution of Case's theory. From the earlier work, which culminated in the book published in 1985, Case outlined a theory of development characterized by the four major stages with a cyclical pattern of substages, a heavy emphasis on detailing the executive control structures, and a WM model in which operational efficiency was thought to influence short-term storage space.

However, Case's theorizing continued to evolve, and the shift begun in the late 1980s (see Case & Sandieson, 1988) was documented in his 1992 book. This book, *The Mind's Staircase*, can be regarded as the first major presentation of the second version of his theory, and it saw the introduction of the notion of central conceptual structures. The shift continued and refinement of the theory was documented in an SRCD Monograph (Case & Okamoto, 1996) and again in another major chapter (Case, 1998). In these and subsequent publications, Case and his colleagues presented empirical evidence regarding the structural and processing elements of the theory, including a solidification of the construct of central conceptual structures.

One of the reasons for the shift was the realization (shared by a number of neo-Piagetian theorists) that children's thinking is far more variable than Piaget had suggested (Case & Edelstein, 1993). To address such variability, Case proposed that children do not develop a single system of logical operations; rather, they develop conceptual structures that influence thinking capabilities within a particular domain, such as number, narrative and space.

Thus, although conceptual development is domain specific, according to Case it can still be characterized as a series of stages (e.g., Case, 1985, 1998). He further proposed that working memory capacity, which is governed by biological maturation, restricts children's ability to acquire complex thinking and reasoning skills, both at the level of executive control structures and of central conceptual structures. In this way, Case places system-wide "upper limits" on what children can accomplish at any particular stage in any CCS domain (Case & Okamoto, 1996; Fischer & Bidell, 1991). Thus, given the role attributable to practice and experience, Case can present his theory as a possible bridge between general and specific constraints on development.

Any theoretical framework is a work in progress, and Case's theory is no exception. Although theories attempt to answer questions, invariably, as some questions are answered, new ones are generated. As we have seen in the chapter, Case's theory provides many answers, but many questions are still open for debate (see Keating, 1996; Siegler, 1996a). Some of these are more critical than others, and in this final section we outline some that call for further research.

A first question concerns the role of working memory. Overall, extensive research has left in place the notion that WM growth strongly influences the development of children's thinking (Case, 1992c, 1995, 1998; Case & Okamoto, 1996) and that it does so because it constrains the complexity of both the executive control structures and conceptual structures that children can acquire. Numerous studies (for example, Case, 1995; de Ribaupierre & Bailleux, 1995; Morra, 1994; Pascual-Leone & Baillargeon, 1994) indicate that during childhood different tests provide converging estimates of mental capacity. Notwithstanding the major role of maturation, individual children could, for various reasons, underperform on working memory measures with respect to their maturational potential and benefit from training and practice. However, their performance will asymptote at their maturational level and not improve with further practice. There seems to be a relationship between capacity and processing speed (Case et al., 1982; Halford, 1993b; Hitch, Halliday, & Littler, 1989), but the precise nature of this relationship is not yet fully clear. Although some studies suggest that both speed and capacity could have a maturational development, recent models (Barrouillet et al., 2004) suggest that speed constraints are involved in complex WM span measures. Although a stronger version of a trade-off between speed and span had to be discarded, it seems unlikely that speed and capacity develop in a completely independent way; and further research seems necessary to clarify their link.

The second question has to do with the inter- and intraindividual variability encountered in most experiments. We have just discussed differences in performance on CCS tasks for a variety of children and situations, though these differences were limited for the most part to a single substage (Case, Okamoto et al., 1996; Marini & Case, 1994). Why are there differences in the level of performance in tasks within a domain and between domains? Why are differences generally more pronounced in older subjects? Answers should consider the interplay between experience, physiological factors, and WM size. The fact that control structures in each stage are proposed as specific to each domain (rather than independent of the domain as with Piaget's logical structures) may account for individual differences. If these can be partly explained by operational efficiency, then two types of factors are called into play. One is variation in the degree of the individual's experience and of social support available. The other type points to maturational variation on which working memory and, consequently, learning of specific domain CCSs are based. Both sources are important: this is why Case generally found that although culture has an influence on the content, it very rarely does so on the structure of CCSs. As already noted by Bruner (1986), culture is understood as the legacy of generations that ensures the transmission of values and tools necessary to face any sort of problem; however, development of conceptual structures resides in other factors that are more stable. This is confirmed by the fact that the form and complexity of the structures are similar in different domains, as also shown, for example, by the even developmental profile of low-SES children just mentioned. Schooling is one culturally based tool; but, although embedded in different contents, at early grades schools tend to propose similar core concepts. With these considerations in mind, Case's assumption is that with age, factors like experience, knowledge, and formal schooling are destined to play a larger role (Okamoto et al., 1996).

Related concerns in need of further research are which components of cognitive development are subject to general limits, which are biological in origin, and which components can overcome those limits. For example, Porath's (1992) study examining talented children showed that although they perform at exceptionally high levels on such measures as graphic competence and attributes of language form, on measures of structural organization (in narratives and in spatial layouts) there was less difference. This disparity was accounted for by introducing the idea that measures of the second type, but not of the first, are subject to central limits of WM. Given the relevance of this issue for the theory, it would be useful to make this theoretical distinction more precise in order to give the base of such disparity and to provide a tool that establishes *a priori* which aspects of cognitive development can produce asynchronies of this type.

The third crucial question for a theory of development pertains to the transition between substages and from one stage to another, the latter signaling the strongest change in CCS development. Three processes, consolidation, differentiation and integration, are proposed to explain progression in types of strategies within a domain; and an additional process of hierarchical integration is proposed to account for stage transition. What is the nature of hierarchical integration? In his later writings Case introduces two mechanisms, iterative feedback loop and hierarchical learning loop, to further elaborate both on the slow changes taking place within a stage and on the rapid changes occurring at a stage transition. His novel idea was to explain change as an iterative feedback passing from specific to general structural levels. Some aspects relating to the functioning of these mechanisms and to the reciprocal influence of specific and general understanding need further clarification. As it provides a possible solution to many otherwise problematic concerns, the proposal is appealing; but it still needs empirical support, for example, through online microgenetic observation of problem solving processes related to aspects of CCS acquisition.

A fourth question concerns how domains are defined and the tasks used to measure them. There is a need to be more precise about the contents of Central Conceptual Structures as a means of better characterizing and delineating them. It is often the case that the problems presented to participants, even though they belong to a given domain (for example, numerical), are contextualized in another area (for example, social), so that their understanding may call for extra knowledge from a different domain. A clearer and more theoretically driven task analysis would permit us to take that knowledge into account when preparing tasks to be used in the evaluation of the developmental progression in a given domain.

Notwithstanding the questions outlined, Case's theory makes a significant contribution to the continuing search for the structures and mechanisms of children's development. We have seen that there is strong support for the idea that development proceeds within specific domains in a stagewise progression and is subject to limits imposed by system-wide constraints that influence general processing capacity. This intermediate position seems to function as a bridge between developmental generality and developmental specificity, a position that is able to explain research data for which other hypotheses, considered individually, do not have the same explanatory power.

7

Cognitive Development
as Change in Representations

This chapter considers representation and representational change as a manifestation and as a potential account of qualitative changes in cognitive development. The issue of representation, generally understood as internal structures and symbols corresponding to aspects of the external world, has already been considered in previous chapters. For instance, the concept of scheme has a major role in the theories of Pascual-Leone and Case. Central Conceptual Structures are also theorized by Case. The distinction between analogical and propositional representations is crucial to the work of Lautrey and colleagues, and Specialized Structural Systems are a basic concept in Demetriou's theory. Siegler's rules and Fischer's skills are largely based on mental representations of a problem situation. Recent developments in Halford's theory have redefined representations and their degree of complexity in a connectionist framework.

Some theories assign a central role to mental representations in explaining the qualitative changes in the cognitive developmental progression. This is the case of some critics of Piaget; for example, consider Bruner's earlier work, discussed in the introduction, or Carey's (1987, 1991, 2000) view of changes in children's "theories" in different domains, whereby a child's previously endorsed theory in a domain is regarded as incommensurable with the new theory that replaces it.

The concept of representation, however, is also crucial for some neo-Piagetian theories, particularly in accounting for the transition from one major stage to the next. In Halford's theory, for instance, increased capacity enables the child to form representations of increased dimensionality; thus, increasing processing capacity and representational change are jointly in-volved in the main qualitative leaps of cognitive development. Also in Case's theory a capacity increase through substages enables the child to form, during the last substage of a stage, a new type of representation that is the base for the next stage. Is it possible to give representations an even more crucial role, without departing too much from Piagetian spirit?

The issue of qualitative changes resulting in major stages also raises a central question, namely whether it possible to appreciate and compre-hend qualitative stage differences without understanding fully the gradual changes that precede the establishment of a new stage.

This chapter focuses especially on Mounoud's theory and some aspects of Karmiloff-Smith's work. We acknowledge that Karmiloff-Smith would not describe herself as a neo-Piagetian, but we consider her research here not only because of her Genevan formation and the importance of her work, but especially because her epistemological and metatheoretical views lead us to consider her, if not a full-fledged neo-Piagetian, at least a very close relative. These two theoretical frameworks are important because they (a) illustrate that qualitative change can be part of a view of development that may be either general or domain-specific, (b) shed light on the possible mechanisms of structural change while claiming the existence of some forms of innate abilities, and (c) show that, in the course of development, children construct types of representation that, under some conditions, cause their performance to regress. A section of the chapter is also devoted to other theoretical orientations in which knowledge and its representation is considered a key to understanding development.

GENERAL CHANGES IN REPRESENTATION: MOUNOUD'S QUALITATIVE DEVELOPMENTAL PROGRESSION

According to Mounoud (see Mounoud, 1990a, 1993, 1996), the role of repre-sentation, understood as an internal organization of contents, is established in early infancy. From birth (on this issue Mounoud does not agree with Piaget) the child possesses a rudimentary form of representation that is pre-formed, the product of evolutionary adaptation. Thus, in certain situations, the child is capable of responding with behaviors organized in stimulus pat-terns. This form of early organization of stimuli is subsequently reorganized in a slow process that leads children to plan in a new way their actions in the environment. Before illustrating the succession of phases and stages of de-velopment, it is relevant to outline the basic concepts of the theory.

For Mounoud, development is accounted for by two hierarchical organi-zations, the first is a "structural organization" that centrally directs coordination of action and activation of representational codes characterizing developmental stages. It permits elaboration of analogical and propositional representations. The second is "functional organization," constrained by the structural one. Although structural organization is characterized by preformed, endogenous structures that are impenetrable, the functional one is characterized by open systems, penetrable to analysis, on which exchanges with the environment play a specific role. The proposal of two hierarchically organized systems accounts for both homogeneity in stagewise development (due to the predetermined constraints), and some variability (due to interchange with the environment).

General Form of Mounoud's Developmental Model

During development, there emerge four types of knowledge organization (Mounoud, 1993) or modes of representation (Mounoud, 1986), which correspond to an equivalent number of stages or levels of development, characterized by type of organization (and level of representations) namely: "Sensorimotor" (sensorial) from birth; "Perceptivomotor" (perceptual) 18–24 months; "Conceptuomotor" (conceptual) 9–11 years; and "Semioticomotor" (formal) 16–18 years. Although the first level of knowledge representation (i.e., Sensorimotor) is assumed to be preformed, subsequent levels are constructed by more advanced elaborations permitted by new codes (Mounoud, 1986; Mounoud & Vinter, 1981), also called "centers" or "structures" (Mounoud, 1993). For example, the transition between the first and second stage (i.e., from Sensorimotor to Perceptivomotor) is achieved by using new coding capacities characterized by the "perceptual" code, which permits the construction of perceptual representations. Similarly, the transition between the second and third stage (i.e., from Perceptivomotor to Conceptuomotor) is achieved by using the new "conceptual" coding capacities, which permit the construction of conceptual representations. Lastly, the transition from the third to the fourth stage (i.e., from Conceptuomotor to Semioticomotor) is achieved by using the new "semiotic" coding capacities, which permit the construction of semiotic representations. Codes, which are assumed to appear in a predetermined way with the child's maturation, are conceived as means of translation "of the different contents with which the child interacts (with objects, people, or his own body)" (Mounoud, 1986, p. 52).

Although Mounoud's early writings assumed that the child's initial knowledge was procedural and only later became declarative, starting from the 1990s, he suggests that the two systems of knowledge representation are simultaneously present in most developmental and learning processes. Further differentiation is made between constituted knowledge, which tends to be implicit and generally below the level of consciousness, and conceptual knowledge, which tends to be explicit knowledge of which the subject has awareness.

In other words, one system consists of what Mounoud calls "constituted knowledge" on which the child can rely without activating conscious procedures. This system allows access to a kind of practical knowledge. These are representations and procedures that have been consolidated to the point of being automatized and are activated directly by stimuli in the environment. The second system, instead, consists of representations in elaboration, and these in turn allow for new procedures to be established. However, this is conceptual, explicit knowledge of which the subject has awareness.

Constituted (practical) and conceptual knowledge[1] are considered to be two forms (or distinct states) of every given system of knowledge (see Mounoud, 1993). For example, at the age of 3–4, a child's behavior is determined by two systems: (a) the Perceptivomotor system, comprising the so-called constituted representations, which is activated without the child's awareness and is expressed in practical terms, and (b) the concrete system, which is in its initial phase and comprises representations in elaboration and is expressed in conceptual terms. However, both practical and conceptual representations are present at the same time at different levels of maturity and form a hierarchical relationship such that, depending on the phase of development reached by the child, one form controls and directs the other. Over the years in his effort to characterize the developmental process, Mounoud has used a number of similar terms, such as revolutionary periods (1986), phases (1988), transitions (1993), or recursive transformation (1996). He suggests that these transitions recur cyclically in development. In addition, two processes are suggested to be used in alternation. One process unpacks, decomposes, and selects components. It breaks down initial global representations and the new total representations achieved at a later phase into elementary or partial actions. Thus, it marks the shift from global representations to representations broken into elementary parts. As we see later, in Mounoud's theory this process assumes a very important role.

The second process, which is complementary to the first, leads to the sedimentation (i.e., "integration" or "consolidation") of knowledge. Knowledge becomes automatized owing to the coordination of subroutines or pieces of information in the form of larger units or "chunks." This allows the subject to consider the object as a whole, but not to analyze its parts. This transition proceeds from elementary representations to a new total representation that in turn, at the end of the learning process, will lead to establishing relationships among the parts.

---

[1]The use of these terms by Mounoud is not always constant, and this creates potential confusion regarding their meaning and applications.

Thus, the developing child passes through cyclical phases of adaptation. Behavior goes from being automatic to intentional; there is temporarily a conscious awareness, and new elaborated knowledge replaces the preceding knowledge (Mounoud, 1990, 1993, 1996). Conscious access to information is considered to be a transitory phenomenon because the knowledge subsequently becomes once again automatized and used without the child's awareness.

The two ways of considering objects—continuous with parts that can be decomposed and placed in relation to one another, or discontinuous, discrete (invariant) and capable of relationships with other objects—constitute two complementary systems. To the first system are ascribed infralogical operations, such as those used in the spatial domain. To the second system are ascribed logical operations that are elaborated, for example, in forming hierarchical classes. It is through these phases and processes that the child becomes able to consider an object in terms of the relations among its parts or as invariant and in relation to other objects, before being able to consider both intra- and interobject relationships.

Phases in Mounoud's Developmental Model

Table 7.1 outlines in some detail the sequence of phases traversed within the four stages of development according to Mounoud (1986). We illustrate the phases of Stage 2 of this model (i.e., Perceptivomotor) by means of a seminal study (Mounoud, 1970) of the development in children aged 4 to 9 of the ability to construct a tool.[2] In brief, the task is to construct from Lego pieces a tool to move a block, initially located in one of four different positions, so that it reaches the home base provided (see Fig. 7.1). In order to complete the task successfully, the form of the child's tool must be such as to avoid two partitions that create an obstacle to movement of the instrument within the apparatus.

The youngest children find themselves in the phase in which knowledge is practical (i.e., pragmatic or concrete). It enables global syncretic representation in which the stimuli are coded as organized units of information. As just indicated, this is "encapsulated" or constituted knowledge that the child is still unable to segment or unpack into its parts, and which the child uses in an automatic way.

In this phase, the instrument is considered merely as an extension of the hand. In fact, the child constructs a rectilinear segment to which he/she im-

---

[2]Regarding the initial phase, it appears that Mounoud (1993) may fall into some degree of circularity by claiming that on one hand conceptual understanding develops new elements based on cognitive systems already developed, and on the other affirming that every developed cognitive system is built on preceding conceptual forms. It is apparent from Figure 7.1 that at least in the initial phase children seem to possess representations that are global in nature.

TABLE 7.1

Phases and Transition Processes in the Elaboration of New Representations and the Ages When They Occur Cyclically

Stage 1	Stage 2	Stage 3	Steps	Process
0–1 month	1½–3 years	10–11 years	Initial global representations: Syncretic	Sampling of object and action properties: By means of new code
1–4 months	3–5 years	11–13 years	New elementary representations: Separated and juxtaposed	Coordination–integration of elementary representations: And establishment of correspondence with objects and situations
4–8 months	5–7 years	13–15 years	New total representations nondecomposable: Rigid with global relationship between them	Decomposition–analysis of new total representations in their components: And establishment of correspondence with objects dimensions
8–14 months	7–9 years	15–16 years	New total representations partly decomposable: With partial relationship between them and their components	Composition–synthesis of the components of new total representations
14–18 months	9–10 years	16–18 years	New complete representations fully decomposable: With complete relationship between them and with their components	

Note. Adapted from Mounoud (1986).

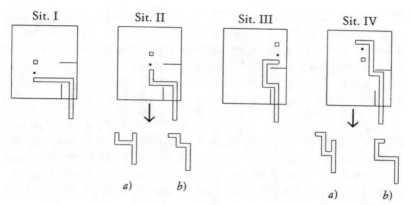

FIG. 7.1. Schematic of four situations arranged for studying the construction and use of a tool. The small black cube is to be moved onto its home base (the larger empty square) by means of a tool constructed for that purpose from Lego blocks. The lower portion of the figure gives examples of constructions that are suitable b) and unsuitable a) for situations II and IV. *Source:* Adapted from Mounoud (1996).

parts circular movements; in the face of failure, the child simply adds or removes pieces at the far end without modifying the structure. The instrument is endowed with a global property that cannot be segmented or disassembled.

The phase of global representation is followed by that of elementary representations that are permitted to emerge by the appearance of a new, more evolved code. Its activation sets off the process of conceptualization in which global representations are analyzed through a process of information selection and become partial representations. The conceptual change operates not only on the declarative representations that become elementary but also on the procedure, which becomes local and partial, directed toward the simple objectives allowed by those representations. This is a kind of conscious construction of knowledge in which the child, starting from knowledge of the object as a whole, selects only those dimensions that are useful for attainment of the goal. The properties of actions and objects are dissociated and treated as independent units of information. One by one, the individual dimensions are noted, and the object is understood differently in accordance with the dimension that stands out at the moment.

The child that makes this basic transition at first assembles a curvilinear segment, averting the obstacle, and modifies its length to adapt to the different situations. At the end of the segment the child then adds a vertical piece for the purpose of pushing the cube toward the desired position. On the basis of constituted knowledge, the child has decomposed the various salient properties (such as length and curvature) to which he or she assigns specific, distinct functions corresponding to fragmented representations of the problem. Thus, a certain length "serves to" approach the cube; the verticality of the last segment "serves to" push the cube; a certain curve "serves to" avoid the obstacle.

In turn, this system of knowledge also undergoes a fundamental change that determines a more complex behavior by the child. Such a shift occurs in phases and enables the child to reconstitute the unity of the object. The first transition allows the child to pass from a partial representation to a new global representation through a juxtaposition of individual dimensions. In this new representation, the object as a whole acquires a new meaning relative to the initial one. This is once again a whole that cannot be decomposed, but in this phase the objects that have become stable entities are considered in an autonomous way, no longer dependent on action.

The change from partial to whole representation is evident in the performance of 6-year-old children for whom the instrument is no longer fragmented into separate properties: its function acquires meaning as a totality and is no longer an emanation of their actions. However, the wholeness of the object having been restored, the children are not able to decompose its parts and, as Mounoud notes, they paradoxically correct the length of the grip to which they attribute the function of moving the object even though it is completely irrelevant in practical terms.

Finally, we come to the phase characterized by whole representations with decomposition and relationships among the parts. Unlike the phase in which constituted knowledge led to a fragmentary analysis with the construction of isolated, local representations, the decomposition of the parts is now carried out without overlooking the object as a whole. Through processes of decomposition, coordination and integration, the child, after 7 years of age, starts to elaborate dimensions simultaneously and reciprocal relations are established among the dimensions (at first only in part, and then in a complete way). The object as whole is placed in relation to other objects and to the actions of the subject, and the units of information are now elaborated simultaneously (Mounoud, 1993, 1996). Thus the child maintains a unified concept of the instrument and at the same time places it in relation to various parts while keeping in mind the properties in relation to the context of the situation. Each part performs a precise function but in relation to and in interdependence with the other parts. For this reason the child now constructs the instrument, anticipating the functions of the various parts, and understands that the same problems can be solved by using instruments that have different configurations because what matters is that, each time, specific relations among the parts are respected.

Mounoud (1993) specifies that cyclically in each stage the child elaborates the object in infralogical and logical ways, in parallel. For instance, at age 6, the child shows, in different situations, the ability to consider the relations between the parts of an object (considered as a continuum) or the relations between the objects (considered as discrete), but uses separate processes or representations to achieve those results. That is, the child is unable to integrate and coordinate infralogical, analogical representations and propositional ones, and has a difficulty (which persists beyond 10 years of age, and occasionally into adulthood) with tasks in which simultaneous infralogical and logical processing is demanded. For instance, a correct classification requires that relations between classes of the same level and classes at different hierarchical levels are simultaneously considered. Mounoud suggests that difficulties in classification tasks may arise because they are performed by means of infralogical processes, in which the superordinate class is considered as a continuous object composed of parts. This enables one to perform tasks that bear on collective classes easily, but it is a source of errors in class inclusion problems.

To summarize, we have seen that new learning and development come from previously sedimented (consolidated or integrated) knowledge and emerge as a product of the elaboration of units of information selected on the basis of the characteristics and constraints encountered in the situation. In turn, this new knowledge being elaborated becomes stabilized and forms the basis on which new elaborations are constructed. These transitions are cyclical and recursive in nature (Mounoud, 1995, 1996) in the sense that, in each of the various stages of development, the child follows these same steps in learning.

Empirical Support for the Model

Mounoud and his colleagues have conducted a number of studies to examine how the model applies to different stages of development and to different contents. For instance, Mounoud and Vinter (1985) examine 3- to 11-year-old children's recognition of their own reflection in the mirror. At first, the mirror has either a concave or convex surface that can be changed by turning a handle so that the degree of distortion varies. The researcher controls the distortions presented to the children 3–6 years of age, whereas the older children turn the handle themselves. Their task is to indicate whether or not the image produced corresponds to the real image.

The 3-year-olds accept a lower degree of distortion than children of 4–5 years of age. The model accounts for this by proposing that at the age of 3 children have a global, relatively undifferentiated image of themselves. At 4–5 years children, instead, choose a wider range of images; in other words they seem to accept "multiple identities." At this age they develop representations with elementary properties based on isolated, uncoordinated facial features, rather than unified holistic representations.

At age 6, as at age 3, children accept a lower degree of distortion of their image than do 4- to 5-year-olds but, unlike the 3-year-olds, they are more consistent in their selections. They have constructed a new global image of themselves, a "unique" image whose various properties are unified; now the image that the children have of themselves is stable. Between the ages of 7 and 9, children show consistency in the selection of their self-image. However, there is a regression in their performance in that this image is more distorted than for 6-year-olds (even though it is less than at the age of 4–5), at least when the mirror is concave. The self-image stabilizes on the basis of one characteristic, with a preference for a wide face. This selection indicates that the different properties of the face reproduced by the curves of the mirror are placed in relation to one another, and the different images are grouped into a single category. They have a "typical" image of themselves, which is a product of the capacity to decompose the totality and place the parts in relation to the whole.

An example of how similar phases are also found in other periods of development is provided by analysis of children's initial language production (Mounoud, 1988). In the phase that precedes the utterance of a word endowed with referential meaning, the child develops elementary segments operating at the level of isolated syllables, which are produced, then duplicated and juxtaposed. These units become increasingly complex at 9 months and culminate in the phase where the child integrates these segments to produce entire words, though imperfectly at first. However, a regression occurs in this phase in that the child is no longer able to make phonetic distinctions that, as shown by Jusczyk (1985), were possible at 2 months. This supports the idea that the word has become a nondecomposable whole for the child. In subsequent phases, the child initially succeeds in segmenting the word into syllables, which are then placed in relation to one another and later segmented into more abstract phonetic units. Thus, the child succeeds in adding or substituting phonemes and can use morphological markers for gender, number, and so on (Dromi, 1986). Now the child is once more able to distinguish phonetic segments, but some phonetic contrasts are lost.

Other interesting research has been conducted on sensorimotor development (Mounoud & Hauert, 1982), focusing on the behavior of grasping an object and the action programs activated when the weight of the objects presented varies; in this study, phases that can be explained by the model have been identified.

Badan, Hauert, and Mounoud (2000) investigate children's and adults' behavior in a speeded sequential pointing task, in which participants are required to touch a series of small rings. The demands and the difficulty of the task are varied in four experiments by manipulating the number and size of the targets and the distances between them. Some discontinuities are found in the motor planning strategies prevalent at different ages. The most interesting point is that 6-year-olds were not planning more than one motor action at a time in advance, an outcome consistent with the theoretical view that children between five and seven tend to encode elementary components and inflexible relations among them. Consistent with the idea of a composition or synthesis of components, 7-year-olds, instead, planned their movements toward at least two targets. They only did so, however, when the task was rather easy, that is, with large and regularly spaced targets. Only from the age of eight did the ability to plan more than one movement in advance become stabilized. Some other qualitative change in planning strategy seems to occur between 10 years and adulthood, but the results of Badan et al. (2000) do not clarify the nature of this later change.

It seems that during certain developmental periods of transition (i.e., in this research, at age seven) a number of strategies are available and the context (for instance, the task difficulty) affects strategy selection. This line of thinking is reminiscent of Siegler's (2004) wave theory that proposes a similar argument to illustrate why children's strategy selection is not uniform (Siegler & Jenkins, 1989).

SPECIFIC CHANGES IN KNOWLEDGE REPRESENTATION IN A. KARMILOFF-SMITH

One can divide Karmiloff-Smith's research career into three phases; during a first period she worked within a Piagetian framework, then in the 1980s and early 1990s she worked out an autonomous theory of representation development, and more recently she has become one of the main proponents of neuroconstructivism. This section focuses mainly on her second period, which is the most relevant to the current discourse on representations. The next section is devoted to her more recent work that is also relevant, not only to representational change, but also to the broader theme of this book and the dialogue between neo-Piagetian and other approaches to cognitive developmental theory.

Unlike Mounoud, who proposes that developmental change occurs in general stages, Karmiloff-Smith (1991, 1993) maintains that development occurs within specific domains. However, as does Mounoud, Karmiloff-Smith intends to reconcile the innate knowledge hypothesis, according to which development occurs like an unfolding of structures of pre-existing knowledge at birth, and the constructivist position. She proposes that: "Nature specifies initial biases or predispositions that channel attention to relevant environmental inputs, which in turn affect subsequent brain development" (Karmiloff-Smith, 1992, p. 5). In the following section, we outline how Karmiloff-Smith (1991, 1992, 1993), through a model based on representational redescriptions, is able to reconcile, for the most part, these positions that at first may appear incompatible with the Piagetian approach of studying development.

A key assumption of Karmiloff-Smith's early model is the notion of the child as "spontaneous theoretician" (Karmiloff-Smith, 1988) for whom, in the course of development, specific representations undergo a transformation from implicit to explicit. This process, which is a most critical feature of the theory and is called "representational redescription," is endogenous and occurs spontaneously, but it is influenced by complex interactions with the environment. In other words, development is a process whereby the child's mind grows in ability to make representations of representations—an idea reminiscent of Piaget's "reflective abstraction," but elaborated in a more explicit way. This process can be found in all domains of knowledge, but it is not a general-domain process; on the contrary, it takes place in each specific domain (or, rather, microdomain; for instance, acquisition of personal pronouns is a microdomain within language). According to Karmiloff-Smith, initial knowledge of a microdomain tends to be procedural in nature, is not easily modified, and is not available to conscious evaluation. By going beyond this level of representation through the process of representational redescription, certain aspects of knowledge become available to other parts of the cognitive system. This process takes place several times during development and also takes place during adulthood, when one learns a new skill.

As we see, in the representational redescription (RR) model, the phase in which knowledge is automatized and inaccessible is the starting point for subsequent redescriptions of knowledge that allow passage from one form of knowledge "in the mind" to another form of knowledge "for the mind," with the possibility that knowledge formed in one part of the system is transmitted to other parts where it may be available and utilized.

From Procedural Knowledge to the Construction of Theories: The RR Model

We can now outline the changes in the organization of knowledge that occur in the course of different acquisitions as illustrated in the model of representational redescriptions (see Karmiloff-Smith, 1991, 1992).

According to this model, there is a shift in knowledge representation from implicit (I) to explicit (E). This shift involves a number of levels, beginning at the implicit level and progressing through increasingly more complex explicit levels (E1, E2, and E3). Although the implicit level is assumed to occur outside the field of awareness and is thus unavailable to other cognitive systems, the three explicit levels are available to consciousness and to other cognitive systems, and thus involve representational redescriptions.[3] As we see, the child passes from knowing "how to" do something, which produces stable but inflexible behaviors that do not permit understanding how the action is done, to the final stage of the process, which allows flexible and creative behaviors. In moving through the different phases, the typical procedural level of knowing "how to" never disappears and, depending on the problem to be solved, can be accessed without other reflections within the rapid, automatized procedures.

To illustrate the sequence of phases we refer to an earlier study conducted in 1974–1975 with Inhelder and discussed in some detail in an initial outline of the theory (Karmiloff-Smith, 1984). The study investigated the ability of children aged from 4 years and 6 months to 9 years and 5 months to balance blocks on a thin beam; the center of gravity of some blocks coincided with the geometric center of the beam, whereas in others (despite apparent similarity) the two centers did not match up because on one side of the blocks heavy material was added, which may or may not have been visible.

Level I (Implicit). Knowledge that starts from an innate base is the product of endogenous processes and acquisition resulting from interaction with the environment. The child focuses on external sources of information and the representations are not integrated in a consistent manner. Procedures activated and guided by this type of data are accessible as a global entity (because they are nondecomposable units). We cannot speak of theoretical knowledge but of knowledge "in the mind" of the implicit type. With practice, the procedures become automatized and the performances more and more efficient to the point of mastery of one's responses to the environment (behavioral mastery).

In regards to research on balancing blocks, in this phase the children pick up each block with their hands and place them on the beam and, using proprioceptive (perceptual) feedback, they find a point at which the blocks are in balance. Success is related directly to their action and each block is a problem to be solved, so much so that what is learned from handling one block is not applied to other similar ones.

Level E-I (Explicit I). Having attained behavioral mastery, the child becomes capable of redescribing the implicit knowledge in procedures of a different kind, manipulating and placing in relation to one another the various representations of the preceding level. Through a process of recognition of patterns, the child eliminates the details of single units of information in an effort to simplify and control the components of the problem,

---

[3]It is worth noting that the three explicit levels (E1, E2, and E3) correspond to phases that previously Karmiloff-Smith (1984) called procedural, metaprocedural and conceptual.

which can no longer be solved by means of isolated bottom-up procedures. The sources of information are the child's internal representations. The child now focuses on these rather than on information from external sources. In fact the child imposes on the input from the environment his own internal representation and, in so doing, may ignore some characteristics and properties. This is "theory in action" that, through analogical procedures, applies to a vast array of problems whose similarities the child has noted (see chap. 4). The child is not as interested in the result as much as in understanding the effect of the use of a given procedure.

Because they are directed by the child's internal organization, performances are even less flexible, do not take into account negative feedback, and show little propensity for self-correction. Thus, the performances are sometimes inferior to those at the preceding phase. However, if we think of the child as a "theoretician," this level of representation constitutes a step forward in that the child is capable of distinguishing between representations that are faithful to reality and those that are not. The child can take into account that what is in mind at a given moment may not correspond to reality.

In the task of balancing the blocks on a beam, the child constructs a theory of which he or she is not necessarily aware and according to which the balancing point coincides with the geometric center. The child applies the theory to all the blocks, even to those to which a weight not visible on the exterior has been added. Thus, the theory directs the behavior of the child, who is not aware of negative feedback, there are failures that do not occur in younger children. This inflexibility is expressed as an incapacity to make use of the informational value of counterexamples or anomalous data. Such children criticize their own procedures, rather than the theory on which they rely, and discard "impossible" blocks.

Levels E-2; E-3 (Explicit 2–3). At these two levels, the child has conscious access to part of the knowledge, which becomes the "object of thought." The child reacquires the capacity to control the feedback from the environment by using processes that mediate external data and internal representation. However, these redescriptions occur slowly.

In the task of balancing the blocks, change occurs after the child has understood the differences associated with balancing blocks of perceptibly different weights and has accumulated a good deal of anomalous information regarding the different balance point of blocks that are apparently similar. Only then does the child interpret the anomalous data as well, by applying a unified theory. The child is prompted in this by an internal tension (a concept similar to Piaget's notion of "disequilibrium").

The information, which in earlier phases was analyzed with a domain-specific code (i.e., spatial), is now interpreted with a linguistic code common to several domains, and this enables a child to communicate representations verbally. This does not mean, however, that consciousness is reducible to verbal description. In fact, we can identify two levels, E-2 and E-3. In E-2, knowledge is conscious but not verbally expressible; and we can see this, for example, when we are able to make a drawing that communicates even though we are not able to express verbally our representation. However, due to the scarcity of studies on knowledge that cannot be verbalized, here the two levels are presented together.

Although these two levels are characterized by the possibility of consciously accessing our internal representations, part of our knowledge (in particular our linguistic knowledge) remains impenetrable to reflection and cannot be reported verbally. In other words, Karmiloff-Smith (1991) hypothesizes the presence of two opposing developmental processes, one that makes part of the knowledge an object of reflection and another that makes part of the knowledge modular, specific and nontransferable across domains.

Empirical Support for the RR Model

Evidence supporting the RR model is provided primarily by language studies. Karmiloff-Smith (1992) presents, for example, two tasks that concern the ability to subdivide a statement into words and to know what a word is. In the first, the experimenter tells a story to a child, interrupting from time to time in order to ask what the last word pronounced was. The aim is to see if the child can recognize as words both those belonging to the open class (chair, child, etc.), that is, words that refer to external reality, and to the closed class (when, for, etc.), which have a function within the language system but lack an external referent. The second task is to read words from both the open and closed class to the child, who is to say whether or not these are words. The results show that, even though they produce language without making errors in word segmentation, children at 3–4 years of age can not perform either task; and this result, according to the author, indicates that their representation is procedural and implicit (Level I).

In the task of identifying the last word pronounced, the 4- and 5-year-olds achieve a high level of success because they are led by their internal representation (Level E-1). However, in the second task few are able to assign words to the closed class because they can not reflect consciously on what a word is. In subsequent Levels E-2 and E-3, instead, children have mastery over this metalinguistic component and are able to perform the second task as well, because they have the capacity to reflect on the fact that words are part of a system whose elements vary in role and function according to certain constraints.

Another study, also on verbal language, deals with the development of the understanding of the difference between the indefinite and definite article (Karmiloff-Smith, 1979). Children show the capacity to make this distinction even before they are able to use it in linguistic production; for example, hearing the words "a dax," a child understands that the words refer to a common noun, but considers "Dax" to be a proper noun, the name of a person. This study investigates whether children who already use both types of articles in their linguistic production can also understand and explain their use. The task involves the presentation of two puppets, each of which is placed behind different numbers of toys, one with only one exemplar of a toy such as "car" and the other with many exemplars of cars. The experimenter makes requests of the kind, "Give me a car" or "Give me the car" and the child has to decide which of the two puppets the request applies to. This is followed by a request to explain the choices made.

The younger children, aged 3–4, are at Level I; that is, they perform very well the task of deciding to which puppet the experimenter is referring, and this indicates that they have proceduralized the distinction between definite and indefinite articles. However, the level of their explanation is quite low as they refer more to the content than to the form of the sentence. The 5-year-olds, instead, show a lower level of performance in that, although they do not have a problem with expressions containing the definite article, they make more errors with the indefinite article than do the younger children. They ascribe the request "Give me an x" to the puppet with only one of the x toys rather than to the puppet with several. They treat the article as if it indicated "a single unit" (number function), rather than "any one of" the objects of the same type (indefinite function), thus collapsing the two functions into the same phonological unit. However, their representation is not flexible and, in assessing the requests of the experimenter, the children are no longer guided only by the distinction between definite and indefinite, as occurs at the previous level, but also by the distinction between indefinite and numerical. This type of understanding can be observed also in production. For example, the expression "a car" is used by the child to indicate the indefinite and "one of the cars" to indicate number. Finally, in the final redescription phase, children aged 7–8 manifest awareness in accessing the definite/indefinite distinction and offer explanations that reveal a metalinguistic ability (Karmiloff-Smith, 1986).

To support the idea that part of the linguistic knowledge remains encapsulated and therefore inaccessible to consciousness—even at the level of final redescription—Karmiloff-Smith considers the analysis that the child performs of the pronoun "he." The child learns to use it correctly, and is also able to offer a definition based on the pronoun's characteristics of masculine gender, singular number, and reference to a person. Despite this capacity for analysis, however, the child can not explain its use in discourse (which is characterized by rules that take into account the mental model of the speaker and the knowledge shared with the listener). This operation escapes consciousness and occurs in adults as well: the speaker uses his mental model, but is not able to explain it verbally (Karmiloff-Smith et al., 1993). This aspect of the process remains modular and, as Karmiloff-Smith (1991) states, is accessible only to linguists because of the change of code, from oral to written, occurring when the analysis is conducted.

Research on children's drawing, at first, also seemed to support the RR model. Karmiloff-Smith (1990) suggested that preschoolers have acquired drawing procedures that enable them to successfully depict many items, such as "a man," but they cannot access their own drawing procedures and redescribe them at a higher level of awareness. They are, therefore, bound to inflexible procedures that produce stereotyped drawings. However, subsequent research (e.g., Berti & Freeman, 1997; Morra, 2005; Spensley & Taylor, 1999) criticizes that study, noting that young children also show some flexibility in drawing and proposing that accounts different from RR explain the increase of flexibility with age. Karmiloff-Smith (1999), too, has recognized that young children's sequence in drawing the various parts of an item is not as rigid as she had initially hypothesized.

DEVELOPMENT: WHAT IS INNATE IN KARMILOFF-SMITH'S THEORY?

As already noted, Karmiloff-Smith's theorizing has evolved considerably over the years. These changes are quite pronounced in the shifting focus of such nativistic concepts as innateness and prespecified modules. For instance, the original theorizing was based on what can be considered a "strong" version of neonativist assumptions; which is to say, that infants are born with many cognitive abilities requiring little or no development. Thus in the early 1990s, although proposing that at birth there is a biological predetermination to attend and process specific classes of stimuli in different domains (Karmiloff-Smith, 1991, 1993), she also showed an acceptance of the presence of a kind of innate knowledge. Innate knowledge was thought to be complex, such as knowledge of some of the physical properties of objects (e.g., Spelke, 1991), or schematic, such as the tendency at birth to follow the stimulus of the human face longer than that of other objects. She reiterates that this is knowledge *in* the mind that is not yet capable of being analyzed *by* the mind, as clarified by her RR model.

Although Karmiloff-Smith may have adopted some version of a neonativist perspective in her early theorizing she did not, however, entirely share Fodor's (1983) innate knowledge hypothesis. This hypothesis states that modules exist at birth (for example the modules relating to language such as morphology, syntax, etc.), but Karmiloff-Smith did not accept the notion that one area of knowledge and the computations performed in that area are encapsulated and impenetrable. Instead, she argued that there had to be a way to explain the role of development and the resulting modularization. In this regard, she proposed that the environment not only has the function of activating one computational parameter rather than another; it also imposes constraints that guide the acquisition of abilities and knowledge. As a matter of fact, some authors known for their nativist view accept that genes do not determine reasoning in specific domains but *guide* it (Carey & Spelke, 1994). For example, concerning language, Pinker (1994) states that genes *help* to wire the grammar in place but acquisition itself of grammar is not only a matter of genes. However Karmiloff-Smith's idea went a step further, stating that nativism and constructivism need not be mutually incompatible concepts. She traced a clearer distinction between the infant's knowledge and subsequent developments. At birth, the child is biologically predisposed or ready to process limited classes of stimuli that are important to human existence, including knowledge of cause and effect, space, and language. However, subsequent achievements, thought to be predominantly constructivist in nature, involve a dynamic interaction between the child and the environment.

Both of these cornerstone concepts—nativism and constructivism—have undergone considerable theorizing and refinement, characterizing Karmiloff-Smith's later way of thinking as is clarified in the following section.

Representation and Neuroconstructivism

Starting from the middle 1990s, the notion of innateness has been rethought in depth by Karmiloff-Smith. Definitely, she opposes a "staunch" version of nativism according to which "a set of genes specifically targets domain-specific modules as the end product of their epigenesis" (Karmiloff-Smith, 1998, p. 389). Moreover, she objects to assigning the environment merely the role of triggering genetically prewired and prespecified modules. Her later theorizing evolved decisively toward neuroconstructivism, and includes a more complex set of assumptions highlighted by—amongst other things—a differentiation between representational and architectural innateness, with the former referring to prespecified knowledge content and the latter referring to prespecified learning mechanisms (see Elman et al., 1996; Karmiloff-Smith, Plunkett, Johnson, Elman, & Bates, 1998).

In recent years, Karmiloff-Smith's research has focused increasingly on atypical cognitive processes, such as those manifested in individuals with Williams syndrome, Specific Language Impairment (SLI), or autism. This is not only due to the clear applied value of such research projects, but also to their importance for answering basic research questions on issues such as innateness, modularity, developmental change. In her account of such disorders, Karmiloff-Smith (1998; Scerif & Karmiloff-Smith, 2005) criticizes the idea that genes exert a *direct* influence on the functioning of pre-specified modules. Instead, she proposes a neuroconstructivist approach that emphasizes interactions between biological and experiential factors.

Karmiloff-Smith (1992) and Elman et al. (1996) have argued that modules are not innately pre-wired, but rather, that modularization arises at a later point as a product of the progressive developmental specialization of cortical pathways. Consistent with this general view, the main assumption of Karmiloff-Smith's research on developmental disorders is that innate biological constraints are not domain-specific, but rather, that they have *indirect* and cascading effects by way of interactions with the environment.

Initial genetic influence regards many aspects relating to brain size, neuronal migration, neurotransmission, and timing of gene expression (Elman et al., 1996; Pennington, 2001), and these aspects progressively constrain the infant's selection and processing of different kinds of input. Thus, developmental processes are "implemented in the available repertoire of mechanisms of brain development" and "the final organization of the cortex depends on the way in which the cortex has been activated from birth" (Thomas & Karmiloff-Smith, 2005, p. 76). In this way, developmental disorders are the result of multiple factors at the brain level and at the cognitive level.

Overall, Karmiloff-Smith's idea is that cognitive performance in genetic disorders is the result of developmental trajectories, rather than of innately impaired and spared modules. In her view, atypical development is not explained by damage to a specific brain region. Dissociations between impaired and spared functions in adult brain-damaged patients (whose brain is characterized by lack of plasticity and of compensatory processes) are often explained in terms of modules. However, selective impairment in atypically developing children does not imply innate modularized brain structures similar to those of adults. Instead, to explain fractionation one should consider that brain developments occur through activities in the cortex taking place in interaction with the environment; the processes of ontogenetic development work on an infant's brain presenting alteration at neurocomputational level (Thomas & Karmiloff-Smith, 2005).

Examples of studies within this framework have considered in detail aspects of cognition in individuals with Williams Syndrome (WS), who are often believed to have intact language and social cognition but impaired spatial cognition and number, and low IQ.[4] In particular, Karmiloff-Smith and collabo-

---

[4]Williams syndrome is a neurodevelopment disorder characterized by an uneven cognitive-linguistic profile where individuals can experience a range of intellectual and behavioral difficulties and, at the same time, exhibit relatively strong linguistic skills (e.g., see Bellugi, Lichtenberger, Jones, Lai, & George, 2001).

rators (2004) examined aspects such as face processing and verb past tense formation (Thomas & Karmiloff-Smith, 2003). A pattern of detailed anomalies, with both strength and weaknesses, emerges from these studies (see Karmiloff-Smith, Brown, Grice, & Paterson, 2003). For example, WS individuals exhibit face processing abilities similar to normal; however, this does not mean that they have an intact module. Instead of using holistic strategies, faces are processed feature-by-feature, in a way that is—as Mounoud would have it—at a lower cognitive level than the ability to integrate a totality. In addition, adults with WS perform less well than WS children in face processing. For these reasons, Karmiloff-Smith (1998) makes a useful distinction between behavioral mastery and intact cognitive functioning, given that a similar behavioral outcome is obtained by different processes. The results lead the author to criticize the "myth" of innate modularity and of residual normality. In other terms, she not only objects to the idea that people are born with brain structures devoted to specific modules; but in addition, she opposes the idea that some genetic anomalies can affect one of those modules while leaving the others intact—the so-called assumption of residual normality of modules not affected by a specific developmental disorder.

In the same vein, fractionation of different aspects of language seems to occur at a very fine-grained level. This result would rule out the existence of broad modules, such as, for instance, a syntax module or a pragmatics module. For example, in WS individuals syntactic and pragmatic scores differ depending on which aspects they are based on.

In normally developing children, native speakers of English, a U-shaped curve is often found in the acquisition of the past tense: children initially use the correct past tense of a small number of verbs, both regular and irregular, then in a subsequent phase they produce over-regularized forms (e.g., *thinked, runned*) of irregular verbs on some occasions, and finally they use again the correct forms. The same sort of over-regularization errors can be found in WS children, and proponents of innate modules have interpreted this finding as supporting evidence for a spared syntactic module in WS. However, detailed analysis and connectionist modeling of their error patterns lead Thomas and Karmiloff-Smith (2003) to conclude that a brain with diffuse damage (e.g., in the connectionist models, anomalous initial parameters in the lexical-semantic component of the architecture) can produce that pattern of errors at a certain stage of learning, at a later age than in normally developing children. Therefore, there is no need of positing a spared syntactic module, because low-level computational constraints in the start state of the system can provide a better account.[5]

---

[5]Occasionally these authors also discuss specific aspects of interaction between representational domains, such as the relation between semantics and phonology in Williams syndrome (Karmiloff-Smith et al., 2003; Thomas & Karmiloff-Smith, 2003). Detailed consideration of these aspects, however, is beyond the scope of this chapter.

At the same time, detailed analysis of Specific Language Impairment suggests that deficits do not reflect a neat fractionation between language and other functions, but rather, they are graded and simply show greater impairment in language than nonlinguistic domains (Thomas & Karmiloff-Smith, 2005). In other terms, the evidence points to both a high degree of specificity and fractionation of representation in different microdomains, and a high degree of interactivity between components, which allow for cascade influences and compensation processes in the course of development.

What do these studies tell us about representation development? Within this framework, representation has a crucial role. The neural basis of developmental disorders "can be best understood in terms of the progressive emergence of representations during ontogeny" (Oliver et al., 2000, p. 7). Dissociations and differences between disorders, as well as associations and similarities between them, are assumed to emerge through developmental trajectories, during which a variety of factors (both internal to the organism and environmental) affect the formation and change of representations, which in turn would explain the pattern of impairments and other anomalies in the cognitive processes of individuals with a given syndrome. Thus, developmental disorders are defined "in terms of their deviation from a dynamic trajectory, rather than a static end state" (Oliver et al., 2000, p. 4).

The choice of a constructivist approach and the emphasis on representation are two aspects that Karmiloff-Smith's recent work shares with the neo-Piagetians. There are also important theoretical differences, however— starting with how representation is conceived.

Development of representations, in Karmiloff-Smith's recent work (starting from Elman et al., 1996), is often modeled in connectionist terms. In those articles that present detailed formal models of representation development (Thomas & Karmiloff-Smith, 2002, 2003) we find, essentially, the classical units of connectionist models of language, such as phonemes and semantic features in the input level, phonemes in the output level, and an intermediate level of hidden units without a specific representational content. The creative contribution of these studies (see also Oliver et al., 2000) is that they simulate atypical development by manipulating specific aspects of the initial state of the network; for instance, they remove a certain proportion of connections between units, or they add a certain degree of random noise to the activation level of each hidden unit. In this way, their simulations show that certain diffuse alterations in the initial state of the network can produce a developmental trajectory of the network itself, which leads to an end state that behaves similarly to the individuals of an atypical population. This is certainly an important achievement; however, the representations that are modeled are very simple ones, and although the network shows a developmental trajectory, this does not include any qualitative change in representation.

In this type of model there is nothing similar to representational redescription, an important feature of Karmiloff-Smith's earlier model of cognitive development. Thus, one may wonder whether Karmiloff-Smith now considers the idea of representational redescription to have been superseded, or is it just too complex for connectionist simulation. Connectionist modeling has its advantages, but it seems to obscure the strong ideas of Karmiloff-Smith's earlier theorizing.

At this point, one may wish to compare Halford's connectionist turn (described in chap. 3) with Karmiloff-Smith's. As we have seen, Halford has recently grounded representations in connectionist models, without losing track of the main ideas presented in earlier versions of his theory; thus, the level of complexity of symbol systems has been reformulated in terms of the dimensionality of a connectionist model, where each dimension of a problem representation (or each variable in a symbol system) is expressed by a separate set of units and the overall representation is expressed as a convolution of various dimensions. A developmentally increasing number of dimensions enables more powerful representations to emerge, and thus, discontinuities in cognitive development are modeled explicitly.

The sort of connectionist models used by Karmiloff-Smith and colleagues, instead, seems to sacrifice important ideas expressed in the RR model, although they are advantageous in modeling developmental trajectories. As noted by Fischer and Connell (2000), Oliver et al. (2000) have set clearly the goal of a neuroconstructivist approach to developmental disorders and proposed a promising broad framework, but their specific models present overly simple and impoverished representations. Fischer and Connell also suggest that multiple components and aspects of emotion, perception, and activity should be represented in more complex models of developmental trajectories. Following up that debate, we may observe that Thomas and Karmiloff-Smith (2002, 2003) have taken some further steps in specifying the content of developmentally plausible representations, but do not yet reach the point of modeling developmental discontinuity. This seems to remain a challenge for the future work of their research group.

COMPARING THE TWO THEORIES

It is useful to make a comparison between Mounoud's and Karmiloff-Smith's theories with respect to such problems as whether developmental change is qualitative or quantitative, and what the mechanisms of development are. The two theories share some similarity; the qualitative aspect of development is a basic principle of both. Furthermore, both of them propose that qualitative change is due to the construction of new forms of knowledge representation.

In terms of types of knowledge, they both maintain the distinction between procedural and declarative knowledge and accept the idea that the former is not accessible to consciousness whereas the latter is, and that from declarative knowledge more complex procedures can ensue (Karmiloff-Smith, 1991; Mounoud, 1990a). However, different theoretical assumptions underlie the two models. For Mounoud, the two systems are interdependent in the sense that one controls the other in alternate phases. New conceptual knowledge generates new procedural knowledge, which, once consolidated, gives rise to another conceptual phase. Meanwhile, consciousness does not appear to be stable from a certain age on, but is a transitory phenomenon limited to the phase of conceptual elaboration (Mounoud, 1992). For Karmiloff-Smith, the two systems are successive forms of the re-elaboration of knowledge. In early infancy and each time afterward that there are new acquisitions, knowledge is of the procedural type and this knowledge then may become explicit and conscious through subsequent redescriptions.

The greatest difference between Mounoud and Karmiloff-Smith lies in the weight given to general and specific factors. For Mounoud, the role attributed to the appearance of predetermined structures (or codes) causes development to be the primary product of general processes that control change across different areas and domains of knowledge. This idea is not weakened by the role assigned to the environment: "the temporal décalages between domains do not undermine the hypothesis of general change in the functioning of cognitive structures" (Mounoud, 1990b, p. 407). For Karmiloff-Smith, instead, representational change is domain-specific. As does Mounoud, she acknowledges the existence of general processes, such as inferential ability and detection of analogy also in young children, when knowledge is still "theory in action." She affirms, however, that the processes are general in the sense that they are the same in all domains. Further, she does not predict that they are activated in synchronic fashion in the various domains. This aspect of the theory is also maintained in the more recent neuroconstructivist approach, where mechanisms for learning and brain development are assumed to be general across the whole network, but specific domains and microdomains are assumed to develop independently of one another—even though they do communicate and interact, so that, for instance, compensation phenomena can occur in the course of atypical development (e.g., Thomas & Karmiloff-Smith, 2005).

Although the two authors have different views about the shape of development, both agree on a role of the environment. Mounoud, who speaks of a functional organization linked to neural development, and Karmiloff-Smith, who proposes a neuroconstructivist position, share the idea that both endogenous and exogenous factors influence development.

Regarding developmental change, Mounoud's theory contains two mechanisms: selection and integration, which are fundamental to the shifts, respectively, from global to elementary representations and from fragmentary to global, decomposable representations. One aspect that should be discussed in greater detail is the proposed maturational base of the shift from one stage to another, because the shift is initiated by the appearance of a new predetermined code. This assumption is indeed necessary because, in the absence of a psychological device or transition mechanism to enable construction of a new type of representation (such as, for instance, the increase of working memory capacity in Case's theory), a developmental account of stage transition is not feasible and one must resort to innate or preformed representations in order to avoid falling into the learning paradox (see chap. 2).

Independently of acceptance of the innate unfolding of new codes during development, however, it would be important to clarify further the psychological mechanisms for developmental transitions. Mounoud discusses such processes as decomposition, composition, selection and integration in the step transitions; however, one might question what enables those processes, how they are actualized, and whether the passage between qualitatively different stages is fully accounted for by maturation of a new code.

On her side, Karmiloff-Smith does not specify a mechanism that enables transition from Level I to Level E-1. This transition seems very relevant in that children pass from procedural knowledge to the first level of explicit, declarative knowledge. It would be valuable to give an account of the type of processes that allow such a transition. She does mention mastery of Level I procedures that enables consistent successful performance, and a process of "appropriation" of stable states that extracts the useful information. However, how procedural mastery permits the passage to the next higher level is not explicitly worked out.

Another common aspect of the two theories is their capability of accounting for regressions in performance. Both authors' theoretical proposals include a phase in which achieving a new ability may bring along a period in which a regression may occur. In Mounoud's proposal, after moving from global representations to a feature-by-feature processing, children represent information again in a holistic form, apparently falling back in some respects to the earlier performance (see Table 7.1). This regression leads them to a gradual construction of a decomposable totality. This pattern is exemplified by the aforementioned research on self-image (Mounoud & Vinter, 1985). In a similar vein, in Karmiloff-Smith's RR model, the child who through knowledge redescription reaches the first explicit level of representation can regress to a lower performance: starting to process information in the mind makes the child temporarily unable to elaborate information coming from external inputs at the same time. As an example, consider Karmiloff-Smith's (1979) study, just described, on the understanding of definite and indefinite articles.

Reference is made to the so-called loss and gain model applied to apparently regressive performance, also discussed by Siegler (1978). As Mounoud (1990b) states, in the study of development neither the model of impoverishment nor that of enrichment should prevail, but rather there should be an intermediate model. For example, when categorization is used, the number of characteristics analyzed is necessarily reduced but this impoverishment serves to produce a more efficient categorization.

Regressions can also be caused by the fact that, during a phase in which effort is directed to unifying data, the child overlooks dimensions previously considered or uses a new strategy, but one that is still in elaboration, in the place of a less efficient one that produced success from time to time. The performances can temporarily become more erratic or even wrong relative to the preceding stage in which a level of automatism was achieved. Thus, as maintained by Mounoud (1993), errors indicate inappropriate use of propositional or analogic representations (or logic and infralogic) rather than lack of logic, and errors prepare future coordinations: variability is productive. As suggested by Karmiloff-Smith (1981), regressions are such only from the point of view of the observer. A more detailed provision of the role of regression in development can be found in chapter 10.

CHANGE OR ENRICHMENT OF CHILDREN'S THEORIES?

Karmiloff-Smith's theory is not the only one that emphasizes domain-specific changes in representation. The issue of representational change has been widely debated in the last decades by researchers of different theoretical orientation—some of whom are quite distant from a neo-Piagetian framework.

The paradigm of comparing the performance of experts and non-experts in domain-specific knowledge (Chi, Glaser, & Rees, 1982) suggests that, due to the increase in knowledge and its different organization in a given domain, such as physics, the problems encountered are elaborated differently. Chi's influential study (1978) in which the memory span of children expert in the domain of chess was compared to that of non-expert adults is a seminal example. Gobbo and Chi (1986) compared two groups of children, one expert and the other not in the domain of dinosaurs. The authors showed that, in a classification problem, the expert children succeeded in inferring the placement of unknown objects in the appropriate class on the basis of attributes used in an exclusive and exhaustive way. Their non-expert peers failed to solve this problem that posed a cognitive load that was too high for them given that they had to keep in mind the attribute used previously while also encoding the characteristics of each dinosaur and deciding to which class it belonged.

This line of research suggests that specific knowledge explains at least in part developmental changes in solving domain-specific tasks. With the increase in knowledge we see not only an increase in the number of concepts, attributes, and connections, but there is also a change in the structure of that knowledge. Concepts begin to acquire defining attributes that modify their causal structure and the network of links that connects them to one another, leading to the formation of different theoretical beliefs. As they become experts in a specific domain, such as physics, children abandon naïve theories (McCloskey, Washburn, & Felch, 1983) in favor of more formal theories even if these are sometimes counterintuitive. In addition, knowledge becomes more accessible and the retrieval of relevant information, along with the implementation of appropriate procedures, becomes more rapid.

But there is no general agreement on the idea of a qualitative change in the organization of knowledge that parallels the increase of knowledge. According to Spelke (1991), development is "a process of enrichment of fundamental principles that remain constant" (p. 135), principles present at birth. For Spelke, knowledge of physics is an enrichment that allows new concepts and beliefs to form starting from the constraints imposed by innate representations: only scientific reasoning is subject to conceptual change in that systematic observations of critical phenomena can cause the subject to reflect on the adequacy or the incompatibility of beliefs constructed on the basis of common sense (see also Shutts & Spelke, 2004; Spelke, 1998).

As opposed to Spelke, for whom conceptual change can only be talked about in the context of the history of science, Karmiloff-Smith has proposed that the child shifts from a phase in which knowledge is non-theoretical, procedural and the product of enrichment of innate abilities, to phases in which knowledge becomes explicit and theoretical. Also for Carey (1985, 2000, 2004) the child constructs theories and beliefs on the basis of personal experience of the world. Like Spelke, she suggests that development flows from innate knowledge and predetermination, but differently from Spelke, she proposes that the change concerns the theory that the child previously had with respect to a given domain of knowledge (see also Keil, 1991).

Drawing on evidence from a variety of sources, including studies in the domains of physics and biology, Carey analyzes how knowledge is restructured during children's development and compares it with how knowledge is restructured by adults and to the ways that conceptual advances have been made in the various fields of science.

According to Carey (1991, 2000), a theory is formed by the mental representations pertaining to one domain of phenomena and to the principles or mechanisms that explain them. The mental representations have, as a base, individual concepts that are units of representation more or less equivalent to a single word (i.e., weight, matter, heat, animal, alive, etc.). Individual concepts can be combined to build propositions, which are complex representational structures (i.e., "all animals are alive" or "air is made of matter"), as well as theories (for instance, natural selection), which express laws regulating these concepts and propositions (Carey, 2000). During development, knowledge in a specific domain is reorganized through introduction of new ontological categories (for example, the earth and the sun are assigned to the class of planets and stars respectively), and as a result the initial theory is modified. A more dramatic conceptual change occurs when "locally incommensurable" concepts are introduced, which is to say, the new concepts no longer have the same meaning they had in the context of the previous theory (see Carey, 1987). This makes the previous theory incompatible with the new one, as occurs in the history of science, in terms of what Kuhn (1962) calls scientific revolutions. For instance, Carey (1991) shows that the knowledge of 4-year-old children is incommensurable with that which they will have at 10, an age at which they attain a conceptualization similar to that of adults.

More recently, Carey continues to address critical aspects of her theory, such as the distinction between knowledge enrichment and conceptual change, and a more explicit outline of the process involved in conceptual change. For example, Johnson and Carey (1998) tested two types of conceptual knowledge acquisition: enrichment (i.e., acquisition of new knowledge related to an existing conceptual base, sometimes referred to as the "accretionist" position) and genuine conceptual change. The sample for their study consisted of three groups; 6-year-olds, 10-year-olds and adolescents and adults with Williams syndrome (with a mean verbal mental age of 11.5 years). Individuals with Williams syndrome can often display considerable conversation proficiency, able to talk in great detail about a topic and at the same time demonstrating only superficial understanding of it. Thus, Johnson and Carey (1998) hypothesized that participants with Williams syndrome could acquire encyclopedic knowledge in the biological domain, consistent with the conceptual repertoire of normally developing preschool children, but not biological concepts that require conceptual change for their construction (e.g., man as an animal among many).

The results showed that the 6-year-olds were able to acquire knowledge such as concepts of animal properties and animal parts, but they were not able to acquire concepts requiring conceptual changes. Ten-year-olds were able to perform well on both conditions. Participants with Williams syndrome did well on the enrichment condition but not on the genuine conceptual change conditions, lending further support to the distinction between the conceptual change and the enrichment position.

Carey has also proposed a learning process that would explain how children create representational systems that are ever more powerful. The process that she calls "Bootstrapping" refers to a uniquely human ability in which ". . . the end point of the process transcends in some qualitative way the starting point" (Carey, 2004, p. 59). This process makes extensive use of the human capability to create and use external symbols: they can be used as placeholders of "meanings" that can change and become richer when previously distinct systems of representation are integrated and combined into new and more powerful conceptual representations (Carey, 2004).

Other researchers have also supported the idea that children possess theories that are subject to conceptual change (see Keil, 1991, 2006). Keil (1991) considers theories pertaining to "natural genders," which are intrinsically endowed with a coherent causal structure that allows inductive inference of properties. For instance, at age 5, children do not accept the idea that an animal can be transformed into an element belonging to another category (e.g., from a porcupine to a cactus), because such a transformation would change a property that is considered essential in their theory. Rather children accept a transformation within the same category (from lion to tiger), which shows that they possess theoretical principles that guide them in maintaining the boundaries between categories but no principles concerning the introduction of different species within the same category. This may not apply to "nominal" genders (e.g., triangle), which are the product of conventions, or to "artificial genders" in which the causal structure is not intrinsic. However, Keil does not agree with Carey that the change involves a differentiation of the initial domains and contends that the biological and psychological theories are already differentiated in the young child.

More recently, expanding on his earlier work on conceptual changes Keil and his colleagues have examined how children of different ages cluster knowledge in terms of features such as goals, topics and principles related to various disciplines such as mechanical and social (Danovitch & Keil, 2004; Keil, 2006). Younger children (i.e., age 5 to 7 years) tend to rely predominantly on topics and goals to cluster knowledge. It is not until the fourth grade (about age 9) that children consistently use principles dependent on specific discipline to cluster knowledge (see Danovitch & Keil, 2004). Although it is not clear the nature of the mechanism involved, it appears that there is a clear shift in the way children cluster their knowledge about the world, namely from topic to discipline based.

CONCLUSION

In this chapter, we have discussed a number of intertwined issues: representations as a basis for explaining qualitative change in development; innatism, constructivism, and neuroconstructivism; the processes of cognitive change and their domain-specific or general nature; normal and atypical development; regressions in behavior and U-shaped curves; and advantages and disadvantages of connectionist modeling of representation.

In the first sections, we have introduced and compared two theories, pointing out how they study qualitative change by analyzing the child's conscious representations in different phases of development. Unlike Karmiloff-Smith, who embraces the idea that acquisitions occur within specific domains, Mounoud thinks of development in terms of cyclical phases that develop across different domains and abilities although not denying that, depending on experience, there can be variations in the performance of tasks or in domains. The merit of his theory is that it suggests how the general stages unfold through phases that bring about qualitative changes, so that the child deals with the external world in a different way.

The neuroconstructivist approach proposes to resolve the debate on the nature of innate knowledge by drawing a clear distinction between prespecified knowledge content and prespecified learning mechanisms. Connectionist modeling seems to suggest that the latter type of innate endowment suffices to account for development of a mature representational system. In this way, emphasis on representation and on the neural bases of cognition is brought together with constructivist assumptions akin to Piaget's. However, the specific connectionist models so far proposed within this framework have not yet offered a solution to the problem of qualitative discontinuity in representation. A typical neo-Piagetian solution to such problem would involve growth in the course of development of the dimensionality of representations (as in Halford's recent proposals) or growth of some other computational mechanism akin to working memory.

Children's representations of some domains may have characteristics similar to theories, or at least they have a certain degree of coherence and systematicity (which is reminiscent of de Ribaupierre's notion of "minimal structuralism"; see chap. 3). Some proposed solutions to the problem of discontinuity consider whether or not development in domain-specific knowledge entails conceptual change with respect to a previously formed theory. Although there is no agreement on the idea that the knowledge that the child has from early life can be called a theory, researchers as Carey or Keil assert that, in development, children construct and modify theories that enable them to understand the world. These theories are guided both by the predetermined constraints on the type of information to be processed and by constraints imposed by the culture in which the child lives. As Carey states, the construction of theories requires the evolution of crucial components, such as causality and the difference between appearance and reality, which in the course of development, change the theory not in general terms but in terms of more specific knowledge of mechanisms. The construction and change of theories occurs spontaneously in the child; more than a solver of problems, as Case thinks, the child appears to be a scientist who, as Karmiloff-Smith contends, being neither a philosopher nor a logician, retains for a long time the theory that is being used until the child can no longer deal with contrasting observations. The theory may be incommensurable with formal theory, as in the cases examined by Carey, but it has explanatory power. This does not mean that we do not also store correlational information that is the basis of future development, but that it is not immediately placed within our theory: "conceptual structures are neither completely guided by information nor completely guided by theory" (Keil, 1991, p. 253).

We remind the reader, to prevent misunderstanding, that most of the theories considered in this chapter are not neo-Piagetian ones. Some of them rely heavily on innatist or empiricist presuppositions, and among the authors only Mounoud sometimes called himself a neo-Piagetian (although he could be regarded as an atypical one because of his strong assumption of predetermined maturational emergence of codes). However, all of these theories propose some answers to questions that are crucial to neo-Piagetian theory, and thus contribute to dialogue among different approaches.

None of the approaches discussed in this chapter denies that there are general mechanisms or processes that intervene in the development of children's conceptual system. At the very least, they make reference to the child's ability to make inductive or analogical inferences and comprehend causality. They also propose, however, that general mechanisms act within acquisitions and conceptual changes that are domain-specific, and that representational change is at the core of cognitive development.

The resulting view of development differs from that described by other theories in which a crucial role is assigned to the capacity to process an increasing load of information (e.g., Pascual-Leone's theory) or to environmental variation (e.g., Fischer's theory). The theories discussed in this chapter use (even though in differentiated ways) the concept of representation, understood as an organization of knowledge that the child constructs from a predetermined base, and for many of them such a knowledge organization has the characteristics of a theory and is domain-specific. For this reason, the organization does not include or permit consideration of all the information. This justifies the presence of partial regressions in performances and the slowness with which the reorganization of knowledge occurs, as well as conceptual change; a child's encounters with information that contradicts his or her theory does not entail that this information is being examined and that it will lead to theory revision.

However, it does not seem necessary to make innatist assumptions concerning representation, because there is evidence (including the results of simulation studies, such as those by Karmiloff-Smith and her colleagues) that a constructivist account of representation formation can be satisfactory. Moreover, constructivist assumptions explain better than nativist approaches both the interactions and compensations that are found in atypical development, and in addition, can account more easily for the widely acknowledged cultural influences.

CHAPTER

8

Cognitive Development
and Emotional Development

Cognition often involves goals and representations that carry an affective quality or tone, whereas emotions often involve cognitive processes—perception, representations, and interpretations of events. Emotion, cognition, and social interaction are not readily dissociated from one another in daily experience; the relationship between cognition and emotion has been the focus of extensive research in the last decades (e.g., Frijda, 1986; Lazarus, 1991) as well as the links between cognitive and emotional development (e.g., Harris, 1989; Izard, 1991; Sroufe, 1995). Neo-Piagetian theorists are no exception in this regard, and offer several contributions to the debate in this field.

Some early contributions (Chapman, 1981; Edelstein, Keller, & Wahlen, 1984) were pioneering studies on egocentrism in social cognition; others (e.g., Fischer & Watson, 1981; White & Pillemer, 1979) can be regarded as contributions to a cognitive critique of psychoanalytical theory. Later, however, more systematic theories have also appeared.

DAGGERS DRAWN WITH PSYCHOANALYTIC ACCOUNTS

Sometimes, criticizing a former paradigm is the starting point of a new, successful theoretical approach. The first neo-Piagetian writings on emotional development were quite speculative, but they suggested plausible and consistent accounts of phenomena that were explained by psychoanalysts in a more problematic way. It seems worthwhile, therefore, to begin with those early models, even though they were limited to explanations of a few specific phenomena.

Fischer's Oedipus Conflict and the Unconscious

In one of the first neo-Piagetian attempts to interrelate cognitive and emotional development, Fischer and Watson (1981) propose a model of the Oedipal conflict. An important problem in the classical Freudian description is the conflict's nonuniversality. In societies where the family structure is not the same as that observed by Freud, children do not necessarily develop the intense attraction for opposite-sex parents or the hostility for same-sexed parents that he described. Nevertheless, such superego components as ideals and conscience, which Freud viewed as deriving from resolution of the Oedipal complex, do develop in these children.

Fischer and Watson's thesis is that the Oedipal conflict results from confusions in the child's understanding of concepts related to familial roles. Clearly these concepts are characterized by strong affective connotations. In Fischer's theory, such confusions would be typical of the representational processes associated with level $Rp2$ (i.e., the second level of the representational tier; see chap. 5). Although the Oedipal conflict may not be universal, some form of cognitive confusion about familial roles might well be universal and be resolved at the $Rp3$ level. In addition, acquisition of the so-called superego components and concomitant understanding of such roles might be universal, without necessarily being the result of castration anxiety or other related psychoanalytic constructs.

In Fischer and Watson's model, 2-year-olds are not expected to show any Oedipal conflict, and this follows from not yet understanding the social relationships involved. However, the $Rp1$-level representation of these relationships does set the stage for such conflict. At age 2, children are capable of symbolic representations and an affective value can be associated with them. Thus, these children can have frightful thoughts—for example, witches that they have heard others talk about, monsters they have seen on TV or personally imagined. They are also able to represent other persons as agents, independent of their own actions. What they lack, however, is knowledge of how to put a representation into relationship with another person's point of view. Thus, although they see that their parents often know their thoughts and desires, they do not appreciate how the parents come to know these (that is, they do not know what aspects of their behavior reveal their thoughts and desires). Although 2-year-olds are able to use terms such as "mommy," "daddy," and "baby," they do not use these in a manner that is congruent with a suitable categorization of the persons to whom they apply, nor do they understand the interconnecting relations among the social roles. Thus, the idea that the same-sex parent knows one's thoughts or the idea that one might be punished by a horrible monster does not contribute to formation of an Oedipal complex. Such a formation is impeded by the child's inability to understand the complementarity of the social roles involved in the conflict.

This ability appears only at level $Rp2$ (about age 4) because complementary polarities such as man–woman, mommy–daddy, and husband–wife presuppose drawing correspondences between representations. At this age it also becomes possible to represent changes that are tied to age, such as the boy becomes a man, the girl becomes a woman. Nevertheless, such correspondences only enable the child to put persons or the social roles into relation along one dimension at a time. For example, a 5-year-old boy knows that he will become older like his father and do the same things that his father does now; but he does not consider that, in the meantime, his mother will grow old. When he considers the male–female dichotomy, he does not simultaneously take account of the child–parent dichotomy. If he considers the correspondence between the roles of husband and wife, he realizes that every wife has a husband. If he could grow to become like his father, and if he could take the role of husband currently occupied by his father, then he would have to get rid of his father's presence. At this point other characteristics of the Oedipal conflict can be manifest: the thought of the father destroyed is itself unpleasant and anxiety provoking, perhaps the father is aware of this thought, the punishment for this thought could be terrible. . . . Thus, a limited understanding of the classification of persons and social roles (which, as seen in chap. 5, is in fact multidimensional) together with an inability to combine the correspondences with respect to social gender roles and social generational roles impedes the 4-year-old's understanding of the impossibility of replacing the same-sexed parent both in the present and in the future. According to Fischer and Watson, it is from such confused representations that incompatible desires, emotional ambivalences and anxieties stem. Children growing up in non-Western family structures will develop confusions of the same conceptual nature, though they might be less distressing.

The solution of the Oedipal conflict requires the representational ability of level $Rp3$. Full comprehension of social roles, such as those of husband and wife, requires simultaneous consideration of additional characteristics of a person. At this level, a child is able to understand that one's parents can occupy more than one role *at the same time*—for example, husband and father, or similarly that, as children become older, adults become older *simultaneously*. The confusions about social roles found at the preceding level are resolved with normal development. And even if castration anxiety may appear in an Oedipal conflict, Fischer (contrary to Freud) excludes it from any role in the conflict's resolution.

Just as the Oedipal conflict's resolution is not based on anxiety, the development of ideals and conscience do not stem from resolution of that conflict. Although level *Rp2* representations do allow a rough understanding of some social rules, according to Fischer and Watson it is only at level *Rp3* that comprehension of a system of behavior rules and comparison of one's behavior with a rule or ideal becomes possible. Thus, in summary, Fischer and Watson's position is that development of the ability to construct systems of representations (level *Rp3*) permits the child *both* to overcome the preceding confusions about familial relations *and* to build ideals and a developed "superego." Although Fischer and Watson's (1981) position is limited in that it does not account for cases of inadequate solution of the Oedipal conflict by a child, more recently Fischer's research group has undertaken studies of anomalous emotional development (see the section entitled "Emotions, Skills, Social Roles, and Attachment," this chapter).

Fischer and Pipp (1984a) suggest that there is no unitary mental structure serving as a repository of impulses and memories, that is, no Unconscious as a system. Rather, they associate unconsciousness and other primary process characteristics (such as wish fulfillment, compensation, displacement) with the thought processes that occur when situation demands are higher than an individual's level of skill. Lack of familiarity with the context, absence of environmental support, or strong arousal can lead children to approach a situation with a lower-than-optimal level of skill; and, therefore, in these situations children can fail to maintain full awareness of their thoughts or actions.

In addition, Fischer and Pipp characterize as unconscious the processes that they term active and passive dissociation. Passive dissociation refers simply to the natural division of skills that have been acquired in different contexts and not actively integrated. Active dissociation consists in actively maintaining a separation between distinct skills (recall the concept of an Interrupt as described in chap. 2). Repression is an example of active dissociation motivated by avoidance of unpleasant emotions. The extreme and more complex forms of active dissociation are found in cases of multiple personality and schizophrenia. Active dissociation is not possible in the early stages of development, as it presupposes the ability to put different representations in relation to each other. To isolate a particular content of consciousness and remove it presupposes a concept of self, the perception of a representation as threatening to the self, and the formation of strategies for pushing the undesirable representation from consciousness. At the very least, this process requires the ability to move from activation of one representation to activation of another, and this becomes easier when one is able to put two representations in relation with each other. Thus, cognitive development makes possible more refined repression strategies.

Another of Fischer and Pipp's ideas is that unconscious processes, although primitive with respect to an individual's optimal level, nevertheless differ in complexity. They maintain that cognitive development leads to manifestations of unconscious and irrational processes, but that progressively they become more elaborated and complex. In the first 18 to 24 months of life, even though most mental processes are unconscious, one can not yet really speak of unconscious *thought*.

Childhood Amnesia

If the solution of the Oedipal conflict doesn't lie in castration anxiety, and if the unconscious is not a network of suppressed memories and drives, then how does one explain childhood amnesia?

Childhood amnesia refers to the universally recognized phenomenon of not being able to recall any of the experiences of the first years of life—the oblivion that Freud says envelops our first age and estranges us from it. According to the Freudian explanation, around the age of 6, a wall of repression rises up and impedes re-emergence in consciousness of emotionally unpleasant and anxiety-producing memories from infancy, thus preventing their secondary processing. However, the childhood impressions and their emotional charge, which remain intact in the unconscious, constitute nuclei for the formation of neurotic symptoms. Analytic therapy seeks to overcome repression, allowing a grasp of consciousness and an emotional catharsis that leads to dissolution of the neuroses.

White and Pillemer (1979) raise facts challenging the Freudian explanation. For example, not even the successful patients of analytic therapies are able to remember the details of their infancy. Various researchers suggest instead that the number of memories relating to the different ages of childhood is a function of the underlying degree of cognitive development: the higher the level of cognitive development at a given age, the greater the likelihood that as an adult one will be able to recall some experience from that time. The data reviewed by White and Pillemer have been corroborated by recent studies (Bruce, Dolan & Phillips, 2000; Multhaup, Johnson, & Tetirick, 2005; Peterson, Grant, & Boland, 2005), which show that older children and adults can remember very little from before the age of three, and that the transition to retrievable autobiographic memory occurs gradually, with a turning point at about 4 and a half years.

A cognitive interpretation of childhood amnesia is possible. If remembering is a process of reconstructing past experiences based on cognitive schemes, and if the cognitive schemes of the young child differ greatly from those of the adult, then an adult will have serious difficulty reconstructing the contents of his or her infant experiences.

White and Pillemer (1979) explain childhood amnesia on the basis of Pascual-Leone's (1976b) distinction between *LM* and *LC* operators, two learning mechanisms described in "Second Level Operators" in chapter 2. Both types of learning processes enable formation of complex knowledge structures. In particular, *LC* learning is based on repeated coactivation of two or more schemes and depends heavily on context and experience, and in everyday experience various sources (including perceptual input) could activate repeatedly the same schemes in the same context. In contrast, *LM* learning consists in fast learning of a structure whose constituents are schemes simultaneously activated by means of the same attentional device, that is, by using *M* capacity.

In order to recall childhood experiences one must activate relevant schemes and connect them in a meaningful symbolic or narrative reconstruction. A child's encoding of an episode in combination with additional conscious knowledge (such as information regarding time or place, verbal labels, or attributions of causality) could lead to formation of an *LM* structure. Subsequently, such a structure would allow the child to use the additional knowledge as a decontextualized memory cue. However, *LM* learning requires at least a minimum degree of *M* capacity, because two (or more) schemes have to be coordinated, coactivating them by means of *M* capacity. Thus, an essential requirement for forming *LM* structures is an *M* capacity of at least $e + 2$, a capacity not acquired until about age 5. Of course, with a greater *M* capacity, the creation of *LM* structures becomes easier.

The young child, however, can not intentionally and readily coactivate, by means of the *M*-operator, a sufficient number of schemes to create recallable memories. The structures of schemes that the young child can form are those learned (*LC*-operator) through repeated experiences in which the same schemes are coactivated without a voluntary investment of mental effort. Subsequent reactivation depends on the presence of external cues (environmental context) or internal ones (the person's cognitive and emotional states) similar to those present when the structure itself was formed. Up to 5 years of age the mental representation of an event or complex situation is most likely to be of the *LC* type,[1] and, therefore, that mental representation will be evoked again only in the presence of contextual cues or the right emotional state. Only in rare cases, with a particularly strong activation of affective origin (*A*-operator), will one form a full representation of a single event experienced only once; and even in this case, the structure is not an *LM* structure and can not be activated independently from the context.

---

[1]Adults are also capable of *LC* learning. They find it easier to employ recently formed *LC* structures than structures formed in childhood for the simple reason that in everyday life the context in which recent *LC* structures were formed is the one more likely to recur.

A recent review (Hayne, 2004) concludes that childhood amnesia is explained by age-related changes in encoding, retention, and retrieval during infancy and early childhood. In particular, Hayne notes that young children need highly specific cues to initiate memory retrieval, and therefore it may be difficult for early memories to be retrieved by cues or in contexts that were not part of the original experience. This account sounds very close to White and Pillemer's emphasis on *LC* learning in early childhood.

According to White and Pillemer, turning one's experience into stories is a means of building *LM* structures. This view is supported to some extent by McKeough's (1992) finding that the creation of a coherent story (a form of secondary processing for psychoanalysts) requires a certain working memory capacity. Someone who can recount an episode or rehearse it when it spontaneously comes to consciousness is thus engaged in reprocessing it as an *LM* structure. As a result of this elaboration, the structure will be more easily evoked in the future. In this way it could also happen, though only occasionally, that an event that occurred at age 3 or 4 comes to mind at age 5 or 6 in a similar context and, therefore, becomes incorporated into a more readily accessible *LM* structure. The finding by Peterson et al. (2005) that children aged 6 to 9 can recall earlier experiences than older children seems consistent with the assumption that they still have enough contextual cues available for retrieving some very early memories.

Other theories explain the wane of childhood amnesia with the role of language and social interaction, particularly early parent–child memory sharing, which would teach children what to remember, how, and why. However, Peterson et al. (2005) found that the largest proportion of their participants' memories described single moments in time, and that most of them were about rather mundane experiences; such facts do not seem to agree with the view of parental scaffolding through conversation.[2] Nevertheless, language acquisition and parent–child memory sharing could have at least a partial role; according to Hayne (2004) early language could serve, like other sorts of stimuli, as a memory attribute or as a retrieval cue.

In summary, the discontinuity in autobiographical memory around age 5 is not due to repression, but rather to a growing use of controlled information-processing operations. This does not imply, however, that there is no point to using psychoanalytic techniques of free association. The suspension of mental effort and critical attitude, the surrender to a state of affective dependence, in some cases can favor lesser use of *LM* structures and the restoration of an emotional state more similar than usual to that experi-

---

[2]Curiously, Peterson et al. (2005) dismiss White and Pillemer's (1979) explanation as no longer credible in light of recent research. Probably this is due to their oversimplification of White and Pillemer's account, which they summarize in terms of "a poor memory system that Changes dramatically" (p. 623), instead of considering the properties of the two learning mechanisms, *LC* and *LM*, posited in the model and of the interaction between them.

enced in childhood. This result could, in turn, favor re-emergence of a child-hood memory (or a subjective reconstruction in a more or less distorted fashion from fragments of memory) that an analyst could discuss with the patient according to any particular therapeutic conviction. Clearly, this kind of process is not a matter of overcoming a suspected repression (if it was, a successful analysis would cast full light on the patient's childhood experience). Rather, it involves the occurrence of conditions (favored by the analytic setting) that permit a sporadic and more or less fragmented re-covery of some memory of *LC* structures formed in early life.

EMOTIONS, SKILLS, SOCIAL ROLES, AND ATTACHMENT

Kurt Fischer and his colleagues (Fischer, Shaver, & Carnochan, 1990; Fischer, Wang, Kennedy & Cheng, 1998; Li et al., 2004; Mascolo & Fischer, 1995; Mas-colo, Harkins, & Harakal, 2000) propose a theory of emotions and their devel-opment, based on the use of prototypes for classifying emotions, and the use of scripts for describing their antecedents. (Also see chap. 5 for some aspects of the role of emotions on social cognition and self perception.)

According to Fischer et al. (1990), emotions start with the detection of a situational change, which is appraised in terms of the person's goals, con-cerns, and coping potential. For instance, anger occurs when an event is ap-praised as threatening for an important goal, and the person feels capable of removing the threat or obstacle. Following each emotion's specific ap-praisal, a person shows an action tendency specific to that emotion. How-ever, there is a large variability within each emotion category. For instance, people speak of a man being angry when he gets into a fist fight or when he fumes about his boss's unreasonableness. Thus, emotions are best de-scribed as prototypes. For instance, the function of anger is to drive an en-ergized reaction against the obstacle that hampers one's goals; it is the overall organization and function of anger that is important to its definition, whereas the presence of certain characteristics (such as a raised voice, a certain facial expression, clenched fists, or verbal claims about legitimacy) is a matter of probability.

Emotions are viewed as prototypes in a hierarchy of categories with a broad positive/negative distinction at the superordinate level; a small num-ber of categories organized around primary emotions at the basic level; and a number of more specific emotions, often complex and socially con-structed, at the subordinate level. For instance, resentment is a subordi-nate-level category; it is included in the basic family of anger and in the broader category of negative emotions. A particular script of antecedents (i.e., appraisal) and consequences (i.e., action tendencies) would characterize each prototypical emotion category at whatever level. Different methods have been used to identify emotion categories or the scripts that characterize them, such as cluster analysis of emotional term sorting (Li et al., 2004), dramatized stories and pretend play (Fischer et al., 1990), or cluster analysis of the features of an angry child's behavior (Mascolo et al., 2000).

The developmental process would move from basic emotions to culture-specific, subordinate-category emotions, and Fischer's skill theory enters the picture by accounting for the different sorts of appraisal that a child can perform at different ages. To keep with examples of anger, Mascolo and Griffin (1998) propose a developmental model of changes in appraisal, according to which, for instance, a 4-month-old infant (level *S1*) could be frustrated over a caregiver's failure to respond when wanted, whereas a 2-year-old child (level *Rp1*) could react to intrusions on objects considered "mine," and a 6-year-old child (level *Rp3*) could be sensitive to unfair violations of rules. Clearly, in these cases, event appraisal involves increasingly complex representations or skills. Even though cognitive development constrains the child's capability to appraise the significance of an event, a number of other factors (e.g., the source of frustration, the social context, cultural norms, individual differences, etc.) would codetermine the specific ways in which anger manifests itself. Mascolo et al. (2000) also emphasize that appraisal does not have a mere causal role in a linear chain of causes and effects; rather, it also receives feedback from affective, motivational and action systems, so that influence is reciprocal.

The same structural levels of skill involved in event appraisal and representation of emotion-laden interactions are also crucial to defining the self and its roles in social interaction. Whereas a child who is acting at skill level *Rp1* can only focus on one role or feature at a time, with the advent of representational mappings (level *Rp2*) a child could, for instance, coordinate parental and professional roles, and understand that his mother is also a pediatrician; or coordinate the domains of nice and mean about himself, seeing that he can be both nice and mean at the same time; or understand the relationship between himself being good and his mother being proud of him. With representational systems, even more complex coordination of roles and personal features is achieved.

On the ground of these assumptions, Fischer et al. (1997) discuss whether psychopathology involves developmental immaturity of the self (e.g., fixation, regression, or retardation). Contrary to widespread views in clinical psychology and psychiatry, Fischer et al. (1997) suggest that people with psychopathology often are not developmentally immature, but instead, have taken a different pathway. Their self-representations and their emotional appraisal are as complex and sophisticated as those of normally developing people; they show, however, specific biases, splittings, and other peculiar forms of adaptation. Fischer et al. (1997) illustrate their views by discussing the personality of children and adolescents who are victims of hidden family violence. Affective splitting (e.g., between what is categorized as positive or negative) is quite normal in young children, and healthy adults also make use of it in more complex ways. However, children who are victims of hidden family violence may push such splitting to the extreme and learn to dissociate the public and private worlds, building separate skills for their adaptation to the two dissociated settings. Thus, at skill level *Rp1*, a child could conceive himself as both a bad agent (in the private domain) and as a good agent (in the public domain), keeping the two separate. At level *Rp2*, that child could understand (in the private domain) a role dyad formed by a bad self and a bossy dad, and (in the public domain) a role dyad formed by a good self and a proud mother. Furthermore, at level *Rp3* the combined roles of boss and follower could emerge in the private sphere, where a bad follower is punished by a boss and the boss places heavy demands on the follower's obedience, whereas in the public sphere the combined roles of child and adult could be characterized by the dynamics of commanding–obeying and being smart–proud. Then, at level *A1* (i.e., when the abstract tier is reached), the (private) personality of a tyrant self and the (public) personality of a competent self could be constructed; and so on. The point of interest—which also has clinical implications—is that despite suffering from violence and notwithstanding the extreme pathological splitting, the skills for representing the self and its interactions with others would follow a developmental course that is not delayed or regressive with respect to the typical one of non-abused children[3] (see also Fischer & Bidell, 2005, and the related discussion in chap. 5).

In a similar vein, Ayoub, Fischer, and O'Connor (2003) suggest that Bowlby's working models of attachment are not static patterns that, once established, remain relatively constant throughout an individual's life, but rather, they develop and change throughout the lifespan, being based on the skills that a person uses to represent the self, the others and their interactions. Hence, also the internal models of close and emotionally significant relationships would follow a developmental course predicted by skill theory—and at the same time, their content would be affected by the quality of relations with caregivers or other significant figures. Thus, trauma would produce not developmental delay or fixation, but the construction of complex and sometimes peculiar models of attachment.

---

[3]Fischer et al. (1997, 1998) also present a technique, the self-in-relationships interview, which explores self-representation and its positivity bias. With this technique, Fischer et al. (1998) demonstrate that in less individualistic cultures (e.g., in Korea or China) self-representation is as complex and as positively biased as in the United States. However, Fischer et al. (1997) show that abused children's self-representation, even though equal in complexity to that of non-abused children, is characterized by a negativity bias, that is, many features of the self that are perceived as highly important are also evaluated negatively.

In line with Fischer's skill theory, the studies reviewed here do not imply that skill levels unfold one from the other in a deterministic way, as predetermined forms. Skills are always the result of an interaction between an individual and an environment; new skills are constructed by integrating or coordinating the previously existing ones, often in a self-organizing process (e.g., see Bidell & Fischer, 2000).

A THEORY OF EMOTIONAL DEVELOPMENT

An equally ambitious line of research on the interconnection of cognitive and emotional development was started by Case, Hayward, Lewis, and Hurst (1988). These authors propose to round out the cognitive theory of Case (1985), which was described in chapter 6.

The Emergence of Emotions and Control Structures

Case et al. (1988) broadly agree with a functional view of emotion, as a system that enables the organism to respond quickly, appropriately, and with suitable intensity to events. Emotions have a neural base; they can directly influence other components of the central nervous system—in particular, cognitive components—and in turn be directly influenced by them. An event can provoke more than one emotion, and these could be more or less compatible with one another. Case et al. (1988) take the assumption from Pascual-Leone's theory that the expressive motor components of compatible emotions combine together, as do their effects on the establishment of goals. In the case of incompatible emotions, however, one of the emotions prevails and inhibits the expression of the other(s). Any such others may, nevertheless, remain active and take the upper hand as soon as the initially stronger emotion dissolves.

An aspect that is particularly emphasized by Case et al. (1988) is the development of control structures for coping with emotional situations. They describe such structures in two categories: (1) external control—action strategies that seek to change or maintain a situation; and (2) internal control—operative schemes (including the defense mechanisms) that seek to modify one's emotional experience rather than the external situation. They argue that the development of such structures of emotional control follows the same laws (see chap. 5) as any other type of control structure.

There is considerable debate as to how many and which emotions should be assumed to be innate. The hypothesis of Case and his collaborators is close to Sroufe's differentiation theory, and only two pairs of affective states are postulated as present at birth: contentment/distress and sensory engagement/disengagement. The more complex emotions that emerge with subsequent development derive from these two pairs by differentiation with a contribution from cognitive factors.

The components of control structures are all modified as a result of cognitive development. The figurative schemes acquired for representing the initial and desired final states of situations become increasingly complex. And the same is true with respect to the operative schemes that permit reaching the goal. After the age of 1 month (when an infant has the ability to maintain one sensorimotor scheme in working memory) these goals begin to assume the form of expectations. Presence in working memory of a sensorimotor scheme representing a desired final state is required by such emotions as anger—following from an unexpected obstacle that blocks goal-directed activities, or happiness—evoked by sudden achievement of an actively pursued goal. Fear also involves anticipation of a feared pain or suffering. For these reasons, Case et al. (1988) argue that joy, fear and anger are not innate emotions, but rather that they emerge with cognitive development in the substage between 1 and 4 months of age.

Jealousy, however, is a response to a situation in which (a) one is aware of an emotional interaction between a loved person and a third person, and (b) one anticipates that this interaction could preclude a similar one between the loved person and oneself. Thus a child needs to coordinate *two relational schemes* (not simply sensorimotor ones) in order to feel jealousy, and from this necessity follows the hypothesis that jealousy will appear around the age of 1½ years old. A similar argument applies to other social emotions, such as shame or pride.

It is interesting to consider the cognitive prerequisites of the control structures known as defense mechanisms. For example, the simplest forms of projection, which involve attributing a negative emotion to another person rather than to oneself, require that one displace attention from signs allowing recognition of one's undesirable emotion to signs permitting its recognition in someone else. According to Case et al., to do so involves displacement of attention from one relational pair to another and this would not be possible until substage 2 of the interrelational stage (between ages 2 and 3½). Rationalization, however, requires evaluation of the motives of one's actions or feelings on a dimension of cultural acceptability and mental construction of an acceptable motive. To shift attention from one criterion or dimension to another more acceptable one is an ability that would rarely appear prior to the second substage of the dimensional stage (7–9 years).

Case (1988) develops this topic, analyzing the ways in which cognitive development influences *object relations* (i.e., relations with one's mother and with other emotionally significant persons) in the first 5 years of life. For example, stranger anxiety is seen as a product of bifocal sensorimotor coordination, in which a child holds in working memory a representation of the interaction with one's own mother while a stranger begins an interaction with him or her. Opposition, displays of autonomy, empathic behavior, and peer conflicts over the possession of objects appear around age 2 because, like jealousy, they involve the coordination of two relational schemes. With acquisition of bifocal coordination, the first compensation strategies with respect to interpersonal conflicts would become possible.

Case (1991b) also analyzes the interplay of cognitive and emotional processes in the development of the self, considering both the "explicit self" (the self as an object of conscious reflection) and the "implicit self" (i.e., the sense of self as an active subject). Sensorimotor activity and its emotional facets between 1 and 4 months would enable infants to develop an implicit sense of their own agency, which becomes fully established with the routines and the interpersonal transactions that are characteristic of sensorimotor coordination, between 4 and 8 months. However, the explicit self would develop only later. Sensorimotor coordination would only afford initial elements of it, such as a perceptual representation of one's hands and their movements. Only the complex patterns of social interaction that are possible during the interrelational stage, the social emotions that come along with them, and the ability to shift from one interrelation to another would finally drive the emergence of an explicit sense of self, which can be inferred from differentiation of the words "I" and "me" in a child's lexicon, as well as from the ability to use a mirror not as a perceptual object but as a perceptual model of one's own body.

Affective experiences, on the other hand, influence cognitive development in various ways (Case et al., 1988). In the first months of life, extreme anomalous conditions impede development of the first control structures and of the basic emotions, and such conditions can result in a chronic apathy that hinders normal epistemic activity. The loss (without adequate replacement) of the mother figure between 4 and 18 months deprives the child of mutual regulation and of imitation; it eliminates a secure base for exploration and independent problem solving. Such a loss can even cause depression resulting in a general reduction of epistemic activity. To give another example, the development of a strong trait anxiety[4] can lead to a slight cognitive delay by reducing available attentional resources by a small, but measurable, amount. Affective factors, related to values, models, and social reinforcers typical of the environment in which the child grows could channel epistemic activity into key domains or favor the development of a particular cognitive style. In general, affective factors could influence the time dedicated to epistemic activity, the content of that activity or the efficiency of cognitive processing.

---

[4]Trait anxiety refers to anxiety that is not connected to any particular circumstance, but rather, has become consolidated as a relatively stable personality trait.

There is empirical evidence supporting these theoretical analyses. Case et al. (1988) present results on the acquisition of jealousy and separation anxiety. As we have seen, they hypothesize that jealousy presupposes a sense of two relations, one between the loved person and oneself and another between the loved person and the rival. This leads to the prediction that clear instances of jealousy will emerge only after 18 months of age. To test it, mothers of children ranging in age from 4 months to 5 years were each asked to initiate a 2-minute interaction with a peer of their child's or with a young infant (according to the experimental condition) who was already present in the room. Manifestations of jealousy were virtually absent in children of 12 months or younger; there were some signs of jealousy in the group of age 16 months, and it was present in the majority of cases for 20-month-olds; and these results held in both experimental conditions. The situation was unchanged with 3-year-olds; after age 4, in the presence of peers jealousy increased, whereas with respect to infants it decreased and was replaced by new coping strategies such as devaluation of the rival or assumption of a role complementary to the adult.

Separation anxiety, according to Case et al. requires a working memory capacity of 2 sensorimotor units and for this reason develops around 4 months of age. This hypothesis was confirmed in a longitudinal study with a group of children ranging from 2 to 6 months in age, observed for 1 minute following a sudden separation from the mother. It was precisely at 4 months that an abrupt increase in separation anxiety was observed. The same children were also given cognitive tasks, which demonstrated an ability to coordinate two sensorimotor schemes at the same age.

Other studies (Bruchkowsky, 1992; Griffin, 1992; Porath, 2003) provide additional evidence that Case's theory can account for the development of empathy and emotion understanding, recognition, and awareness during early and middle childhood. Also, Pons, de Rosnay, and Philipona (2005) demonstrate that working memory capacity is predictive of emotion understanding in children between 4 and 7 years of age.

Appraisals, Moods, and Personality Development

Lewis (2001) develops further the theoretical analysis of appraisal processes, by connecting Case's theory with a dynamic systems approach and the study of individual differences. In particular, the appraisal dimensions of goal conduciveness, coping potential, and norm compatibility are examined in terms of the schemes that can afford them. The earliest appraisals described by Lewis (2001) regard anger or sadness displayed by 4-month-olds when they wish to be picked up and their mothers are visible but out of reach. A perceptual configuration recognized as mother-at-a-distance would be appraised as obstructing goal conduciveness, and motor expectations of mother's approach would suggest high coping potential (thus triggering anger). Sadness can result from the same situations that produce anger in early infancy—suggesting, however, an appraisal of low coping potential. If appraisal dimensions have any meaning at this age, Lewis argues, they must be equated with processes within the capabilities of an infant's sensorimotor schemes. In these cases, two dimensions of appraisal would be produced by distinct sensorimotor schemes.

With the qualitative shift to the interrelational stage, symbols, language, and the formation of scripts enable toddlers to consider not only states or actions, but relationships between kinds of things or agendas. For instance, low goal conduciveness appraisal occurs whenever the mother's goals and wishes are perceived as clashing with the child's own. Threatening a child's possession (e.g., taking a bottle of juice), even in case no immediate action (e.g., drinking) is intended, would lead to a low goal conduciveness appraisal, because possessions now symbolize the potential for action, and goal conduciveness now resides also in availability of resources for future use.

Ability to shift from one script to another, at the age of about two and a half, would be a necessary basis for taking control of emotional experience. For instance, in the case of a child who recites to herself "Babies can cry, but big kids like Emmy don't cry," it seems that high coping potential is involved, as well as a first appearance of norm compatibility—afforded by one of the two scripts that this child is coordinating. A further advance in complexity of appraisals can be observed at the following substage; when a child realizes that other people hold opinions; thus, norm compatibility becomes a focus of appraisal, and shame becomes a more frequent and powerful emotion than it was earlier. A child might also feel incapable of controlling a belief in another person's mind, that is, appraise a low coping potential, and, thus, conceive only one control strategy to get rid of the evaluation, namely, to remove the self from the other's attention.

Dimensional and vectorial thinking would lead to even deeper levels of processing in children's appraisal; for instance, with dimensional thinking goal conduciveness can be assessed in terms of one's rights, the violation of norms is rapidly evaluated thanks to the understanding of rules, and fairness may be linked with coping potential, because one can appeal to fairness to regain one's rights.

This analysis of appraisal is fully consistent with Case's theory. However, Lewis (2001) notes that even though cognitive development sets clear structural limits on which appraisals are possible, a considerable degree of individual variability exists. For example, some children seem impervious to shame and others are painfully dominated by it. Personality differences can be defined as differences in appraisals and the emotions that accompany them. People tend to show a stylistic consistency within (but not necessarily across) types of situations; for example, a child could be aggressive when confronted by peers but meek in response to adult authority. Emergence and development of such individual differences has to be explained.

In addition, Lewis (2000, 2001) points out that appraisal is likely not to be "the" cause of emotion in a linear chain of causes and effects. Rather appraisal and emotion can be seen to cause one another. They consolidate or amplify each other in recursive feedback cycles until the system converges to a stable state on a time scale of a few seconds. In other terms, appraisal would be "the cognitive aspect of a larger self-organizing process" (Lewis, 2001, p. 215; see also Scherer, 2000). These assumptions state the case for a strong complementarity between neo-Piagetian views such as Case's theory and dynamic systems approaches.

Lewis (2000) proposes that three different time-scales are nested within each other: emotional interpretations, which occur in real time and develop on a time scale of seconds or minutes, moods that last for hours or days, and personality patterns that persist for years. Processes on these three time scales would interact and influence each other, so that, on the one hand, personality differences would affect moods and emotional episodes, but on the other, personality differences would evolve and consolidate through recurrent patterns of appraisals (cognitive–emotional interactions) and episodes at the middle time-scale of cognition–emotion resonance, that is, moods. Thus, "personality development can be described as change and stabilization in the state space of cognition–emotion interactions" (Lewis, 2000, p. 54). According to Lewis (2000, 2001), this nesting of time scales makes dynamic system theory an ideal bridge between real-time processes such as appraisals and developmental processes such as personality formation.

Each developmental stage has different "rules" or sets of schemes to make sense of situations, including those that are appraised in relation to emotion. A 4-year-old may think that a child who receives the biggest present is the happiest, but a school-aged child comes to understand that happiness depends on what is wished for (see Case, Marini, et al., 1986). Or, when a mother extends her shopping past the limits of her tired preschooler, she is faced with the distress that accompanies the violation of a script for going home; whereas in the same situation an older child may focus on the violation of compromise and fairness principles, and thus appraise the unfairness of having to remain at the store for mother to buy nonessential items—an appraisal that resonates with feelings of indignation rather than distress. But, Lewis (2001) notes, the stage-specific constraints do not act on some objective read-out of situations in the world; rather, they act on what has already become meaningful and emotional to a particular child through previous experience. Thus, in the late preschool period, through repeated appraisal–emotion events of a similar sort, a particular child may develop a tendency to appraise the self as bad, whereas another child may develop a tendency to blame others. The cognitive characteristics of that age do not dictate any of these two particular outcomes, but permit them both.

Such complementarities between cognitive schemes, appraisal features, and emotions solidify through recurrent appraisals, and shape a child's particular developmental path through a given stage or substage. However, when cognitive developmental parameters change at the beginning of the next stage, those complementarities are bound to be modified. Thus, cognitive stage transitions necessitate the development of new appraisals, and these new appraisals, although partly constrained by existing complementarities, inevitably differ from anything that preceded them.

THE HORIZON OF WISDOM

Pascual-Leone and coworkers have devoted considerable attention to the intertwining of cognitive and affective processes in lifespan development. Moral reasoning is one field of interaction of these processes, and Stewart and Pascual-Leone (1992) present an experimentally supported model of its development in preadolescence and adolescence.[5]

Pascual-Leone (1983, 1984, 1990a, 1990b) considers the developmental stages of the self from adolescence to old age. His theoretical work draws heavily on philosophy (particularly from existentialist authors); he also takes up concepts and terms originally proposed by William James and reinterprets some themes found in psychoanalytic schools. In particular, Pascual-Leone (1990b, 1991, 2000b; Pascual-Leone & Irwin, 1994, 1998) considers themes that have often been neglected by cognitive developmentalists, such as the will, wisdom and the organization of primary emotions in dynamic systems.

"There is no ego in the sense of an organismic faculty or homunculus. . . . The ego is only a particular collection of schemes," claims Pascual-Leone (1990a, p. 269). He considers both the "actual Self" structures and those that constitute the "ego milieu" (i.e., representations of others and objects that are relevant to the self, ideals and values, and ideologies). In particular, he conceptualizes the self as a vast repertoire of schemes, which tend to reach a state of consciousness when activated; any of them might be complex and formed by a coordinated totality of simpler component schemes, some of which might be cognitive in nature and others affective. Broadly speaking the repertoire of schemes constituting the self can be subdivided into five constituents. The first, called *I-self*, includes mental representations of one's own feeling and acting, which also carry the individual's sense of agency and sub-

---

[5]For converging evidence, see also Pasupathi and Staudinger (2001).

jectivity. The second, called *Me-self* or figurative self, contains objectified representations of oneself and one's personal history, which are figurative schemes and fluents;[6] it provides the texture of phenomenal continuity of the self. A third category, *Body-self*, involves personal bodily experiences, such as the output of the somatic senses and motor feedback, as well as their integration in the experience of one's own body as a whole. The fourth repertoire, *Identity*, contains representations of one's different identities within the changeable contexts of life, and of those characteristics or traits that a person regards as stable and essential to one's definition.

The contours of the fifth component, *Ego-synthesis*, are perhaps less clearly defined; it can be understood as a set of personality integration functions. It includes schemes that serve the purposes of self-evaluation, metacognition, ethical conscience, defense mechanisms, and aesthetic awareness, as well as the "collectives of the Self" (a type of representation to be discussed further in the following section).

This subdivision into five components is speculative and, largely, a matter of convenience. It is actually assumed that the schemes form a highly interconnected network, all relating to representations of self. The subrepertoires are connected to one another, and each one could, in turn, be repartitioned into more circumscribed areas according to the connections and similarities among the schemes of which it is made up. The important point is the conception of the self as a set of schemes.

The repertoire, of course, is not static; accommodations and acquisitions are made continuously. Many self schemes are acquired in childhood, and by adolescence a high level of organization is reached, which allows one an awareness of self in daily life and a degree of autonomy in interactions across many different contexts. The Ego synthesis functions themselves require a certain level of development. From here Pascual-Leone (1983, 1990a) puts forward an account of the stages of adult ego development, taking into account both a growth in experience and a deterioration of attentional resources.

In the so-called late formal stage (from about 17 to 25), advanced explorations of interpersonal relations enrich and consolidate two I-self structures— the I-agent, a system that governs relations of interpersonal power and of environmental control; and the I-soul, a system of relations and feelings of love (in a broad sense). In this stage the emerging contradictions among affective goals and among schemes (*partial-selves*) acquired in different contexts are sharper than at earlier ages. That sharpness could release a new awareness of contradictions in the self and, therefore, a new coordinated structure, in which the various partial-selves are represented and controlled. This struc-

---

[6]Fluents are defined as schemes with an intrinsic time structure (see chap. 2). Thus, a figurative fluent is a scheme that carries representations or expectations of how certain events have taken place or will unfold in time.

ture would be a "collective Self" or *ultraself*; however, it is limited to what Jaspers called "empirical existence." Pascual-Leone calls "existential self" the typical ultraself of the late formal stage.

The subsequent "predialectical" stage (up to 35–40 years) features the consolidation of a lifestyle and philosophy, including theories regarding certain experiential domains. These structures, together with the person's defense mechanisms and the I-operator, serve the function of keeping a sense of coherence, by inhibiting those contradictory Ego schemes that are not dominant (i.e., are not part of the current contextually variable identity). The theories of life of this stage correspond to the self-awareness that Jaspers called "conceptual existence." However, they could be too global and idealized to encompass the evolving diversity of true empirical existence. At this point in development it is possible that one creates a dual system in which an ultraself of empirical existence is to be found just beside an ultraself of conceptual existence, whose respective structures cannot be directly integrated.

Based in part on a functional decline in the cognitive resources ($M, I, C,$ and A-operators),[7] it is to be expected that a crisis would occur at age 35–40. Attentional energy becomes less easy to mobilize, and irrelevant information is less easily inhibited; spontaneous learning of new content is slower; emotions are less intensely felt, or rather, their power of activation decreases. The processes regulated by conceptual existence schemes (which make heavy attentional demands) begin to lose their predominance; and, as a result, one is less able to suppress affective goals and values, which up to that time had been inhibited in the name of efficiency and faithfulness to the principles of one's philosophy of life. On the other hand, greater life experience and a new uncertainty regarding the future allow one to notice contradictions among one's dominant theories. These theories become more elastic, less static and more attentive to changes with respect to both one's personal history and the times. An awareness of "temporal existence" emerges.[8] One can, so to speak, discover dialectic. More precisely, it is the

---

[7]Abundant evidence (e.g., Salthouse, 1996; Schonfield & Wenger, 1975) suggests that decline in some cognitive functions starts prior to age 40 and accelerates after age 60. However, not all cognitive functions decline and some are even capable of continuing development at an advanced age (Baltes & Baltes, 1990).

[8]In some persons, based on the style of life (e.g., a person dedicated to caring for a family) or on other individual differences, the ultraself of the predialectical stage might assume the form of a temporal existence, based on awareness of the processes of change in others and an ethic of interpersonal responsibility. Those people who in the previous stage had acquired a temporal ultraself could now commit themselves, conversely, to develop the conceptual aspects of existence. For example, it sometimes happens that, when one's children have grown up a bit, a parent who had previously been devoted to childcare decides to initiate a program of study or some professional activity. In the process such parents would develop not only their cognitive competencies but also new self and existential schemes.

COGNITIVE AND EMOTIONAL DEVELOPMENT

organization of the ultraself that, in coordinating the empirical, conceptual and temporal awareness of existence, tends to become dialectical. It is from this development that the name "dialectical stage" derives (Pascual-Leone, 1990a).

The main thesis of Pascual-Leone (1983, 1990a) is precisely that the decline of cognitive resources (in particular, of the I-operator—see chap. 2), along with the internalization of greater life experience and awareness of one's multiple, often contradictory roles and goals, makes it difficult to suppress awareness of the contradictions in the self, thus opening the way to dialectical thinking—in the sense that one becomes more aware of contradictions in one's own ego-schemes and world views, and one can use this awareness in thinking about the constraints and challenges of life. As Pascual-Leone and Irwin (1998) note, young adolescents may study dialectical philosophy and understand dialectical thinking well, but only in an "external" manner. Dialectical thinking becomes actually rooted in the self only with the "positive hermeneutics" of this stage of life, during which a person is likely to actively pursue one's contradictions in search of new dynamic syntheses that might resolve the experienced conflicts.

After age 55–60, the deterioration of attentional resources can result in a lessened capacity for action; however, greater experience, reduced planning of the future, further reduction of the inhibition of contradictory "theories" and ego-schemes, and reminiscence (which is facilitated by reduced interruption) can lead to the emergence of a form of "meditative thinking." Detached from the tie to action and from pressing affective goals, thought is able to take up the ego structures (i.e., one's selves, ultraself and "theories" of life and the world) as objects of dialectical reflection, thereby freely exploring the actual or possible evolution of one's mind as a whole or of one's life. Now the ultraself or self collective stretches to include the operative schemes of the "meditative existence," coordinating them with the other forms of self-awareness and self-regulation. This stage is called "transcendental" by Pascual-Leone (1983).

Of course, the sequence of adult stages outlined here is not rigid. The decline of attentional resources is even less determined by chronological age than is their development, and environmental opportunities are probably more unequal for adults than they are for children. As well, there are experiential and social factors to consider; for example, the family models and career models that are prominent in a society. Not only is the age of passage from one stage to another approximate, but neither can it be taken for granted that every person acquires the forms of organization and self-awareness that are proposed to be associated with each stage. As we have emphasized, the focus is on the possibilities that arise in the different phases of one's life, but they do not necessarily arise in the same way for everyone. Though cautious with respect to these points, Pascual-Leone is certainly speaking of proper stages. He proposes transitions from one stage to the next that are characterized by crises and disequilibria and followed by a phase of variations from which emerge new structures involving general aspects of self. The similarity to the Piagetian conception of equilibration is clear.

In addition to social factors and personal experiences in family life and professional career, some particular sorts of experience are likely to affect adult development—and deliberately aim to do so. One of these is psychotherapy. Greenberg and Pascual-Leone (2001) discuss how conceptual and experiential schemes (see chap. 2, footnote 10) interact in the process of constructing personal meaning. Much emotional experience is driven initially by dynamic syntheses among automatic processes, which can be followed by deeper levels of processing. In particular in the context of psychotherapy, emotions are evoked; and, thus, affects, bodily perceptions and feelings can be targeted for attention and reflection. The authors discuss the dialectic between experiential and conceptual schemes, and between automatic processes and attentional control, in three important moments of personal meaning construction during a psychotherapy session, that is, emotional arousal, symbolization, and reflection. Another activity that purposely affects adult development and the emergence of wisdom is meditation, in its various forms of practice, mostly originating from Eastern cultures. Pascual-Leone (2000b) offers an interesting neuropsychological analysis of the consciousness processes and phenomena that occur during meditation, and of their neural substratum.

In this lifespan developmental context Pascual-Leone (1990b; Pascual-Leone & Irwin, 1994, 1998) reintroduce the theme of will into the psychological discussion. They relate classical philosophical analyses of will to TCO models, describing the contribution of the various operators to will as expressed in acts and judgments. An act of will is a choice brought about by dynamic syntheses made possible by the resources of mental attention and inhibition monitored by suitable executives of a high level of abstraction.

In the transcendental stage, the I-agent and the ultraself are characterized, in part, by a "will-not-to-will." In the previous stages, however, especially at the younger ages, the individual has only the "will-to-will"; that is, a desire to make choices and pursue goals. At more advanced ages a desire for harmony could prevail and lead one to "will" only if necessary for existential, ethical, or life-threatening reasons. The "will-not-to-will" would seem an essential aspect of wisdom. Another important aspect would be a capacity for empathy and justice, deriving from a full dialectical integration between the I-agent and I-soul. For example, wise counsel can be differentiated from counsel that is simply expert and competent by the fact that it not only calls on the authority of reason (or of a reasoned tradition), but also, almost paradoxically, emphasizes the freedom of the person to whom it is addressed. Pascual-Leone (1990b) illustrates the paradoxical nature of wise counsel with a verse from Antonio Machado (1964, p. 269), *"Doy consejo a fuer de viejo: / Nunca sigas un consejo."*[9]

Within this lifespan stage system (though, as we have said, not a rigid one), wisdom is conceptualized as "the rarely attained, *asymptotic* state of normal human growth toward maturity" (Pascual-Leone, 1990b, p. 272).

CONCLUSION

A first, important conclusion that we can draw is that numerous studies, carried out within different neo-Piagetian theories (e.g., Case et al., 1988; Fischer et al., 1990, 1997; Lewis, 2001; Mascolo et al., 2000; Pascual-Leone, 1991), converge in their regard of emotions as constrained by cognitive development. All these authors would agree that the degree of coordination among schemes, skills or representations that a child can achieve at a certain stage or substage of cognitive development places an upper limit on the type of appraisal of which that child is capable. Emotions and coping strategies seem to emerge according to a time schedule that depends on the time schedule of cognitive development.

Of course, there can also be differences among specific models because of the assumptions made by different neo-Piagetian theories on the basic units of cognition and the development of working memory and attentional resources. However, in most cases, it would not seem difficult to "translate" models from the language of one theory to another, for example, to translate the models of Mascolo et al. (2000) into Case's theoretical language, or those of Lewis (2001) into Pascual-Leone's. Though interested readers could try for themselves, we do not carry out this exercise here due to space limitations.

The approaches reviewed here depart from each other in a few important details, and these reflect to some extent the broader debate on the psychology of emotions. Although Case et al. (1988) essentially accept Sroufe's differentiation point of view, Pascual-Leone (1991) takes up aspects of the differential theory of discrete emotions and the hypothesis that these are innate. More precisely, he suggests that the pure *affective schemes* (physiological modifications, predispositions to goal generation and to action) are innate, whereas *emotions* (combinations of pure affective schemes with cognitive schemes, which permit activation and, eventually, interpretation of the affective schemes) become manifest in the course of development. Thus, although the numerous primary emotions may have an innate neurological base, this does not mean that they are displayed at birth. Debate on

---

[9]As I am an old man I give you counsel: / Never follow any counsel.

what components of emotions are innate is likely to continue among psychologists of different orientations for the foreseeable future.

An original idea of Pascual-Leone (1991) is that affects and emotions constitute *dynamic regulatory systems*. By this account the primary emotions are not constituted of isolated affective schemes, but by dynamic systems of affects that allow a person to react to situations with alternative strategies (that is, with different, sometimes incompatible, emotional responses that are, nevertheless, all adaptive in some respect). For example, he hypothesizes two dynamic systems that predispose a person's action toward objects in the environment. One of these systems is composed of the emotions of attraction, non-attraction, disgust and tolerance; the other of courage, cowardice, fear and trusting acceptance. Within both systems, for each of the four constitutive emotions there is another emotion that is highly compatible (e.g., cowardice and fear can easily mix in a single emotional state) and two that are incompatible. Weaker relations of compatibility or of incompatibility are found between emotions belonging to different systems (e.g., there is some compatibility between disgust and fear). The possible alternatives for adapting to a situation through different emotional reactions derive from these relations of compatibility or reciprocal inhibition among the emotions.

More recently, the idea of emotions as dynamic systems has been developed and pushed further by other authors. Lewis (2000, 2002) views emotions as self-organizing systems and proposes to apply the principles of nonlinear dynamic systems theory to each of three time-scales of emotion development. Also Mascolo et al. (2000) regard emotions as composed by multiple processes or subsystems, which mutually regulate each other and self-organize into a series of patterns or attractors. Similarly, Scherer (2000) describes different emotions as attractors in a response surface that can be modeled according to the functions of catastrophe theory. Scherer's idea of emotions as attractors in a nonlinear response space seems akin to Pascual-Leone's concept of dynamic systems of emotions that are more or less compatible with one another—even though these two authors might disagree on some of the variables that control and regulate the space of emotions.

More generally, Fischer and Bidell (1998, 2006) consider emotions as a psychological domain that can be analyzed by combining structuralistic and dynamic principles. They also note that emotion and cognition affect each other's development so extensively that they are difficult to separate, and many of the major developmental reorganizations occur concurrently for emotion and cognition. In a similar vein, Lewis (2005) sees not only emotions, but also perceptual categories, motor coordinations, linguistic categories, cognitive skills, and belief systems as attractors in a psychological state space. Lewis proposes that some self-organizing cognition–emotion patterns converge with increasing likelihood and become characteristic responses to particular kinds of situations. These emerging attractors can be viewed as a source of individual differences, but at the same time they can be considered as stage-specific constellations that characterize a particular period of development and then break down at the onset of a stage transition. Lewis (2005) also suggests that positive and negative emotions may have an important role in the selection and reinforcement of a child's cognitive strategies in the periods of fluctuation that characterize stage transitions.

Thus, emotional development and its intertwining with cognitive development seems an area that offers major opportunities for a comparison, and probably an integration, of neo-Piagetian and dynamic system approaches. More precisely, in the field of emotion research it becomes apparent that neo-Piagetian and dynamic system approaches at least share certain epistemological assumptions and could usefully complement each other.

CHAPTER

9

Applications

We have considered neo-Piagetian theory and basic research in the earlier chapters. Now we turn to some applications of the theory to testing and educational practice. We also consider methods for task analysis, which though not totally formalized, appear useful for both research and application.

PSYCHOMETRIC APPLICATIONS

Neo-Piagetian theories assign a central role to constructs such as working memory, attentional resources, or central computing space. As a result, the studies undertaken to test those theories have also created measurement instruments for such constructs. By developing and refining these measures the neo-Piagetians have also contributed to the technology of testing. However, not all the theories have contributed in equal measure. As discussed in chapter 3, Halford initially worked with the traditional concept of short-term memory understood as a storage site for information in the course of processing. As that concept became problematic, Halford turned to the dual-task, easy-to-hard method, which is valid, but does not provide a capacity measure. Others, like Fischer or Siegler, have been interested in the construction of scales of cognitive development in specific domains, but have not worked on measures of general information-processing capacity. The main contributions in this area come instead from the work of Pascual-Leone and, above all, Case.

APPLICATIONS

285

The CSVI (Compound Stimuli Visual Information task) was the first measure proposed by Pascual-Leone (1970). Numerous studies (e.g., Globerson, 1983a; Miller, Pascual-Leone et al., 1989; Pascual-Leone, 1978) validate this task and another similar one, the SSVI (Serial Stimuli Visual Information task; "serial" because each figure's characteristics are presented in sequence, one at a time) as measures of M-capacity. Some details of this work were presented in chapter 2. In the years since the tasks' origin the availability of computers enabled improvements of the tasks in terms of controlling stimuli presentation and provision of a special response keyboard. A practical disadvantage of these measures, however, is that they require a rather long time to administer. Despite other merits of these tasks (e.g., the possibility of using them over a wide range of ages) they seem more likely to continue to be used for research purposes than for diagnosis.

The advantage of simple, rapid administration is to be found in other tests such as the Counting Span (Case et al., 1982), the Mr. Cucumber Test (De Avila et al., 1976), and the Backward Digit Span. Case (1985) discusses these tests and proposes their use with children up to age 11.

The Counting Span involves displaying cards with a number of differently colored dots. The child must count out loud only those dots that are of a specified color, and do so rapidly while pointing to each one (so that the counting is quick and mechanical and does not leave time for enacting other strategies). For the initial items, which involve a single card, the child needs only to repeat the result of the counting. As the test proceeds, however, each item involves the presentation of two cards, then of three, and so on; and the child must remember the number of colored dots on each card in the item. It is not required that the count totals are repeated in strict order, and a certain tolerance is allowed for any counting errors. Item difficulty depends mainly on the number of cards presented; the test score is based on the number of counts that the child is able to recall (Case, 1985).

The Mr. Cucumber Test uses the outline of an extraterrestrial character to which colored stickers have been attached; the number and position of the stickers vary with each item. Each figure is displayed for 5 seconds before an identical outline is presented without stickers and the child must point to the places where stickers had been attached. The score on this test depends on the item's principal source of difficulty, namely the number of colored stickers for which the child must reproduce the positions (Case, 1985; De Avila et al., 1976; de Ribaupierre & Bailleux, 1994).

The Backward Digit Span consists simply of repeating back a series of digits in the opposite order of their presentation. Tasks of this type are found in various intelligence tests, including the Wechsler battery. In Wechsler's test, forward and backward digit span are taken together to yield a single score. This is an unfortunate confounding given that the two types of task involve different mental processes (Case, 1972; Morra et al., 2001; Schofield & Ashman, 1986). Case and Globerson (1974) were among the first to propose the use of the Backward Digit Span as a measure of the "central computing space," arguing that it entailed the mental representation of a series of numbers as distinct units and the transformation of their order.

In the FIT (Figural Intersection Test) each item involves the display of a number of separate geometric figures on the right side, and on the left side the same figures (often rotated, enlarged or reduced, and in some items also an additional, irrelevant figure) in a manner such that they overlap and intersect. The essential task is to place a mark in that area of the compound figures where all of the relevant figures intersect. The task becomes more complex as the number of component figures increases (Pascual-Leone & Baillargeon, 1994; Pascual-Leone & Ijaz, 1989). The FIT can be used with individuals from age 7 up through adulthood; children younger than 7 could have difficulty understanding the instructions. The test can be group-administered, with considerable savings in time. Recent research (e.g., Pascual-Leone et al., 2005) suggests that the FIT is also useful for identifying "latent-gifted" children, that is, gifted children who are not identified by traditional testing. However, a disadvantage of the FIT is that its score is also influenced to some extent by spatial ability and field independence (e.g., Baillargeon et al., 1998).

Neo-Piagetian research has also produced other tests that have not, however, been frequently used. These include the digit placement task (Case, 1972), a backward word span (Morra & Scopesi, 1988), a Raven matrices adaptation (Bereiter & Scardamalia, 1979; Pennings & Hessels, 1996), the mental-attention memory task (a measure of memory for strings of consonants in dual-task conditions, such as alternating recall of each single consonant with items of a pointing task or the Stroop task; see Pascual-Leone & Johnson, 2005) and the direction following task (similar in method to the Token test, but with items carefully graded for M capacity demand; see Cunning, 2003; Pascual-Leone & Johnson, 2005). In chapter 6, we have already considered Case's construction of tasks appropriate for preschoolers (Case, 1985; Case & Khanna, 1981). Alp's (1994, 1996) Imitation Sorting Task involves, in its first items, imitating an adult who drops an object in a container, and in following items, imitating the adult's sorting of a group of objects that are dropped in two separate containers. This task should be mentioned as the only M capacity test that can be used with very young children, from 12 to 42 months.

The value of using the tests just described with children, and perhaps with elderly or cognitively impaired adults, becomes evident when one considers that, traditionally, cognitive diagnosis has involved either intelligence tests, which provide a useful but rather global measure, or tests of particular abilities intended to detect rather specific deficits. It is not common practice to evaluate whether the quantity of information children are able to process simultaneously is normal for their age. This lack may stem from the fact that such hypothetical constructs as short-term memory store (Atkinson & Shiffrin, 1968) or central executive (Baddeley, 1986) were either inadequate or insufficiently specified. In this regard, neo-Piagetian research is able to provide a more adequate theoretical framework as well as the measuring instruments that stem from it.

An important methodological problem that the neo-Piagetian approach had to solve concerns the definition of a measurement unit. If a theory conceptualizes information-processing capacity as the number of schemes (or cognitive units) that the child is able to keep in mind simultaneously and coordinate, then a technical difficulty is how to make well-grounded assumptions on which pieces of information should be regarded as distinct schemes in a test. Furthermore, the test must not lend itself to a strategic variability that permits the shrewder children to reduce the information load. Case (1985) recommends the use of tests in which (a) all the stimuli constitute distinct units and are unrelated, (b) all the items have the same content and are presumably approached with the same strategy, and (c) the only difference among the items is the number of stimuli presented (and, therefore, the number of figurative schemes employed). Even though these criteria may oversimplify the problem somewhat, they are certainly useful as a practical guide to the construction of items.

Another important methodological problem concerns the construct validity of the tests, that is, whether or not the tests assess the construct they are intended to assess. Though not numerous, the studies concerned with this issue do provide converging data (Case, 1985; Case & Globerson, 1974; Globerson, 1983a; Morra, 1994; Morra et al., 2001; Morra & Camba, 2005; Pascual-Leone & Johnson, 2005; see also Pulos, 1997, and related commentaries). In general terms, the important questions are whether the measures demonstrate the predicted progression relative to age and whether they are positively correlated with one another. Although very high correlations are not to be expected among tests that involve such different materials and tasks, without substantial correlations among them it would not be possible to consider the tests to be measures of the same psychological construct.

The cited studies show that the tests have the same age trends, are positively correlated and that it is possible to identify (by means of factor analysis) a common dimension among them. This dimension can be interpreted as information-processing capacity. At the same time, however, the correlations are not very large and, in general, the test scores seem to reflect not only a general ability to keep information in mind, but also specific abilities related to the type of material and the type of information used in the test.

For this reason, it is advisable both for research and diagnostic purposes to employ a battery of several tests rather than to rely on any one alone.

Though not designed within a specifically neo-Piagetian framework, studies have also shown that some of these tests are good predictors of reasoning and mathematical ability (e.g., Barrouillet & Lecas, 1999; Bull & Scerif, 2001; Handley et al., 2004), thus providing additional evidence for their construct validity.

It should also be noted, however, that some tests (in particular, the Counting Span and the Mr. Cucumber Test) seem to yield valid measures of capacity only in children up to about age 11, or in elderly people; these tests probably underestimate the capacity of older children and normal young adults. Why can these people not recall the larger sets of items that, in principle, their M capacity should afford? For the counting span, there is clear evidence that memory performance is highly prone to interference from counting (Halford et al., 1994; Ransdell & Hecht, 2003). Therefore, with larger sets, interference from extended counting as well as some output interference (e.g., Cowan et al., 1992) could hinder participants' performance. Because younger children are only able to count and correctly recall items with few sets of dots, the counting activity can only interfere minimally with recall of those digits. However, as soon as one reaches items with four or more sets to count—as occurs with older children and adults—performance appears to be affected not only by limited capacity, but also by a stronger interference of counting on digit recall. For the Mr. Cucumber test, there is some evidence (de Ribaupierre, Lecerf, & Bailleux, 2000) that adults tend to encode stimuli verbally, even though this strategy is not particularly efficient. Also for the backward digit span, both output interference and strategy development may restrict the age range to which it is validly applicable as a measure of capacity. These issues could be clarified by a research program—so far, still missing—that compares and tests detailed task analyses of all these tests.

EDUCATIONAL APPLICATIONS

Education is a major field of application for neo-Piagetian theories. Mascolo, Kanner, and Griffin (1998) suggest that a neo-Piagetian approach can break down the dichotomies that separate constructivist and sociocultural approaches. Major neo-Piagetian contributions to education concern individualization of instruction and the promotion of broad cognitive skills. The term *individualization* refers to the adaptation of a curriculum or instructional sequence according to the characteristics of the students. Instruction of broad skills involves the teaching of conceptual structures that cross over several domains, executive schemes, and metacognitive skills that can be used in various contexts.

The most general principle of neo-Piagetian work on education (e.g., Case, 1978b) is based in an analysis of the cognitive operations that the proposed instructional situation requires and of the cognitive operations of which the students are capable. From this point of view, teachers plan instructional activities that favor students' acquisition of operational abilities (strategies, executive schemes) and application of these to the given situation.

Curriculum Planning and Individualized Instruction

Neo-Piagetian theories, as we have seen, incorporate a number of different constructs; this implies that the difficulty in learning any particular concept or skill could have a variety of different causes. Early studies by Case (1975b, 1978b, 1980) provide useful suggestions for diagnostic strategies and associated instructional interventions.

For diagnostic purposes, one may want to detect the causes of a child's failure on a task. A child could approach a topic with a pre-established conception or strategy that is simplistic or inadequate and hinders acquisition of more appropriate concepts or strategies. Some aspect of an exercise or of the instructional material may be particularly salient and strongly activate inadequate knowledge. It is also possible that the content or the way in which it is presented poses an excessive information load for the student's processing capacity. Even if after identifying (in the manner of Gagné, 1970) the information and procedures that the child must integrate in order to acquire a new skill and having found that the child already has all of these, it is still possible that the child might lack the necessary processing capacity to integrate them. Still another possibility is that such base knowledge is lacking, or that for lack of sufficient practice it is not yet automatized to the point of becoming a scheme that can be activated as a single unit.

The presence of inadequate conceptions or strategies in the child's repertoire leads to errors that are systematic (see Case, 1975b, for examples). In this situation the problem is not the lack of some basic information or skill that has to be activated in order to gain success. Rather the skill the child lacks is the ability to *avoid* activation of inappropriate knowledge. Often an expanded explanation of the correct procedure and a bit of practice will not be sufficient. Even if rewarded, after a short period the correct response will begin to be displaced by the original spontaneous response.

Whenever a task carries an information load beyond the child's capacity (or when the relevant knowledge is not yet sufficiently automatized)[1] the

---

[1] It is useful to evaluate whether the problem's cause lies in a reduced processing capacity or in an insufficient automatization of the fundamental operations. In the first case individualization of the instruction would involve a reduction of the information load, whereas in the second it would require practicing the component operations so as to consolidate the associated schemes.

child is likely to fluctuate among different errors depending on which aspect of the information essential for success is neglected by the child.

Case suggests that a teacher's first goal should be to determine precisely the strategy with which the child is approaching the problem, that is, to determine the informational and operational base of the child's response. Sometimes the nature of systematic errors is obvious and shows the child's approach clearly, but more often it is necessary for the teacher to consider whether there is some similar problem for which the child's procedure would be correct, or whether there is some more restricted set of information for which the response would be appropriate. Also, Case suggests, it may prove useful to observe the sequence of actions or eye movements carried out by the child while engaged with the task. And although the student's metacognitive awareness might be slight, it could still be helpful to ask directly about the procedure followed.

A second goal for the teacher is to define precisely the strategy that is to be taught. Appropriate knowledge of the topic and consideration of how one might proceed are only starting points. It is valuable to observe some students who are able to complete the task successfully, to note their actions or what they look at and to ask them about their procedure. As accomplished students are likely to describe fairly sophisticated strategies, it might be more helpful to speak with those students who have most recently become successful with respect to the task in question. The task analysis techniques that we discuss later in this chapter are also useful.

The instructional intervention must not overload the child with information. Having determined the cognitive skills or units that constitute the appropriate strategy, the teacher must also take care not to introduce more than one new component at a time, nor to ask the student to coordinate too many units of information simultaneously (Case, 1975b, 1978b, 1980). If a particular step in a proposed instructional sequence would require the student to hold too many pieces of information in mind, it would be better to divide it into successive steps.

The first phase of an intervention should engage the learner in some situation that facilitates awareness of the ineffectiveness of his or her strategy. As becomes clearer from the example in the next section, such situations are characterized by having only a few units of relevant information, and these should be familiar to the child as well as salient. The verbal portion of the explanation should refer to only one aspect of the task at a time, and it should be expressed in brief phrases using concrete nouns and active verbs. The explanation should be supported with (simple and salient) visual or tactile information. Pointing out the difference between the presented situation and those other contexts in which the student's response might be suitable is also recommended.

The teacher then demonstrates the appropriate strategy, once again limiting the information presented to the minimum necessary while attending to its familiarity and salience. In this phase as in the first, the accompanying explanation could be preceded by guided discovery and completed with modelling (the teacher demonstrating the strategy while thinking out loud). Most important at this point is taking care to reduce to a minimum both the number of distinct units of information employed and the number of new units introduced in each step. The explanation concludes with a demonstration of how the new strategy functions better than the one spontaneously applied by the student, and the explanation should be presented in a manner that facilitates discriminating between the two strategies.

Finally, the teacher provides situations and time for practice in using the new strategy. Gradually the relevant information in these situations can be made less salient or more numerous. In the event of continuing errors, feedback and suggestions that review the preceding activities and explanations should be provided.

An Example: The Missing Addend Problem

It isn't possible to report here on all the numerous examples to be found in the early educational work of Case (1975b, 1978b, 1980). We must limit ourselves to a brief description of a type of arithmetic problem that causes considerable difficulty for first-graders. These children, though able to count, read numbers and add, often fail to complete operations of the form: $4 + \_ = 7$. Frequently their response is to add the two numbers that are present in the equation, writing for example: $4 + 11 = 7$.

There are two different correct strategies for solving problems of this type. The first, which is the one typically followed by adults, is to calculate the appropriate difference (in the example, $7 - 4$) and then to write the result in the position of the missing addend. The second strategy, and the one generally followed by first-graders who do succeed with the problem, is to start counting from the first addend[2] (e.g., "five, six, seven") while keeping track of the number of units required to reach the given total (three in this case), which they then write down. Case (1980) points out that the first strategy requires understanding of the inverse relation between addition and subtraction and also places a higher load on working memory; therefore, he rejects the first approach in favor of the alternative.

It is not difficult to show students, for example, that $4 + 11 = 15$ and, therefore, that there is something wrong with $4 + 11 = 7$. It is more difficult, however, to teach a correct strategy and to show how to differentiate it

---

[2]In Italy we have often informally observed the use of this strategy by shopkeepers, to calculate a purchaser's change.

from the mistaken one. Using preliminary exercises that clarify for students the meaning of the = and + signs, Case shows them the nature of the problem and explains what goal they are trying to achieve. Rather than using numbers, he presents schematic faces made up of two semicircles joined side by side to make a full circle; various small shapes are used to represent the eyes, nose and mouth. Children are presented with one of these faces together with the = symbol, for example, and then asked to construct another face that is just the same. The next step is to present in sequence from left to right: one half of a face (one semicircle with the curve to the left), a + sign, a second half-face (a semicircle with the curve to the right) and an = sign. The children are asked to construct a full face that would be the same as the one that would result from combining the two half-faces shown in the sequence. All the explanations and instructions are given in very simple terms.

The goal of the first phase is to be certain that children clearly understand the + and = symbols as meaning "put together" and "make the same," respectively—rather than simply interpreting them as "do addition." Once this goal is accomplished, then a problem that uses the same materials and is analogous to the Missing Addend problem can be presented. For example: given a half-face plus an empty semicircle, place appropriate shapes in the semicircle so that the result of putting together the two half-faces will make the same full-face as a particular one that is presented. The faces used in the problems are generally asymmetric; thus, a shortcut of simply selecting the same shapes that are in the given half-face is not viable. The children have to search more carefully to determine the correct shapes that will complete the face. They typically learn these tasks easily and with pleasure.

At this point in the instructional sequence, an intermediate step toward the numeric problem is taken while continuing to capitalize on the salience of visually presented figures. The faces and half-faces are replaced with configurations of dots, and the children are asked to count these. Analogous to the Missing Addend problem, one configuration is missing and the children must determine how many dots are needed in that set. Case (1980) provides the following example of the verbal explanation:

> The question asks how many dots to add on to these dots to make seven. We have four dots here now, so let's keep adding until we get seven. What's the first number after four? Right, five (advancing a token). Keep counting. Six (adding a token), seven (adding a token). Now we have seven dots, just like we're supposed to. So let's count up and see how many we added. Go ahead. These are the dots we added up (indicating the set). Right, we added three. So that's the answer. (p. 173)

These instructions demonstrate how each step presents one piece of information or one request at a time. When it is necessary to coordinate two pieces of information, their salience is maximized. The subsequent steps in the instruction are equally simple. According to Case (1978b, 1980) this sequence for teaching children how to solve the numerical Missing Addend problem is effective not only with first-graders but also with nursery school children and with children who are at higher grades but have a learning disability in mathematics.

Note that, after using schematic faces to help children get rid of misconceptions about the meaning of the signs + and =, Case does not leap immediately to number symbols. Rather he takes the intermediate step of using very concrete and visually salient dot configurations; these help children to construct an intuitive representation of the meaning of the task. In a similar vein, Schwartz and Fischer (2004) describe adults' attempts to solve a problem about an electric circuit and note their frequent attempts to test concretely the behaviour of the circuit, even in those cases where they expected that a certain solution would not work; as these authors remark,

> Students need to build representations based on their own sensorimotor understandings. The advantage of testing the design is that the sensorimotor outcome provides direct information, not information coming from an outside authority (such as a teacher or book). Once students have created their own sensorimotor understanding, they are usually ready to accept the resulting representations as their own. This is an important point for educators who believe that representational knowledge can be transferred to students by simply telling it to them—a process that forces them to "borrow" representations instead of "building" their own. (p. 177)

Thus, both Case (1980) and Schwartz and Fischer (2004) emphasize the role of direct experience and very concrete representations in constructing more abstract concepts or skills. In addition, Case is particularly attentive to describe how to reduce properly the information load at each step of the instruction sequence, and how to use highly salient information at the beginning of the process and progressively reduce the saliency of relevant information.

Teaching Central Conceptual Structures

A paper by Case, Sandieson, and Dennis (1986) is a turning point in Case's applied work, because it is the first educational research that considers central conceptual structures. The authors compare two short curricula for teaching two separate groups of intellectually handicapped teenagers how to tell time. Both curricula were planned according to the suggestions reported here, but the instructional path to be followed differed between them. In the first group the strategy taught involved the mental operations followed by normal adults in telling time. The instructional intervention provided practice with respect to the component skills, coordinating them a few at a time, using them with the help of stimuli that gradually reduced in salience, and developing their significance in contexts encountered in daily life, according to the principles for strategy teaching presented in "Curriculum Planning and Individualized Instruction" (e.g., strong prompts for the minutes were used in the first steps of the training).

In the second group, however, the aim was to recapitulate the acquisition of conceptual skills as they are normally gained (according to a preliminary study) in the course of development from age 4 to adulthood. Like other physical and mathematical concepts (see Case & Okamoto, 1996), the concept of time is usually predimensional at age 4. Children can only grasp time in global terms (short or long), recognise some familiar patterns of the clock hands, and treat them as signals of expected events. Around age 6, most children can understand time in a unidimensional way, similar to the number line; they can also compare two measures of time, but only if the comparison is limited to a single variable (such as hours or minutes). Usually around age 8 they can take into account both of these time scales. A full integration of these dimensions, also including the 5-minute and the 1-minute intervals that are represented on the clock dial, only takes place in normal children between 9 and 11.

The curricula used with the two groups were comparable with respect to their duration and their use of the techniques suggested by Case (1975b, 1980) and described here. The activities were different in that one steered the students toward learning the adult strategy, whereas the other led them through a series of competencies that focused on the conceptual structures underlying the development of quantification. Following the instruction the first group evidenced considerable learning, but the improvement of the second was even greater. Thus in deciding on strategy objectives to pursue, the authors recommend use of a developmental, conceptual model (even if it is based on the performance of normal children only).

The basic and applied research work of Case's group remained closely intertwined in the following years (see also Griffin, 2004, for a review), and other articles proposed educational methods in various fields such as narrative language (Case & McKeough, 1989), scientific thinking (Case & Sandieson, 1988), and spatial abilities (Case, Stephenson, Bleiker & Okamoto, 1996).

However, mathematical education is certainly the domain in which there has been the most extensive work to design curricula based on central conceptual structures (e.g., Case & Sowder, 1990; Griffin et al., 1995; Griffin et al., 1994). Specific curricula, each of which extends over several years, have been proposed for teaching the conceptual structures of whole numbers (Griffin & Case, 1997; Griffin et al., 1994), rational numbers (Moss & Case, 1999), and functions (Kalchman & Case, 1998).

Each of these curricula is basically organised around the four levels of complexity or developmental substages that were presented in chapter 6. For whole numbers, it is assumed that initially children have a sequential, analytic scheme with a major verbal component, the counting scheme, and another scheme for global quantity comparison, with a major perceptual component. These two schemes are at first uncoordinated and thus do not form a conceptual structure proper, but they are its precursors. During the following substage, the two primitive schemes become coordinated into a simple, unidimensional conceptual structure, such as the number line, which enables the child to make fine-grained comparisons and arithmetic operations, not yet possible in the previous substage. A third achievement is the understanding of numbers with two component dimensions, such as tens and units; also the distinction between number as representation of a quantity and as an operator would belong to this substage. Finally, a full understanding of positional value in whole numbers would be achieved.

Understanding of rational numbers would also start with separate, uncoordinated schemes—a propositional one for operations like doubling or halving a number and an analogic one for global perceptual evaluation of proportionality. Subsequently, a sort of mental number line would be constructed, but quite a rudimentary one. One that would only hold, for instance, the results of a sequence of halvings (e.g., $1/2$, $1/4$, $1/8$, etc.), or very simple decimal numbers, such as .1, .2, .3, . . . In a third phase, the conceptual structure would involve representation of rational numbers that derive from different ratios, like 1:2, 1:3, 1:10, and so on. Finally, a full understanding of the rational number system would be acquired, which coordinates such different forms of representation as decimal numbers, fractions, percentages, and the relations among them; however, with a lack of appropriate education, not all children would spontaneously achieve this final substage.

In the case of functions, the two initially uncoordinated schemes would be a digital, sequential procedure for iterative computation of numeric expressions (such as $5 \times 1 + 2$, $5 \times 2 + 2$, $5 \times 3 + 2$, etc.) and an analogic representation of a series of numbers, for example by means of a bar graph. In our culture, most 10-year-olds can master those prerequisites of the function concept, and also understand arithmetic operations, Cartesian axes, some concrete instances of quantitative variables, and relations between them. A subsequent achievement would be putting into relation the two abstract elements (the variables) of a function, by means of a numeric table, or a graph, or a formula (that represents the computations to be run iteratively). Thus, the line graph of a function could be understood as a representation that connects the various results of a series of iterative computations, for different values of x. Further, the relationship between two variables could be grasped in more sophisticated ways later (between about 13 and 15 years), by, for instance, understanding parameters like the slope and the intercept of a linear function, or by clearly differentiating confusable functions, like "$y = 2x$" and "$y = x^2$." Finally, usually after age 15 or 16, one can acquire an ability to understand polynomials, that is multicomponent functions, in which different components could have different properties, so that understanding the properties of the whole function involves understanding not only the properties of each component, but also the relations among them and how they combine in a particular function.

As the reader may note, these ideas keep with the cyclic view of development presented in chapter 6. The proposed sequences of substages, however, are not meant as deterministic. Development involves constructive processes by which simpler representations are coordinated into more and more complex structures. Such increasing complexity relies on both increasing working memory capacity, and progressive automatization of basic components. The latter frees up attentional resources that can be devoted to relations among components. Educational intervention plays a role in the natural developmental process by promoting learners' discovery of relevant dimensions and links among components, and by promoting learners' construction of a semantic and conceptual network rich in connections between various verbal and analogic representations, between figurative and operative schemes. Thus, instruction can facilitate, broaden, and refine cognitive development through activities aimed at constructing, differentiating, and integrating novel schemes, so that pupils can move seamlessly among different forms of representation of the same type of concepts (e.g., the many different instantiations of rational number).

Education is a construction of bridges—not only the large bridges that connect one developmental stage to the next, but also the smaller bridges that connect different meanings and forms of representation.[3] Without these (that is, without construction of a conceptual network in which different procedures and different representations enrich the meaning of one another) education could promote acquisition of routine strategies for solving "standard" tasks, but would not aid transition to conceptual structures of a higher level. The proposed curricula (e.g., Griffin & Case, 1997; Kalchman & Case, 1998; Moss & Case, 1999) are grounded not only in rigorous cognitive developmental research but also in extensive know-how on the art of teaching. For instance, mathematical conceptual structures are usually approached within a nonmathematical context (e.g., playing board games, or using containers for liquids) that has an analogical structure that "will serve as a conceptual bridge between the schemes that are already avail-

---

[3]Case's metaphor of "bridges" for connections that should be constructed among similar or related representations should not be confounded with Fischer's construct of "bridging" as a transitional process that prepares a "leap into the unknown" (see chap. 5).

able in isolation and the more elaborate and integrated structure that is the ultimate target" (Kalchman & Case, 1998, p. 15).

Social class differences in school achievement are a major educational issue. Case, Griffin, and Kelly (1999) note that social class differences in arithmetical knowledge exist in all the *first world*, are particularly dramatic in certain countries including the United States, and can be found as early as age 3. The economic trend of the 1990s toward increasing income differences within Western countries, a trend that so far does not seem to have changed in the new millennium, carries the likely risk of an increase in cognitive ability differences among preschoolers and school children. Case et al. (1999) present the results of a study that spanned four school years starting from kindergarten, and in which low-SES children received an educational treatment with the curriculum "Rightstart." The treatment was designed to foster acquisition of the central conceptual structure of whole numbers (Griffin et al., 1994; Griffin & Case, 1997). These children were compared with a control group of low-SES children and with a "normative" group of children who were not socially disadvantaged. The results showed that at the end of kindergarten the Rightstart group scored much higher in understanding number concepts than the low-SES control group and had nearly caught up with the normative group. At the end of grade one the gap with the normative group was closed, and after grades two and three the average score of the Rightstart group was higher than that of the normative group. As one might expect, there was no reduction in the delay of the low-SES control group with respect to the normative group.

Case et al. (1999) claim that these results "are stronger than any others that have been reported in the literature to date" (p. 143). They also discuss the features of the Rightstart curriculum that make it so effective in treating socioculturally disadvantaged children. They also note, however, that their research was carried out on a limited scale, and that replication on a larger scale would be advisable before proposing a generalised use of this curriculum in schools. This would demand a quite large investment of funds on educational research, but such an economic cost would likely be compensated not only by benefits for the pupils involved, but also by savings in special or compensatory education for those children. Thus, once more, one faces the problem of gaining acceptance for innovative ideas within conservative institutions, which are often concerned especially with immediate financial costs.

Other Broad Educational Goals

Educational theorists often insist on representing not only the specific skills and concepts to be taught, but also on structuring lists of explicit and measurable objectives. The language of neo-Piagetian theories offers a fairly precise means of expressing such objectives, for example, in terms of executive schemes, conceptual structures and other related concepts.

Pascual-Leone et al. (1978) and Case and Sandieson (1988) consider the benefits and costs of instructional sequences designed to facilitate learning particular skills. Pascual-Leone notes that, although such instruction does facilitate acquisition of the skills of interest, excessive use of those forms of teaching limits children's opportunities to gain experience with misleading situations (cognitive conflict) or distracting situations (which activate irrelevant information). Important in curricular content and daily life, such situations also have a general educational importance because of the opportunity they provide for the construction of executive schemes (see chap. 2). Case and Sandieson (1988) also warn that although structured instructional methods can be useful and effective, they are limited in that the transfer of learning beyond the specific, expressly taught skill is not significant.

Pascual-Leone et al. (1978) discuss a variety of control functions that can only be practiced or consciously trained in the context of misleading or distracting situations. Such control functions include the executive schemes that control the use of M operator and I operator resources; decentration (as Piaget called it), which involves moving from activation of level-zero schemes to activation of higher or lower order ones; memory retrieval and metamemory functions in general; and even defense mechanisms and cognitive styles. Rather than gaining practice with these functions, a child who regularly experiences facilitating instructional strategies at home and at school may well, in their place, learn such strategic executive and operative schemes as seeking peer assistance, seeking indulgence from teachers, or withdrawing in the face of difficulties. Pascual-Leone et al. (1978) present examples of two methods for educating executive control schemes.

The "graded learning loops" involve tasks for which the degree of difficulty associated with cognitive conflict or distraction can be adjusted. Children are exposed to a sequence of exercises, all of which involve a similar problem-solving process structure, and that are sufficiently variable in difficulty that each student is able to solve at least a few of them. Suppose that one wishes to teach a sequence of topics A, B, C, D, E, and let us represent a series of exercises as A_1, A_2, A_3, B_1, C_1, C_2, C_3, D_1, E_1, where A_1, A_2, A_3, and C_1, C_2, C_3, are used to create graded loops. The features of these loops are: (a) the first exercise is more difficult than the second, that, in turn, is more difficult than the third, and so on; and (b) whenever students succeed with an easier exercise, they loop back to the slightly more difficult one that they previously failed.

In general, the last item of each sequence is made as easy as possible, facilitated by field effects and familiar content. The first item, on the other hand, is formulated in a more misleading manner. Spontaneous solutions to the simplest items constitute informative feedback that (in addition to maintaining interest) favors acquiring executive and operative schemes that will be useful for solving the more difficult exercises. The teacher returns as often as necessary to these difficult items; and if the acquisition of relevant schemes from working with the simpler exercises is not sufficient, he or she can intervene in a way that guides the students to compare the strategies they have used. The teacher might, for example, ask for explanations of the exercises and for comparisons between them. Because the topics A, B, C, D, . . . are ordered by increasing difficulty, the graded loops encountered early in the sequence assist students to spontaneously develop (that is, without explicit instruction) the executive control schemes and plans needed for tackling problems later in the series.

The "executive time sharing" method is one designed to favor development of I operator controls (interruption and disinterruption executives, which one might also call regulation of attentional filters). Within the context of a game, children are asked to rapidly alternate between (or to carry out concurrently) two tasks that present competing demands to the I operator. One task requires strong inhibition of field effects or particularly salient information, whereas the other relies on such factors for good performance and, thus, inhibition is not desirable for that task. By alternating between such tasks the children exercise control over inhibitory processes, particularly over the movement back and forth between interruption and disinterruption.[4]

Another educational goal that cuts across disciplines is fostering the ability to use analogy in reasoning. A number of applied studies from different theoretical orientations fit well into the debate on enhancing analogical reasoning (see chap. 4). Among these, we mention here Clement and Steinberg (2002), who used a combination of various favorable conditions to help students' use of analogy to change their mental models of electric circuits. They made students go through a series of increasingly complex models, each time presenting their similarities and then their limitations in explaining the target phenomenon. For example, in the first lesson the tutor discussed naïve analogies spontaneously used by students. Then, an analogy was presented and students were led to adopt a more refined model that, in turn, had to be revised in light of conflicting evidence. This process continued until gradually students would revise and reconstruct their knowledge. Also, observing the errors in forming analogies may help the teacher to notice possible problems in students' knowledge and strategic processing. In this respect a hierarchical categorization of error types was identified by Alexander et al. (1998) in a study of learning in two diverse do-

---

[4]It is conceivable that control over the M operator might be practiced in an analogous manner, that is, by alternating between one task that imposes a heavy load on working memory and another that requires use of no more than a small amount of highly salient information.

mains, biology and educational psychology, with fourth grade and under-graduate students, respectively. Using such a categorization may help teachers to tailor adequate instructional interventions.

Teachers should be aware of the relevance of using well-designed analo-gies following instructions derived from research. When a textbook in-cludes an analogy, the teacher may supply operational steps, leading them to identify similar features and consider whether they are surface or struc-tural, to map the critical features, and to draw inferential information for the target concept, while making explicit the limits of the analogy.

We close this section with a brief mention of motivation, a central theme in educational psychology. The role of what neo-Piagetians call executive schemes in the motivational processes is widely recognized; representation of goals and certain aspects of metacognition provide relevant examples of executive schemes. Case's group always paid attention to children's moti-vation in developing curricula such as those described in the previous sec-tion. However, motivation in educational context has not been widely inves-tigated by neo-Piagetian authors. Some implications for motivation can be found in discussions of the will by Pascual-Leone and Irwin (e.g., 1998) and in research work by Shafrir and Pascual-Leone (1990) on the effect of cogni-tive styles on children's errors in problem solving.

Toward a New Foundation of Cognitive Educational Research?

The studies just described contribute to educational practice in important ways; however, Fischer and Immordino-Yang (2002) set an even more ambi-tious goal, that is, founding a new kind of educational science. This science would be based on the recognition that skills develop independently within domains (see chap. 5 for Fischer's web metaphor), but at the same time, processes of cognitive development are similar across strands in the devel-opmental web, and can be described according to a single scale—the levels of skill complexity described by Fischer (1980a; Fischer & Bidell, 2006). Based on these general theoretical views of development, on broad psycho-logical constructs such as Case's central conceptual structures, and on re-cent methodological improvements such as the microdevelopmental ap-proach, Fischer and Immordino-Yang (2002) propose to use detailed data on learning in specific contexts to assess learning for each student or group of collaborating students (see also chap. 5). For instance, they discuss how the detailed observation of a dyad of students who try to understand the functioning of a robot (Granott, 2002) can illustrate acquisition of a new skill. The process starts from primitive sensorimotor actions on the robot, but does not progress along a straight line. Rather, there are different phases of skill acquisition involving disruption when the context changes even minimally and reconstruction of knowledge. The study of word reading by Knight and Fischer (1992) also provides an interesting example of how different skills (such as letter identification, rhyme recognition, and word reading) may merge into the same strand for some children, and remain as separate strands for other children (in particular, for those with reading difficulties). Schwartz and Fischer (2004), on the same line of reasoning, discuss students' use of skills at different levels, from simple sensorimotor actions to systems of representations (level $Rp3$) in solving problems on electric circuits.

All these examples illustrate how learning and skill acquisition can be described in terms of non-linear progress along different strands of skills, strands that are interconnected but to some extent independent of one another. Fischer and Immordino-Yang (2002) suggest that intensive collection of detailed data, according to the microdevelopmental method prescriptions, and the use of nonlinear dynamic mathematical tools for modeling complex growth curves, can bring about a radical change in describing and predicting learning, and designing educational intervention. In this sense they set the goal of founding a new cognitive science of learning and development.

Certainly the link between development and learning is a major feature not only of Fischer's, but of all neo-Piagetian approaches to education. The suggestion of using microdevelopmental methods and nonlinear mathematical modelling also seems very promising, in that it has already provided valuable descriptive accounts. Attainment of the most ambitious goal of refounding cognitive educational science depends, however, on a critical assumption, namely, that Fischer's scale of developmental levels (described in chap. 5) is not only valid, but also that it can be applied with equal ease across all domains and content areas of educational interest.

With this caveat, one might suggest that alternatively other scales, less universal in scope than Fischer's skill complexity levels but still sufficiently general, could be used to assess students' understanding and learning; for instance, the developmental levels in each of Case's central conceptual structures.[5] Also in this case, using microdevelopmental methods and nonlinear mathematical models could still prove very fruitful.

On the other hand one might object that, although microdevelopmental studies are very important for accurate modelling of the skill acquisition process, they could be too time-consuming for the applied purposes of everyday educational assessment. For these clearly applied goals, educators might be especially interested in psychological models of the optimal conditions

---

[5]Or, at an even more domain-specific level, the scale proposed by Niaz (1987) for understanding chemical equations—a scale, based on Pascual-Leone's theory, of the solution complexity of chemistry problems.

and ways of acquiring core concepts and skills. Neo-Piagetian models such as those presented in this chapter seem to be quite useful in this regard.

It also seems important to note that all main neo-Piagetian authors who consider educational applications have emphasized a dialectic between facilitating or supporting conditions and misleading, problematic or unfamiliar contexts.[6] This is evident in Fischer's discussion of optimal versus functional levels of performance and of how a skill has to be reconstructed when the context changes (e.g., Fischer & Immordino-Yang, 2002), in Pascual-Leone's discussion of graded learning loops (Pascual-Leone et al., 1978), and in Case's care about creating connections between different representations of a concept (e.g., Griffin & Case, 1997) and assessing the extent of transfer that a training procedure affords (Case & Okamoto, 1996). The message that seems to emerge from these different contributions is that educational intervention should exploit both highly supportive contexts (which, in Fischer's terms, enable optimal performance to emerge) and more problematic or even misleading contexts that challenge students to rework and generalize their skills, applying them in a novel situation or in the face of misleading factors.

HEURISTIC TOOLS FOR TASK ANALYSIS

Whether for research or for applied work, use of a neo-Piagetian theoretical framework requires at least some creativity in task analysis. One has to formulate an explicit, detailed model of the mental processes involved in the psychological performance that one wishes to explain, produce, or remediate. Because neo-Piagetian theories are general theories of mental development, they cannot be applied directly to specific situations or tasks. They must be applied indirectly, that is, with the mediation of a specific model that is constrained by the constructs and propositions of the general theory as well as by an accurate representation of the task and its context. For a clear discussion of the relationship between general theories and specific models see Pascual-Leone and Sparkman (1980). The specific model can not be derived deductively from the general theory like a theorem, and the theory obviously does not represent the infinite number of specific situations that are possible. Instead, it is necessary to use the theoretical concepts to create one or more models that are suitable for the demands of the given situation.

Classical discussions of task analysis distinguish between rational and empirical methods. The former refer to a theoretical assessment of what

---

[6]Performance and understanding in misleading or unfamiliar contexts can also be hindered by students' misconceptions; for example, see Schwartz and Fischer (2004) regarding misconceptions of electricity.

knowledge and processes are required by the task; the latter involve the use of data collected from the situation under consideration (for example, typical errors, detailed behavioral observations, think-aloud protocols, or interviews with those who are skilled or expert in the task). Neo-Piagetian authors generally use both rational and empirical methods in carrying out their task analyses.

Pascual-Leone and Johnson (1991) lay out some steps for a psychologist engaged in the creative process of task analysis. They define task analysis as a collection of heuristic methods that is able to yield a specific model of the processes leading to an individual's final performance, given a particular situation and the adoption of a particular strategy. The account given in the following section is based on papers that specifically describe methods for task analysis (e.g., Pascual-Leone & Johnson, 1991, 2005) as well as on research seminars, recurrent personal communication, and informally shared research experience.

Identifying the Cognitive Units

Objective analysis is a first, necessary step in task analysis. One begins with a description of the objective aspects of the situation in which the task takes place—for example, the materials, the instructions, and the physical and social environment. An objective description of the performance of interest is also required; for instance, the relevant aspects of the behavior of any prior participants who performed the task in this manner might be described. Objective analysis of this sort has long been expected from psychologists in the area of applied behavior analysis. This first level of analysis is necessary in order to have a clear representation of the constraints and the situational opportunities to which the participant might respond, as well as of the required features of an individual's performance. Up to this point, the units of analysis need not represent the participant's cognitive structures. For example, one could describe the physical environment using standard units of measure or the participants' behavior in terms of a purely observer's language.

An *introspective and phenomenological analysis* could follow the objective analysis. In this case one might ask what one's own behavior would be in the same situation; or better, ask what that behavior would be if he or she were a person of the sort that is of interest in the research.[7] "Phenomenological reduction" suggests taking account of the experience of a generic task participant from the point of view of an ideal observer. If one is skepti-

---

[7]Though we are not sure of the anecdote's source, it seems that Edward Tolman, the father of "subjective behaviorism" in the thirties, would ask himself when planning animal experiments, "What would I do, if I were a rat?"

cal about phenomenological methods, however, or doesn't feel competent in their use, there are also empirical means that can be used—for example, interviewing participants who are experienced in the task's general domain, or watching the participants for signs of insight and paying particular attention to the actions that precede and follow it. The goal of this second step in the task analysis is to identify participants' goals, intentions, or interpretations of the task that might orient or guide their praxis.

Subjective analysis, the third step in task analysis, goes beyond the objective elements of the situation and the behavior in it, as well as beyond the aspects of experience that are consciously accessible. The subjective level of analysis involves psychological aspects of which the participant may be unaware. Conventional or arbitrarily selected units of analysis are not satisfactory at this level, as the units must be appropriate to the theory that is adopted: schemes, skills, productions or whatever else is defined as basic information processing units. There is broad agreement among diverse cognitive theories that schemes (or other basic cognitive units) are hierarchical—that is, complex units are seen as constituted of simpler units. However, if in a task analysis one takes the position that a person is using a scheme of a certain level of complexity, because the more complex cognitive representation takes on the unitary character of a well constituted whole, it is not necessary to determine the simpler units of which it is composed.

It is not typically easy to determine what subjective information units (what schemes, in the case of most neo-Piagetian theories) are involved in a given mental process. In fact, most of the criticism of the neo-Piagetian approach points to the difficulty or arbitrariness of this determination[8] (e.g., Flavell, 1978). The first steps of the analysis, that is, the identification of the objective situation's obstacles and opportunities, the identification of the basic characteristics of the analyzed performance, and the identification of goals and task features likely to be salient for participants, constitute a series of useful pointers toward a preliminary, hypothetical list of the schemes that those individuals employ. The participants' errors are a further source of useful information for this purpose.

Systematic errors on a task may be indicative of erroneous strategies, or they may indicate inefficient use of an appropriate strategy.[9] In the first

---

[8] Such criticism, however, often comes from an empiricist epistemological conception and has a familiar ring echoing the behaviorists' criticism of mentalism. Nevertheless, it is a useful reminder that the process of identifying the schemes employed in a task should not be arbitrary.

[9] To discriminate these two cases, Case (1975b) suggests a valuable heuristic, namely to ask whether there is some similar problem for which the participants' procedure would be appropriate, or whether there is some more limited set of information for which their responses would be correct.

case, the psychologist could consider such questions as: what schemes (what condition–effect pairs) are involved in the erroneous strategy? What factors tend to activate such schemes? What other schemes would have to be activated in order to overcome the erroneous strategy? In the interesting case of an appropriate strategy inappropriately applied, each systematic error is actually a direct pointer to information that is necessary for efficient use of the strategy in question. The failure to activate or use such information leads to a certain type of error. Different errors are indicators of distinct information units that are required for use of the strategy of interest.[10]

Having carried out the steps described thus far and having drafted a list of schemes or units likely involved in the task, the psychologist should briefly check that they are actually *subjective*, that is, to make sure that his or her own schemes have not been put in the place of the participants' schemes. Pascual-Leone and Johnson (1991) provide some criteria that are useful for this purpose. First, one can carry out an "ecological assessment," asking oneself if it is plausible that the environment in which the participants live has provided them the opportunity to acquire the designated scheme. An additional question is whether it is credible that the participants' praxis or interests have led them to actually form such schemes. And if the participants are children, then a "psychogenetic assessment" is advisable. In this case one would ask whether the schemes in question have generally been acquired at the age level of the children involved. If there is evidence that they have, one can continue the analysis more comfortably. However, if there is evidence to the contrary, or if the complexity of the schemes is such that the children are not yet likely to have the ability to acquire them, then it would be necessary to split the more complex schemes into their components, which are more likely to have been acquired.

We have dwelt in particular on the subjective phase of the analysis because it is the most delicate. One is identifying cognitive units that are connected not only to the task or to the described performance, but also to the "subjects" who produce that performance. The difficulties and problems are obvious; one must remember, however, that task analysis is a heuristic method. The psychologist is not seeking to *verify* a model of cognitive proc-

---

[10]Note that the procedures described are appropriate for developing a model of the subjective units employed by a *generic* participant who belongs to a certain population. If the task analysis is undertaken for study of or intervention with an *individual*, it could be difficult and laborious to conceptually reconstruct that person's repertoire of schemes. It would be advisable to begin with a detailed behavioral observation in the situation of interest, or with techniques (verbal, graphic, etc.) for eliciting the person's related knowledge. However, the problem remains of identifying the cognitive *units* or schemes. In addition to the assessments described in the remainder of the text, it is possible to design minitests in which those who do possess a particular scheme would be able to produce a rapid response.

esses, but rather simply to propose one. Verification is a matter for the application of other means, for example, experimental methods. Nevertheless, the importance of a well conducted task analysis is clear: the more the use of these heuristic methods leads to valid hypotheses, the more one is spared the laborious revisions that accompany unsatisfactory attempts at verification.[11]

Process Modeling

Structural analysis is the fourth phase of task analysis. Its purpose is to identify, from among all the information units involved in the task, which set of units that must necessarily be coactivated and coordinated lest the described strategy be impossible to enact effectively. It is not a matter of adding to or building on the knowledge obtained in the previous steps of the analysis, but rather of drawing attention to one part of it. When a theory like Pascual-Leone's is adopted, the structural analysis is a rather important step because it provides an estimate of the information load associated with the task. On the other hand, if the theory adopted is that of Case, Fischer or Halford, then the structural analysis is absolutely decisive because of the structural nature of their explanatory models.

Just as the cognitive abilities associated with each stage are expressed formally with algebraic or logical structures in Piaget's theory, so it is that in some of the neo-Piagetian theories each stage or substage is defined by a category of relations, which specifies a finite set of cognitive units and the form of the functional relation among them. Consider, for example, the second level of Case's dimensional stage. It is defined by the presence of four cognitive units of the dimensional type, and the relationship among these units is pairs. This substage is further defined by an index that allows a child to focus on one relation without forgetting the other. Similar examples could be drawn from Halford's or Fischer's theories with differences only in the types of units and the forms of relationships that they propose (see, e.g., Andrews & Halford, 2002; Fischer & Bidell, 1998). Therefore, a psychologist using one of these theories must give maximum attention to the structural analysis phase. It is not enough to determine the cognitive units or schemes that a strategy requires. The psychologist must also specify the interrelation among these units and how it corresponds to the relations (structures) posited by the theory.

The structural analysis is often followed by a *temporal* or *computational analysis* of the information processing. An advantage of considering the

---

[11]If the test of a model leads to its falsification, and if revision and correction turn out to be impossible, then at that point it must be concluded that the theory used to construct the model is false, or at least that it is not able to explain the phenomenon of interest.

temporal flow of information is a "sharpening" of the results of the structural analysis. It could happen that a rational structural analysis indicates that a certain set of cognitive units are all equally necessary for implementing a strategy, and yet a temporal analysis of the processing might reveal that although these units are indeed all necessary, they are activated at different steps of the mental processing.

Given that cognitive science has already developed numerous techniques, many based on empirical data, for analyzing the temporal flow of processing, we do not dwell on the details of this aspect of task analysis. We mention only that even if the task analysis does consider the temporal aspects of the cognitive processing, it is still necessary to consider information load and the structural relationships among the cognitive units. At this point, these are not expressed with respect to the strategy as a whole. Rather, the concern is with the particular step of the processing that is characterized by the maximum information load or by the maximum degree of structural complexity. Thus, one will not state that the overall task carries a certain information load or a given structural complexity, but rather that these are associated with a critical step of the process.

For psychologists who choose to work with the TCO, there is a final basic part of task analysis, the *metasubjective analysis*. This analysis involves formulating explicit and plausible assumptions about the sources of activation of each scheme in each moment in the flow of processing. By doing so, quantitative or qualitative predictions of the sort we have seen in previous chapters become possible. Recall that a scheme can be activated directly by perceptual input, or it can be activated by one or more metasubjective operators; but a scheme may also remain partially active after having been activated in an earlier moment of the cognitive process. In this case, however, its partial activation will be ineffective in the presence of other fully activated and incompatible schemes. One of the purposes of the metasubjective analysis is to point out the temporal sequence of sets of schemes activated by the M operator in order to be able to derive predictions from it regarding the possibility of succeeding on a task. Another important purpose is to point out the role of learning, or of the F and I operators in activating and inhibiting schemes. It is from these that predictions of individual differences derive.

Given the nature of the TCO's constructs, it is evident that the metasubjective analysis is essential to its use. In principle, however, this analysis is not exclusive to the TCO. Any theory that postulates the existence of a set of general information processing mechanisms at the psychological (or neuropsychological) level requires assumptions, implicit or explicit, on the role of such mechanisms in each moment of processing.

The directions we have given here assume an ideal task analysis, one in which the psychologist has access to all the necessary information and faces no practical restrictions (time, availability of suitable participants, etc.) In reality, however, all sorts of practical problems may arise. If, for example, there is no sufficient basis for an adequate temporal processing analysis, then one will have to make do with a structural analysis (which often represents a critical aspect of the processing) and possibly apply the metasubjective analysis to that. If one lacks empirical evidence regarding what cognitive units the participants use, then one must proceed with conjectures.

Task analytic methods are a debated topic and some authors see them as a weak point or a limitation of neo-Piagetian research programs. For instance, Siegler (1996a) criticizes Case's research program on the grounds of a lack of explicit principles by which types of reasoning are assigned to levels. According to Siegler, the degree of difficulty of an item could depend on some combination of conceptual structure, working memory capacity, specific knowledge (possibly taught at school) and practice at a given skill (such as mental arithmetic), and the theory does not specify clearly how a conceptual structure is involved in understanding or solving a particular problem. Case (1996d) answers that one can never make a prediction about a specific task only on the basis of a general theory; one must also always develop a specific model for that task. In other words, a theory with explicit, formal rules for analysing a certain class of tasks would no longer be a general theory, but rather, a specific theory for that class of tasks. Such specific theories and models can be generated within the frame of a general theory, but only on the condition that additional assumptions are made, for instance, on the experiential factors that affect children's representation and response to certain tasks. These *specific* assumptions are not a part of a *general* theory of cognitive development. On such relationships between general theories and specific models see also Fischer and Immordino-Yang (2002), Pascual-Leone (1994), Pascual-Leone and Sparkman (1980). One might argue whether certain heuristics or analytic procedures are better than others and more likely to yield a valid model of a task—and the aim of this section has been to guide the reader to use heuristics that we believe to be useful—but it remains a fact that they are heuristics, not algorithms.

Therefore, obviously, even a task analysis conducted under optimal conditions can not be guaranteed to result in success. And yet, sometimes an analysis conducted by purely rational means can give good results. However, the more one has to do without empirical evidence, controls, and other research precautions, the more one risks rash assumptions and hypotheses. If one thinks of a theory as the conceptual scaffolding for a specific model, then good heuristic methods for task analysis can be considered the safety standards intended to prevent falling off of it.

CONCLUSION

In this chapter we have presented some psychometric applications of neo-Piagetian theories, and a range of educational applications. These fields of application are quite natural for cognitive developmental theories. We have also presented some heuristic tools for task analysis that the readers can use to shape their own theoretical models or to plan their own applied research.

Although cognitive testing and education are the most natural fields of application for neo-Piagetian theories, one can also conceive of potential applications to other fields. For instance, one might attempt to use neo-Piagetian theories and task analytic techniques to examine human factors, expertise and cognitive load in working situations (for a pioneering study in this field, see Boag, Neal, Loft, & Halford, 2006). As well, neo-Piagetian contributions to the study of emotions could be a starting point for future applications in the study of personality differences, atypical emotional development, and perhaps even clinical intervention. Basic research, in psychology as in any other science, need always be ahead of application, but the fact that several applications of neo-Piagetian theories are already available is also a promise that more and more applications can be invented in the future.

10

In Conclusion

Our discussion of neo-Piagetian theories concludes with a review of the various theories in terms of some of the fundamental questions of developmental psychology. We consider the response of each theory to those questions and evaluate the extent to which they do or do not succeed. In the final section, we make some suggestions for future work toward their theoretical integration with one another.

THE SHAPE OF DEVELOPMENT

One justification for associating the adjective "neo-Piagetian" with the theories we have discussed is their retention of Piaget's idea that development advances in stages, the idea that cognitive changes associated with subsequent levels or phases permit resolution of successively more complex problems and tasks. Another idea is that the same processes underlie progress in different domains, and that it is for this reason that development takes the same shape in different domains.

The Issue of Generality and Specificity in Stage Development

We can make a first distinction among the theories by establishing what it is that advances. Pascual-Leone, Case, Halford, de Ribaupierre, and Demetriou propose that the change is structural. They associate progress with the type of operations and with the complexity of the schemes. For Case, progress is related to conceptual structures that the child is able to apply across different problems. Karmiloff-Smith and Mounoud argue that it is the child's representations of the world that advance from phase to phase. Karmiloff-Smith points to changes in the child's level of awareness of specific pieces of knowledge. Mounoud explains representational change introducing both structural and functional organizations. Finally, for Fischer and Siegler the change is the result of patterns of variability and stability. Fischer proposes a dynamic structuralism according to which the advance is to be found in the child's skills, that is, in a dynamic organization of behaviors. For Siegler the change involves increasingly complex rules and processes of strategy discovery and selection.

Associated with these differences is the important issue of generality versus specificity. Is there a development of general processes and operations that apply across knowledge domains, as proposed by Piaget; or is there, instead, an acquisition of specific knowledge and skills in relation to particular knowledge domains?

The answers provided by the neo-Piagetian theories include theoretical constructs that assume (at least to some extent) general development while also including constructs that account for developmental progress in each set of tasks separately. The difference lies in the relative emphasis of the constructs. Some theorists (Halford, Mounoud, and Pascual-Leone) give major emphasis to the general aspects, although they also include learning processes that can account for lack of synchrony across different domains. Others emphasize specific acquisitions (Demetriou, Fischer, Karmiloff-Smith, Lautrey, and Siegler), so that a child is not expected to be at the same level in different domains nor on all tasks within a domain. Case focuses on general as well as on specific aspects.

Although some of the proposals we have considered do view progress as occurring primarily within knowledge domains, it bears noting that none of these fall into the extreme nativist position of prewired modules. As Karmiloff-Smith (1993) states, "Modules, where they exist, may turn out to be the developmental *product* of a gradual process of modularization" (p. 10).

The issue of generality is also linked to the concept of a constraint on the level of progress during development. There is an effort in all theories to account for the common impression that children at certain ages typically show a general increase in a range of abilities. A shared idea among theories that give a stage account of development is placement of an upper limit on the child's performance in a given stage, a sort of ceiling that performance cannot exceed. The upper limit concept appears not only in those theories that emphasize generality over specificity, but also in those for which the emphasis is reversed. One might ask how this concept can feature in theories with such different bases. One consideration is that a theory may acknowledge the involvement of general processes in the acquisition of domain-specific knowledge, for example, analogy (Karmiloff-Smith) or processes of strategy selection (such as explaining why to use a strategy, as in Siegler; see Crowley & Siegler, 1999). Another is that theories may assign an explicit role to maturation, which places an upper limit on the rate of development, a limit that applies in all fields of knowledge.

In the case of Mounoud, a maturational limit is based in a predetermined type of code that marks a genetic mechanism and marks a new general stage. A general process of conceptualization or thematization (Mounoud, 1988) permits the child to represent through cyclical phases the transactions between organism and its environment in any domain, according to the symbolic level allowed by the new code (see chap. 7). Structural organizations are general and relate to central processes (Lautrey, 1990) controlling activation of basic reasoning structures. Environment plays a specific role only on the functional organizations.

In the case of the theories of Pascual-Leone, Halford and Case one finds a parameter relating to mental capacity in terms of information load and/or working memory. This is M-power in Pascual-Leone, WM in Case, and processing capacity in Halford. For Fischer, an upper limit is set by the system's carrying capacity. The different labels suggest different views on the nature of the upper limit. For example, WM for Case is a quantitative parameter defined by the number of units and relations among them that a child is able to operate at a given time. The parameter concerns the executive structures, but Case indicates that WM sets a limit as well on the level of the conceptual structures. For Fischer, carrying capacity refers to quantitative aspects such as frequency of an activity and complexity of a level, as well as to qualitative aspects such as appearance of a new level or coordination of two abilities (Fischer & Bidell, 2006). Although his model considers the number of skill components and type of relations among them, Fischer does not emphasize a quantitative measurement of the upper limit.

To exemplify differences in the ways generality and specificity are addressed we refer to two perspectives, represented by the theories of Fischer and Case. Each includes basic concepts and processes to account for both specific and general developments in their theories.

Fischer maintains that behaviors relating to a single skill display patterns of variability and stability. Concerning specificity, the child builds a skill by acting on specific tasks within each specific domain, through processes such as shift of focus and bridging. These processes lead to differentiation and integration and to hierarchical skill coordination. Within his dynamic systems approach, growth is influenced both by continuous biological changes and by ever changing physical and social environments. An increase in specific skill performance, when associated with temporary optimal support, creates instability, and performance soon drops by way of a backward transition process that permits rebuilding of the skill. This fact indicates that consolidation may trail the first appearance of a higher level performance considerably. Siegler's notion of rate of change, relating to the first use of a strategy, is similar (see chap. 4; Siegler & Stern, 1998; Siegler & Svetina, 2002). As Fischer states, "The human capacity to move down to such elementary levels provides enormous flexibility for intelligent adaptation"; thus regression of performance on a specific task domain reflects "the need to build and rebuild a skill with variations so that the person can eventually sustain it in the face of changes in context and state" (Fischer, in press, p. 17). A change in one variable of the context affects the others; but perturbation of the system creates the conditions for consolidation of a task domain skill via simple rules like substitution and repetition. These involve *within-domain* generalization, which first occurs in tasks sharing more component features (see chap. 5).

Furthermore, for Fischer development is constrained by maturation and controlled by features of a dynamic system. For example, many brain measures show growth in cycles of spurts and drops, which appears to relate to skill progress (Fischer & Bidell, 2006; Fischer & Rose, 1994; Thatcher, 1994). Discontinuities occur in concurrent clusters produced by dynamic regulatory processes; this points to the concept of equilibration (inspired by Piaget). Fischer introduces the concept of an "attractor" functioning as a point toward which skill performances tend to converge. The system is "attracted" by stable configurations and when it is lost, as in the case of a rapid spurt in a task domain, for example, the system seeks equilibrium (Fogel, 1993; Thelen & Smith, 1998; van der Maas & Molenaar, 1992; van Geert, 1998). If the system is ready, processes of skill construction lead to a macrodevelopment, showing concurrent spurts of (relatively independent) skill clusters. However, when the system does not have the "carrying capacity" needed to move up the other skills, a process of backward transition is activated, the level of the spurting skill drops and equilibrium is reached again.

In sum, Fischer pays attention to the need to explain generality and does so without renouncing the idea that psychological development is primarily a matter of skills constructed in specific task domains. In fact, his theory allows some generalization within a skill domain, but does not allow the so-called general abilities. General changes marked by hierarchical levels and tiers occur because the system is self-regulated and self-organized and stability is a temporary phase obtained by concurrent skill clustering through the mechanism previously described.

Other theorists share Fischer's idea of the importance of variability for generalization. For example, for Goldin-Meadow and Alibali (2002) a regression eventually leads to a more stable performance predicting generalization. In particular, Siegler proposes that generalization is slow and benefits from the use of various strategies. In his computer simulation model of strategy discovery, the system learns which strategies are useful for a specific task and which can have a more general application (Shrager & Siegler, 1998).

Case, whose focus was originally on generality, modified his theory in an important attempt to mediate (or, as he says, to create a "compromise") between general and specific perspectives on development (Case, 1992a; Case et al., 1993; Case & Okamoto, 1996). The modified perspective is the result of a long process of elaboration undertaken in the course of his study of development (see chap. 6). He attributes great importance to maintaining a stage concept that can explain the considerable synchrony found across domains, a crucial inheritance from Piaget. However, he also takes account of domain specificity views. In addition to executive control structures (ECSs, the procedural operational level of the organism), children develop central conceptual structures (CCSs), integrated networks of concepts and relations among concepts. They are applicable to a broad range of domain-specific tasks (like the specific structural systems [SSS] of Demetriou et al., 1993) as indicated by high within-task-domain correlations and by the finding that different task domains load different factors. This supports both specificity and within domain generalization.

How does Case preserve the possibility of both specificity and generality? Could CCSs account for specificity with generality guaranteed by ECSs? This is not the case: both ECS and CCS structures present specificity in their acquisition: executive structures are tailored on specific tasks and different ECSs are built in service of the same domain-specific CCS (Case, 1996). Factors such as culture, experience with the task, and motivation influence, to some extent, the level of performance and contribute to variability. Yet, development follows a stage-like pattern of progress with similar levels of performance shown in tasks belonging to different domains and with influence of factors such as culture, when present, limited to one substage (with rare exceptions: Fiati, 1992; Porath, 1992). Further, they involve activities focused differently in different cultures rather than general understandings common to a task domain. Case notes a general correspondence between levels of acquisition of executive and conceptual structures: increases in one can foster increases in the other: in Case's terms, they are reciprocally coupled.

Generality in development depends on a general quantifiable constraint, the size of working memory. WM slowly increases with age, controls the complexity of relations that executive structures can handle at a given point, and has a facilitating effect on conceptual components. Consequently, WM sets a limit on the highest performance achieved at a given age in any task domain, but training that has improved a conceptual structure does not exert an influence on size of WM (Griffin, 1994). The constraint has a maturational origin that also involves neurological growth: Case (like Fischer) is very interested in carefully examining studies on different aspects of cortical changes in the brain. Cyclical advancements (levels within a stage and major stage transitions) are controlled by multiple maturational factors that constrain the processing capabilities of an individual and contribute to synchronous developments (see the following section). According to Case, the interplay between maturation and children's experience permits developmental changes to take place in different domains at about the same time. Lewis (1994) noted a difficulty in this solution given the problem of measuring experience. However, studies in which experience is manipulated (e.g., Fischer & Pipp, 1990; Griffin & Case, 1996) do encourage introduction of this factor. Experience may take different forms and children may be variably exposed to it, creating a source of asynchrony. However, Case notes that any cultural and social context offers some experience useful to build basic concepts in any domain. This narrows the extent of variability across task domains and, given the required processing capabilities, may lead to different forms of developmental generalization.

In elaborating a deeper account of specificity and generality, Case introduces different levels of psychological processes (see chap. 6) such as processes of differentiation and structure integration supported by associative (C-learning) and attentionally mediated (M-learning) processes (borrowed from Pascual-Leone), working together in an "iterative feedback loop" (Case, 1996b, 1998). New associations among schemes, formed with awareness, are consciously applied in different task contexts through processes of differentiation and integration. Their consolidation frees attention that, in turn, is useful to learn yet new associations improving some aspects of a CCS, in an iterative fashion. A hierarchical feedback loop connects this new specific learning to a more general structure, advancing through the abstractions of basic principles that possess, in Case's terms, some commonalties in form, leading to further generalization of the conceptual structures to include other specific situations. Clearly, the hierarchical learning loop has an important role in mediating general and specific advances.

Thus, new structures formed in specific domains contribute to general advances in learning and, in turn, these advances influence progress in specific task domains, including those in which a child does not have much experience. By proposing such an interaction, Case aims at supporting the idea of an "averaging" effect in performance levels. In particular, Case suggests two ways in which even profiles can be obtained with the mediation of general structures. A high frequency of learning experience in many tasks can be passed on to those situations less frequently experienced: this accelerates their progress, favoring a leveled performance. This way is connected to the small (non significant) effect on development exerted by cultural difference in the case where a culture may offer low exposure to some task domain. The other way is connected to the more diffuse negative effect of a low socioeconomic environment. That is, relatively little experience in most of the tasks in a CCS decelerates the rate of development and results in a significantly lower CCS level. These conclusions are further supported by a mathematical model: This model has a dynamic component in that the growth rate is the mediation of two opposing tendencies. One is toward dispersion and the other toward holding different developmental pathways together, via connections posed by a hierarchical feedback loop controlled by the system's capacity. The interaction between generality and specificity is supported by the finding that the best fit to Case's data is obtained for growth curves derived by modeling a process in which a hierarchical system is characterized by reciprocity between general and specific variables (Case, 1996b).

The positions taken in Case's and Fischer's theories, although starting from different premises share some similarity regarding the importance attributed to task-specific acquisition and generalization within a domain. However, the contrast is considerable between the nature of the executive control and conceptual structures in Case and the task-specific skills in Fischer. For Case generalization is theoretically predicted within each broad conceptual domain. For Fischer, variability is expected whereas generality seems procedurally grounded (based on processes or rules such as substitution, shift of focus and bridging) and it is predicted mainly on the basis of shared components only within specific tasks.

Some similarity is present also, however, in the way they explain stage-like development. Fischer utilizes the notion of "attractor" suggested by the dynamic systems approach. It relates to the convergent spurts shown by skill clusters; for example, the process of bridging is considered an attractor (see chap. 5). Case speaks of a "standardizing" or "averaging" mechanism, a hierarchical feedback loop as previously described.

Furthermore, for both theorists maturation is an ultimate, but indirect, basis from which general stage-like change derives. Both seek to determine how brain growth controls acquisition of specific abilities in mental development, and both attribute the stage or tier development to a general constraint ((having a maturational origin) on processing capabilities that controls development in different specific task domains. A difference is found in the specification of how such a general constraint operates during development: Fischer introduces the notion of the system's carrying capacity, a somewhat vague concept that has limited predictive power (although, as mentioned in chap. 5, he occasionally speaks of working memory [Bidell & Fischer, 1994]). Case is more precise in this regard, and speaks of a quantifiable size of working memory as a psychological constraint to which executive control and conceptual structures are subjected, thus limiting the role of experience in increasing the level of performance. However Fischer explains variability directly, Case views it as the effect of fluencing performance rather than as a phenomenon helping to ex predict development.

Continuity and Discontinuity in Stage Development

A proposal that development proceeds in stages is bound to involve discontinuity. Stage change is viewed as qualitative: with attainment of a new stage the performance of the prior stage is no longer recognizable as the child's method of thought and form of representation become different. Many neo-Piagetians have noticed that when children have moved to a new stage, they still approach some tasks at the level of ability characterizing the previous stage. For example, Fischer shares with Siegler the observation that when children are learning new skills or strategies they also have at their disposal less advanced ways of thinking (see the following section).

Furthermore, recall that one of the criticisms directed to Piaget's theory related to his lack of clarity and precision regarding the developmental processes leading to stage changes. The neo-Piagetian theories, inspired by the information processing and dynamic systems approaches, have attempted to avoid this problem by describing structural changes with quantitative parameters and/or with sophisticated qualitative processes. Some theorists (namely, Case, Fischer, Halford, Pascual-Leone, de Ribaupierre, and Demetriou) employ task analyses for the purpose of characterizing the complexity of ability at the new stage transition. In so doing, they determine processing load required in task performance, considering both the number of elements and the relations among them that must be kept active in order to solve a given problem. As a matter of fact, some have questioned whether, for the purpose of assessing these theories, it is sufficient to compare the cognitive level actually required to solve a task with the level predicted by the theory for that task. The concern is that both the observed and predicted values result from analyses based in the same theory. Whatever one's position on this matter, however, one must acknowledge that a task analysis, even with these limitations, gives greater precision to a theory and permits an account of the effects of the variables introduced. In fact, Mounoud and Karmiloff-Smith have not formulated analyses capable of making accurate predictions and they lack the ability to anticipate the role of task-relevant variables despite having attested to their importance.

Some theories resolve the continuity/discontinuity problem by proposing substages within each Piagetian-type stage. This construct permits theorists to hold on to the idea that progress occurs through partial achievements so that minor spurts do not await the stage transition to occur. The theories of Fischer, Mounoud and Case all include this construct, and they also share a cyclical conception of development as a recursive progression of phases within each stage. Stage change is presented as resulting from the attainment of greater structural complexity and more complex skills through the recursive levels or substages. The precise form of the substages differs among proponents. In Case and Fischer, on the basis of a task analysis, the four successive substages involve an increase in the number of schemes and in the complexity of their relations. The first level is characterized by single units, used and elaborated independently of one another. In the last substage (featuring the highest complexity reached in a skill or concept in that stage) consolidation of performance permits compacting the skills into higher order single units, at the expense, however, of the single components. These units constitute the basis for further developments, that is to say, they become the minimal unit (of skill, ability, concept) constituting the first level of the next stage, and the cycle of substages is repeated.

For Mounoud, it is the mode of representing the world that varies with each phase. Initially global and syncretic, a representation becomes partial, decomposed into its constituent features. Then, through unification of the elementary representations, representation of the totality becomes possible, first without the ability to represent its features, subsequently with the ability to represent both the totality and the relations among the parts. Compared to Fischer or Case, Mounoud's cyclically recurring phases have a more qualitative nature.

These theories represent a step forward in our understanding of development by suggesting how to conceptualize the minor changes that precede stage changes. Yet, although these proposals are certainly more explicit about changes between substages, they seem to provide a less precise account for the qualitative nature of stage to stage progression. Certainly their various stages have labels similar to those used by Piaget, but although Piaget explicates how a new stage differs from the preceding one in terms of his (problematic) conception of change in logical structure, for Fischer and Case the new stage results from a major change in structural complexity, in terms of reciprocal relations among a greater number of elements that are compacted (or chunked) to become the basic units of the new stage. Mounoud's theory also shows limitations in explaining how children pass to the type of representation permitted by the code of the new stage. It is not clear, in particular, how the child renders the most advanced representation formed at the end of the preceding stage (a representation that considers the relation among the parts alongside the totality) into the least advanced representation (a syncretic global mode) characterizing the new stage.

Overall, these theories seem to concentrate more on the characteristics of continuity or, more precisely, of minor quantitative changes, than on the discontinuity of development at a stage level. For example, Halford (1993b) notes that Case, the only theorist assigning a quantitative value to substage developments, defines the working memory load for the within stage transitions but does not do the same for the stages. As a matter of fact, stage transition is presented by Fischer, Case and Mounoud as having a qualitative nature, and by definition such a change cannot be accounted in terms of quantitative processing load alone. The three theorists do address the question of how a major qualitative change occurs and share the proposal of processes such as differentiation and integration (introduced also in substage transition) as a partial answer to the question. In particular, whereas Mounoud resorts to a new predetermined symbolic code to take account of stage changes versus changes between phases, stage transition has been reworked by Case and Fischer. They have done so by turning to more precise psychological processes and to general constraints of the system processing capabilities. This reworking has been facilitated by Case's sharing of some aspects of a dynamic view of the system and basic concepts of Pascual-Leone, and by Fischer's elaborations based on features of dynamic systems models, such as catastrophe and hysteresis. As just mentioned with respect to generalization, processes such as bridging, hierarchical integration, and hierarchical feedback loop at the time of stage transition work along with a system's tendency to "standardize" (Case) or "attract" (Fischer) performance at an equivalent level to reestablish equilibrium, and they do so either by pulling task performances toward the highest limit or decelerating toward a lower point. This new proposal appears a very useful contribution on the path to explaining discontinuity at the stage level also. Despite these promising efforts, it seems that stage transitions are still less specified than transitions between substages in any proposals of the cyclical type, and they would benefit from further specification of how the mechanisms work.

Cyclic phases within stages are not the only resolution of the continuity/discontinuity problem; other neo-Piagetian theories offer alternatives, and we briefly consider each. Pascual-Leone proposes an increase with age in M capacity (from 1 to 7 units; see chap. 2). That increase has a maturational base and even though maturation can be described as gradual, a qualitative leap (i.e., a new stage) can take place only when enough mental energy has accumulated to afford activation of one additional scheme. A discontinuity in the theory is seen, for example, in the transition from sensorimotor to symbolic processing, which requires the construction of more abstract (in Piaget's terms, *representational*) schemes, using a certain mental capacity quantified by Pascual-Leone and Johnson (1991, 1999, 2005). In addition, using symbols to think and to understand some simple but misleading task requires that at least one symbolic scheme is activated in the service of a task executive. Given the number of units required for this endeavor, symbolic thought takes a long time to appear, and the process of biological maturation would offer sufficient M capacity for the child to take this step not earlier than at age 3.

The Theory of Constructive Operators also includes constructs that account for gradual aspects of mental development. These are the two operators of associative learning (C and LC) that enable, respectively, scheme differentiation and scheme coordination due to context-bound experiential coactivation. Little neo-Piagetian research has focused explicitly on these mechanisms but they are assumed to be important, for example, in those situations that are facilitative because of overlearning. Although Pascual-Leone does take gradual changes into consideration to some extent, the processes permitting transitions remain to be detailed.

In Halford's theory, based on a structural analysis, the two concepts of processing capacity and learning have a prominent role—though in many respects it is quite different from Pascual-Leone's. In the current version, discontinuous stages are defined by the ability to process relations of increasing complexity: unary, binary, and so on (see chap. 3). Processing capacity is an attentional resource that undergoes maturation and thus accounts for the ability to process increasingly complex relations. Successful processing in a task requires that an adequately complex representation of that task be constructed.[1] This is achieved through some specific experience with the task (or with sufficiently similar tasks) and, consequently, constructions of representations may vary depending on experience offered by the environment across various domains. Thus, Halford's theory is general and discontinuous in its broad relational complexity stages, but it allows some degree of specificity. Learning can also be involved in shortcuts that enable a child to simplify the relational complexity of a problem and thus reduce its processing load. One such learning mechanism is chunking. For instance, if two variables relevant to a task can be compressed into a single, higher order piece of information, then the way is open for an increase in one's ability in that task and in other tasks permitting similar chunking (see chap. 4).

Halford's proposal has attracted some criticisms in the way it determines the cognitive load of tasks and related processes. For example, Zelazo et al. (2003) note that the load is attributed in terms of number of relations or dimensions, disregarding the role that executive functions exert on task complexity.

---

[1]Halford's analysis of processing load involved in cognitive tasks is supported by connectionist models. For instance, a convolution of two vectors can not afford Piagetian conservation, whereas a convolution of three vectors can. To solve a conservation problem of any sort, the child has to construct a representation that interconnects three dimensions relevant to that type of conservation problem.

In contrast to the theorists mentioned with respect to general stage development, Karmiloff-Smith proposes that successively more advanced ways of representing knowledge develop in each concept domain. She is not interested in quantitative change; her theory focuses on qualitative change—a relevant matter for those who consider the qualitative an essential characteristic of Piaget's theory. However, as already noted, relying on a purely qualitative change makes the theory less precise on constraints of a psychological type, and she introduces maturational constraints. Recent consideration of neuroconstructivism has specified multiple influences from biological factors, which also permits graduality in development; but, to our knowledge, the development of qualitative phases of representational redescriptions has not been further elaborated in her later work.

Finally, Siegler's approach to task-specific development does not focus on general stage-like development. His earlier proposal characterizes development in terms of an acquisition of rules of increasing complexity. Siegler's interest in the processes of acquiring more potent rules leads him to focus on the strategies children use to solve more difficult and novel tasks or problems, studying quantitative reasoning and arithmetic primarily but also such domains as spelling (e.g., Rittle-Johnson & Siegler, 1999; Siegler & Jenkins, 1989). He proposes that development proceeds in patterns of "overlapping waves" (see chap. 4), referring to children's use of a variety of strategies from both lower and more advanced levels.

Siegler acknowledges the role of WM, although he does not use a quantitative measure: for example, Shrager and Siegler (1998) indicate that automatization of a problem-solving strategy increases the system's resources, allowing better evaluation of efficient processing and new strategy discovery. Based in his adoption of fine grain analyses of microgenetic observations of children's behavior, Siegler proposes that variation is an important feature of strategy discovery (as we have seen for Fischer). Within-child variability can be accompanied by mechanisms that make possible adaptive choices, allowing the child to anticipate the usefulness of more advanced strategies even before knowing how to use them. For Siegler, development is both qualitative and quantitative: qualitative changes are observed in discovery of new strategies and quantitative changes are found in measures of frequency and efficiency of strategy use (Siegler, 2006).

In sum, Piaget's inheritance has been taken up by neo-Piagetians and elaborated in different forms and within different theoretical frameworks. Differences in the number of stages or substages proposed, for example, point to different views regarding how development takes place and suggest different research goals. We believe, however, that such diversity is a benefit, rather than a limit, of their contributions. We have seen theorists emphasizing general stages (Pascual-Leone and Halford), others mediating between general levels and minor changes associated with cyclical substages or levels (Fischer, Case, and Mounoud), and still others focusing on specific abilities, concepts or theories without interest in building on the notion of broad general stages (Karmiloff-Smith, Siegler, and Demetriou). Halford does not detail minor steps in the broad general stages and is unable to account for gradual advances leading to major transitions. By contrast, Karmiloff-Smith and Siegler, though mentioning generality, focus on how children construct specific abilities and avoid the problem of giving a big picture of child development. Whereas Siegler includes both qualitative and quantitative changes, Karmiloff-Smith and Mounoud focus on qualitative change (although, occasionally Mounoud also speaks of quantitative changes in performance on motor behavior). They give a good picture of children's representation in the different phases but at the expense of a predictive power of the theory.

In turn, cyclical theories provide the most equilibrated proposals with respect to the issue of continuity and discontinuity, and those of Case and Fischer also take account of both qualitative and quantitative aspects of development. As do the other theories, these have some weaknesses in addition to their strengths. The quantitative aspects are well described and explained, and the qualitative changes have been greatly elaborated lately in terms of cognitive and maturational processes. Yet their proposals lack a deeper justification of the qualitatively different type of thought implied in stage transition.

VARIABILITY IN DEVELOPMENT

Varying hand in hand with the neo-Piagetian theorists' position on stage development and generality is their explanation of *horizontal décalage*. Piaget's explanation of *décalage* has often been regarded as unsatisfactory. Recently, researchers have addressed the issue of *décalage* in a more sophisticated way and extended their discussion to other forms of variability as well. Some authors point out that variability speaks against a linear, monotonic view of development, and they do so with different strength and with appeals to different sources and theoretical explanations (Branco & Valsiner, 1997; Case, 1996; 1998; Fischer, 1980; Fischer & Bidell, 2006; Fogel & Lyra, 1997; Karmiloff-Smith, 1979b; Pascual-Leone & Goodman, 1979; Siegler, 1994, 2006; van Geert, 2002).

Those theories that emphasize developmental specificity tend to draw from studies that emphasize differences in performance, by comparing either tasks belonging to different domains or multiple performances on a task presenting some degree of novelty. In line with Klahr and Wallace (1976), they consider *variability* to be the rule rather than the exception in that minimal task variations lead to differences in performance. Those theories that propose synchronous progress across knowledge domains tend, however, to evaluate performance in a manner that emphasizes its homogeneity. Their analyses either do not emphasize minor differences in level or explain them with situational variation. Furthermore, they suggest that differences in performance level may result from the use of tasks that, though based on the same content, are actually suited to different ages.

Today variability is a generally accepted feature of development; how it is conceptualized and the role assigned to it within a theory can take two forms. In one case, variability is a temporary regression predicted by a theory: it appears consistently at a particular phase of ability acquisition in which achieving a higher phase is accompanied by a decrease in performance. In the second, variability is seen in the form of instability. It characterizes performance on tasks presenting some novelty and it may also be related to particular personal and external circumstances in which performance takes place. Although more marked in certain phases of ability acquisitions, it is nonetheless diffuse and could appear as either regression or progression.

U-Shaped Behaviors

In the first case just described, variability takes the form of the letter U, a phenomenon already described by Strauss in 1982. Performance regresses to a lower level (time 2), after having already exhibited (time 1) a higher level on the same type of task or ability, the latter being shown again at a successive phase of development (time 3). According to Goldin-Meadow (2004), it is not necessary that the two behaviors (time 1 and 3) coincide, to be called U-shaped (see Alibali & Goldin-Meadow, 1993). From a theoretical point of view, the important point about identification of a U-shaped behavior is to observe whether it is consistently found at a specific phase of development such that it might be considered a characteristic pattern in the development of certain abilities or concepts.

Siegler addresses the possibility of U-shaped patterns in development by constructing a sequence of problems scaled according to the six levels corresponding to the rule acquisition model (see chap. 4). A good example of a U-shaped behavior is drawn from studies on children's acquisition of rules to solve two-dimensional problems such as the balance scale problem (Siegler, 1981). At 3 years, children consider neither the dimension of weight nor that of distance from the fulcrum; rather, independently of problem type, they choose which arm of the balance goes down at random. When at 6 years children become able to consider the dimension of weight, they decide that the arm with a greater number of weights goes down. Thus, in "conflict" problems where the arm with a fewer number of weights placed at a greater distance from the fulcrum goes down, they show 0% accuracy. The new ability to handle the weight dimension decreases performance because the child, disregarding distance, consistently decides for the arm that has more weight. Then, at 9 years, the child begins to consider the dimension of distance, but still separately from weight: accuracy reaches chance level again, but for a different reason. In this intermediate phase, according to Siegler, the child is not yet able to combine the two dimensions (calculating a ratio) and decides at random between the two arms, the one showing more weight or the one with more distance.

Also Karmiloff-Smith's (1981a, 1981b, 1992) specific-domain RR theory (see chap. 7) predicts regression in phases of development where progress in knowledge acquisition does not reach awareness such as to allow flexible consideration of both internal and external inputs (1991, 1992). In particular, regression occurs with a redescription of implicit, procedural knowledge into the first explicit level. However, in this new, more advanced phase in which the children begin to reflect on the information stored in their minds, they rely solely on their newly formed internal representations and interpret external information to fit such representations. To use Karmiloff-Smith's terms, when the child reorganizes implicit knowledge (after consolidation), his or her theory is imposed on the input and incoming data is thereby simplified. Overgeneralizations are likely to occur: the child's lack of awareness of the theory leading their thought and actions makes the child temporarily unable to take into account negative feedback from the environment. Examples of U-shapes observed by Karmiloff-Smith with the aid of a microgenetic method come from diverse domains such as language and route map drawing (Karmiloff-Smith, 1981b).

U-shapes are predicted also in Mounoud's model (chap. 7), which involves a developmental phase (occurring cyclically at each general stage) in which the child loses the ability to elaborate an object in terms of the relations between its parts (continuous) once the capability to recompose them into a new (discontinuous, discrete) totality has been achieved. This regression is overcome in the subsequent phase when new representation permits consideration of both the different features of the object and its totality. Regressions are observed also in development of visuomanual tracking (Mounoud et al., 1985) and the author comments that a regression from the level previously reached is the price to be paid when an old, familiar strategy not working in certain situations is replaced with a new one that will become effective only at a later stage (a notion recently re-elaborated and refined by Siegler).

Recently, there has been a surge of interest in U-shaped behavior, and testifying to its theoretical relevance, studies of this phenomenon were discussed in a 2004 issue of the *Journal of Cognition and Development*. From these studies it also appears that different instances of U-shape behaviors may derive from different sources. In some cases U-shapes are attributed to improvement in abilities unaccompanied by full understanding (Namy, Campbell, & Tomasello, 2004). Another source of U-shape is the different rate of progress achieved by two strictly related (allied) abilities, one growing faster than the other. Both abilities increase monotonically but at different pace, in such a way as to allow some progress but also to cause a regression. An example by Gershkoff-Stove and Thelen (2004), relating to motor development, is found in the decrease of infants' stepping ability when leg weight increases faster than leg strength. Rule overregularization is another source of U-shapes. In a simulation by Rogers, Rakison, and McClelland (2004) the model initially exhibits a correct response, but when the transition from association to rule-governed cognition begins, an overgeneralization causes a U-shaped behavior, before learning finally occurs. In children's language acquisition a common example is overgeneralization of the past-tense rule to irregular verbs after showing correct production of past-tense for a (smaller) number of regular and irregular verbs (a phenomenon that is variously explained, for example, by Marcus, 2004, and Marcovitch & Lewkowicz, 2004).

Each of these examples of U-shaped behavior refers to a phenomenon consistently observed in children at a certain phase of development, and sheds new light on ability acquisitions. The inferior level of performance is not only temporary, but also, rephrasing Karmiloff-Smith (1981), it is only "in the eye of the beholder" (Goldin-Meadow, 2004).

The regressions just cited focus on development of concepts and strategies for which variability is found to positively correlate with their subsequent progress. To complete the picture, it is worth mentioning a different type of regression shown by adults with Williams syndrome and concerning face processing. This aspect is only apparently intact during infancy in that infants elaborate faces using different processes (see chap. 7), suitable to some tasks but not to others. However, with adulthood age performance decreases to a lower level compared to infancy (Karmiloff-Smith, 1998; Paterson, Brown, Gsödl, Johnson & Karmiloff-Smith, 1999). Differently from U-shapes, which are temporary regressions functional to a further progress, this regression seems a later phase of a specific path taken by atypically developing individuals.

Variability as a Cue to Multiple Levels of Cognitive Functioning

U-shaped behaviors have a different theoretical status from the apparently less coherent, unstable variations typical of the second form of variability just mentioned. This latter type is ubiquitous: while trying to solve a problem, children (but also adults) resort to various strategies and they do so even during a single trial; both advances and temporary regressions take place. Oscillations in performance may occur in various contexts and for different reasons, such as when the child is trying to cope with a novel task before the required new ability is acquired, or when there is a change in the degree of environmental support (e.g., Fischer & Bidell, 1998; 2006; Granott, 2002; Karmiloff-Smith, 1981b; Karmiloff-Smith & Inhelder, 1974; Mounoud 1993; Mounoud & Vinter, 1985; Parziale, 2002; Pascual-Leone. 1994; Siegler, 1996; 2006; Siegler & Munakata, 1993; van Geert, 2002).

We examine, in particular, Fischer and Siegler's positions, given that both scholars study development of specific concepts and assign to variability a very relevant role in problem solving and skill acquisition (Fischer, 1980; 2006; Fischer & Bidell, 1998; 2006; Fischer & Kennedy, 1997; Siegler, 1987; 1994; 1995; 1996; 2006; Siegler & Jenkins, 1989; Siegler & Munakata, 1993; Yan & Fischer, 2002). Variability is considered a feature of nonmonotonic development at both intra- and interindividual levels: thus, development is not a sequence of ever increasing abilities as suggested by Case's representation of development as a "staircase." Variability is the tip of the iceberg with a base in the possession of multiple strategies situated at either lower or higher cognitive levels. Appearance of a new way of thinking does not replace all of the previous, less developed strategies or reasoning modalities; to the contrary, multiple representations and strategies are typically available and used, as shown by closer observations of children's behaviors (actions, moves) and/or verbal explanations in successive trials in microdevelopmental studies. These authors maintain, on the basis of their own and others' studies, that variability is more pronounced in transitional phases of acquisition of a new concept or strategy, but that it is also present to a lesser extent during periods of consolidation that are thought of as relatively stable.

In particular, Siegler's (1996) model of "overlapping waves" points to variation in ways of thinking; for example, in arithmetic problems the child shows multiple numerical representations (Siegler & Opfer, 2003) available at each acquisition, particularly in time of transitions. Children's progress results not only from the construction of new strategies but also from changes in the choice from the already practiced strategies. As Siegler and Munakata (1993) state, "transcending the tyranny of the old ways of thinking seems to be as much a part of change as the discovery of new ways of thinking" (p. 10).

Also Fischer speaks of variability in terms of "waves" or "scallops" (Fischer & Bidell, 2006). He further specifies that there is a limit to variations in terms of levels of regressions and progressions: the lowest and the highest performance levels exhibited in any phase of skill acquisition fall within a developmental range (see chap. 5). In particular, a process of "backward transition" in problem solving is identified, meaning that a regression may follow a spurt in performance, under certain circumstances

(Granott, 2002; Parziale, 2002). A typical case for regression is a rapid progress occurring without true understanding such as when a high environmental support is quickly withdrawn before allowing much experience.

In Fischer's theory, variability in development is explained within a dynamic system approach. Performance (and its variations) is placed within a system involving many components relating to people, physical environment, and characteristics of the person (cognitive and emotional states), all interacting with one another (see also Demetriou & Raftopoulos, 2004). Due to a continuous change of variables in each component, the system is not stable, and stability is re-established by processes of self-regulation and self-organization. In the same vein as Siegler, it is stated that the system is perturbed the most when going through a qualitative change. External factors are important: low environmental support may determine regressions in performance whereas optimal support can temporarily push performance to a higher level. Moreover, the path taken by development is affected by the previous learning history (a notion shared also by Case and Siegler). It is this idea that leads Fischer to state that variability is the rule rather than the exception. Congruently, variation is so pervasive that stability is viewed as a special case of variation.

Why is variability useful? Variability is a positive, adaptive feature of development. It presents some characteristic patterns that afford the researcher a better understanding of learning and development. For example, Dixon and Bangert (2002) found that the trials immediately preceding discovery have a longer solution time compared to earlier trials. As Siegler comments, longer solution time before a discovery reflects intense cognitive activity, Moreover, use of multiple strategies in a single trial and number of different types of explanations is predictive of learning in various domains, both in children and adults (Schlagmüller & Schneider, 2002; Siegler, 1995, 1996). According to Siegler, it is being successful rather than the perception of failure that is crucial to an advance; that is to say, it is not observation of a strategy's failure that leads to its dismissal, but rather observation of a good strategy's success that leads to its choice.

However, Siegler also points out that not all patterns of variability correlate positively with performance. In fact, initial variability is critical for discovery of a new strategy in learning and problem solving, and this is particularly true when extended experience is provided. Instead, when variability occurs at a later point after starting with an initially stable performance, the strategy choice would take longer (Siegler, 2006; Thornton, 1999). Thus, success is the highway to improvement, but it has to be the result of a search rather than of initial performance correct by chance. Over-regularization also depends on the learning conditions. A greater number of correct extensions or generalizations are observable when a strategy is discovered in problems for which it is consistently appropriate—but there are also more overextensions—compared to when learning takes place with problems on which the strategy is not always appropriate (Siegler & Stern, 1998).

Another positive aspect of variability is linked to the reason why a regression occurred. As predicted by Fischer's theory, when a higher performance is achieved too rapidly, this improvement causes a regression because it is obtained at the expenses of consolidating the new skill or, even worse, at the price of bypassing a phase of construction of the basic components of understanding. "Commonly, mastering a task requires moving down to primitive levels of representations of even actions (similar to those of infants) so that the person can figure out the action characteristics of the task or situation" (Fischer, in press). Thus, regression is very useful because it permits reconstruction and reorganization of the needed components in order to generalize to the peculiarities of the new task and to facilitate a more stable, consolidated advance, through a process of self-organization of the system. Fischer and Bidell (2006) propose that a property of catastrophe accounts for unstable effects exerted by important factors such as contextual support and emotional state: variability determined by these factors depends on the phase of development and their influence is higher during a phase of transition than during a period of consolidation (van der Maas & Molenaar, 1992).

What conditions best allow a researcher to observe variability? Siegler and Fischer, among others (e.g., van Geert & van Dijk, 2002), maintain that it is useful to analyze performance not only in terms of group average but also of individual growth curves. The microgenetic method is very useful in that, to use Siegler's metaphor, it provides not just snapshots of development, but videos, highlighting variations and relevant factors in ability acquisitions. For example, Siegler and Chen (1998), using a microgenetic method, show that developmental differences in rule learning on the balance scale problem are due jointly to the type of processes 4- and 5-year-olds use throughout the learning trials, and to initial knowledge (in terms of initial rule use, initial encoding of the dimensions).

Siegler (1994, 2006) retraces the study of short-term variability back to Werner (1948) and Vygotsky (1934/1962). Microgenetic method was used very early by Flavell (Flavell & Draguns, 1957) and it was adopted also within the Geneva school (Inhelder et al., 1976; Karmiloff-Smith & Inhelder, 1974/1975). Piaget (1975/1985) proposed recurrent phases showing different level of variability and stability in development, although eventually a new stage (*structure d'ensemble*) would replace old levels of thinking. Recently, microgenetic method has been widely used by Siegler (e.g., Chen & Siegler, 2000; Siegler, 1995: Siegler, 2002; Siegler & Crowley, 1991; Siegler & Jenkins, 1989), Mounoud (e.g., Mounoud & Vinter, 1985; Mounoud, Viviani, Hauert, & Guyon, 1985), as well as by Karmiloff-Smith (e.g., 1979b, 1981b, 1993a) and Lautrey (1993). It has also been widely adopted within dynamic systems approaches (e.g., Fischer & Bidell, 2006; Fischer & Granott, 1995; Fischer & Yan, 2002; Granott & Parziale, 2002; Thelen & Corbetta, 2002; van Geert & van Dijk, 2002), and by other scholars within various theoretical frameworks (e.g., Alibali, 1999; Branco & Valsiner, 1997; Coyle & Bjorklund, 1997; Fogel & Lyra, 1997; Kuhn, Garcia-Mila, Zohar, & Anderson, 1995).

This microgenetic method is consistent with various designs—single subject, a small number of individuals, or a group, including prolonged or dense observations during a certain time, which could be as short as a single session presenting multiple trials of a problem or many sessions within a critical time period. It may also involve collaborative work (Granott, 2002; Parziale, 2002); working in pairs reduces time of strategy discovery. The crucial point is to begin observations slightly before spontaneous transition to the target acquisition and continue until a relative stability in performance is reached.

Data analysis may involve trial-by-trial analysis to observe such aspects as the strategies used, adaptiveness of the choice, and types of changes with trials (Rittle-Johnson & Siegler, 1999; Siegler, 1995). Ruhland and van Geert (1998), analyzing performances related to acquisition of function words, compare the first half of the trials with the second half and note intra- and interindividual variability. Siegler and Stern (1998) propose a backward graphing technique of reaction time data that (along with overt behaviors and verbal reports) permits inferring unconscious discovery of a new strategy before the child would use it consciously (in arithmetic problems by second graders, for example). van Geert and van Dijk (2002) propose techniques based on the "critical frequency method" (to calculate how large are the fluctuations, useful to notice when the system has lost stability); they also propose plotting time-series scores to visualize the minimum and maximum performance within given time periods (useful to specific hypothesis testing), whereas Molenaar, Huizenga, and Nesselroade et al. (2000) suggest analysis of time-series data by means of a dynamic factor analysis, rather than a standard analysis.

The variety of designs and analyses in microgenetic studies points to continuous attempts to implement suitable methodologies that avoid methodological flaws such as hidden interference from repeated trials or misconstruing measurement errors and random noise as meaningful variations. Microgenetic studies are a leap forward on the path of acknowledging and taking variability into account, with a view to better understanding development and learning.

Role of Variability in General Developmental Theories

In general, all the theories that emphasize homogeneity (Pascual-Leone, Case, Halford, and Mounoud) admit (to different degrees) that variability may arise in adaptation to a task: the content of the schemes and the order in which a child constructs them are specific to and may vary according to domain or to situational factors. For perspectives of this sort, which do allow for some degree of variability, the shape of development and its speed are nevertheless similar across individuals and across domains, allowing few exceptions. Variability is limited by central-level restrictions.

These theorists can account for *décalage* by employing a task analysis that identifies the type and number of schemes in a task according to the variables at play within it. For example, Pascual-Leone analyzes two conservation problems already known for revealing a *décalage*—substance and weight—and finds that the second requires keeping one more scheme active than does the first. Thus his theory, contrary to Piaget's, predicts that conservation of weight will be accomplished later and only at the point that the child has attained the necessary mental capacity. Along the same line, Case also reasons that *décalage* may result with different versions of what appears to be tasks of the same level: his theory predicts that apparently similar problems, in fact, pose different cognitive demands in terms of the number of schemes and relations between them that need to be kept in WM.

Case states that the presence of variability may often be more appearance than reality. Although unable to solve the more complex problems indicative of a concept's complete acquisition, a child may still be able at a relative early age to solve the simpler problems typical of a lower substage. Such a solution cannot be taken as an indication of preformed knowledge. Conversely, finding a lower performance on a given task than that expected for a given stage sometimes could be the result of using a version of the task that requires a greater capacity than do other versions typically employed at that stage; that is, variability could be due to a methodological artifact. Also in this case variability is only apparent in that the observed performance is anticipated on the basis of an appropriate task analysis. However, Case did find some *décalages* involving different performances on tasks of the same level within a given stage and either belonging to the same CCS or to two CCSs (quantity and social); and, of course, he acknowledges them. But he also noted that overall *décalage* is typically limited to one substage and regards mainly older children (adolescents). He attributes such variability to the influence of domain knowledge that may show more marked differences at older ages (see chap. 6).

Halford (1993b), however, admonishes Case for considering a deviation of one or two substages to be minor and unworthy of regard as a true gap. Halford considers this means of maintaining the idea of synchrony to be purely arbitrary, pointing out that elsewhere Case himself considers as successful training that improves performance by only a single substage. It should be noted, however, that Halford himself seems not to give much emphasis to small changes when discussing his own data on intra- and inter-domain variability, probably due to his methodology.

In his later writing, Case gave greater consideration to the presence of variability, although he typically mentioned environmental factors as a possible source of temporary performance differences. On the one hand, he further specifies that the components of executive control structures are tailored to the task: this creates a basis for some variability in that it leaves open the possibility of small differences in the early phases of their acquisition, depending on the type of task. On the other hand there are also factors affecting CCS that result from experience with the domain and with specific task contents.

Thus, altogether, sources of variations include factors relating to task material and instruction, as well as familiarity with the material experience with type of task and specific domain, as derived from cultural differences. Culture poses some differences on values and tools offered, constraining a child's approach to particular domains. In fact Lewis (1994) argues that the appearance of homogeneous, stage-like progress across domains can result from the use of tasks that exemplify cultural norms. Case proposes that cultural differences are in part compensated by much similarity between cultures, at an abstract level: every culture offers a type of experience useful for the child to develop the basic concepts on which cognitive development is built. For this reason, the difference may amount to about one substage, rather than marking absence or extremely high developments. For example, a greater ability in Japanese children compared to U.S. children was found in some tasks of numerical conceptual structure (Case et al., 1996). According to Case, this may be due to a higher parental support compared to North American culture. Indeed, higher math scores in Japanese children are pronounced only in early schooling when parents' emphasis on math achievement may play a great role; in later years, greater experience and knowledge supersede cultural influence. An exception is represented by Fiati's (1992) research with children from a subculture of Ghana: they were far behind compared to Western standard but only in the number domain (balance task) and only if unschooled. Moreover, none of the older participants performed lower than the 6-year-old level, and this confirms Case's idea that any culture allows the building of basic concepts in any domain.

As a matter of fact, other theorists focusing on variability are also aware of the influence of culture in development. For example, Siegler found higher math scores among Japanese fifth-graders and specifies that it is attributable to specific instructions emphasizing self-explanations, a strategy that plays a role in acquisition (Siegler, 2002; Stigler & Hiebert, 1999; chap. 4). Fischer, in his study on self-concept with Korean and U.S. adolescents, found that optimal support conditions fostered Korean advancement to the point of displaying the same complexity of self as another cultural group just 1 year later. Thus, with the right support compensating some cultural distinctions, development showed the same pattern across cultures and differences were limited to a delay in time. These examples suggest that although cultural differences do affect some aspects of development, they do not determine the presence or absence of an ability, nor do they affect the shape of its development. The only influence is on the time of acquisition and this is typically small. Other indications from these studies is that cultural influence can be moderated or nullified by factors (linked also to motivation) such as greater exposure, domain knowledge and schooling, environmental support and appropriate instructions. Overall, Case's idea is that although culture is a source of variability, it is of a type that is handled by his theory.

Despite important modifications to his theory, Case continues to maintain in his later work the idea that one substage is a small difference. One may wonder why he does so. The fact that Case devotes little attention to studying small fluctuations around the time of transition does not mean that he does not recognize them as a feature intrinsic to the child's striving toward development. The presence of such variability does not determine its theoretical importance, and it does not necessarily mean that variability represents the central feature of development. Case feels that in the end, dedicated processes lead achievements to a sort of (imperfect) synchronicity in transitions. His efforts are directed to showing the existence of (almost) synchronous advancement in the various areas of development. More specifically, although CCSs are specific, his goal is to show that through important developmental mechanisms such as hierarchical integration and the maturational constraints posed by working memory, acquisitions may take somewhat different paths within and across domains but in the end that they will converge and show a qualitative change at the same period of time (what Fischer would attribute to an attractor). Thus, notwithstanding the fact that he occasionally found one substage differences concerning some specific tasks in targeted individuals, he chose not to focus on what he called "minor variations."

Some Notes on Individual Differences

Individual differences represent another fundamental form of variability. Contributions to the study of individual differences come from scholars of different orientations, although the role they play in the theory differs depending on the approach. Several factors have been identified as responsible for individual differences.

Pascual-Leone has studied differences in cognitive style extensively, in particular field dependence, and he has often reported interactions between M capacity and cognitive style in performance on Piagetian and other tasks (Baillargeon et al., 1998; Globerson, 1983b), also including physiological measures (Goode et al., 2002). As discussed in chapter 2, the Theory of

Constructive Operators accounts for field dependence as the outcome of the interaction among the operators F, L, M, I, and the executive schemes (Pascual-Leone, 1989). The F operator (field effects) and the I operator (inhibition) can act differently on performance across individuals depending on whether they are more or less subject to their effects (some people are more sensitive to field effects, others have more efficient inhibitory processes, and so on). Thus, cognitive style also becomes a source of variability; for example, field dependent subjects are expected to perform well in facilitating situations[2] and on tasks in which the misleading cues are not particularly strong. They should underscore only on those tasks in which the misleading cues are particularly salient. In such cases individual performance may show oscillations: for example, considering field dependence, for various items of Piaget's water-level task, some adults could go back and forth between correct performance, lower level responses, and also unusual errors (Pascual-Leone & Morra, 1991). It is worth noting that physical knowledge, field independence and M capacity all predict performance in the water-level task, although their effect may vary according to the children's M capacity (Morra, in press).

Reflectivity–impulsivity is another cognitive style leading to performance differences. These differences are explained by the TCO in terms of children's executive schemes (Shafrir & Pascual-Leone, 1990). In the same vein, individual differences due to giftedness are explained in terms of M and I operators and executive schemes (Johnson et al., 2003; Johnson et al., 2004).

Case has great interest in individual differences that, in fact, become a sort of test of his theory. Individual differences are found in such cases as gifted children and writing prodigies (Porath, 1992), in children with reading and/or arithmetic disabilities (Crammond, 1992), and in children with low socioeconomic status (Okamoto et al., 1996). For example, in verbally or spatially gifted children, performance is higher in measures relating to their specific domain of talent (e.g., story telling or drawing complexity, respectively). The difference is present only in some of the children and is almost always limited to one substage, confirming what has been found with cultural differences. Children with low SES show a significantly lower performance from those with high SES in a number of developmental measures in which acquisition is the result of a social construction (Demetriou et al., 1988; Okamoto et al., 1996). As just described in "The Shape of Development," the low frequency of certain experiences in low-SES children can decelerate performance in skills that are socially constructed. To be noted, the asymmetries are not found in structural tasks drawing on children's ba-

---

[2]For instance, Johnson, Prior, and Artuso (2000) report that field-dependent adults perform better on a communication task in the second language.

sic developmental capacity; these appear to be influenced neither by low SES nor by specific talents. Rather they are found in those tasks devised to measure construction of conceptual structures that are culturally bounded (Case, 1996c).

Individual differences can be obscured by the type of methodology adopted in homogeneity-oriented theories and by the type of data analysis. Indeed, these theories typically do not favor information about minor acquisition steps; they include fewer details about processes and strategies employed to prepare transitions, and these could well be a source of individual differences. To reveal interindividual differences, both within age and across ages, one should consider the individual scores at each age rather than the average score of different groups (van Geert & van Dijk, 2002).

A proposal compatible with theories considering variability an important aspect of development has been made by de Ribaupierre et al. (1991) and Lautrey (1993). Because processes are multiple, their accessibility in part depends on the type of situation and on the type of child. The mode of elaboration is one factor that accounts for variability, for example: elaboration could be propositional or analogical depending on the type of problem and/or the type of participant (see also Larivée et al., 2000; Mounoud, 1993).

Siegler indicated some relevant factors for individual differences, including conceptual domain knowledge and encoding of problem dimensions. For example, he considers what accounts for individual differences in pure numerical estimation tasks that concern ability to approximate quantitative values of entities and for which real-world knowledge is not required. Booth and Siegler (2006) ask children to place numbers on an unmarked number line with 0 and 100 (or 0–1,000) at the extremities. Individual differences are attributed to representing either linear patterns of estimates (that is evenly spacing the numbers on the 0–100 line) or logarithmic representation (spacing the lower numbers further apart than the higher ones). Differences are not simply age-related because older children fall back to logarithmic patterns with the 1–1,000 number line. Accounts for individual differences include numerical knowledge that grows with age and correlates with mathematical achievement scores. Another is working memory, which may control children's ability to relate the number to be estimated to the lower and the higher ends, that is, keeping in mind simultaneously the number and both ends of the number line.

Fischer displays a great interest in individual differences. In one study on interindividual variability in reading single words (Knight & Fischer, 1992), he was able to capture the pathway followed by normal readers and two different pathways exhibited by children with reading disorders in building this skill. Each shows a well-ordered sequence of acquisition of the ability components (see chaps. 5 and 8). Fischer has also conducted various studies on children with negative life histories. For example, maltreated children are able to tell complex stories; however, compared to non-maltreated, they show a specific bias toward mean stories. If explicitly asked to tell a positive one, they soon switch the content to the negative (Fischer, Hencke, Hand, Ayoub, & Russell, 2001). In contrast, children with an inhibited temperament show a bias toward telling positive interaction stories, and this bias is even more pronounced when the story's main character has to be the child her/himself (Fischer & Ayoub, 1994). More generally, Fischer's theory represents an important approach to individual differences in that it offers the possibility to reveal alternative pathways to development, not only in the field of cognition but also in those of personality development and emotional disorders (Ayoub & Fischer, 2006; see chaps. 5 and 8).

Interindividual variability studied within a dynamic systems approach may also highlight different transitions. For example, Ruhland and van Geert (1998) observe some aspects of syntactic development in young children. In addition to intraindividual variations shown by every child, individual curves reveal great differences, with one child showing more abrupt transitions than another, for example. It is worth noting that some scholars within a dynamic systems approach note that the expression "individual differences" points to fixed characteristics; thus, given the multiple forms that individual variations may take in a given time, they prefer to speak of interindividual variability rather than of individual differences.

In sum, in this section we have discussed various forms of variability in the performance of single individuals while they are trying to solve a new problem; these include horizontal *décalage*, U-shaped curves, and cognitive styles. Different theories have different points of strength and give better accounts of one or another type of variability. Furthermore, variability is more important in some theories than in others. Particularly in the case of Fischer, the emphasis is on asynchronous developments and his focus is on intraindividual differences. However, in his case, too, performance is controlled by central constraints such as the system carrying capacity, and level of variability is restricted within a developmental range. Overall, it seems that synchronous and asynchronous approaches to development are, in a sense, complementary in terms of ways of addressing the question of variability.

Unfortunately not all the neo-Piagetians we consider assign a precise role to variability, leaving the impression that their theory is not yet able to account for it. Unsatisfied with proposals focused on general development, Lewis (1994) asked if homogeneity might originate from the implicit conventionality of the tasks used, a procedure that results in measuring only an ideal development and in minimizing variability. However, the type of homogeneity proposed by most theorists allowing for general development seems defendable. As de Ribaupierre (1994) states, "similar processes may operate in different individuals, explaining why behavior tends to take the same form; yet ... the products—that is, the mental representations or schemes built by the individual—might differ almost endlessly" (p. 174).

Overall, it seems that synchronous and asynchronous theories are, in a sense, complementary in terms of ways of addressing the issue of variability versus homogeneity. We believe that the efforts made by neo-Piagetians, in particular Fischer, Siegler and Case, with their different ways to acknowledge and explain variability, are fruitful not only in supporting the idea of generality in development, but also in strengthening the consideration of variability as a basic feature of development rather than as an accident of peculiar environmental conditions. The richness of methods and findings encourage consideration of variability as fertile ground on which to work toward integration among the theories.

INFORMATION LOAD
AND WORKING MEMORY

According to the neo-Piagetian theories, the ability to process an increasingly larger and more complex information load is one of the main explanatory mechanisms of cognitive development, especially of its discontinuous aspects. The theories that we have discussed vary in the degree to which they are explicit about this ability. All theories include explanatory concepts that refer to the ability to process a limited information load—such as working memory, M capacity, processing capacity, or carrying capacity, and they elaborate on these concepts often in great detail, as discussed in previous chapters. However, not all such concepts have been operationalized with measurement procedures. This would seem a necessary step for testing a particular model of working memory. For this reason, this section focuses particularly on those theories that have proposed specific measures of working memory or related concepts.

Fischer, for example, models the complexity of relations among the pieces of information considered; such complexity would explain the level transitions within the cycles. However, he does not indicate criteria for evaluating the degree of complexity of the information that a subject can process. Also, the concept of an individual's optimal level is not assessed in a manner that is independent of the specific task studied. Notwithstanding the assumptions that development results from domain-specific acquisitions and *décalage* is "the rule rather than the exception," Fischer is greatly interested in general processing models and introduces a concept of "carrying capacity" of the system; however, so far, no specific measure has been proposed for that capacity.

Other authors formulate theories in which the growing complexity of the information processed is implicit. For example, Mounoud's processes of decomposition–selection and construction of new total representations, underlying different developmental phases, involve an increase in the child's field of attention. However, this is a general statement and there is no explicit model of the complexity of the relations among the pieces of information considered in relation to a child's attentional capacity. For Demetriou, storage is one of the three dimensions of the processing system, along with speed and control; recently, Demetriou, Christou et al. (2002) also proposed a set of new measures of working memory. However, he does not put forward explicit claims or models of how development of the processing system affects children's performance on specific tasks.

Finally, in other theories (particularly those of Pascual-Leone, Case, and Halford) the model is explicit about the increase in the information load that can be processed at each stage or substage. In addition, the model is also accompanied by an attempt to define measures of the child's processing capacity, to analyze tasks and evaluate their processing requirements, and to examine the relationship of these measures with an individual's performance on other tasks.

As reported in chapter 3, Halford initially hypothesized that short-term memory span could index children's processing capacity and therefore their cognitive level, but this hypothesis proved unsatisfactory. Subsequently, Halford and colleagues used the easy-to-hard method to demonstrate the role of capacity limitation in cognitive development. This attempt has been successful but does not enable measurement of individual children's capacity. Thus, more recently, Halford has resorted to prediction of children's reasoning in a given task from their level of reasoning in other tasks (without an independent measurement of processing capacity).

The efforts of Pascual-Leone and Case to devise capacity measures seem to be more successful (see chaps. 2, 6, and 9), and their results quite consistent, at least with participants in the age range from 4 years to adolescence (e.g., see de Ribaupierre et al., 1990; de Ribaupierre & Bailleux, 1995; Case, 1985, 1995; Morra, 1994; Pascual-Leone, 1978; Pascual-Leone & Baillargeon, 1994; Pascual-Leone & Johnson, 2005; Pulos, 1997). A study by Foley and Berch (1997) also confirms with the easy-to-hard method the validity of the Digit Placement Task, one of the measures devised by Case. Two studies by de Ribaupierre et al. (1997) and by Morra et al. (2001) yield promising results for capacity measurement in ageing people.

The fact that Case, differently from Pascual-Leone, distinguishes a dimensional and a vectorial stage is not a problem from the point of view of consistency among their proposals for capacity measurement, because the substages of these two stages, according to Case, coincide with the ages of the M-capacity stages proposed by Pascual-Leone. The linear progress, hypothesized by both theories, of one unit every second year in age-appropriate capacity tests has so far resisted well the test of extensive research. It still remains to be tested, at a more fine-grained level and with an adequately large data base, whether the increase in this age range is actually linear or whether, perhaps, it follows a slightly decelerating curve, as may be suggested also by recent microgenetic studies by Siegler and Fischer. Were this to be the case, however, there are reasons to expect that such a curve would not depart very much from a linear function that, so far, has proved correct within the degree of approximation that is appropriate for most research or applied purposes.

Research on capacity measurement in young children has been less extensive (Alp, 1994, 2006; Case, 1985; Case & Khanna, 1981) and this is a limitation. On the one hand there is a slight age difference between Case's substages of the interrelational stage and Pascual-Leone's corresponding M-capacity stages; on the other, the units of analysis adopted by the two theories during that age range—and consequently, the units involved in the measures devised in the two labs—are qualitatively different (interrelational schemes for Case, sensorimotor schemes for Pascual-Leone, even though the sensorimotor schemes in the second year of life can already be quite complex and acquire a status of symbols) More research is needed to compare the capacity measures associated with the two theories during the preschool years.

In a perspective of comparing and integrating neo-Piagetian theories, it would also be interesting to pursue further Halford's research program on the easy-to-hard paradigm, as well as to follow up Foley and Berch's study that used Halford's methods to validate a measure proposed by Case. Furthermore, it would be interesting to test how well Case's and Pascual-Leone's capacity measures predict performance on tasks studied by other neo-Piagetian theorists—say, on Mounoud's task on instrument use or on Fischer's task on understanding social roles. If those capacity measures turn out to be predictive, it would count as evidence that—despite differences in how each theory conceives the increase of behavior complexity throughout developmental stages—the concepts of information load and limited capacity are not tied to one or another neo-Piagetian theory, but rather have an explanatory power that extends beyond the phenomena originally covered by a given theory.

It is worth noting that, although often short-term memory span measures are not regarded as valid indicators of processing capacity or cognitive-developmental level in older children and adults, Case (1985; Case & Khanna, 1981) proposes that during the interrelational stage (but not during other stages) short-term memory span is predictive of other cognitive performances. This, however, takes us to the broader issue of clarifying the nature of working memory capacity and related concepts.

Models of Working Memory

Often a distinction is made in the literature between short-term memory and working memory tasks, the former involving mere recall or recognition of an input, the latter also involving some additional, concurrent and usually deeper processing. This distinction is sound and empirically supported (Engle, Tuholski, et al., 1999; Kail & Hall, 2001; Lanfranchi & Swanson, 2005; Swanson, 1994) but merely describes a general characteristic of different types of tasks; it does not shed light on the architecture of the mind that underlies performance on those different tasks. It is generally acknowledged that short-term memory tasks are simpler and afford specific strategies for information maintenance (e.g., rehearsal), strategies that cannot be carried out in the more complex "working memory" tasks.

Furthermore, to complicate the scenario of task features, one should consider that some of Pascual-Leone's measures of M capacity have very minimal memory requirements. For instance, in the Figural Intersection Test (FIT; see chap. 9), the stimuli are constantly in view of the participant, who must, however, attend simultaneously to various shapes in order to find the appropriate overlapping area. One could call this an attentional load, rather than a memory load. Yet, the FIT correlates with tests traditionally labelled as working memory measures (e.g., Morra, 1994). Keeping the discussion only at the level of task features would be superficial and confusing. We need to enter the controversial field of theoretical models of working memory and mental attention.

Early models of human information processing proposed that the mind includes three types of memory systems, that is, sensory buffers, a short-term store and a long-term store; in particular, Atkinson and Shiffrin (1968) proposed that short-term memory[3] carries out the functions of working memory or processing space for the higher cognitive processes. If there were such a system, then it would be possible to use children's performance on short-term-memory tasks to predict performance on Piagetian tasks, on reasoning tasks, and on other cognitive tasks with a high information load (McLaughlin, 1963). Halford entertained this possibility until his research results contradicted it (see chap. 3). The results of classic adult re-

---

[3]Note that here the expression "short-term memory" is not used to describe the features or demands of a task, but to indicate a hypothetical component of the human information processing system. It is always important to consider whether expressions like *short-term memory* or *working memory* are used in a descriptive way (to specify task features or demands) or in an explanatory way (to identify a component of the mind). As Crowder (1993) noted, people need to remember information in the short term, but this does not imply the existence of specific memory receptacles that carry out that function. We would like to add that a term like *working memory* is legitimate not only to label a class of tasks but also to characterize a wide class of functions of the mind; its explanatory use, however, could be misleading unless one provides an adequate account of the complex system that carries out those functions.

search (e.g., Baddeley & Hitch, 1974; Klapp et al., 1983) also fail to support the hypothesis that a short-term memory store is the processing space for higher cognitive processes.

The failure of the early hypothesis that a short-term store serves the function of working memory has opened the way for the proposal of more complex models. A very well-known one is presented by Baddeley (1986); his model, instead of a single store, includes multiple components. One component, called "central executive," would supervise, control, coordinate other components, and on occasion also store information. The other components are conceived as "slave" storage systems specialized for specific types of information (an articulatory loop, a passive phonological store, and a visuospatial sketchpad—a sort of mental blackboard, perhaps with distinct visual and spatial components). This model has an elegant simplicity in accounting for short-term memory of different types of information by distinct stores. Those distinct stores are the proposed explanation for an often-replicated finding concerning dual tasks: Two cognitive tasks performed simultaneously interfere with each other more if both involve the same type of information (two spatial tasks, or two verbal tasks, e.g., as compared with one spatial and one verbal task).

However, Baddeley's model also has several weak points. In the first place, the existence of a unitary central executive is unlikely (Allport, Styles, & Hsieh, 1994). On the contrary, current research tends to distinguish different types or dimensions of executive functions (e.g., Lehto et al., 2003). It is also unclear how the central executive component, which is attention-based, interfaces with the various specific stores and coordinates them.

Another important problem is that, if specific capacity-limited stores do exist, then one should be able to estimate their capacity. For visuospatial storage, a number of different and conflicting estimates have been proposed, for instance in terms of pattern complexity, number of positions, or fidelity and complexity of a single unparsed representation. Doubts have even been raised that the visuospatial sketch pad has a storage capacity of its own, distinguishable from the central executive resources (Logie & Marchetti, 1991). The difficulty of defining the limits of visuospatial short-term storage has long been acknowledged (Cornoldi, 1995; Logie, 1995) and the problem does not appear to have been clarified in the last years.[4]

---

[4]Baddeley (2000) has proposed a new component, called "episodic buffer"—a store connected with the central executive that would hold, for a short time, information that cuts across modalities and domains. The concept of short-term formation of episodic memories seems an important theoretical insight. So far, however, we still lack an operational definition and capacity measures of the episodic buffer, as well as adequate specification of its properties, except that it is supposed to function as the store of the central executive and hold some chunks of information.

For some time, it seemed that the capacity of the articulatory loop had been identified; Baddeley, Thomson and Buchanan (1975) examined short-term memory for word lists as a function of the spoken duration of words (called the word-length effect), and suggested that people can store as many words or other verbal materials as they can pronounce in about 2 seconds. However, more recent research showed that, in addition to spoken duration, many other variables (such as semantic, syntactic, lexical variables, and also the language in which the experiment is made, as well as various aspects of the experimental procedure) affect verbal short-term memory, and more important, they also modulate the word-length effect (for reviews see Morra, 1998, 2001). Thus, it seems that the only supposedly precise estimate of a specific storage capacity—that of the articulatory loop—could have been an artefact, obtained fortuitously from supra-span lists of English words. Several other explanations, alternative to the time-limited articulatory loop, have been proposed for the word-length effect (Brown & Hulme, 1995; Cowan et al., 1992; Henry, 1991; Morra, 2000; Nairne, Neath, & Serra, 1997; Service, 1998). Now, in short, the idea of a time-limited specialized store, such as the articulatory loop is also often regarded as too simplistic.

Baddeley's model is probably the most elegant among the working memory models based on the metaphor of short-term storage, but now this metaphor itself is going out of fashion. An alternative metaphor has long been available in the literature—activation. Various authors, such as Anderson (1983) and Cowan (1988), conceive working memory as the currently activated subset of long-term memory. Activation-based models can be quite complex (e.g., Anderson & Matessa, 1997; Just & Carpenter, 1992), in part because they cannot simply posit different stores to account for a given data pattern. They often, instead, include constructs at different levels. For instance, Engle, Tuholski et al. (1999) propose that working memory consists of (a) long-term memory representations active above a threshold, (b) processes for achieving and maintaining that activation, and (c) controlled attention. Similarly, Cowan (1999) defines a hierarchy that includes (a) long-term memory, (b) the subset of long-term memory that is currently activated, and (c) the subset of activated memory that is in the focus of attention and awareness. Cowan (2005) emphasizes that only the focus of attention is capacity-limited. The amount of memory information activated at a given time would not have a capacity limit, but would only be limited by interference and, possibly, by decay of activation with time.

Activation-based models of working memory not only account for extensive experimental data, but are also supported by a growing body of brain imaging evidence (e.g., Campo et al., 2005; Jonides, Lacey, & Nee, 2005; Majerus et al., 2006; Ruchkin, Grafman, Cameron, & Berndt, 2003). Research in that field suggests that, during a working memory task, the same brain structures are activated as in tasks that involve perceiving, representing in long-term memory, or acting on the same sort of information. In addition, other brain structures are also activated (usually in the frontal cortex) and these are involved in attentional control processes. As Ruchkin et al. (2003) point out, the fact that the same brain structures of long-term memory are activated suggests that it is not necessary to posit separate short-term stores in the brain; their results strongly agree with a view of working memory as activated long-term memory assisted by attentional resources.

As the reader has probably realized, there is a consistency between the activation view of working memory that is currently becoming predominant and the neo-Piagetian developmental models—in particular, those presented by Pascual-Leone, the latest writings of Case, and (perhaps to a lesser extent) recent theorizing by Halford. For instance, Pascual-Leone (1987, 1997) presents a model of mental attention, according to which the operators located in the prefrontal lobes (M and I operators and executive schemes) would enhance or suppress the activation of the currently active schemes, the set of which constitutes working memory. The conceptual consistency between the main tenets of this model and Cowan's (1988, 1999) is remarkable (e.g., see the discussion of neo-Piagetian models of capacity by Cowan, 2002, 2005).

Thus, we can speak of a clear convergence of experimental and developmental psychology and neuroscience on an emerging view of working memory and mental attention. However, there are issues that deserve further clarification. One concerns the units of analysis. For Pascual-Leone, Case, and some other authors in the Piagetian tradition, the cognitive units whose activation constitutes working memory are Piagetian schemes. Cowan (1999, 2001) uses more neutral terms, such as "items" or "chunks"; this could open a debate on the extent to which the concepts of "chunk" and "scheme" overlap or differ. Halford's view of relational complexity is based on the number of arguments that occur in a relation. An argument is a logical variable, that is, a concept at a higher level of abstraction than chunks or schemes. However, the degree of abstraction of the specific values that fill in those variables in a given relational instance is comparable to that of chunks or schemes.

One point of difference among these models is that Pascual-Leone's and Case's task analyses consider both operative and figurative schemes and count either of them as loading working memory or M capacity. Instead, when identifying the content of working memory, Cowan only considers declarative knowledge (or, in Piagetian terminology, disregards operative schemes; see Cowan, 2002). Also arguments in Halford's relations represent declarative or figurative knowledge; this is an aspect in which Cowan's model seems closer to Halford's than to Pascual-Leone's or Case's.

Also permeating the debate on working memory is the issue of generality versus specificity (e.g., Hambrick, Kane, & Engle, 2005). For instance,

Baddeley's model includes a domain-general central executive and a number of domain-specific stores, and one of its main strengths is ability to account for interference patterns in dual-task paradigms, as just mentioned; interference would be larger when two concurrent tasks involved the same specialized store. Kemps, de Rammelaere, and Desmet (2000), on the basis of experiments with children who performed various working memory tasks, suggested that Pascual-Leone's and Baddeley's models should be integrated, because the former would account better for developmental differences and the latter for differences in level of performance between verbal and spatial tasks. That article raised some debate; in a commentary article, Pascual-Leone (2000) rejoined that one need not posit separate short-term stores to account for differences between content domains, because the existence of different domain-specific repertoires in long-term memory, and factors in the structure of intelligence, has long been known. Those structures in the long-term organization of knowledge and abilities would suffice to account for domain specificity.[5] Moreover, de Ribaupierre and Bailleux (2000) note that differences in the level of performance can also be observed between tasks in the same domain (e.g., two spatial tasks) and this calls for an accurate task analysis of the measures that one uses. The conclusion that we can draw from that debate is that not only storage-based, but also activation-based theories of working memory can account well for domain specificity in performance on working memory measures (or in dual-task interference for that matter); however, they are able to do so at the price of a detailed task analysis, which is likely to introduce a certain degree of complexity in the models.

For instance, the importance of subvocal rehearsal in verbal short-term memory tasks has long been known, and Baddeley's model accounts for it in terms of a time-limited articulatory loop. What alternative, from the point of view of neo-Piagetian modeling, could there be to this account of a specificity in the phonological domain? Morra (2000) provides an answer to this question[6] through a complex model involving operative schemes that carry out the encoding, rehearsal, and retrieval operations and that need M capacity to be activated (with the exception of auditory encoding that occurs automatically). Rehearsal is conceptualized as an operative scheme that keeps track of information order, and it is assumed that people only use it if advantageous (e.g., children below 7 years are unlikely to rehearse, given

---

[5]A similar argument is made by Cowan (2002): "We propose only one processing capacity limit, namely the limit in the focus of attention, which is general across modalities; but processing within activated memory may be susceptible of interference that depends on the similarity between stimuli, thus allowing for apparently modality-specific and materials-specific resources" (p. 11).

[6]The Morra (2000) model is an elaboration upon previous work by Burtis (1982), who models free recall of consonant lists within the framework of the Theory of Constructive Operators.

that it would take too large a portion of their narrowly limited M capacity). The model also includes figurative schemes representing the stimuli to be remembered. Available M capacity is allocated to operative and figurative schemes, and a free parameter expresses loss of activation of those figurative schemes that exceed M capacity. Also the number of schemes that are currently losing activation, and therefore interfere with each other, is assumed to affect recall probability. This model, with only one free parameter, accounts well for primary school children's recall of word lists presented visually or auditorily, either with a span procedure or in a supra-span condition. It also promises to be generalizable to other, similar tasks; for instance, Pascual-Leone, Romero, Johnson, and Morra (2006) extend this model to account for consonant recall under varying interference conditions.

Capacity and Speed

One further issue merits attention in this section—the relationship between working memory or attentional capacity and speed of processing. Extensive evidence from children, adults, and ageing people shows a correlation between capacity and speed (e.g., Case et al., 1982; Fry & Hale, 1996; Kail & Salthouse, 1994; for a discussion, see also Heitz, Unsworth, & Engle, 2005). The problem, however, is how to interpret that correlation in causal terms: is greater capacity a by-product of faster processing? As we have seen in chapter 6, a particular version of this hypothesis (the efficiency–storage tradeoff) has been ruled out, but speed could cause capacity in other ways. Or, on the contrary, can people with a larger capacity use that resource to process information faster? Or, as still another possibility, are larger capacity and faster speed two consequences of a same, so far undiscovered underlying causal factor?

The issue, at present, is controversial. On the one hand, Johnson et al. (2003) replicate the finding of a correlation between speed and capacity; however, they also find that speed of processing and inhibition efficiency do not explain age or group differences on M capacity. On the other hand, Demetriou and colleagues (Demetriou, Christou et al., 2002; Demetriou & Mouyi, 2006) present supporting evidence for structural equations models in which the age-related increases in processing speed and control of interference account for a substantial part of the variance of executive control in working memory, which in turn contributes to reasoning ability. Although processing speed (and interference control) would explain working memory development, individual differences in working memory account for some variance in reasoning ability independently of processing speed or interference control. A lifespan study by de Ribaupierre (2001) reports a significant, but not exclusive influence of speed on working memory, especially in children. One should note that the capacity measures used in those lines of research are not the same, and that some of the speed measures and most of the inhibition-interference measures are also different. Most likely, extensive research will be needed to settle this controversy.

Other approaches do not consider general speed of processing, but rather, the speed of specific operations. For instance, in research on verbal short-term memory, individual participants' articulation rate has long been considered an indicator of the efficiency of their articulatory loop (Baddeley et al., 1975). Rehearsal speed could still be a relevant factor even when the articulatory loop model is abandoned. For instance, Morra (2000) reports that both M capacity and articulation rate account for separate components of variance in children's verbal short-term memory. Similarly, Cowan et al. (1998) report that both the rate of articulation and the duration of interword pauses during the response (an indicator of the speed of memory search) account for separate components of variance in verbal short-term memory. From the point of view of neo-Piagetian models, all these findings should be interpreted in terms of individual differences in the efficiency of the operative schemes for both rehearsal and retrieval.

In chapter 6, we briefly introduced the idea, recently proposed by Barrouillet and colleagues, that performance on a task is constrained both by the difficulty of the required operations and by the number of such operations per unit of time. In neo-Piagetian terms this idea could be rephrased, suggesting that capacity might be limited *not only* by the number of schemes that must be activated simultaneously, but *also* by the rate at which that scheme activation must take place. Broadly speaking, in the studies reviewed in this section there is nothing that contradicts that idea. Because classical Piagetian tasks are not speeded, and most neo-Piagetian measures of capacity are self-paced or present stimuli at a rather slow rate, such hypothetical time constraints on processing could not have appeared in a prominent way in much Piagetian and neo-Piagetian research.

One can conclude that neo-Piagetian research has already provided extensive information about working memory or attentional capacity and its development, but we can still expect exciting progress in the next years. The relationship between capacity and speed of processing, and the possibility of elaborating models that integrate time and resource constraints, is a field that clearly deserves deeper investigation.

Such integration may also involve some dialogue between neo-Piagetian researchers and their closest neighbors. For instance, Cowan (2002) proposes to take into account three types of parameters in the study of working memory development: the capacity limit of the attentional focus, retrieval rates, and decay rates, with due caution against a simplistic view that the three are by definition independent of each other. However, no existing study takes into account all three parameter types. Cowan et al.

(1998) only consider rehearsal rate and search rate. Morra (2000) considers capacity and interference, and also finds a significant effect of rehearsal rate, but does not integrate speed considerations into the model. Barrouillet and colleagues demonstrate that capacity increases with age (Gavens & Barrouillet, 2004), and their model integrates capacity and time constraints (e.g., Barrouillet et al., 2004); however, it does not yet provide a metric for either the individual's attentional capacity and processing rate, or the processing load imposed by tasks of different difficulty.[7] Therefore, given the respective strengths and limitations of these and other models of capacity and speed development, there seems to be ample scope for comparing and possibly integrating them.

Research on capacity and speed also involves some methodological problems, however. Some researchers measure speed on very simple tasks; others, instead, measure speed on tasks that bear a more considerable processing load. As noted by Conway et al. (2002), the correlation between measures of speed and working memory capacity measures tend to be larger when the speed measures are taken from tasks that involve a larger amount of information. In this case, the supposed correlation between capacity and speed could actually be due to a correlation between capacity and capacity (that is, between an explicit measure of working memory capacity and a disguised measure of the capacity required by the speed measure obtained in a high-load condition). To that argument we can add that, similarly, if the working memory task involves—for instance—encoding stimuli at a fast rate, then its correlation with processing speed could actually be due to a correlation between speed and speed.[8] Although theoretical models usually specify with enough clarity the presumed nature of working memory or attentional capacity, often processing speed is taken for granted conceptually, and only defined in operational terms. Those operational definitions may be quite different from one study to another (Heitz et al., 2005). As often is the case, progress of research on the capacity-speed relationship may need not only more extensive empirical research, but also conceptual clarification: speed of what? In which components of the system? For which processing goals?

---

[7]A similar conceptual problem can be found in Tombu and Jolicœur (2005), who provide very interesting evidence for a capacity-sharing model (as opposed to structural bottleneck models) of the psychological refractory period. However, in their model, capacity is expressed in terms of time available for processing; thus, by that definition, capacity becomes indistinguishable from speed.

[8]Some of the measures proposed by Cowan et al. (2005) might be problematic for this reason. For instance, they consider recognition of colour patterns presented for 250 msec, and memory for strings of digits presented acoustically at a rate of 250 msec per digit. Those fast presentation rates are used to prevent grouping or rehearsal strategies. They could have, however, the potential drawback of requiring considerable speed of multiple encoding operations.

Capacity and Its Interaction With Other Constructs

Finally we would like to add that although neo-Piagetian research on capacity development and its effects on performance on various tasks is extensive, the same can not be said of studies that consider the interactions between capacity and other mechanisms of the processing system. It seems advisable that future research be oriented toward the study of the *interactions*, in children and across the lifespan, among the various mechanisms or processes posited by neo-Piagetian theories. The ability to maintain an increasing amount of information active is a very important element, but only an element, of this set of constructs. Such research would be valuable for gaining a better understanding of the whole complexity of the child's developing cognitive system.

MATURATION AND ENVIRONMENT

We now consider another classic developmental issue, namely the role of maturational and environmental factors. The intent of this section is to evaluate the neo-Piagetian theories with respect to a debate in which nativism and empiricism are two polar opposites.

The Issue of Precocious Abilities

Methodological progress in the last decades has brought about a wealth of discoveries on newborns' and infants' competencies (for reviews, see Cohen & Cashon, 2003; Haith & Benson, 1998). For instance, it has been claimed that infants achieve object permanence earlier than Piaget believed (Baillargeon, 1987) and that they know a lot about the solidity of objects, their unity when partially occluded, and their relation to the surrounding space (e.g., Baillargeon 1993; Johnson & Nañez, 1995; Saxe, Tzelnic, & Carey, 2006; Spelke, Breinlinger, Macomber, & Jacobson, 1992). Long since, Leslie (1988) has argued that 7-month-old infants perceive causality in simple events and proposed that a causality module is present and operating at that age. Small numbers such as "2" and "3" can be discriminated by 4-month-olds (Starkey & Cooper, 1980) and even by newborns (Antell & Keating, 1983), whereas 5-month-olds can engage in very simple addition and subtraction (Wynn, 1992). Face processing is quite sophisticated. Even though some perceptual mechanisms are very simple and merely bias newborns to attend to faces (Johnson & Morton, 1991; Simion, Macchi Cassia, Turati, & Valenza, 2001), after a few hours of exposure newborns show a preference for their mother's face over a stranger's (Bushnell, 2001), and they can also learn about other individual faces or parts of faces and recognize them (Turati, Macchi Cassia, Simion, & Leo, 2006). On such grounds, Slater (2002) concludes that, at birth, visual cortex is already endowed with efficient learning mechanisms. Three-month-old babies also seem to be able to categorize pictures at the level of superordinate categories (Mandler, 2004).

Some of these claims have been criticized on the grounds of insufficient methodological control. For instance, in Baillargeon's "impossible event' paradigm, infants look longer at the impossible event such as the passage of a rotating screen through a solid box; however, Schilling (2000) manipulated carefully the duration and the content of the habituation phase, and concluded that children could look longer at the impossible event not because they find it impossible, but because they find it familiar. Similarly, early discrimination of cardinal numbers 2 and 3 could be an artefact due to insufficient control of the physical parameters of the stimuli (e.g., Xu, Spelke, & Goddard, 2005). Nevertheless, contemporary methods for the study of infant perception, unavailable at the time of Piaget, have revealed that young infants have a much richer cognitive competence than was held to be the case a few decades ago.

One important issue is how that competence should be characterized. Haith and Benson (1998) offer a brilliant critique of "precocism," that is, the tendency to attribute mature cognitive abilities to infants (also using terms like expectation, theory, belief, surprise, understanding, inference), and in some cases to also suggest that such abilities are innate—on the grounds only of infants' looking behavior. We cannot restate here all of their arguments, but the essential point is that, often, the reported patterns of differential looking behavior could also be explained by perceptual mechanisms and perceptual learning. "Differential looking in the habituation paradigm tells us only that an infant discriminates two events, not about why," and in addition, "the familiarization phase of an habituation procedure is an experience in its own right" (Haith & Benson, 1998, p. 202). Thus, one should refrain from attributing high-level cognitive abilities to infants, unless the alternative perceptual explanations can be confidently ruled out.[9]

Haith and Benson (1998) also note that sometimes, to demonstrate that infants of a few months of age can represent nonvisible objects, researchers use a procedure in which the objects are only occluded for a pair of seconds. Thus, it seems unwise to assume that all perceptual information about the crucial objects is immediately lost; rather, Heath and Benson find it more likely that it decays at some unspecified rate and could still be available, at least partly, after a few seconds. Indeed, a recent study (Ross-Sheehy, Oakes,

---

[9] Indeed, as Slater (2002) argued, the visual perceptual system is quite efficient at birth. For instance, as shown by Turati et al. (2006), various components both at the feature and configuration analysis levels are involved in the newborns' processing of individual faces. Three-month-olds can make sophisticated categorizations on a perceptual basis (Mandler, 2004). Therefore, the argument that differential patterns of infants' looking behavior could be explained in perceptual terms must be taken very seriously.

& Luck, 2003) shows that infants aged 4 to 13 months can remember some visual information in the short term—and that indeed, during that age range, their short-term memory capacity increases at a rate that is broadly compatible with the neo-Piagetian models of working memory in infancy.

It should also be noted that, occasionally, researchers interpret the finding of children's looking behavior toward an occluded object as an evidence for object permanence, and a challenge to Piaget's views. As Fischer and Bidell (1991) remark, such a finding is actually *consistent* with Piaget's description of sensorimotor substage 3 children (aged 4 to 8 months), who look at the point where an object has disappeared, although they do not yet try to retrieve it. For Piaget, object permanence was a concept constructed through partial achievements in various substages, and not an all-or-none category, as nativist psychologists sometimes seem to consider it.

The nativist position holds that the skills that have been identified in infants are evidence of innate knowledge and abilities. For example, Spelke (1994) argues on the basis of her research that the child shows some precocious concepts relative to the world of physics and that these can therefore be considered innate. By this view development is a maturational unfolding over the years of structures or modules, and the effect of learning and of the environment is simply to provide opportunities for the structures to unfold.

These assumptions have raised important debates in the last decades (see also chap. 7). Only a few researchers take extreme nativist or empiricist positions (some, but not all, connectionist models can be labelled as empiricist). A third position in the debate on early abilities is the constructivist—one that included Piaget among its pioneers, and to which the various neo-Piagetian researchers adhere either fully or in part. In a constructivist view, increasingly complex abilities are constructed out of simpler ones through a dynamic process, in which the individual (with its biological and cognitive structures) interacts with the environment and meets problems and contradictions. Many researchers, however, take intermediate positions among these three poles.

One clear example of a constructivist position is Karmiloff-Smith's neuro-constructivism, discussed in chapter 7. Cohen, Chaput, and Cashon (2002) also take a clearly constructivist position. They propose a constructivist learning architecture based on a multilayered connectionist network where unsupervised learning takes place (technically called a Kohonen network), which enables the individual to construct a hierarchy of representations at various levels of complexity.[10]

---

[10]However, one limitation in the constructivist approach of Cohen et al. (2002) is that it does not seem to tackle the problem of how novel responses are produced when the input offers misleading cues. That approach is clearly constructivist as far as representation is concerned, but it seems moot regarding executive processes. Until this limitation is resolved, that model may still fall under the learning paradox.

We have mentioned the existence of intermediate positions. One of these is Mounoud's proposal that from birth children have preformed categorical representations of the external world and of themselves (Mounoud & Vinter, 1985). These permit early behaviors such as imitation but they are temporary because, then, during development, categorization goes through a long process by means of propositional and infralogical structures and the construction of the categories is necessarily dependent on the environment.

Carey (1985, 1991, 2000) is often regarded as a strong proponent of nativism, because of her emphasis on the domain-specific core conceptual knowledge that constitutes the basis of children's theories; such core knowledge is assumed to be innate. However, Carey's nativism is mitigated by her view that children's theories undergo radical restructuring; in particular, the concept of "bootstrapping" (Carey, 2004) introduces a touch of constructivism in her nativist view. To limit ourselves to her main example, Carey (2004) describes natural numbers as a representational system that derives from various building blocks, which include an approximate analog representation of magnitude, an exact representation of very small quantities (from 1 to 3), the semantics of quantifiers in natural language (i.e., words like "a," "some," "two," or morphological markers for plural), and the ability to remember an ordered list of words (such as "one, two, three, four . . ."). But, Carey notes, there are various necessary stages in the construction of number[11] because children first understand the meaning of "one," then after several months they acquire the meaning of "two," then "three," and in all it takes a year and a half until they induce how counting works. Until this point it is easy for us to agree. However, why is it so difficult for children to acquire the meaning of the counting words that are present in their linguistic environment; why is it so laborious for them to come to understand that the last word uttered in the counting routine indicates unambiguously the cardinality of a set? The notion of bootstrapping, like Piaget's notion of reflective abstraction, describes a constructive process but only has a descriptive value. It does not account for why children who have long been unable to coordinate various "building blocks" of information suddenly come to put them together.

The neo-Piagetian theories, described in this book, have a particular status in the constructivist camp. Not only do they assume that more complex schemes, skills, or strategies are constructed by assembling or differentiating simpler ones; but they also specify the information load that is imposed by such constructions, and they set clear criteria about children's capacity to process simultaneously that amount of information.

---

[11]In turn, we note that this rules out Gelman and Gallistel's (1978) claim that the principles of counting are innate.

Neo-Piagetian theories often assume that there are maturational constraints on the development of children's capacity to process an amount of information that increases with age. However, we do not agree with Karmiloff-Smith's (1993) opinion that "the focus of most neo-Piagetian approaches is on maturation rather than on epigenesis" (p. 3). Rather, we think that, in neo-Piagetian theories, maturation of the system's capacity (working memory, or similar constructs) sets *necessary but not sufficient conditions* for epigenesis (i.e., construction) to take place. In our opinion, the neo-Piagetian theories discussed in this book are still faithful in spirit to Piaget's (1964) suggestion that maturation has an undeniable, though partial, role in accounting for mental development. Maturation of the nervous system opens a range of possibilities, whereas lack of maturation sets a range of impossibilities.

Neurological Maturation and Limits of Environmental Influence

The neo-Piagetian theories seek to place in a constructive perspective the influence of maturational factors in the child's cognitive development. Although neo-Piagetian authors generally agree that such influence must be posited, the proposals on exactly how it takes place are still somewhat speculative. Recent reviews, both from a neo-Piagetian perspective (Fischer, in press) and from a theoretically more neutral perspective (Nelson, Thomas, & de Haan, 2006), agree that spurts in cognitive development and increases in working memory performance coincide with the timing of several neurodevelopmental processes. These include myelination, axonal and synaptic pruning—changes in cerebral metabolism, changes in brain activity, and so on. However, we do not have clear evidence about how any of these neural developments would constrain cognitive development.

A problem in the current state of knowledge is that, although much evidence is available on both cognitive development and neural development, fewer studies directly examine the relationship between changes in cognition and in the brain. Much reasoning on such relationship, therefore, is an indirect attempt to connect different data bases—and is, thus, necessarily speculative. It is also important to bear in mind that brain changes cannot be understood in a mechanistic way as an outcome of pure maturation, but they usually involve some combination of maturation and experience. We return to this point in the following section.

In addition, as Fischer (in press) notes, much research on brain development has focused on microscopic anatomy and physiology—on how single neurons or synapses function. The big picture of how the working brain changes in the course of development, however, is needed. For instance, given the role of contradictions in Piagetian and neo-Piagetian theories, it seems particularly important to gather information about developmental change in the interactions between dialectically complementary systems in the brain—for instance, about changes in the interaction between anterior and posterior cortex, in the interaction between the hemispheres, or in the interactions between systems regulated by different neurotransmitters (e.g., Pascual-Leone, 1995).

Until a few decades ago, there were few relevant studies and these were focused on very specific aspects of neural development; therefore, the earliest hypotheses were necessarily constrained by this state of available knowledge. One early and simple hypothesis (Fischer, 1987; Goldman-Rakic, 1987) states that at least the first phases of development are related with *synaptogenesis*, that is, with an overproduction of synapses in the first months of life and the subsequent pruning of the synapses in excess. For instance, Goldman-Rakic (1987) suggested that the excess of synapses in the prefrontal cortex could account for children's perseverance errors in object permanence tasks: at 8 months an object hidden in position A with the child watching is successfully found; but if subsequently hidden in position B, the child may again search for it at A. Synaptic density is reduced to the adult level at 4–6 years of age in the occipital cortex, but only around 13–14 years in the prefrontal cortex (Huttenlocher, 1979; Nelson et al., 2006). The synaptic development in various areas of the cortex would account for the fact that in key periods of development the child demonstrates improvement in a series of different abilities.

Another early, simple hypothesis (Case, 1985) concerns the role of *myelination*, which permits an increase in the speed of connection among the neurons while diminishing lateral transmission. Myelination occurs in waves between birth and adolescence; it takes place subsequently in the cortical areas called primary, secondary, tertiary, and high-tertiary. The degree of myelination of those areas would offer an explanation for the increasing efficiency of sensorimotor, relational and dimensional operations.

Pascual-Leone (1987, 1989) accepts, as a first approximation, the view that different cortical areas can be involved in increasingly abstract processes, but complements it by pointing at the role of the prefrontal lobes. As mentioned in chapter 2, Pascual-Leone suggests that the *M* operator is based on circuits connecting the prefrontal lobes, through subcortical structures, to other cortical areas; thus, as a function of prefrontal lobe maturation, an increased activation would be induced in the primary, secondary areas, and so on, beyond that already permitted by their current state.[12]

---

[12]Pascual-Leone and Johnson (1991) also suggest that the infants' behavior in Piaget's object permanence tasks becomes increasingly sophisticated with age because it involves coordination of an increasing number of sensorimotor schemes, and that the initial maturation of the prefrontal lobes would be the neural basis for the *M* operator to activate all those schemes.

Because of widespread agreement that the prefrontal lobes are involved in the development of various kinds of executive processes (as discussed in previous chapters), several authors of differing theoretical orientations have discussed their maturation. The prefrontal lobes are clearly involved in working memory in adults (e.g., Ruchkin et al., 2003) and developmental and individual differences have been reported that could account for working memory development. For instance, Klingberg, Forssberg, and Westerberg (2002) and Kwon, Reiss, and Menon (2002) report that participants (in the age range, respectively, from 9 and from 7 years to adulthood), who were scanned with fMRI while performing a spatial working memory task, showed age-related and ability-related differences in the activation of a frontal-parietal network.

Prefrontal lobes are also involved in inhibitory control. Adult fMRI studies with various tasks involving inhibition of a prepotent response (e.g., Konishi et al., 1999) or selection of conflicting stimulus information (e.g., Fan et al., 2003) consistently find prefrontal cortex activation. Whereas dorsolateral prefrontal cortex is usually involved in working memory tasks, inhibitory control most often seems to involve ventral prefrontal cortex (although in this respect there are a few inconsistencies in the literature). Konishi et al. (1999) report involvement of the right prefrontal lobe in response inhibition, whereas Fan et al. (2003) find that the left prefrontal lobe is involved in information selection. In addition, Fan et al. report a lack of correlation between the pattern of areas activated while controlling conflict in different tasks and a lack of significant interactions when tasks were combined so that two different types of conflict could occur in the same trial. These results seem to point to a specificity of each type of inhibitory control process, although all of them tend to involve neural circuitry that involves the ventral prefrontal cortex. Recent, systematic research (Jonides, 2006; Jonides & Nee, 2006) suggests that there is not a single mechanism for conflict resolution, but rather that brain activation is idiosyncratic with respect to different tasks and stages of processing. However, one frontal area (the left inferior frontal gyrus) does seem consistently involved in resolving proactive interference in working memory—an outcome broadly consistent with Fan et al. (2003).

If adult studies present a complex picture of the brain substratum of inhibitory control and conflict resolution, the developmental picture seems even more complex—and the available evidence far less extensive. Both Casey et al. (1997) and Durston et al. (2002) compare adults and school children on Go-No-Go paradigms (in which participants must refrain from responding when a particular stimulus is presented). Both studies find activation in the prefrontal areas, and that the interference-related activation is greater in children than adults. However, the areas that emerge as relevant in these two studies do not coincide exactly. Durston et al. conclude that children's cognitive processes are more susceptible to interference, and this seems to be related to maturational differences in the underlying fronto-striatal circuitry. In a follow-up study, Durston et al. (2006) report that focal activation in ventral prefrontal regions increases with age. Bunge et al. (2002), instead, compare children and adults on a flanker task (in which the target stimulus is flanked by irrelevant distracters, either congruent or incongruent with the target), and find ventrolateral prefrontal activation at both ages. However, this activation occurs in the right hemisphere with adults and in the left hemisphere with children. Some important (and so far unspecified) transformation would seem to take place during adolescence.

The finding by Janice Johnson and colleagues of different inhibitory mechanisms, discussed in chapter 2, seems to fit well the pattern emerging from recent studies that show a plethora of specific inhibitory mechanisms in the brain, located mostly, but not exclusively, in the prefrontal lobes.

Some authors are trying to draw a unitary coherent picture from the available findings. Casey, Tottenham, and Fossella (2002) present a model of brain mechanisms for cognitive control, based on circuitry that connects the frontal cortex, the basal ganglia, and the thalamus. This network would have a developmental course; for instance, the basal ganglia could have a more prominent role in young children than adults, because of relative immaturity of the frontal lobes. The basal ganglia thalamo-cortical circuitry would develop throughout childhood and adolescence, as evidenced by "the prolonged development of prefrontal regions in synapse elimination and myelination and by the maturation of the dopamine system" (Casey et al., 2002, p. 249). Atypical development of that circuitry (for instance, neonatal basal ganglia insults) would account for the clinical problems (for instance, attentional deficit and hyperactivity disorder) that emerge in some atypical populations with impaired inhibitory functions. Future research will tell whether Casey's model offers an adequate account of the neuropsychological and maturational basis of inhibitory control that is so important in Pascual-Leone's theory and also discussed to some extent in other neo-Piagetian theories.

As noted in chapter 2, field factors are one of the sources of cognitive conflict in the TCO. Pascual-Leone (personal communication, July 2004; Pascual-Leone & Johnson, in preparation) believes that the F operator has its neuropsychological basis in the lateral inhibition that takes place especially in the granular layer (i.e., the fourth of six layers of which the cortex is composed) and is enhanced by the acetylcoline system. It should also be mentioned in this context that, in visual processing of hierarchical stimuli, adults show a right-hemisphere advantage for the global level and a left-hemisphere advantage for the local level. The global advantage in the right hemisphere, which could underlie field effects, is already present in 7-year-olds, the youngest age tested so far (Moses et al., 2002). The left hemisphere advantage for the local level starts to emerge between 12 and 14 years, and continues to develop during adolescence (Mondloch et al., 2003, Experiment 3; Moses et al., 2002).

Other important data have been provided by studies of *EEG coherence*, that is, the degree to which the electrical activity of different cortical areas shows phase synchrony in a given frequency band (see also chap. 5). A high coherence between two areas indicates that they are functionally connected, which of course is an important aspect of the "big picture" of the working brain. Research by Thatcher (1992, 1994a, 1994b, 1996, 1997; Hanlon, Thatcher, & Cline, 1999; Thatcher et al., 1987) as well as by other groups (Bell & Fox, 1994, 1996; Bell & Wolfe, 2007; Mundy, Fox, & Card, 2003; Ross & Segalowitz, 2000; see also Stauder, Molenaar, & van der Molen, 1999; Somsen et al., 1997, for consistent results with other brain imaging techniques) provide illuminating data that have attracted much attention by neo-Piagetian researchers.

The developing brain must accomplish two transformations that have contradictory effects on EEG coherence. On the one hand, the various parts of the cortex must specialize. That is the modularization process (proposed, e.g., by Karmiloff-Smith and discussed in chap. 7), which involves a change from diffuse to more focal activity in the brain. This process manifests itself as a reduction of EEG coherence in the course of development. On the other hand, the parts of the brain must communicate and achieve integration with one another, so that different specialized parts can collaborate effectively and smoothly in complex tasks. Such growing integration among modules manifests itself as an increase of EEG coherence. The outcome of these two complementary processes of differentiation and integration is that EEG coherence does not simply increase or decrease linearly with age, but goes up and down again and again. Such a pattern has been reported by Thatcher on the basis of large samples of participants ranging from infants to young adults (for discussions see also Barry et al., 2004; Bell, 1998). However, analyzing the details of those ups-and-downs, Thatcher noted a recursive pattern in the age range between 3 years and adolescence, which suggested to him a model of cyclic reorganization of the cortex.

In brief, spurts of coherence growth take place in the brain every few years (slightly different timing of the cycles has been suggested by Thatcher, 1992, 1994a, 1997; Thatcher et al., 1987), but one can say approximately that a cycle from one growth spurt to the next takes between 2 and 4 years. During those cycles, one can observe first a growth of long-distance prefrontal-occipital connections, then the leading edge of connection growth moves around the cortex, starting from frontal-parietal connections in the right hemisphere, followed by shorter right frontal-temporal-occipital pathways. Growth of connections then takes place especially in the frontal lobes, followed by shorter and then longer connections in the left hemi-sphere, until the leading edge of connection growth returns to the longest frontal-occipital connections, and a new cycle of growth can begin. Thus, the process is modeled as a developmental spiral where brain structures are periodically revisited and results in stepwise increases in differentiation and integration. Those stepwise increases of cortical integration are as-sumed to underlie the periods of growth of the major skills represented in those cortical areas.

The frontal lobes play a special role in this process, because they are supposed to be responsible for the selection and pruning of synapses in the other cortical areas. Thatcher metaphorically describes the frontal lobes as acting as a predator toward the posterior cortical areas, but the outcome of such "predation" is actually a more ordered landscape with better orga-nized connections. Growth of EEG coherence, regulated by the frontal lobes according to Thatcher (1994b), turns out into cognitively more advanced behavior (e.g., Bell & Wolfe, 2007; Mundy et al., 2003).

Neo-Piagetian authors (e.g., Case, 1992b, 1995, 1998; Fischer, in press; Fischer & Rose, 1999; Pascual-Leone, 2006a, 2006b) have commented exten-sively on Thatcher's model. It proposes that the cortex develops according to a pattern of cyclic reorganization, with stepwise improvements that, broadly speaking, resemble the stages and substages of Piaget's theory and the neo-Piagetian theories. In some cases, the EEG measures indeed grow with age at a rate similar to that proposed by some neo-Piagetian theory. For instance, as mentioned in chapter 5, the spurts of alpha-waves power in the occipito-parietal area, reported by Matousek and Petersen (1973), are congruent with the levels of Fischer's abstract tier, and those reported by Mizuno et al. (1970) with the spurts during the sensorimotor tier. On the other hand, the development of theta-waves coherence between left frontal and left parietal cortex (Thatcher, 1994, 1997) coincides closely with Pascual-Leone's M capacity stages. And, indeed, it seems plausible that the regulating role of the frontal lobes in reorganizing the connections in other parts of the cortex, proposed by Thatcher, can provide a neuropsycho-logical account of the psychological mechanisms proposed by Case (1998) for the construction of Central Conceptual Structures. At this point, how-ever, we would also like to take a prudent stance and remind the reader that, even though the processes and the chronological patterns reported by Thatcher and other scholars bear a striking resemblance with those pro-posed by neo-Piagetian theories, much more research is needed on the re-lationship between physiological and behavioral measures before one can come to strong conclusions on the neuropsychological substratum of cogni-tive development.

The last point to be mentioned briefly before concluding our discussion of maturational influences, regards the role of processing speed in cognitive development (Demetriou et al., 2002) and in the lifespan (de Ribau-pierre, 2001). Although the relationship between processing speed and working memory still needs to be clarified, as just discussed in this chapter, it has been argued persuasively that practice and experience alone cannot account for developmental changes in processing speed (Case, 1995). This suggests that speed is affected by maturational constraints, although the mechanisms controlling speed development are not yet clear.

Conversely, maturation alone is not enough to account for changes in the brain—let alone for cognitive development. Maturation is directly integrated with the contribution of environmental factors. For example, Mounoud (1993) speaks of structural organization of the nervous system ruled by endogenous factors and of a functional organization relating to neural activities that are in part influenced by external, exogenous factors and thus, dependent on experience. Practice and experience influence brain changes, both at the level of synaptic overproduction and with respect to the selection of synapses to preserve (Greenough, Black, & Wallace, 1987; Greenough & Schwark, 1984). For example, in studies in which a single eye of a newborn kitten is sutured, one finds that the portion of the cortex corresponding to the nondeprived eye is favoured in cortical development. If the sutured eye is reopened after the sensitive period, that is, the time in which experience affects maturation, one finds a visual deficit. Demonstrated in this way is the existence of a period in which the environment exerts its maximum influence.

Synaptic overproduction is associated with a greater neural plasticity and is typical of systems highly responsive to environmental input. During a relatively restricted period, an expected experience participates in the organization of the neural pattern. The neural manifestation of expectation or sensitivity appears to be the production of an excess number of synapses, a subset of which will be selectively preserved by experience-generated neural activity (Greenough et al., 1987).

This phenomenon occurs in the first phases of child development, on the basis of experiences that are expected at that age to usually take place, and also occurs in more advanced stages. And even with adults, synaptic formations could occur in response to events that provide information for coding by the nervous system.

More generally, adults and even elderly people maintain some potential for neural plasticity, and this plasticity enables both brain change due to extensive experience and some compensatory processes after brain lesions. One remarkable illustration of adults' neural plasticity and of the effects of expertise on the brain is provided by Maguire et al. (2000), who examine structural MRI scans of the brains of experienced London taxi drivers with a mean professional experience of over 14 years, plus 2 of training. They find that, in comparison with a control group, the taxi drivers have a significantly larger volume of grey matter in the posterior region of both the left and the right hippocampus (which is believed to store spatial representations). In the anterior hippocampi, instead, the control group shows a larger grey matter volume than the taxi drivers. Furthermore, the amount of experience of the taxi drivers correlates positively with the volume of the posterior right hippocampus, and negatively with the volume of their anterior right hippocampus. The authors conclude that the increasing expertise on navigational skills in London taxi drivers is associated with a relative redistribution of grey matter in the hippocampus, particularly in the right one. Studies such as this demonstrate persuasively that a healthy adult human brain still has considerable potential for plasticity as a function of exposure to environment, and more generally, that the brain structure is not a mere product of maturation, but is sculpted by both maturation and experience.

Research using fMRI also shows adults' neural plasticity, and a role of expertise in the process of modularization. Stiles, Moses, Passarotti, and Dick (2003) review some of those studies, and mention that the fusiform area that in most people is specialized for face processing becomes active when experts of cars or birds perceive not only faces, but also cars or birds, respectively. They also discuss the finding that bilinguals represent their second language either in a diffuse and bilateral way or, if they are highly proficient, in a more focal and left-lateralized way. Such proficiency-related shift in the brain representation of second language takes place irrespective of the age of second language acquisition.[13] One can conclude that our brains do not have innate, fixed modules, but the modularization process is affected by experience and continues in adult age, as also suggested by Karmiloff-Smith (see chap. 7).

A few EEG coherence studies also provide valuable information on the relationship between maturation and experience in shaping the connections in the brain. Bell and Fox (1996) record EEGs for a sample of 8-month-old infants, who vary in their crawling experience. Frontal-occipital coherence is low in the group of infants who have not yet started to crawl, increases in the novice crawlers (less than 4 weeks experience), remains high in the group with intermediate crawling experience (5 to 8 weeks experience) and decreases again in the most experienced group (9 weeks or more). A similar pattern, though just short of significance, is also found for parietal-occipital coherence. These results suggest that onset of locomotion is associated with changes in cortical organization, that is, with an (experi-

---

[13] In Greenough's terms, these are experience-dependent changes that take place on top and beyond the experience-expectant changes (that is, those changes that normally take place along a course predisposed by maturation, but that needs some appropriate input to unfold).

ence-expectant) overproduction of connections. However, increased loco-motor experience leads to a pruning of those connections.

These results are important because they guide the interpretation of Thatcher's findings also. Although it seems reasonable to interpret the cy-cles of increasing and decreasing EEG coherence described by Thatcher as essentially due to maturation, results like those reported by Bell and Fox (1996) draw our attention to the essential role that experience also has in shaping the changes in cortical connectivity.

Summary

To summarize this section, the neo-Piagetian theories have not followed the fashion of "precocism"; neo-Piagetian authors are happy to acknowledge the remarkable abilities recently discovered in infants, but refrain from in-terpreting them in terms of mature cognitive abilities, and rather seek for constructivist explanations based on activation and coordination of percep-tual-motor schemes or skills.

The neo-Piagetian theories also exclude nativist assumptions, such as in-nate representations or knowledge. The assumption is generally made that representations, strategies, skills, and executive control structures are con-structed—on the grounds of and within the constraints placed by innate en-dowment and maturational changes. Of course, for neo-Piagetian theories, one important change controlled by maturational constraints is the growth of working memory or processing capacity.

Even though the content of Karmiloff-Smith's neuroconstructivism is dif-ferent from that of neo-Piagetian theories, at a more abstract, epistemo-logical level they are quite similar in their emphasis on representation, on constructive processes, and in the role assigned to innate, maturational, and experiential factors.

All neo-Piagetian theories, as argued throughout this book, posit an im-portant role (although in subtly different terms from one another) for expe-rience and learning, which interact with aspects of maturation in shaping cognitive development. Several times in our discussion of the various theo-ries we have pointed to the environment as a medium of practical experi-ence, a source of feedback that regulates the organism and as a support for reducing the cognitive load. Given the intertwined nature of maturation and experience, positing the influence of environment on performance is com-patible with the idea that discontinuous cognitive development is the mani-festation of several underlying developmental variables, including physio-logical changes, which in themselves are sometimes gradual and relatively continuous, and sometimes occur in spurts. Experience also yields the con-solidation or even the automatization of various abilities, which can be regarded as a relatively continuous aspect in the otherwise discontinuous pattern of cognitive development.

TOWARD AN INTEGRATION

The reader who has patiently reached this point may wonder whether the various neo-Piagetian theories could be integrated into a more comprehensive theory of cognitive development. Throughout the book we have highlighted specific aspects by means of which some theories could be compared and sometimes integrated, sometimes scrutinized with further research to resolve a controversy. We have also presented, in chapter 3, Chapman's early and probably premature attempt at integrating Pascual-Leone's and Halford's theories. Moreover, we have mentioned both Case's proposal for integrating some concepts of Pascual-Leone and Fischer, in view of a unified theory, and Fischer's integration of constructivist and dynamic concepts. In this final section, we wish to recap the main points of agreement and of ongoing debate, outline the chances of achieving a broader integration, and suggest the emerging prospects within the neo-Piagetian field.

Points of Agreement

Although certainly different from one another, the theories discussed in this book share several foundational elements. All seek to surpass Piaget's theory while maintaining some of its basic ideas. Case (1987, 1991, 1992d) outlined the points of agreement and disagreement among the neo-Piagetian authors, and several of the points that he made are still valid, because they concern the very foundations of neo-Piagetian theories.

They agree that the child possesses *cognitive structures*, constructed through interaction with the environment, that assimilate and interpret experience. Thus they are united in rejecting an empiricist view of mental development. Different accents are found in the pattern of cognitive structures assumed as units of analysis, but the neo-Piagetian theories are not incompatible in this regard. For example, a cognitive process could consist in successive or simultaneous activation of schemes (Pascual-Leone) that in their totality can be described as an executive strategy (Case) which in certain cases could be called a skill (Fischer).

Initially cognitive development is predominated by sensorimotor structures, whereas in successive phases the cognitive structures become more symbolic and abstract. However, the neo-Piagetian authors also agree that the processes that produce new structures do not involve the child's entire cognitive repertoire, but rather act in a circumscribed way, on a specific set of structures.

Because the neo-Piagetian theories do not follow Piaget in explaining cognitive structures in terms of logical competencies, it is also possible for them to extend their analyses to emotional, motor and linguistic development in greater depth than Piaget did. However, although abandoning the Piagetian explanation of stages in terms of logic, the notion of stage is still recognized as a first approximation having descriptive value. During development there are typical periods or ages for the most important cognitive acquisitions[14] affected to a certain degree by social and cultural factors. According to some neo-Piagetian authors (i.e., Case, Fischer, Mounoud) the succession of stages has a cyclical, recursive nature. Neo-Piagetian theorists also propose, with Piaget, that the cognitive structures of one stage are the fruit of a restructuring and re-elaboration of the less abstract structures of the previous stage.

Most neo-Piagetian authors also take up the Piagetian distinction between *development* and *learning*. For instance, Halford considers them the two basic explanatory factors of cognitive development, and assumes that acquiring the processing capacity for representations at a new level of complexity is the precondition for learning those representations. Fischer distinguishes the processes (for instance, coordination) that produce changes across levels of a cognitive structure from processes of differentiation and integration that produce greater complexity within a given level. Pascual-Leone distinguishes learning due to cumulative experience, that is, due to repeated co-activation of schemes (operators C and LC) from another more rapid type of learning (operator LM). The latter involves symbolic processing cognitive effort and the use of attentional resources, which are more abundant in older children. For Case learning is involved in development: his theory includes the processes L- and M-learning (similar to Pascual-Leone's) that iteratively feed into each other in the construction of a new conceptual structure and hierarchical feedback loops that interconnect the acquisition of new schemes and the construction of new executive control structures and central conceptual structures. In each of these theories, a combination of development and learning produces new cognitive structures that are applicable in increasingly complex contexts with a minimal attentional effort. In general, neo-Piagetian theories distinguish the general factors that foster and constrain development from the specific factors involved in acquiring new structures. This reconciles according a descriptive value to stages (such as the "minimal structuralism" of which de Ribau-

---

[14]Of course, in different societies and cultures those cognitive acquisitions considered primary would be different. For instance, the formal structure of mathematics and science is a cultural patrimony that provides Western children with the content of advanced conceptual structures, but these are not a universal finish line for cognitive development. In any case, the content of the most advanced cognitive structures manifest within a society have a cultural origin.

pierre, 1993, speaks) with the idea that cognitive structures have a specific content and a specific genesis (making horizontal *décalage* an unexceptional phenomena).

With respect to Piaget's two souls (logical and dialectical) as discussed in chapter 1, although the neo-Piagetians certainly abandon the former, in general they follow the latter and contribute to clarifying the processes involved in the "equilibration of cognitive structures." In our view there is at least what might be called a "minimal dialectic" in each neo-Piagetian theory. Most theories consider the interaction between a child endowed with cognitive structures and the environment, and each recognizes that the child has the potential to transform (when having the necessary resources) his or her preexisting cognitive structures through interaction with the environment. Examples of dialectical aspects are found in Case's interplay between differentiation and integration in building up hierarchical learning loops, Demetriou's interaction between his "hypercognitive system" and the SSSs, Mounoud's decomposition and recomposition processes, and Fischer's transitional processes. They all constitute proposals intended to specify the mechanisms of mutual regulation, and in this sense they exemplify this minimal dialectic. We return to the issue of dialectic in the section "Again on Dialectic."

Controversies and Possible Solutions

Despite agreement on the points considered so far, clearly each theory defines differently the cognitive units, the stages of development, and the relevant aspects of individual differences. The main points of disagreement among theorists concern the defining criteria of stages and the processes that underlie changes in the cognitive structures.

There are two types of difference among the models of developmental stages discussed throughout this book. One type of difference (cyclical vs. noncyclical) is not irreconcilable in terms of the proposed ages for transitional changes. For instance, Case proposes four major stages, and a sequence of substages that repeats itself cyclically in each stage, whereas Pascual-Leone marks only one major difference between sensorimotor and symbolic processing, and proposes that developmental stages from 3 years to adolescence are due to a linear increase in capacity. However, these two models are compatible with each other, because the ages posited for each transition are basically the same and, moreover, one can translate Case's structural account and Pascual-Leone's functional account of each stage into each other (e.g., Pascual-Leone & Johnson, 2005). The same, however, cannot be said of the other two theories involving cyclical phases. This takes us directly to the second (related) difference, which concerns the ages posited for stage transitions and that is more difficult to reconcile. No doubt, all proposals of typical ages for stage transitions are only approximate indications of when a transition should occur in an "average" child; however, the important point here is that there are considerable differences in the ages proposed by various theories.

A first difference worth mentioning regards the three cyclical theories. Mounoud and Fischer, although presenting some phases in which ages coincide with those of Case, propose cyclical phases recurring within 3 major stages (or tiers) instead of four. Mounoud does not present an analogue of Case's relational stage. Thus, in not providing transitional phases, the first qualitative change after 18 months takes place at 5 years. Fischer unites Case's relational and dimensional in one tier from 2–10 years, thus identifying only three transitional levels and sacrificing most of the phases of Case's latter stage.

Furthermore, as just noted, Pascual-Leone and Case indicate very similar ages in their staircases of cognitive development; Halford and Demetriou also propose very similar ones, but they differ from those of Pascual-Leone and Case. And Fischer (although criticizing the staircase metaphor and preferring that of a web with many strands) actually proposes a sequence of ages representing the development of optimal levels of performance that is different from both Pascual-Leone's and Halford's. Mounoud's developmental progression is similar to Halford's for the main stages, but also includes a more fine-grained subdivision, similar to Fischer's. Thus, we must consider why these differences arise and what sort of research would be necessary to resolve the controversy.

One reason for such differences is that some theories base their stages on the format (or the level of abstraction) of representations. In particular, Halford considers the dimensionality of relations that are involved in representation of a problem, and suggests that, at different ages, children can learn concepts that involve unary, binary, ternary, or quaternary relations. However, solving a problem or performing a task involves more than representing relations. If we consider, for instance, Case's executive control structures or Fischer's skills, they involve not only representations of concepts, objects, and the relations among them, but also operations, processes, and actions. Thus, one feasible research strategy could be modeling the cognitive tasks studied by Halford in the terms of, for instance, Case's or Fischer's theory. If one of those theories (that are more fine-grained than Halford's regarding progress with age) is able to account for Halford's data, and eventually also to generate new predictions, then the contradiction would be resolved. If, instead, it turns out that they cannot account for Halford's results, then one would conclude that Halford's view of representational development is irreducible to other theories, and a truly general cognitive developmental theory should keep it as a basic construct.

Another important reason for differences among the proposed stage progressions lies in the conditions under which children's performance is typically studied. On this issue, Pascual-Leone and Fischer have rather extreme positions. On the one hand, Pascual-Leone holds that developmental stages only emerge from novel performance in misleading tasks. This is because the presence of several different sources of activation for relevant schemes in facilitating or overlearned tasks does not permit isolation of the M capacity component of activation, and thus it becomes impossible to detect the developmental pattern of M capacity increase. On the other hand (and simplifying his argument on synchrony somewhat) Fischer claims that different tasks show synchronous development only with sufficient practice and in conditions of optimal support. In these conditions one can observe children's optimal performance, at the tiers and levels predicted by his theory; whereas in conditions of non-optimal support, he believes children are likely to perform less well, in a more variable way, and in ways that are not univocally predicted by the theory.

Possibly, the picture of cognitive development offered by Pascual-Leone and Fischer differs also as a consequence of their different emphasis on novel, misleading tasks versus practice and optimal support. Research is needed to clarify this issue, and all the more needed because Pascual-Leone's and Fischer's theories have never been compared directly. One feasible research strategy could be to concentrate on a few selected tasks and manipulate the experimental conditions so that they vary systematically for presence of misleading cues, amount of practice, and environmental support. If the developmental pattern proposed by Pascual-Leone only emerges in misleading conditions, and that proposed by Fischer only in the most facilitating and supportive conditions, then both of them would be right (even though one-sided). The two theories should then be deemed complementary and both of them retained within an integrated neo-Piagetian theory. If, instead, the predictions of either theory were not satisfied, then at least one of them should be superseded in the process of constructing an integrated theory.

Manipulating the degree of misleadingness of a task may not be simple; however, there are instructive examples that can be taken as starting points. Let us consider briefly the balance scale task, just as a case study. It is a task for which many versions exist (see chaps. 4 and 6 in this book). Halford et al. (2002) devised a version suitable for preschoolers, with the two sides of the scale made salient by a large duck or rabbit at each end, a very small number of weights (no more than 3 per side) made salient by a line drawn around their edge, and only 3 pegs per side. Distance between the pegs is made salient by means of wide spacing; the first peg is very close to the fulcrum and the last one very close to the toy animal that marks the end of the beam. In one experiment with this apparatus a group of children of mean age 2 years 8 months responded better than chance on items where a correct response could be made on the basis of the number of weights (Siegler's rule 1). After training, the same group of children could also answer better than chance on items with an equal number of weights per side, but different distance from the fulcrum (Siegler's rule 2). In another experiment, a group of mean age 6 years, after training, could integrate with some success weight and distance on items where the two dimensions were in conflict (Siegler's rule 3). Such early success is indeed remarkable, and Halford et al. (2002) note that it suggests earlier emergence of balance scale rules than predicted by Case (1985). One might object that Case used stricter criteria for success, or that age-groups should be compared under more similar conditions, but that is not the point we want to make here. Rather, we wish to point out that manipulations like those used by Halford et al. (2002) seem to be very successful in creating a highly facilitating and supportive version of the balance scale task—which yields quite a different pattern of results from those obtained under more misleading conditions. A systematic use of such manipulations, with a few selected tasks and several, properly selected age groups, could be very appropriate for anyone who wishes to test the hypothesis that Pascual-Leone's and Fischer's developmental sequences reflect children's performance under misleading and supportive conditions, respectively.

Again on Dialectic

As just mentioned, the processes that underlie changes in cognitive structures are another controversial matter. We have outlined throughout the book the developmental processes proposed in various theories, noting their similarities and differences, and we have also discussed them at some length in this final chapter. However, it remains to consider how they relate to "the dialectical Piaget"—to his ideas on contradiction, regulation and equilibration in cognitive development.

Useful points on the dialectical Piaget have already been made in previous discussions of neo-Piagetian theories. Case (1987) contrasts Piaget's structuralist notions of schematic differentiation and coordination with his dialectical notion of equilibration. Pascual-Leone (1987) reviews the main philosophical principles of dialectic and their relevance for psychology. In this context, he criticizes those developmental theories that lack mechanisms for the child's dynamic or creative synthesis of new schemes or cognitive structures and that "focus too exclusively on the logical characteristics of the to-be-produced correct response" (p. 538), disregarding the influence of misleading schemes that are also activated in a problem situation and that conflict with the activation of the relevant ones. Thus, Pascual-Leone (1987) argues that to have explanatory power a neo-Piagetian theory needs an explicit dialectical model of attentional resources. Juckes (1991) makes a similar argument with regard to stage transitions. He argues that any theory that involves qualitative differences among stages, and for which behavior associated with the new stage cannot be explained simply in terms of learning, must hypothesize one or more generative mechanisms integral to the organism capable of explaining the qualitative changes. Otherwise (and this is the learning paradox) one must assert that the new behavior is based in learning that could not yet have taken place.

Pascual-Leone and Case had a pioneering role in highlighting the dialectical side of Piaget's theory and in stimulating other neo-Piagetian theorists to investigate the information processing mechanisms that enable humans to cope with contradiction, cognitive conflict and equilibration. It should also be noted, however, that in the last 10 or 15 years most of the main neo-Piagetian theories have been greatly enriched in their dialectical content. This is also true of Case's and Pascual-Leone's work. For instance, we remind the reader of the processes invoked by Case (1998; Case & Okamoto, 1996) to account for children's synthesis of new concepts and more advanced central conceptual structures (see chap. 6), and of the distinction between different inhibitory mechanisms in Pascual-Leone's theory (Johnson et al., 2003; see chap. 2).

The dialectical enrichment has been even more remarkable in some theories that had initially developed this facet to a lesser extent. A very important step has been taken by Fischer, who accepts the dynamic systems approach as a framework for the study of development (e.g., Fischer & Bidell, 2006; Fischer & Kennedy, 1997; see chap. 5). Similarly, other authors who have studied emotional development in connection with a neo-Piagetian approach to cognition (Lewis, 2000, 2001; Mascolo et al., 2000; see chap. 8) also take a dynamic system perspective in their account of the cognition–emotion relationship. Dynamic systems involve functions with several variables and parameters, which represent features either of the organism or of the environment. Those variables are irreducible to each other, because they represent different constructs and can be varied independently; however, even a small change in one variable can directly or indirectly affect the others, often in nonlinear ways. Contradictions can be represented in a dynamic system, because two variables can be varied simultaneously in ways that have opposite effects on the (dependent) variable representing the behavioral or cognitive state that one intends to explain. Although attractors are often described metaphorically as a sort of entity with a pulling force (a metaphor that is indeed appropriate), speaking more technically, an attractor is defined as a local minimum point in the dependent variable(s), and for that reason it works as a point of equilibrium where the system tends to stabilize, because only a large change in other variables (e.g., a strong Piagetian "perturbation," a notable change in experimental conditions or in the environment, or a sizable increase in the developing child's working memory capacity) could move the system away from an attractor. Thus, the concept of attractor fits very well the Piagetian concepts of equilibration and disequilibrium.

Thus we see that the concepts of the dialectical Piaget (equilibrium, perturbation, contradiction) can be represented by means of dynamic systems. The concept of equilibration can also be represented, provided that the system includes one or more variables that refer to the organism's adaptive reactions (e.g., executive control processes, attentional resources). The particular dialectical models adopted by Fischer and by Lewis are different from those of Pascual-Leone, especially because they do not refer to the same attentional constructs. However, a common language has been established, and it is a matter for empirical research to determine which particular variables are needed in a dynamic system model of a given psychological phenomenon.

Similar considerations also apply to Demetriou's proposal of mutual constraints and influences among components of a child's mind. These components may develop at different rates, and at certain points a change in one component may trigger dramatic changes and reorganization of other components (Demetriou et al., 1993; Demetriou & Raftopoulos, 1999; see chap. 3). Such a proposal is fully compatible with a dynamic system approach (as highlighted by Demetriou & Raftopoulos, 2004); it differs from the previous ones in that it models the dialectic of long-term development of the mind's components, rather than the dialectic of ongoing mental processes.[15]

Among the main neo-Piagetian theoreticians, Halford is the one whose assumptions place great importance on structuralism, but not on dialectic. In principle, connectionist models could have some dialectical features, for instance, if separate parts of the network were used to represent contradictory processes or components. However, the main feature of Halford's connectionist models of relational concepts is that more complex models (i.e., models based on the convolution of a larger number of dimensions; see chap. 3) are capable of learning more complex relations. Learning, of course, can be modeled very well in a connectionist model. However, learning depends on experience and feedback, and the problem remains of how to account for novel performance. A connectionist network does respond to the input of a new stimulus, but its response depends on generalization from previous learning. Even in case a part of the network were to be dedicated to representation of control processes (a feature missing so far in

---

[15]Some other proposals regarding interactions among components of the processing system are more specific. Lautrey (1993) points to the distinction between symbolic and analogic processing modes, and suggests that the analogic processes can generate expectations and heuristics that in turn guide usage of symbolic processes. This theoretical proposal refers above all to those tasks in which analogic processes can have a facilitative role, and to those individuals who have greater ability in the analogic domain.

Halford's models), those control processes would have to be either pre-wired in the network or learned by it. How would one account for problem solving in situations where previous learning is not helpful, or is even misleading? It appears that the critical analysis of Juckes (1991) is applicable here, that is, Halford's theory (even after his connectionist turn) may still fall under the learning paradox; a developmental increase in a child's processing capacity is represented in the model as an increase of the number of dimensions of the relational concepts that the child can learn, but the model is still moot with regard to contradictions, equilibration processes and novel solutions to problems.

Prospects

Throughout this book we have pointed out that the neo-Piagetian theories share many basic tenets and that, overall, they have produced a considerable body of experimental results and new explanations. In this final chapter we have also discussed points of agreement, ideas for specific comparisons, and possibilities for partial integration. However, it must also be acknowledged that, so far, an adequate integration of neo-Piagetian theories that overcomes the various aspects on which they differ has not yet been achieved.

An integration would certainly be desirable, in view of the shared goal of formulating a general theory of cognitive development. However, in our view, a simple juxtaposition of pieces of different theories is not a viable possibility for a satisfactory integration. Rather, a suitable research strategy would consist (a) in verifying which constructs among those that are present in one theory, but not in others, are actually necessary to account for developmental evidence; and (b) in considering whether two theories that make different predictions for a particular situation are reconcilable at a higher level, or whether at least one of them needs to be modified.

An example of case (a) would be to assess, as just suggested, whether Case's or Fischer's theories, which are not based on the dimensionality of relations among the variables in a problem, can account for Halford's results. If they do not, then one should conclude that dimensionality of relations is not reducible to the concepts specified by those other theories; and, therefore, it must be kept as a specific construct in an integrated and more general theory. Similarly, one could investigate whether Pascual-Leone's construct of the I operator is necessary to explain his data or whether other theories can account for the same findings without resorting to it.

An example of case (b) would be investigating, as also just suggested, whether the developmental progressions proposed by Pascual-Leone's and Fischer's theories are compatible at a higher level, as might happen, for instance, if the former pattern were to be found in misleading conditions and the latter in facilitating, supportive ones. If, however, the empirical results were to found inconsistent with this hypothesis, then one of the theories (or possibly both) should be modified.

Given the range of topics that are still controversial among neo-Piagetian theorists, we suggest that at least three large-scale projects would be needed, before an adequate theoretical integration could be achieved. A first project should focus on the development of working memory or processing capacity, also including individual-difference and lifespan perspectives, and comparing the measures proposed by different authors such as Case, Pascual-Leone, Demetriou, and de Ribaupierre. Their predictive validity should be assessed, as well as their adequacy on strict criteria such as those set by the easy-to-hard paradigm that some authors—most notably, Halford—have already used successfully. The relation of capacity to processing speed should also be investigated further. To enjoy the full benefits of dialogue between general-experimental and developmental research, the neo-Piagetian models of working memory development should be compared (and perhaps integrated) with models of working memory such as Cowan's and Engle's, as well as with Barrouillet's hypothesis that the rate of operations is one component of a formula that expresses a task's processing load (and an individual's processing capacity).

A second large-scale project that seems necessary concerns the role of structural learning in cognitive development. As just mentioned, all neo-Piagetian theories make a clear distinction between development of the processing system and learning of new cognitive structures; however, each theory does so in a different way. Case's theoretical proposal about the acquisition of central conceptual structures has been supported by fairly extensive research (e.g., Case & Okamoto, 1996), both basic and applied, and it can be regarded as a promising reconciliation of generality and specificity in cognitive development and a plausible solution to the problem of developmental constraints on learning capabilities. Moreover, it also offers very promising results in the applied field, for instance, with respect to the mathematics curriculum. However, with the untimely death of Robbie Case (May 19th, 2000), research on the CCS model seems, with very few exceptions, to have stopped. A collaborative study with Demetriou's research group (Case et al., 2001) reveals remarkable agreement between the domains of Case's CCSs and Demetriou's SSSs. Yet, much work remains to be done by way of integrating theories. For instance, could Case's initial effort to put the model of central conceptual structures into relation with the multiple intelligences perspective (Gardner, 1983) be pursued further to account for structural learning in other domains (e.g., music)? In Fischer's theory, strands in the dynamic constructive web of development represent skill domains (see chap. 5), which seem to be task-specific and more circumscribed than Case's CCSs; one could ask whether the skill domains can be subsumed or be put into relation with the domains of CCSs and SSSs. In any event, it would seem important to employ the microdevelopmental methods, widely used by Siegler, Fischer, and their colleagues, to study the details of the construction of central conceptual structures and the different pathways taken by individuals of the same or different age in CCS development. Despite evident similarities between Case's and Fischer's theories, we are not aware of empirical research that attempts to integrate their contributions regarding structural learning—a gap that it is time to fill.[16]

In the same vein, Halford and Pascual-Leone's theories would also benefit from use of microgenetic methods to identify different courses taken by development of different concepts and to better observe intra- and interindividual variability. Moreover, also in the field of structural learning, it would be valuable to assess whether Halford's relational complexity can contribute to an account of conceptual learning beyond what Case's or Fischer's theories can explain. Halford et al. (2002) suggest that Case's theory might underestimate young children's capabilities. Would that claim be supported by further research? In that case, could one model acquisition of central conceptual structures and skill generalization within the framework of relational complexity?[17]

Formal modeling is a third domain for research prior to integration of neo-Piagetian theories. As noted in previous chapters, both Pascual-Leone and Halford have emphasized, from the very beginning of neo-Piagetian research, the importance of detailed formal models of specific tasks. In the following decades, newer approaches to formal modeling have also been undertaken by other researchers. For instance, Halford and Karmiloff-Smith have used connectionist modeling; Fischer and Lewis often invoke dynamic systems (even though they tend not to formalize them in mathematical terms). We have highlighted the advantages of those models, as well as their limitations—for instance, the connectionist models of Thomas and Karmiloff-Smith give a powerful demonstration of the potential of a neuroconstructivist approach, but tend to obscure the qualitative changes in representations. Those of Halford and colleagues provide an elegant frame-

---

[16] We do not discuss integration between Case's and Pascual-Leone's ideas on learning here as that task has already been performed by Case (1998) and Pascual-Leone and Johnson (2005); see also "Points of Agreement" in this chapter.

[17] In this regard, it would also be interesting to consider Zelazo's Cognitive Complexity and Control theory as a possible alternative to Halford's. Zelazo and colleagues acknowledge the similarities but also note the differences between the two theories. For instance, Zelazo and Müller (2002; Zelazo et al., 2003) raise important questions regarding the importance of reflective abstraction, the role of executive function, and the difference between processing a number of dimensions simultaneously and creating a hierarchy among them. between them. The field of structural learning could be a ground for assessing those differences between the two theories.

work for the study of the development of thinking, but are also liable to fall under the "learning paradox." Increased effort in the way of formal modeling could not only make the testing of neo-Piagetian models more stringent, but could also aid in comparing the different theories by providing a common formal language. For instance, the concept of schemes as structures of hierarchically organized components (see chap. 2) and that of central conceptual structures as networks of heterogeneous representations (see chap. 6) seem to lend themselves well to connectionist modeling, in particular of a localist type. However, Pascual-Leone's and Case's concepts of executive control structures, executive schemes, M and I operators, do not lend themselves equally well to that sort of model. Perhaps a solution could lie in hybrid modeling, with domain-specific knowledge represented in a connectionist network and executive control provided by a rule-based system.[18] Of course, that sort of solution is not simple to achieve; yet one can speculate that hybrid, partly connectionist models could provide a common formal language to compare, and possibly integrate, the predictions from different theories. In any case, more specific research using formalized or mathematical models seems to be a potentially useful instrument on the way toward detailed comparison and possible integration of neo-Piagetian theories.[19]

CONCLUSION

We have highlighted here some lines of research that we would consider useful for further theoretical progress. Of course, the future could take quite different directions. For instance, the various research groups might prefer to develop their own lines of research, rather than concentrating

---

[18] The (speculative) suggestion being made here is that a connectionist network could represent the domain-specific knowledge (conceptual structures, schemes at different hierarchical levels), susceptible to data-driven bottom-up activation of its units and endowed with all the properties of an ordinary neural network, whereas another part of the system could represent, probably in a symbolic way, not only the task goal but also rules for processing the information relevant to that goal (i.e., executive control processes). The two components of the system would have to communicate: given a task goal and a certain input, executive-control rules could be cued and in turn activate or inhibit (to a variable degree, within the limits of their available resources) units in the connectionist representational component—until a response is produced, and so that learning occurs in the process. Limited capacity constraints could be embedded in such models by specifying the amount of activation/inhibition resources available to the executive-control rules (or by varying that amount, to simulate development). Such hybrid connectionist versions of neo-Piagetian models have not yet been implemented, but we think that it would be worthwhile to try them.

[19] See also Case (1996b; Case & Serlin, 1979) regarding comparison of different mathematical models of cognitive growth.

much effort on possible integration. Perhaps the dialogue will be particularly intense between neo-Piagetian and other cognitive researchers on the basis of common interests or methodological approaches. Thus, for example, Fischer's group might interact especially with dynamic system oriented researchers, Pascual-Leone's group with scholars of inhibitory control, Demetriou's group with students of individual differences in abilities, and de Ribaupierre's group with those who study cognition in the lifespan. In this way, both the influence of neo-Piagetian theories in the current scientific debate and their mutual influence among the neo-Piagetian theories themselves would be more indirect and, so to say, distributed.

Of course, the future does not depend on researchers' intentions and plans alone; the support received from scientific funding institutions is also influential. Research projects like those we have suggested will certainly be costly, and one may wonder whether, in the present world, funding organizations will be willing to support such large-scale, theoretically oriented research on children's cognitive development.

Nevertheless, we keep our faith that research on cognitive development is important for both theoretical and applied reasons and that it is worthwhile to continue working toward an integration of neo-Piagetian theories. We are aware that it is a considerable undertaking, involving analysis of epistemological presuppositions, task analysis and formal modeling, reanalysis of existing data in the light of different assumptions, perhaps redefinition of theoretical concepts, and of course, extensive empirical research. As we have argued, much remains to be done prior to achievement of a mature, integrated theory. Such an endeavor will certainly be arduous, but such are the intellectual enterprises that mark out the progress of a science.

References

Agostino, A., Im-Bolter, N., Johnson, J., & Pascual-Leone, J. (2005, April). *Developmental changes in children's multiplication reasoning abilities.* Paper presented to the meeting of the Society for Research in Child Development, Atlanta, GA.

Alexander, P. A., Murphy, P. K., & Kulikowich, J. M. (1998). What responses to domain-specific analogy problems reveal about emerging competence: A new perspective on an old acquaintance. *Journal of Educational Psychology, 90*(3), 397–406.

Alibali, M. W. (1999). How children change their minds: Strategy change can be gradual or abrupt. *Developmental Psychology, 35*(1), 127–145.

Alibali, M. W., & Goldin-Meadow, S. (1993). Gesture-speech mismatch and mechanisms of learning: What the hands reveal about the mind? *Cognitive Psychology, 25*, 468–523.

Allard, F., & Burnett, N. (1985). Skill in sport. *Canadian Journal of Psychology, 39*, 294–312.

Allport, D. A., Styles, E. A., & Hsieh, S. (1994). Shifting intentional set: Exploring the dynamic control of tasks. In C. Umiltà & M. Moscovitch (Eds.), *Attention and performance XV: Conscious and nonconscious information processing* (pp. 421–452). Hillsdale, NJ: Lawrence Erlbaum Associates.

Allport, A., & Wylie, G. (2000). Task switching, stimulus–response bindings, and negative priming. In S. Monsell & J. Driver (Eds.), *Control of cognitive processes: Attention and performance XVIII* (pp. 35–70). Cambridge, MA: MIT Press.

Alp, I. E. (1988). *Mental capacity and working memory in one- to three-year-olds.* Unpublished doctoral thesis, York University, Toronto.

Alp, I. E. (1991, July). *Development of working memory in very young children.* Paper presented at the International Conference on Memory, Lancaster, UK.

Alp, I. E. (1994).Measuring the size of working memory in very young children. *International Journal of Behavioral Development, 17*, 125–141.

Alp, I. E. (1996, July). *The imitation sorting task: A replication study.* Paper presented at the Second International Conference on Memory, Abano, Italy.

Alp, I. E. (2006, June). *Working memory in very young children: A comparison of two imitation tasks.* Paper presented at the meeting of the 3rd European Working Memory Symposium, Genoa, Italy.

Amann Gainotti, M. (1980). Piaget e Marx: Alcune convergenze e differenze [Piaget and Marx: Some convergences and differences]. *Psicologia Contemporanea, 39,* 18–21.

Amin, T. G., & Valsiner, J. (2004). Coordinating operative and figurative knowledge: Piaget, Vygotsky, and beyond. In J. I. M. Carpendale & U. Muller (Eds.), *Social interaction and the development of knowledge* (pp. 87–109). Mahwah, NJ: Lawrence Erlbaum Associates.

Anderson, J. R. (1983). *The architecture of cognition.* Cambridge, MA: Harvard University Press.

Anderson, J. R., & Bower, G. H. (1973). *Human associative memory.* Washington, DC: Winston.

Anderson, J. R., Greeno, J. G., Kline, P. L., & Neves, D. M. (1981). Acquisition of problem-solving skill. In J. R. Anderson (Ed.), *Cognitive skills and their acquisition* (pp. 191–230). Hillsdale, NJ: Lawrence Erlbaum Associates.

Anderson, J. R., & Matessa, M. (1997). A production system theory of serial memory. *Psychological Review, 104,* 728–748.

Andrews, G., & Halford, G. S. (1998). Children's ability to make transitive inferences: The importance of premise integration and structural complexity. *Cognitive Development, 13,* 479–513.

Andrews, G., & Halford, G. S. (2002). A cognitive complexity metric applied to cognitive development. *Cognitive Development, 45,* 153–219.

Antell, S. E., & Keating, D. P. (1983). Perception of numerical invariance in neonates. *Child Development, 54,* 695–701.

Astington, J. W. (1994). *The child's discovery of mind.* New York: Cambridge University Press.

Atkinson, R. C., & Shiffrin, R. M. (1968). Human memory: A proposed system and its control processes. In K. W. Spence & J. T. Spence (Eds.), *The psychology of learning and motivation* (pp. 89–195). New York: Academic Press.

Ayoub, C. C., & Fischer, K. W. (2006). Developmental pathways and intersections among domains of development. In K. McCartney & D. Phillips (Eds.), *Blackwell handbook on early childhood development* (pp. 62–81). Malden, MA: Blackwell.

Ayoub, C. C., Fischer, K. W., & O'Connor, E. E. (2003). Analyzing development of working models for disrupted attachments: The case of hidden family violence. *Attachment and Human Development, 5,* 97–119.

Badan, M., Hauert, C. A., & Mounoud, P. (2000). Sequential pointing in children and adults. *Journal of Experimental Child Psychology, 75,* 43–69.

Baddeley, A. D. (1986). *Working memory.* Oxford, UK: Oxford University Press.

Baddeley, A. D. (2000). The episodic buffer: A new component of working memory. *Trends in Cognitive cience, 4,* 417–423.

Baddeley, A. D., & Hitch, G. (1974).Working memory. In G. Bower (Ed.), *The psychology of learning and motivation: Advances in research and theory* (pp. 47–89). New York: Academic Press.

Baddeley, A. D., Thomson, N., & Buchanan, M. (1975). Word length and the structure of short term memory. *Journal of Verbal Learning and Verbal Behaviour, 14,* 575–589.

Baillargeon, R. (1987). Object permanence in 3.5- and 4.5-month-old infants. *Developmental Psychology, 23,* 655–664.

Baillargeon, R. (1993). The object concept revisited: New direction in the investigation of infants' physical knowledge. In C. Granrud (Ed.), *Perception and cognition in infancy* (pp. 265–315). Hillsdale, NJ: Lawrence Erlbaum Associates.

Baillargeon, R. H., Pascual-Leone, J., & Roncadin, C. (1998). Mental-attentional capacity: Does cognitive style make a difference? *Journal of Experimental Child Psychology, 70,* 143–166.

Baldwin, J. M. (1968). *Mental development in the child and the race* (3rd ed.). New York: A. M. Kelley. (Original work published 1906)

Baltes, P. B., & Baltes, M. M. (1990). Psychological perspectives on successful aging: The model of selective optimization with compensation. In P. B. Baltes & M. M. Baltes (Eds.), *Successful aging: Perspectives from the behavioral sciences* (pp. 1–34). Cambridge, UK: Cambridge University Press.

Barrouillet, P., Bernardin, S., & Camos, V. (2004). Time constraints and resource sharing in adults' working memory spans. *Journal of Experimental Psychology: General, 133*, 83–100.

Barrouillet, P., & Camos, V. (2001). Developmental increase in working memory span: Resource sharing or temporal decay? *Journal of Memory and Language, 45*, 1–20.

Barrouillet, P., & Lecas, J. F. (1999). Mental models in conditional reasoning and working memory. *Thinking and Reasoning, 5*, 289–302.

Barry, R. J., Clarke, A. R., McCarthy, R., Selikowitz, M., Johnstone, S. J., & Rushby, J. A. (2004). Age and gender effects in EEG coherence: Developmental trends in normal children. *Clinical Neurophysiology, 115*, 2252–2258.

Bassok, M. (1990). Transfer of domain-specific problem-solving procedures. *Journal of Experimental Psychology: Learning, Memory, and Cognition, 16*(3), 522–533.

Beilin, H. (1971). Developmental stages and developmental processes. In D. R. Green, M. P. Ford, & G. P. Flammer (Eds.), *Measurement and Piaget* (pp. 172–197). New York: McGraw-Hill.

Beilin, H. (1992a). Piaget's new theory. In H. Beilin & P. B. Pufall (Eds.), *Piaget's theory: Prospects and possibilities* (pp. 1–17). Hillsdale, NJ: Lawrence Erlbaum Associates.

Beilin, H. (1992b). Piaget's enduring contribution to developmental psychology. *Developmental Psychology, 28*, 191–204.

Bell, M. A. (1998). The ontogeny of the EEG during infancy and childhood: Implications for cognitive Development. In B. Garreau (Ed.), *Neuroimaging in child psychiatric disorders* (pp. 97–111). Berlin: Springer-Verlag.

Bell, M. A., & Fox, N. A. (1994). Brain development over the first year of life: Relations between electroencephalographic frequency coherence and cognitive and affective behaviors. In G. Dawson & K. W. Fischer (Eds.), *Human behavior and the developing brain* (pp. 314–345). New York: Guilford.

Bell, M. A., & Fox, N. A. (1996). Crawling experience is related to changes in cortical organization during infancy: Evidence from EEG coherence. *Developmental Psychobiology, 29*, 551–561.

Bell, M. A., & Wolfe, C. D. (2007). Changes in brain functioning from infancy to early childhood: Evidence from EEG power and coherence during working memory tasks. *Developmental Neuropsychology, 31*, 21–38.

Bell, T. S., & Kee, D. W. (1984). Individual differences in cognitive synthesis: An *M*-capacity analysis. *Contemporary Educational Psychology, 9*, 323–332.

Bellugi, U., Lichtenberger, L., Jones, W., Lai, Z., & George, M. S. (2001). *The neurocognitive profile of Williams Syndrome: A complex pattern of strengths and weaknesses.* Cambridge, MA: The MIT Press.

Benson, N. (1989). *Mental capacity constraints on early symbolic processing: The origin of language from a cognitive perspective.* Unpublished doctoral dissertation, York University, Toronto.

Bentley, A. M., Kvalsvig, J., & Miller, R. (1990). The cognitive consequence of poverty: A neo-Piagetian study with Zulu children. *Applied Cognitive Psychology, 4*, 451–459.

Bereiter, C. (1985). Toward a solution of the learning paradox. *Review of Educational Research, 55*, 201–226.

Bereiter, C., & Scardamalia, M. (1979). Pascual-Leone's *M* construct as a link between cognitive developmental and psychometric concepts of intelligence. *Intelligence, 3*, 41–63.

Berthoud, I., & Ackermann-Valladao, E. (1980). How can themes suggested by genetic epistemology be translated into problems that lend themselves to experimental research? *Cahiers de la Fondation Archives Jean Piaget, 1*, 9–22.

Berti, A. E., & Freeman, N. H. (1997). Representational change in resources for pictorial innovation: A three-component analysis. *Cognitive Development, 12*, 501–522.

Bickhard, M. H., Cooper, R. G., & Mace, P. E. (1985). Vestiges of logical positivism: Critiques of stage explanations. *Human Development, 28*, 240–258.

Bidell, T. (1988). Vygotsky, Piaget and the dialectic of development. *Human Development, 31*, 329–348.

Bidell, T. R., & Fischer, K. W. (1994a). Developmental transitions in children's early online planning. In M. M. Haith, J. B. Benson, R. J. J. Roberts, & B. F. Pennington (Eds.), *The development of future-oriented processes* (pp. 141–176). Chicago: University of Chicago Press.

Bidell, T. R., & Fischer, K. W. (1994b). Beyond the stage debate: Action, structure, and variability in Piagetian theory and research. In R. Sternberg & C. Berg (Eds.), *Intellectual development* (pp. 100–140). New York: Cambridge University Press.

Bidell, T. R., & Fischer, K. W. (2000). The role of cognitive structure in the development of behavioral control: A dynamic skills approach. In A. Grob &W. J. Perrig (Eds.), *Control of human behavior, mental processes, and consciousness* (pp. 183–201). Mahwah, NJ: Lawrence Erlbaum Associates.

Bjorklund, D. F., Miller, P. H., Coyle, T. R., & Slawinski, J. L. (1997). Instructing children to use memory strategies: Evidence of utilization deficiencies in memory training studies. *Developmental Review, 17*(4), 411–441.

Blumberg, P. (1978, April). *Developmental differences in solution strategies on problems involving alternative choices.* Presentation to the Annual Meeting of the American Educational Research Association, Toronto.

Boag, C., Neal, A., Loft, S., & Halford, G. S. (2006). An analysis of relational complexity in an air traffic control conflict detection task. *Ergonomics, 49*, 1508–1526.

Bond, T. G. (1998). Fifty years of formal operational research: The empirical evidence. *Archives de Psychologie, 66*, 221–238.

Booth, J. L., & Siegler, R. S. (2006). Developmental and individual differences in pure numerical estimation. *Developmental Psychology, 42*(1), 189–201.

Borella, E., & de Ribaupierre, A. (2006, June). *Reading comprehension, working memory, inhibition, and processing speed: A lifespan perspective.* Paper presented to the 3rd European Working Memory Symposium, Genoa.

Brainerd, C. J. (1978). The stage question in cognitive-developmental theory. *The Behavioural and Brain Sciences, 2*, 173–182.

Brainerd, C. J., & Kingma, J. (1984). Do children have to remember to reason? A fuzzy trace theory of transitivity development. *Developmental Review, 4*, 311–377.

Branco, A. U., & Valsiner, J. (1997). Changing methodologies: A co-constructivist study of goal orientations in social interactions. *Psychology & Developing Societies, 9*, 35–64.

Bronckart, J. P., & Parot-Locatelli, F. (1977). Introduction. *Cahiers du Centre d'Etudes et de Recherches Marxistes. Special issue "Sur la Théorie Opératoire"* [On operational theory], *140*, 15-22.

Brown, A. L. (1978). Knowing when, where andhow to remember: A problem of metacognition. In R. Glaser (Ed.), *Advances in instructional psychology* (pp. 77–165). Hillsdale, NJ: Lawrence Erlbaum Associates.

Brown, A. L., Bransford, J. D., Ferrara, R. A., & Campione, J. C. (1983). Learning, remembering and understanding. In J. H. Flavell & E. M. Markman (Eds.), *Handbook of child psychology* (pp. 77–166). New York: Wiley.

Brown, A. L., Kane, M. J., & Echols, C. H. (1986). Young children's mental models determine analogical transfer across problems with a common goal structure. *Cognitive Development, 1*, 103–121.

Brown, G. D. A., & Hulme, C. (1995). Modeling item length effects in memory span: No rehearsal needed? *Journal of Memory and Language, 34*, 594–621.

Brown, T., & Weiss, L. (1987). Structures, procedures, heuristics, and affectivity. *Archives de Psychologie, 55*, 59–94.

Bruce, D., Dolan, A., & Phillips, G. K. (2000). On the transition from childhood amnesia to the recall of personal memories. *Psychological Science, 11*, 360–364.

Bruchkowsky,M. (1992). The development of empathic cognition in middle and early childhood. In R. Case (Ed.), *The mind's staircase: Exploring the conceptual underpinnings of children's thought and knowledge* (pp. 153–170). Hillsdale, NJ: Lawrence Erlbaum Associates.

Bruner, J. (1986). *Actual minds, possible worlds.* Cambridge, MA: Harvard University Press.

Bruner, J., & Anglin, J.M. (1973). *Beyond the information given. studies in the psychology of knowing.* New York: Norton.

Bruner, J., Goodnow, J. J., & Austin, G. A. (1956). *A study of thinking.* New York: Wiley.

Bruner, J., Olver, R. R., & Greenfield, P.M. (1966). *Studies in cognitive growth.* New York: Wiley.

Bryant, P. E. (1972). The understanding of invariance by very young children. *Canadian Journal of Psychology, 26,* 78–96.

Bryant, P. E., & Trabasso, T. (1971). Transitive inferences and memory in young children. *Nature, 232,* 456–458.

Buck-Morss, S. (1975). Socioeconomic bias in Piaget's theory and it's implication for cross culture studies. *Human Development, 18,* 35–49.

Bull, R., & Scerif, G. (2001). Executive functioning as a predictor of children's mathematical ability: Inhibition, switching, and working memory. *Developmental Neuropsychology, 19,* 273–293.

Bunge, S., Dudukovic, N., Thomason, M., Vaidya, C., & Gabrieli, G. (2002). Immature frontal lobe contributions to cognitive control in children: Evidence from fMRI. *Neuron, 33,* 301–311.

Burtis, P. J. (1982). Capacity increase and chunking in the development of short-term memory. *Journal of Experimental Child Psychology, 34,* 387–413.

Bushnell, I. W. R. (2001). Mother's face recognition in newborn infants: Learning and memory. *Infant and Child Development, 10,* 67–74.

Buss, A. R. (1977). Piaget, Marx, and Buck-Morss on cognitive development: A critique and a reinterpretation. *Human Development, 20,* 118–128.

Byrnes, M. A., & Spitz, H. (1977). Performance of retarded adolescents and nonretarded children on the tower of Hanoi problem. *American Journal of Mental Deficiency, 81,* 561–569.

Calverley, R., Fischer, K. W., & Ayoub, C. (1994). Complex splitting of self-representations in sexually abused adolescent girls. *Development and Psychopathology, 61*(1–2), 195–213.

Campo, P., Maest, F., Ortiz, T., Capilla, A., Fernandez, S., & Fernandez, A. (2005). Is medial temporal lobe activation specific for encoding long-term memories? *Neuroimage, 25,* 34–42.

Carey, S. (1985). *Conceptual change in childhood.* Cambridge, MA: MIT Press.

Carey, S. (1987). Theory change in childhood. In B. Inhelder, D. de Caprona, & A. Cornu-Wells (Eds.), *Piaget today* (pp. 141–163). Hillsdale, NJ: Lawrence Erlbaum Associates.

Carey, S. (1991). Knowledge acquisition: Enrichment or conceptual change? In S. Carey & R. Gelman (Eds.), *The epigenesis of mind. Essay on biology and cognition* (pp. 257–291). Hillsdale, NJ: Lawrence Erlbaum Associates.

Carey, S. (2000). The origin of concepts. *Journal of Cognition and Development, 1,* 37–41.

Carey, S. (2004). Bootstrapping and the origins of concepts. *Daedalus, 133*(11), 59–68.

Carey, S., & Spelke, E. (1994). Domain-specific knowledge and conceptual change. In L. A. Hirschfeld & S. A. Gelman (Eds.), *Mapping the mind: Domain specificity in cognition and culture* (pp. 169–200). New York: Cambridge University Press.

Case, R. (1972). Validation of a neo-Piagetian mental capacity construct. *Journal of Experimental Child Psychology, 14,* 287–302.

Case, R. (1974a). Structures and strictures: Some functional limitations on the course of cognitive development. *Cognitive Psychology, 6,* 544–573.

Case, R. (1974b). Mental strategies, mental capacity, and instruction: A neo-Piagetian investigation. *Journal of Experimental Child Psychology, 18,* 382–397.

Case, R. (1975a). Social class differences in intellectual development: A neo-Piagetian investigation. *Canadian Journal of Behavioural Science, 7,* 244–261.

Case, R. (1975b). Gearing the demands of instruction to the developmental capacities of the learner. *Review of Educational Research, 45,* 59–87.

Case R. (1977). Responsiveness to conservation training as a function of induced subjective uncertainty, M-space, and cognitive style. *Canadian Journal of Behavioral Science, 9,* 12-25.

Case, R. (1978). Piaget and beyond : Toward a developmentally based theory and technology of instruction. In R. Glaser (Ed.), *Advances in instructional psychology* (pp. 167–228). Hillsdale, NJ: Lawrence Erlbaum Associates.

Case, R. (1978a). Intellectual development from birth to adulthood: A neo-Piagetian interpretation, in R. Siegler (Ed.), *Children's thinking: What develops?* (pp. 37–71). Hillsdale, NJ: Lawrence Erlbaum Associates.

Case, R. (1980). Implications of a neo-Piagetian theory for improving the design of instruction. In J. R. Kirby & J. B. Biggs (Eds.), *Cognition, development, and instruction* (pp. 161–186). New York: Academic Press.

Case, R. (1985). *Intellectual development: Birth to adulthood*. New York: Academic Press.

Case, R. (1987). Neo-Piagetian theory: Retrospect and prospect. *International Journal of Psychology, 22*, 773–791.

Case, R. (1988). The whole child: Towards an integrated view of young children's cognitive, social, and emotional development. In A. Pellegrini (Ed.), *Psychological bases of early education* (pp. 155–184). Chichester: Wiley.

Case, R. (1991a). Neo-Piagetian theories of child development. In R.J. Sternberg & C.A. Berg (Eds.) *Intellectual development* (pp. 161-197). New York: Cambridge University Press.

Case R. (1991b). Stages in the development of the young child's first sense of self. *Developmental Review, 11,* 210-230.

Case, R. (1992a). The mind and its modules: Toward a multilevel view of the development of human intelligence. In R. Case (Ed.), *The mind's staircase: Exploring the conceptual underpinnings of children's thought and knowledge* (pp. 343–376). Hillsdale, NJ: Lawrence Erlbaum Associates.

Case, R. (1992b). The role of the frontal lobes in the regulation of cognitive development. *Brain and Cognition, 20,* 51–73.

Case, R. (Ed.). (1992c). *The mind's staircase: Exploring the conceptual underpinnings of children's thought and knowledge.* Hillsdale, NJ: Lawrence Erlbaum Associates.

Case, R. (1992d). Neo-Piagetian theories of child development. In R. Sternberg & C. A. Berg (Eds.), *Intellectual development* (pp. 1–41). New York: Cambridge University Press.

Case, R. (1993). Theories of learning and theories of development. *Educational Psychologist, 28,* 219–233.

Case, R. (1995). Capacity based explanations of working memory growth: A brief history and a reevaluation. In F. M. Weinert & W. Schneider (Eds.), *Memory performance and competencies: Issues in growth and development* (pp. 23–44). Hillsdale, NJ: Lawrence Erlbaum Associates.

Case, R. (1996a). Introduction: Reconceptualizing the nature of children's conceptual structures and their development in middle childhood. *Monographs of the Society for Research in Child Development, 61*(1-2), 1–26. Case, R. (1996b). Modeling the dynamic interplay between general and specific change in children's conceptual understanding. *Monographs of the Society for Research in Child Development, 61*(1-2), 156–188.

Case, R. (1996c). Summary and conclusion. *Monographs of the Society for Research in Child Development, 61*(1-2), 189–214.

Case, R. (1996d). Reply: Modeling the process of conceptual change in a continuously evolving hierarchical system. *Monographs of the Society for Research in Child Development, 61*(1-2), 283–295.

Case, R. (1998). The development of conceptual structures. In D. Kuhn & R. S. Siegler (Eds.), *Handbook of child psychology, Vol. 2: Cognition, perception, and language* (5th ed.; pp. 745–800). New York: Wiley.

Case, R., Demetriou, A., Platsidou, M., & Kazi, S. (2001). Integrating concepts and tests of intelligence from the differential and developmental traditions. *Intelligence, 29,* 307–336.

Case, R., & Edelstein, W. (Eds.). (1993). *The new structuralism in cognitive development: Theory and research on individual pathways.* Basel: Karger.

Case, R., & Globerson, T. (1974). Field dependence and central computing space. *Child Development, 45,* 772–778.

Case, R., Griffin, S., & Kelly, W. M. (1999). Socioeconomic gradients in mathematical ability and their responsiveness to intervention during early childhood. In D. P. Keating & C. Hertzman (Eds.), *Developmental health and the wealth of nations* (pp. 125–149). New York: Guilford.

Case, R., & Hayward, S. (1984). *Understanding causality in the sensorimotor period: The infant balance beam test.* Unpublished manuscript, University of Toronto (OISE).

Case, R., Hayward, S., Lewis, M., & Hurst, P. (1988). Toward a neo-Piagetian theory of cognitive and emotional development. *Developmental Review, 8*(1), 1–51.

Case, R., & Khanna, F. (1981). The missing links: Stages in children's progression from sensorimotor to logical thought. *New Directions for Child Development, 12,* 21–32.

Case, R., Krohn, C., & Bushey, B. (1992, April). *The acquisition of fractional number knowledge: A developmental analysis.* Paper presented at the meeting of the American Educational Research Association, San Francisco.

Case, R., & Kurland, M. (1978). Construction and validation of a new test of children's M-space. Unpublished manuscript, University of Toronto (OISE).

Case, R., Kurland, M., & Daneman, M. (1979, March). *Operational efficiency and the growth of Mspace.* Paper presented at the meeting of the Society for Research in Child Development, San Francisco.

Case, R., & Kurland, M. D. (1980). A new measure for determining children's subjective organization of speech. *Journal of Experimental Child Psychology, 30,* 206–222.

Case, R., Kurland, M., & Goldberg, J. (1982). Operational efficiency and the growth of short term memory. *Journal of Experimental Child Psychology, 33,* 386–404.

Case, R., Marini, Z., McKeough, A., Dennis, S., & Goldberg, J. (1986). Horizontal structure in middle childhood: Cross-domain parallels in the course of cognitive growth. In I. Levin (Ed.), *Stage and structure: Reopening the debate* (pp. 1–39). Norwood: Ablex.

Case, R., & McKeough, A. (1989). Schooling and the development of central conceptual structures: An example from the domain of children's narrative. *International Journal of Educational Research, 8,* 835–855.

Case, R., & McKeough, A. (1990). Schooling and the development of central conceptual structures: an example from the domain of children's narrative. *International Journal of Educational Psychology, 8,* 835-855.

Case, R., & Mueller, M. P. (2001). Differentiation, integration, and covariance mapping as fundamental processes in cognitive and neurological growth. In J. L. McClelland& R. S. Siegler (Eds.), *Mechanisms of cognitive development: Behavioral and neural perspectives* (pp. 185–219). Mahwah, NJ: Lawrence Erlbaum Associates.

Case, R., & Okamoto, Y. (1996). The role of central conceptual structures in the development of children's thought. *Monographs of the Society for Research in Child Development, 61*(1–2, Serial No. 246).

Case, R., Okamoto, Y., Henderson, B., & McKeough, A. (1993). Individual variability and consistency in cognitive development: New evidence for the existence of central conceptual structures. In R. Case & W. Edelstein (Eds.), *The new structuralism in cognitive development: Theory and research on individual pathways* (pp. 71–100). Basel: Karger.

Case, R., Okamoto, Y., Henderson, B., McKeough, A., & Bleiker, C. (1996). Exploring the macrostructure of children's central conceptual structures in the domains of number and narrative. *Monographs of the Society for Research in Child Development, 61*(1-2), 59–82.

Case, R., & Sandieson, R. (1988). A developmental approach to the identification and teaching of central conceptual structures in middle school mathematics and science. In J. Hebert & M. Behr (Eds.), *Research agenda in mathematics education: Number concepts in the middle grades* (pp. 236–270). Hillsdale, NJ: Lawrence Erlbaum Associates.

Case, R., & Sandieson, R. (1992). Testing for the presence of a central quantitative structure: Use of the transfer paradigm. In R. Case (Ed.), *The mind's staircase: Exploring the conceptual underpinnings of children's thought and knowledge* (pp. 117–132). Hillsdale, NJ: Lawrence Erlbaum Associates.

Case, R., Sandieson, R., & Dennis, S. (1986). Two cognitive-developmental approaches to the design of remedial education. *Cognitive Development, 1*, 293–333.

Case, R., & Serlin, R. (1979). A new processing model for predicting performance on Pascual-Leone's test of *M*-space. *Cognitive Psychology, 11*, 308–326.

Case, R., & Sowder, J. (1990). The development of computational estimation: A neo-Piagetian analysis. *Cognition and Instruction, 7*, 79–104.

Case, R., Stephenson, K. M., Bleiker, C., & Okamoto, Y. (1996). Central spatial structures and their development. *Monographs of the Society for Research in Child Development, 61*(1-2), 103–130.

Casey, B. J., Tottenham, N., & Fossella, J. (2002). Clinical, imaging, lesion, and genetic approaches Toward a model of cognitive control. *Developmental Psychobiology, 40*, 237–254.

Casey, B. J., Trainor, R., Orendi, J., Schubert, A., Nystrom, L., Giedd, J. N., et al. (1997). A developmental functional MRI study of prefrontal activation during performance of a go-no-go task. *Journal of Cognitive Neuroscience, 9*, 835–847.

Cashon, C. H., & Cohen, L. B. (2004). Beyond U-shaped development in infants' processing of faces: An information-processing account. *Journal of Cognition and Development, 5*, 59–80.

Cellérier, G. (1979). Structures cognitives et schemes d'action, I et II [Cognitive structures and action schemes, I and II]. *Archives de Psychologie, 47*, 87–122.

Chapman, M. (1981). Egocentrism and mental capacity: A neo-Piagetian analysis. In A. J. Meacham & N. R. Santilli (Eds.), *Social development in youth: Structure and content* (pp. 47–63). Basel: Karger.

Chapman, M. (1987). Piaget, attentional capacity, and the functional implications of formal structure. In H. W. Reese (Ed.), *Advances in child development and behaviour* (pp. 289–334). Orlando, FL: Academic Press.

Chapman, M. (1990). Cognitive development and the growth of capacity: Issues in neo-Piagetian theory. In J. T. Enns (Ed.), *The development of attention: Research and theory* (pp. 263–287). Amsterdam: Elsevier.

Chapman, M., & Lindenberger, U. (1988). Functions, operations, and décalage in the development of transitivity. *Developmental Psychology, 24*, 542–551.

Chapman, M., & Lindenberger, U. (1989). Concrete operations and attentional capacity. *Journal of Experimental Child Psychology, 47*, 236–258.

Chapman, M., & Lindenberger, U. (1992a). Transitivity judgments, memory for premises, and models of children's reasoning. *Developmental Review, 12*, 124–163.

Chapman, M., & Lindenberger, U. (1992b). How to detect reasoning–remembering dependence (and how not to). *Developmental Review, 12*, 187–198.

Chase, W. G., & Ericsson, K. A. (1982). Skill and working memory. In G. H. Bower (Ed.), *The psychology of learning and motivation, Vol. 16* (pp. 1–58). New York: Academic Press.

Chase, W. G., & Simon, H. A. (1973). Perception in chess. *Cognitive Psychology, 4*, 55–81.

Chen, Z. (1999). Schema induction in children's analogical problem solving. *Journal of Educational Psychology, 91*(4), 703–715.

Chen, Z. (2003). Worth one thousand words: Children's use of pictures in analogical problem solving. *Journal of Cognition and Development, 4*(4), 415–434.

Chen, Z., & Daehler, M. W. (1992). Intention and outcome: Key components of causal structure facilitating mapping in children's analogical transfer. *Journal of Experimental Child Psychology, 53*(3), 237–257.

Chen, Z., & Doehler, M. W. (1989). Positive and negative transfer in analogical problem solving by 6-year-oldchildren. *Cognitive Development, 4*, 327–344.

Chen, Z., & Klahr, D. (1999). All other things being equal: Acquisition and transfer of the control of variables strategy. *Child Development, 70*(5), 1098–1120.

Chen, Z., Sanchez, R. P., & Campbell, T. (1997). From beyond to within their grasp: The rudiments of analogical problem solving in 10- and13-month-old s. *Developmental Psychology, 33*(5), 790–801.

Chen, Z., & Siegler, R. S. (2000). Across the great divide: Bridging the gap between understanding of toddlers' and older children's thinking. *Monographs of the Society for Research in Child Development, 65*(2), 1–96.

Cheng, P. W., Holyoak, K. J., Nisbett, R. E., & Oliver, L. M. (1986). Pragmatic versus syntactic approaches to training deductive reasoning. *Cognitive Psychology, 18*, 293–328.

Chi, M. T. H. (1978). Knowledge structures and memory development. In R. S. Siegler (Ed.), *Children's thinking: What develops?* (pp. 73–96). Hillsdale, NJ: Lawrence Erlbaum Associates.

Chi, M. T., Bassok, M., Lewis, M. W., & Reimann, P. (1989). Self-explanations: How students study and use examples in learning to solve problems. *Cognitive Science, 13*(2), 145–182.

Chi, M. T. H., de Leeuw, N., Chiu, M., & LaVancher, C. (1994). Eliciting self-explanations improves understanding. *Cognitive Science, 18*(3), 439–477.

Chi, M., Feltovich, P., & Glaser, R. (1981). Categories and representation of physics problems by experts and novices. *Cognitive Science, 5*, 121–152.

Chi, M., Glaser, R., & Rees, T. (1982). Expertise in problem solving. In R. Stenberg (Ed.), *Advances in the psychology of human intelligence, Vol. 1* (pp. 1–75). Hillsdale, NJ: Lawrence Erlbaum Associates.

Chi, M., & Koeske, R. D. (1983). Network representation of a child's dinosaur knowledge. *Developmental Psychology, 19*, 29–39.

Chomsky N. (1977). A review to B.F. Skinner's "Verbal Behavior". *Language, 35*, 26-58.

Christ, S. E., White, D. A., Mandernach, T., & Keys, B. A. (2001). Inhibitory control across the life span. *Developmental Neuropsychology, 20*, 653–669.

Clement, J. J., & Steinberg, M. S. (2002). Step-wise evolution of mental models of electric circuits: A "learning-aloud" case study. *Journal of the Learning Sciences, 11*(4), 389–452.

Cohen, L. B., & Cashon, C. H. (2003). Infant perception and cognition. In R. M. Lerner, M. A. Easterbrooks, & J. Mistry (Eds.), *Handbook of psychology: Developmental psychology* (pp. 65–89). Hoboken, NJ: Wiley.

Cohen, L. B., Chaput, H. H., & Cashon, C. H. (2002). A constructivist model of infant cognition. *Cognitive Development, 17*, 1323–1343.

Collins, A. M., & Loftus, E. F. (1975). A spreading activation theory of semantic processing. *Psychological Review, 82*, 407–428.

Conway, A. R. A., Cowan, N., Bunting, M. F., Therriault, D. J., & Minkoff, S. R. B. (2002). A latent variable analysis of working memory capacity, short-term memory capacity, processing speed, and general fluid intelligence. *Intelligence, 30*, 163–183.

Corbett, K. E., & Pulos, S. M. (1999, June). *Motor development and attentional capacity in the young child: A neo-Piagetian perspective.* Paper presented at the 29th Conference of the Jean Piaget Society, Mexico City.

Cornoldi, C. (1995). La memoria di lavoro visuo-spaziale [Visuo-spatial working memory]. In F. Marucci (Ed.), *Le immagini mentali* [Mental images] (pp. 147–183). Firenze, Italy: La Nuova Italia.

Cornoldi, C., Gobbo, C., & Mazzioni, G. (1991). On metamemory–memory relationship: Strategy availability and training. *International Journal of Psychology, 14*, 101–121.

Corrigan, R. (1978). Language development as related to stage 6 object permanence development. *Journal of Child Language, 5*, 173–189.

Cowan, N. (1988). Evolving conceptions of memory storage, selective attention, and their mutual constraints within the human information-processing system. *Psychological Bulletin, 104*, 163–191.

Cowan, N. (1999). An embedded-processes model of working memory. In A. Miyake & P. Shah (Eds.), *Models of working memory* (pp. 62–101). Cambridge, UK: Cambridge University Press.

Cowan, N. (2001). The magical number 4 in short-term memory: A reconsideration of mental storage capacity. *Behavioral and Brain Sciences, 24*, 87–185.

Cowan, N. (2002). The search for what is fundamental in the development of working memory. In R. V. Kail & H.W. Reese (Eds.), *Advances in child development and behavior* (pp. 1–49). Amsterdam: Elsevier.

Cowan, N. (2005). *Working memory capacity.* Hove, UK: Psychology Press.

Cowan, N., Day, L., Saults, J. S., Keller, T. A., Johnson, T., & Flores, L. (1992). The role of verbal output time in the effects of word length on immediate memory. *Journal of Memory and Language, 31,* 1–17.

Cowan, N., Elliott, E. M., Saults, J. S., Morey, C. C., Mattox, S., Hismjatullina, A., et al. (2005). On the capacity of attention: Its estimation and its role in working memory and cognitive aptitudes. *Cognitive Psychology, 51,* 42–100.

Cowan, N., Wood, N. L., Wood, P. K., Keller, T. A., Nugent, L. D., & Keller, C. V. (1998). Two separate verbal processing rates contributing to short-term memory span. *Journal of Experimental Psychology: General, 127,* 141–160.

Cox, M. V. (1991). *The child's point of view: The development of cognition and language* (2nd ed.). London: Harvester Press.

Coyle, T. R., & Bjorklund, D. F. (1997). Age differences in, and consequences of, multiple- and variable-strategy use on a multitrial sort-recall task. *Developmental Psychology, 33*(2), 372–380.

Crammond, J. (1992). Analyzing the basic cognitive-developmental processes of children with specific types of learning disability. In R. Case (Ed.), *The mind's staircase: Exploring the conceptual underpinnings of children's thought and knowledge* (pp. 285–302). Hillsdale, NJ: Lawrence Erlbaum Associates.

Crowder, R. G. (1993). Short-term memory: Where do we stand? *Memory and Cognition, 21,* 142–145.

Crowley, K., & Siegler, R. S. (1999). Explanation and generalization in young children's strategy learning. *Child Development, 70*(2), 304–316.

Cunning, S. A. (2003). *The direction-following task: Assessing mental capacity in the linguistic domain.* Unpublished dissertation, York University.

Daneman, M., & Carpenter, P. A. (1980). Individual differences in working memory and reading. *Journal of Verbal Learning and Verbal Behavior, 19,* 450–466.

Danovitch, J. H., & Keil, F. C. (2004). Should you ask a fisherman or a biologist?: Developmental shifts in ways of clustering knowledge. *Child Development, 75*(3), 918–931.

Dasen, P. R. (1975). Concrete operational development in three cultures. *Journal of Cross-Cultural Psychology, 6,* 156–172.

Dasen, P. R., & Heron, A. (1981). Cross-cultural tests of Piaget's theory. In H. C. Triandis & A. Heron (Eds.), *Handbook of cross-cultural psychology* (pp. 295–341). Boston: Allyn & Bacon.

Dawson-Tunik, T. L., Commons, M., Wilson, M., & Fischer, K. W. (2005). The shape of development. *European Journal of Developmental Psychology, 2*(2), 163–195.

Dawson-Tunik, T. L., Fischer, K. W., & Stein, Z. (2004). Do stages belong at the center of developmental theory? A commentary on Piaget's stages. *New Ideas in Psychology, 22*(3), 255–263.

De Avila, E., Havassy, B., & Pascual-Leone, J. (1976). *Mexican-American school children: A neo-Piagetian analysis.* Washington, DC: Georgetown University Press.

de Groot, A. (1966). Perception and memory versus thought: Some old ideas and recent findings. In B. Kleinmutz (Ed.), *Problem solving* (pp. 19–50). New York: Wiley.

Dehaene, S., & Cohen, L. (1994). Dissociable mechanisms of subitizing and counting: Neuropsychological evidence from simultanagnosis patients. *Journal of Experimental Psychology: Human Perception and Performance, 20,* 958–975.

DeLoache, J. S., Miller, K. F., & Pierroutsakos, S. L. (1998). Reasoning and problem solving. In D. Kuhn & R. Siegler (Eds.), *Handbook of child psychology, 5th Ed., Vol 2: Cognition, perception, & language* (pp. 801–850). New York: Wiley.

Demetriou, A. (1987). Preface. *International Journal of Psychology, 22,* 501-505.

Demetriou, A., Christou, C., Spanoudis, G., & Platsidou, M. (2002). The development of mental processing: Efficiency, working memory, and thinking. *Monographs of the Society for Research in Child Development, 67*(1), 1–154.

Demetriou, A., & Efklides, A. (1987). Experiential structuralism and neo-Piagetian theories: Toward an Integrated model. *International Journal of Psychology, 22,* 679–728.

Demetriou, A., & Efklides, A. (1989). The person's conception of the structures of developing intellect: Early adolescence to middle age. *Genetic, Social, and General Psychology Monographs, 115*(3), 371–423.

Demetriou, A., Efklides, A., & Platsidou, M. (1993). The architecture and dynamics of developing mind: Experiential structuralism as a frame for unifying cognitive developmental theories. *Monographs of the Society for Research in Child Development, 58*(5–6), 1–167.

Demetriou, A., Kazi, S., & Georgiou, S. (1999). The emerging self: The convergence of mind, personality, and thinking styles. *Developmental Science, 2,* 387–409.

Demetriou, A., Kui, Z. X., Spanoudis, G., Christou, C., Kyriakides, L., & Plastidou, M. (2005). The architecture, dynamics, and development of mental processing: Greek, Chinese, or universal? *Intelligence, 33,* 109–141.

Demetriou, A., & Mouyi, A. (2006, June). *Processing efficiency, working memory, and reasoning: Deciphering their relations.* Paper presented to the 3rd European Working Memory Symposium, Genoa, Italy.

Demetriou, A., Pachaury, A., Metallidou, Y., & Kazi, S. (1996). Universals and specificities in the structure and development of quantitative-relational thought: A cross-cultural study In Greece and India. *International Journal of Behavioral Development, 19,* 255–290.

Demetriou, A., Platsidou, M., Efklides, A., Metallidou, Y., & Shayer, M. (1991). Structure and sequence of the quantitative-relational abilities and processing potential from childhood to adolescence. *Learning and Instruction, 1,* 19–44.

Demetriou, A., & Raftopoulos, A. (1999). Modeling the developing mind: From structure to change. *Developmental Review, 19,* 319–368.

Demetriou, A., & Raftopoulos, A. (2004). The shape and direction of development: Teleologically but erratically lifted up or timely harmonious? *Journal of Cognition and Development, 5*(1), 89–95.

Demetriou, A., Shayer, M., & Perez, M. (1988). The structure and scaling of concrete operational thought: Three studies in four countries. *Genetic, Social, and General Psychology Monographs, 114,* 307–376.

Demetriou, A., Spanoudis, G., Christou, C., & Platsidou, M. (2002).Modeling the Stroop phenomenon: Processes, processing flow, and development. *Cognitive Development, 16,* 987–1005.

Dempster, F. M. (1981). Memory span: Sources of individual and developmental differences. *Psychological Bulletin, 89,* 63–100.

Dempster, F. M. (1992). The rise and fall of the inhibitory mechanism: Toward a unified theory of cognitive development and aging. *Developmental Review, 12,* 45–75.

de Ribaupierre A. (1980). Application d'un modèle neo-Piagetien à l'étude du stade des opérations formelles [Application of neo-Piagetian model to the study of the formal operations stage]. *Bulletin de Psychologie, 33,* 699-709.

de Ribaupierre, A. (1989). Cognitive style and cognitive development: A review of French literature and a neo-Piagetian reinterpretation. In T. Globerson & T. Zelniker (Eds.), *Cognitive style and cognitive development* (pp. 86–115). Norwood, NJ: Ablex.

de Ribaupierre, A. (1993). Structural invariants and individual differences: On the difficulty of dissociating developmental and differential process. In R. Case & W. Edelstein (Eds.), *The new structuralism in cognitive development: Theory and research on individual pathways* (pp. 11–32). Basel: Karger.

de Ribaupierre, A. (1994). Commentary. *Human Development, 37,* 170–176.

de Ribaupierre, A. (2001). Working memory and attentional processes across the lifespan. In P. Graf & N. Otha (Eds.), *Lifespan development of human memory* (pp. 59–80). Cambridge, MA: MIT Press.

de Ribaupierre, A., & Bailleux, C. (1994). Developmental change in a spatial task of attentional capacity: An essay toward an integration of two working memory models. *International Journal of Behavioural Development, 17*, 5–35.

de Ribaupierre, A., & Bailleux, C. (1995). Development of attentional capacity in childhood: A longitudinal study. In F. E. Weinert & W. Schneider (Eds.), *Memory performance and competencies: Issues in growth and development* (pp. 45–70). Hillsdale, NJ: Lawrence Erlbaum Associates.

de Ribaupierre, A., & Bailleux, C. (2000). The development of working memory: Further note on the comparability of two models of working memory. *Journal of Experimental Child Psychology, 77*, 110–127.

de Ribaupierre, A., Keizer, I., Sancho, A., Spira, A., & Thomas, L. (1990). *Etude longitudinale de la capacité d'attention mentale chez l'enfant de 5 à 12ans* [A longitudinal study of mental attention capacity in 5- to 12-year-old children]. Unpublished research report for the FNRS, University of Geneva.

de Ribaupierre, A., Lecerf, T., & Bailleux, C. (2000). Is a nonverbal working memory task necessarily nonverbally encoded? *Cahiers de Psychologie Cognitive* [Current Psychology of Cognition], *19*, 135–170.

de Ribaupierre, A., Lecerf, T., Leutwyler, J., & Poget, L. (1997). *Mémoire de travail et attention sélective au cours du lifespan* [Working memory and selective attention in the life span]. Unpublished paper, University of Geneva.

de Ribaupierre, A., & Pascual-Leone, J. (1979). Formal operations and M-power: A neo-Piagetian investigation. *New Directions for Child Development, 5*, 1–43.

de Ribaupierre, A., Rieben, L., & Lautrey, J. (1985). Horizontal *décalages* and individual differences In the development of concrete operations. In V. L. Shulman, L. C. R. Restaino-Baumann, & L. Butler (Eds.), *The future of Piagetian theory* (pp. 175–200). New York: Plenum.

de Ribaupierre, A., Rieben, L., & Lautrey, J. (1991). Developmental change and individual differences: A longitudinal study using Piagetian tasks. *Genetic, Social and General Psychology Monographs, 117*, 285–311.

Desrochers, S. (2003). Les balbutiements de la causalité chez le nourisson: Piaget accomodé [The babbling of causality in infants: Piaget revisited]. *Archives de Psychologie, 70*, 97-119.

de Weerth, C., van Geert, P., & Hoitink, H. (1999). Intraindividual variability in infant behavior. *Developmental Psychology, 35*(4), 1102–1112.

Diamond, A. (2002). Normal development of prefrontal cortex from birth to young adulthood: Cognitive functions, anatomy, and biochemistry. In D. T. Stuss & R. T. Knight (Eds.), *The frontal lobes* (pp. 466–503). London: Oxford University Press.

Dixon, J. A., & Bangert, A. S. (2002). The prehistory of discovery: Precursors of representational change in solving gear system problems. *Developmental Psychology, 38*(6), 918–933.

Dromi, E. (1986). The one-word period. In I. Levin (Ed.), *Stage and structure* (pp. 220–245). Norwood, NJ: Ablex.

Duit, R., Roth, W., Komorek, M., & Wilbers, J. (2001). Fostering conceptual change by analogies—between Scylla and Charybd is. *Learning and Instruction, 11*(4–5), 283–303.

Dunbar, K. (2001). The analogical paradox: Why analogy is so easy in naturalistic settings yet so difficult in the psychological laboratory. In D. Gentner, K. J. Holyoak, & B. N. Kokinov (Eds.), *The analogical mind: Perspectives from cognitive science* (pp. 313–334). Cambridge, MA: The MIT Press.

Durston, S., Davidson, M. C., Tottenham, M., Galvan, A., Spicer, J., Fossella, J. A., et al. (2006). A shift from diffuse to focal cortical activity with development. *Developmental Science, 9*, 1–8.

Durston, S., Thomas, K., Yang, Y., Ulug, A., Zimmerman, R., & Casey, B. (2002). A neural basis for the development of inhibitory control. *Developmental Science, 5*(4), F9–F16.

Edelstein, W., Keller, M., & Schröder, E. (1990). Child development and social structure: A longitudinal study of individual differences. In P. B. Baltes, D. L. Featherman, & R. M. Lerner (Eds.),

Life-span development and behavior (pp. 151–185). Hillsdale, NJ: Lawrence Erlbaum Associates.

Edelstein, W., Keller, M., & Wahlen, K. (1984). Structure and content in social cognition: Conceptual And empirical analyses. *Child Development, 55*, 1514–1526.

Efklides, A., Demetriou, A., & Metallidou, Y. (1994). The structure and development of prepositional reasoning ability: Cognitive and metacognitive aspects. In A. Demetriou & A. Efklides (Eds.), *Intelligence, mind and reasoning: Structure and development* (pp. 151–172). Amsterdam: North Holland.

Elman, J. L. (1993). Learning and development in neural networks: The importance of starting small. *Cognition, 48*, 71–99.

Elman, J. L., Bates, E. A., Johnson, M. H., Karmiloff-Smith, A., Parisi, D., & Plunkett, K. (1996). *Rethinking innateness: A connectionist perspective on development.* Cambridge, MA: MIT Press.

Engle, R. W., Conway, A. R., Tuholski, S. W., & Shisler, R. J. (1995). A resource account of inhibition. *Psychological Science, 6*, 122–125.

Engle, R. W., Kane, M. J., & Tuholski, S. W. (1999). Individual differences in working memory capacity and what they tell us about controlled attention, general fluid intelligence and functions of the prefrontal cortex. In A. Miyake & P. Shah (Eds.), *Models of working memory: Mechanisms of active maintenance and executive control* (pp. 102–131). Cambridge, UK: Cambridge University Press.

Engle, R. W., Tuholski, S. W., Laughlin, J. E., & Conway, A. R. A. (1999). Working memory, short term memory and general fluid intelligence: A latent variable approach. *Journal of Experimental Psychology: General, 128*, 309–331.

Ennis, R. H. (1978). Description, explanation, and circularity. *The Behavioral and Brain Sciences, 2*, 184–185.

Evans, J. S. B. T. (2002). Logic and human reasoning: An assessment of the deduction paradigm. *Psychological Bulletin, 128*, 978–996.

Fagan, J. F., & Singer, L. T. (1979). The role of simple feature differences in infants' recognition of faces. *Infant Behavior and Development, 2*, 39–45.

Fan, J., Flombaum, J., McCandliss, B., Thomas, K., & Posner, M. (2003). Cognitive and brain consequences of conflict. *NeuroImage, 18*, 42–57.

Fan, N., Mueller, J., & Marini, A. (1994). Solving difference problems: Wording primes coordination. *Cognition and Instruction, 12*, 355–369.

Farrell, M. J., & Robertson, I. H. (1998).Mental rotation and automatic updating of body-centered spatial relationships. *Journal of Experimental Psychology: Learning, Memory and Cognition, 24*, 227–233.

Feller, W. (1968). *An introduction to probability theory and its applications* (3rd ed.). New York: Wiley.

Felsten, G., & Wasserman, G. S. (1980). Visual masking: Mechanisms and theories. *Psychological Bulletin, 88*, 329–353.

Fiati, T. A. (1992). Cross-cultural variation in the structure of children's thought. In R. Case (Ed.), *The mind's staircase: Exploring the conceptual underpinnings of children's thought and knowledge* (pp. 319–342). Hillsdale, NJ: Lawrence Erlbaum Associates.

Field, D. (1987). A review of preschool conservation training: An analysis of analyses. *Developmental Review, 7*, 210–251.

Fischer, K. W. (1980a). A theory of cognitive development: The control and construction of hierarchies and skills. *Psychological Review, 87*, 477–531.

Fischer, K. W. (1980b). Learning as the development of organized behavior. *Journal of Structural Learning, 6*(3), 253–267.

Fischer, K. W. (1987). Relations between brain and cognitive development. *Child Development, 58*, 623–633.

Fischer, K. W. (in press). Dynamic cycles of cognitive and brain development: Measuring growth In mind, brain, and education. In A. M. Battro & K.W. Fischer (Eds.), *The educated brain.* Cambridge, UK: Cambridge University Press.

Fischer, K. W., & Ayoub, C. (1994). Affective splitting and dissociation in normal and maltreated children: Developmental pathways for self in relationships. In D. Cicchetti & S. L. Toth (Eds.), *Disorders and dysfunctions of the self* (pp. 149–222). Rochester, NY: University of Rochester Press.

Fischer, K. W., Ayoub, C., Singh, I., Noam, G., Maraganore, A., & Raya, P. (1997). Psychopathology as adaptive development along distinctive pathways. *Development and Psychopathology, 9*, 749–779.

Fischer, K. W., & Bidell, T. (1991). Constraining nativist inferences about cognitive capacities. In S. Carey & R. Gelman (Eds.), *The epigenesis of mind: Essays on biology and cognition* (pp. 199–235). Hillsdale, NJ: Lawrence Erlbaum Associates.

Fischer, K. W., & Bidell, T. (1993). Beyond the stage debate: Keeping the constructor in constructivism. *SRCD Newsletter*, (Autumn).

Fischer, K. W., & Bidell, T. R. (1998). Dynamic development of psychological structures in action and thought. In R. M. Lerner (Ed.), *Handbook of child psychology, Volume 1: Theoretical models of human development* (5th ed., pp. 467–561). New York: Wiley.

Fischer, K. W., & Bidell, T. R. (2006). Dynamic development of action, thought and emotion. In R. M. Lerner (Ed.), *Handbook of child psychology, volume 1: Theoretical models of human development.* (6th ed., pp. 313–399). New York: Wiley.

Fischer, K. W., & Canfield, R. L. (1986). The ambiguity of stage and structure in behaviour: Person and environment in the development of psychological structures. In I. Levin (Ed.), *Stage and structure: Reopening the debate* (pp. 246–267). Norwood, NJ: Ablex.

Fischer, K. W., & Connell, M. W. (2000). Using neuroconstructivist tools to understand developmental pathways to disorders. *Developmental Science, 3*(1), 24–26.

Fischer, K. W., & Corrigan, R. (1981). A skill approach to language development. In R. Stark (Ed.), *Language behaviour in infancy and early childhood* (pp. 245–273). Amsterdam: Elsevier.

Fischer, K. W., & Farrar, M. J. (1987). Generalizations about generalization: How a theory of skill development explains both generality and specificity. *International Journal of Psychology, 22*, 643–677.

Fischer, K. W., & Granott, N. (1995). Beyond one-dimensional change: Parallel, concurrent, socially distributed processes in learning and development. *Human Development, 38*(6), 302–314.

Fischer, K., Hencke, R., Hand, H., Ayoub, C., & Russell, C. (2001). *Mean and nice interaction scale: Peers* (Test Manual). Cambridge, MA: Harvard University Graduate School of Education, Cognitive Development Laboratory.

Fischer, K. W., & Immordino-Yang, M. H. (2002). Cognitive development and education: From dynamic general structure to specific learning and teaching. In E. Lagemann (Ed.), *Traditions of scholarship in education.* Chicago: Spencer Foundation.

Fischer, K. W., & Kennedy, B. P. (1997). Tools for analyzing the many shapes of development: The case of self-in-relationships in Korea. In E. Amsel & K. A. Renninger (Eds.), *Change and development: Issues of theory, method, and application* (pp. 117–152). Mahwah, NJ: Lawrence Erlbaum Associates.

Fischer, K. W., Kenny, S. L., & Pipp, S. L. (1990). How cognitive processes and environmental conditions organize discontinuities in the development of abstractions. In C. N. Alexander & E. J. Langer (Eds.), *Higher stages of human development: Perspectives on adult growth* (pp. 162–187). New York: Oxford University Press.

Fischer, K. W., & Knight, C. C. (1990). Cognitive development in real children: Levels and variations. In B. Z. Presseisen (Ed.), *Learning and thinking styles: Classroom interaction* (pp. 43–67). Washington, DC: National Education Association.

Fischer, K. W., Knight, C. C., & Van Parys, M. (1993). Analyzing diversity in developmental pathways: Methods and concepts. In R. Case & W. Edelstein (Eds.), *The new structuralism in cognitive development: Theory and research on individual pathways* (pp. 33–56). Basel: Karger.

Fischer, K. W., & Lazerson, A. (1984). *Human development from conception through adolescence.* New York: Freeman.

Fischer, K. W., & Pipp, S. L. (1984a). Development of the structures of unconscious thought. In K. Bowers & D. Meichenbaum (Eds.), *The unconscious reconsidered* (pp. 88–148). New York: Wiley.

Fischer, K. W., & Pipp, S. L. (1984b). Processes of cognitive development. In R. J. Sternberg (Ed.), *Mechanisms of cognitive development* (pp. 45–80). San Francisco, CA: Freeman.

Fischer, K. W., & Pruyne, E. (2002). Reflective thinking in adulthood: Development, variation, and consolidation. In J. Demick & C. Andreoletti (Eds.), *Handbook of adult development* (pp. 169–197). New York: Plenum.

Fischer, K. W., & Rose, S. P. (1994). Dynamic development of coordination of components In brain and behavior: A framework for theory and research. In G. Dawson & K. W. Fischer (Eds.), *Human behavior and the developing brain* (pp. 3–66). New York: Guilford.

Fischer, K. W., Rotenberg, E. J., Bullock, D. H., & Raya, P. (1993). The dynamics of competence: How context contributes directly to skill. In R. H. Wozniak & K. W. Fischer (Eds.), *Development in context: Acting and thinking in specific environments* (pp. 93–117). Hillsdale, NJ: Lawrence Erlbaum Associates.

Fischer, K. W., Shaver, P. R., & Carnochan, P. (1990). How emotions develop and how they organize development. *Cognition and Emotion, 4*, 81–127.

Fischer, K. W., Wang, L., Kennedy, B., & Cheng, C. L. (1998). Culture and biology in emotional development. *New Directions for Child Development, 81*, 21–43.

Fischer, K. W., & Watson, M. W. (1981). Explaining the Oedipus conflict. *New Directions for Child Development, 12*, 79–92.

Flavell, J. H. (1963). *The developmental psychology of Jean Piaget.* Princeton, NJ: Van Nostrand.

Flavell, J. H. (1970). Developmental studies of mediated memory. In L. P. Lipsitt (Ed.), *Advances in child development and behaviour* (pp. 181–211). New York: Academic Press.

Flavell, J. H. (1978). Comments. In R. S. Siegler (Ed.), *Children's thinking: What develops?* (pp. 97–105). Hillsdale, NJ: Lawrence Erlbaum Associates.

Flavell, J. H. (1982). On cognitive development. *Child Development, 53*, 1–10.

Flavell, J. (1996). Piaget's legacy. *Psychological Science, 7*, 200–203.

Flavell, J. H., & Draguns, J. (1957). A microgenetic approach to perception and thought. *Psychological Bulletin, 54*, 197–217.

Flavell, J. H., & Wellman, H. M. (1977). Metamemory. In R. V. Kail & J.W. Hagen (Eds.), *Perspectives on the development of memory and cognition* (pp. 3–33). Hillsdale, NJ: Lawrence Erlbaum Associates.

Fodor, J. A. (1983). *The modularity of the mind.* Cambridge, MA: MIT Bradford Books.

Fodor, J. A., & Pylyshyn, Z.W. (1988). Connectionism and cognitive architecture: A critical analysis. *Cognition, 28*, 3–71.

Fogel, A. (1993). *Developing through relationships: Origins of communication, self, and culture.* Chicago: University of Chicago Press.

Fogel, A., & Lyra, M. (1997). Dynamics of development in relationships. In F. Masterpasqua &P. A. Perna (Eds.), *The psychological meaning of chaos: Translating theory into practice* (pp. 75–94). Washington, DC: American Psychological Association.

Foley, E. J., & Berch, D. B. (1997). Capacity limitations in a classical*M*-powermeasure: A modified dual-task approach. *Journal of Experimental Child Psychology, 66*, 129–143.

Freeman, N. H. (1980). *Strategies of representation in young children.* London: Academic Press.

French, K. E., & Thomas, J. R. (1987). The relation of knowledge development to children's basketball performance. *Journal of Sport Psychology, 9*, 15–32.

Friedman, N. P., & Miyake, A. (2004). The relations among inhibition and interference control functions: A latent-variable analysis. *Journal of Experimental Psychology: General, 133*, 101–135.

Frijda, N. H. (1986). *The emotions.* Cambridge, UK: Cambridge University Press.

Frith, C. D., & Frith, U. (1978). Feature selection and classification: A developmental study. *Journal of Experimental Child Psychology, 25*, 413–428.

Fry, A. F., & Hale, S. (1996). Processing speed, working memory, and fluid intelligence. *Psychological Science, 7*, 237–241.

Furman, I. (1981). *The development of problem solving strategies: A neo-Piagetian analysis of children's performance in a balance task.* Unpublished dissertation, University of California, Berkeley.

Gagné, R. M. (1970). *The conditions of learning.* New York: Holt, Rinehart and Winston.

Garcia, R., Piaget, J., Davidson, P. M., & Easley, J. (1991). *Toward a logic of meanings.* Hillsdale, NJ: Lawrence Erlbaum Associates.

Gardner, H. (1983). *Frames of mind: The theory of multiple intelligence.* New York: Basic Books.

Gauvain, M., & Rogoff, B. (1989). Collaborative problem solving and children's planning skills. *Developmental Psychology, 25*(1), 139–151.

Gavens, N., & Barrouillet, P. (2004). Delays of retention, processing efficiency, and attentional resources In working memory span development. *Journal of Memory and Language, 51*, 244–257.

Gelman, R. (1978). Counting in the preschooler: What does and does not develop. In R. S. Siegler (Ed.), *Children's thinking: What develops?* (pp. 213–241). Hillsdale, NJ: Lawrence Erlbaum Associates.

Gelman, R., & Gallistel, C. R. (1978). *The child's understanding of a number.* Cambridge, MA: Harvard University Press.

Gentner, D. (1983). Structure-mapping: A theoretical framework for analogy. *Cognitive Science, 7*, 155–170.

Gentner, D. (1988). Metaphor as structure mapping: The relational shift. *Child Development, 59*(1), 47–59.

Gentner, D., & Toupin, C. (1986). Systematicity and surface similarity in the development of analogy. *Cognitive Science, 10*, 277–300.

Gershkoff-Stowe, L., & Thelen, E. (2004). U-shaped changes in behavior: A dynamic systems perspective. *Journal of Cognition and Development, 5*(1), 11–36.

Gerson, R. F., & Thomas, J. R. (1977). Schema theory and practice variability within a neo-Piagetian framework. *Journal of Motor Behaviour, 9*, 127–134.

Gerson, R. F., & Thomas, J. R. (1978). A neo-Piagetian investigation of the serial position effect In children's motor learning. *Journal of Motor Behavior, 10*, 95–104.

Gick, M. L., & Holyoak, K. J. (1983). Schema induction and analogical transfer. *Cognitive Psychology, 15*, 1–38.

Globerson, T. (1983a). Mental capacity, mental effort and cognitive style. *Developmental Review, 3*, 292–302.

Globerson, T. (1983b). Mental capacity and cognitive functioning: Developmental and social class differences. *Developmental Psychology, 19*, 225–230.

Globerson, T. (1985). Field dependence/independence and mental capacity: A developmental approach. *Developmental Review, 5*, 261–273.

Globerson, T. (1987). Confusing developmental and individual differences: A reply to Anderson. *Developmental Review, 7*, 142–144.

Globerson, T. (1989). What is the relationship between cognitive style and cognitive development? In T. Globerson & T. Zelniker (Eds.), *Cognitive style and cognitive development* (pp. 71–85). Norwood, NJ: Ablex.

Gobbo, C. (1991a). Logica e psicologia dello sviluppo [Logic and developmental psychology]. *Sistemi Intelligenti, 2*, 285–303.

Gobbo, C. (1991b). Alcuni aspetti dello sviluppo della teoria della mente: Attribuzione di conoscenza [Some aspects of the development of theory of mind: Knowledge attribution]. *Età Evolutiva, 40*, 61–66.

Gobbo, C., & Chi, M. (1986). How knowledge is structured and used by experts and novice children. *Cognitive Development, 1*, 221–237.

Gobbo, C., & Morra, S. (1997). *Lo sviluppo mentale: Prospettive neopiagetiane* [Mental development: Neo-Piagetian perspectives]. Bologna: Il Mulino.

Goldberg-Reitman, J. (1992). Young girls' conception of their mothers' role: A neo-structural analysis. In R. Case (Ed.), *The mind's staircase: Exploring the conceptual underpinnings of children's thought and knowledge* (pp. 135–151). Hillsdale, NJ: Lawrence Erlbaum Associates.

Goldin-Meadow, S. (2004). U-shaped changes are in the eye of the beholder. *Journal of Cognition and Development, 5*(1), 109–111.

Goldin-Meadow, S., & Alibali, M. W. (2002). Looking at the hands through time: A microgenetic perspective on learning and instruction. In N. Granott & J. Parziale (Eds.), *Microdevelopment: Transition processes in development and learning* (pp. 80–105). New York: Cambridge University Press.

Goldmann, L. (1966). Jean Piaget et la philosophie [Jean Piaget and philosophy]. In *Jean Piaget et les sciences sociales* [Jean Piaget and the social sciences] (pp. 5-23). Geneva: Droz.

Goldmann, L. (1970). *Marxisme et sciences humaines* [Marxism and human sciences]. Paris: Gallimard.

Goldman-Rakic, P. S. (1987). Development of cortical circuitry and cognitive function. *Child Development, 58,* 601–622.

Goode, P. E., Goddard, P. H., & Pascual-Leone, J. (2002). Event-related potentials index cognitive style differences during a serial-order recall task. *International Journal of Psychophysiology, 43,* 123–140.

Gopnik, A. (1996). The post-Piaget era. *Psychological Science, 7,* 221–225.

Goswami, U. (1989). Relational complexity and the development of analogical reasoning. *Cognitive Development, 4,* 251–268.

Goswami, U. (1995). Phonological development and reading by analogy: What is analogy, and what is not? *Journal of Research in Reading, 18*(2), 139–145.

Goswami, U. (2001). Cognitive development: No stages please—we're British. *British Journal of Developmental Psychology, 92,* 257–277.

Goswami, U., & Pauen, S. (2005). The effects of a "family" analogy on class inclusion reasoning by young children. *Swiss Journal of Psychology, 64*(2), 115–124.

Granott, N. (2002). How microdevelopment creates macrodevelopment: Reiterated sequences, backward transitions, and the zone of current development. In N. Granott & J. Parziale (Eds.), *Microdevelopment: Transition processes in development and learning* (pp. 213–242). New York: Cambridge University Press.

Granott, N., Fischer, K. W., & Parziale, J. (2002). Bridging to the unknown: A transition mechanism In learning and development. In N. Granott & J. Parziale (Eds.), *Microdevelopment: Transition processes in development and learning* (pp. 131–156). New York: Cambridge University Press.

Granott, N., & Parziale, J. (2002a). Micro-development: A process-oriented perspective for studying development and learning. In N. Granott & J. Parziale (Eds.), *Microdevelopment: Transition processes in development and learning* (pp. 1–28). Cambridge, UK: Cambridge University Press.

Granott, N., & Parziale, J. (Eds.). (2002b). *Microdevelopment: Transition processes in development and learning.* New York: Cambridge University Press.

Greenberg, L. S., & Pascual-Leone, J. (2001). A dialectical constructivist view of the creation of personal meaning. *Journal of Constructivist Psychology, 14,* 165–186.

Greeno, J. G. (1978). Natures of problem-solving abilities. In W. K. Estes (Ed.), *Handbook of learning and cognitive processes: V. Human information* (pp. 239–270). Hillsdale, NJ: Lawrence Erlbaum Associates.

Greenough, W. T., Black, J. E., & Wallace, C. S. (1987). Experience and brain development. *Child Development, 58,* 539–559.

Greenough, W. T., & Schwark, H. D. (1984). Age related aspects of experience effects upon brain structure. In N. Emde & R. J. Harmon (Eds.), *Continuities and discontinuities in development* (pp. 69–91). Hillsdale, NJ: Plenum.

Griffin, S. (1992). Young children's awareness of their inner world: A neo-structural analysis of the development of intrapersonal intelligence. In R. Case (Ed.), *The mind's staircase: Ex-*

ploring the conceptual underpinnings of children's thought and knowledge (pp. 89–206). Hillsdale, NJ: Lawrence Erlbaum Associates.

Griffin, S. A. (1994, June). Working memory capacity and the acquisition of mathematical knowledge: Implications for learning and development. Paper presented at the meeting of the International Society for the Study of Behavioral Development, Amsterdam.

Griffin, S. (2004). Contribution of central conceptual structure theory to education. In A. Demetriou & A. Raftopoulos (Eds.), Cognitive developmental change: Theories, models and measurement (pp. 264–295). Cambridge, UK: Cambridge University Press.

Griffin, S., & Case, R. (1996). Evaluating the breadth and depth of training effects when central conceptual structures are taught. Monographs of the Society for Research in Child Development, 61(1-2), 83–102.

Griffin, S., & Case, R. (1997). Rethinking the primary school math curriculum: An approach based on cognitive science. Issues in Education, 3, 1–65.

Griffin, S., Case, R., & Capodilupo, A. (1995). Teaching for understanding: The importance of the central conceptual structures in the elementary mathematics curriculum. In A.Mc Keough & J. Lupart (Eds.), Teaching for transfer: Fostering generalization in learning (pp. 125–151). Mahwah, NJ: Lawrence Erlbaum Associates.

Griffin, S., Case, R., & Siegler, R. (1994). Rightstart: Providing the central conceptual prerequisites for first formal learning of arithmetic to students at risk for failure. In K. McGilly (Ed.), Classroom lessons: Integrating cognitive theory and classroom practice (pp. 25–49). Cambridge, MA: MIT Press.

Hagen, J. W., Hargrave, S., & Ross, W. (1973). Prompting and rehearsal in short-term memory. Child Development, 44(1), 201–204.

Haith, M. M., & Benson, J. B. (1998). Infant cognition. In W. Damon, D. Kuhn, & R. S. Siegler (Eds.), Handbook of child psychology. volume two: Cognition, perception, and language, 5th ed. (pp. 199–254). New York: Wiley.

Halford, G. S. (1969). An experimental analysis of the criteria used by children to judge quantities. Journal of Experimental Child Psychology, 8, 314–327.

Halford, G. S. (1970a). A classification learning set which is a possible model for conservation of quantity. Australian Journal of Psychology, 22(1), 11–19.

Halford, G. S. (1970b). A theory of acquisition of conservation. Psychological Review, 77, 302–316.

Halford, G. S. (1978a). Toward a working model of Piaget's stages. In J. A. Keats, K. F. Collis, & G. S. Halford (Eds.), Cognitive development: Research based on a neo-Piagetian approach (pp. 169–220). London: Wiley.

Halford, G. S. (1978b). Cognitive development stages, emerging from levels of learning. Journal of Behavioural Development, 1, 341–354.

Halford, G. S. (1978c). An approach to the definition of cognitive developmental stages in school mathematics. British Journal of Educational Psychology, 48, 298–314.

Halford, G. S. (1982). The development of thought. Hillsdale, NJ: Lawrence Erlbaum Associates.

Halford, G. S. (1984). Can young children integrate premises in transitivity and serial order tasks? Cognitive Psychology, 16, 65–93.

Halford, G. S. (1987). A structure-mapping approach to cognitive development. International Journal of Psychology, 22, 609–642.

Halford, G. S. (1989). Reflections on 25 years of Piagetian cognitive developmental psychology, 1963–1988. Human Development, 32, 325–357.

Halford, G. S. (1993a). Children's understanding: The development of mental models. Hillsdale, NJ: Lawrence Erlbaum Associates.

Halford, G. S. (1993b). Central conceptual structures: Achievements and challenges: Essay review of The Mind's Staircase: Exploring the Conceptual Underpinnings of Children's Thought and Knowledge by Robbie Case. Human Development, 36, 300–308.

Halford, G. S. (1998). Development of processing capacity entails representing more complex relations: Implications for cognitive development. In R. H. Logie & K. J. Gilhooly (Eds.), Working memory and thinking (pp. 139–157). Hove, UK: Psychology Press.

Halford, G. S. (1999). The properties of representations used in higher cognitive processes: Developmental implications. In I. E. Sigel (Ed.), *Development of mental representation: Theories and applications* (pp. 147–168). Mahwah, NJ: Lawrence Erlbaum Associates.

Halford, G. S., & Andrews, G. (2004). The development of deductive reasoning: How important is complexity? *Thinking and Reasoning, 10,* 123–145.

Halford, G. S., Andrews, G., Dalton, C., Boag, C., & Zielinski, T. (2002). Young children's performance on the balance scale: The influence of relational complexity. *Journal of Experimental Child Psychology, 81,* 417–445.

Halford, G. S., Bain, J. D., & Maybery, M. T. (1984). Working memory and representational process: Implications for cognitive development. In H. Bouma & D. G. Bouwhuis (Eds.), *Attention and performance* (pp. 459–470). Hillsdale, NJ: Lawrence Erlbaum Associates.

Halford, G. S., Bain, J. D., Maybery, M. T., & Andrews, G. (1998). Induction of relational schemas: Common processes in reasoning and complex learning. *Cognitive Psychology, 35,* 201–245.

Halford, G. S., Baker, R., McCredden, J. E., & Bain, J. D. (2005). How many variables can humans process? *Psychological Science, 16,* 60–76.

Halford, G. S., & Boyle, F. M. (1985). Do young children understand conservation of number? *Child Development, 56,* 165–176.

Halford, G. S., Brown, C. A., & Thompson, R. M. (1986). Children's concepts of volume and floatation. *Developmental Psychology, 22,* 218–222.

Halford, G. S., & Fullerton, T. (1970). A discrimination task which induces discrimination of number. *Child Development, 41,* 205–213.

Halford, G. S., & Kelly, M. E. (1984). On the basis of early transitivity judgments. *Journal of Experimental Child Psychology, 38,* 42–63.

Halford, G. S., & Leitch, E. (1989). Processing load constraints: A structure-mapping approach. In M. A. Luszcz & T. Nettelbeck (Eds.), *Psychological development: Perspectives across the lifespan* (pp. 151–159). Amsterdam: Elsevier.

Halford, G. S., Maybery,M. T., & Bain, J. D. (1986). Capacity limitations in children's reasoning: A dual-task approach. *Child Development, 57,* 616–627.

Halford, G. S., Maybery, M., O'Hare, T. & Grant, P. (1994). The development of memory and processing capacity. *Child Development, 65,* 1338–1356.

Halford, G. S., & McCredden, J. E. (1998). Cognitive science questions for cognitive development: The concepts of learning, analogy, and capacity. *Learning and Instruction, 8*(4), 289–308.

Halford, G. S., & Wilson, W. H. (1980). A category theory approach to cognitive development. *Cognitive Psychology, 12,* 356–411.

Halford, G. S., Wilson, W. H., & Phillips, S. (1998). Processing capacity defined by relational complexity: Implications for comparative, developmental, and cognitive psychology. *Behavioral and Brain Sciences, 21,* 803–831.

Hambrick, D. Z., Kane, M. J., & Engle, R. W. (2005). The role of working memory in higher-level cognition: Domain-specific versus domain-general perspectives. In R. J. Sternberg & J. E. Pretz (Eds.), *Cognition and intelligence: Identifying the mechanisms of the mind* (pp. 104–121). New York: Cambridge University Press.

Handley, S. J., Capon, A., Beveridge, M., Dennis, I., & Evans, J. (2004).Working memory, inhibitory control, and the development of children's reasoning. *Thinking and Reasoning, 10,* 175–195.

Hanlon, H. W., Thatcher, R. W., & Cline, M. J. (1999). Gender differences in the development of EEG coherence in normal children. *Developmental Neuropsychology, 16,* 479–506.

Harris, P., & Nunez, M. (1996). Understanding of permission rules by preschool children. *Child Development, 67,* 1572–1591.

Harris, P. L. (1989). *Children and emotion. the development of psychological understanding.* Oxford, UK: Blackwell.

Hayne, H. (2004). Infant memory development: Implications for childhood amnesia. *Developmental Review, 24,* 33–73.

Hayward, S. (1986). *The development of jealousy: The social triangle, and its effect on the developing child*. Unpublished doctoral dissertation, University of Toronto (OISE).

Heitz, R. P., Unsworth, N., & Engle, R. W. (2005).Working memory capacity, attention control, and fluid intelligence. In O. Wilhelm & R. W. Engle (Eds.), *Handbook of understanding and measuring intelligence* (pp. 61–79). Thousand Oaks, CA: Sage.

Henry, L. (1991). Development of auditory memory span: The role of rehearsal. *British Journal of Developmental Psychology, 9*, 493–511.

Heron, A., & Dowel, W. (1973). Weight conservation and matrix-solving ability in Papuan children. *Journal of Cross-Cultural Psychology, 4*, 207–219.

Heron, A., & Dowel, W. (1974). The questionable unity of the concrete operations stage. *International Journal of Psychology, 9*, 1–9.

Hitch, G., Halliday, M. S., & Littler, J. E. (1989). Item identification time and rehearsal rate as predictors of memory span in children. *Quarterly Journal of Experimental Psychology, 41*, 321–337.

Hochberg, J. (1988). Visual perception. In R. C. Atkinson, R. J. Hernstein, G. Lindzey, & R. D. Luce (Eds.), *Stevens' handbook of experimental psychology* (pp. 195–276). New York: Wiley.

Hofstadter, D. R. (2001). Analogy as the core of cognition. In D. Gentner, K. J. Holoyoak, & B. N. Kokinov (Ed.), *The analogical mind: Perspectives from cognitive science* (pp. 449–538). Cambridge, MA: MIT Press.

Holyoak, K. J., Junn, E. N., & Billman, D. O. (1984). Development of analogical problem-solving skill. *Child Development, 55*(6), 2042–2055.

Holyoak, K. J., & Koh, K. (1987). Surface and structural similarity in analogical transfer. *Memory & Cognition, 15*(4), 332–340.

Holyoak, K. J., & Thagard, P. (1989). Analogical mapping by constraint satisfaction. *Cognitive Science, 13*, 295–355.

Holyoak, K. J., & Thagard, P. (1995). *Mental leaps: Analogy in creative thought*. Cambridge, MA: The MIT Press.

Houghton, G., & Tipper, S. P. (1994). A model of inhibitory mechanisms in selective attention. In D. Dagenbach & T. Carr (Eds.), *Inhibitory mechanisms in attention, memory, and language* (pp. 53–112). New York: Academic Press.

Howard, I. P. (1978). Recognition and knowledge of the water-level principle. *Perception, 7*, 151–160.

Hughes, C. (1998). Executive function in preschoolers: Links with theory of mind and verbal ability. *British Journal of Developmental Psychology, 16*, 233-253.

Hunt, E., & Lansman, M. (1982). Individual differences in attention. In R. J. Sternberg (Ed.), *Advances in the psychology of human intelligence* (pp. 207–254). Hillsdale, NJ: Lawrence Erlbaum Associates.

Huteau, M. (1980). Dépendance–indépendance a l'égard du champ et développment de la pensée opératoire [Field independence-dependence and the development of operational thought]. *Archives de Psychologie, 48*, 1–40.

Huttenlocher, P. R. (1979). Synaptic density in human frontal cortex: Developmental changes and effects of aging. *Brain Research, 163*, 195–205.

Im-Bolter, N., Johnson, J., & Pascual-Leone, J. (2006). Processing limitations in children with specific language impairment: The role of executive function. *Child Development, 27*, 1827–1846.

Inhelder, B. (1978). New currents in genetic epistemology and developmental psychology. In J. Bruner & A. Garton (Eds.), *Human growth and development: Wolfson College lectures 1976* (pp. 121-138). Oxford, UK: Clarendon.

Inhelder, B. (1982). Sulle ultime ricerche di Jean Piaget [On Jean Piaget's latest research]. In L. Camaioni (Ed.), *La teoria di Jean Piaget* [Jean Piaget's theory]. (pp. 17–28). Firenze, Italy: Giunti-Barbera.

Inhelder, B., & Piaget, J. (1958). *The growth of logical thinking from childhood to adolescence*. (A. Parsons & S. Milgram, Trans.). New York: Basic Books. (Original work published 1955)

Inhelder, B., & Piaget, J. (1979). Procedures et structures [Procedures and structures]. *Archives de Psychologie, 47*, 165–176.

Inhelder, B., Sinclair, H., & Bovet, M. (1974). *Learning and development of cognition.* Cambridge, MA: Harvard University Press.

Izard, C. E. (1991). *Psychology of emotions.* New York: Plenum.

Jalley, E. (1977). Untitled paper. *Cahiers du Centre d'Etudes et de Recherches Marxiste. Special issue "Sur la théorie opératoire"* [On operational theory], *140*, 56–67.

Jamison, W. (1977). Developmental inter-relationships among concrete operational tasks: An investigation of Piaget's stage concept. *Journal of Experimental Child Psychology, 23*, 235–253.

Johnson, J. (1989). Factors related to cross-language transfer and metaphor interpretation in bilingual children. *Applied Psycholinguistics, 10*, 157–177.

Johnson, J., Fabian, V., & Pascual-Leone, J. (1989). Quantitative hardware stages that constrain language development. *Human Development, 32*, 245–271.

Johnson, J., Im-Bolter, N., & Pascual-Leone, J. (2003). Development of mental attention in gifted and mainstream children: The role of mental capacity, inhibition, and speed of processing. *Child Development, 74*(6), 1594–1614.

Johnson J., Im-Bolter N., & Pascual-Leone J. (2005). *Central inhibitory processes: Are they one or many?* Unpublished manuscript.

Johnson, J., & Pascual-Leone, J. (1989a). Developmental levels of processing in metaphor interpretation. *Journal of Experimental Child Psychology, 48*, 1–31.

Johnson, J., & Pascual-Leone, J. (1989b). Reply. *Human Development, 32*, 276–278.

Johnson, J., Pascual-Leone, J., Im-Bolter, N., & Verrilli, E. (2004, July). *Executive functions and mental attention in cognitively gifted children.* Paper presented to the meeting of the International Society for the Study of Behavioral Development, Ghent, Belgium.

Johnson, J., Prior, S., & Artuso, M. (2000). Field dependence as a factor in second language communicative production. *Language Learning, 50*(3), 529–567.

Johnson, M. H., & Morton, J. (1991). *Biology and cognitive development: The case for face recognition.* Oxford, UK: Blackwell.

Johnson, S., & Carey, S. (1998). Knowledge enrichment and conceptual change in folk biology: Evidence from Williams Syndrome. *Cognitive Psychology, 37*, 156–200.

Johnson, S. P., & Nanez, J. E. (1995). Young infants' perception of object unity in two-dimensional displays. *Infant Behavior and Development, 18*, 133–143.

Johnson-Laird, P. N. (1983). *Mental models.* Cambridge, MA: Cambridge University Press.

Jonides, J. (2006, June). *Resolving interference in working memory.* Paper presented to the 3rd European Working Memory Symposium, Genoa, Italy.

Jonides, J., Lacey, S. C., & Nee, D. E. (2005). Processes of working memory in mind and brain. *Current Directions in Psychological Science, 14*, 2–5.

Jonides, J., & Nee, D. E. (2006). Brain mechanisms of proactive interference in working memory. *Neuroscience, 139*, 181–193.

Juckes, T. J. (1991). Equilibration and the learning paradox. *Human Development, 34*, 261–272.

Jusczyk, P. W. (1985). On characterizing the development of speech perception. In J. Mehler & R. Fox (Eds.), *Neonate cognition: Beyond the blooming buzzing confusion* (pp. 199–229). Hillsdale, NJ: Lawrence Erlbaum Associates.

Just, M. A., & Carpenter, P. A. (1992). A capacity theory of comprehension: Individual differences in working memory. *Psychological Review, 99*, 122–149.

Kahneman, D. (1973). *Attention and effort.* Englewood Cliffs, NJ: Prentice-Hall.

Kail, R. (1991). Development of processing speed in childhood and adolescence. In H. W. Reese (Ed.), *Advances in child development and behavior, Vol. 23* (pp. 151–185). San Diego, CA: Academic Press.

Kail, R. (2000). Speed of information processing: Developmental change and links to intelligence. *Journal of School Psychology, 38*, 51–61.

Kail, R., & Hall, L. K. (2001). Distinguishing short-term memory from working memory. *Memory and Cognition, 29,* 1–9.

Kail, R., & Salthouse, T. A. (1994). Processing speed as a mental capacity. *Acta Psychologica, 86,* 199–255.

Kalchman, M., & Case, R. (1998). Teaching mathematical functions in primary and middle childhood: An approach based on neo-Piagetian theory. *Scientia Paedagogica Experimentalis, 35,* 7–53.

Kanizsa, G. (1979). *Organization in vision: Essays on gestalt perception.* New York: Praeger.

Karmiloff-Smith, A. (1978). On stage: The importance of being a nonconserver. *The Behavioural and Brain Sciences, 2,* 188–190.

Karmiloff-Smith, A. (1979). Micro- and macrodevelopmental changes in language acquisition and other representational systems. *Cognitive Science, 3*(2), 91–117.

Karmiloff-Smith, A. (1981a). Getting developmental differences or studying child development? *Cognition, 10*(1), 151–158.

Karmiloff-Smith, A. (1981b). *A functional approach to child language.* Cambridge, UK: Cambridge University Press.

Karmiloff-Smith, A. (1984). Children's problem solving. In M. E. Lamb, A. L. Brown, & B. Rogoff (Eds.), *Advances in developmental psychology* (pp. 39–90). Hillsdale, NJ: Lawrence Erlbaum Associates.

Karmiloff-Smith, A. (1986). From metaprocesses to conscious access: Evidence from children's metalinguistic and repair data. *Cognition, 23,* 95–147.

Karmiloff-Smith, A. (1988). The child is a theoretician not an individualist. *Mind and Language, 3*(3), 183–195.

Karmiloff-Smith, A. (1989). Commentary. *Human Development, 32,* 272–275.

Karmiloff-Smith, A. (1990). Constraints on representational change: Evidence from children's drawing. *Cognition, 34,* 57–83.

Karmiloff-Smith, A. (1991). Beyond modularity: Innate constraints and developmental change. In S. Carey & R. Gelman (Eds.), *The epigenesis of the mind. Essay on biology and cognition* (pp. 171–197). Hillsdale, NJ: Lawrence Erlbaum Associates.

Karmiloff-Smith, A. (1992). *Beyond modularity: A developmental perspective on cognitive science.* Cambridge, MA: MIT Press.

Karmiloff-Smith, A. (1993). Neo-Piagetians: A theoretical misnomer? *SRCD Newsletter,* (Spring).

Karmiloff-Smith, A. (1998). Development itself is the key to understanding developmental disorders. *Trends in Cognitive Science, 2,* 389–398.

Karmiloff-Smith, A. (1999). Taking development seriously. *Human Development, 42,* 325–327.

Karmiloff-Smith, A., Brown, J. H., Grice, S., & Paterson, S. (2003). Dethroning the myth: Cognitive dissociations and innate modularity in Williams Syndrome. *Developmental Neuropsychology, 23,* 227–242.

Karmiloff-Smith, A., & Inhelder, B. (1974/1975). If you want to get ahead, get a theory. *Cognition, 3*(3), 195–212.

Karmiloff-Smith, A., Johnson, H., Grant, J., Jones, M. C., Karmiloff, Y. N. Bartrip, J., & Cuckle, P. (1993). Rethinking metalinguistic awareness: Representing and discussing knowledge about what acounts as a word. *Discourse Processes, 16,* 565–589.

Karmiloff-Smith, A., Plunkett, K., Johnson, M. H., Elman, J. L., & Bates, E. A. (1998). What does it mean to claim that something is 'innate'? Response to Clark, Harris, Lightfoot and Samuels. *Mind and Language, 13,* 558–597.

Karmiloff-Smith, A., Thomas, M., Annaz, D., Humphreys, K., Ewing, S., & Brace, N., et al. (2004). Exploring the Williams Syndrome face-processing debate: The importance of building developmental trajectories. *Journal of Child Psychology and Psychiatry, 45,* 1258–1274.

Keating, D. P. (1979). Thinking processes in adolescents. In J. Adelson (Ed.), *Handbook of adolescent psychology* (pp. 211–246). New York: Wiley.

Keating, D. P. (1996). Central conceptual structures: Seeking developmental integration. *Monographs of the Society for Research in Child Development, 61*(1-2), 276–282.

Keil, F. (1991). The emergence of theoretical belief as constraints on concepts. In S. Carey & R. Gelman (Eds.), *The epigenesis of the mind. Essay on biology and cognition* (pp. 237–256). Hillsdale, NJ: Lawrence Erlbaum Associates.

Keil, F. C. (2006). Explanation and understanding. *Annual Review of Psychology, 57,* 227–254.

Kemps, E., de Rammelaere, S., & Desmet, T. (2000). The development of working memory: Exploring the complementarity of two models. *Journal of Experimental Child Psychology, 77,* 89–109.

Kirkham, N. Z., Cruess, L., & Diamond, A. (2003). Helping children apply their knowledge to their behavior on a dimension-switching task. *Developmental Science, 6,* 449–467.

Kirkham, N. Z., & Diamond, A. (2003). Sorting between theories of perseveration: Performance In the conflict task requires memory, attention and inhibition. *Developmental Science, 6,* 474–476.

Kitayama, S., Markus, H. R., & Matsumoto, H. (1995). Culture, self, and emotion: A cultural perspective on "self-conscious" emotions. In J. P. Tangney & K. W. Fischer (Eds.), *Self-conscious emotions: The psychology of shame, guilt, embarrassment, and pride* (pp. 439–464). New York: Guilford.

Kitchener, K. S., Lynch, C. L., Fischer, K. W., & Wood, P. K. (1993). Developmental range of reflective judgment: The effect of contextual support and practice on developmental stage. *Developmental Psychology, 29*(5), 893–906.

Klahr, D. (1978a). Goal formation, planning and learning by pre-school problem solvers or: "My socks are in the dryer." In R. Siegler (Ed.), *Children's thinking: What develops?* (pp. 180–212). Hillsdale, NJ: Lawrence Erlbaum Associates.

Klahr, D. (1978b). Rages over stages. *The Behavioural and Brain Sciences, 2,* 191–192.

Klahr, D., & Nigam, M. (2004). The equivalence of learning paths in early science instruction: Effects of direct instruction and discovery learning. *Psychological Science, 15*(10), 661–667.

Klahr, D., & Robinson, M. (1981). Formal assessment of problem-solving and planning processes In preschool children. *Cognitive Psychology, 13,* 113–148.

Klahr, D., &Wallace, J. G. (1976). *Cognitive development: An information processing view.* Hillsdale, NJ: Lawrence Erlbaum Associates.

Klapp, S. T., Mashburn, E. A., & Lester, P. T. (1983). Short-term memory does not involve the "working memory" of information processing: The demise of a common assumption. *Journal of Experimental Child Psychology, 112,* 240–264.

Klingberg, T., Forssberg, H., & Westerberg, H. (2002). Increased brain activity in frontal and parietal cortex underlies the development of visuospatial working memory capacity during childhood. *Journal of Cognitive Neuroscience, 14,* 1–10.

Knight, C. C., & Fischer, K. W. (1992). Learning to read words: Individual differences in developmental sequences. *Journal of Applied Developmental Psychology, 13*(3), 377–404.

Konishi, S., Nakajima, K., Uchida, I., Kikyo, H., Kameyama, M., & Miyashita, Y. (1999). Common inhibitory mechanism in human inferior prefrontal cortex revealed by event-related functional MRI. *Brain, 122,* 981–999.

Kornblum, S., Hasbroucq, T., & Osman, A. (1990). Dimensional overlap: Cognitive basis for stimulus–response compatibility. A model and a taxonomy. *Psychological Review, 97,* 253–270.

Kosslyn, S. M. (1980). *Image and mind.* Cambridge, MA: Harvard University Press.

Kotovsky, L., & Gentner, D. (1996). Comparison and categorization in the development of relational similarity. *Child Development, 67*(6), 2797–2822.

Kreutzer, M. A., Leonard, S. C., & Flavell, J. H. (1975). An interview study of children's knowledge about memory. *Monographs of the Society for Research in Child Development, 40*(1), n. 159.

Kuhn, T. S. (1962). *The structure of scientific revolutions.* Chicago: University of Chicago Press.

Kuhn, D., Garcia-Mila, M., Zohar, A., & Andersen, C. (1995). Strategies of knowledge acquisition. *Monographs of the Society for Research in Child Development, 60*(4), 1–128.

REFERENCES

Kurtines, W. M. (1978). Measurability, description, and explanation: The explanatory adequacy of stage model. *The Behavioral and Brain Sciences, 2,* 192–194.

Kurtz, K. J., Miao, C., & Gentner, D. (2001). Learning by analogical bootstrapping. *Journal of the Learning Sciences, 10*(4), 417–446.

Kwon, H., Reiss, A. L., & Menon, V. (2002). Neural basis of protracted developmental changes In visuo-spatial working memory. *Proceedings of the National Academy of Science, USA, 99,* 13336–13341.

Kyllonen, P. C. (2002). g: Knowledge, speed, or working memory capacity? A systems perspective. In R. J. Sternberg & E. L. Gregorienko (Eds.), *The general factor of intelligence: How general is it?* (pp. 415–445). Mahwah, NJ: Lawrence Erlbaum Associates.

Lakatos, I. (1970). Falsification and the methodology of scientific research programmes. In I. Lakatos & A. Musgrave (Eds.), *Criticism and the growth of knowledge* (pp. 91–195). Cambridge, UK: Cambridge University Press.

Lanfranchi, S., & Swanson, H. L. (2005). Short-term memory and working memory in children as a function of language-specific knowledge in English and Spanish. *Learning and Individual Differences, 15,* 299–319.

Lange, G. (1978). Organization-related processes in children's recall: Maintenance and generalization effects. *Child Development, 56,* 643–653.

Larivée, S., Normandeau, S., & Parent, S. (2000). The French connection: Some contributions of French-language research to the post-Piagetian era. *Child Development, 71,* 823–839.

Lautrey, J. (1990). From unitary to pluralist conceptions of cognitive development. *Archives de Psychologie, 58*(225), 185–196.

Lautrey, J. (1993). Structure and variability: A plea for a pluralistic approach to cognitive development. In R. Case & W. Edelstein (Eds.), *The new structuralism in cognitive development: Theory and research on individual pathways* (pp. 101–114). Basel: Karger.

Lautrey, J., de Ribaupierre, A., & Rieben, L. (1985). Intraindividual variability in the development of concrete operations: Relations between logical and infralogical operations. *Genetic, Social and General Psychology Monographs, 111,* 167–192.

Lautrey, J., de Ribaupierre, A., & Rieben, L. (1987). Operational development and individual differences. In E. De Corte, H. Lodewijks, R. Parmentier, & P. Span (Eds.), *Learning and instruction* (pp. 19–30). Oxford, UK: Leuven University Press-Pergamon Press.

Lawler, J. (1975). Dialectical philosophy and developmental psychology: Hegel and Piaget on contradiction. *Human Development, 18,* 1–17.

Lazarus, R. (1991). *Emotion and adaptation.* New York: Oxford University Press.

Le Ny, J. F. (1977). Untitled paper. *Cahiers du Centre d'Etudes et de Recherches Marxistes. Special issue "Sur la théorie opératoire"* [On operational theory], *140,* 68–75.

Legrenzi, P. (1975). *Forma e contenuto dei processi cognitivi* [Form and contents of cognitive processes]. Bologna: Il Mulino.

Legrenzi, P., & Murino, M. (1974). Falsification at the pre-operational level. *Italian Journal of Psychology, 1,* 363–368.

Lehto, J. E., Juujärvi, P., Kooistra, L., & Pulkkinen, L. (2003). Dimensions of executive functioning: Evidence from children. *British Journal of Developmental Psychology, 21*(1), 59–80.

Lesgold, A. M. (1985, October). *Expertise in complex skills.* Paper presented at the ONR Nature of Expertise Conference, Pittsburgh.

Leslie, A.M. (1988). The necessity of illusion: Perception and thought in infancy. In L.Weiskrantz (Ed.), *Thought without language* (pp. 185–210). New York: Clarendon Press.

Lewis, M. D. (1994). Reconciling stage and specificity in neo-Piagetian theory: Self-organizing conceptual structures. *Human Development, 37,* 143–169.

Lewis, M. D. (1995). Cognition–emotion feedback and the self-organization of developmental paths. *Human Development, 38,* 71–102.

Lewis, M. D. (2000). Emotional self-organization at three time-scales. In M. D. Lewis & I. Granic (Eds.), *Emotion, development, and self-organisation* (pp. 37–69). Cambridge, UK: Cambridge University Press.

Lewis, M. D. (2001). Personal pathways in the development of appraisal. In A. Schorr & K. R. Scherer (Eds.), *Appraisal processes in emotion: Theory, methods, research* (pp. 205–220). London: Oxford University Press.

Lewis, M. D. (2002). Interacting time scales in personality (and cognitive) development: Intentions, emotions, and emergent forms. In N. Granott & J. Parziale (Eds.), *Microdevelopment: Transition processes in development and learning* (pp. 183–212). Cambridge, UK: Cambridge University Press.

Lewis, M. D. (2005). The emergence of mind in the emotional brain. In A. Demetriou & A. Raftopoulos (Eds.), *Cognitive developmental change: Theories, models and measurement* (pp. 217–240). Cambridge, UK: Cambridge University Press.

Li, J., Wang, L., & Fischer, K. W. (2004). The organization of Chinese shame concepts. *Cognition and Emotion, 18*, 767–797.

Liu, P., & Case, R. (1981, January). *Quantitative and qualitative changes in preschool development.* Paper presented to the Annual Conference on Piaget and the Helping Professions, Los Angeles.

Logan, G. D., & Irwin, D. E. (2000). Don't look! Don't touch! Inhibitory control of eye and hand movements. *Psychonomic Bulletin & Review, 7*, 107–112.

Logie, R. H. (1995). *Visuo-spatial working memory.* Hillsdale, NJ: Lawrence Erlbaum Associates.

Logie, R. H., & Denis, M. (Eds.). (1991). *Mental images in human cognition.* Amsterdam: North Holland.

Logie, R. H., & Marchetti, C. (1991). Visuo-spatial working memory: Visual, spatial, or central executive? In R. H. Logie & C. Marchetti (Eds.), *Mental images in human cognition* (pp. 105–115). Amsterdam, North Holland: Luchins, A. S. (1942). Mechanization in problem solving—the effect of einstellung. *Psychological Monographs, 54, no, 6*, 95.

Machado, A. (1964). Proverbios y cantares [Proverbs and songs]. In A. de Albornoz & G. de Torre (Eds.), *Obras: Poesia y prose/Antonio Machado* [Collected works: Poetry and prose/Antonio Machado]. Buenos Aires: Ediotrial Losada.

Maguire, E. A., Gadian, D. G., Johnsrude, I. S., Good, C. D., Ashburner, J., Frackowiak, R., et al. (2000). Navigation-related structural change in the hippocampi of taxi drivers. *Proceedings of the National Academy of Sciences, USA, 97*, 4398–4403.

Maier, N. R. (1931). Reasoning in humans: The solution of a problem at its appearance in consciousness. *Journal of Comparative Psychology, 12*, 181–194.

Majerus, S., Poncelet, M., Collette, F., Maquet, P., & van der Linden, M. (2006, June). *Verbal working memory as the result of attentional modulation of networks involved in language and serial order processing: Evidence from fMRI.* Paper presented to the 3rd European Working Memory Symposium, Genoa, Italy.

Mandler, J. M. (1983). Representation. In P. H. Mussen (Ed.), *Handbook of child development* (pp. 420–494). New York: Wiley.

Mandler, J. M. (1992). The precocious infant revisited. *SRCD Newsletter, Spring.*

Mandler, J. M. (2004). *The foundations of mind: Origins of conceptual thought.* New York: Oxford University Press.

Marcovitch, S., & Lewkowicz, D. J. (2004). U-shaped functions: Artifact or hallmark of development? *Journal of Cognition and Development, 5*(1), 113–118.

Marcus, G. F. (2004). What's in a U? The shapes of cognitive development. *Journal of Cognition and Development, (5)*, 113–118.

Marini, Z. (1984). *The development of social and non-social cognition in childhood and adolescence.* Unpublished doctoral dissertation. University of Toronto.

Marini, Z. (1992). Synchrony and asynchrony in the development of children's scientific reasoning. In R. Case (Ed.), *The mind's staircase: Exploring the conceptual underpinnings of children's thought and knowledge* (pp. 55–73). Hillsdale, NJ: Lawrence Erlbaum Associates.

398 REFERENCES

Marini, Z., & Case, R. (1994). The development of abstract reasoning about the physical and social world. *Child Development, 65*, 147–159.

Marx, K. (1976). Theses on Feuerbach. In Marx, K., *Karl Marx, Frederick Engels: Collected Works: Vol. 5* (pp. 3-8). New York: International Publishers. (Original work published 1845)

Mascolo, M. F., & Fischer, K. W. (1995). Developmental transformations in appraisals for pride, shame, and guilt. In K. W. Fischer & J. P. Tangney (Eds.), *Self-conscious emotions: The psychology of shame, guilt, embarrassment, and pride* (pp. 64–113). New York: Guilford.

Mascolo, M. F., & Griffin, S. (1998). Alternative trajectories in the development of anger. In M. F. Mascolo & S. Griffin (Eds.), *What develops in emotional development?* (pp. 219–249). New York: Plenum.

Mascolo, M. F., Harkins, D., & Harakal, T. (2000). The dynamic construction of emotion: Varieties In anger. In M. D. Lewis & I. Granic (Eds.), *Emotion, development, and self-organisation* (pp. 125–152). Cambridge, UK: Cambridge University Press.

Mascolo, M. F., Kanner, B. G., & Griffin, S. (1998). Neo-Piagetian systems theory and the education of young children. *Early Child Development and Care, 140*, 31–52.

Mason, L. (1994). Analogy, metaconceptual awareness and conceptual change: A classroom study. *Educational Studies, 20*(2), 267–291.

Matousek, M., & Petersén, I. (1973). Automatic evaluation of EEG background activity by means of age-dependent EEG quotients. *Electroencephalography and Clinical Neurophysiology, 35*(6), 603–612.

McCloskey, M., Washburn, A., & Felch, L. (1983). Intuitive physics: The straight-down belief and its origin. *The Journal of Experimental Psychology: Learning, Memory and Cognition, 9*, 636–649.

McKeough, A. (1992). A neo-structural analysis of children's narrative and its development. In R. Case (Ed.), *The mind's staircase: Exploring the conceptual underpinnings of children's thought and knowledge* (pp. 171–188). Hillsdale, NJ: Lawrence Erlbaum Associates.

McKeough, A., & Genereux, R. (2003). Transformation in narrative thought during adolescence: The structure and content of story compositions. *Journal of Educational Psychology, 95*, 537–552.

McLaughlin, G. H. (1963). Psycho-logic: A possible alternative to Piaget's formulation. *British Journal of Educational Psychology, 33*, 61–67.

McLeod, C.M. (1991). Half a century of research on the Stroop effect: An interpretive review. *Psychological Bulletin, 109*, 163–203.

McPherson, S. L., & Thomas, J. R. (1989). Relation of knowledge and performance in boys' tennis: Age and expertise. *Journal of Experimental Child Psychology, 48*, 190–211.

Miall, D. S. (1989). Beyond the schema given: Affective comprehension of literary narratives. *Cognition and Emotion, 3*, 55–78.

Miller, G. A. (1956). The magical number seven plus or minus two: Some limits on our capacity for processing information. *Psychological Review, 63*, 81–97.

Miller, R., Bentley, A., & Pascual-Leone, J. (1989, July). *Executive training and mental capacity.* Paper Presented to the Tenth Biennial Meeting of the International Society for the Study of Behavioral Development, Jyväskylä, Finland.

Miller, R., Pascual-Leone, J., Campbell, C., & Juckes, T. (1989). Cross-cultural similarities and differences on two neo-Piagetian cognitive tasks. *International Journal of Psychology, 24*, 293–313.

Milliken, B., Tipper, S. P., & Weaver, B. (1994). Negative priming in a spatial localization task : Feature mismatching and distractor inhibition. *Journal of Experimental Psychology: Human Perception and Performance, 20*, 624–646.

Mitchell, J. P., Macrae, C. N., & Gilchrist, I. D. (2002).Working memory and the suppression of reflexive saccades. *Journal of Cognitive Neuroscience, 14*, 95–103.

Mizuno, T., Yamauchi, N., Watanabe, A., Komatsushiro, M., Takagi, T., Iinuma, K., et al. (1970). Maturation of patterns of EEG: Basic waves of healthy infants under 12 months of age. *Tohoku Journal of Experimental Medicine, 102*, 91–98.

Moessinger, P. (1977). Piaget on contradiction. *Human Development, 20*, 178–184.

Molenaar, P., Huizenga, H., & Nesselroade, J. (2003). The relationship between the structure of interindividual and intraindividual variability: A theoretical and empirical vindication of Developmental Systems Theory. In U. M. Staudinger & U. Lindenberger (Eds.), *Understanding human development: Dialogues with lifespan psychology* (pp. 339–360). Dordrecht: Kluwer Academic Publishers.

Mondloch, C., Geldart, S., Maurer, D., & de Schonen, S. (2003). Developmental changes in the processing of hierarchical shapes continue into adolescence. *Journal of Experimental Child Psychology, 84*, 20–40.

Morra, S. (1994). Issues in working memory measurement: Testing for *M* capacity. *International Journal of Behavioural Development, 17*, 143–159.

Morra, S. (1995). A neo-Piagetian approach to children's drawings. In C. Lange-Kuettner & G. V. Thomas (Eds.), *Drawing and looking: Theoretical approaches to pictorial representation in children* (pp. 93–106). London: Harvester.

Morra, S. (1998). Magazzini di memoria? Pronti per l'oblio! [Memory stores? Ready for forgetting!]. *Giornale Italiano di Psicologia, 25*, 695–730.

Morra, S. (2000). A new model of verbal short-term memory. *Journal of Experimental Child Psychology, 75*, 191–227.

Morra, S. (2001a). On the information-processing demands of spatial reasoning. *Thinking and Reasoning, 7*, 347–365.

Morra, S. (2001b). Nothing left in store . . . but how do we measure attentional capacity? *Behavioral and Brain Sciences, 24*, 132–133.

Morra, S. (2002). On the relationship between partial occlusion drawing, *M* capacity, and field independence. *British Journal of Developmental Psychology, 20*, 421–438.

Morra, S. (2005). Cognitive aspects of change in drawings: A reconsideration and a theoretical account *British Journal of Developmental Psychology, 23*, 317–341.

Morra, S. (in press-a). A test of a neo-Piagetian model of the water level task. *European Journal of Developmental Psychology.*

Morra, S. (in press-b). Spatial structures in children's drawings: How do they develop? In C. Lange-Küttner & A. Vinter (Eds.), *Drawing and non verbal intelligence.* Cambridge, UK: Cambridge University Press.

Morra, S., Angi, A., & Tomat, L. (1996). Planning, encoding, and overcoming conflict in partial occlusion drawing: A neo-Piagetian model and an experimental analysis. *Journal of Experimental Child Psychology, 61*, 276–301.

Morra, S., Caloni, B., & D'Amico, M. R. (1994). Working memory and the intentional depiction of emotions. *Archives de Psychologie, 64*, 71–87.

Morra, S., & Camba, R. (2005, August). *Non-word learning in school children: A causal analysis.* Paper presented to the XII European Conference on Developmental Psychology, Tenerife.

Morra, S., Moizo, C., & Scopesi, A. (1988).Working memory (or the *M* operator) and the planning of children's drawings. *Journal of Experimental Child Psychology, 46*, 41–73.

Morra, S., Pascual-Leone, J., Johnson, J., & Baillargeon, R. H. (1991). Understanding spatial descriptions: A test of a mental capacity model. In R. H. Logie & M. Denis (Eds.), *Mental images in human cognition* (pp. 241–254). Amsterdam: North-Holland.

Morra, S., & Scopesi, A. (1988). La memoria operativa e la sua misurazione [Working memory and its measurement]. *Età Evolutiva, 31*, 22–33.

Morra, S., Tressoldi, P., Mazzoni, G., Sava, D., & Zucco, G. (1988). *Span di memoria a breve termine e lunghezza delle parole: Probabile falsificazione del modello "loop articolatorio"* [Short-term memory and word length: Probable falsification of the "articulartory loop" model]. Paper presented to the VII Congress della Divisione SIPs Ricerca di Base, Palermo, Italy.

Morra, S., Vigliocco, G., & Penello, B. (2001). *M* capacity as a lifespan construct: A study of its decrease In ageing subjects. *International Journal of Behavioral Development, 25*, 78–87.

Moses, P., Roe, K., Buxton, R. B., Wong, E. C., Frank, L. R., & Stiles, J. (2002). Functional MRI of global and local processing in children. *NeuroImage, 16*, 415–424.

Moss, J., & Case, R. (1999). Developing children's understanding of the rational numbers: A new model and an experimental curriculum. *Journal for Research in Mathematics Education, 30,* 122–147.

Mounoud, P. (1970). *Structuration et utilisation d'instruments chez l'enfant* [Children's structuring and use of tools]. Neuchâtel: Delachaux et Niestlé.

Mounoud, P. (1986). Similarities between developmental sequences at different age periods. In I. Levin (Ed.), *Stage and structure* (pp. 40–58). Norwood, NJ: Ablex.

Mounoud, P. (1988). The ontogenesis of different types of thought: Language and motor behaviors as non-specific manifestations. In L. Weisenkrantz (Ed.), *Thought without language* (pp. 40–58). Oxford, UK: Clarendon Press.

Mounoud, P. (1990a). Consciousness as a necessary transitional phenomenon in cognitive development. *Psychological Inquiry, 1,* 248–277.

Mounoud, P. (1990b). Cognitive development: Enrichment or impoverishment? How to conciliate psychological and neurobiological models of development. In C. A. Hauert (Ed.), *Developmental psychology: Cognitive, perceptuo-motor and neuropsychological perspectives* (pp. 389–414). Amsterdam, North Holland.

Mounoud, P. (1992). Coscienza e intenzionalità nello sviluppo cognitivo [Consciousness and intentionality in cognitive development]. In M. Ceruti (Ed.), *Evoluzione e conoscenza: L'epistemologiagenetica di Jean Piaget e le prospettive del costruttivismo* [Evolution and consciousness: Jean Piaget's genetic epistemology and the prospects of constructivism] (pp. 197–209). Bergamo, Italy: Lubrina.

Mounoud, P. (1993). The emergence of new skills: Dialectic relations between knowledge systems. In Savelsbergh, G. J. P. (Ed.), *The development of coordination in infancy* (pp. 13–46). Amsterdam: North Holland.

Mounoud, P. (1995). From direct to reflexive (self-) knowledge: A recursive model. In P. Rochat (Ed.), *The self in infancy: Theory and research* (pp. 141–160). Amsterdam: Elsevier Science Publishers.

Mounoud, P. (1996). A recursive transformation of central cognitive mechanisms: The shift from partial to whole representations. In A. Sameroff & M. Haith (Eds.), *The five to seven year shift: The age of reason and responsibility* (pp. 85–110). Chicago: University of Chicago Press.

Mounoud, P., & Hauert, C. A. (1982). Development of sensorimotor organization in young children: Grasping and lifting objects. In G. E. Horman (Ed.), *Action and thought: From sensorimotor schemes to symbolic operations* (pp. 3–35). New York: Academic Press.

Mounoud, P., & Vinter, A. (1981). Representation and sensorimotor development. In G. Butterworth (Ed.), *Infancy and epistemology: An evaluation of Piaget's theory* (pp. 200–235). Brighton: Harvester.

Mounoud, P., & Vinter, A. (1985). The development of self-image in 3 to 11 years old children. In V. Shulman, L. C. Restaino, & L. Butler (Eds.), *The future of Piagetian theory: The neo-Piagetians* (pp. 37–69). New York: Plenum.

Mounoud, P., Viviani, P., Hauert, C. A., & Guyon, J. (1985). Development of visuomanual tracking In 5- to 9-years-oldboys. *Journal of Experimental Child Psychology, 40,* 115–132.

Multhaup, K. S., Johnson, M. D., & Tetirick, J. C. (2005). The wane of childhood amnesia for autobiographical and public event memories. *Memory, 13,* 161–173.

Mundy, P., Fox, N., & Card, J. (2003). EEG coherence, joint attention, and language development In the second year. *Developmental Science, 6,* 48–54.

Nairne, J. S., Neath, I., & Serra, M. (1997). Proactive interference plays a role in the word-length effect. *Psychonomic Bulletin & Review, 4,* 541–545.

Namy, L. L., Campbell, A. L., & Tomasello, M. (2004). The changing role of iconicity in non-verbal symbol learning: A U-shaped trajectory in the acquisition of arbitrary gestures. *Journal of Cognition and Development, 5*(1), 37–57.

Neimark, E. D. (1979). Current status of formal operational research. *Human Development, 22,* 60–67.

Neimark, E. D. (1981). Confounding with cognitive style factors: An artifact explanation for the apparent nonuniversal incidence of formal operations. In I. E. Sigel, D. M. Brodzinky, & R. M. Golinkoff (Eds.), *New directions in Piagetian theory and practice* (pp. 177–189). Hillsdale, NJ: Lawrence Erlbaum Associates.

Nelson, C. A., Thomas, K. M., & de Haan, M. (2006). Neural bases of cognitive development. In D. Kuhn & R. S. Siegler (Eds.), *Handbook of child psychology. volume two: Cognition, perception, and language, 6th edition* (pp. 3–57). New York: Wiley.

Nelson, K. (1986). *Event knowledge: Structure and function in development.* Hillsdale, NJ: Lawrence Erlbaum Associates.

Nelson, K. (1988). Constraints on word meaning. *Cognitive Development, 3,* 221–46.

Newell, A., & Simon, H. A. (1972). *Human problem solving.* Englewood Cliffs, NJ: Prentice-Hall.

Niaz, M. (1987). Relation between *M*-space of students and *M*-demand of different items of general chemistry. *Journal of Chemical Education, 64,* 502–505.

Niaz, M. (1998). The epistemological significance of Piaget's developmental stages: A Lakatosian interpretation. *New Ideas in Psychology, 16,* 47–59.

Norman, D. A., & Shallice, T. (1986). Attention to action: Willed and automatic control of behavior. In R. J. Davidson, G. E. Schwartz, & D. Shapiro (Eds.), *Consciousness and self-regulation* (pp. 1–18). New York: Plenum.

Normandeau, S., Larivée, S., Roulin, J., & Longeot, F. (1989). The balance-scale dilemma: Either the subject or the experimenter muddles through. *Journal of Genetic Psychology, 150*(3), 237–250.

Novick, L. R. (1988). Analogical transfer, problem similarity, and expertise. *Journal of Experimental Psychology: Learning, Memory, and Cognition, 14*(3), 510–520.

Okamoto, Y., & Case, R. (1996). Exploring the microstructure of children's conceptual structures in the domain of number. *Monographs of the Society for Research in Child Development, 61*(1-2), 27–58.

Okamoto, Y., Case, R., Bleiker, C., & Henderson, B. (1996). Cross-cultural investigations. *Monographs of the Society for Research in Child Development, 61*(1-2), 131–155.

Oliver, A., Johnson, M. H., Karmiloff-Smith, A., & Pennington, B. (2000). Deviations in the emergence of representations: A neuroconstructivist framework for analyzing developmental disorders. *Developmental Science, 3,* 1–23.

Ornstein, P. A., Naus, M. J., & Liberty, C. (1975). Rehearsal and organizational processes in children's memory. *Child Development, 26,* 818–830.

Page, M. (2000). Connectionist modeling in psychology: A localist manifesto. *Behavioral and Brain Sciences, 23,* 443–512.

Parker, S. T. (1978). Species-specific acquisition vs. universal sequence of acquisition. *Behavioural and Brain Sciences, 2,* 199–200.

Parziale, J. (2002). Observing the dynamics of construction: Children building bridges and new ideas. In N. Granott & J. Parziale (Eds.), *Microdevelopment: Transition processes in development and learning* (pp. 157–180). New York: Cambridge University Press.

Pascual-Leone, J. (1969). *Cognitive development and cognitive style: A general psychological integration.* Unpublished doctoral dissertation, University of Geneva.

Pascual-Leone, J. (1970). A mathematical model for the transitional rule in Piaget's developmental stages. *Acta Psychologica, 63,* 301–345.

Pascual-Leone, J. (1974). *A neo-Piagetian process-structural model of Witkin's differentiation.* Paper presented at the International Association for Cross-Cultural Psychology, Kingston.

Pascual-Leone, J. (1976a).Metasubjective problems of constructive cognition: Forms of knowing and their psychological mechanisms. *Canadian Psychological Review, 17,* 110–125.

Pascual-Leone, J. (1976b). On learning and development, Piagetian style. *Canadian Psychological Review, 17,* 270–297.

Pascual-Leone, J. (1978). Compounds, confounds and models in developmental information processing: A reply to Trabasso and Foellinger. *Journal of Experimental Child Psychology, 26*, 18–40.

Pascual-Leone, J. (1980). Constructive problems for constructive theories: The current relevance of Piaget's work and a critique of information-processing simulation psychology. In R. Kluwe & H. Spada (Eds.), *Developmental models of thinking* (pp. 263–296). New York: Academic Press.

Pascual-Leone, J. (1983). Growing into human maturity: Toward a meta-subjective theory of adulthood stages. In P. B. Baltes & O. G. Brim (Eds.), *Lifespan development and behavior* (pp. 117–155). New York: Academic Press.

Pascual-Leone, J. (1984). Attentional dialectic and mental effort: Toward an organismic theory of life stages. In M. L. Commons, F. L. Richards, & C. Armon (Eds.), *Beyond formal operations: Late adolescent and adult cognitive development* (pp. 182–215). New York: Praeger.

Pascual-Leone, J. (1987). Organismic processes for neo-Piagetian theories: A dialectical causal account of cognitive development. *International Journal of Psychology, 22*, 531–570.

Pascual-Leone, J. (1988). Affirmations and negations, disturbances and contradictions in understanding Piaget: Is his later theory causal? *Contemporary Psychology, 33*, 420–421.

Pascual-Leone, J. (1989). An organismic process model of Witkin's field dependence–independence. In T. Globerson & T. Zelniker (Eds.), *Cognitive style and cognitive development* (pp. 36–70). Norwood, NJ: Ablex.

Pascual-Leone, J. (1990a). Reflections on life-span intelligence, consciousness and ego development. In C. N. Alexander & E. Langer (Eds.), *Higher stages of human development* (pp. 258–285). Oxford:, UK: Oxford University Press.

Pascual-Leone, J. (1990b). An essay on wisdom: Toward organismic processes that make it possible. In R. Sternberg (Ed.), *Wisdom: Its nature, origins, and development* (pp. 244–278). Cambridge, UK: Cambridge University Press.

Pascual-Leone, J. (1991). Emotions, development, and psychotherapy: A dialectical-constructivist perspective. In J. Safran & L. Greenberg (Eds.), *Emotion, psychotherapy and change* (pp. 302–325). New York: Guilford.

Pascual-Leone, J. (1994). An experimentalist's understanding of children: Essay review of children's understanding: The development of mental models by Graeme S. Halford. *Human Development, 37*, 370–384.

Pascual-Leone, J. (1995). Learning and development as dialectical factors in cognitive growth. *Human Development, 38*, 338–348.

Pascual-Leone, J. (1996a). Piaget, Vygotski, y la función del sìmbolo [Piaget, Vygotsky, and the function of the symbol]. *Substratum, 3*, 63–87.

Pascual-Leone, J. (1996b, September). *Organismic processes of mental attention: Their role in life-span development.* Paper presented to The Conference for the Centennial of Piaget's Birth. Geneva.

Pascual-Leone, J. (1997). Metasubjective processes: The missing lingua franca of cognitive science. In D. M. Johnson & C. E. Erneling (Eds.), *The future of the cognitive revolution* (pp. 75–101). New York: Oxford University Press.

Pascual-Leone, J. (2000a). Reflections on working memory: Are the two models complementary? *Journal of Experimental Child Psychology, 77*, 138–154.

Pascual-Leone, J. (2000b). Mental attention, consciousness, and the progressive emergence of wisdom. *Journal of Adult Development, 7*, 241–254.

Pascual-Leone, J. (2006a, June). *Is working memory a product of mental/executive attention?* Paper presented to the 3rd European Working Memory Symposium, Genoa, Italy.

Pascual-Leone, J. (2006b). Mental attention, not language, may explain evolutionary growth of human intelligence. *Behavioral and Brain Sciences, 29*, 19–21.

Pascual-Leone, J., & Baillargeon, R. H. (1994). Developmental measures of mental attention. *International Journal of Behavioral Development, 17*, 161–200.

Pascual-Leone, J., & Bovet, M. C. (1966). L'apprentissage de la quantification de l'inclusion et la théorie opératoire [Inclusion quantification learning and operational theory]. *Acta Psychologica, 25*, 334–356.

Pascual-Leone, J., & Goodman, D. (1979). Intelligence and experience: A neo-Piagetian approach. *Instructional Science, 8*, 301–367.

Pascual-Leone, J., Goodman, D., Ammon, P., & Subelman, I. (1978). Piagetian theory and neo-Piagetian analysis as psychological guides in education. In J. Gallagher & J. A. Easley (Eds.), *Knowledge and development* (pp. 243–289). New York: Plenum.

Pascual-Leone, J., & Ijaz, H. (1989). Mental capacity testing as a form of intellectual-developmental assessment. In R. Samuda, S. Kong, J. Cummins, J. Pascual-Leone, & J. Lewis (Eds.), *Assessment and placement of minority students* (pp. 143–171). Toronto: Hogrefe.

Pascual-Leone, J., & Irwin, R. R. (1994). Noncognitive factors in high-road/low-road learning: The will, the self, and modes of instruction in adulthood. *Journal of Adult Development, 1*, 153–168.

Pascual-Leone, J., & Irwin, R. R. (1998). Abstraction, the will, the self, and modes of learning In adulthood. In M. C. Smith & T. Pourchot (Eds.), *Adult learning and development: Perspectives from educational psychology* (pp. 35–66). Mahwah, NJ: Lawrence Erlbaum Associates.

Pascual-Leone, J., & Johnson, J. (1991). The psychological unit and its role in task analysis: A re-interpretation of object permanence. In M. Chandler & M. Chapman (Eds.), *Criteria for competence: Controversies in the assessment of children's abilities* (pp. 153–187). Hillsdale, NJ: Lawrence Erlbaum Associates.

Pascual-Leone, J., & Johnson, J. (1999). A dialectical constructivist view of representation: Role of mental attention, executives, and symbols. In I. E. Sigel (Ed.), *Development of mental representation: Theories and applications* (pp. 169–200). Mahwah, NJ: Lawrence Erlbaum Associates.

Pascual-Leone, J., & Johnson, J. (2005). A dialectical constructivist view of developmental intelligence. In O. Wilhelm & R. Engle (Eds.), *Handbook of understanding and measuring intelligence* (pp. 177–201). Thousand Oaks, CA: Sage.

Pascual-Leone, J., & Johnson, J. (in preparation). *Organismic processes in cognitive development: A dialectical constructivist essay.* Unpublished manuscript.

Pascual-Leone, J., Johnson, J., Goodman, D., Hameluck, D., & Theodor, L. H. (1981). *Interruption effects in backward pattern masking: The neglected role of fixation stimuli.* Proceedings of the Third Annual Conference of the Cognitive Science Society, Berkeley.

Pascual-Leone, J., Johnson, J., Hameluck, D., Skakich, S., & Jedrzkiewicz, J. (1987). *A fixation centration effect in central backward masking and its implications for theories of attention.* Unpublished manuscript.

Pascual-Leone, J., Johnson, J., Verrilli, E., & Calvo, A. (2005, April). *In search of latent giftedness: Do M-capacity measures detect it?* Paper presented to the meeting of the Society for Research In Child Development, Atlanta.

Pascual-Leone, J., & Morra, S. (1991). Horizontality of water level: A neo-Piagetian developmental review. In H. W. Reese (Ed.), *Advances in child development and behaviour* (pp. 231–276). Orlando, FL: Academic Press.

Pascual-Leone, J., Romero, E. M., Johnson, J., & Morra, S. (2006, June). *Mathematical modeling of free recall in the mental attention memory task.* Paper presented to the International Meeting of the Psychometric Society, Montreal.

Pascual-Leone, J., & Smith, J. (1969). The encoding and decoding of symbols by children: A new experimental paradigm and a neo-Piagetian model. *Journal of Experimental Child Psychology, 8*, 328–355.

Pascual-Leone, J., & Sparkman, E. (1980). The dialectics of empiricism and rationalism: A last methodological reply to Trabasso. *Journal of Experimental Child Psychology, 29*, 88–101.

Pasupathi, M., & Staudinger, U. M. (2001). Do advanced moral reasoners also show wisdom? Linking moral reasoning and wisdom-related knowledge and judgment. *International Journal of Behavioral Development, 25*, 401–415.

Paterson, S. J., Brown, J. H., Gsödl, M. K., Johnson, M. H., & Karmiloff-Smith, A. (1999). Cognitive modularity and genetic disorders. *Science, 286,* 2355–2358.

Pauen, S., & Wilkening, F. (1997). Children's analogical reasoning about natural phenomena. *Journal of Experimental Child Psychology, 67*(1), 90–113.

Pears, R., & Bryant, P. (1990). Transitive inferences by young children about spatial position. *British Journal of Psychology, 81,* 511–525.

Peluffo, N. (1967). Culture and cognitive problems. *International Journal of Psychology, 2,* 187–198.

Pennings A. H. (1991). Altering strategies in the embedded-figures and water-level tasks through instruction: A neo-Piagetian learning study. *Perceptual and Motor Skills, 72,* 639-660.

Pennings A. H., & Hessels M. G. P. (1996). The measurement of mental attentional capacity: A neo-Piagetian developmental study. *Intelligence, 23,* 59-78.

Perry, M., Church, R. B., & Goldin-Meadow, S. (1988). Transitional knowledge in the acquisition of concepts. *Cognitive Development, 3*(4), 359–400.

Perry, M., & Lewis, J. L. (1999). Verbal imprecision as an index of knowledge in transition. *Developmental Psychology, 35*(3), 749–759.

Peterson, C., Grant, V. V., & Boland, L. D. (2005). Childhood amnesia in children and adolescents: Their earliest memories. *Memory, 13,* 622–637.

Piaget, J. (1923). *Le langage et la pensée chez l'enfant* [The language and thought of the child]. Neuchâtel: Delachaux et Niestlé.

Piaget, J. (1952). La logistique axiomatique ou 'pure', la logistique opératoire ou psychologique et les réalités auxquelles elles correspondent [Axiomatic or 'pure' logic, operational or psychological logic and the reality to which they correspond]. *Methodos, 4,* 72-84.

Piaget, J. (1952). *The origins of intelligence in children.* (M. Cook, Trans.). New York: International Universities Press. (Original work published 1936)

Piaget, J. (1954). Le langage et la pensée du point de vue génétique [Language and thinking from a genetic point of view]. *Acta Psychologica, 10,* 51–60.

Piaget, J. (1957). *Logic and psychology.* (W. Mays & F. Whitehead, Trans.). New York: Basic Books. (Original lectures 1952)

Piaget, J. (1959). *The construction of reality in the child.* (M. Cook, Trans.). New York: Basic Books. (Original work published 1937)

Piaget, J. (1962). *Play, dreams and imitation in childhood.* (C. Gattegno & F. Hodgson, Trans.). London: Routledge & Kegan Paul. (Original work published 1945)

Piaget, J. (1964). Problèmes de psychologie gènètique [Problems of genetic psychology]. In J. Piaget (Ed.), *Six ètudes de psychologie.* Geneva, CH: Gonthier.

Piaget, J. (1965). *Judgement and reasoning in the child.* (M. Warden, Trans.). London: Routledge & Kegan Paul. (Original work published 1924) Piaget, J. (1967). *Biologie et connaissance* [Biology and knowledge]. Paris: Gallimard.

Piaget, J. (1967). Genesis and structure in the psychology of intelligence. In J. Piaget (Ed.), *Six psychological studies* (pp. 143-158). (A. Tenzer & D. Elkind, Trans.). New York: Random House. (Original work published 1964)

Piaget, J. (1968). *Le structuralisme* [Structuralism]. Paris: Puf.

Piaget, J. (1970a). Piaget's theory. In P. H. Mussen (Ed.), *Carmichael's manual of child psychology* (pp. 703–732). New York: Wiley.

Piaget, J. (1970b). *Genetic epistemology.* New York: Columbia University Press.

Piaget, J. (1972). *Essai de logique opératoire* [An essay on operational logic]. Paris: Dunod.

Piaget, J. (1974). *La prise de conscience* [The grasp of consciousness]. Paris: Puf.

Piaget, J. (1977). Essai sur la necessité [An essay on necessity]. *Archives de Psychologie, 45,* 235–251.

Piaget, J. (1978). *Success and understanding.* (A. Pomerans, Trans.). Cambridge, MA: Harvard University. (Original work published 1974)

Piaget, J. (1980). The constructivist approach: Recent studies in genetic epistemology. *Cahiers de la Fondation Archives Jean Piaget, 1,* 3–7.

Piaget, J. (1985). *The equilibration of cognitive structures: The central problem of intellectual development*. (T. Brown & K. Thampy, Trans.). Chicago: University of Chicago. (Original work published 1975)

Piaget, J., & Garcia, R. (1991). *Towards a logic of meanings*. Hillsdale, NJ: Lawrence Erlbaum Associates. (Original work published 1987)

Piaget, J., Grize, J. B., Szeminska, A., & Vinh Bang, D. (1977). *Epistemology and psychology of functions*. (F. Castellanos & V. Anderson, Trans.). Dordrecht, Holland: D. Reidel . (Original work published 1968)

Piaget, J., & Inhelder, B. (1959). *La genèse des structures logiques élémentaires* [The early growth of logic in the child]. Neuchâtel: Delachaux et Niestlé.

Piaget, J., & Inhelder, B. (1963). Les opérations intellectuelles et leur développement [Intellectual operations and their development]. In P. Fraisse & J. Piaget (Eds.), *Traité de psychologie expérimentale, Vol. VII, L'intelligence* (pp. 109–155). Paris: Puf.

Piaget, J., & Inhelder, B. (1966). *L'image mentale chez l'enfant* [Mental imagery in the child]. Paris: Puf.

Piaget, J., & Inhelder, B. (1967). *The child's conception of space*. (F. Langdon & J. Lunzer, Trans.). London: Routledge &Kegan Paul. (Original work published 1947)

Piaget, J., & Inhelder, B. (1974). *The child's construction of quantities: Conservation and atomism*. (A. Pomerans, Trans.). London: Routledge and Kegan Paul. (Original work published 1941)

Piaget, J., & Inhelder, B. (1975). *The origin of the idea of chance in children*. (L. Leake, Jr., P. Burrell, & H. Fishbein, Trans.). New York: Norton. (Original work published 1951)

Piaget, J., Inhelder, B., & Szeminska, A. (1948). *La géometrie spontanée chez l'enfant* [The child's conception of geometry]. Paris: Puf.

Piaget, J., Montangero, J., & Billeter, J. (1977). La formation des correlates [The formation of correlations]. In J. Piaget (Ed.), *Recherches sur l'abstraction reflechissante I* (pp. 115-129). Paris: Presses Universitaires de France. Piaget, J., & Szeminska, A. (1952). *The child's conception of number*. (C. Gattegno & F. Hodgson, Trans.) London: Routledge & Kegan Paul. (Original work published 1941)

Pinker, S. (1994). *The language instinct*. New York: William Morrow & Co.

Pons, F., de Rosnay, M., & Philipona, M. T. (2005, August). *Lag between theory of mind and emotion understanding in young children: Impact of language and working memory*. Paper presented to the 12th European Conference on Developmental Psychology, Tenerife.

Porath, M. (1992). Stage and structure in the development of children with various types of "giftedness." In R. Case (Ed.), *The mind's staircase: Exploring the conceptual underpinnings of children's thought and knowledge* (pp. 303–317). Hillsdale, NJ: Lawrence Erlbaum Associates.

Porath, M. (2003). Social understanding in the first years of school. *Early Childhood Research Quarterly, 18*, 468–484.

Pulos, S. (1997). Divergent validity and the measurement of processing capacity. *International Journal of Behavioral Development, 20*, 731–734.

Rabinowitz, F. M., Howe, M. L., & Lawrence, J. A. (1989). Class inclusion and working memory. *Journal of Experimental Child Psychology, 48*(3), 379–409.

Ransdell, S., & Hecht, S. (2003). Time and resource limits on working memory: Cross-age consistency In counting span performance. *Journal of Experimental Child Psychology, 86*, 303–313.

Rattermann, M. J., & Gentner, D. (1998). More evidence for a relational shift in the development of analogy: Children's performance on a causal-mapping task. *Cognitive Development, 13*(4), 453–478.

Reese, H. W. (1993). Developments in child psychology from the 1960s to the 1990s. *Developmental Psychology, 13*, 503–524.

Richards, I. A. (1936). *The philosophy of rhetoric*. Oxford, UK: Oxford University Press.

Rieben, L., & de Ribaupierre, A. (1988, August). *Developmental change and individual differences: A structural approach*. Paper presented to the 3rd European Conference on Developmental Psychology, Budapest.

Rieben, L., de Ribaupierre, A., & Lautrey, J. (1986). Une définition structuraliste des formes du développement cognitif: Un projet chimérique? [A structuralist definition of the different forms of cognitive development: A dream?]. *Archives de Psychologie, 54*, 95–123.

Rieben, L., de Ribaupierre, A., & Lautrey, J. (1990). Structural invariants and individual modes of processing: On the necessity of a minimally structuralist approach of development for education. *Archives de Psychologie, 58*, 29–53.

Riegel, K. F. (1979). *Foundations of dialectical psychology.* New York: Academic Press.

Rittle-Johnson, B., & Siegler, R. S. (1999). Learning to spell: Variability, choice, and change in children's strategy use. *Child Development, 70*(2), 332–348.

Rogers, T. T., Rakison, D. H., & McClelland, J. L. (2004). U-shaped curves in development: A PDP approach. *Journal of Cognition and Development, 5*(1), 137–145.

Ross, G. S. (1980). Categorization in 1- to 2-years-old. *Developmental Psychology, 16*, 391–396.

Ross, P., & Segalowitz, S. J. (2000). An EEG coherence test of the frontal dorsal versus ventral hypothesis In N-back working memory. *Brain and Cognition, 43*, 375–379.

Ross-Sheehy, S., Oakes, L. M., & Luck, S. J. (2003). The development of visual short-term memory capacity in infants. *Child Development, 74*, 1807–1822.

Roth, D., Slone, M., & Dar, R. (2000). Which way cognitive development? An evaluation of the Piagetian and the domain-specific research programs. *Theory & Psychology, 10*, 353–373.

Ruchkin, D. S., Grafman, J., Cameron, K., & Berndt, R. S. (2003). Working memory retention systems: A state of activated long-term memory. *Behavioral and Brain Sciences, 26*, 709–728.

Ruhland, R., & van Geert, P. (1998). Jumping into syntax: Transitions in the development of closed class words. *British Journal of Developmental Psychology, 16*(1), 65–95.

Rumelhart, D. E., & Norman, D. A. (1981). Analogical processes in learning. In J. R. Anderson (Ed.), *Cognitive skills and their acquisition* (pp. 335–359). Hillsdale, NJ: Lawrence Erlbaum Associates.

Rumelhart, D. E., & Ortony, A. (1977). The representation of knowledge in memory. In R. C. Anderson, R. J. Spiro, & W. E. Montague (Eds.), *Schoolgoing and the acquisition of knowledge* (pp. 99–136). Hillsdale, NJ: Lawrence Erlbaum Associates.

Russell, J. (1999). Cognitive development as an executive process—in part: A homeopathic dose of Piaget. *Developmental Science, 2*, 247–270.

Russell, J., Mauthner, N., & Tidswell, T. (1991). The "windows task" as a measure of strategic deception In preschoolers and in autistic subjects. *British Journal of Developmental Psychology, 9*, 331–349.

Russell, S. J. (1990). Athlete's knowledge in task perception: definition and classification. *International Journal of Sport Psychology, 21*, 85–101.

Salthouse, T. A. (1996). The processing-speed theory of adult age differences in cognition. *Psychological Review, 103*, 403–428.

Saxe, R., Tzelnic, T., & Carey, S. (2006). Five-month-old infants know humans are solid, like inanimate objects. *Cognition, 101*, B1–B8.

Scardamalia, M. (1977). Information-processing capacity and the problem of horizontal décalage: A demonstration using combinatorial reasoning tasks. *Child Development, 48*, 28–37.

Scerif, G., & Karmiloff-Smith, A. (2005). The dawn of cognitive genetics? Crucial developmental caveats. *Trends in Cognitive Science, 9*, 126–135.

Schank, R. C., & Abelson, R. P. (1977). *Scripts, plans, goals, and understanding.* Hillsdale, NJ: Lawrence Erlbaum Associates.

Scherer, K. R. (2000). Emotions as episodes of subsystem synchronization driven by nonlinear appraisal processes. In M. D. Lewis & I. Granic (Eds.), *Emotion, development, and self-organisation* (pp. 70–99). Cambridge, UK: Cambridge University Press.

Schilling, T. H. (2000). Infants' looking at possible and impossible screen rotations: The role of familiarization. *Infancy, 1*, 389–402.

Schlagmüller, M., & Schneider, W. (2002). The development of organizational strategies in children: Evidence from a microgenetic longitudinal study. *Journal of Experimental Child Psychology, 81*(3), 298–319.

Schofield, N. J., & Ashman, A. F. (1986). The relationship between digit span and cognitive processing across ability groups. *Intelligence, 10*, 59–73.

Schonfield, D., & Wenger, L. (1975). Age limitation of perceptual span. *Nature, 253*, 377–378.

Schumann-Hengsteler, R. (1992). The development of visuo-spatial memory: How to remember location. *International Journal of Behavioral Development, 15*, 455–471.

Schwartz, M., & Fischer, K. W. (2004). Building general knowledge and skill: Cognition and microdevelopment in science learning. In A. Demetriou & A. Raftopoulos (Eds.), *Cognitive developmental change: Theories, models, and measurement* (pp. 157–184). Cambridge, UK: Cambridge University Press.

Service, E. (1998). The effect of word-length on immediate serial recall depends on phonological complexity, not articulatory duration. *Quarterly Journal of Experimental Psychology, 51a*, 283–304.

Shafrir, U., & Pascual-Leone, J. (1990). Postfailure reflectivity-impulsivity and spontaneous attention to errors. *Journal of Educational Psychology, 82*, 378–387.

Shallice, T. (1988). *From neuropsychology to mental structure.* Cambridge, UK: Cambridge University Press.

Shallice, T., & Burgess, P. (1993). Supervisory control of action andthought selection. In A. Baddeley & L. Weiskrantz (Eds.), *Attention: Selection, awareness, and control. A tribute to Donald Broadbent* (pp. 171–187). Oxford, UK: Clarendon.

Shayer, M. (2003). Not just Piaget, not just Vygotsky, and certainly not Vygotsky as alternative to Piaget. *Learning and Instruction, 13*, 465–485.

Shayer, M., Demetriou, A., & Pervez, M. (1988). The structure and scaling of concrete operational thought: Three studies in four countries. *Genetic, Social, and General Psychology Monographs ,114*(3), 307–375.

Sheppard, J. L. (1978). A structural analysis of concrete operations. In J. Keats, K. Collis, & G. Halford (Eds.). *Cognitive Development: Research based on a neo-Piagetian approach* (pp. 47–85). London: Wiley.

Shrager, J., & Siegler, R. S. (1998). SCADS: A model of children's strategy choices and strategy discoveries. *Psychological Science, 9*(5), 405–410.

Shutts, K., & Spelke, E. S. (2004). Straddling the perception–conception boundary. *Developmental Science, 7*, 507–511.

Siegler, R. S. (1976). Three aspects of cognitive development. *Cognitive Psychology, 8*, 481–520.

Siegler, R. S. (1978). The origins of scientific reasoning. In R. S. Siegler (Ed.), *Children's thinking: What develops?* (pp. 109–149). Hillsdale, NJ: Lawrence Erlbaum Associates.

Siegler, R. S. (1981). Developmental sequences within and between concepts. *Monographs of the Society for Research in Child Development, 46*(2), 84.

Siegler, R. S. (1987a). The perils of averaging data over strategies: An example from children's addition. *Journal of Experimental Psychology: General, 116*(3), 250–264.

Siegler, R. S. (1987b). Some general conclusions about children's strategy choice procedures. *International Journal of Psychology, 22*, 729–749.

Siegler, R. S. (1994). Cognitive variability: A key to understanding cognitive development. *Current Directions in Psychological Science, 3*, 1–5.

Siegler, R. S. (1995). Children's thinking: How does change occur? In F. E. Weinert &W. Schneider (Eds.), *Memory performance and competencies: Issues in growth and development* (pp. 405–430). Hillsdale, NJ: Lawrence Erlbaum Associates.

Siegler, R. S. (1996a). A grand theory of development. *Monographs of the Society for Research in Child Development, 61*(1-2), 266–275.

Siegler, R. S. (1996b). *Emerging minds: The process of change in children's thinking.* New York: Oxford University Press.

Siegler, R. S. (2002). Microgenetic studies of self-explanation. In N. Granott & J. Parziale (Eds.), *Microdevelopment: Transition processes in development and learning* (pp. 31–58). New York: Cambridge University Press.

Siegler, R. S. (2004). U-shaped interest in U-shaped development—and what it means. *Journal of Cognition and Development, 5*(1), 1–10.

Siegler, R. S. (2006). Microgenetic analyses of learning. In D. Kuhn & R. S. Siegler (Eds.), *Handbook of child psychology: Volume 2: Cognition, perception, and language* (6th ed., pp. 464–510). Hoboken, NJ: Wiley.

Siegler, R. S., & Chen, Z. (1998). Developmental differences in rule learning: A microgenetic analysis. *Cognitive Psychology, 36*(3), 273–310.

Siegler, R. S., & Chen, Z. (2002). Development of rules and strategies: Balancing the old and the new. *Journal of Experimental Child Psychology, 81*(4), 446–457.

Siegler, R. S., & Crowley, K. (1991). The microgenetic method. A direct means for studying cognitive development. *American Psychologist, 46,* 606–620.

Siegler, R. S., & Jenkins, E. (1989). *How children discover new strategies*. Hillsdale, NJ: Lawrence Erlbaum Associates.

Siegler, R. S., & Klahr, D. (1982). When do children learn? The relationship between existing knowledge and the acquisition of new knowledge. In R. Glaser (Ed.), *Advances in instructional psychology* (pp. 121–211). Hillsdale, NJ: Lawrence Erlbaum Associates.

Siegler, R. S., & Liebert, R. M. (1975). Acquisition of formal scientific reasoning by 10- and 13-years old: Designing a factorial experiment. *Developmental Psychology, 11,* 401–402.

Siegler, R. S., & Munakata, Y. (1993). Beyond the immaculate transition: Advances in the understanding of change. *SRCD Newsletter (Winter),* pp. 3, 10–11, 13.

Siegler, R. S., & Opfer, J. E. (2003). The development of numerical estimation: Evidence for multiple representations of numerical quantity. *Psychological Science, 14*(3), 237–243.

Siegler, R. S., & Stern, E. (1998). Conscious and unconscious strategy discoveries: A microgenetic analysis. *Journal of Experimental Psychology: General, 127*(4), 377–397.

Siegler, R. S., & Svetina, M. (2002). A microgenetic/cross-sectional study of matrix completion: Comparing short-term and long-term change. *Child Development, 73*(3), 793–809.

Simion, F., Macchi Cassia, V., Turati, C., & Valenza, E. (2001). The origins of face perception: Specific vs. non-specific mechanisms. *Infant and Child Development, 10,* 59–65.

Simon, H. A. (1979). The functional equivalence of problem-solving skills. In H. A. Simon (Ed.), *Model of thought* (pp. 230–244). New Haven, CT: Yale University Press.

Simon, H. A., & Hayes, J. R. (1979). Psychological differences among problem isomorphs. In H. A. Simon (Ed.), *Model of thought* (pp. 498–512). New Haven, CT: Yale University Press.

Simone, P. M., & McCormick, E. B. (1999). Effect of a defining feature on negative priming across the life span. *Visual Cognition, 6,* 587–606.

Sinclair, H. (1967). *Acquisition du langage et développement de la pensée.* [Language acquisition and the development of thought]. Paris: Dunod.

Sinclair, H. (1978). Note on Piaget and dialectics. *Human Development, 21,* 211–213.

Singer-Freeman, K. E. (2005). Analogical reasoning in 2-year-olds: The development of access and relational inference. *Cognitive Development, 20*(2), 214–234.

Slater, A. (2002). Visual perception in the newborn infant: Issues and debates. *Intellectica, 34,* 57–76.

Smith, C., Carey, S., & Wiser, M. (1985). On differentiation: A case study of the development of the concepts of size, weight, and density. *Cognition, 21,* 177–237.

Smith, L. (1993). Concluding assessment. In L. Smith (Ed.), *Jean Piaget: Critical assessments* (pp. 435–467). London: Routledge.

Smith, L. (1996). The social construction of rational understanding. In A. Tryphon & J. Voneche (Eds.), *Piaget–Vygotsky: The social genesis of thought* (pp. 107–122). Hove, UK: Psychology Press.

Smith, L. B., & Thelen, E. (1993). *A dynamic systems approach to development: Applications.* Cambridge, MA: The MIT Press.

Smyth, M. M., & Pendleton, L. R. (1990). Space and movement in working memory. *Quarterly Journal of Experimental Psychology, 42a*, 291–304.

Somsen, R. J. M., van't Klooster, B. J., van der Molen, M. W., van Leeuwen, H. M. P., & Licht, R. (1997). Growth spurts in brain maturation during middle childhood as indexed by EEG power spectra. *Biological Psychology, 44*, 187–209.

Southgate, V., Gomez, J. C., & Meints, K. (2005, August). *The gravity bias: A looking-reaching dissociation in two-year-olds.* Paper presented to the 12th European Conference on Developmental Psychology, Tenerife.

Spelke, E. S. (1991). Physical knowledge in infancy: Reflections on Piaget's theory. In S. Carey & R. Gelman (Eds.), *The epigenesis of mind: Essay on biology and cognition* (pp. 133–169). Hillsdale, NJ: Lawrence Erlbaum Associates.

Spelke, E. S. (1994). Initial knowledge: Six suggestions. *Cognition, 50*, 431–445.

Spelke, E. S. (1998). Nativism, empiricism, and the origins of knowledge. *Behavior & Development, 21*, 181–200.

Spelke, E. S., Breinlinger, K., Macomber, J., & Jacobson, K. (1992). Origins of knowledge. *Psychological Review, 99*, 605–632.

Spensley, F., & Taylor, J. (1999). The development of cognitive flexibility: Evidence from children's drawings. *Human Development, 42*, 300–324.

Spitz, H. H., Minsky, S. K., & Bessellieu, C. L. (1985). Influence of planning time and first-move strategy on tower of Hanoi problem-solving performance of mentally retarded young adults and nonretarded children. *American Journal of Mental Deficiency, 90*(1), 46–56.

Sroufe, L. A. (1995). *Emotional development.* Cambridge, UK: Cambridge University Press.

Starkes, J. L., Caicco, M., Boutilier, C., & Sevsek, B. (1990). Motor recall of experts for structured and unstructured sequences in modern dance. *Journal of Sport and Exercise Psychology, 12*, 317–321.

Starkey, P., & Cooper, R. G. (1980). Perception of numbers by human infants. *Science, 210*, 1033–1035.

Stauder, J. E. A., Molenaar, P. C. M., & van der Molen, M. W. (1999). Brain activity and cognitive transition during childhood: A longitudinal event-related brain potential study. *Child Neuropsychology, 5*, 41–59.

Sternberg, R. J. (1985). *Beyond IQ: A triarchic theory of intelligence.* New York: Cambridge University Press.

Sternberg, R. (1987). A day at Developmental Downs: Sportscast for race #2—Neo-Piagetian theories of cognitive development. *International Journal of Psychology, 22*, 507–529.

Stewart, L., & Pascual-Leone, J. (1992). Mental capacity constraints and the development of moral reasoning. *Journal of Experimental Child Psychology, 54*, 251–287.

Stigler, J., & Hiebert, J. (1999). *The teaching gap.* New York: The Free Press.

Stiles, J., Moses, P., Passarotti, A., & Dick, F. K. (2003). Exploring developmental change in the neural bases of higher cognitive functions: The promise of functional magnetic resonance imaging. *Developmental Neuropsychology, 24*, 641–668.

Strauss, S. (Ed.). (1982). *U-shaped behavioral growth.* New York: Academic Press.

Strauss, S., Stavy, R., & Opraz, N. (1979). Implications of developmental psychology for education. *Israeli Journal of Psychology & Counseling in Education, 11*, 5–23.

Stroop, J. R. (1935). Studies of interference in serial verbal reactions. *Journal of Experimental Psychology, 18*, 643–661.

Stuss, D. T. (1992). Biological and psychological development of executive functions. *Brain and Cognition, 20*, 8–23.

Swanson, H. L. (1994). Short-term memory and working memory: Do both contribute to our understanding of academic achievement in children and adults with learning disabilities? *Journal of Learning Disabilities, 27*, 34–50.

Tallir, I. B., Musch, E., Valcke, M., & Lenoir, M. (2005). Effects of two instructional approaches for basketball on decision-making and recognition ability. *International Journal of Sport Psychology, 36*, 107–126.

Thatcher, R. W. (1992). Cyclical cortical reorganization during early childhood. *Brain and Cognition, 20*, 24–50.

Thatcher, R. W. (1994a). Cyclic cortical reorganization: Origins of human cognitive development. In G. Dawson & K. W. Fischer (Eds.), *Human behavior and the developing brain* (pp. 232–266). New York: Guilford.

Thatcher, R. W. (1994b). Psychopathology of early frontal lobe damage: Dependence on cycles of development. *Developmental Psychopathology, 6*, 565–596.

Thatcher, R. W. (1996). Neuroimaging of cyclic cortical reorganization during human development. In R. W. Thatcher, G. R. Lyon, J. Rumsey, & N. Krasnegor (Eds.), *Developmental neuroimaging: Mapping the development of brain and behavior* (pp. 91–106). San Diego: Academic Press.

Thatcher, R. W. (1997). Human frontal lobe development: A theory of cyclical cortical reorganization. In N. A. Krasnegor, G. R. Lyon, & P. S. Goldman-Rakic (Eds.), *Development of the prefrontal cortex* (pp. 85–113). Baltimore: Paul H. Brookes.

Thatcher, R. W., Walker, R. A., & Giudice, S. (1987). Human cerebral hemispheres develop at different rates andages. *Science, 236*, 1110–1113.

Thelen, E., & Corbetta, D. (2002). Microdevelopment and dynamic systems: Applications to infant motor development. In N. Granott & J. Parziale (Eds.), *Microdevelopment: Transition processes in development and learning* (pp. 59–79). New York: Cambridge University Press.

Thelen, E., & Smith, L. B. (1998). Dynamic systems theories. In R. Lerner (Ed.), *Handbook of child psychology, Vol. 1: Theoretical models of human development* (5th ed.; pp. 563–634). Hoboken, NJ: Wiley.

Thomas, M., & Karmiloff-Smith, A. (2002). Are developmental disorders like cases of adult brain damage? Implications from connectionist modeling. *Behavioral and Brain Sciences, 25*, 727–750.

Thomas, M., & Karmiloff-Smith, A. (2003). Modeling language acquisition in atypical phenotypes. *Psychological Review, 110*, 647–682.

Thomas, M., & Karmiloff-Smith, A. (2005). Can developmental disorders reveal the component parts of the human language faculty? *Language Learning and Development, 1*, 65–92.

Thornton, S. (1999). Creating the conditions for cognitive change: The interaction between task structures and specific strategies. *Child Development, 70*(3), 588–603.

Tipper, S. P. (2001). Does negative priming reflect inhibitory mechanisms? A review and integration of conflicting views. *Quarterly Journal of Experimental Psychology, 54*, 321–343.

Tipper, S. P., Bourque, T. A., Anderson, S. H., & Brehaut, J. C. (1989). Mechanisms of attention: A developmental study. *Journal of Experimental Child Psychology, 48*, 353–378.

Todor, J. I. (1975). Age differences in integration of components of a motor task. *Perceptual and Motor Skills, 41*, 211–215.

Todor, J. I. (1977). Cognitive development, cognitive style, and motor ability. *Proceedings of the 9th Canadian Psycho-Motor Learning and Sports Symposium*, 26–28.

Todor, J. I. (1979). Developmental differences in motor task integration: A test of Pascual-Leone's theory of constructive operators. *Journal of Experimental Child Psychology, 28*, 314–322.

Tombu, M., & Jolicoeur, P. (2005). Testing the predictions of the central capacity sharing model. *Journal of Experimental Psychology: Human Perception and Performance, 31*, 790–802.

Toussaint, N. A. (1974). An analysis of synchrony between concrete-operational tasks in terms of structural and performance demands. *Child Development, 45*, 992–1001.

Toussaint, N. A. (1976).Mental processing capacity, anticipatory and retroactive abilities and development of concrete-operational structures. *Canadian Journal of Behavioral Science, 8*, 363–374.

Towse, J. N., Hitch, G. J., & Hutton, U. (1998). A reevaluation of working memory capacity in children. *Journal of Memory and Language, 39*, 195–217.

Trabasso, T. (1978). On the estimation of parameters and the evaluation of mathematical models: A reply to Pascual-Leone. *Journal of Experimental Child Psychology, 26*, 41–45.

Trabasso, T., & Foellinger, D. B. (1978). Information processing capacity in children: A test of Pascual-Leone's model. *Journal of Experimental Child Psychology, 26*, 1–17.

Tunteler, E., & Resing, W. C. M. (2002). Spontaneous analogical transfer in 4-year-olds: A microgenetic study. *Journal of Experimental Child Psychology, 83*(3), 149–166.

Turati, C., Macchi Cassia, V., Simion, F., & Leo, I. (2006). Newborns' face recognition: Role of inner and outer facial features. *Child Development, 77*, 297–311.

van der Maas, H. L., & Jansen, B. R. (2003). What response times tell of children's behavior on the balance scale task. *Journal of Experimental Child Psychology, 85*(2), 141–177.

van der Maas, H. L., & Molenaar, P. C. (1992). Stagewise cognitive development: An application of catastrophe theory. *Psychological Review, 99*(3), 395–417.

van Geert, P. (1994). Vygotskian dynamics of development. *Human Development, 37*(6), 346–365.

van Geert, P. (1998). A dynamic systems model of basic developmental mechanisms: Piaget, Vygotsky, and beyond . *Psychological Review, 105*(4), 634–677.

van Geert, P. (2002). Developmental dynamics, intentional action, and fuzzy sets. In N. Granott &J. Parziale (Eds.), *Microdevelopment: Transition processes in development and learning* (pp. 319–343). New York: Cambridge University Press.

van Geert, P., & van Dijk, M. (2002). Focus on variability: New tools to study intra-individual variability In developmental data. *Infant Behavior & Development. Special Issue: Variability in Infancy, 25*(4), 340–374.

van Maanen, L., Been, P., & Sijstma, K. (1989). The linear logistic test model and heterogeneity of cognitive strategies. In E. Roskam (Ed.), *Mathematical psychology in progress* (pp. 267–288). Berlin: Springer-Verlag.

van Sommers, P. (1984). *Drawing and cognition*. Cambridge, UK: Cambridge University Press.

Vosniadou, S. (1987). Children and metaphors. *Child Development, 58*, 870–885.

Voss, J., Greene, T. R., Post, T. A., & Perner, B. C. (1983). Problem solving skill in the social sciences. In G. H. Bower (Ed.), *The psychology of learning and motivation: Advances in research and theory* (Vol. 17; pp. 165–213). New York: Academic Press.

Voyat, G. (1980). Piaget on schizophrenia. *Journal of the American Academy of Psychoanalysis & Dynamic Psychiatry, 8*(1), 93–113.

Vygotsky, L. S. (1962). *Thought and language*. (E. Hanfmann & G. Vakar, Trans.). Cambridge, MA: MIT Press. (Original work published 1934)

Walker, P., Hitch, G. J., Doyle, A., & Porter, T. (1994). The development of short-term visual memory In young children. *International Journal of Behavioral Development, 17*, 73–89.

Wason, P. C. (1968). Reasoning about a rule. *Quarterly Journal of Experimental Psychology, 20*, 273–281.

Watson, M. W., & Fischer, K. W. (1980). Development of social roles in elicited and spontaneous behavior during the preschool years. *Developmental Psychology, 16*(5), 483–494.

Wellman, H. M. (1983). Metamemory revisited. In M. Chi (Ed.), *Trends in memory development research* (Vol. 9; pp. 31–51). Basel: S. Karger.

Wellman, H. M. (1990). *The child's theory of mind*. Cambridge, MA: MIT Press.

Wellman, H. M., Cross, D., &Watson, J. (2001).Meta-analysis of theory-of-mind development: The truth about false belief. *Child Development, 72*(3), 655–684.

Welsh, M. C., Pennington, B. F., & Groisser, D. B. (1991). A normative-developmental study of executive function: A window on prefrontal function in children. *Developmental Neuropsychology, 7*(2), 131–149.

Werner, H. (1948). *Comparative psychology of mental development*. Oxford, UK: Follett.

Wertheimer, M. (1945). *Productive thinking*. New York: Harper & Row.

Wetherick, N. E. (1978). In defense of circularity. *The Behavioral and Brain Sciences, 2*, 205.

White, S. H., & Pillemer, D. B. (1979). Childhood amnesia and the development of a socially accessible memory system. In J. F. Kihlstrom & F. J. Evans (Eds.), *Functional disorders of memory* (pp. 29–73). Hillsdale, NJ: Lawrence Erlbaum Associates.

Wilkinson, A. (1976). Counting strategies and semantic analysis as applied to class inclusion. *Cognitive Psychology, 8*, 64–85.

Willats, J. (1987). Marr and pictures: An information-processing account of children's drawings. *Archives De Psychologie, 55*, 105–125.

Williams, A. M., Ward, P., Knowles, J. M., & Smeeton, N. J. (2002). Anticipation skill in a real-world task: Measurement, training, and transfer in tennis. *Journal of Experimental Psychology: Applied, 8*, 259–270.

Winer, G. A. (1980). Class-inclusion in children: A review of the empirical literature. *Child Development, 52*, 309–328.

Witkin, H. A. (1974). Social conformity and psychological differentiation. *International Journal of Psychology, 9*(1), 11–29.

Witkin, H. A., Dyk, R. B., Faterson, H. F., Goodenough, D. R., & Karp, S. A. (1974). *Psychological differentiation*. Hillsdale, NJ: Lawrence Erlbaum Associates.

Witkin, H. A., Goodenough, D. R., & Oltman, P. K. (1979). Psychological differentiation: Current status. *Journal of Personality and Social Psychology, 37*, 1127–1145.

Witkin, H. A., Lewis, H. B., Hertzmann, M., Machover, K., Meissner, P. B., & Wapner, S. (1954). *Personality through perception*. New York: Harper.

Wolfe, C. D., & Bell, M. A. (2004).Working memory and inhibitory control in early childhood: Contributions from physiology, temperament, and language. *Developmental Psychobiology, 44*, 68–83.

Wozniak, R. H. (1975). Dialecticism and structuralism: The philosophical foundation of Soviet psychology and Piagetian cognitive developmental theory. In K. F. Riegel & G. C. Rosenwald (Eds.), *Structure and transformation: Developmental and historical aspects* (pp. 25–49). New York: Wiley.

Wynn, K. (1992). Addition and subtraction by human infants. *Nature, 358*, 749–750.

Xu, F., Spelke, E. S., & Goddard, S. (2005). Number sense in human infants. *Developmental Science, 8*, 88–101.

Yan, Z., & Fischer, K. (2002). Always under construction: Dynamic variations in adult cognitive microdevelopment. *Human Development, 45*(3), 141–160.

Zelazo, P. D., Craik, F. I. M., & Booth, L. (2004). Executive function across the life span. *Acta Psychologica, 115*, 167–183.

Zelazo, P. D., & Müller, U. (2002). The balance beam in the balance: Reflections on rules, relational complexity, and developmental processes. *Journal of Experimental Child Psychology, 81*, 458–465.

Zelazo, P. D., Müller, U., Frye, D., & Marcovitch, S. (2003a). The development of executive function. *Monographs of the Society for Research in Child Development, 68*(3), 11–27.

Zelazo, P. D., Müller, U., Frye, D., & Marcovitch, S. (2003b). The development of executive function: Cognitive complexity and control—revised. *Monographs of the Society for Research in Child Development, 68*, 93–119.

Author Index

A

Abelson, R., 26
Ackermann-Valladao, E., 19
Agostino, A., 87
Alexander, P., 146, 299
Alibali, M., 125, 313, 329
Allard, F., 77
Allport, A., 5
Allport, D., 340
Alp, I., 53, 286, 338
Amann Gainotti, M., 9
Amin, T., 5
Ammon, P., 47, 48, 49, 56, 298, 302
Andersen, C., 329
Anderson, J., 25, 48, 133, 143, 341
Anderson, S., 83, 84
Andrews, G., 97, 98, 103, 106, 129, 131, 138,
    140, 141, 306, 364, 365, 370
Angi, A., 74, 75, 76
Anglin, J., 27, 28
Annaz, D., 247, 248
Antell, S., 347
Arakawa, T., 356
Artuso, M., 333
Ashburner, J., 357
Ashman, A., 286

Astington, J., 216
Atkinson, R., 53, 287, 339
Austin, G., 30
Ayoub, C., 154, 174, 176, 268, 269, 281, 335

B

Badan, M., 238, 239
Baddeley, A., 49, 100, 287, 340, 341, 345
Baillargeon, R. H., 60, 76, 226, 286, 332, 337
Baillargeon, R. L., 347
Bailleux, C., 226, 285, 288, 337, 343
Bain, J., 97, 99, 101
Baker, R., 97
Baltes, M., 278
Baltes, P., 278
Bang, V., 7, 159
Bangert, A., 327
Barrouillet, P., 207, 226, 288, 346
Barry, R., 355
Bartrip, J., 245
Bassok, M., 130, 135
Bates, E., 3, 37, 246, 247, 249
Been, P., 139
Beilin, H., 5, 21, 60
Bell, M., 164, 182, 355, 356, 358, 359
Bell, T., 73

Bellugi, U., 247
Benson, J., 29, 347, 348
Benson, N., 53
Bentley, A., 44, 45, 52, 53
Berch, D., 102, 337
Bereiter, C., 60, 73, 286
Bernardin, S., 207, 226, 346
Berndt, R, 341, 342, 353
Berthoud, I., 19
Berti, A., 245
Bessellieu, C., 124
Beveridge, M., 288
Bickhard, M., 19
Bidell, T., 9, 33, 36, 123, 138, 149, 150, 158,
    164, 165, 168, 175, 176, 177, 178, 180,
    181, 184, 188, 202, 226, 269, 270, 282,
    300, 306, 312,
313, 316, 322, 326, 328, 329, 349, 366
Billeter, J., 130
Billman, D., 126, 129, 133
Bjorklund, D., 204, 329
Black, J., 357
Bleiker, C., 217, 218, 219, 224, 226, 227, 294,
    331, 333
Blumberg, P., 122
Boag, C., 97, 138, 140, 141, 364, 365, 370
Boland, L., 264, 266
Bond, T., 21
Booth, L., 4, 334
Borella, E., 87
Bourque, T, 83, 84
Boutilier, C., 81
Bovet, M., 2, 57, 135
Bower, G., 25
Boyle, F., 97
Brace, N., 247, 248
Brainerd, C., 19, 105
Branco, A., 322, 329
Bransford, J., 32
Brehaut, J., 83, 84
Breinlinger, K., 347
Bronckart, J., 9
Brown, A., 31, 32, 144
Brown, C., 101
Brown, G., 19, 341
Brown, J., 248, 325
Bruce, D., 264
Bruchkowsky, M., 218, 273
Bruner, J., 27, 28, 30, 217, 226
Bryant, P., 97, 98, 183
Buchanan, M., 341, 345
Buck-Morss, S., 9

Bull, R., 288
Bullock, D., 155
Bunge, S., 354
Bunting, M., 4, 346
Burgess, P., 4
Burnett, N., 77
Burtis, P., 62, 343
Bushey, B., 200
Bushnell, I., 347
Buss, A., 9
Buxton, R., 355
Byrnes, M., 119

C

Caicco, M., 81
Caloni, B., 76
Calverley, R., 176
Calvo, A., 286
Camba, R., 87, 287
Cameron, K., 341, 342, 353
Camos, V., 207, 226, 346
Campbell, A., 325
Campbell, C., 52, 245
Campbell, R., 247, 248
Campbell, T., 131
Campione, J., 32
Campo, P., 341
Capilla, A., 341
Capodilupo, A., 225, 294
Capon, A., 288
Card, J., 355, 356
Carey, S., 35, 209, 229, 246, 254, 255, 256, 347,
    350
Carnochan, P., 171, 177, 267, 268, 281
Carpenter, P., 205, 341
Case, R., 4, 17, 23, 33, 35, 36, 38, 44, 60, 63, 64,
    69, 73, 90, 106, 112,
113, 158, 179, 183, 184, 190–209, 211–227,
    270–273, 275, 281, 285, 286, 287,
    289–294, 296, 297, 298, 302, 304, 308,
    314, 315, 316, 322, 331, 333, 334, 337,
    338, 344, 352, 356, 357, 360, 365, 366,
    369, 370, 371
Casey, B., 353, 354
Cashon, C., 347, 349
Castellanos, F., 353
Cellérier, G., 29, 30
Chapman, M., 15, 23, 69, 104, 105, 106, 113,
    260

Chaput, H., 349
Chase, W., 31, 117
Chen, Z., 125, 127, 130, 131, 134, 138, 139, 146, 147, 328
Cheng, C., 267, 269
Cheng, P., 17
Chi, M., 34, 134, 135, 203, 253
Chiu, M., 135
Chomsky, N., 88
Christ, S., 56
Christou, C., 4, 112, 113, 337, 344, 357
Church, R., 167
Clarke, A., 355
Clement, J., 299
Cline, M., 355
Cohen, J., 353
Cohen, L., 222, 347, 349
Collette, F., 341
Collins, A., 25
Commons, M., 153, 163, 185, 186
Connell, M., 250
Conway, A., 3, 4, 85, 339, 341, 346
Cooper, R., 19, 347
Corbett, K., 81
Corbetta, D., 329
Cornoldi, C., 31, 340
Corrigan, R., 162, 179
Cowan, N., 4, 288, 341, 342, 343, 345, 346
Cox, M., 74
Coyle, T., 204, 329
Craik, F., 4
Crammond, J., 333
Cross, D., 184
Crowder, R., 339
Crowley, K., 135, 312, 328
Cruess, L., 4, 5
Cuckle, P., 245
Cunning, S., 286

D

Daehler,Marvin W., 134
Dahl, R., 353
Dalton, C., 97, 138, 140, 141, 364, 365, 370
D'Amico, M., 76
Daneman, M., 205
Danovitch, J., 256
Dar, R., 5, 11
Dasen, P., 17
Davidson, M., 354

Dawson-Tunik, T., 153, 163, 185, 186
Day, L., 288, 341
De Avila, E., 68, 285
de Groot, A., 117
de Haan, M., 351, 352
De Loache, J., 138
de Leeuw, N., 135
de Rammelaere, S., 343
de Ribaupierre, A., 14, 15, 44, 45, 58, 60, 69, 87, 106, 107, 108, 109, 110, 113, 226, 285, 288, 334, 336, 337, 343, 344, 357, 361, 362
de Rosnay, M., 273
de Schonen, S., 355
de Weerth, C., 154
Dehaene, S., 222
Demetriou, A., 4, 37, 39, 90, 106, 110, 111, 112, 113, 221, 314, 327, 333, 337, 344, 357, 367, 369
Dempster, F., 56, 203
Denis, M., 107
Dennis, I., 288
Dennis, S., 218, 275, 293
Desmet, T., 343
Desrochers, S., 5
Diamond, A., 4, 5
Dick, F., 358
Dixon, J., 327
Dolan, A., 264
Dowel, W., 17
Doyle, A., 58
Draguns, J., 328
Dromi, E., 238
Dudukovic, N., 354
Duit, R., 135
Dunbar, K., 125
Durston, S., 56, 353, 354
Dyk, R., 41

E

Echols, C., 144
Edelstein, W., 90, 106, 225, 260
Efklides, A., 37, 90, 106, 110, 111, 112, 314
Elliott, E., 346
Elman, J., 3, 37, 246, 247, 249
Engle, R., 3, 4, 85, 205, 339, 341, 342, 344, 346
Ennis, R., 19
Ericcson, K., 31
Evans, J., 14, 16, 288
Ewing, S., 247, 248

F

Fabian, V., 69, 70, 73
Fagan, J., 29
Fan, J., 353
Fan, N., 215
Farrar, M., 178
Farrell, M., 58
Faterson, H., 41
Felch, L., 254
Feller, W., 44
Felsten, G., 81
Feltovich, P., 134
Fernandez, A., 341
Fernandez, S., 341
Ferrara, R., 32
Fiati, T., 314, 331
Field, D., 16
Fischer, K., 2, 15, 33, 123, 138, 147–160,
    162–165, 167, 168, 169, 171, 173–188,
    202, 208, 226, 250, 260, 261, 263, 267,
    268, 269, 270, 281, 282, 293, 300, 301,
    302, 306, 308, 312, 313, 315, 316, 322,
    326, 328, 329, 334, 335, 349, 351, 352,
    356, 366
Flavell, J., 6, 7, 11, 14, 15, 18, 21, 30, 31, 32,
    33, 304, 328
Flombaum, J., 353
Flores, L., 288, 341
Fodor, J., 3, 110, 209, 245
Foellinger, D., 45
Fogel, A., 313, 322, 329
Foley, E., 102, 337
Forman, S., 353
Forssberg, H., 353
Fossella, J., 354
Fox, N., 182, 356, 358, 359
Frackowiak, R., 357
Frank, L., 355
Freeman, N., 73, 245
French, K., 81
Friedman, N., 56
Frijda, N., 260
Frith, C., 23, 24, 25, 357
Frith, U., 23, 24, 25
Fry, A., 344
Frye, D., 4, 5, 370
Fullerton, T., 97
Furman, I., 198

G

Gabrieli, G., 354
Gadian, D., 357
Gagné, R., 289
Gallistel, C., 350
Galvan, A., 354
Garcia, R., 14
Garcia-Mila, M., 329
Gardner, H., 209, 369
Gauvain, M., 32
Gavens, N., 346
Geldart, S., 355
Gelman, R., 211, 350
Genereux, R., 219
Gentner, D., 127, 128, 129, 133, 145, 146
George, M., 247
Georgiou, S., 112
Gershkoff-Stowe, L., 325
Gerson, R., 80
Gick, M., 134, 145
Giedd, J., 353
Gilchrist, I., 56
Giudice, S., 208, 355
Glaser, R., 134, 135, 253
Globerson, T., 44, 60, 190, 285, 285, 287, 332
Gobbo, C., 14, 31, 253
Goddard, P., 60, 333, 348
Goldberg, J., 205, 207, 226, 275, 285, 344
Goldberg-Reitman, J., 218
Goldin-Meadow, S., 167, 313, 323, 325
Goldmann, L., 9
Goldman-Rakic, P., 352
Gomez, J., 4
Good, C., 357
Goode, P., 60, 333
Goodenough, D., 41
Goodman, D., 45–49, 51, 52, 54, 56, 60, 81,
    298, 302, 322
Goodnow, J., 30
Gopnik, A., 33
Goswami, U., 33, 132, 145
Grafman, J., 341, 342, 353
Granott, N., 2, 154, 167, 168, 169, 178, 180,
    182, 300, 326, 327, 329
Grant, J., 245
Grant, P., 4, 100, 206, 288
Grant, V., 264, 266
Greenberg, L., 280
Greene, T., 117
Greenfield, P., 30

Greeno, J., 125, 133, 143
Greenough, W., 357
Grice, S., 247, 248, 248
Griffin, S., 211, 218, 225, 268, 273, 288, 294, 296, 297, 302, 314, 315
Grize, J., 7, 159
Groisser, D., 123
Gsödl, M., 325
Guyon, J., 324, 328

H

Hagen, J., 32
Haith, M., 29, 347, 348
Hale, S., 344
Halford, G., 3, 4, 16, 17, 21, 23, 37, 90–101, 103, 106, 113, 125–129, 131, 132, 135, 138, 140–143, 206, 226, 288, 306, 309, 319, 330, 364, 365, 370
Hall, L., 339
Halliday, M., 226
Hambrick, D., 342
Hameluck, D., 81
Hand, H., 335
Handley, S., 288
Hanlon, H., 355
Harakal, T., 267, 268, 281, 282, 366
Hargrave, S., 32
Harkins, D., 267, 268, 281, 282, 366
Harris, P., 17, 260
Hasbroucq, T., 57
Hauert, C., 238, 239, 324, 328
Havassy, B., 68, 285
Haxby, J., 353
Hayes, J., 121, 135
Hayne, H., 266
Hayward, S., 194, 270, 271, 272, 273, 281
Hecht, S., 288
Heitz, R., 344, 346
Hencke, R., 335
Henderson, B., 209, 217, 218, 219, 224, 226, 227, 314, 331, 333
Heron, A., 17
Hertzmann, M., 41
Hessels, M., 286
Hiebert, J., 331
Hismjatullina, A., 346
Hitch, G., 58, 100, 206, 226, 340
Hochberg, J., 57
Hofstadter, D., 125

Hoitink, H., 154
Holyoak, K., 17, 125, 126, 129, 133, 134, 145
Houghton, G., 55
Howard, I., 68
Howe, M., 16
Hsieh, S., 340
Hughes, C., 5
Huizenga, H., 329
Hulme, C., 341
Humphreys, K., 247, 248
Hunt, E., 100
Hurst, P., 270, 271, 272, 273
Huteau, M., 43
Huttenlocher, P., 352
Hutton, U., 206

I

Iinuma, K., 356
Ijaz, H., 286
Im-Bolter,N., 5, 83, 84, 85, 86, 87, 333, 344, 366
Immordino-Yang, M., 2, 178, 300, 301, 302, 308
Inhelder, B., 2, 7, 8, 13, 15, 16, 23, 29, 42, 48, 65, 98, 107, 108, 135, 198, 241, 326, 328
Irwin, D., 5
Irwin, R., 276, 279, 280, 300
Izard, C., 260

J

Jacobson, K., 347
Jalley, E., 9
Jamison, W., 14
Jansen, B., 2, 139
Jedrzkiewicz, J., 81
Jenkins, E., 125, 321, 326, 328
Johnson, H., 245
Johnson, J., 4, 5, 38, 45, 47–49, 52–54, 56–59, 69, 70, 72, 73, 76, 81, 83–87, 286, 287, 303, 305, 319, 333, 337, 344, 352, 354, 362, 366, 370
Johnson, M. D., 264
Johnson, M. H., 3, 37, 246, 247, 249, 250, 325, 347
Johnson, S. C., 255
Johnson, S. P., 347
Johnson, T., 288, 341
Johnson-Laird, P., 16, 107

Johnsrude, I., 357
Johnstone, S., 355
Jolicœur, P., 346
Jones, M., 245
Jones, W., 247
Jonides, J., 341, 353
Juckes, T., 52, 60, 245, 365, 368
Junn, E., 126, 129, 133
Jusczyk, P., 238
Just, M., 341
Juujärvi, P., 4, 5, 340

K

Kahneman, D., 53
Kail, R. V., 4, 208, 339, 344
Kalchman, M., 215, 219, 294, 296, 297
Kameyama, M., 353
Kane, M., 4, 144, 205, 342
Kanizsa, G., 57
Kanner, B., 288
Karmiloff, Y., 245
Karmiloff-Smith, A., 2, 3, 20, 29, 37, 69, 239,
    240, 241, 243, 244, 245, 246, 247, 247,
    248, 249, 250, 251, 253, 311, 322, 324,
    325, 326, 328, 351
Karp, S., 41
Kazi, S., 112, 113, 221, 369
Keating, D., 16, 226, 347
Kee, D., 73
Keil, F., 254, 256, 258
Keizer, I., 337
Keller, C., 345, 346
Keller, M., 260
Keller, T., 288, 341, 345, 346
Kelly, M., 97, 98, 106
Kelly, W., 297
Kemps, E., 343
Kennedy, B., 156, 157, 176, 180, 267, 269, 326,
    366
Kenny, S., 156
Keys, B., 56
Khanna, F., 204, 286, 338
Kikyo, H., 353
Kingma, J., 105
Kirkham, N., 4, 5
Kitayama, S., 176
Kitchener, K., 156
Klahr, D., 15, 20, 60, 119, 120, 121, 122, 136,
    141, 142, 147, 322

Klapp, S., 100, 340
Kline, P., 133, 143
Klingberg, T., 353
Knight, C., 148, 153, 155, 156, 173, 184, 301,
    334
Koeske, R., 34
Koh, K., 129
Komatsushiro, M., 356
Komorek, M., 135
Konishi, S., 353
Kooistra, L., 4, 5, 340
Kornblum, S., 57
Kosslyn, S., 107
Kotovsky, L., 133, 146
Kreutzer, M., 32
Krohn, C., 200
Kuhn, D., 329
Kuhn, T., 14, 19, 255
Kui, Z., 113
Kulikowich, J., 146, 299
Kurland, M., 205, 206, 207, 226, 285, 344
Kurtines, W., 19
Kurtz, K., 145
Kvalsvig, J., 53
Kwon, H., 353
Kyllonen, P., 3
Kyriakides, L., 113

L

Lacey, S., 341
Lai, Z., 247
Lakatos, I., 5
Lanfranchi, S., 339
Lange, G., 32
Lansman, M., 100
Larivée, S., 106, 108, 114, 139, 334
Laughlin, J., 3, 339, 341
Lautrey, J., 14, 106, 107, 108, 109, 110, 312,
    328, 334, 367
LaVancher, C., 135
Lawler, J., 9
Lawrence, J., 16
Lazarus, R., 260
Le Ny, J., 9
Lecas, J., 288
Lecerf, T., 288, 337
Legrenzi, P., 15, 17, 33
Lehto, J., 4, 5, 340
Leitch, E., 101

Lenoir, M., 81
Leo, I., 347, 348
Leonard, S., 32
Lesgold, A., 117
Leslie, A., 347
Lester, P., 100, 340
Leutwyler, J., 337
Lewis, H., 41
Lewis, J., 125
Lewis, M. D., 270, 271, 272, 273, 274, 275, 281, 282, 283, 315, 331, 335, 366
Lewis, M. W., 135
Lewkowicz, D., 325
Li, J., 176, 267, 268
Liberty, C., 31
Licht, R., 355
Lichtenberger, L., 247
Liebert, R., 32
Lindenberger, U., 15, 105, 106
Littler, J., 226
Loft, S., 309
Loftus, E., 25
Logan, G., 5
Logie, R., 107, 340
Longeot, F., 139
Luchins, A., 146
Luck, S., 348–349
Lynch, C., 156
Lyra, M., 322, 329

M

Macchi Cassia, V., 347, 348
Mace, P., 19
Machado, A., 281
Machover, K., 41
Macomber, J., 347
Macrae, C., 56
Maest, F., 341
Maguire, E., 357
Maier, N.R., 116
Majerus, S., 341
Mandernach, T., 56
Mandler, J., 26, 29, 348
Maquet, P., 341
Maraganore, A., 174, 268, 269, 281
Marchetti, C., 340
Marcovitch, S., 4, 5, 325, 370
Marcus, G., 325
Marini, A., 215

Marini, Z., 192, 198, 199, 200, 218, 219, 226, 275
Markus, H., 176
Marx, K., 11
Mascolo, M., 267, 268, 281, 282, 288, 366
Mashburn, E., 100, 340
Mason, L., 144
Matessa, M., 341
Matoušek, M., 181, 356
Matsumoto, H., 176
Mattox, S., 346
Maurer, D., 355
Mauthner, N., 5
Maybery, M., 4, 97, 99, 100, 101, 206, 288
Mazzioni, G., 31
McCandliss, B., 353
McCarthy, R., 355
McClelland, J., 325
McCloskey, M., 254
McCormick, E., 84
McCredden, J., 97, 125, 126, 127
McKeough, A., 183, 209, 216, 217, 218, 219, 226, 266, 275, 294, 314, 331
McLaughlin, G., 99, 339
McLeod, C., 54
McPherson, S., 81
Meints, K., 4
Meissner, P., 41
Menon, V., 353
Metallidou, Y., 112, 221
Miall, D., 59
Miao, C., 145
Miller, G., 23, 31, 44, 103
Miller, K., 138
Miller, P., 204
Miller, R., 45, 52, 53
Milliken, B., 84
Minkoff, S., 4, 346
Minsky, S., 124
Mitchell, J., 56
Miyake, A., 56
Miyashita, Y., 353
Mizuno, T., 356
Moessinger, P., 9
Moizo, C., 62
Molenaar, P., 2, 153, 313, 328, 329, 355
Mondloch, C., 355
Montangero, J., 130
Morey, C., 346
Morra, S., 43, 54, 62, 66, 68, 73, 74, 75, 76, 87, 226, 245, 285, 286, 287, 333, 337, 339, 341, 343, 345, 346

Morton, J., 347
Moses, P., 355, 358
Moss, J., 215, 294, 296
Mounoud, P., 230–234, 236, 237, 238, 239, 251,
    252, 253, 312, 324, 326, 328, 334, 350,
    357
Mouyi, A., 344
Mueller, J., 215
Mueller, M., 207
Müller, U., 4, 5, 370
Multhaup, K., 264
Munakata, Y., 326
Mundy, P., 355, 356
Murino, M., 17
Murphy, P., 146, 299
Musch, E., 81

N

Nairne, J., 341
Nakajima, K., 353
Namy, L., 325
Nanez, J., 347
Naus, M., 31
Neal, A., 309
Neath, I., 341
Nee, D., 341, 353
Neimark, E., 16, 43
Nelson, C., 351, 352
Nelson, K., 26, 216
Nesselroade, J., 329
Neves, D., 133, 143
Newell, A., 46, 117, 118
Niaz, M., 5, 301
Nigam, M., 142, 147
Nisbett, R., 17
Noam, G., 174, 268, 269, 281
Noll, D., 353
Norman, D., 4, 5, 126, 133
Normandeau, S., 106, 108, 114, 139, 334
Novick, L., 134
Nugent, L., 345, 346
Nunez, M., 17
Nystrom, L., 353

O

O'Connor, E., 269
O'Hare, A., 4, 100, 206, 288

Oakes, L., 348–349
Okamoto, Y., 4, 179, 190, 191, 192, 203, 209,
    211, 215, 217, 218, 219, 224–227, 294,
    302, 314, 331, 333, 366, 369
Oliver, A., 37, 249, 250
Oliver, L., 17
Oltman, P., 41
Olver, R., 30
Opfer, J., 326
Opraz, N., 170
Orendi, J., 353
Ornstein, P., 31
Ortiz, T., 341
Ortony, A., 26
Osman, A., 57

P

Pachaury, A., 112, 221
Parent, S., 106, 108, 114, 334
Parisi, D., 3, 37, 246, 247, 249
Parker, S., 17
Parot-Locatelli, F., 9
Parziale, J., 2, 123, 149, 167, 168, 169, 180, 326,
    327, 329
Pascual-Leone, J., 4, 5, 13, 23, 36, 37, 38, 40,
    42–49, 51, 52, 53, 54, 56–60, 66–70, 72,
    73, 76, 78, 80–88, 106, 226, 265, 276,
    277, 279–282, 285, 286, 287, 298, 300,
    302, 303, 305, 308, 319, 322, 326, 332,
    333, 337, 342, 343, 344, 352, 354, 356,
    362, 365, 366, 370
Passarotti, A., 358
Pasupathi, M., 276
Paterson, S., 248, 325
Pauen, S., 132, 144
Pears, R., 98
Peluffo, N., 17
Pendleton, L., 77
Penello, B., 54, 285, 287, 337
Pennings, A., 68, 286
Pennington, B., 37, 123, 247, 249, 250
Perez, M., 333
Perner, B., 117
Perry, M., 125, 167
Petersén, I., 181, 356
Peterson, C., 264, 266
Philipona, M., 273
Phillips, G., 264

Phillips, S., 3, 91, 92, 93, 94, 99, 101, 103, 113, 143
Piaget, J., 6–16, 23, 26, 29, 42, 43, 48, 63, 65, 69, 88, 89, 90, 98, 107, 108, 119, 130, 135, 136, 159, 198, 328, 351
Pierroutsakos, S., 138
Pike, G., 247, 248
Pillemer, D., 260, 264, 265, 266
Pinker, S., 246
Pipp, S., 156, 157, 165, 167, 263, 315
Platsidou, M., 4, 90, 110, 111, 112, 113, 314, 337, 344, 357, 369
Plunkett, K., 3, 37, 246, 247, 249
Poget, L., 337
Poncelet, M., 341
Pons, F., 273
Porath, M., 218, 219, 223, 227, 273, 314, 333
Porter, T., 58
Posner, M., 353
Post, T., 117
Prior, S., 333
Pruyne, E., 156
Pulkkinen, L., 4, 5, 340
Pulos, S., 60, 81, 204, 287, 337
Pylyshyn, Z., 3

R

Rabinowitz, F., 16
Raftopoulos, A., 110, 111, 327, 367
Rakison, D., 325
Ransdell, S., 288
Rapoport, J., 353
Rattermann, M., 133
Raya, P., 155, 174, 268, 269, 281
Rees, T., 253
Reese, H., 18, 20, 33
Reimann, P., 135
Reiss, A., 353
Resing, W., 142
Richards, I., 69
Rieben, L., 14, 107, 108, 109, 110, 114, 334
Riegel, K., 20
Rittle-Johnson, B., 321, 329
Robertson, I., 58
Robinson, M., 119, 121, 122
Roe, K., 355
Rogers, T., 325
Rogoff, B., 32

Romero, E., 344
Roncadin, C., 60, 286, 332
Rose, S., 152, 164, 181, 313, 356
Ross, G., 29
Ross, P., 355
Ross, W., 32
Ross-Sheehy, S., 348–349
Rotenberg, E., 155
Roth, D., 5, 11
Roth, W., 135
Roulin, J., 139
Ruchkin, D., 341, 342, 353
Ruhland, R., 180, 329, 335
Rumelhart, D., 26, 126, 133
Rumsey, J., 5
Rushby, J., 355
Russell, C., 335
Russell, J., 37
Russell, S., 80

S

Salthouse, T., 278, 344
Sanchez, R., 131
Sancho, A., 337
Sandieson, R., 183, 209, 211, 218, 225, 293, 294, 298
Saults, J., 288, 341, 346
Saxe, R., 347
Scardamalia, M., 23, 24, 25, 69, 73, 286
Scerif, G., 37, 247, 288
Schank, R., 26
Scherer, K., 275, 282
Schilling, T., 348
Schlagmüller, M., 327
Schneider, W., 327
Schofield, N., 286
Schonfield, D., 278
Schröder, E., 106
Schubert, A., 353
Schumann-Hengsteler, R., 58
Schwark, H., 357
Schwartz, M., 147, 293, 301, 302
Scopesi, A., 62, 286
Segalowitz, S., 355
Selikowitz, M., 355
Serlin, R., 44, 371
Serra, M., 341
Service, E., 341
Sevsek, B., 81

Shafrir, U., 106, 300, 333
Shallice, T., 4, 5, 56
Shaver, P., 171, 177, 267, 268, 281
Shayer, M., 5, 36, 112, 333
Sheppard, J., 7
Shiffrin, R., 53, 287, 339
Shisler, R., 85
Shrager, J., 314, 321
Shutts, K., 254
Siegler, R., 2, 15, 32, 34, 125, 135, 136, 137,
        138, 139, 140, 149, 154, 168, 182, 198,
        199, 211, 218, 226, 239, 253, 294, 297,
        308, 312, 313, 314, 321, 322, 323, 326,
        327, 328, 329, 331, 334
Sijstma, K., 139
Simion, F., 347, 348
Simon, H., 46, 117, 118, 119, 135
Simone, P., 84
Sinclair, H., 2, 9, 57, 69, 135
Singer, L., 29
Singer-Freeman, K., 131
Singh, I., 174, 268, 269, 281
Skakich, S., 81
Slater, A., 347, 348
Slawinski, J., 204
Slone, M., 5, 11
Smeeton, N., 81
Smith, J., 23, 44, 73, 86
Smith, L., 22, 33, 36, 152, 180, 313
Smyth, M., 77
Somsen, R., 355
Southgate, V., 4
Sowder, J., 294
Spanoudis, G., 4, 112, 113, 337, 344, 357
Sparkman, E., 37, 45, 302, 308
Spelke, E., 245, 246, 254, 347, 348, 349
Spensley, F., 245
Spicer, J., 354
Spira, A., 337
Spitz, H., 119, 124
Sroufe, L., 260
Starkes, J., 81
Starkey, P.,347
Stauder, J., 355
Staudinger, U., 276
Stavy, R., 170
Steinberg, M., 299
Stephenson, K. M., 294
Stern, E., 125, 313, 328, 329
Sternberg, R., 39, 127
Stewart, L., 69, 276
Stigler, J., 331

Stiles, J., 355, 358
Strauss, S., 170, 323
Stroop, J., 54
Stuss, D., 208
Styles, E., 340
Subelman, I., 47, 48, 49, 56, 298, 302
Svetina, M., 125, 313
Swanson, H.L., 339
Szeminska, A., 7, 107, 159

T

Takagi, T., 356
Tallir, I., 81
Taylor, J., 245
Tetirick, J., 264
Thagard, P., 125, 129
Thatcher, R., 181, 208, 313, 355, 356
Thelen, E., 152, 180, 313, 325, 329
Theodor, L., 81
Therriault, D., 4, 346
Thomas, J., 80, 81
Thomas, K., 351, 352, 353
Thomas, L., 337
Thomas, M., 3, 247, 248, 249, 250, 251
Thomason, M., 354
Thompson, R., 101
Thomson, N., 341, 345
Thornton, S., 327
Tidswell, T., 5
Tipper, S., 55, 83, 84
Todor, J., 77, 78, 79
Tomasello, M., 325
Tomat, L., 74, 75, 76
Tombu, M., 346
Tottenham, M., 354
Toupin, C., 128, 129, 133
Toussaint, N., 14, 69
Towse, J., 206
Trabasso, T., 45, 98, 183
Trainor, R., 353
Tuholski, S., 3, 4, 85, 205, 339, 341
Tunteler, E., 142
Turati, C., 347, 348
Tzelnic, T., 347

U

Uchida, I., 353

Ulug, A., 353
Unsworth, N., 344, 346

V

Vaidya, C., 354
Valcke, M., 81
Valenza, E., 347
Valsiner, J., 5, 322, 329
van der Linden, M., 341
van der Maas, H., 2, 139, 153, 313, 328
van der Molen, M., 355
van Dijk, M., 152, 180, 328, 329, 334
Van Duuren, M., 247, 248
van Geert, P., 36, 152, 154, 180, 185, 313, 322, 326, 328, 329, 334, 335
van Leeuwen, H., 355
van Maanen, L., 139
Van Parys, M., 148, 153, 155, 156, 184
van Sommers, P., 74
van't Klooster, B., 355
Verrilli, E., 87, 286, 333
Vigliocco, G., 54, 285, 287, 337
Vinter, A., 231, 237, 252, 326, 328, 350
Viviani, P., 323, 328
Vosniadou, S., 70
Voss, J., 117
Voyat, G., 20
Vygotsky, L., 27, 35, 156, 328

W

Wahlen, K., 260
Walker, P., 58
Walker, R., 208, 355
Wallace, C., 357
Wallace, J., 15, 60, 141, 322
Wang, L., 176, 267, 268, 269
Wapner, S., 41
Ward, P., 81
Washburn, A., 254
Wason, P., 16
Wasserman, G., 81
Watanabe, A., 356
Watson, M., 165, 260, 261, 263
Watson, J., 184

Weaver, B., 84
Weiss, L., 19
Wellman, H., 31, 32, 184, 216
Welsh, M., 123
Wenger, L., 278
Werner, H., 328
Wertheimer, M., 143
Westerberg, H., 353
Wetherick, N., 19
White, D., 56
White, S., 260, 264, 265, 266
Wilbers, J., 135
Wilkening, F., 144
Wilkinson, A., 16
Willats, J., 73
Williams, A., 81
Wilson, W., 3, 91, 92, 93, 94, 96, 99, 101, 103, 113, 143
Wilson, M., 153, 163, 185, 186
Winer, G., 16
Witkin, H., 41
Wolfe, C., 355
Wong, E., 355
Wood, N., 345, 346
Wood, P., 156, 345, 346
Wozniak, R., 9
Wylie, G., 5
Wynn, K., 347

X

Xu, F., 348

Y

Yamauchi, N., 356
Yan, Z., 174, 326, 329
Yang, Y., 353

Z

Zelazo, P., 4, 5, 320, 370
Zielinski, T., 97, 138, 140, 141, 364, 365, 370
Zimmerman, R., 353
Zohar, A., 329

Subject Index

A

Abstract tier, 157–158, 162, 173, 182, 269, 356
Abstraction, 19, 48–49, 90, 133, 142, 162–163,
    202, 221, 240, 280, 315, 342, 350, 363,
    370
Adolescence, 7, 15–16, 25, 27, 32, 156, 164,
    176, 181, 200, 219, 255, 269, 276–277,
    330–331, 337, 352, 354–355
Activation of schemes, 53, 59, 342, 345,
    360–361
Ageing, 4, 56, 269, 276, 278–281, 337, 344, 347,
    357, 369, 372
Analogy, 52–54, 80, 191, 204–205, 296, 321, 359
    see also relational complexity
Appraisal, 267–268, 273–276, 281
Attention, 3–5, 13, 22–23, 28, 42, 45, 48–49,
    52–54, 56–58, 60, 72, 78, 81, 86, 97,
    105–106, 114, 123, 142, 167, 195, 208,
    221–222, 271–272, 277–281, 284, 286,
    296, 299, 315, 320, 337, 339–346, 354,
    361, 365, 367
Attractor, 180, 182, 222, 282–283, 313, 316,
    332, 366–367
Autobiographic memory, 264
Automatization, 52–54, 80, 191, 204–205, 296,
    321, 359

B

Backward digit span, 106, 285–286, 288
Backward transition, 167, 170–172, 180, 313,
    326
Balance Beam Task, 194, 198, 364–365
Bottom-up procedures, 242
Brain imaging, 56, 164, 181, 208, 341, 353,
    355–356, 358–359
Bridging process, 170, 186

C

Catastrophe theory, 2, 152, 282
Capacity measurement, 102, 284, 287, 309,
    337–338
Central Conceptual Structures (CCS), 110,
    201–202, 208–211, 214–229, 293–294,
    300–301, 314–316, 331, 356, 361,
    369–371
    see also Specialized Structural Systems
Central Narrative Structure, 150, 209,
    212–213, 215–216, 218–219, 294
Central Numerical Structure, 210–211, 213,
    215, 294–296, 350
Childhood amnesia, 264–266
Children's theories, 240, 253, 350

Chunk, 23, 31–32, 43, 77, 103, 127, 188, 203,
    232, 318, 320, 342
Classification, 24–25, 47–48, 100–101, 106, 132,
    141, 237, 254, 262
Cognitive conflict, 42–43, 82, 298, 354, 366
Cognitive structures, 2, 6, 11, 13, 36, 93, 106,
    209, 251, 349, 360–362, 365, 369
Cognitive style, 2, 6, 11, 13, 36, 93, 106, 209,
    251, 303, 349, 360–362, 365, 369
Compounding rule, 133, 167–168, 183
Comprehension (text, reading, etc.), 59,
    69–70, 72–73, 87, 94, 163, 262–263
Concepts or conceptual categories, 3, 10, 15,
    17, 20, 25, 29, 31, 33, 35, 37, 48, 52, 58,
    90, 93, 97, 106, 108, 116, 127, 156, 184,
    188, 200, 209–212, 215–220, 223,
    245–246, 251–255, 261, 276, 293–294,
    296, 302, 315, 319, 325, 331, 336, 349,
    363, 366–368, 371
Conceptuomotor, 231
Concrete operations, 8, 11, 14, 17, 43, 90, 97,
    107–108
Connectionist models or networks, 3, 38, 87,
    181, 221, 248–250, 257, 320, 349,
    370–371, 367
Consciousness/unconscious, 18, 217, 231,
    240, 243–244, 251, 261, 263–264, 266,
    276, 280, 329
Conservation, 15, 17, 37, 42, 58, 60–61, 97–98,
    108, 153, 159, 162, 168, 173, 184, 320,
    330
Consolidation, 124, 152, 157, 163–164,
    182–183, 185, 189, 192, 196–198,
    201–202, 220, 227, 232, 237, 278, 313,
    315, 318, 324, 326, 328, 359
Constructivism, 22, 29, 37, 89, 92, 239,
    246–247, 249–252, 257, 259, 288, 321,
    349–350, 359
Continuity/discontinuity of development,
    2–3, 10, 53, 107, 151–153, 155, 157–158,
    165, 177, 266, 317–319–320, 322, 324,
    336, 359–360
Control structures for coping: 270, 273–274,
    281
Cortex: 53, 181, 247, 352–357
Counting Span, 205–207, 223, 285, 288
CSVI: 44–45, 52–53, 72, 285
Culture; influence and variation, 17–18, 20,
    35–36, 112–113, 149–150, 176, 210, 227,
    258, 268–269, 271, 280, 295, 314–316,
    331–333, 361
Curricula, 293–296, 298, 300

Cycles, 62, 78, 118, 123, 133, 152–153, 157–158,
    172–173, 180, 182–183, 185–188,
    232–233, 238, 241, 257, 312–313,
    318–321, 328, 336–337, 355–356, 363

D

Décalage, 14–15, 105, 107–109, 137, 170, 177,
    183–184, 187, 251, 322, 330, 335–336
Decomposition, 118, 234, 236, 252, 337
Defense mechanisms, 270–271, 277–278
Developmental path, 174, 189, 325, 327
Developmental web or strand, 151–152, 184,
    300–301, 369
Dialectic, 6, 8–11, 18–22, 33–34, 38, 278–280,
    362, 365–367
Differentiation, 45, 165–166, 201–202, 220–221,
    227, 270, 312, 315, 361–362
Digit Placement Task, 102, 203, 286, 337
Dimensional, 93, 111, 127, 187, 192 198–202,
    211–214, 218–219, 271, 274, 352, 363
Domain specific, 36, 112, 125, 130, 148, 178,
    186, 209, 217–218, 240, 246, 251, 253,
    257–258, 311, 313–314, 350, 371
Drawing, 31, 44, 62, 72–76, 245, 333
Dynamic systems, 3, 36–37, 149, 152, 180, 185,
    188, 273, 275, 282, 316–317, 319, 327,
    366–367

E

Easy-to-hard paradigm, 101–102, 284,
    337–338, 369
Emotional development, 5, 260–261, 267–268,
    270–272, 278, 280–283, 309, 366
Empiricism, 20, 33–37, 258, 304, 347, 349
Encoding, 58–59, 75–76, 127, 139–140, 142,
    145, 265–266, 343
Environmental factors, 147, 149, 177–179, 297,
    327, 331, 347, 357
    see also social class differences
Epigenesis, 10, 18, 90, 148, 182, 184, 186, 351
Equilibration, 10–14, 18–19, 58, 61, 90, 149,
    180–181, 242, 313, 319, 365–367
Errors, 10–14, 18–19, 58, 61, 90, 149, 180–181,
    242, 313, 319, 365–367
Executive function, 4–5, 31, 38, 49, 52–54, 56,
    64, 67, 80, 191, 200–201, 208, 220–222,
    225–226, 298, 300, 314, 320, 331, 333,
    340, 367, 371

Executive Control Structures (ECS), 191–192, 194–198, 200–201, 208, 220–221, 225–227, 270–272, 312, 314
Experience, versus maturation, 23, 32, 42, 45, 50–51, 57, 59, 64, 66, 110–111, 117, 125, 136, 140, 146–147, 185–186, 222–225, 227, 254, 264–265, 277–280, 293, 298, 315–317, 320, 357–361
Expertise, 30, 34–35, 117, 156, 174, 253–254, 357–358
Explanation, scientific, 20, 34–35, 88, 103, 106, 206–207, 222, 290–291, 322, 327, 341, 361

F

Feedback loop (hierarchical / iterative), 7, 26, 28, 52, 119, 153, 185–186, 202, 221–222, 224, 227, 230–233, 295, 304, 312–313, 315–316, 319, 361–362
Field dependence / independence, 40–43, 56, 60, 75–76, 332–333
Field effect, 57, 68, 298–299, 333, 354
Figurative knowledge or schemes, 29, 48–50, 54, 57, 63, 69–71, 75, 78, 107, 231, 251–252, 277, 296, 342, 344
FIT, 73, 83, 106, 286, 339
Formal operations, 8, 15–16, 23, 63, 65, 90
Fractionation, 247–249
Frontal and prefrontal lobes, 53, 56, 208, 222–223
Functional level, 154–157, 163, 172–173, 176–180, 186–187, 302, 363

G

General theories, 39, 94, 281, 302, 308
Generalization, 23, 135, 152, 177–179, 183–187, 217–219, 313–314, 319
Genetic, 246–248, 312
Genetic epistemology, 18–20, 29
Gestalt theory, 115
Giftedness, 18–20, 29
Graded learning loops, 298, 302
Graduality, 9, 70, 52, 165, 167, 169, 177, 252, 311, 319–320, 321–322
Growth curves, 1–3, 151–153, 157, 186, 316, 322, 326, 328

H

Hemispheres, 48, 80, 207, 354–356
Heuristic, 36, 116–119, 302–308
Hierarchical or sequential development, 29, 52, 61, 138, 148, 153, 166–167, 180, 184–187, 190, 202, 221–222, 227, 230–233, 312–316
Hysteresis, 319

I

Imitation Sorting Task, 286
Individual differences, 3, 40–41, 56, 86, 106, 109–111, 114, 152–153, 173, 223, 226, 283, 332–335, 362
Individualized instruction, 288–289, 294
Infant competencies, 16–17, 26–29, 121, 159–161, 194–196, 245, 271–274, 325, 347–349, 359
Information load, 22, 24–25, 32, 99, 287, 289, 306–307, 312, 336–338
Infralogical, 107–109, 233, 236–237, 350
Inhibitory processes, 2–5, 54–56, 81, 83–86, 263, 270–282, 333, 344–345, 355
Insight, 115–117, 304
Instructional intervention, 135, 288–290, 292–293, 297–298
Integration, 12, 51, 78–79, 166–170, 199–202, 217, 220–221, 227, 232, 252, 280, 315, 319
Intelligence, 3, 9, 26, 70, 109, 343, 361, 369
Intentions, 37, 209, 216–218, 233, 265, 304
Interrelational structures, 196–198, 204, 271–274, 338

K

Knowledge
    constituted, 231–236
    declarative, 26, 251–252, 342
    implicit/explicit, 232, 241, 324
    procedural, 5, 26, 29, 48, 240, 251–252, 324
    scripted, 150

L

Language development, 27, 73, 162–164, 243–246

Learning
  (C-, M-, LM, etc.), 51–52, 80, 221, 265–266,
    320, 361, 369–371
  difficulties, 173–174, 246–249, 301
  paradox, 60, 252, 366, 368, 371
Levels of skill complexity, 48, 123, 149–152,
    157–165, 268–270, 300–301
Limited capacity, 2–5, 22–23, 25, 43–45,
    53–56, 62, 64–72, 75–76, 78–80, 147,
    164, 177, 180–181, 202–208, 284–289,
    312, 314, 316, 319–320, 336–351,
    361–362, 369
  attentional capacity, 23, 105–106, 337,
    344–346
  carrying capacity, 164, 177, 180–181, 187,
    189, 312–313, 316, 335–336
  M capacity, 53–56, 62, 64–72, 75–76, 78–80,
    86, 105, 203, 265, 285–288, 312,
    319–320, 336–338, 344–345
  of central computing space, 44, 51–53, 100,
    284, 286
  of processing, 2–3, 22–23, 25, 4–45, 92–93,
    99–106, 114, 125, 127, 129–130,
    132–133, 229–230, 320, 336, 337
  of short-term storage space (STSS),
    204–207, 225, 284 of storage, 111, 337,
    340–341
  of total processing space (TPS), 204
  of working memory, 2–5, 38, 194–195, 199,
    202–208, 210, 222–227, 252, 266, 271,
    273, 296, 308, 312, 314, 319, 345–346,
    359, 366, 369
Logical competence or structure, 7–8, 10,
    13–16, 21, 33–34, 39, 43, 60, 89–90, 150,
    209, 227, 253, 306, 318, 361

M

Mathematical ability, 288
Mathematical education, 294
Maturation, 53–55, 86, 163–164, 181, 207–208,
    222–223, 225–227, 252, 258, 312–316,
    319–322, 347–359
Metacognition, 31–32, 110, 186, 244, 277, 288,
    290, 298, 300, 362
Metasubjective operators, 45, 50–61, 74,
    86–87, 307
  F operator, 58, 61, 62, 67, 68, 75, 82, 333,
    354

I operator, 54–58, 61–62, 81–82, 86–87,
    278–279, 298–299, 307, 333, 342, 368,
    371
L operator, 52, 62, 333
LC operator, 51–52, 72, 265, 361
LM operator, 51–52, 74, 265, 361
M operator, 52–62, 68, 74, 82, 86, 88, 104,
    278, 298, 299, 307, 333, 342, 368, 371
S operator, 58
Microdevelopment/macrodevelopment, 124,
    149, 151, 157, 164–167, 300–301, 313, 370
Microgenetic study or method, 125, 138, 142,
    228, 321, 324, 328–329, 338, 370
Misleadingness, 42–43, 56, 58, 74, 76, 84, 105,
    298, 302, 319, 333, 364–365, 369
Missing addend problem, 291–293
Modularity, 28, 35, 110, 187, 210, 222,
    243–248, 311, 355, 358
  see also knowledge, modular
Moods, 273–275
Motor abilities or tasks, 49, 67–68, 77–81,
    239, 325
Mr. Cucumber test, 285, 288
Myelination, 207, 351–354

N

Nativism and endogenous processes, 37, 89,
    110, 148, 186, 210, 231, 239, 241,
    245–250, 254, 257–259, 270–271,
    281–282, 311, 349–350, 359
Negative priming, 55, 83–85
Neural development, 164, 222, 351–359
Neuroconstructivism, 37, 239, 246–252, 257,
    321, 349, 359, 370
Nonlinear models, 1–3, 151–154, 180, 185,
    282, 301
Nonverbal measures, 72–73, 204
Number concept, 210–215, 297, 334

O

Object permanence, 179, 349
Oedipal conflict, 261–264
Operating Space (OS), 204
Operational efficiency, 191, 204–206, 225, 227
Operative knowledge or schemes, 48–49, 57,
    71–72, 74–75, 270–271, 279, 296,
    298–299, 342–345
  see also Knowledge, procedural

Overlapping waves, 125, 138, 321, 326
Over-regularization, 248, 325, 327, 328

P

Perceptivomotor, 231–233
Personality development, 59, 269, 273–276, 309
Planning, development of, 32, 62, 73–74, 119–124, 239
Praxis, 10–11, 36–37, 161, 196, 241, 304–305, 328
Predicates, 71–72, 93–94
Preoperational, 7–8, 43, 162, 211
Primary emotions, 267, 271, 273–274, 276, 281–282
Processing speed, 4–5, 83, 103, 111, 207, 223, 226, 337, 344–346, 356–357, 369
Psychopathology, 268

Q

Qualitative/quantitative changes, 8–11, 35, 53, 113, 123–124, 151, 157–159, 163–166, 178, 188, 192, 197–198, 201, 209, 229–230, 239, 250–251, 254, 257, 274, 312, 317–322, 363, 366, 370
Quantitative concepts, 112, 199, 209–215, 217–219, 224, 288, 293–296, 321

R

Rationalism, 33–38
Reasoning, 6–9, 16–17, 23–24, 30, 34, 99–105, 108, 112–113, 116, 125–136, 142–147, 163, 200, 225–226, 254, 276, 299, 337, 339, 344
Regression in performance, 125, 138–139, 154, 170–172, 174, 181, 183, 189, 238, 248, 252–253, 257–259, 313, 323–328
Relational or structural complexity, 91–99, 102–103, 106, 113–114, 127–133, 141, 143, 147, 226–227, 250, 307, 318, 320, 336–337, 342, 363, 370
Representational tier, 157–162, 166, 182, 188, 261
Representation
  analogical, 27, 49–50, 52, 107–108, 110, 114, 222, 229, 231, 237, 253, 295, 334

mental, 27, 49–50, 66–67, 93, 196, 229, 255, 265, 276, 336
  propositional, 48, 50, 107–108, 110, 114, 229, 231, 237, 253, 255, 295, 334, 350
Representational change, 3, 229–231, 251, 253, 258, 311
Representational codes, 231–239, 242–245, 251–252, 258, 312, 318–319
Representational development, 232–236, 252
Representational Redescription (RR), 240–245, 250, 252, 324
Retarded children, 124, 293
Retrieval, 254, 266, 298, 343, 345
Rules, 3–5, 27–28, 49–50, 52, 56, 60–61, 94–96, 107, 110, 136–142, 146, 168, 185–186, 229, 275, 311, 313, 316, 321, 323, 371

S

Scaffolding, 156, 169–170, 176–177, 266
Scallop, 174, 326
Scheme coordination, 6, 11–13, 43–45, 47, 50, 52, 59, 78–79, 192, 195–196, 199–200, 202, 220–221, 265, 270–282, 287, 295–296, 320, 359, 361, 365
Schemes, 6, 11–13, 23, 27, 37, 43–68, 71–76, 78–82, 86, 103–104, 107, 109, 126, 132–134, 142–144, 147, 149, 191–192, 194–196, 198–200, 202, 220–221, 229, 264–265, 270–282, 287, 295–300, 304–307, 318–320, 330, 333, 338, 342–345, 359–361, 365, 371
Selection mechanism, 252, 337
Self, 111, 156, 263, 269, 272–280, 331
Self-regulation or organization, 89, 111, 150, 155, 279, 282, 313, 327–328
  see also Transition processes
Semioticomotor, 231
Sensorimotor, 8, 10, 26, 29, 53–54, 91, 157–163,194–197, 202, 231, 238, 271–274, 293, 338, 349
Seriation, 8, 12, 15–16, 106
Short-term memory, 21, 31, 44–45, 86, 99–100, 102, 204–205, 207, 225, 284, 287, 337–343
Shift of focus, 167–169, 202, 312, 316
  Similarity of analogies, 128–134, 142–143, 147
Skills, 123–124, 148–189, 229, 263, 267–270, 300–304, 311–313, 316–318, 326, 350, 360, 363, 369–370

Social class differences, 52, 297, 316, 333
Social emotions, 174–176, 271–273
Social roles, 163–167, 209, 261–263, 267–269, 338
Sociohistorical approach, 35–38
Space representation, 8, 17, 58, 65–67, 74–76, 83–85, 107–110, 224, 340, 353
Specialized Structural Systems (SSS), 110–113, 314, 362, 369–370
Specific Language Impairment, 87, 246, 249
Specific models, 37, 94, 302–303, 308
Spurt or discontinuity, 123–124, 151–155, 157, 163–164, 171, 176, 179–181, 185, 208, 313, 316–317, 351, 355–356
Stability, 19, 150, 152, 154, 158, 178, 180, 311–313, 327–329
Stages, 2–3, 6–8, 10, 17–19, 33–39, 43, 88, 99, 114, 136, 148, 158–159, 172, 188, 190–204, 208–220, 225–228, 229–237, 241–243, 252–253, 257, 271–283, 306, 310–325, 337–338, 356, 361–365
Strategies, 16, 29–32, 42, 60–67, 74–75, 115–126, 147, 184, 190–191, 197–204, 215, 227, 239, 272–274, 281, 289–291, 293–294, 298–299, 304–307, 311–314, 321, 324–329, 359–360
Stroop effect, 54–55, 83–85, 112, 286
Structuralism, 10, 37, 88–114, 282, 311, 365, 367
minimal structuralism, 113, 257, 361
Structure, psychological, 90, 149, 187
Substages, 192–202, 209–220, 225, 230, 295–296, 306, 317–319, 330–333, 337–338, 349, 362
Support, 132, 141–142, 146–147, 150–157, 163, 166, 171, 173, 176–189, 312–313, 326–332, 364–365, 369
Symbol systems, 36, 91–92, 95–96, 99, 202, 220, 250
Symbolic representation, 8, 21, 26–27, 73, 91–94, 319
Synapse(s), 351–357
Synchrony/asynchrony, 14–15, 109, 148–151, 178–189, 227, 311, 314–315, 323, 330, 333–336, 364
Systematicity, 93, 127–130

T

Task analysis, 59–68, 70, 74, 78, 105, 111, 114, 179, 184, 228, 302–309, 330, 343, 372
Tiers, 157–163, 181, 189, 313, 363–364

Time concept, 58–59, 293–294
Tower of Hanoi, 116–124
Training, 97–98, 134, 139–142, 181, 183, 218–219, 223–224, 226, 302, 314, 365
Transfer of learning, 133–134, 144–147
Transition processes or mechanisms, 133–134, 144–147
coordination, 165–169, 185, 192, 361
distributed cognition, 167, 172
hierarchical feedback loop, 221, 224, 315–316, 319, 361
hierarchical integration, 166, 202, 221, 227, 319
recast, 167, 169
reiteration, 124, 167, 170–172, 178
substitution, 167–168, 178, 313, 316
Transitivity, 11, 94, 97–98, 105, 126, 129, 132, 141, 183

U

Units of cognition, 23, 31, 43, 46, 80, 110, 188, 192, 221, 232–233, 237–238, 249–250, 255, 281, 303–308, 338, 342, 360

V

Variability, 68, 139, 148–158, 174, 177–178, 187–189, 225, 253, 311–317, 322–336
Vectorial stage, 192, 200, 204, 219, 274, 337

W

Well-defined and ill-defined problems, 115–119
Whole, laws of the, 45, 89, 103
Will, 280, 300
Williams Syndrome, 246–248, 255–256, 325
Wisdom, 276–281
Working memory, 3–5, 77, 86, 124, 164, 188–192, 201–208, 210, 226, 257, 281, 286, 316, 332, 334, 336, 339–346, 349, 351, 353, 357, 369

Y

Young adulthood, 149, 277–278

Z

Zone of proximal development, 35